Automating Windows Administration

STEIN BORGE

Apress™

Automating Windows Administration

ISBN (pbk): 1-59059-397-9

Printed and bound in the United States of America 9 8 7 6 5 4 3 2 1

Lead Editor: Jim Sumser
Technical Reviewer: Eric Lippert
Editorial Board: Steve Anglin, Dan Appleman, Ewan Buckingham, Gary Cornell, Tony Davis, Jason Gilmore, Chris Mills, Steve Rycroft, Dominic Shakeshaft, Jim Sumser, Gavin Wray
Project Manager: Beth Christmas
Copy Edit Manager: Nicole LeClerc
Copy Editor: Nicole LeClerc
Production Manager: Kari Brooks
Production Editor: Kelly Winquist
Compositor: Diana Van Winkle, Van Winkle Design Group
Proofreader: Liz Welch
Indexer: Kevin Broccoli
Cover Designer: Kurt Krames
Manufacturing Manager: Tom Debolski

Distributed to the book trade in the United States by Springer-Verlag New York, Inc., 233 Spring Street, 6th Floor, New York, New York 10013 and outside the United States by Springer-Verlag GmbH & Co. KG, Tiergartenstr. 17, 69112 Heidelberg, Germany.

In the United States: phone 1-800-SPRINGER (1-800-777-4643), fax 201-348-4505, e-mail orders@springer-ny.com, or visit `http://www.springer-ny.com`. Outside the United States: fax +49 6221 345229, e-mail `orders@springer.de`, or visit `http://www.springer.de`.

For information on translations, please contact Apress directly at 2560 Ninth Street, Suite 219, Berkeley, CA 94710. Phone 510-549-5930, fax 510-549-5939, e-mail `info@apress.com`, or visit `http://www.apress.com`.

The source code for this book is available to readers at `http://www.apress.com` in the Downloads section. You will need to answer questions pertaining to this book in order to successfully download the code.

To my beautiful wife Alison and children Heidi and Christopher.

Contents at a Glance

Foreword xv
About the Author xvii
About the Technical Reviewer xix
Acknowledgments xx

Chapter 1 Introduction 1
Chapter 2 Shell Operations 39
Chapter 3 Logon Scripts and Scheduling 71
Chapter 4 Networking Resources 107
Chapter 5 File Operations 121
Chapter 6 Input/Output Streams 157
Chapter 7 Registry Operations 175
Chapter 8 Regular Expressions 195
Chapter 9 Application Automation 215
Chapter 10 Network Administration/WMI 249
Chapter 11 Internet Applications 359
Chapter 12 Messaging Operations 403
Chapter 13 Data Access 477
Chapter 14 System Administration 575
Chapter 15 Internet Information Server 655
Chapter 16 Exchange Server 695
Chapter 17 Security 739
Index 793

Contents

Foreword .... *xv*
About the Author .... *xvii*
About the Technical Reviewer .... *xix*
Acknowledgments .... *xx*

Chapter 1 Introduction *1*

What Is WSH? *1*
COM Automation *2*
Version 2.0 Features *4*
Scripting Components *12*
Streams, Standard Input and Output, and Piping *35*
Additional Resources *37*

Chapter 2 Shell Operations *39*

2.1 Reading the Command-Line Arguments *39*
2.2 Reading an Environment Variable *46*
2.3 Creating or Updating an Environment Variable *48*
2.4 Deleting an Environment Variable *51*
2.5 Running Applications *52*
2.6 Accessing Windows-Related Folders *58*
2.7 Creating a Windows Shortcut *60*
2.8 Displaying a Message Prompt *63*
2.9 Sending Keystrokes to Applications *65*

Chapter 3 Logon Scripts and Scheduling *71*

3.1 Connecting Network Resources at Logon *71*
3.2 Scheduling Scripts *79*
3.3 Displaying a Logon Message *86*
3.4 Performing Operations Based on Group Membership *95*
3.5 Creating an Inventory of Computers at Logon *102*

Chapter 4 Networking Resources ... 107

4.1 Identifying a User ... 107
4.2 Finding an Available Network Drive ... 108
4.3 Mapping Network Drives ... 110
4.4 Migrating File Services from One Server to Another Server ... 112
4.5 Connecting to a Network Printer ... 115
4.6 Listing Connected Network Printers ... 117
4.7 Disconnecting Network Printers ... 118

Chapter 5 File Operations ... 121

5.1 Determining the Readiness of a Floppy Drive ... 122
5.2 Listing the Drives on a System ... 124
5.3 Finding the Size of a User Directory ... 125
5.4 Determining the Size of a File ... 127
5.5 Reading and Changing File Attributes ... 128
5.6 Determining the Existence of a File or Folder ... 131
5.7 Renaming a File or Folder ... 132
5.8 Comparing Files by Version Number ... 133
5.9 Creating a Folder ... 135
5.10 Finding and Deleting Temporary Files ... 137
5.11 Finding Files That Meet Criteria ... 140
5.12 Deleting a Folder ... 144
5.13 Copying a File ... 145
5.14 Copying and Moving a Folder ... 147
5.15 Deleting a File ... 148
5.16 Creating and Writing to a Text File ... 149
5.17 Opening and Reading a File ... 151
5.18 Updating a Text File ... 153

Chapter 6 Input/Output Streams ... 157

6.1 Using Regular Expressions to Filter the Contents of an Input Stream ... 157
6.2 Reading Keyboard Input ... 163
6.3 Generating Template-Based Data ... 164
6.4 Creating Multiple-User Prompts ... 170

Chapter 7 Registry Operations 175

7.1 Reading a Value from the Registry 176
7.2 Writing a Value to the Registry 180
7.3 Deleting a Registry Entry 184
7.4 Listing the Registry Key Values 186
7.5 Searching and Replacing Registry Values 188
7.6 Accessing the Remote Registry 192

Chapter 8 Regular Expressions 195

8.1 Validating a String 196
8.2 Matching Multiple Patterns 203
8.3 Matching Subexpressions 206
8.4 Replacing Values 211

Chapter 9 Application Automation 215

9.1 Creating Formatted Word Documents 215
9.2 Identifying Office Documents by Their Properties 227
9.3 Importing Data into Excel 231
9.4 Generating Thumbnail Images for Web Pages 240
9.5 Building Web Page Rollover Images 244
9.6 Generating Electronic Copies of Access Reports 246

Chapter 10 Network Administration/WMI 249

10.1 Accessing Information about a Computer 251
10.2 Determining the Role of a Computer 263
10.3 Obtaining IP Information 265
10.4 Changing the Location of an NT Dump File 275
10.5 Setting TCP/IP Information 279
10.6 Inventorying Computer Components 288
10.7 Executing Generic WMI Queries 292
10.8 Changing Environment Variables 298
10.9 Terminating a System Process 300
10.10 Starting an Application on a Remote Computer 304
10.11 Compressing Folders and Files 309
10.12 Copying Files on a Remote Computer 312
10.13 Rebooting a Computer 316
10.14 Checking the Event Viewer for Unauthorized Access 320
10.15 Backing Up Event Viewer Events 327

10.16 Processing Event Viewer Events ... 329
10.17 Changing NT Service Account Information ... 333
10.18 Changing System Time ... 336
10.19 Defragging a Drive ... 338
10.20 Listing DNS Resources ... 341
10.21 Creating a DNS Zone ... 345
10.22 Modifying DNS Zone Properties ... 350
10.23 Creating DNS Address ... 351
10.24 Deleting DNS Resources ... 355
10.25 Modifying DNS Addresses ... 356

Chapter 11 Internet Applications ... 359

11.1 Retrieving HTML Data ... 359
11.2 Displaying HTML ... 364
11.3 Displaying an HTML Logon Message ... 369
11.4 Creating an HTML Form ... 373
11.5 Enumerating HTML Elements ... 378
11.6 Creating a GUI Menu ... 387
11.7 Transferring Files Using FTP ... 390
11.8 Domain Name Resolution ... 396
11.9 Pinging a Computer ... 398

Chapter 12 Messaging Operations ... 403

12.1 Logging On ... 405
12.2 Determining the Default Profile ... 409
12.3 Sending Anonymous Mail ... 411
12.4 Running Message Scripts Using NT Scheduler Service ... 413
12.5 Creating a Mail Message ... 416
12.6 Setting Message Properties ... 417
12.7 Creating Message Recipients ... 419
12.8 Sending the Message ... 422
12.9 Using a Command-Line Script to Send E-mail ... 426
12.10 Checking the Event Log ... 432
12.11 Getting Computer Status Notification ... 433
12.12 Using the Performance Monitor Event ... 435
12.13 Attaching Files to a Message ... 436
12.14 Processing Messages ... 439
12.15 Filtering Mail ... 441
12.16 Extracting Attachments ... 444

12.17 Using a WSH Script Mail Agent 446
12.18 Retrieving a Folder 451
12.19 Posting Messages to an Exchange Server Public Folder 456
12.20 Creating Folders 457
12.21 Copying or Moving Messages 459
12.22 Copying and Moving Folders 462
12.23 Deleting Messages and Folders 464
12.24 Creating New Message Fields 465
12.25 Retrieving an Address Book Recipient 468
12.26 Creating Recipient Entries 472
12.27 Adding a Distribution List 474

Chapter 13 Data Access 477

ODBC 477
OLE DB 477
Using ADO 478
13.1 Data Source Name Connection Strings 480
13.2 File DSN Connection 485
13.3 DSN-Less Connection Strings 487
13.4 Opening a Secure Database 492
13.5 Compacting Access Databases 495
13.6 Querying a Table 500
13.7 Opening a Table for Writing 504
13.8 Manipulating a Text File 508
13.9 Accessing Excel Data 510
13.10 Querying the Index Server 513
13.11 Adding Data 515
13.12 Updating Data 518
13.13 Accessing HTML Data 520
13.14 Deleting Data 524
13.15 Accessing Internet Resources 525
13.16 Exporting Data 535
13.17 Importing Data 537
13.18 Executing a Stored Procedure 552
13.19 Executing an Access Parameter Query 556
13.20 Processing Multiple Recordsets 558
13.21 Modifying Command Results 559
13.22 Returning a Parameter Value from a Stored Procedure 561
13.23 Transaction Processing 571

Chapter 14 System Administration 575

14.1 Setting Domain Properties 576
14.2 Determining a Computer's OS 582
14.3 Listing Users 584
14.4 Creating a New User 586
14.5 Listing Object Properties 589
14.6 Setting Object Properties 592
14.7 Setting Multivalued Properties 605
14.8 Deleting a User 607
14.9 Setting User Logon Time 608
14.10 Limiting Computer Access 614
14.11 Setting User Flags 615
14.12 Listing Groups 619
14.13 Creating or Deleting a User Group 620
14.14 Adding a User or Group to a Group 622
14.15 Determining Group Membership 624
14.16 Querying Active Directory Values 625
14.17 Controlling NT Services 630
14.18 Listing Connected Resources 636
14.19 Determining User RAS Access 638
14.20 Listing Network Shares 642
14.21 Creating or Deleting a Network Share 643
14.22 Print Queue Operations 645
14.23 Listing Print Jobs 647
14.24 Setting Windows Terminal Services Properties 651

Chapter 15 Internet Information Server 655

15.1 Backing Up and Restoring IIS Configuration Information 656
15.2 Listing Web Sites 662
15.3 Creating a Site 666
15.4 Starting an IIS Site 674
15.5 Deleting a Site 675
15.6 Creating Virtual Web Directories 677
15.7 Setting File and Directory Properties 679
15.8 Creating a Web Directory Application 685
15.9 Maintaining Server Bindings 689
15.10 Setting IP Security 691

Chapter 16 Exchange Server 695

16.1 Creating a Mailbox 695
16.2 Setting Mailbox Properties 710
16.3 Setting Mailbox Limits 717
16.4 Creating a Custom Recipient 719
16.5 Maintaining Mailbox E-mail Addresses 722
16.6 Creating a Distribution List 725
16.7 Enumerating a Distribution List 727
16.8 Creating a Recipients Container 729
16.9 Deleting an Exchange Object 732
16.10 Searching an Exchange Server 733

Chapter 17 Security 739

17.1 Setting NT Share Security 740
17.2 Setting File Permissions 751
17.3 Setting Directory Security 759
17.4 Changing User Access to the Exchange 5.5 Recipients Container 773
17.5 Copying a File with Its Security Settings 777
17.6 Taking Ownership of Files 780
17.7 Setting Active Directory Permissions 781

Index 793

Foreword

"Things are more like they are now than they ever have been before. . ."

I've always wanted to see that statement in print. In the monolithic data centers of yesteryear it was an amusing sarcasm because change wasn't really all that rapid. Today, it rings with too much truth to really be humorous anymore. With more and more layers appearing monthly to the world of software and servers, this once comic remark has become merely a fair comment of the pace we are moving at.

After nearly 30 years of facility management, I never cease to be amazed at the administrators who rush in early on Monday morning to restart certain services in order to clear up memory leaks or change the announcement screens activated by login scripts. The first coffee of the morning is enjoyed while poring diligently over the event logs of the night before and accompanied by frantic typing to clear out the scratch file space chewed up by the scheduled procedures from last night's processes and flashing e-mail windows sending out updates and notices to the rest of the crew advising them of points of interest they should delve into as first-priority tasks for the day. With powerful operating systems that promise shortened development cycles and more visual access to the inner world of electronic processing we still seem to be stuck in the mind rut of clicking and typing.

As a consultant of many years I would drag around my backup tape of evolutionary timesaving utilities developed under the Digital Equipment Corporation operating system known as VMS. These utilities were a series of scripts I wrote under the DCL scripting language. They performed a variety of normal facility management tasks. These were embodied into simple and short symbols that allowed me the freedom to perform far-reaching administrative feats with very little sweat. "Who tried to intrude on the system last night?" "Which batch queues were still running jobs that had been started the day before or at least longer than 6 hours ago?" I didn't want to see all the fluff that had only been paying their way for less than 15 minutes. It never ceased to amaze me how many colleagues still typed the full DCL commands. Most of them with all those long-winded switches that took longer to tap out than they did to execute. God forbid if they made a typing mistake that forced them to start all over again on the laborious finger trek they had embarked on. I was accustomed to automated scripting with more power available in a single script than three consultants working under a blank purchase order.

When I first encountered Windows, it was a joy to play what I call "mouse hockey" on the setup screens and configure the system to operate efficiently and smoothly to a fine degree of granularity. But disks filled up. Services would just stop running and told you so in the event log because alerts didn't make it through to me while I was logged out. I wanted to quickly create 50 user accounts, create their directories, and assign security and an Exchange e-mail account from a text file. There was a piece of Windows missing—DOS didn't send mail to me as a result of an event in the event log and I couldn't control the Task Scheduler without being armed with a mouse.

Windows Script Host (WSH) promised to make all this stuff automated and possible to do. I have been enjoying the process of relearning the language of automation and reduced administration under the Windows operating system. In his book, Stein has opened up, and shed light on, a number of dark and scary places for me. I have started to understand VBScripting and some of the powerful facilities that Windows has to offer, such as Active Directory Services Interface (ADSI), Collaborative Data Objects (CDO), and Windows Management Instrumentation (WMI). The real value in reading this book is learning the diversity with which you can deploy WSH to do the grunt work for you. The enjoyable part will be realizing that, in using WSH, the only limitation you will encounter is your imagination.

Mike Rouleau
Director, Information Services
H.Y. Louie Co. Ltd.

About the Author

Stein Borge has worked in the IT industry for the last 10 years. He's developed applications using Visual Basic, Access, and SQL Server, and he's developed web applications using Active Server Pages. Along the way, he has also performed Windows NT administrative tasks, including implementing Exchange and IIS servers.

About the Technical Reviewer

Eric Lippert has been a member of the Microsoft Scripting Technologies Team for the last 5 years. Most of that time was spent working on the Windows Script Host, the VBScript engine, and the forthcoming JScript .NET engine. He tries to write at least one line of bug-free code every day.

Acknowledgments

I WOULD LIKE to acknowledge Dan Appleman and Apress for making the publication of this book a reality. Also, Eric Lippert for very forthcoming views and opinions on the book's content. And a competent, professional, and very patient production team, especially when I didn't meet my deadlines (which was most of the time).

CHAPTER 1

Introduction

Windows Script Host (WSH) provides a powerful environment for hosting scripting languages. It is Microsoft's replacement for MS-DOS batch files, and it provides a modern, 32-bit environment for developing Windows scripts.

MS-DOS batch files have long been available to perform repetitive task automation, such as file manipulation, but they are limited in performing complex conditional logic evaluation and repetitive loops. Batch files are not very extendible; they do not provide any access to Windows internal operations. The only way to access these operations from a batch file is to have a command-line program to perform the operation.

WSH provides programmatic enhancements such as looping, conditional expressions, and the ability to create subroutines and functions, as well as the ability to perform complex operations through external objects. Using these objects, WSH scripts can automate almost any task that can otherwise be performed through a Windows user interface. These tasks include (but are not limited to) user administration, database access, e-mail operations, and Windows server administrative tasks, such as Internet Information Server (IIS) and Exchange server.

WSH is installed with Windows 98, ME, 2000, 2003, and XP. It is available as a separate installation for Windows 95 and NT 4.0.

What Is WSH?

WSH provides a hosted environment for scripting engines. WSH is not a language, and it doesn't rely on any particular language to implement scripts. The default WSH installation provides Visual Basic Scripting Edition (VBScript) and JScript scripting engines.

On their own, these scripting engines can't do anything—they require a host such as WSH to execute scripts. These scripting engines are used by Internet Explorer (IE) for client-side scripts and Active Server Pages (ASP) for server-side scripts.

In WSH, the scripting engines are manipulated by `wscript.exe` and `cscript.exe` applications. Scripts executed using `cscript.exe` send output to the console. Scripts executed using `wscript.exe` send output to the Windows graphical user interface.

COM Automation

The WSH scripting languages provide a huge improvement over the old MS-DOS batch scripts by providing conditional expression evaluation, loops, and the ability to create subroutines. However, the scripting engines do not provide any access to Windows operations.

For example, the VBScript and JScript engines do not have any built-in methods to copy a file or modify a registry value. Because the scripting engines are used by IE and ASP, you wouldn't want to be able to do this, as there wouldn't be anything stopping somebody from creating a Web page to delete all your files. This wouldn't make IE very popular.

Fortunately, scripting engines hosted by WSH allow you to create COM automation objects. COM objects are "black box"–like libraries that can manipulate data, call other executables, or manipulate the operating system on your behalf. COM objects are themselves typically written in languages such as Visual Basic, Delphi, or C++, though they can also be written in VBScript or JScript using the Windows Script Component technology (described later in this section).

Using WSH, you can create instances of these objects. For example, you could create an instance of a `File` object that represents the file `d:\data\report.doc` (specific details on how to do this are covered in Chapter 5). You can have multiple instances of an object, so you could have a `File` object that represents the file `d:\data\report.doc` and another that represents `d:\data\budget.xls`. Each object instance is independent of other instances.

COM objects tasks are performed by calling *methods*. A method is a procedure that performs a specific operation, similar to a subroutine that can be created in VBScript or JScript. An example of a method for the `File` object is `Delete`, which deletes the file represented by the object instance.

Information about the objects is stored in *properties*. Information about the file size represented by a `File` object can be read from the `Size` property. Properties can be read-only or read/write. In the case of the `File` object, the `Size` property is read-only. The `File` object's `Name` property is read/write, which allows you to read the filename as well as write to it, which would rename the file.

WSH includes a number of objects, which are listed in Table 1-1.

Table 1-1. WSH Objects

OBJECT	TASKS	CHAPTER
`WScript.Shell`	Run applications and manipulate environment variables and the Windows registry	Chapter 2 and Chapter 6
`WScript.Network`	Manipulate network resources, such as shares and printers	Chapter 4
`Scripting.FileSystemObject`	Perform file operations	Chapter 5

These objects allow you to perform basic Windows operations. If you want to perform more complex operations, you must rely on other COM objects. Microsoft provides many objects to perform more complicated tasks. Table 1-2 lists tasks and the appropriate objects to perform the tasks.

Table 1-2. Tasks and Appropriate Objects

TASK	OBJECT	CHAPTER
System administration	Windows Management Instrumentation (WMI)	Chapter 10
Network administration	Active Directory Services Interface (ADSI)	Chapter 14
Exchange administration	ADSI	Chapter 16
IIS administration	ADSI	Chapter 15
Database support	ActiveX Data Objects (ADO)	Chapter 13
Mail operations	Collaborative Data Objects (CDO)	Chapter 12
Security operations	ADSI/WMI	Chapter 17

Using these objects, you can build sophisticated administrative scripts. You could have a script that creates a new user account, Exchange mailbox, and user share, and applies appropriate security, all in one step.

You could also create a script that monitors event logs and disk space and sends an e-mail to the appropriate user when a certain condition occurs, such as a locked-out account or a user directory exceeding a space limit. The possibilities are endless.

If you are using Windows 2000, 2003, or XP, the objects listed in Table 1-2 are installed by default (except CDO). Windows 98 and ME include older versions of WMI and ADO. All of the components are available as (free) separate installations for Windows 9*x*/ME and NT 4.0.

In addition to these components, you can automate common Windows applications. All Office applications can be automated, so you can use WSH to build Word documents, Excel spreadsheets, or Visio diagrams. Internet Explorer is also a COM component, and WSH can use it to build user interfaces or manipulate Web pages. Microsoft Messenger can be automated to perform instant messaging operations.

If all of this is not enough, there are thousands of third-party components that perform all ranges of operations. Examples in this book include the ping and FTP components (discussed in Chapter 11).

And if you can't find an object to perform a particular operation, you can write your own objects using a programming language such as Visual Basic or C++.

Version 2.0 Features

By nature, the WSH environment is very extensible as a result of its capability to create COM components. There are a large number of free and third-party components to perform various operations. Furthermore, any new capabilities can be added by writing a component.

However, there are a number of scripting environment features that cannot be implemented using COM components and that require changes to the internal workings of the WSH hosting engine.

The main problem stems from the fact that WSH doesn't depend on any given scripting language. There have been improvements in the VBScript and JScript scripting engines, and new WSH functionality has been added. Because the scripting engines are used by other applications, such as IIS and especially IE, there are many considerations that have to be taken into account when making changes to the engines. For example, JScript conforms to the ECMAScript language specification, an international standard for Web scripting, and making major changes to the engine might render Web pages noncompliant to these standards. The main feature missing from WSH version 1.0 is reusability. There was no way of reusing code libraries in WSH scripts. While kludges could be implemented, they never promoted easy and effective code reuse.

WSH version 2.0 introduces code reusability features in Windows Script Files (WSF) and Windows Script Components (WSC). These features provide language-independent code reusability enhancements. WSF implements include files, which allow for script libraries to be included in other files, while WSC allows COM components to be created using scripting languages.

WSF Files

WSH version 2.0 introduces the Windows Script File (WSF) file format, which adds many enhancements, such as including files and the ability to interface COM object type libraries without losing the language-independent nature of WSH.

WSF files "encapsulate" script logic in Extensible Markup Language (XML). XML is a markup language that resembles HTML.

XML is built up of elements. Each element requires an opening and closing tag. An opening tag is the name of the element surrounded in angle brackets (< and >). A closing tag is the same as the opening tag except the element name is prefixed with a forward slash (/). Information stored between the tags is called the *body* of the element. An example of an XML element is `<greeting>Hello</greeting>`, where `<greeting>` is the opening tag, `Hello` is the body and `</greeting>` is the closing tag.

A WSF script is composed of a number of elements. The minimum requirements for a successful WSF script are a `<job>` element and a `<script>` element.

A WSF script can contain multiple "jobs." Think of a job as a stand-alone script. Each job runs independently. The `<job>` element identifies the job(s) in the file. Using the `<job>` element, you can group multiple programs within a WSF file. The body of the job must contain one or more `<script>` elements to execute a script. The `<script>` element contains the actual script code. The following code snippet displays "Hello World":

```
<job>
 <script language="VBScript">
   'display hello world
   WScript.Echo "Hello World"
 </script>
 </job>
```

You can execute WSF scripts by double-clicking them from Explorer or entering the script name from the command line.

The `<script>` element identifies the script language using an XML element attribute. An XML attribute allows additional information to be associated with an element tag. The `<script>` element's `language` attribute identifies the scripting language for the job, such as VBScript, JScript, PerlScript, or whatever scripting engines are installed on your machine. An XML element may have more than one attribute, and attributes may be optional.

The `<script>` element supports an optional `src` attribute. The `src` attribute implements *include* files. The include file is common throughout all mainstream programming languages and was a much-requested addition to WSH, because it provides code sharing and reuse.

The include file is a separate script file whose contents become accessible from the main script. This is extremely useful for commonly used code and program constants. The include file must be in the script dialect specified by the language attribute and it cannot be a WSF file. The following file, `include.vbs`, contains code to be included in a WSF file:

```
'include.vbs
Sub HelloWorld
   WScript.Echo "Hello World"
End Sub
```

The file is included in the following WSF script file:

```
<job>
 <script language="VBScript"
 src="include.vbs">
   'display a message
```

```
  HelloWorld
</script>
</job>
```

If a directory path is omitted, the include file must reside in the same directory as the WSF script. Directory paths can be either a local path or a UNC path.

If you want to use multiple include files within a job, add an additional <script> element for each file you want to include:

```
<job>
<script language="VBScript" src="include1.vbs"/>
<script language="VBScript" src="include.vbs">
  'display a little message
 HelloWorld
 HelloWorld2
</script>
</job>
```

The HelloWorld2 subroutine is stored in the include1.vbs file. Note the first <script> element does not have a corresponding </script> tag, but rather is terminated with a forward slash (/). This is a valid method of representing an XML element, but it only applies if there is no element body.

A job can contain multiple <script> elements. The <script> elements are executed sequentially, and they can be composed of different script dialects:

```
<job>
  <script language="VBScript">
   Wscript.Echo "Hello World from VBScript"
 </script>
 <script language="JScript">
   var strMsg = "Hello World from JScript";
   WScript.Echo(strMsg);
 </script>
</job>
```

Variables declared in <script> elements become available to following <script> elements, even if they are declared in a different script language. In the following snippet, the variable strMessage is declared in a VBScript script element, and it is used in the following element implemented in JScript:

```
<job>
  <script language="VBScript">
   Dim strMessage
```

```
   strMessage = "Hello World"
   Wscript.Echo strMessage & " from VBScript"
 </script>
 <script language="JScript">
   var msg2 = "hello";
   WScript.Echo(strMessage + " from JScript");
 </script>
</job>
```

While variables and constants can be shared through different script blocks, they are only available in the order they are declared, so a variable declared in the second script block would not be available in the first.

As mentioned earlier, there can be multiple jobs in a WSF file. Jobs can be used to group related scripts into one file. For example, you could have a backup script and a restore script in one file. If there are multiple jobs in a script, the `<package>` element must be included in the script. The body of the `<package>` element contains all of the jobs in the script. When you include more than one job, each job must be given a unique ID to identify the job within the package. The ID is assigned by setting an `id` attribute in each `<job>` element, as demonstrated by the following script, `2job.wsf`:

```
<package>
 <job id ="Display Job 1">
   <script language="VBScript" >
   'display a little message
   Wscript.Echo "This is job 1"
   </script>
 </job>
 <job id ="display2">
  <script language="VBScript">
   'display a little message
   Wscript.Echo " This is job 2"
  </script>
 </job>
</package>
```

To execute a specific job, use the `//job` switch with either `cscript` or `wscript`:

```
wscript | cscript //job:jobname scriptfile.wsf
```

where `jobname` is the name of the job and `scriptfile.wsf` is the `.wsf` script file where the job is located. For example:

```
cscript //job:display2 2job.wsf
```

would execute the job named display2 from the job2 script. If the job ID contains spaces, the //job parameter and job name must be enclosed by double quotes:

```
cscript "//job: Display Job 1" 2job.wsf
```

WSF jobs can contain a number of optional XML elements. While the ability to use include files makes the creation and use of constant files easier, it still can be tedious to build and maintain include files. The <reference> element provides support for referencing COM object type libraries. A type library contains information on all methods, properties, and constants exposed by an object. Referencing a type library in a WSF file makes all constants available to the script. The syntax is as follows:

```
<reference object="ProgID"|guid="GUID" [version="versnum"]/>
```

Specify either the ProgID or guid for the object type library you want to reference. The ProgID is a "friendly" alias for a COM object. The version attribute is optional and specifies the version number of the type library. The default value is 1.0.

In the following example, a reference to the type library for the File System Object (FSO) component object is made, using the ProgID Scripting.FileSystemObject:

```
<job>
<reference object="Scripting.FileSystemObject" />
<script language="VBscript">
  Const strFile = "c:\autoexec.bat"
  Dim objFSO, objTS

  Set objFSO = CreateObject("Scripting.FileSystemObject")
  Set objTS = objFSO.OpenTextFile(strFile, ForReading, False, TristateFalse)

  WScript.Echo objTS.ReadAll
  objTS.Close
</script>
</job>
```

All constants exposed through the object's type libraries are made available to the script. See Solution 9.1 for information on using the Word automation object.

Many type libraries do not have a ProgID and must be referenced by a globally unique identifier (GUID), which uniquely identifies the object and is also known as a class ID (CLSID):

```
<job>
<comment>Reference the Excel type library</comment>
<reference guid="{00020813-0000-0000-C000-000000000046}"/>
<script language="VBScript">
  </script>
</job>
```

Another WSF element is `<object>`. The `<object>` element creates an instance of a COM object, similar to the VBScript `CreateObject` methods or the JScript new `ActiveXObject` methods:

```
<object id="objID" classid="GUID"|progid="ProgID"  [events="Yes|No"]/>
```

The `objID` parameter is used to identify the object in the script.

Use either `ProgID` or `GUID` to identify the COM object you want to create. These parameters are the same as those used by the `<reference>` element:

```
<job>
 <comment>Create FSO object and show temp file name</comment>
 <object id="objFSO" progid="Scripting.FileSystemObject"/>
  <script language="VBScript">
    'show a temporary file name
    WScript.Echo objFSO.GetTempName
  </script>
</job>
```

The optional `events` attribute allows object events to be "sinked." If this attribute is set to `Yes` or `True`, the script will receive any events fired by the object. See the "Events" section of this chapter for more information.

WSF files support a `<resource>` element that can be used as an alternative to script constants. The information stored by the `<resource>` element is available to all `<script>` elements within a WSF job and is scripting-language independent:

```
<resource id=strResourceID>resource text</resource>
```

The `strResourceID` parameter identifies the resource and can contain alphanumeric characters, including spaces. The body of the element is the resource.

Resources are accessed using the `getResource` function:

```
strResource = getResource(strResourceID)
```

`strResourceID` is the `<resource>` element ID and is case-sensitive.

While the <resource> element does not provide any great advantage over program constants, it is very useful for multiline string messages. The <resource> element's body can span as many lines as required, and it does not require any carriage returns to be added at the end of each line:

```
<job>
 <comment>Create FSO object and show temp file name</comment>
   <script language="VBScript">
    Wscript.Echo getResource("Welcome Message")
  </script>
<resource id="Welcome Message">The advantage of using the resource element
is that resource text can span multiple lines,
so you can avoid multi-line statements. </resource>
</job>
```

The XML version of the script file is determined by version argument, and it should be set to 1.0. The optional DTDflag parameter identifies if a reference to a Document Type Definition (DTD) is made in the script. This does not apply to WSF scripts and should not be set.

If used, the <?XML> element must appear in the first line of your WSF script:

```
<?XML version="1.0" ?>
 <job>
  <script language="VBScript">
   'display hello world
   Wscript.Echo "Hello World"
  </script>
 </job>
```

Adding the <?XML> element instructs the script interpreter to check all elements for XML syntax, including the body of the <script> element. If any XML characters are included in the script body, they will be checked for valid XML syntax:

```
<?XML version="1.0" ?>
 <job>
  <script language="VBScript">
   'display hello world
   Wscript.Echo "<Hello World>"
  </script>
 </job>
```

Including the angle brackets in the "Hello World" message will generate an error because the element is parsed for valid XML syntax. Use the ![CDATA[section element to encapsulate any script code:

```
<?XML version="1.0" ?>
 <job>
   <script language="VBScript">
   <![CDATA[
    'display hello world
    Wscript.Echo "<Hello World>"
   ]]>
  </script>
 </job>
```

Using CDATA ensures that the XML parser ignores any text that appears in the body of the <script> element.

```
<?XML version="1.0" ?>
 <job>
   <script language="VBScript">
   <![CDATA[
    'display hello world
    Wscript.Echo "<Hello World>"
   ]]>
  </script>
</job>
```

You can add comments to WSF jobs and packages using the XML comment tag sequence <!-- and --> or a <comment> element. Anything that appears between the <!-- and --> tags or <comment> element is ignored by the interpreter:

```
<?XML version="1.0" ?>
<package>
 <!--comment
  Script:hello.wsf
  Description:displays a nice message
 -->
 <comment>Another comment</comment>
  <job>
   <script language="VBScript">
    <![CDATA[
      Wscript.Echo "Hello World"
    ]]>
   </script>
 </job>
<package>
```

Scripting Components

COM components have traditionally been developed using languages such as Visual Basic, Visual C++, and Delphi. WSH 2.0 introduced Windows Script Components (WSC), which allows COM components to be implemented using scripting languages.

Window Script Components use the scripting engines included with WSH, such as VBScript or JScript, as well as third-party scripting engines, such as ActivePerl. The components do not use the WSH commands `cscript` or `wscript` to execute the scripts. Script components do not have access to the `WScript` object exposed by the WSH environment.

Script components can be used by any programming environment that supports the creation of COM objects. This pretty much covers any Windows programming language that is available, and includes Visual Basic, C++, Delphi, and the Microsoft Office Visual Basic programming environment.

Script components require the `scrobj.dll` file as well as the script engines the component was developed in to be used. As long as the component was developed using VBScript or JScript, all you require is a recent version (2.0 or later) of WSH. Script components also don't require any development environment to be installed to maintain them; all you need is a simple text editor such as Notepad.

It's important to note that script components are not suitable for all purposes. Because they're not compiled, there is a performance hit when using them, and the lack of an integrated development environment makes creating and debugging large components tedious.

Script Wizard

Before you create a component, you should determine what the component is going to do. You should plan what *properties*, *methods*, and *events* the component will expose.

Windows Script Components encapsulate the component logic using XML, similar to WSF files. WSC uses XML elements to expose the operations performed and information about the component, such as properties and methods.

Components can be built using a text editor, as with any WSH script. A WSC "wizard" is included with the WSH installation that simplifies the construction of a component by asking a number of questions about the component, such as the name, description, properties, and methods, and then generates the "skeleton" code that you can populate with the support script logic.

To use the wizard, start the Windows Script Component Wizard (see Figure 1-1), which you can find by clicking the Start button and selecting Programs > Microsoft Windows Script.

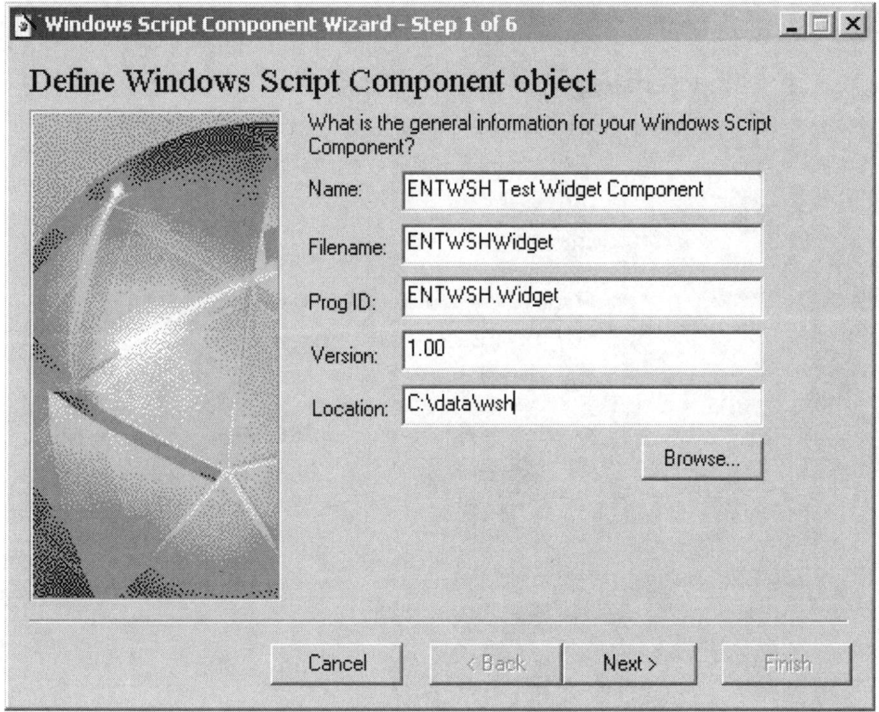

Figure 1-1. The Windows Script Component Wizard

The Name is the name or description of the component.

The Filename is the name of the file that contains the component and is created with a WSC extension.

The Prog ID (henceforth "`ProgID`") is used to identify the object when creating instances of it. There are no technical restrictions on naming `ProgID`s—they can be any string that you like that does not contain any spaces. However, there are some commonly used conventions. Usually a `ProgID` is a description of the company or class of functionality, followed by a period, followed by the name of the object, which is optionally followed by a period and then a version number. For instance, `Word.Document.8`. This convention helps guarantee uniqueness. Version is a number associated with the component, and it defaults to 1.0.

Location is the directory where the Windows Script Component will be created.

The next screen (see Figure 1-2) displays options related to the scripting language and additional options.

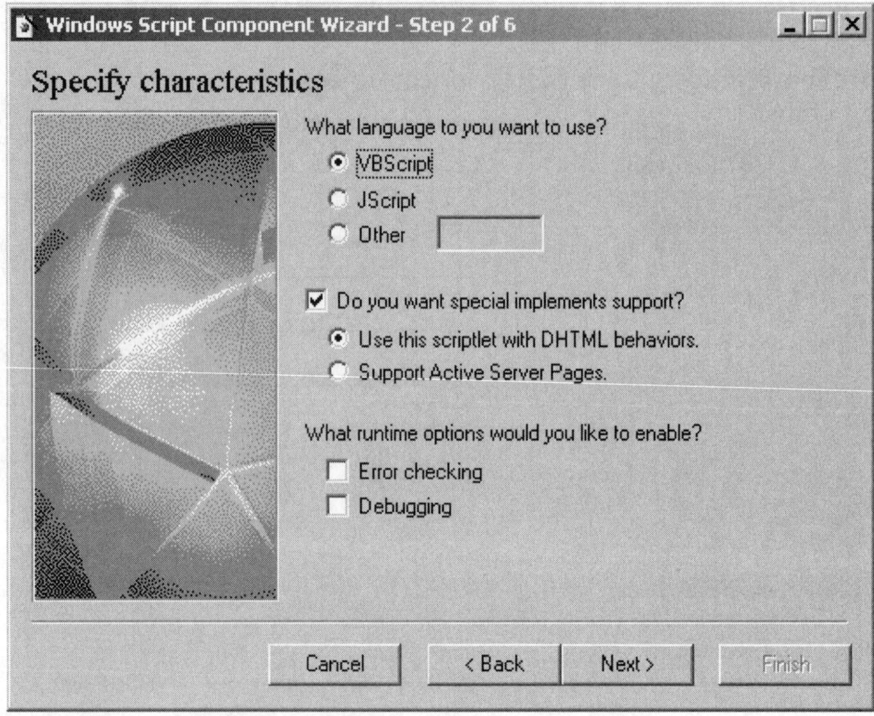

Figure 1-2. Options related to the scripting language

Select the scripting language the component will be implemented in. The DHTML and ASP options should not be set if you do not intend to use the component within a Web page or an Active Server Pages page. Set the "Error checking" and/or "Debugging" check boxes if you want to debug your component (see the "Advanced Script Component Topics" section for more information).

The next dialog box (see Figure 1-3) allows you to specify component properties.

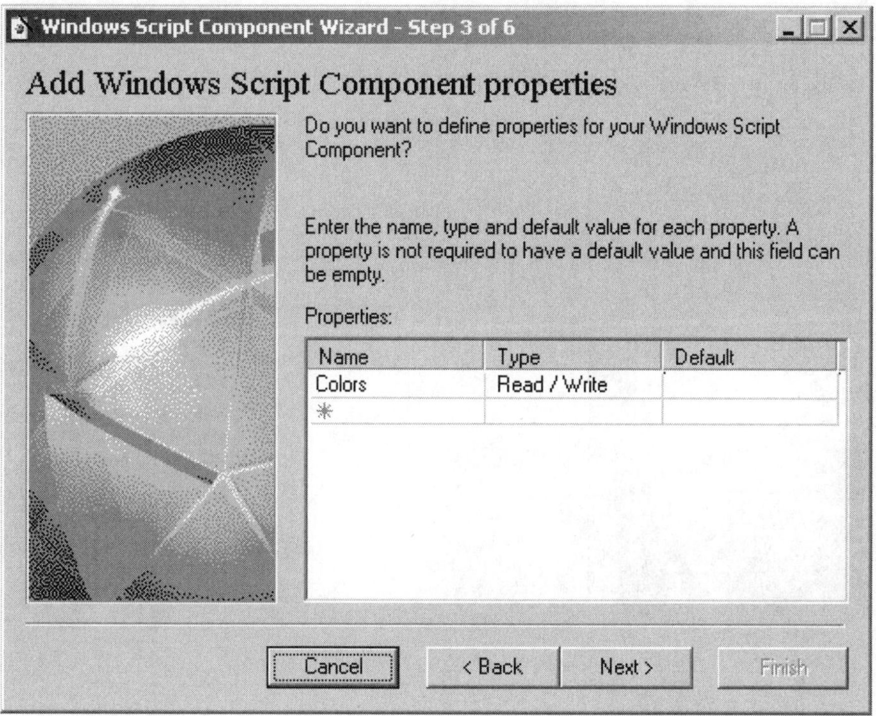

Figure 1-3. Specifying component properties

Property names cannot contain spaces. For each property, you must select if it can be read from and/or written to, and optionally you can assign a default value, which determines the initial value the property will contain when an instance of the object is first created.

After the properties have been determined, you can set the methods that are exposed by the object, as shown in Figure 1-4.

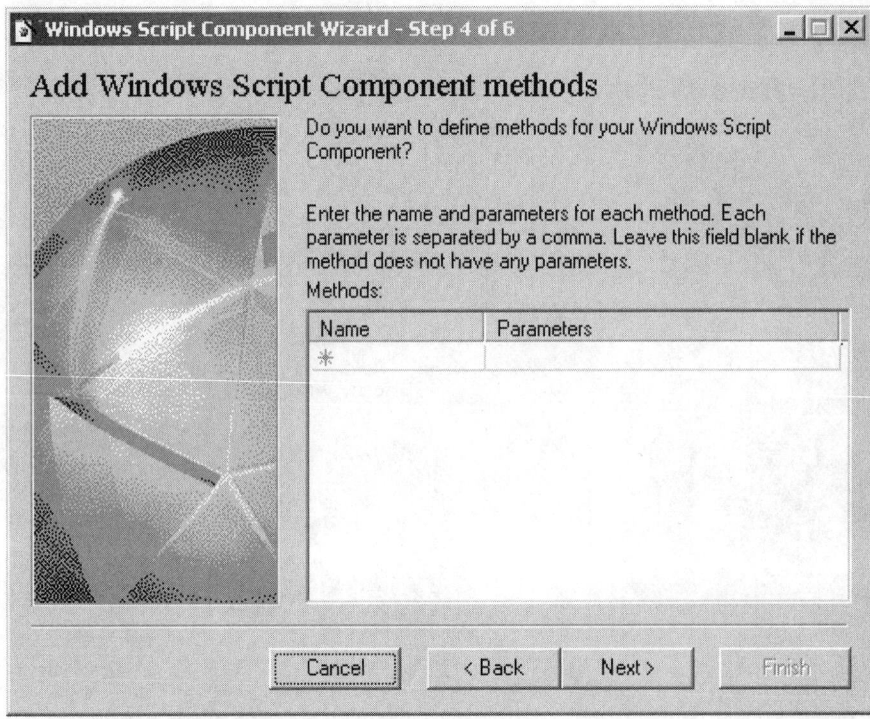

Figure 1-4. Setting the methods that are exposed by the object

Enter the name of each method (if there are any), and if the methods require parameters list them in the Parameters text box. Separate each method parameter by a comma.

Finally, you are prompted to specify any events exposed by the component. This doesn't seem to work in the current version of the WSC Wizard. See the "Events" section later in the chapter for more details on events and how to add them.

The last screen (see Figure 1-5) lists the information that you have specified for the component. When you click the Finished button, the component file is created.

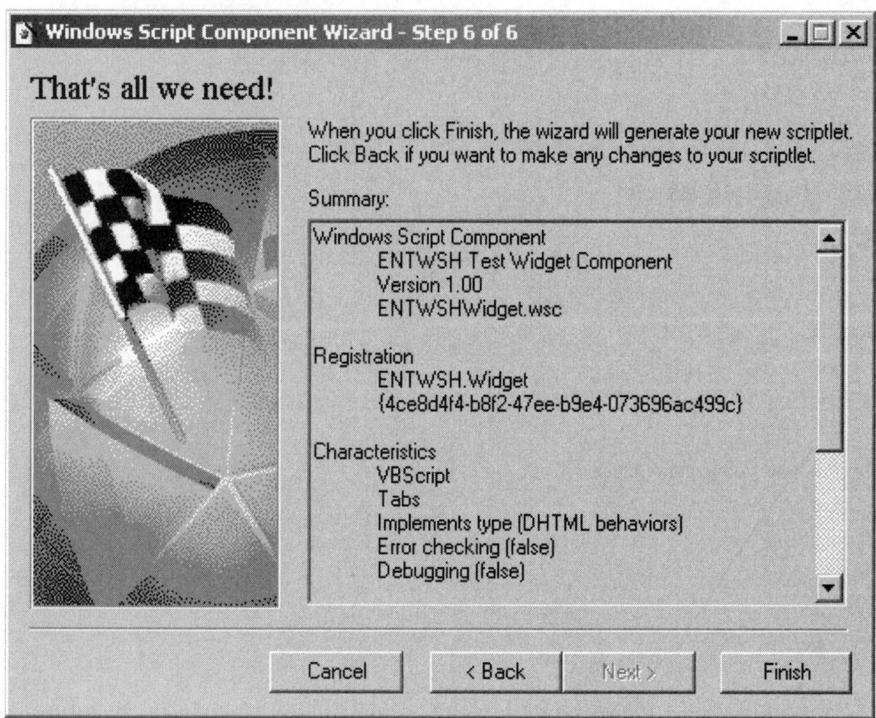

Figure 1-5. Listing of the information that you specified for the component

> **NOTE** *A component created using the WSC Wizard can be modified and extended at any time using a text editor; however, you cannot use the wizard to modify existing components.*

You now have a "skeleton" to add program logic to:

```
<?xml version="1.0"?>
<component>

<registration
    description="ENTWSH Test Widget Component"
    progid="ENTWSH.Widget"
    version="1.00"
    classid="{35f5fa40-6ace-11d4-bce1-00104b164591}"
>
</registration>
<public>
```

```
    <property name="Color">
        <get/>
        <put/>
    </property>
</public>
<script language="VBScript">
<![CDATA[
dim Color

function get_Color()
    get_Color = Color
end function

function put_Color(newValue)
   Color = newValue
end function
]]>
</script>
</component>
```

You can use the code generated by the wizard to look at what script components are composed of.

A WSC file consists of XML elements. A WSC file must have at least one `<component>` element. The body of the `<component>` element contains the component logic.

The `<registration>` element contains information used to register the component:

```
<registration
    description="ENTWSH Test Widget Component"
    progid=" ENTWSH.Widget"
    version="1.00"
    classid="{35f5fa40-6ace-11d4-bce1-00104b164591}"
>
```

The `description` attribute corresponds to the Name field in the first WSC Wizard dialog box. The `ProgID` and `version` attributes correspond to the fields with the same names in the first WSC Wizard dialog box. The `classid` attribute is generated by the WSC Wizard and is a unique identifier used to identify the component. Do not change the value of `classid` unless you are familiar with how it is used. The `<public>` element contains the public interface, which lists all properties and methods exposed by the component.

Each property is contained in a <property> element. The name of the property is set using a name attribute. The <property> element's body contains <put/> if the property can be written to and/or <get/> if the property can be read:

```
 <property name="Color">
        <get/>
        <put/>
</property>
```

Any methods exposed by the component are defined by the <method> element. The name of the method is identified by the name attribute. Any method parameters are identified by <parameter> elements in the body of the <method> element. The parameter names are specified by a name attribute. Each method parameter requires a parameter attribute:

```
<method name="CreateFile">
  <parameter name="filepath"/>
  <parameter name="bOverWrite"/>
</method >
```

The actual code is contained in a <script> element, which is the same as the script element used in WSF files. The element requires a language attribute to identify the scripting language the component is implemented in and an optional <src> element, which contains the path name to an include file.

You can add any code to the body of the <script> element. You will notice that the WSC Wizard has added code to the body of the element. Functions are created for each property defined in the <public> element.

For each "read" property, there is a corresponding function identified by the property name and prefixed with get_. The value returned by the get_ function is the value that the component property will return.

Each "write" property has a corresponding function identified by the property name prefixed with put_. Each put_ function contains one parameter, which is used to assign the value to the property variable.

The WSC Wizard creates a variable for each property. The name of the variable is the same as the property name. This variable is automatically inserted into the corresponding get_ and put_ functions. You are not constrained by this convention, and you can rename the variables to match any naming convention that suits you. In the following code snippet, the Color variable created by the WSC Wizard is renamed to comply with a naming convention:

```
Dim strColor
Function get_Color()
    get_Color = strColor
End Function
```

```
Function put_Color(newValue)
    strColor = newValue
End Function
```

You may be required to rename property variables if they clash with standard scripting language–reserved keywords, one example being `Date`. To perform XML compliance checking, add a `?xml` declaration element as the first line in the script as you would with a WSF file. The WSC Wizard automatically adds the element to the file.

Component Registration

Once the component has been completed, it can be registered. Registering a component makes it available to other COM object consumers, such as Visual Basic, C++, Delphi, VBA, or WSH scripts.

A script can be registered by using the `regsvr32.exe` command-line registration program. The syntax for `regsvr32.exe` is as follows:

```
regsvr32.exe filename
```

where `filename` represents the name of the file to register.

Script components can also be registered through Explorer. To register a component using this method, find the component file in Explorer. Right-click the file to display a context-sensitive menu. From the menu, select Register.

Components may be unregistered. Unregistering a component removes any reference to it from the registry and prevents any instances from being created using the `ProgID`. To unregister a component using `regsvr32`, repeat the steps to register a component but add `/u` to the command line:

```
regsvr32.exe filename/u
```

To unregister through Explorer, find the component, right-click the file, and select the Unregister menu option.

Component code can be executed when a component is registered or unregistered by adding a `Register` or `Unregister` function to the component, respectively.

These functions can perform one-off installation operations when the component is registered, such as creating registry entries for storing component-related information, or in the case of unregistering the component, removing registry entries.

The code must reside in the registration event and be contained in a <script> element:

```
<registration
    description=" ENTWSH Register Sample"
    progid=" ENTWSH.RegIT"
    version="1.00"
    classid="{a2e51600-6ce5-11d4-bce1-00104b164591}"
>
<script language="VBScript">
<![CDATA[
'execute at registration, setup registry entries
Function Register()
Dim objShell
  Set objShell = CreateObject("WScript.Shell")
  objShell.RegWrite "HKCU\SOFTWARE\WSHWidget\Path", _
                    "d:\data\wsh"
  Set objShell = Nothing
  Register = False
End function

'execute at component is unregistered, delete registry entries
Function unregister()
 Dim objShell
  On Error Resume Next
  Set objShell = CreateObject("WScript.Shell")
  objShell.RegDelete  "HKCU\SOFTWARE\WSHWidget\Path"
  objShell.RegDelete  "HKCU\SOFTWARE\WSHWidget\"
End function
   ]]>
   </script>
</registration>
```

The preceding <registration> element contains `Register` and `Unregister` functions that are executed when the component is registered/unregistered.

Using Script Components

To use a script component you must create an instance of it by using either the `CreateObject` or `GetObject` methods.

There are two `CreateObject` methods available to WSH scripts: One is exposed through the WScript WSH object and the other is part of the VBScript environment. They are functionally identical for the creation of general objects, but they vary in relation to event sinking and remote object creation. The WScript `CreateObject` method allows for sinking of events (see the "Events" section for more information) and the VBScript method can create remote instances of COM objects (see the "Remote Automation" section for more information).

To create an object, call the `CreateObject` method (either the WScript or VBScript one) and pass the `ProgID` as a parameter:

```
Set objWSC = CreateObject(strProgID)
```

If successful, the methods will return an instance of the object; otherwise, a runtime error will be generated.

To create an instance of a script component using the `GetObject` method instead of the `CreateObject` method, call `GetObject` and pass the path to the component prefixed with `script:`:

```
Set obj = GetObject("script:strPath")
```

`strPath` identifies the path to the component and can be a local path, UNC, or URL. The advantage of using `GetObject` over `CreateObject` is the Windows Script Component does not need to be registered. The following snippet creates an instance of the `ENTWSH.Widget` component using the `script:` prefix:

```
Set objWidget = GetObject("script:\\odin\wsc$\ENTWSHWidget.wsc")
```

This method cannot be used with compiled COM components written in languages such as VB or C++.

Events

A component can be considered a "black box" that exposes predefined operations and information through properties and methods. An event allows an instance of a component to perform a "call back" to the code that created it. This allows the component to call functions in the host script based on operations that occur in the component.

To create an event, add an `<event>` element to the body of the `<public>` element in your script component. An event can contain parameters passed from the component. For each parameter, add a `<parameter>` element to the body of each `<event>` element:

```
<event name="FoundFile">
  <parameter name="filepath"/>
 </event>
```

In this sample, an event called `FoundFile` is defined. The `FoundFile` event has one parameter called `filepath`.

No additional code is required in the component itself to support the event—the actual processing of the event operation occurs in the host script.

The following script component, `ENTWSH.ListFiles`, provides a simple demonstration of events:

```
<?xml version="1.0"?>
<component>
<registration
    description=" ENTWSH List Files"
    progid=" ENTWSH.ListFiles"
    version="1.00"
    classid="{997c9d40-6d12-11d4-bce1-00104b164591}"
>
</registration>
<public>
    <property name="Path">
        <put/>
    </property>
    <method name="Search">
    </method>
    <event name="FoundFile">
      <parameter name="filepath"/>
     </event>
</public>
<?component error="true" debug="true"?>
<script language="VBScript">
<![CDATA[
Dim Path
Function put_Path(newValue)
    Path = newValue
End Function

Function Search()
 Set objFSO = CreateObject("Scripting.FileSystemObject")
 Set objFolder = objFSO.GetFolder(Path)
```

```
 Set objFiles = objFolder.Files
 'fire FoundFile event for each file found
 For Each objFile In objFiles
  fireEvent "FoundFile", objFile.Path
 Next
 Set objFSO = Nothing
End Function
]]>
</script>
</component>
```

The component searches a specified directory and "fires" an event for each file found. A Path property is exposed that identifies the path to search. To perform the search, call the Search method.

The Search method enumerates each file in the specified directory and fires the FoundFile event, which executes a function in the host script. Events are fired using the fireEvent subroutine:

```
fireEvent strEventName[, parameter1, parameter2, parameterx]
```

strEventName is the name of the event to fire. The event must be defined in the component's <public> element. If an event requires parameters, they are passed through the parameters parameter1, parameter2, and so on.

To use events in a script, which is known as *sinking*, use the WScript object's CreateObject method. The term "sinking" refers to the relationship between the object and host script and is analogous to real-world plumbing, where a source supplies water and the sink sucks it away. The object acts as the source, and the host acts as a sink, processing the events from the object. The WScript.CreateObject method takes a second parameter that is used to prefix sinked event function names in the host script.

You want to sink the FoundFile event from the ENTWSH.ListFiles component. If you specify the event prefix to be lf_, you need to create a function called lf_FoundFile in the host script:

```
'create an instance of the ListFiles component
Dim objListFiles
Set objListFiles = Wscript.CreateObject ("ENTWSH.ListFiles","lf_")
objListFiles.Path = "d:\data" 'set the path to search
'call the search method
Call objListFiles.Search
```

```
Set objListFiles = Nothing
'FoundFile event, this is called for each file found in the search
'directory
Sub lf_FoundFile(strPath)
  Wscript.Echo strPath
End Sub
```

The sample script creates an instance of the `ListFiles` object. Any event subroutines are prefixed with `_lf`. The directory `d:\data` is searched, and for each file found the `FoundFile` event is fired. This calls the `lf_FoundFile` routine in the host script, which displays the name of the file.

Event-driven environments can add a layer of complexity to scripts because events may execute segments of code in any given order. An event may call a subroutine that sets a termination flag, signaling the script to terminate, but it's possible another event may fire after that, changing the termination state.

To stop events from being fired through a specific component, use the `WScript.DisconnectObject` method:

```
WScript.DisconnectObject object
```

The `object` parameter identifies the object you want to disconnect events from.

Disconnecting an object does not terminate the operation of the component. All properties and methods are still available, but events fired from the object will not be handled in the host script. You can find another event script in Chapter 5, Solution 5.10. It's a more powerful version of the `ListFiles` object that allows file criteria to be passed as well as performing subdirectory searches.

WSH is not limited to event sinking from script components. Many application objects expose events that WSH can sink. This is demonstrated in Chapter 11, using Internet Explorer events.

Remote Automation

Remote instances of script components (or any other COM component) can be created using WSH, so an instance of script component that resides on computer X can be created from computer Y. This functionality is performed through Distributed COM (DCOM), which is installed with Windows NT, 98, 2000, XP, and 2003. Windows 95 requires a separate installation for DCOM.

Creating remote instances does not require any local support objects the component requires. For example, a component may require database support objects or other components not installed on all computers, or a component may require a great deal of processing ability not available on all machines.

To make a component accessible from remote computers, add a `remoteable` attribute to the `<registration>` element of your script component:

```
<registration
    description=" ENTWSH Test Widget Component"
    progid=" ENTWSH.Widget"
    version="1.00"
    classid="{35f5fa40-6ace-11d4-bce1-00104b164591}"
    remotable="true"
>
</registration>
```

The `remotable` attribute is a Boolean attribute, and if it is set to `True` it indicates that remote instances of the component can be created. No special method is required to register the component.

Once registered, the component becomes available through DCOM. A DCOM-enabled object acts like a normal COM component locally, but instances can also be created remotely. There are a number of steps required to create an object on a remote computer. First you need to ensure the component is configured to work correctly under DCOM.

To configure DCOM components, run the DCOM configuration utility `dcomcnfg.exe`. `Dcomcnfg` allows different levels of permissions to be assigned to components. `Dcomcnfg` is included with all recent Windows operating systems except Windows 95, where it is available as a separate download from `http://www.microsoft.com/com/dcom/dcom95/dcom1_3.asp`.

`Dcomcnfg` is located under the `<Windows>\System32` directory for Windows NT, Windows 2000, Windows 2003, and Windows XP, or `<Windows>\System` for Windows 9*x*. When run, the program lists all components that are available through DCOM, as shown in Figure 1-6.

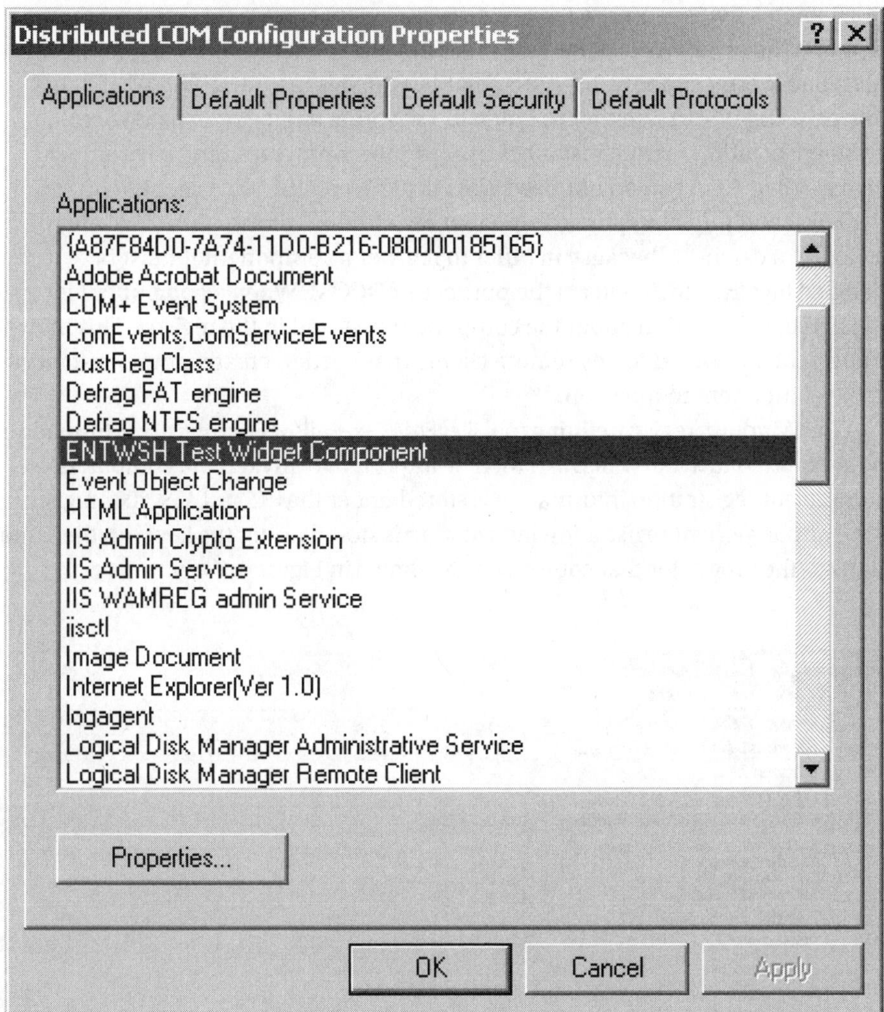

Figure 1-6. Listing all components that are available through DCOM

Script components are stored by their description. You can set permissions to determine who can create remote instances.

NOTE *Windows 9x/ME machines have limited security settings compared to Windows NT/2000/XP.*

Remote clients require a scripting engine or programming language that supports the creation of remote objects. The latest versions of VBScript (5.0 or later) and JScript support this functionality, which is included with WSH 2.0. If you are using WSH 1.0, either upgrade the scripting engine or install WSH 5.6. If you are creating remote instances using another programming environment, such as VB or C++, you do not need WSH installed on the local client.

Local computers require component registration information. This might seem like a catch-22, because in order to register a component it must be installed locally, which defeats the purpose of DCOM. When a component is registered, information about the component is stored in the registry. This information can be copied to any remote clients that need to create remote instances of the component in question.

The Windows registry editing tool, `RegEdit.exe`, allows for registry information to be exported to a file, which can then be imported to any remote computers. Component registration information is stored under the `HKEY_CLASS_ROOT` registry key. The component registration information is stored under the key with the same name as the `ProgID` for that component, as shown in Figure 1-7.

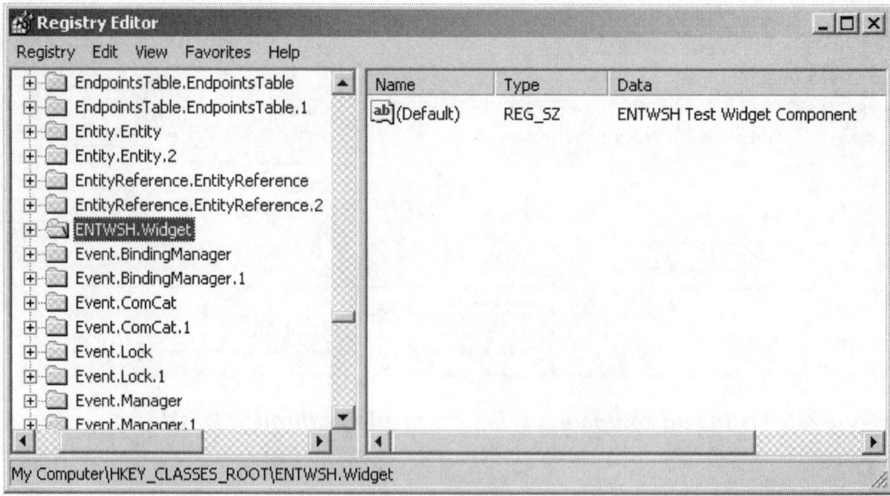

Figure 1-7. Component registration information

To create a registry text file with component registration information, follow these steps:

1. Start RegEdit.

2. Select the key you want to export and select File > Export Registry File.

3. Specify the file to which you want to export the entries. This creates a text file with a `.reg` extension.

To import the registration information from the `.reg` file on the client computer, double-click the file from Explorer. You can also run RegEdit from the command prompt by specifying the `.reg` file as a parameter. Remote instances can be created once the component registration information is stored on the local computer.

Remote instances can only be created using the VBScript `CreateObject` method. If you require events to be fired, use the `WScript.ConnectObject` method to sink to the remote object. When you create an instance, specify the name of the remote computer as the second parameter:

```
'create remote instance of Widget object on computer Odin
Set objRem = CreateObject("ENTWSH.Widget", "\\Odin")
'set property and display value
objRem.Color = "Red"
Wscript.Echo objRem.Color
Set objRem = Nothing
```

The component functions exactly like a locally created instance. There can be performance issues as a result of the additional overhead of network traffic and authentication, but if the remote computer is a more powerful machine than the remote client it might run quicker as a result of the increased processing power available on the remote computer.

Advanced Script Component Topics

The WSC Wizard is capable of creating a functional script component quickly, but you may want to tweak the contents of the component logic or bypass the WSC Wizard altogether and manually create script components.

For component properties, you may want to change the name of functions associated with the property. By default, the name is the property name prefixed with either `get_` or `put_`. Setting the `internalName` attribute for either the `<get>` or `<put>` element will change the associated function name:

```
<property name="Color">
 <get internalName="ReadColor"/>
 <put internalName="WriteColor"/>
</property>
```

In this sample, the name of the property exposed through the component is Color, while the internal function associated with the read (get) operation becomes ReadColor, and the write (put) function becomes WriteColor. If the internalName attributes had been omitted, a get_Color and put_Color function would have been used.

If you want to expose a variable as a property for read/write access through the component without any corresponding get_ or put_ function, add a <property> element with a name attribute but no body:

```
<property name="Age"/>
```

This line would expose a property called Age that would make a script variable of the same name accessible. This needs less code, because it doesn't require any get or put functions, but you cannot perform any of the validation or calculations you could if you used the corresponding get and put functions.

You can assign a different internal variable to the property using the internalName attribute:

```
<property name="Age" internalName="nAge"/>
```

Components often return a "default" property or method. If you create a default property, you do not have to specify the property name when retrieving the property value from code.

If you want to make a property or method the default item for a component, assign a dispid attribute to the <property> or <method> element:

```
<property name="Color" dispid="0">
```

The dispid attribute must be set to 0, and it can only be assigned to one property or method per component.

When an error occurs in a script component, a general runtime error is generated from the host script the component was created in. This doesn't give any detailed information about the cause or location of the error. An XML ?component declaration can be added to the component to allow debugging:

```
<?component [error="bEFlag"] [debug="bDflag"] ?>
```

The declaration enables/disables error and debug functionality. The element can take optional error and debug attributes. Both attributes accept Boolean values. If the error attribute is set to True, detailed error checking is enabled, and when an error occurs in a component, error information is displayed together with the line number on which the error occurred, which is very useful in tracking down the error.

Setting the debug attribute to True enables debugging. Using the component debugging options is useful during development, but they should be removed when the component is deployed for production use. Window Script Components can use many of the same elements as WSF, such as the reference, resource, comment, package, and object elements.

The "package" element performs similarly in WSF files, allowing multiple components to be stored in a single WSC file.

When storing multiple components in a single WSC file, each component element must include an id attribute identifying the component. This id attribute is not used when creating instances of the component using CreateObject.

WSC can use other XML elements, such as reference, resource, comment, and object, and these elements function the same way they do in WSF files. The following sample component demonstrates the use of these elements:

```
<?xml version="1.0"?>
<component>
<registration
    description="ENTWSH XML Element example"
    progid="ENTWSH.XMLExamples"
    version="1.00"
    classid="{23cb7610-6eae-11d4-bce2-00104b164591}"
>
</registration>
<public>
    <method name="WriteFile">
          <parameter name="strPath"/>
    </method>
</public>
 <comment>
  Set debugging on, reference the FSO type library,
  create an instance of the FSO object and create a resource.
 </comment>
 <?component error="true" debug="true"?>
 <reference object="Scripting.FileSystemObject"/>
 <object id="objFSO" progid="Scripting.FileSystemObject"/>
 <resource id="Message">This is a message to write to the file
to test a few additional XML elements that can be used
 </resource>
<script language="VBScript">
  <![CDATA[
Function WriteFile(strPath)
   'write the Message resource to a file specified by the
   'strPath parameter
```

```
  Set objTS = objFSO.OpenTextFile(strPath, ForWriting, True)
  objTS.Write getResource("Message")
  objTS.Close
End Function
]]>
 </script>
</component>
```

The elements must be outside the script element(s). See the “WSF Files” section for details on the syntax and use of these elements.

Creating Type Libraries

If you intend to use script components in other programming environments, such as Visual Basic or Microsoft Office, it can be useful to create a *type library.* A type library contains information about a component's properties, methods, and events. The information contained in the type library can be accessed through development environments using object browsers. Some development environments, such as Visual Basic and VBA, provide IntelliSense programming features that allow autocompletion of statements for objects, methods, and properties.

While type libraries make your life easier when you view an object's methods and properties, in some cases type libraries are required in order to implement certain features—for example, if you want to sink component events in Visual Basic.

A type library is easy to create for a script component. From Explorer, right-click the WSC file you want to create a type library for and select the Generate Type Library option.

This action generates a `scriptlet.tlb` file in the same directory that the WSC file resides. The file should be renamed because it will be overwritten the next time a type library is generated, and this can be a problem as you might overwrite the type library for one component with the contents for another component.

To use the type library from VB, select Project > References. From the VBA development environment, such as recent versions of Microsoft Office applications, select Tools > References (see Figure 1-8).

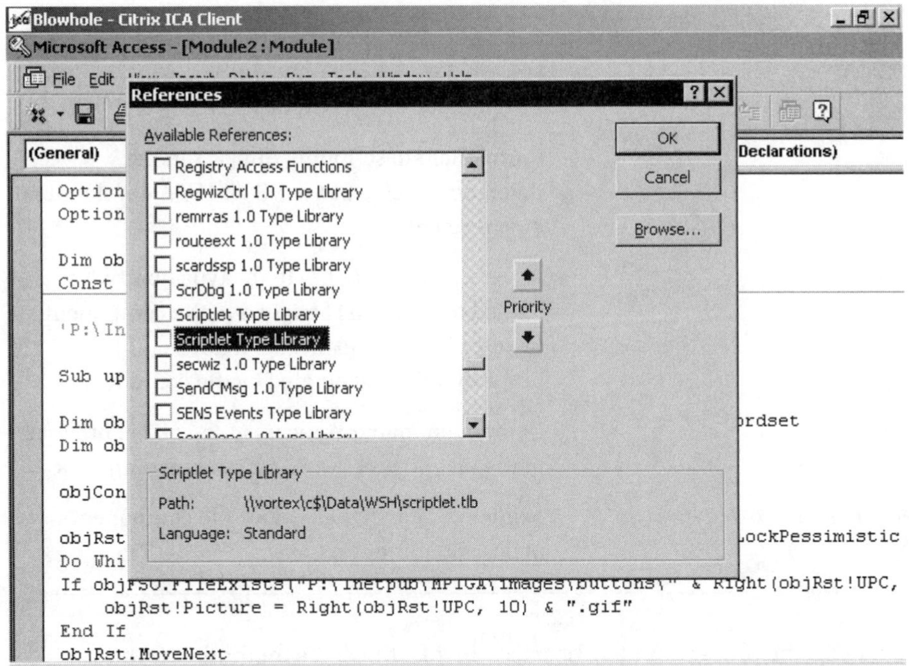

Figure 1-8. Using the type library

If you look at the References dialog box in Figure 1-8, you will see a problem. If you create a type library for more than one component, multiple instances of the Scriptlet Type Library appear in the References dialog box for each component.

While you can use the file path to determine what object the type library is associated with, it is more convenient to be able to assign a specific name with the type library. Script component type libraries can be created programmatically using methods exposed through the `Scriptlet.TypeLib` component.

The programming interface allows more control over information associated with the type library, such as description and version information.

To create a type library, create an instance of the object using the `ProgID` `Scriptlet.TypeLib`.

Add each component you want to include in the type library using the `AddURL` method:

```
objTypeLib.AddURL strURL
```

The `strURL` parameter specifies the path to the script component file. It can be a local path, UNC, or URL. Call the method for each script component you want to include. `AddURL` will not generate any errors if an invalid file path is added, but an error will occur when the type library is generated.

Table 1-3 lists the properties that can be set for the type library.

Table 1-3. Type Library Properties

PROPERTY	DESCRIPTION
Path	File path for the type library to create.
Doc	Component description. Appears in the References dialog box in VB and VBA development environments.
GUID	Assigns a unique GUID to the type library. Not related to the GUID assigned to the component(s) the type library is exposing. If not set, this property will be generated by the component.
Name	Component name. Appears in the object browser in the VB and VBA development environments.
MajorVersion, MinorVersion	Numeric value that identifies the component's major and minor versions.

Once the properties have been set, invoke the `Write` method. The `Write` method attempts to create the type library entry in the registry. If any properties have been set incorrectly (or not set), errors will occur:

```
Set objTypeLib = CreateObject("Scriptlet.TypeLib")
objTypeLib.AddURL "d:\data\wsh\ENTWSHWidget.wsc"

objTypeLib.Path = "d:\data\wsh\ENTWSHWidget.tlb" 'set path to type library

objTypeLib.Guid = "{fb50eb50-7032-11d4-bce3-00104b164591}"
'the Doc property sets description that appears in References dialog

objTypeLib.Doc = "ENTWSH Widget Sample Type library Registry"
'Name sets property that appears in application object browser
objTypeLib.Name = "ENTWSHWidget"
' Create the type library
objTypeLib.Write
```

This sample code generates a type library for the WSH Widget component. Adding type library generation code to the `Register` function of a component's `<registration>` element can automatically create type library information when a component is registered on a computer (see the "Component Registration" section).

It's wise to prefix the `Doc` and `Name` properties with a simple, consistent identifier, such as company or component information, because this can make it easier to identify groups of components in the object browser and References dialog box. All WSC components created in this book are prefixed with `ENTWSH` (Enterprise WSH).

Type libraries can be generated for the same component(s) as many times as you want, and this is often required if additions have been made to the component(s), such as new methods or events that need to be reflected in the object browser.

If you intend to regenerate type libraries, it is wise to set a GUID, even though this is optional. If a GUID is not specified, one is generated by the component, and this will occur each time you regenerate the type library. Every time a type library is added, it adds a new entry to the registry. Even though the old type library registry entries are ignored, they clutter the registry.

If you assign a GUID to a type library, any updates will update the existing type library registry entries. To generate a GUID (never try to guess!) use the WSC Wizard to generate a "dummy" component and copy and paste the GUID into the code.

Streams, Standard Input and Output, and Piping

The ability to manipulate streams is a new feature introduced in WSH 2.0. It is not promoted to the same degree as the WSF files or script components, but it is quite a useful feature that in many ways is as important in providing script reusability.

A *stream* allows access to file contents and the input or output generated by a physical device, such as a keyboard, or a program. Streams have always been a part of Windows and DOS operating systems, but very few command-line applications use streams. The ability to work with streams has always been an important part of the UNIX environment, where data can be manipulated by stringing together commands such as `grep` and `sed`.

Streams are available through the command-line DOS console interface, and they allow data to be passed between files, physical devices, scripts, and other console applications.

To demonstrate how streams work, you will look at how an application would handle streams in WSH 1.0 (which also will work in WSH 2.0) and how it would function if implemented using streams.

You may create a command-line script to perform a specific task. For example, you may want to extract or filter information from a file. In WSH 1.0, you would create a script that would open a file specified by a command-line parameter and send the results to an output file, also specified by a command-line parameter. An example of this could be as follows:

```
Filter.vbs inputfile outputfile
```

In the preceding sample, the first parameter represents the input file and the second parameter represents the output file to store the results.

In WSH 2.0, you can send the results to the *standard output* (StdOut), which is the output stream. Instead of sending the results to an output file, it is written to the standard output instead, which is very similar to writing to a file.

The previous sample program would require no output file as a second parameter—the processed results would be sent to standard output instead. By default, the standard output appears on the standard output device, which is the screen.

If you wanted to send the results to a file, you would redirect them. Redirection is performed by using the redirection symbol, the greater-than sign (>), from the command line:

```
Filter.vbs inputfile > outputfile
```

Using ">>" instead of ">" would append the results to a file.

You can *pipe* standard output results to another command-line application for further processing. Piping allows streams to be passed from one program to another. To pipe information, separate each command with a vertical bar (|). The DOS command-line environment includes a few commands, such as the `more` and `sort` programs:

```
Dir *.* | sort | more
```

In this example, the results of the `dir` command are piped to the DOS `sort` program. The `sort` program reads the results from the `dir` command through the standard input stream and sends the sorted results to the `more` command through standard output. The `more` command pauses at each full screen of information.

In the filter sample, instead of specifying the contents to filter as a file, you could pipe the results to the filter script:

```
type inputfile | cscript Filter.vbs inputfile > outputfile
```

The contents of the input file are piped to the `filter.vbs` script. The results of the script are then redirected to an output file.

Using pipes, you can string together a number of programs that perform specific tasks to perform sophisticated operations. Pipes are used throughout this book as a method of passing information between scripts. Chapter 6 provides more detailed information on how to work with streams.

Additional Resources

No one book or publication can cover all topics. There are a large number of resources available on the Internet that can complement the information provided in this book. Book errata will be available at the Apress Web site (`http://www.apress.com/`) as well as `http://www.EnterpriseWSH.com/`.

Newsgroups are probably the most important source of up-to-date information. The `microsoft.public.scripting.wsh` newsgroup is your best bet for WSH-related postings. This newsgroup is commonly hosted by ISP news servers, but you can also access it directly by pointing your newsreader at `news://msnews.microsoft.com`, which guarantees the speediest replies to any queries posted.

Chances are any question you may have has been answered before. Use the newsgroup search engines at `http://groups.google.com/` to search newsgroup archives.

The Microsoft Developers Network (MSDN) is an enormous resource for Microsoft-related development material. There's a never-ending supply of articles on the latest technologies, including a scripting-specific site at `http://msdn.microsoft.com/scripting`.

Finally, there are a number of excellent Web sites that contain large amounts of additional information and scripting samples. The two standouts are Ian Morrish's site `http://www.windows-script.com` and Clarence Washington's Win32Scripting site at `http://cwashington.netreach.net/`.

CHAPTER 2

Shell Operations

THE WSH SHELL OBJECT provides the ability to create Windows shortcuts, read environment variables, manipulate registry settings, and run external programs.

To create an instance of the WSH Shell object, pass the argument "WScript.Shell" to the CreateObject method:

```
Set objShell =CreateObject("WScript.Shell")
```

2.1 Reading the Command-Line Arguments

Problem

You want to read the command-line arguments.

Solution

All versions of WSH support the WScript object's Arguments property to get the command-line arguments. The following script attempts to set the read-only attribute for a file that is specified by a command-line argument:

```
'hidefile.vbs
Dim objFileSystem, objFile

'check if the parameter count is a single parameter.
' If not then show the command syntax
If WScript.Arguments.Count<>1 Then
WScript.Echo " Syntax: " & WScript.ScriptName &  _
"  FileName " & vbCrLf & _
          " Filename: the path of the file you wish to hide"
        WScript.Quit
End If

 'create FileSystem object
 Set objFileSystem = CreateObject("Scripting.FileSystemObject")
 On Error Resume Next
```

```
'get the file specified in command line
Set objFile = objFileSystem.GetFile(WScript.Arguments(0))
'check if error occurred - file not found
If Err Then
    WScript.Echo "Error:File:'" & WScript.Arguments(0) & "' not found"
Else
    objFile.Attributes = 2
End If
```

WSH 5.6 introduces new elements to the WSF file format that allow for greater control in argument creation as well as a consistent method of script documentation. The following script performs the same operation as the first solution script using these new elements:

```
<job>
<runtime>
<description>
The hidefile.wsf filename script sets the hidden attribute
for a specified file
</description>
<named
      name="FileName"
      helpstring="Name of file to hide."
      type="string"
      required="True"
/>
<example>
This is an example of how to use this script:
 Hidefile.wsf Filename:data.doc
</example>
</runtime>
<script language="VBScript">
If Not WScript.Arguments.Named.Exists("FileName") Then
  WScript.Arguments.ShowUsage
  WScript.Quit
 End If

Set objFileSystem = CreateObject("Scripting.FileSystemObject")
 On Error Resume Next
 'get the file specified in command line

 strFile = WScript.Arguments.Named("FileName")
 Set objFile = objFileSystem.GetFile(strFile)
```

```
    'check if error occurred - file not found
    If Err Then
        WScript.Echo "File:'" & strFile & "' not found"
    Else
        objFile.Attributes = 2
    End If

</script>
</job>
```

Discussion

The Arguments collection contains the parameters that are passed to the script.

The Arguments collection is returned from the WScript object, which is a root WSH object and does not need to be created using CreateObject. The collection has a Count property that returns the number of items in the collection. The argument count is also accessible through the length property, which is included for JScript compatibility.

The Arguments collection is represented as an array with a 0 offset. The first argument would be stored as element 0, the second as 1, and so on. In the following command line, Fred is the first argument and Smith is the second:

```
Test.vbs Fred Smith
```

The following snippet represents the test.vbs script:

```
'test.vbs
WScript.Echo "Argument 1 is " & WScript.Arguments(0)
WScript.Echo "Argument 2 is " & WScript.Arguments(1)
```

If you want Fred Smith to be read as a single argument, it must be surrounded by double quotes (" "):

```
test.vbs "Fred Smith"
```

If you attempt to obtain an argument from the collection that has not been passed in the command line, an error will occur. In the previous example, passing "Fred Smith" to the test.vbs script will generate an error because the script attempts to display a second argument and "Fred Smith" is considered to be one argument.

The following example lists all parameters passed to the script:

```
'get a reference to the arguments collection
'output the first argument
WScript.Echo WScript.Arguments(0)

'show each command line argument
For Each arg in WScript.Arguments
   WScript.Echo arg
Next
```

WSH version 2.0 and later supports drag-and-drop argument passing. Any files dragged onto a script file using Explorer can be obtained through the `Arguments` collection.

WSH version 5.6 (the version after 2.0) provides a more sophisticated command-line parameter handling using XML constructs in WSF files. This is provided through the XML `<runtime>` element.

The advantage of this new element is that it provides a consistent method of documenting WSH scripts, as well as easier parsing of command-line arguments, which leads to less code.

The `<runtime>` element appears at the beginning of a WSF file, inside the body of the job element. It can contain a number of elements that describe the script's arguments and provide examples.

The first element is the `<description>` element. Any text between the beginning and end element is used for a script description, or whatever you want to put there. This is much easier than attempting to format a large block using `WScript` Echo statements.

```
<description>
Anything that appears between the description
elements will appear as a script description.
</description>
```

Following the `<description>` element is the `<named>` element. There can be one or more occurrences of this element, and it is used to describe parameters that can be passed to the script.

The `<named>` element contains a number of attributes, as listed in Table 2-1.

Table 2-1. `<Named>` *Element Attributes*

CONSTANT	TYPE	DESCRIPTION
Name	String	Argument name
Helpstring	String	Argument description
Type	String	Argument type: string, Boolean, or simple
Required	Boolean	Indicates whether parameter is required or not

The name attribute identifies the command-line parameter, while the helpstring attribute describes the parameter's function.

The type attribute identifies the parameter type. If the type is a string, the argument is expected to appear as /argumentname:stringvalue in the command line, where the argumentname represents the name of the argument as described with the name attribute and stringvalue is the argument value.

The following <named> element defines the parameter user, which is a string type and is required:

```
<named
        name="user"
        helpstring="The name of the user to modify."
        type="string"
        required="true"
/>
```

In the following command-line sample, FredS is passed as the user argument:

```
Deluser.wsf /user:FredS
```

If the string argument contains spaces, surround the argument in double quotes:

```
Deluser.wsf /user:"Fred Smith"
```

If the argument is Boolean, it is toggled using /argumentname+ to indicate True, or /argumentname- to indicate a False argument value:

```
Deluser.wsf /Update+
```

Setting the type to simple indicates that no value is required for the argument.

Once all arguments have been defined, an <example> element can be added to provide script usage samples. The <example> element is similar to the <description> element, where text can flow over multiple lines.

The following code snippet contains a complete sequence of argument elements that provides a script description, defines three command-line arguments, and displays example text on how to use the script:

```
<runtime>
<description>
This script is a sample script that demonstrates how to
define command line arguments.
```

```
</description>
<named
      name="StringArg"
      helpstring="Sample string argument."
      type="string"
      required="True"
/>
<named
      name="SimpleArg"
      helpstring="Sample simple argument"
      type="simple"
      required="false"
/>
<named
      name="BooleanArg"
      helpstring="Boolean argument"
      type="Boolean"
      required="false"
/>

<example>
This is an example of how to use this script:
 Argex.wsf StringArg:testing /SimpleArg  BooleanArg+
</example>
</runtime>
```

> **NOTE** *No validation is performed against the arguments defined using the named and unnamed elements. No error message is returned if a "required" argument is not passed or an invalid data type is passed for an argument. Checking if an argument is passed and is the correct data type should be performed in code. The* `<runtime>` *element is intended more for documentation than data validation purposes.*

The named arguments are accessed through the `WScript.Arguments.Named` object. Use this object's `Exists` method to determine if an argument has been passed. The syntax is as follows:

```
bExists = WScript.Arguments.Named.Exists(strArgument)
```

`strArgument` is the argument you want to check. It is not case-sensitive. The function returns `True` if the argument has been passed and `False` if not:

```
'check if name user argument has been passed
If Not WScript.Arguments.Named.Exists("User") Then
   WScript.Echo "You must specify a user name"
   WScript.Quit
End If
```

Named arguments are accessed through the `WScript.Arguments.Named` object's collection:

```
Value =WScript.Arguments.Named(strArgument)
```

`strArgument` is the argument you want to reference and it is not case-sensitive. If the argument does not exist, an empty string is returned and no error is generated.

> **TIP** *Any argument prefixed with a forward slash (/) can be referenced using the* `Named` *object, regardless if it has been defined in the* `<runtime>` *elements using the* `<named>` *tags.*

Information defined in the `<runtime>` elements makes the script self-documenting, but it can also be displayed at script execution. If a script containing the `<runtime>` element is executed and `/?` is passed as a command-line parameter, the script information is displayed.

This information can be displayed by calling the `WScript.Arguments.ShowUsage` method from within a script. The solution script demonstrates this by executing this method if the argument count is 0.

WSH 5.6 also allows for "unnamed" arguments to be defined. An unnamed argument is an argument that does not have a corresponding named argument. In the following command line, the arguments `joeb` and `123456` are considered unnamed:

```
/name:freds joeb /flag+ /phone:5551234 123456
```

Any argument that does not have an associated argument name is stored in the `Unnamed` collection.

Unnamed arguments are useful when you have a mixture of arguments that might take an unknown number of values. To access unnamed arguments, reference the `WScript.Arguments.Unnamed` collection using a numeric value:

```
Value =WScript.Arguments.Unnamed(nArgument)
```

`nArgument` represents the argument position in the command line with a 0 offset.

Attempting to access the `Unnamed` collection when no unnamed arguments have been passed will generate an error. To determine if any unnamed arguments have been passed, use the `WScript.Arguments.Unnamed.Count` property, which returns the number of unnamed arguments in the command line.

2.2 Reading an Environment Variable

Problem

You need to be able to read an environment variable.

Solution

Use the `Shell` object's `ExpandEnvironmentStrings` method:

```
Dim objShell
Set objShell = WScript.CreateObject("WScript.shell")
WScript.Echo _
     objShell.ExpandEnvironmentStrings("Your temp directory is %TEMP%")
```

Discussion

Environment variables are information stored by the Windows operating system. You can enumerate and create environment variables currently by executing the `Set` command from the command prompt. You can read their values using the Shell object's `ExpandEnvironmentVariables` method. The syntax is as follows:

```
strValue = objShell.ExpandEnvironmentStrings(strString)
```

Any strings in the `strString` argument that are enclosed between percent symbols (%) will be expanded with the corresponding environment variable value.

Whenever a new process is created, it is assigned a copy of the parent environment variables, which are known as the *process environment variables*. The ExpandEnvironmentStrings method looks in the process environment variable "block" when expanding the strString parameter.

Under Windows NT/2000/XP/2003, environment variables can be system, user, or volatile. These are copied to the process environment block for each new process—when you are reading a variable using ExpandEnvironmentStrings it might be System, Volatile, or User.

Changes made to environment variables outside of the process to which they are referenced are not reflected in the process environment because it is only a copy.

Environment variables with the same name may exist in system, user, or volatile. One example is the temp environment variable, which usually exists for each user profile as well as the system.

If you read a Process environment variable that has duplicate values, such as existing in the system and user environment, it will return the User variable.

Use the Shell object's Environment collection to access variables of specific environment types. The syntax is as follows:

```
objCollection = objShell.Environment([strType])
```

The optional strType parameter can be system, user, process, or volatile. Under Windows NT/2000/XP/2003, it defaults to system. Windows 9*x*/ME defaults to Process, but it can also be User or Volatile, although these operating systems don't normally use these environments.

Any changes made to the System, Volatile, or User variables outside the running script will be reflected using the Environment collection for the appropriate environment type. The following code outputs the User and System temp environment variables:

```
Dim objShell
Set objShell = CreateObject("WScript.shell")

WScript.Echo "Temp variable for user is : " & _

objShell.ExpandEnvironmentStrings(objShell.Environment("User")("Temp"))

WScript.Echo "Temp variable for system is : " & _
      objShell.ExpandEnvironmentStrings(objShell.Environment("System")("Temp"))
```

Environment variables returned from the Environment collection are not "expanded." Some environment variables are a combination of other environment variables. For example, the system Temp environment variable may be stored as %SystemRoot%\TEMP. This is why in the previous example the ExpandEnvironmentStrings method is used to expand any environment variables.

Under Windows NT, you may be limited to what keys you can access. If you are logged on as a nonadministrative user account, you will not be able to access System environment variables.

```
'this runs on Windows NT only
Dim objShell, objEnv, strEnv
Set objShell = WScriptCreateObject("WScript.shell")
'get the user environment variables
Set objEnv = objShell.Environment("User")
For Each strEnv In objEnv
  WScript.Echo strEnv
Next
```

2.3 Creating or Updating an Environment Variable

Problem

You want to create an environment variable.

Solution

Use the WScript.Shell object's Environment collection to create a new environment variable in this way:

```
Dim objShell, objEnv
Set objShell = WScript.CreateObject("WScript.shell")
'get the User environment variables
Set objEnv = objShell.Environment("User")
objEnv("username") = "Fred Smith"
```

Discussion

The Environment collection that is described in Problem 2.3 can be used to update or create environment variables. The example script sets the value for the environment variable user name for the User environment.

This method works fine for Windows NT/2000/XP/2003. You can update the Process, User, or Volatile environments. You can also update the system environment if you have the appropriate security access. If you want the changes to take effect globally, apply the changes to the appropriate environment type. Any changes made to the process environment block are lost when the script exits.

If you are using Windows 9*x* or ME, it's not so straightforward.

If you set the environment variable using this method under Windows 9*x*/ME, the variable will be set under the process environment block and exist during the execution of the script, but once the script terminates the environment variable will disappear.

There are a couple of ways to get past this problem. Under Windows 9*x*/ME, you can set an environment variable `User` or `Volatile`, even though the WSH documentation specifies that this works under Windows NT/2000/XP/2003 only:

```
'this works under Windows 9x
Dim objShell, objEnv
Set objShell = WScript.CreateObject("WScript.shell")
'get the User environment variables
Set objEnv = objShell.Environment("User")
objEnv("username") = "Fred Smith"
```

The problem with this is that it is not available to the Windows environment. If you execute a SET statement from the command prompt, the variable will not appear. Furthermore, it will not be available to applications that read environment variables.

Using `Volatile` or `User` under Windows 9*x*/ME can be appropriate if you require a place to store values to be read by WSH scripts only; that is, you don't need to read the values from other applications.

The `User` environment variables are stored under the `HKEY_CURRENT_USER\Environment` registry key. The `Volatile` variables are stored under `HKEY_CURRENT_USER\Volatile Environment`.

If you require the variables to be visible to the Windows environment under Windows 9*x*/ME, you can use the Winset.exe application to set the variable. `Winset.`exe is available from the Windows 9*x*/ME CD. It is a command-line utility that sets an environment variable. The syntax is as follows:

```
winset.exe variable=value
```

Use the `Shell` object's `Run` method to execute `Winset`:

```
Set objShell = CreateObject("WScript.Shell")

objShell.Run "c:\winset datapath=d:\data", WshHide, True
```

Even `Winset` isn't perfect, though. `Winset` will set the environment variable for the duration of your Windows 9*x*/ME session. Once you shut down or log off your Windows 9*x*/ME machine, you will lose any environment variables set using `Winset`.

The only real way to solve this problem is to manipulate the `Autoexec.bat` command file. `Autoexec.bat` is executed upon start-up of Windows 9*x*/ME, and any SET statements will assign an environment variable with a value.

The following script updates the global environment using `Winset` and updates the `Autoexec.bat` file with the environment variable using a `SET` statement. If the `SET` statement for the specified environment variable doesn't exist, it will add it to the file:

```
'UpdateEnvironment
'Description
'updates autoexec.bat file with environment variables and sets
'the environment variable
'Parameters:
'strVariablename of environment variable
'varValue       value to set
Sub UpdateEnvironment(strVariable, varValue)

Const ForWriting = 2
Const WshHide = 0
Dim objFSO, objTextFile, strFileText, aDataFile, nF
Dim bFoundSet

'open autoexec.bat
Set objFSO = CreateObject("Scripting.FileSystemObject")
Set objTextFile = objFSO.OpenTextFile("C:\autoexec.bat")

strFileText = objTextFile.ReadAll

'read the file into an array
aDataFile = Split(strFileText, vbCrLf)

bFoundUser = False

'search for the SET statement for the specified variable
For nF = 0 To UBound(aDataFile)
    'if it's found, then update line
    If InStr(1, aDataFile(nF), "set " & strVariable, vbTextCompare) >0 Then
        bFoundSet = True
        aDataFile(nF) = "SET " & strVariable & "=" & varValue
```

```
        Exit For
    End If
Next

objTextFile.Close

'open autoexec.bat for writing
Set objTextFile = objFSO.OpenTextFile("C:\autoexec.bat", ForWriting)
strFileText = Join(aDataFile, vbCrLf)

'write back contents of file
objTextFile.Write strFileText
'if set statement not found, then
If Not bFoundSet Then
objTextFile.WriteLine
    objTextFile.WriteLine "SET " & strVariable & "=" & varValue
End If

objTextFile.Close

Set objShell = CreateObject("WScript.Shell")
'run Winset. This assumes it is in the path
objShell.Run "winset " & strVariable & "=" & varValue, WshHide, True

End Sub
```

2.4 Deleting an Environment Variable

Problem

You want to delete an environment variable.

Solution

Use the Environment collection's Remove method to delete an environment variable:

```
Dim objShell, objEnv

Set objShell = CreateObject("WScript.shell")

Set objEnv = objShell.Environment("User")
objEnv.Remove "username"
```

Discussion

The Shell object's Environment object has a Remove method that removes environment variables. The syntax is as follows:

```
objEnvironment.Remove(strEnvironmentVariable)
```

The strEnvironmentVariable parameter represents the environment variable to remove.

Under Windows NT/2000/XP/2003, invoking the Remove method deletes the specified environment variable. Under Windows 9*x*/ME it removes User and Volatile environment variables, which are stored under registry locations like NT/2000/XP/2003, but do not appear as standard Process environment variables that are accessible by MS-DOS and Windows applications.

Process environment variables, such as TEMP, PATH, and COMSPEC, are only removed from the script process. They are not removed from the global environment. To permanently remove a Windows 9*x*/ME environment variable, the SET statement that creates the variable must be removed from the appropriate location (autoexec.bat, config.sys, and so on). The location may vary depending on the variable.

2.5 Running Applications

Problem

You want to run an application.

Solution

You can create an instance of the WScript.Shell object and invoke the Run method. All versions of WSH support the WScript.Shell object's Run method:

```
'notepad.vbs
Const WshNormalFocus = 1
Dim objShell

Set objShell = WScript.CreateObject("WScript.shell")
objShell.Run "Notepad.exe", WshNormalFocus ,True
```

Discussion

The Run method executes applications. These can be any Windows or command-line applications. The syntax is as follows:

```
objShell.Run(strCommand, [nStyle], [nWaitOnReturn])
```

The strCommand parameter contains the name of the application you want to execute. If the application is not found in the current directory, the directory path specified in the PATH environment variable is searched.

The nStyle parameter determines what type of window to run the program in. Table 2-2 lists the Window-style values.

Table 2-2. Window-Style Values

CONSTANT	VALUE	DESCRIPTION
WshHide	0	Hide window
WshNormalFocus	1	Create normal window with normal focus
WshMinimizedFocus	2	Create minimized window with focus
WshMaximizedFocus	3	Create maximized window with focus
WshNormalNoFocus	4	Create normal window with no focus
WshMinimizedNoFocus	6	Create minimized window with no focus

If the nWaitOnReturn parameter is set to True, the script will not continue execution until the executed program has completed execution. The default is False.

The Run command does not provide the ability to return the results of the application that is being executed. You cannot add a redirection symbol (>) in the statement you are executing:

```
objShell.Run "dir > dir.txt",1 , True
```

To redirect output from a console application, you must execute the command shell and specify the command line together with any redirection. The command shell for Windows NT/2000/XP/2003 is CMD.EXE, while for Windows 9*x*/ME it is COMMAND.COM.

The path to the command shell is stored in the COMSPEC environment variable in all Windows operating systems. For both shells, a /C parameter specifies that you want the shell to execute a command.

The Run method automatically expands any environment variables, so you do not have to use the ExpandEnvironmentStrings method to expand the string:

```
Const WshHide = 0

'run an application and redirect the output to a text file
Dim objShell

Set objShell = CreateObject("WScript.shell")
objShell.Run "%Comspec% /c tree > c:\tree.txt", WshHide, True
```

WSH 5.6 introduces the Exec method, which functionally is the same as the Run method except that it allows full access to the standard input and output, which is the data entered and generated by the executed program. The Exec method also passes a copy of the process environment variables to the new program.

The Exec method is a WScript.Shell object method and takes one parameter, which is the command to execute. This is the same as the command parameter for the Run method. The Exec method does not support the optional windowstyle argument like the Run method.

This functionality allows the results of the executed program to be retrieved within the script. An example of this is the previous sample script that executes the MS-DOS tree command and redirects the results to the file tree.txt. Instead of redirecting to a separate file, the Exec command allows the output to be referenced directly from within the script:

```
'extree.vbs
Set objShell = CreateObject("WScript.shell")

'execute the DOS tree command
Set objRun = objShell.Exec ("%Comspec% /c tree e:\")

'loop while application executes
  'build output text with results of tree command
  strText =  strText & objRun.StdOut.ReadAll


'output results
WScript.Echo strText

Set objShell = Nothing
```

The Exec method returns a WshScriptExec object. This object exposes Stdin, Stdout, and StdErr streams. Chapter 6 contains information on how to manipulate these streams.

The application executed using the Exec method runs *asynchronously,* which means the application the Exec method used continues running and doesn't wait for the executed application to finish.

To determine if the spawned application is still running, query the Status property. This property returns 0 if the application is still running, and it returns 1 if the application has completed running.

The Exec method provides the ability to terminate a spawned application by invoking the Terminate method, although using this method can result in the loss of data.

WSH 5.6 provides support for executing scripts on remote computers. This offers you the ability to run scripts on client computers that perform administrative tasks, such as housecleaning or system inventory.

WSH 2.0 has the ability to create remote components (see the Introduction); WSH 5.6 can execute whole command-line scripts, not just individual components on a remote machine. Like remote components, WSH uses the Distributed Component Object Model (DCOM) to execute scripts on remote machines.

Running scripts on remote computers poses a number of issues: What about security? Could a malicious script be executed on a remote computer? To limit the possibility of such activity occurring, by default remote scripts can only be run from a computer where the user is logged in as a member of the Administrators group.

Because Windows 9*x* and Windows ME provide limited domain user authentication capabilities in their DCOM implementation, remote scripting does not work on these platforms—it works only on Windows NT 4, Windows 2000, Windows 2003, and Windows XP.

And to further limit any malicious activity, by default remote scripting is disabled. To enable the ability to run scripts sent from another machine, the Remote registry value (which can be found under the HKLM\SOFTWARE\Microsoft\Windows Script Host\Settings key in the registry) must be set to 1. By default this value is 0.

To create a remote script, create an instance of an object using the ProgID WshController. This returns an instance of a WSHController object, which is used to create instances of remote scripts.

Use the WSHController object's CreateScript method to execute the remote script. This method can take two parameters.

The first parameter is the path to the script. The file executed must be a WSH script, such as a VBS, JS, or WSF file. The path points to the locally stored script. This is not the location on the remote computer, but the location on the computer that's invoking the remote script. The script is uploaded from the local computer to the remote computer for execution, which saves having to have the script stored on all clients. An error will not occur if the script is not found in the specified location.

The CreateScript method's second parameter is the name of the remote computer where the script is to be executed. This can be passed as the computer name or IP address. The computer name can be passed in UNC format—that is, prefixed with two back slashes (\\).

The remote computer parameter is optional. If it is not specified, the script is executed on the local computer similar to the Run method. This is useful for testing remote scripts.

The CreateScript method does not execute the script. Rather, it attempts to connect and load a specified script on a remote computer. It returns a WshRemote object, which represents the remote instance of the script. To execute the script, invoke the remote object's Execute method.

Remotely executed scripts function similarly to scripts executed using the Exec method described earlier. The script runs asynchronously and you must query the Remote object's Status property to determine if the remote script is running.

The Status property will return 0 if no remote script is running, 1 if the script is running, and 2 when the script finishes execution on the remote computer.

The following script executes a remote script called inv.vbs on the remote computer Odin:

```
<job>
<script language="VBScript">
'remex1.wsf
Const WshFailed = 2
Set objController = CreateObject("WshController")

'create an instance of the remote object for script inv.vbs
'to execute on computer odin
Set objRemote = _
  objController.CreateScript("e:\wsh\chpt1\inv.vbs", "odin")
'execute the remote script
objRemote.Execute

'loop while the remote script is running
Do While Not objRemote.Status =  WshFailed
   WScript.Sleep 100
Loop
WScript.Echo "remote script finished execution"
</script>
</job>
```

The script assumes the remote script executed successfully, which might not always be the case (only in a perfect world). The Remote object exposes an Error property, which returns a WshRemoteError object. This object details information on any errors that occurred in the remote script. Table 2-3 lists the WshRemoteError object properties.

Table 2-3. `WshRemoteError` *Object Properties*

PROPERTY	DESCRIPTION
Description	Short description of error
Line	Line error occurred on
Character	Column error occurred at
SourceText	Line of source code that caused the error
Source	Name of COM object that caused error (if applicable)
Number	Error number

Not all properties may be set for a given WshRemoteError object when an error occurs.

To effectively trap errors, you can "sink" WshRemote object events that are fired during the execution of the remote script. When an error occurs in the remote script, an Error event is fired. In order to trap this event you must "connect" to the WshRemote object. This can be done using the WScript object's ConnectObject method, which sinks any events fired by a specific object. In order to uniquely identify the events within the script, a prefix is passed with the ConnectObject method. This prefix is added to the event name.

The WshRemote object can fire a Start and End event as well as the Error event. These events fire when the remote script starts and ends execution.

The following script demonstrates these events:

```
<job>
<script language="VBScript">
'remex.wsf
Const WshFailed = 2
Set objController = CreateObject("WshController")

'create an instance of the remote object for script
Set objRemote = _
  objController.CreateScript("e:\wsh\chpt1\inv.vbs", "odin")

'connect to the remote object. The second parameter is
'used to prefix local event functions
WScript.ConnectObject objRemote , "rem_"

objRemote.Execute

'loop while the script is running
```

```
Do While objRemote.Status <>  WshFailed
    WScript.Sleep 100
Loop


'error event fires if an error occurs in remote script
Function rem_Error
 Set objErr = objRemote.Error
 WScript.Echo "Description " & objErr.Description
 WScript.Echo "Line " & objErr.Line & " at character " & objErr.Character
 WScript.Echo "Code that caused error " & objErr.Source
 WScript.Quit
End Function

'start event fires when remote script starts execution
Function rem_Start
 WScript.Echo "Remote script started execution"
End Function

'end event fires when remote script starts execution
Function rem_End
 WScript.Echo "Remote script ended"
End Function

</script>
</job>
```

The script creates a remote script using the `inv.vbs` script and attempts to execute it on the remote computer Odin.

The `ConnectObject` method is used to synch events from the remote script object to the local script. Any events called from the remote script are identified in the local script by the event name prefixed with "rem_."

2.6 Accessing Windows-Related Folders

Problem

You need to access the paths of Windows-related folders.

Solution

You can use the `WScript.Shell` object's `SpecialFolders` collection:

```
Set objShell = WScript.CreateObject("WScript.Shell")
strDesktop = objShell.SpecialFolders("Desktop")
```

Discussion

The SpecialFolders collection returns the path to a specified Windows folder. The syntax is as follows:

```
strPath = objShell.SpecialFolders(strFolderName)
```

The strFolderName parameter identifies the folder to return. This parameter is not case-sensitive. Table 2-4 lists valid SpecialFolders parameters.

Table 2-4. SpecialFolders *Parameters*

PARAMETER	DESCRIPTION
AppData	Location of user application data.
Desktop	Location of desktop folders.
Favorites	Internet Favorites folder.
Fonts	Folder where system fonts are stored.
MyDocuments	Default documents/personal folder.
NetHood	Location of Network Neighborhood folder.
PrintHood	Location of Printer Neighborhood folder.
Programs	Location of shortcuts that appear on the Programs menu under the Start menu.
Recent	Location of folder containing shortcuts for recently accessed resources.
SendTo	Send to menu folder location.
StartMenu	Location of shortcuts that appear on Start menu.
Startup	Location of start-up folder under Start menu.
Templates	Default template folder.
AllUsersStartMenu	All Users Start menu folder. Contains shortcuts that appear for all users under the Start menu. Only available under Windows NT/2000/XP/2003.

Continued

Table 2-4. SpecialFolders *Parameters (continued)*

PARAMETER	DESCRIPTION
AllUsersDesktop	All Users desktop folder. Contains desktop shortcuts that appear for all users. Only available under Windows NT/2000/XP/2003.
AllUsersPrograms	All Users Start menu Programs folder. Contains shortcuts that appear for all users under the Start menu's Programs folder. Only available under Windows NT/2000/XP/2003.
AllUsersStartup	All Users Startup folder. Shortcuts in this folder are executed upon start-up. Only available under Windows NT/2000/XP/2003.

If the folder name is not found, SpecialFolders will return an empty string.

2.7 Creating a Windows Shortcut

Problem

You want to create a Windows shortcut.

Solution

Use the WScript.Shell object's CreateShortcut method:

```
'create a shortcut on desktop linked to hello script

Set objShell = CreateObject("WScript.Shell")
strDesktop = objShell.SpecialFolders("Desktop") 'get the path to desktop
Set objShortcut = objShell.CreateShortcut(strDesktop & "\Hello World.lnk")
objShortcut.TargetPath = "D:\hello.vbs" 'script to execute
objShortcut.Save ' save shortcut
```

Discussion

The WScript.Shell object can create shortcuts using the CreateShortcut method. The syntax is as follows:

```
objShortCut = objShell.CreateShortcut(strPath)
```

The `strPath` parameter represents the path to the shortcut. The shortcut must end in either a .lnk or .url extension. Specifying .lnk indicates you are creating a Windows shortcut, while .url will create a URL shortcut. A different `Shortcut` object is returned depending on the extension that you use.

The method returns a `WshShortCut` object.

The object provides the same settings that are available when creating shortcuts using Explorer. Table 2-5 lists the properties that can be set for the `Shortcut` object.

Table 2-5. `Shortcut` *Object Properties*

PARAMETER	TYPE	DESCRIPTION
`Arguments`	String	Arguments to pass the application specified in TargetPath.
`Description`	String	Shortcut description. Doesn't work.
`Hotkey`	String	Keyboard combination used to execute shortcut (e.g., Alt+Ctrl+F).
`IconLocation`	String	Sets the icon based on an existing application or library. The format is the path to the application or library followed by a comma and the icon number. The icon number starts at 0. For example, `objShortCut.IconLocation = "c:\winnt40\system32\SHELL32.dll,9"` would set the tenth icon of the SHELL32.dll resource DLL as the icon that would appear associated with the shortcut.
`TargetPath`	String	Path of the application to execute or document to open.
`WindowStyle`	Integer	Window type to display application or document. Valid values are 1 for a normal, 2 for a minimized, and 3 for a maximized window.
`WorkingDirectory`	String	Default application working directory.
`FullName`	String	Read-only property. The location of the shortcut.

It can be easier to determine certain settings such as shortcut hot key keystrokes and icons by reading the properties of existing shortcuts using Windows Explorer. The following sample creates a shortcut on the desktop that points to the Autoexec.bat file:

```
'create a shortcut on desktop that starts Notepad with Autoexec.bat
'as parameter
Dim objShell, strDesktop, objShortCut
'create a shortcut on desktop
Set objShell = CreateObject("WScript.Shell")
strDesktop = objShell.SpecialFolders("Desktop") 'get the path to desktop
Set objShortCut = objShell.CreateShortCut(strDesktop & "\Show AutoExec.lnk")
objShortCut.IconLocation = "c:\winnt\system32\SHELL32.dll,9"
objShortCut.TargetPath = "notepad.exe" 'script to execute
objShortCut.Arguments = "c:\autoexec.bat" 'argument to pass
objShortCut.HotKey =  "ALT+CTRL+N" 'hotkey to start
objShortCut.Save ' save and update shortcut
```

Once you have set the parameters for the shortcut, invoke the Save method to save and update the shortcut.

If you call the CreateShortCut method with a path to a shortcut that already exists, the settings for the shortcut are loaded into the Shortcut object. This allows you to modify existing shortcuts without needing to reapply the existing properties.

WSH also supports the creation of URL shortcuts. These shortcuts are similar to file shortcuts except they point to an Internet URL.

```
Dim objShell, strDesktop, objURLShortCut
'create a URL shortcut on desktop linked to company homepage
Set objShell = CreateObject("WScript.Shell")
strDesktop = objShell.SpecialFolders("Desktop") 'get the path to desktop
Set objURLShortCut = _
       objShell.CreateShortcut(strDesktop & "\Company Home Page.url")
objURLShortCut.TargetPath = "www.acompany.com"
objURLShortCut.Save ' save and update shortcut
```

The URL shortcut supports the TargetPath and FullName properties. TargetPath is the URL to point to, and FullName returns the path to the shortcut and is read-only.

2.8 Displaying a Message Prompt

Problem

You need to display a message that prompts a user to choose Yes or No, which results in an action being performed that is based on the user's choice.

Solution

You can use the following script to display a pop-up window that prompts the user to choose Yes or No:

```
Const YesButton = 6
Const QuestionMark = 32
Const YesNo = 4
'display a pop-up with yes/no buttons and question mark icon
Set objShell = CreateObject("WScript.Shell")
intValue = objShell.Popup("Do you wish to continue?", _
    , , QuestionMark + YesNo)
'test if the Yes button was selected
If intValue = YesButton Then
    'do something
End If
```

The result of the Solution script is shown in Figure 2-1.

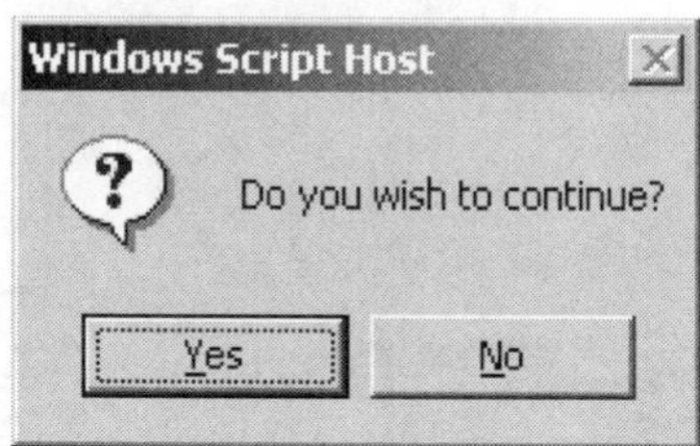

Figure 2-1. Pop-up window that prompts the user to choose Yes or No

Discussion

The Popup method displays a Windows pop-up message and then returns a value depending on the button that was selected. The syntax is as follows:

```
intButton = objShell.Popup(strMessage, [nSecondsWait], [strTitle], [nType])
```

Table 2-6 details the Popup method's parameters.

Table 2-6. Popup *Method Parameters*

PARAMETER	DESCRIPTION
strMessage	Message to display.
nSecondsWait	Optional parameter. If passed, the pop-up waits a specified number of seconds and then closes.
strTitle	Optional title for pop-up window.
nType	Optional numeric value that determines the number of buttons to show and icon. This is determined by combining a value from Table 2-7 and Table 2-8. For example, the value 65 would display an OK button and the Information icon.

Popup returns an integer value depending on what button was selected. Table 2-7 lists the button selection values.

Table 2-7. Button Selection Values

VALUE	BUTTONS SHOWN
0	OK
1	OK and Cancel
2	Abort, Retry, and Ignore
3	Yes, No, and Cancel
4	Yes and No
5	Retry and Cancel

Table 2-8 lists the icon types.

Table 2-8. Icon Types

VALUE	ICON TO SHOW
16	Stop Mark
32	Question Mark
48	Exclamation Mark
64	Information

Table 2-9 lists the `Popup` return values.

Table 2-9. `Popup` *Return Values*

VALUE	DESCRIPTION
1	OK button
2	Cancel button
3	Abort button
4	Retry button
5	Ignore button
6	Yes button
7	No button

2.9 Sending Keystrokes to Applications

Problem

You need to automate the process of creating text button images for Web pages. To accomplish this, you want to write a routine that enables you to drag a selection of files into a script, which results in creating text images automatically.

Solution

You can use the WScript.Shell object's SendKeys method to send keystrokes to an application. For example, the following script uses Microsoft PhotoDraw to create text buttons:

```
Dim objShell
Dim strText, strFontSize, strFont, strFileName

strFont = "Arial"
strFontSize = 12

If Not Wscript.Arguments.Count = 2 Then
    WScript.Echo "mkbutton creates text image buttons" & vbCrLf & _
    "Syntax:"  &  vbCrLf & _
    "mkimage.vbs buttontext filename" &  vbCrLf & _
    "buttontext  Text forcreate button" &  vbCrLf & _
    "filename    File name for text button image" &  vbCrLf & _
    "Example:" & vbCrLf & _
    "mkbutton Home d:\data\images\homebutton"
  WScript.Quit
End If

strText = Wscript.Arguments(0)
strFileName = Wscript.Arguments(1)

Set objShell = CreateObject("WScript.Shell")

objShell.Run "Photodrw.exe"
Wscript.Sleep 100
objShell.AppActivate "Microsoft Photodraw"
Wscript.Sleep 1000 'wait for PhotoDraw to start

objShell.SendKeys "{ESC}^n" 'new document
Wscript.Sleep 100
objShell.SendKeys "^t" 'text mode
objShell.SendKeys strText
objShell.SendKeys "{tab}"
objShell.SendKeys strFont
objShell.SendKeys "~{tab}"
objShell.SendKeys strFontSize
objShell.SendKeys "{tab}"
```

```
objShell.SendKeys "%oes" 'Format menu - Effects - Shadow
objShell.SendKeys "{tab}{down 3}{right}&~"

objShell.SendKeys "%oei" 'Format menu - Effects - Designer Text
objShell.SendKeys "{tab}" '{down 3}{right}"
objShell.SendKeys "~"

objShell.SendKeys "%vf" 'fit picture to selection
objShell.SendKeys "^s"
objShell.SendKeys strFileName
objShell.SendKeys "{tab}"
objShell.SendKeys "j~~~"
objShell.SendKeys "%fcn" 'close
objShell.SendKeys "%fx" 'quit
```

The result of the Solution script appears in Figure 2-2.

Figure 2-2. New button

Discussion

WSH 2.0 provides a SendKeys method to send keystrokes to other applications. The SendKeys method sends keystrokes to the current active application.

To assure the correct application is set to send keystrokes to, use the AppActivate method. The syntax is as follows:

```
objShell.AppActivate strTitle
```

strTitle identifies the window that you want to activate. If more than one occurrence of the application is running, one of the occurrences is activated.

The keystrokes are sent using the SendKeys method. The syntax is as follows:

```
objShell.SendKeys strKeys
```

The strKeys parameter represents the keystrokes sent to the application. This can be any combination of characters.

```
objShell.SendKeys "Fred" '
```

Noncharacter keys, such as function keys, directional keys, and the Enter key, are represented by keystroke codes surrounded by curly braces ({}).

```
objShell.SendKeys "{F2}test~" '
```

Table 2-10 lists the keystroke codes.

Table 2-10. Keystroke Codes

KEYSTROKE	SENDKEYS CODE
Backspace	{BACKSPACE}, {BS}, or {BKSP}
Break	{BREAK}
Caps Lock	{CAPSLOCK}
Del or Delete	{DELETE} {DEL}
Down/up/left/right arrows	{DOWN} {UP} {LEFT} {RIGHT}
Home or End	{END} {HOME}
Enter	{ENTER} or ~
Esc	{ESC}
Help	{HELP}
Insert	{INSERT} or {INS}
Num Lock	{NUMLOCK}
Page Up and Page Down	{PGUP} {PGDN}
Print Screen	{PRTSC}
Scroll Lock	{SCROLLLOCK}
Tab	{TAB}
Function keys F1–F16	{F1} – {F16}

To repeat keystrokes a set number of times, enclose the keystroke followed by the repetition count in braces.

```
objShell.SendKeys strKeys "{a 10}" 'press the a key 10 times
objShell.SendKeys strKeys "{Down 10}" 'press the down arrow key 10 times
```

To perform keystroke combinations with the Ctrl, Alt, or Shift keys, prefix the keystroke with ^, %, or +.

```
objShell.SendKeys strKeys "%fs" 'press Alt-F then S (File - Save)
objShell.SendKeys strKeys "^s" 'press Ctrl-S
```

If you want to press Ctrl, Shift, or Alt with a multiple combination of keystrokes, surround the keystrokes with brackets.

```
objShell.SendKeys strKeys "^(%f)" 'press Ctrl-Alt-F
```

Note that you can't use SendKeys to send keystrokes to an application that is not designed to run in Microsoft Windows. Furthermore, SendKeys can't send the Print Screen key {PRTSC} to any application.

CHAPTER 3

Logon Scripts and Scheduling

THE ABILITY TO EXECUTE LOGON scripts has always been available in the Windows NT networked environment. The scripts relied on batch files, which could perform operations such as connecting to network resources and file operations.

Although you can connect to a networked resource by using a batch file, there is not a way for you to check if you're already connected or for you to test for a specific condition. Batch files cannot perform operations such as checking user group membership or enumerating shared drives and printers.

Batch files provide a very primitive method of using environment variables, simplistic flow control, and limited error handling. Furthermore, they are not very expandable, and they are limited to the command-line programs on the system.

Windows Script Host (WSH) changes all of this. WSH has native support for enumeration and manipulation of network resources such as network shares and printers. The various scripting engines that are available to WSH provide flexible flow control and error handling.

Most important, however, is the expandability of WSH through COM objects. The Windows environment provides interfaces to perform common logon operations. Group membership checking can be performed using Active Directory Services Interface (ADSI), and database operations can be performed through ActiveX Data Objects (ADO). Windows Management Instrumentation (WMI) can be used to query the system information. Graphical logon messages can be implemented using Internet Explorer.

3.1 Connecting Network Resources at Logon

Problem

You want to connect a user to a home directory and enable the person to share a public network at logon.

Solution

You can use the `WScript.Network` object's `MapNetworkDrive` method:

```
'get logged on user name to display in greeting. Loop to ensure
Dim objNetwork, strUser
Set objNetwork = CreateObject("WScript.Network")
strUser =""


'get logged on user name to display in greeting. Loop to ensure
' user ID is returned correctly on Win 9x/ME computers
 Do While strUser =""
strUser = objNetwork.UserName

Loop

'map user to home drive - assumes home drive share is combination of
'user-id and $ sign (hidden share)
objNetwork.MapNetworkDrive "H:", _
      "\\THOR\" & strUser & "$" , True
'connect to public area
objNetwork.MapNetworkDrive "P:", _
             "\\THOR\PublicArea", True
```

Discussion

Logon scripts often connect networked file server and printer resources.

WSH scripts have a number of advantages over the corresponding command-line connection programs such as `net use`. WSH scripts provide more error handling and provide better control flow.

Configuring your network to execute WSH scripts depends on the clients on the network. Windows 2000/2003/XP and Windows 98/ME can execute scripts natively by entering the script name in the Logon Script Name field under the User Profiles option, as shown in Figure 3-1, or the Profile dialog box in the Windows 2000/2003/XP Active Directory Users and Computers snap-in (`dsa.msc`).

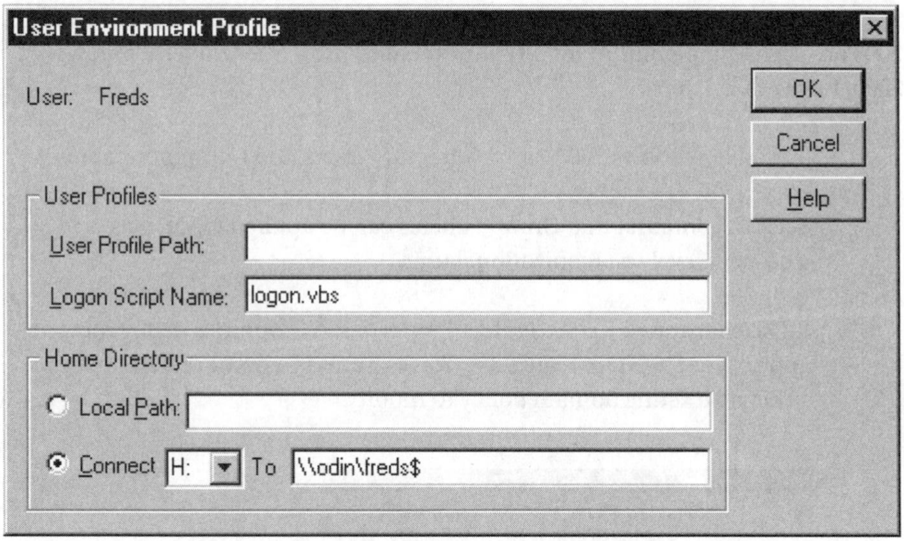

Figure 3-1. Windows NT 4 User Environment Profile dialog box

The default location Windows NT 4.0 logon scripts is the `%systemroot%\system32\repl\import` directory on domain controllers. This is automatically assigned the Netlogon share. Under Windows 2000 and 2003 Active Directory domains, the default logon directory is located under `%systemroot%\Sysvol\Sysvol\domain_name\Scripts`. For the domain `acme.com`, the location would be `%systemroot%\Sysvol\Sysvol\acme.com\Scripts`.

Both NT 4.0 and Windows 2000/2003 have file replication mechanisms that replicate logon scripts between domain controllers. This allows for redundancy, since a client may be authenticated by any domain controller and the logon scripts have to be synchronized when changes are made.

If you are working in an Active Directory–enabled Windows 2000/2003/XP environment, you can use *Group Policies* to execute scripts. Group Policies determine settings that apply to objects within Active Directory. Examples of Active Directory objects include groups, containers, and users.

Using Group Policies, scripts can be executed at user logon and logoff as well as at computer start-up and shutdown. Group Policies can be set at the domain and container (organizational unit) level, allowing specific policies to be applied to different groups of users.

For example, users within the finance organizational unit could run a different logon script than users within the accounting organizational unit.

The steps required to manipulate Group Policies under Windows 2000 and 2003 are slightly different. To modify Group Policy properties under Windows 2000, follow these steps:

1. Start the Windows 2000 Active Directory Users and Computers snap-in.

2. Select a container that Group Policies can be applied to, such as a domain level or organizational unit.

3. Right-click the object and select Properties. A Properties dialog box appears, as shown in Figure 3-2. You can create a new domain policy or select an existing domain policy to modify.

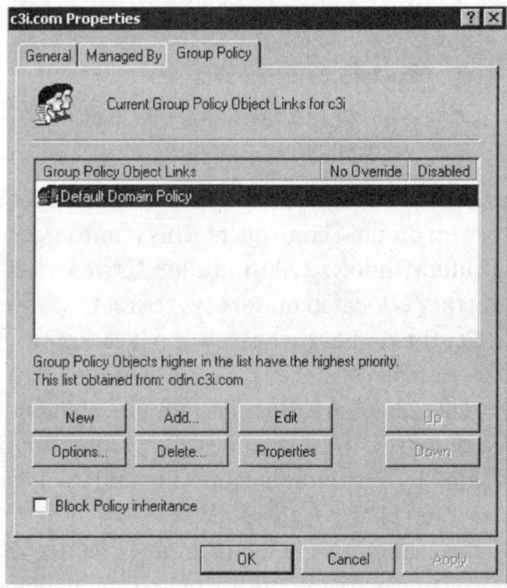

Figure 3-2. Group Policy Object Links list displaying a Default Domain Policy

4. Click the Edit button. A Group Policy window similar to the one in Figure 3-3 appears, displaying all available policy properties. As you can see, Startup and Shutdown scripts are set under the `Computer Configuration\Windows Settings\Scripts (Startup/Shutdown)` entry, while user logon and logoff scripts are configured under `User Configuration\Windows Settings\Scripts (Logon/Logoff)`.

5. After you've set all the properties, exit out of the Group Policy window.

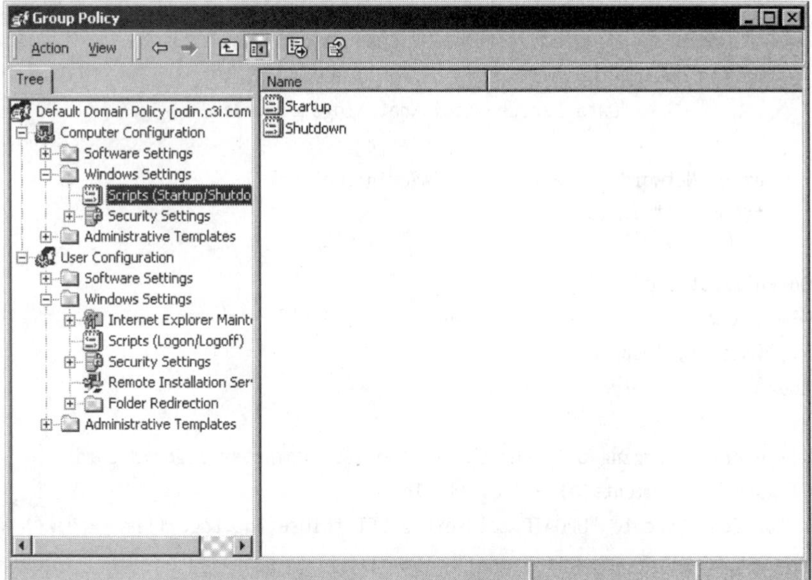

Figure 3-3. Group Policy Startup and Shutdown scripts

Under Windows 2003, follow these steps:

1. Start the Windows 2003 Group Policy Management plug-in.

2. Right-click the policy object you wish to modify.

Follow steps 4 and 5 from Windows 2000 Group Policy instructions.

To use Group Policies effectively, you must be using Windows 2000/2003/XP with an Active Directory–enabled domain. The clients must also be running Windows 2000/2003/XP, which limits the application in a mixed Windows client environment. Individual logon scripts assigned to users will execute together with Group Policy scripts.

If you have multiple scripts assigned to you, they will each run in order, with the domain-level script executing first. For example, you may have a domain and organizational unit Group Policy login script assigned to a user. The domain-level script will run first, followed by the organizational unit script.

Group Policies also provides logoff scripts. These scripts are executed when a user logs off and is set through policies in a similar matter as logon scripts. The following script provides user logon and logoff logging:

```
'logonoff.vbs
Dim objConn, objNetwork, strCmp
```

```
   'create a ADO connection and open a Access database
   Set objConn = CreateObject("ADODB.Connection")
   objConn.Open "Provider=Microsoft.Jet.OLEDB.4.0;" & _
                "Data Source=\\odin\data\logonoff.mdb"

   Set objNetwork = CreateObject("WScript.Network")
   strCmp = ""

Do While strCmp = ""
    strCmp = Trim(objNetwork.ComputerName) & ""
    Wscript.Sleep 10
Loop

'if user is logging off then update the last computer logon record
If Wscript.Arguments(0) = "Logoff" Then
   objConn.Execute "UPDATE tblUserLog SET tblUserLog.LogoffTime = Now() WHERE "
& _

"tblUserLog.LogEntryID=DMax(""LogEntryID"",""tblUserLog"",""UserName = '" & _
                    "Administrator" & "' And LogOffTime Is Null"");"

Else 'add new logon record
   objConn.Execute "INSERT INTO tblUserLog (UserName,LogonTime,LogonComputer)
VALUES (""" _
                 & objNetwork.UserName & """,#" & Now & "#,""" & strCmp &
""")", nF
End If

objConn.Close
```

To use the script, add it to both logon and logoff Group Policy events. Set the parameters to `Logon` for the logon event and `Logoff` for the logoff event. When a user logs on, it adds a record to the database for the logon start time. When the user logs off, the record is updated with the logoff time.

Windows 2000/2003/XP computers that are not part of an Active Directory domain can apply Group Policies to a local computer. This is done using the Group Policy editor. While you can apply the same script settings (logon, logoff, start-up, and shutdown), you cannot centrally control these settings, so it becomes impractical for a large number of computers. The Group Policy editor usually doesn't appear in the menus of a non-Active Directory computer, but you can access it by executing the `gpedit.msc` application located in the System32 directory.

If there are Windows NT 4.0 or Windows 9*x*/ME clients on the network, any WSH logon script must be executed from a batch file. Configure a batch file as the logon script, which calls the WSH script(s) you want to run at logon. Windows 2000, 2003, and XP clients do not require this step.

A problem that can occur with Windows 95 and NT 4.0 clients is not having WSH installed, and this can be checked by the logon script and installed if required.

The following logon batch file checks the client type and determines if WSH is already installed by searching for the `cscript.exe` file:

```
REM Logon.bat
REM Checks if WSH is installed on client and attempts to install it
REM then executes WSH logon script.
@ECHO OFF

IF "%OS%" == "Windows_NT" goto WIN_NT

IF NOT EXIST %WINDIR%\CSCRIPT.EXE %0\..\WSHBIN\STE50EN.EXE /Q
GOTO ENDSCRIPT
:WIN_NT
IF NOT EXIST %WINDIR%\SYSTEM32\CSCRIPT.EXE %0\..\WSHBIN\STE50EN.EXE /Q
GOTO ENDSCRIPT

:ENDSCRIPT
REM execute WSH script
 cscript login.vbs
```

If WSH is not found, it is installed. The WSH install file can take a `/Q` switch that performs a "silent" install, which doesn't display any install information or display any user prompts. The installation file `STE50EN.EXE` used in the batch is the name of a recent WSH installation—it may be different on newer (or older) installation packages.

> **NOTE** *Depending on the WSH installation version, the user may be prompted to reboot his or her machine after the installation of WSH is complete (even if it's a "silent" installation). This might not be desirable upon logon and may require user education.*

An issue that will arise when providing software distribution in logon scripts is the location of the source files. A central network share is an option, but this might not be as desirable in WAN environments where a computer might reside in a remote location and the data share is only accessible over a low bandwidth connection. A more flexible way to handle this issue is to locate files in the logon directory the script is executed from.

The location of a logon directory can vary (unless you only have a single domain controller), because Windows clients authenticate on the "closest" domain controller it finds. Using NT replication, the logon scripts and any associated support files can be replicated between the domain controllers.

When the logon batch file is executed, the path of the batch file is passed as a "zero" parameter. This can be referenced through the %0 variable in the DOS batch. To pass this to a WSH script, set an environment variable with the value `%0\..\`:

```
REM get path for logon script
SET LDIR=%0\..\

cscript logon.vbs
```

The value stored in the temporary `LDIR` environment variable can be retrieved using the `ExpandEnvironmentStrings` method in your WSH script:

```
Set objShell = WScript.CreateObject("WScript.Shell")
strPath = objShell.ExpandEnvironmentStrings("%LDIR%")
```

The following script copies a number of files to a client's desktop and fonts directory and updates flags identifying that the operation has completed:

```
'updfiles.vbs
'copy files upon logon
Dim strPath, objFSO, strVal, objShell, strCopyPath

Set objFSO = CreateObject("Scripting.FileSystemObject")
Set objShell = CreateObject("WScript.Shell")

strPath = objShell.ExpandEnvironmentStrings("%LDIR%")
On Error Resume Next
'get reference to registry flag
strVal = _
   objShell.RegRead("HKCU\SOFTWARE\WSHUpdates\DeskTopShortcutsUpdate1")
'if registry key didn't exist, then copy files to desktop
If IsEmpty(strVal) Then
```

```
 strCopyPath = objShell.SpecialFolders("Desktop") & "\"
 objFSO.CopyFile strPath & "E-mail Policy.doc.lnk", strCopyPath, True
 objFSO.CopyFile strPath & "Phone List.doc.lnk", strCopyPath, True
 'update registry entry to reflect the operation has been performed
 objShell.RegWrite "HKCU\SOFTWARE\WSHUpdates\DeskTopShortcutsUpdate1", _
                   Date
End If
strVal = Empty
'get reference to font update flag under local machine
strVal = objShell.RegRead("HKLM\SOFTWARE\WSHUpdates\TreFontUpd")

'if registry key didn't exist, then copy files to desktop
If IsEmpty(strVal) Then
  strCopyPath = objShell.SpecialFolders("Fonts") & "\"
  objFSO.CopyFile strPath & "Trebucbd.ttf", strCopyPath, True
  objShell.RegWrite "HKLM\SOFTWARE\WSHUpdates\TreFontUpd", Date
End If
```

The script performs the operations and updates a registry entry. This registry entry is checked at the execution of the script and the operations are not performed if a value has been set for the particular key.

The script assumes it has been called from a batch file and the `LDIR` environment variable has been set to the directory path of the logon script. The files copied to the desktop are stored in this path.

See Also

Solution 4.3, Solution 5.13, Solution 7.1, and Solution 7.2.

3.2 Scheduling Scripts

Problem

You want to schedule a WSH script.

Solution

You can use the Scheduled Tasks feature to implement script scheduling. Scheduled Tasks is integrated into Windows 2000/XP and Windows 98/ME. It is also an optional component of Internet Explorer, so it can be installed on

Windows 95 and Windows NT. If Schedules Tasks is installed on Windows NT, it replaces the scheduler service.

To schedule a task, follow these steps:

1. From My Computer, select the Scheduled Tasks icon.

2. Double-click the Add Scheduled Task icon. The Scheduled Task Wizard dialog box appears, as shown in Figure 3-4.

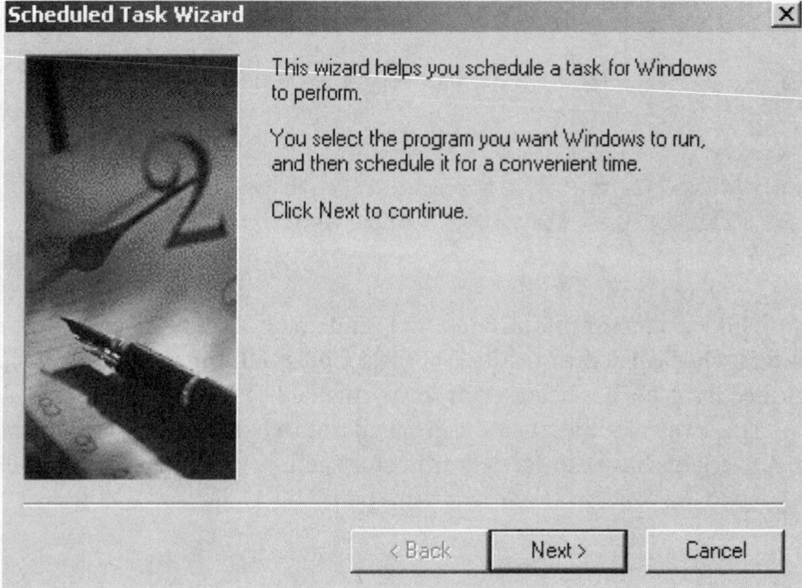

Figure 3-4. Scheduled Task Wizard dialog box

3. Click the Next button to continue.

4. You are prompted to select an application to run, as shown in Figure 3-5.

5. Click the Browse button. A file dialog box appears.

6. Select the script you want to schedule.

7. Enter a name for the scheduled task and select the time to perform the task, as shown in Figure 3-6.

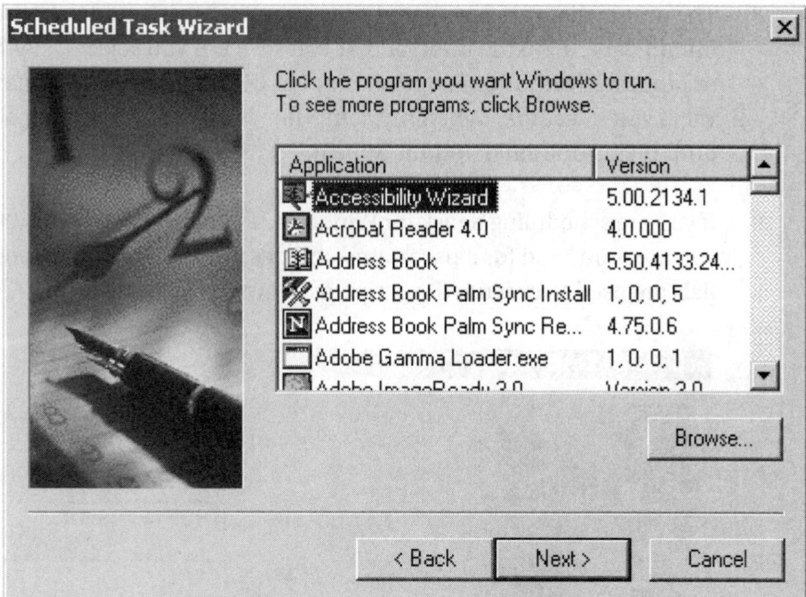

Figure 3-5. Scheduled Task Wizard application selection

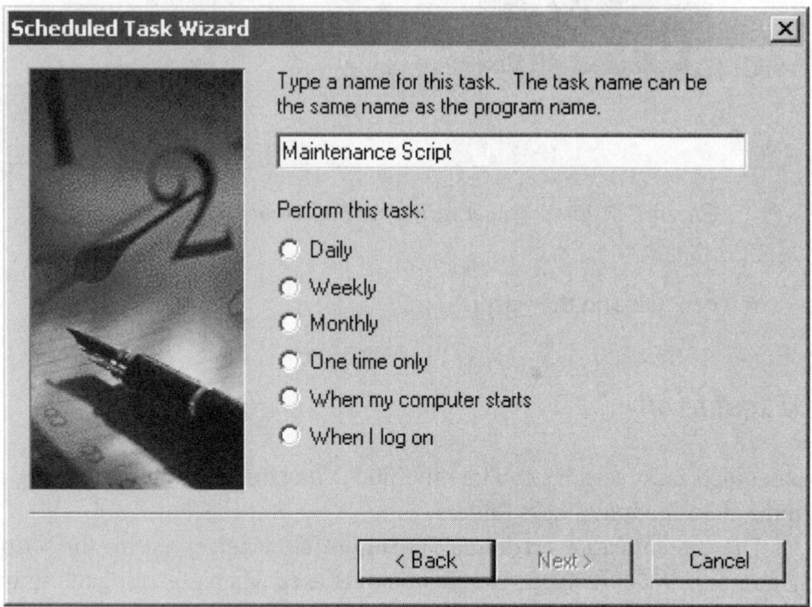

Figure 3-6. Enter a task name and select a performance interval.

8. The option dialog boxes that appear after you've selected the scheduled option depend on the interval that you select. If you select Daily, Weekly or Monthly, various time options appear that determine the time interval; if you select the "When my computer starts" or "When I log on" option, no additional options appear.

9. If you are scheduling a task for Windows NT or Windows 2000/2003/XP, you are prompted for a user name and password. These logon credentials are used to execute the script, as shown in Figure 3-7.

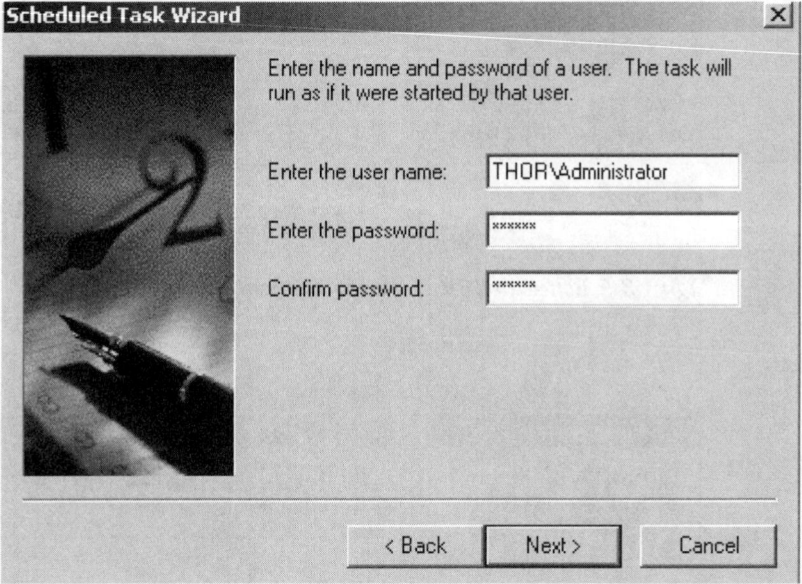

Figure 3-7. Enter a user name and password.

You can now run the script.

Discussion

Scheduled Tasks settings can be modified at any time by double-clicking any task under the Scheduled Tasks folder.

The authentication credentials are important when executing the script under Windows NT/2000/2003. The credentials are used when executing the script, and any resources accessed by the script are authenticated using these credentials. Do not use an account with excess security rights if possible, because the contents of a script could be replaced with a malicious script and executed in a security context where it could perform damaging operations.

Windows NT/2000/XP/2003 includes native scheduling capability using the DOS `AT` command and scheduling service. See Solution 10.10 for how to create jobs using the AT command through Windows Management Interface (WMI). The native NT scheduling service is less flexible than Scheduled Tasks for scheduling items, especially for executing scripts at mixed intervals. Scheduled Tasks also allows tasks to be executed by different user accounts, whereas the NT scheduling services are limited to the logon account set for the scheduler service, which by default is a local system account. If you install the Scheduled Tasks feature under Windows NT, all existing tasks scheduled using the `AT` command are kept.

Scripts that are scheduled to run on Windows NT/2000/2003 when the user is not logged on should be executed using `cscript.exe`; if graphical prompts are displayed while the user is not logged in, unpredictable operations may result. Either set cscript as the default script host or explicitly configure the scheduled script to use `cscript.exe`, as shown in Figure 3-8.

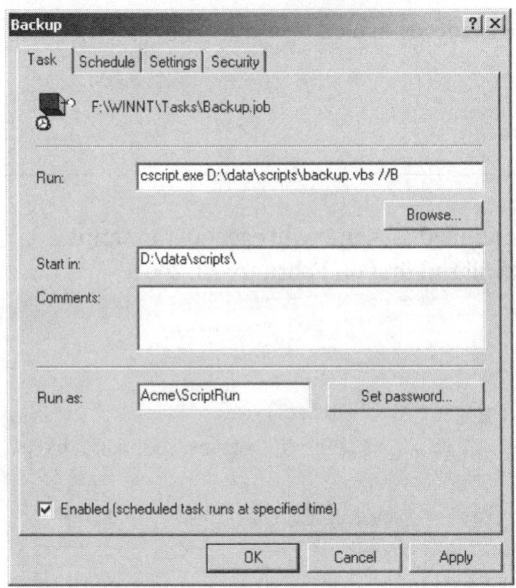

Figure 3-8. Set cscript to execute a scheduled script.

There is no method included with WSH or Scheduled Tasks to automate the creation of tasks. Microsoft has a free component that provides limited Scheduled Tasks creation functionality. To download the component, search for the phrase "Task Scheduler Using VBScript" at `http://technet.microsoft.com`. Download and install the component. To use the component, create an instance of an object using the class ID `SchedulingAgent.NTScheduler`.

The component exposes the method `ISchedulingAgent_ScheduleTask`. The syntax is as follows:

```
objShell.ISchedulingAgent_ScheduleTask strName, strApp, strParam _
, strUser, strPassword, strDate, strTime
```

Table 3-1 lists the `ISchedulingAgent_ScheduleTask` method parameters.

Table 3-1. ISchedulingAgent_ScheduleTask Method Parameters

PARAMETER	DESCRIPTION
strName	Scheduled task job name
strApp	Scheduled application
strParam	Parameters
strUser	User ID to execute scheduled task
strPassword	User password to execute scheduled task
strDate	Scheduled start date
strTime	Scheduled start time

The following script creates a scheduled task that will execute the script `dbackup` daily at 8:10 p.m. The script will run first on February 23, 2004:

```
Dim objAgent

Set objAgent = CreateObject("SchedulingAgent.NTScheduler")
objAgent.ISchedulingAgent_ScheduleTask "Daily Backup", "c:\scrupts\dbackup.vbs",
_
                    "", "Acme\Administrator", "ZXcvBNm,", "2/23/2004", "8:10 PM"
```

The scheduling component edits existing jobs or creates varying execution schedules. If you wanted to set up scheduled operations on a number of computers, such as at logon, you could distribute the Scheduled Tasks file.

Scheduled Tasks are stored as .job files under the `%windir%\Tasks` folder. If these files are copied to the Tasks folders on remote computers, they automatically appear as scheduled items on that computer.

Scheduled Tasks implemented through this method should be thoroughly tested before being distributed, especially if the tasks are being used by different operating systems, such as Windows 95, 2000, and 2003.

The following script copies a `.job` file from a central location to the `Windows\Tasks` directory:

```
'updatejob.vbs
'copy job file from logon location to Tasks folder
Const WindowsFolder = 0
Dim objShell, strPath, objFSO, strVal

Set objFSO = CreateObject("Scripting.FileSystemObject")
Set objShell = CreateObject("WScript.Shell")


Set objShell = CreateObject("WScript.Shell")
'set the directory to find the job file to copy
strPath = "\\odin\jobfiles\"

On Error Resume Next
'get reference to registry flag
strVal = _
    objShell.RegRead("HKCU\SOFTWARE\WSHUpdates\AddJob1")
'if registry key didn't exist, then copy files to Windows Tasks folder
If IsEmpty(strVal) Then
 strCopyPath = objFSO.GetSpecialFolder(WindowsFolder) & "\Tasks\"

 objFSO.CopyFile strPath & "maintenance.job", strCopyPath , True
'update registry entry to reflect the operation has been performed
 objShell.RegWrite "HKCU\SOFTWARE\WSHUpdates\AddJob1", Date
End If
```

The script can be called from a logon script to update clients' Scheduled Tasks. The registry is updated with a flag so the file is not copied again at next logon.

If the Scheduled Task is being used by Windows 2000/2003/XP or Windows NT 4.0 as well as Windows 9*x*/ME computers, it should be created on the Windows NT/2000/2003/XP platforms. Tasks created by Windows NT/2000/2003 will run under Windows 9*x*, but tasks created under Windows 9*x* will be missing the Windows NT/2000/2003 account authentication information that Windows 9*x* does not require.

Task Scheduler logs the execution of scheduled operations. You can view the log by selecting the View Log option from the Advanced menu under Scheduled Tasks.

See Also

Task Scheduler Help file `mstask.chm`, which is located under the Windows Help directory.

3.3 Displaying a Logon Message

Problem

You want to display a graphical welcome message upon logon. Figure 3-9 shows an example of a "welcome" screen that appears when a user logs on.

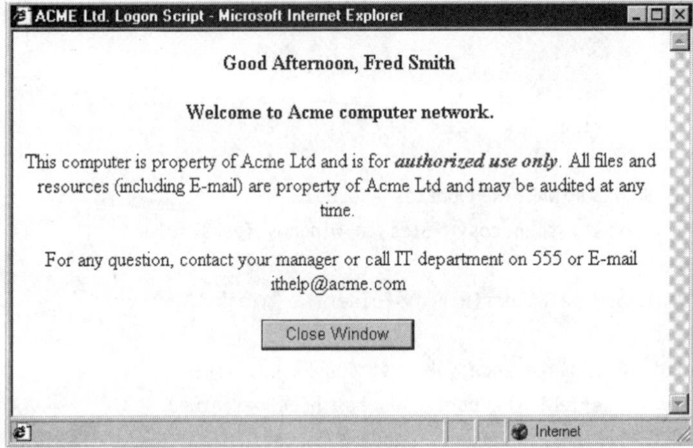

Figure 3-9. Logon "welcome" message

Solution

You can use the `ENTWSH.HTMLGen` scripting component from Chapter 11 to build a graphical dialog box using Internet Explorer 5.*x* or later:

```
'logon.vbs
Const DOMAIN = "Acme"

Set objShell = CreateObject("WScript.Shell")
Set objNetwork = CreateObject("WScript.Network")
Set objFSO = CreateObject("Scripting.FileSystemObject")
```

```
'create a ENTWSH.HTMLGen component
Set objHTMLGen = GetObject("script:\\odin\wsc$\htmlgen.wsc")

On Error Resume Next
objHTMLGen.StartDOC "ACME Ltd. Logon Script", True

'get logged on user name to display in greeting. Loop to ensure
' user ID is returned correctly on Win 9x/ME computers
Do While strUser =""
 strUser = objNetwork.UserName
 WScript.Sleep 100
Loop

'get ADSI User object from domain
Set objUser = GetObject("WinNT://" & DOMAIN & "/" & strUser & ",User")
'if no error occurred getting ADSI user object, set user ID to
'user full name
If Not Err Then strUser = objUser.FullName

Set objIE = objHTMLGen.Object
objIE.MenuBar = 0
objIE.Toolbar = 0

strMsg = "Good "

If Hour(Time)>=17 Then
  strMsg = strMsg & "Evening, "
ElseIf Hour(Time)>=12 Then
  strMsg = strMsg & "Afternoon, "
Else
  strMsg = strMsg & "Morning, "
End If

Err.Clear
'if OS Windows 9x/ME map home directory
If Not objShell.Environment("OS") = "Windows_NT" Then
 objNetwork.RemoveNetworkDrive "H:", True
 Err.Clear
 objNetwork.MapNetworkDrive "H:", "\\Odin\" & objNetwork.UserName _
                                & "$", True
End If
```

```
objHTMLGen.WriteLine "<center><b>" & strMsg & strUser & _
                     "</center></b><br>"
Set objTS = objFSO.OpenTextFile("\\odin\d$\data\messages\hello.htm")
objHTMLGen.WriteLine objTS.ReadAll
objHTMLGen.WriteLine "<center><input type=""submit"" value=""" & _
                  "Close Window"" onClick=""window.close()""></center>"

objHTMLGen.EndDOC
```

Discussion

Messages displayed at logon can be used to provide general information to users as well as to display system information.

The solution script uses the Active Directory Services Interface (ADSI) to get the connected user's name. ADSI is covered in more detail in Chapter 14. The solution script and other scripts in this chapter use the ADSI WinNT provider to connect to a domain and retrieve user details from the provider's `User` object. This provider was originally developed for Windows NT 4.0, but it also works under native Active Directory modes under Windows 2000 and Windows 2003.

There may be times when you'll want to retrieve user information from a native or mixed mode Active Directory domain running under Windows 2000 or 2003. In these instances, you need to get a reference to the Active Directory `User` object using LDAP, which is tricky since the user may reside in different containers and you need to know the user's location before you can connect.

The following sample displays the current user's default Web page set in Active Directory:

```
Dim objConn, objRS, objRoot, objDomain
Dim strFilter, objNetwork

Set objNetwork = CreateObject("WScript.Network")

'get logged on user name
 strUser = objNetwork.UserName

'get current domain
Set objRoot = GetObject("LDAP://rootDSE")
Set objDomain = GetObject("LDAP://" & _
        objRoot.Get("defaultNamingContext"))

'build a query to find user object's samAccountName property for logon name
strFilter = "(&(objectCategory=person)(objectClass=user)(samAccountName=" _
  & strUser & "))"
```

```
strQuery = "<" & objDomain.ADsPath & ">" _
      & ";" & strFilter & ";adsPath;subTree"

'connect to OLEDB Active directory provider
Set objConn = CreateObject("ADODB.Connection")

objConn.Open _
  "Data Source=Active Directory Provider;Provider=ADsDSOObject"

Set objRS = objConn.Execute(strQuery)

'if user object found display
If Not objRS.EOF Then
    Set objUser = GetObject(objRS("adsPath"))

Set objIE = CreateObject("InternetExplorer.Application")
    'go to the page
    objIE.Navigate objUser.wWWHomePage

    'wait to load page
    While objIE.Busy
    Wend
    objIE.Visible = True
End If
```

The script searches the default domain for the current user using ADO. See Solution 14.16 for more information on how to search Active Directory. The default Web page can be set for each user and is available only in Active Directory–enabled domains. The Solution script uses Internet Explorer (IE) to build a logon message. An instance of IE is created through the `WSHENT.HTMLGen` component, which is discussed in Chapter 11.

An instance of the `HTMLGen` component is created using the `GetObject` method. Windows Script components can use either `CreateObject` or `GetObject` to create new instances. Creating new instances by using `GetObject` only applies to WSC objects and is implemented by calling the method and then passing the path to the component prefixed with `script:`. The following snippet creates an instance of the `HTMLGen` component using the `script:` prefix:

```
Set objHTMLGen = GetObject("script:\\odin\wsc$\ HTMLGen.wsc")
```

The path to the component can be a local path or UNC. The advantage of using `GetObject` over `CreateObject` is the WSC object does not need to be registered. This is useful in logon scripts because you may not be guaranteed that all clients that log on to the network have the appropriate WSC objects registered.

This method cannot be used with compiled COM components written in languages such as VB or C++. These components must be registered before being used, which can be difficult to guarantee on all client computers.

If you are implementing logon scripts that require the use of components, you can check if the component is registered and install and register it before executing the WSH script. The following sample checks if the `regobj.dll` registry component exists in the Windows system directory, and if not, copies it over and registers it:

```
IF "%OS%" == "Windows_NT" goto WIN_NT

IF NOT EXIST %WINDIR%\regobj.dll GOTO REG9X
GOTO ENDSCRIPT
:REG9X
Copy %0\..\DLL\regobj.dll %WINDIR%\system
%0\..\exe\regsvr32 /s %WINDIR%\system\regobj.dll
GOTO ENDSCRIPT

:WIN_NT
IF NOT EXIST %WINDIR%\system32\regobj.dll GOTO REGNT
GOTO ENDSCRIPT
:REGNT
Copy %0\..\DLL\regobj.dll %WINDIR%\system32
%0\..\exe\regsvr32 /s %WINDIR%\system32\regobj.dll

:ENDSCRIPT
 cscript login.vbs
```

The logon script checks for the existence of `regobj.dll` in the client's system directory. If it is not in the directory, it is copied over and registered using `regsvr32`. The `regsvr32` application is not a standard Windows-installed application, so it is executed from the logon directory. The `/s` (silent) switch is used when registering the component to ensure no prompts appear to the user.

You can check for the existence of and register components through a WSH script upon logon. Additional checking can be performed in the script, such as version checking, error trapping, and logging, which can't be easily implemented through a batch file.

The following script contains the logic to check for the existence of a specific file and copy and register it if it does not exist:

```
'regit.vbs
'checks for existence of specified DLLs and registers
'them if required
```

```
Const ForAppending = 8
Dim objShell, strComputer, strSource, strDest
Dim strLogFile,  objNetwork, strUser

Set objNetwork = CreateObject("WScript.Network")

'loop until user id is retrieved, required for Win9x
Do While strUser =""
 strUser = objNetwork.UserName
Loop

'set the log file name - ensure uniqueness by combining
'user id and date and time
strLogFile = "\\thor\e$\" & strUser & " " &  Month(date) & "-" & _
              Day(date) & "-" & Year(date) & " " & _
              Hour(time) & "_" & Minute(time) & "_" _
              & Second(time) & ".txt"

Set objShell =CreateObject("WScript.Shell")

'set destination directory depending on OS
If objShell.ExpandEnvironmentStrings("%OS%") = "Windows_NT" Then
  strDest = objShell.ExpandEnvironmentStrings("%windir%") _
                & "\system32\"
Else
  strDest = objShell.ExpandEnvironmentStrings("%windir%") _
                & "\system\"
End If

'get the source directory to find the components to register
strSource = objShell.ExpandEnvironmentStrings("%LDIR%")

CheckRegister "regobj.dll", False


'CheckRegister
'Checks for existence of specified file and copies and registers it
'if it does not exist.
'Parameters
'strFile   Name of file to check for
'bReplace  Boolean value. If True then file will be updated if newer
'           version exists
Sub CheckRegister(strFile, bReplace)
```

```
Dim strPath
Dim objFSO
Dim bRegister, strDstVer, strSrcVer

strComputer = ""

strDest = strDest & strFile
strSource = strSource & strFile

Set objFSO = CreateObject("Scripting.FileSystemObject")
 bRegister = False

 'check if specified file exists
 If Not objFSO.FileExists(strDest) Then
    objFSO.CopyFile strSource, strDest
    bRegister = True
 Else
  'file exists.. replace?
  If bReplace Then

   On Error Resume Next
   'attempt to get file version of specified files
   strSrcVer = objFSO.GetFileVersion(strSource)
   strDstVer = objFSO.GetFileVersion(strDest)
   'error occurred.. unable to get version, use file size instead
   If Err Then
    strSrcVer = objFSO.GetFile(strSource).Size
    strDstVer = objFSO.GetFile(strDest).Size
   End If
   Err.Clear
   'check if the destination file version is less than source
    If Val(strSrcVer) > Val(strDstVer) Then
     'copy over existing file
     objFSO.CopyFile strSource, strDest
      'error copying file?
      If Err Then
       'error copying source to destination..
         LogIt strLogFile, "Error copying file " & strSource & _
                " to " & strDest & " on computer " & strComputer _
                & vbCrLf & Err.Description & " " & Err
        CheckRegister = False
       Exit Sub
      End If
     bRegister = True
```

```
    Else
     'more recent version of file, exit function
     LogIt strLogFile, "File " & strSource & _
          " is more recent than " & strDest & " on computer " & _
          strComputer
     Exit Sub
    End If
  End If

 End If

 'register the file?
 If bRegister Then
    objShell.Run strSource & "regsvr32 /s " & strDest, 0, True
 End If

End Sub

'Procedure Logfile
'Logs text to specified file
'Parameters
'strFile   Path to log file
'strMsg    Message to log
Sub LogIt(strFile, strMsg)
Dim objTS, objFSO

Set objFSO = CreateObject("Scripting.FileSystemObject")
Set objTS = objFSO.OpenTextFile(strFile, ForAppending, True)
objTS.WriteLine Now & " " & strMsg

objTS.Close
End Sub
```

The script also compares versions of the specified component or library and attempts to replace it if the current version is older than the one to be copied. The file version is determined by the File Scripting object's `GetFileVersion` method.

Operation results are written to a log file, which allows for the rollout and updating of components to be monitored. Because the operating system does not allow more than one process to open and write to a file at the same time, a unique filename is used to ensure that conflicts don't occur. The file name consists of the user ID followed by the date and time—for example, `FredS 7-16-2001 20_32_28.txt`. An alternative method of logging is to use the event log. This is useful in a Windows NT4/2000/XP-only environment, because it allows for information to be logged in a central location.

WSH version 2.0 and later provides the ability to write events to the Windows NT/2000/2003/XP event log using the `WScript.Shell` object's `LogEvent` method. The syntax is as follows:

```
objShell.LogEvent(intType, strMessage [,strTarget])
```

Table 3-2 lists the LogEvent method parameters.

Table 3-2. LogEvent Parameters

PARAMETER	DESCRIPTION
`intType`	Type of the event. Table 3-3 lists the event types.
`strMessage`	Message to log.
`strTarget`	Optional. Applies to Windows NT4/2000/2003/XP only. The name of the system where the event should be logged. Default is local system. Parameter is ignored on Windows 9*x*/ME.

Table 3-3. LogEvent Types

PARAMETER	DESCRIPTION
1	Success
2	Error
4	Warning
8	Information
16	Audit_Success

On Windows NT4/2000/2003/XP the method logs an event in the event log. The logged message is stored in an application log with the Source as WSH. The following code sample logs an information message to the event log on the remote computer Odin:

```
Const Information = 8
Set objShell = CreateObject("WScript.Shell")
objShell.LogEvent Information, "Error occurred when sending mail", "Odin"
```

On Windows 9*x*/ME the information is logged to the file `WSH.log`, which will be in the user's Windows directory. The `WSH.log` file will contain a timestamp, the event type, and the text of the log entry.

The method returns `True` if the event is successfully logged; otherwise, it returns `False`.

The Solution script displays a salutation to the user at logon. The salutation displays Good Morning/Afternoon/Evening followed by the user name. The user name is referenced from the Full Name field from NT User Manager or Display Name field from the Active Directory Users and Computer plug-in under an Active Directory domain. The property is retrieved using ADSI (which must be installed on the client workstation as well as domain controllers). If ADSI is not installed, the user's logon user ID is used instead.

Additional information is stored in an external html file, `hello.htm`, and loaded into the browser at logon. This makes for easier editing of the logon message.

See Also

Solution 11.2, Solution 14.3, and Solution 14.5.

3.4 Performing Operations Based on Group Membership

Problem

You want to check group membership upon logon.

Solution

You can get a reference to the ADSI group object that you want to check and then use the ADSI Group object's `IsMember` method to determine group membership:

```
'chkmember.vbs
Const Domain = "ACME"
Dim strUser, objGroup, strGroup, objUser

Set objNetwork = CreateObject("WScript.Network")

'get name of logged on user - loop until user id is retrieved, required for Win9x
Do While strUser = ""
  strUser = objNetwork.UserName
  WScript.Sleep 100
Loop
```

```
If CheckGroup(Domain, "Accounting", strUser) Then
   'connect to accounting share
   objWshNetwork.MapNetworkDrive "P:", "\\THOR\Accounting", True
End If

Function CheckGroup(strDomain, strGroup, strUser)
Dim objGroup
'get ADSI User object from domain
Set objGroup = GetObject("WinNT://" & strDomain & "/" _
                 & strGroup & ",Group")

If objGroup.IsMember("WinNT://" & strDomain & "/" & strUser) Then
  CheckGroup = True
Else
  CheckGroup = False
End If

End Function
```

Discussion

Performing actions that are based on user ID or group membership has traditionally been hard to accomplish using normal batch file logon scripts in a Windows NT networked environment.

Active Directory Services Interface (ADSI) provides a mechanism to test for group membership in a WSH script. ADSI is included in Windows 2000, XP, and 2003, but you must install it on Windows 95, 98, ME, and NT 4.0 clients to use this feature. See Chapter 14 for more information on how to use ADSI and the `IsMember` method.

Testing for group membership for a large number of groups can be time-consuming. Each reference made to a `Group` object requires another call to a server. Instead, get a reference to the user that is being checked and enumerate the groups the account is a member of, adding each group account to a string. The following script demonstrates this method and connects drives based on group membership:

```
Dim strGroups, objGroup, objUser, strUser, objNetwork
Const Domain = "acme"

Set objNetwork = CreateObject("WScript.Network")
```

```
'get logged on user name
'get name of logged on user - loop until user id is retrieved, required for Win9x
Do While strUser = ""
 strUser = objNetwork.UserName
 WScript.Sleep 100
Loop

'get ADSI User object from domain
Set objUser = GetObject("WinNT://" & Domain & "/" & strUser & ",User")

strGroups = ";"
'enumerate all user groups
For Each objGroup In objUser.Groups
  strGroups = strGroups & objGroup.Name & ";"
Next

'check if member of Accounting or Finance group
MapGroup "Accounting", "\\THOR\Accounting", "P:"
MapGroup "Finance", "\\THOR\Finance", "O:"


Sub MapGroup(strName, strShare, strDrive)
'check if member of specified group
   If InStr(strGroups, ";" & strName & ";", vbTextCompare) > 0 Then
    objNetwork.MapNetworkDrive strDrive,  strShare, True
   End If
End Sub
```

If you are using Windows 2000/2003/XP with Active Directory enabled and Windows 2000/XP clients, logon scripts can be assigned to organizational units via Group Policies. This allows scripts to be executed depending on the organizational unit to which a user belongs. See Solution 3.2 for information on setting Group Policies.

Login scripts that perform operations based on group membership and/or network user IDs can be tedious to maintain. Whenever a change is made, the script must be replicated to all domain controllers to ensure the script is available when a user logs on.

The following application, Quick and Dirty Network Administration (QADNA), provides an administrative interface that allows user accounts and groups to be assigned network resources and set registry values. Figure 3-10 illustrates the graphical user interface that is used to associate resources to a user.

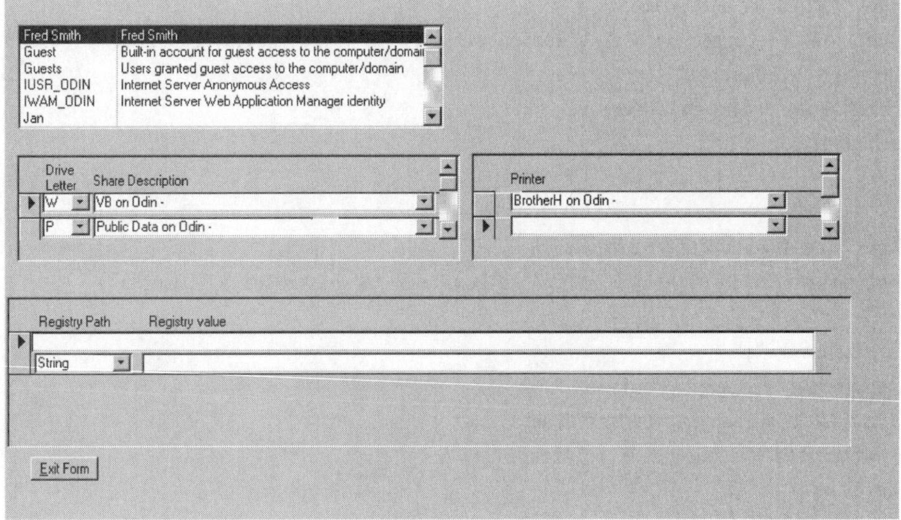

Figure 3-10. QADNA User configuration

QADNA is implemented using Microsoft Access 97 and can be found in the Downloads area of the Apress Web site (`http://www.apress.com`). The application provides a simple interface to associate resources with a particular user or group.

Users and groups are maintained through an administrative screen that uses ADSI to search for all users, groups, and computers on the network. These are added to the Access database. The database must be manually refreshed each time a new resource (user, group, or computer resource) is added.

You can use the following script as a client logon script:

```
'qadna.vbs
'Quick and Dirty Network Administration interface
Const Domain = "c3i"
Const ForAppending = 8
Const DataFile="Provider=Microsoft.Jet.OLEDB.4.0;DataSource=\\odin\Data\qadna.mdb"
Const ConnectShare = 5
Const ConnectPrinter = 4
Const UpdateRegistry = 100

Dim objConn, objRst, objNetwork
Dim strGroups, strUser, objGroup
Dim strQuery, strComputer, objShell, strLogFile

Set objShell = CreateObject("WScript.Shell")
```

```
Set objNetwork = CreateObject("WScript.Network")

'set the log filename - ensure uniqueness by combining
'user id and date and time
strLogFile = "\\odin\logfiles\" & strUser & " " &  Month(date) & "-" & _
             Day(date) & "-" & Year(date) & " " & _
             Hour(time) & "_" & Minute(time) & "_" _
             & Second(time) & ".txt"

'get name of logged on user - loop until user id is retrieved
'required for Win9x
Do While strUser = ""
 strUser = objNetwork.UserName
 WScript.Sleep 100
Loop

strComputer = objNetwork.ComputerName

On Error Resume Next

'get ADSI User object from domain
Set objUser = GetObject("WinNT://" & Domain & "/" & strUser & ",User")

If Err Then
  LogIt strLogFile,"Error getting ADSI user object for " & strUser & _
        vbCr & Err.Description & " " & Err
  WScript.Quit -1
End If

'build query to execute against QADNA database
strQuery = "Select * From qryLinkAccountsWithActions WHERE " & _
           "(AccountName In ("

'enumerate all user groups
For Each objGroup In objUser.Groups
  strQuery = strQuery & "'" & objGroup.Name & "',"
Next

'add user name to query
strQuery = Left(strQuery, Len(strQuery) - 1) & _
           ")) Or AccountName ='" & strUser & "'"

'create ADO object and open QADNA database
```

```
Set objConn = CreateObject("ADODB.Connection")
objConn.Open DataFile

If Err Then
  LogIt strLogFile,"Error opening database " & DataFile & _
        " on computer " & strComputer & vbCrLf & _
        Err.Description & " " & Err
  WScript.Quit -1
End If

Set objRst = objConn.Execute(strQuery)

 'loop through each record and perform specified operation
 Do While Not objRst.Eof
   Select Case objRst("ActionType")
     Case ConnectShare
        'remove any existing connected drive
        objNetwork.RemoveNetworkDrive objRst("DriveLetter") & ":", True
        'clear any errors occurred, such as removing nonconnected drive
        Err.Clear
       'connect drive
        strPath = "\\" & objRst("ObjectSource") & "\" _
                  & objRst("ObjectName")
        objNetwork.MapNetworkDrive objRst("DriveLetter") & ":", _
                                        strPath, True

       If Err Then
        LogIt strLogFile,"Error connecting to  " & strPath & _
              " on computer " & strComputer & vbCrLf  & _
              Err.Description & " " & Err

       End If

     Case ConnectPrinter 'add printer
        Err.Clear
        strPath = "\\" & objRst("ObjectSource") & "\" & _
                   objRst("ObjectName")
        objNetwork.AddWindowsPrinterConnection strPath

       If Err Then
        LogIt strLogFile,"Error adding printer " & strPath & _
              " on computer " & strComputer & vbCrLf & _
              Err.Description & " " & Err
```

```
        End If

      Case UpdateRegistry

          'write registry value
         strPath = objRst("Path1")
         'check if DWORD type value

      If objRst("DriveLetter") = "D" Then
          objShell.RegWrite strPath, objRst("Path2"),"REG_DWORD"
         Else
          objShell.RegWrite strPath, objRst("Path2")
         End If
        If Err Then

          LogIt strLogFile,"Error setting registry key  " & strPath & _
               " on computer " & strComputer & vbCrLf & _
               Err.Description & " " & Err
        End If

    End Select
    objRst.MoveNext
  Loop

objRst.Close
objConn.Close
```

When a client logs on and the script is executed, the database is checked for any resources associated with the user or any groups the user belongs to and they are set accordingly. Printer resources are added, network shares are connected, and registry values are set depending on the values set in the QADNA program.

Each client must have ADO version 2.0, which includes the OLEDB provider required to read the Access database. For more information on database manipulation using ADO, see Chapter 13.

File locations stored in the DSN file need to be changed to reflect locations in your environment. A recent version of ADSI must also be installed on the client machine to use the script.

See Also

Solution 3.1 and Solution 14.15.

3.5 Creating an Inventory of Computers at Logon

Problem

You want to inventory a computer at logon and store the details in a database.

Solution

WMI provides a large number of classes that expose system-related information. The following script uses WMI to inventory major system components and stores the information in the Access QADNA database introduced in Solution 3.5 to store and manage the information. ADO is used within the script to populate the database. The `SysInfo.ENTWSH` Windows script component created in Solution 10.1 is used to query O/S, memory, serial number, and CPU information:

```
'invcom.vbs
'inventories computer upon logon
Option Explicit

Const DataFile = "Provider=Microsoft.Jet.OLEDB.4.0;DataSource=\\odin\Data\qadna.mdb

Const adOpenDynamic= 2
Const adLockOptimistic= 3

Dim objSysInfo, objService, objNetwork, objRst, objConn
Dim strComputerName, nCompID, bUpdate, bNew

Set objNetwork = CreateObject("WScript.Network")
strComputerName = objNetwork.ComputerName

'create ADO object and open QADNA database
Set objConn = CreateObject("ADODB.Connection")
Set objRst = CreateObject("ADODB.Recordset")
objConn.Open DataFile

bUpdate = False
bNew = False

'open tblcomputers table and determine if computer exists
objRst.Open "tblComputers", objConn, adOpenDynamic, adLockOptimistic
objRst.Find "ComputerName='" & strComputerName & "'"
```

```
bUpdate = False
'if computer does not exist, add to inventory
If objRst.EOF Then
    objRst.AddNew
    objRst("ComputerName") = strComputerName
    bNew = True
Else
   'check if computer record needs updating..
   If Date>= Cdate(objRst("UpdateDate")) Then bUpdate = True
End If


If bUpdate Or bNew Then

 Set objService = _
    GetObject("winmgmts:{impersonationLevel=impersonate}!root\cimv2")

 'create an instance of the SysInfo object
 Set objSysInfo = GetObject("script:\\odin\wsc$\SysInfo.wsc")

 objRst("BIOSVersion") = objSysInfo.BIOSVersion
 objRst("CPU") = objSysInfo.CPU
 objRst("Memory") = objSysInfo.Memory
 objRst("OSVersion") = objSysInfo.OS
 objRst("RegisteredUser") = objSysInfo.RegisteredUser
 objRst("OSSerialNum") = objSysInfo.SerialNumber
 objRst("VirtualMemory") = objSysInfo.VirtualMemory
 objRst("UpdateDate") = Date  + 180
 nCompID = objRst("ComputerID")

 objRst.Update
 objRst.Close

 'if new computer record get record ID
 If bNew Then
  Set objRst = objConn.Execute("SELECT Max(ComputerID) FROM tblComputers")
  nCompID = objRst(0)
 End If

 'delete any existing computer inventory
 objConn.Execute "Delete From tblComputerItems " & _
                "Where ComputerID = "  & nCompID
```

```
 WMIInv "Select Description, Size From Win32_DiskDrive" _
        , Array("Description" , "Size"),1, nCompID

 WMIInv "Select AdapterType, AdapterRAM From " & _
        "Win32_VideoConfiguration" _
        ,Array("AdapterType", "AdapterRAM"), 2, nCompID

 WMIInv "Select Description, MacAddress From " & _
        "Win32_NetworkAdapterConfiguration Where IPEnabled = True" _
        , Array("Description", "MacAddress"), 3, nCompID

 WMIInv "Select Model, ProviderName From " & _
        "Win32_POTSModem", Array("Model", "ProviderName"), 4, nCompID

 WMIInv "Select Description, Manufacturer From " & _
        "Win32_SCSIController" , Array("Description", _
        "Manufacturer"), 5, nCompID

End If

objConn.Close

'WMIInv
'returns specified information from WMI query
'Parameters:
'strQuery     SQL query to execute against WMI service
'aFields      Array of fields to store
'nType        Type of item
'nCompID      Unique computer identifier
Sub WMIInv(strQuery, aFields, nType, nCompID)
Dim objInstance, objResults, objProp
Dim nF, strSQL, strText

Set objResults = objService.ExecQuery(strQuery)

'loop through each instance and build the output lines
For Each objInstance In objResults
strSQL="INSERT INTO tblComputerItems (ComputerID,ItemType, Item1,Item2)" _
        & " Values (" & nCompID & "," & nType & ","

'loop through each property
 For nF = LBound(aFields) To UBound(aFields)
  Set objProp = objInstance.Properties_(aFields(nF))
```

```
  strText = objProp.Value
  strSQL = strSQL & "'" & strText & "',"
 Next

 strSQL = Left(strSQL, Len(strSQL) - 1) & ");"
 objConn.Execute strSQL
Next
End Sub
```

Discussion

Keeping an up-to-date inventory of client hardware is a never-ending, time-consuming, but important task for any IT departments.

This Solution uses Windows Management Instrumentation (WMI) to inventory the resources on the client computer. The information is stored in the QADNA Access database that was introduced in Solution 3.4. Figure 3-11 shows the computer information that has been inventoried after running the script.

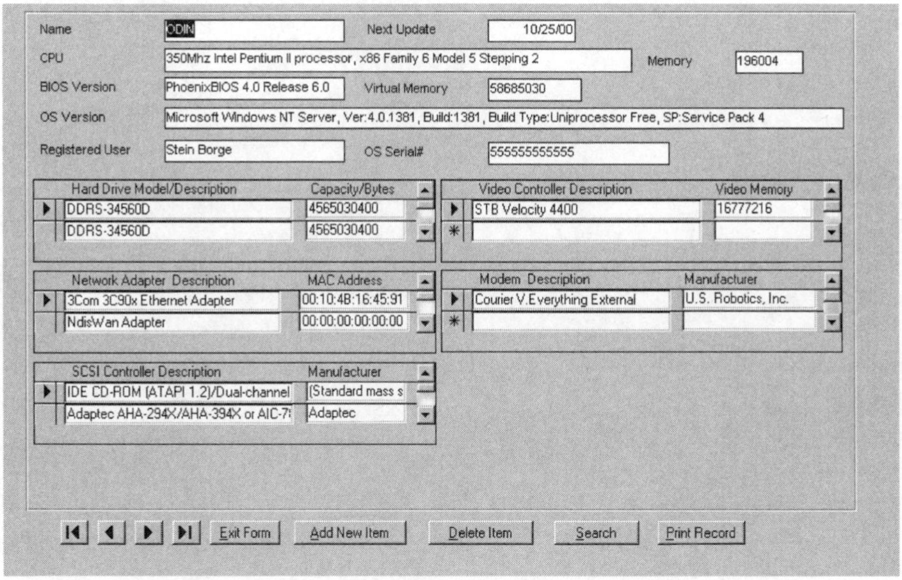

Figure 3-11. QADNA computer inventory screen

Upon logon, the script checks the database to see if a record for the computer exists. If not, the computer is added and inventoried. Each computer record also includes a Next Update date field, which controls when the next update occurs. This can be manually changed to force an update; otherwise, it will reinventory the machine after a 180-day interval. Each client must have ADO version 2.0 or later to read and write the database, ODBC drivers for Microsoft Access 97, and WMI to read system information.

See Also

Solution 3.4, Solution 10.1, Solution 13.8, and Solution 13.13.

CHAPTER 4

Networking Resources

NETWORKED ENVIRONMENTS PLAY an important role in today's corporate computer systems. WSH provides the ability to programmatically manipulate network resources. This functionality allows for operations to be performed that would be impossible using the old command-line programs, such as `net use`.

These operations are exposed through the `WScript.Network` object. This object provides methods that can perform network-related functions, such as network share and printer connection, and they can also query network-related information, such as user name and computer name.

4.1 Identifying a User

Problem

You want to find out who is currently logged on the local computer.

Solution

You can create an instance of the `WScript.Network` object and reference the `UserName` property:

```
'create an instance of the Wscript.Network object
Set objNetwork = CreateObject("Wscript.Network")
'output user name
Wscript.Echo "You are logged on as " & objNetwork.UserName
```

Discussion

The `WScript.Network` object exposes a number of properties that can be used to determine the computer, user, and domain information for the local computer. Table 4-1 lists `Network` object properties.

Table 4-1. `Network` *Object Properties*

PROPERTY	DESCRIPTION
ComputerName	Name of the local computer.
UserName	Name of the user logged into the local computer.
UserDomain	Name of the domain the user is currently logged into. Returns the computer name if it is not a member of the domain.

On the Windows 9*x*/ME platforms you may encounter problems referencing the UserName property in logon scripts. The problem is that the user ID doesn't get assigned immediately during the logon process.

To ensure the user name of the logged-on user is returned correctly in these instances, create a loop that continuously assigns the `UserName` property to a variable until it returns a valid user ID, as demonstrated in the following code snippet:

```
'create an instance of the Wscript.Network object
Dim objNetwork, strName
Set objNetwork = CreateObject("Wscript.Network")
On Error Resume Next
'loop until a user ID is assigned
While strName = ""
    strName = objNetwork.UserName
    Wscript.Sleep 100
WEnd
```

4.2 Finding an Available Network Drive

Problem

You want to find the next available network drive.

Solution

You can use the Scripting File System Object's `DriveExists` method to determine if a drive exists. The following function returns the next available drive:

```
'ReturnNextDrive.vbs
Function ReturnNextDrive()
```

```
Dim nF, objFSO
Set objFSO = CreateObject("Scripting.FileSystemObject")

'loop through drives starting from D:
For nF = ASC("d")  To ASC("z")
'if drive doesn't exist, it's available
 If Not objFSO.DriveExists(Chr(nF) & ":") Then
    ReturnNextDrive = Chr(nF) & ":"
    Exit Function
 End If
Next


End Function
```

Discussion

The ReturnNextDrive function listed in the Solution script returns the next available drive letter. If all drives are connected, it returns a Empty variant. It assumes the first potentially available drive starts at the D: drive.

The function uses the FSO library to determine if the drives exist. See Chapter 5 for more information on FSO-related operations.

The WScript.Network object's EnumNetworkDrives property returns a collection of connected network drives. The collection returned is a WSH collection, which operates in a slightly different manner than other object collections. The collection is represented as an array with items starting at 0 offset. For each connected drive, the array contains an element for the drive letter and an element for the share name. If you have two connected network drive shares (H: and P:), the collection array would contain four elements: the first element contains the H: drive, the second element contains the share H: is connected to in UNC format, the third element contains the P: drive, and the fourth element contains the share P: is connected to.

Use the EnumNetworkDrives property's Count property to determine the number of elements in the collection. The number represents double the number of connected shares.

The following code snippet demonstrates how to list details on the first share as well as listing details on all connected shares:

```
'listshares.vbs
'lists connected network shares
Dim objNetwork, objShares, nf
Set objNetwork = CreateObject("Wscript.Network")
```

```
Set objShares = objNetwork.EnumNetworkDrives
'output the first connected share and associated drive letter
Wscript.Echo "Drive " & objShares(0) & " is connected to " & objShares(1)

'loop through all connected shares and output details
For nf = 0 To objShares.Count - 1 Step 2
  Wscript.Echo objShares(nf) & " is connected to " & objShares(nf + 1)
Next
```

4.3 Mapping Network Drives

Problem

You need to connect clients to their home directory on a server and then to an applications and public data area when they log on.

Solution

You can use the WScript.Network object's MapNetworkDrive method to connect drives to network shares. Add the following code to their logon scripts:

```
'logon.vbs
Dim objNetwork, strName
Set objNetwork = CreateObject("Wscript.Network")

On Error Resume Next
  'get user name
While strName = ""
    strName = objNetwork.UserName
    Wscript.Sleep 100
WEnd
'map user to home drive
objNetwork.MapNetworkDrive "H:",
                "\\THOR\" & strName & "$", True
'connect to public area
objNetwork.MapNetworkDrive "P:", "\\THOR\PublicArea", True
'connect to apps share
objNetwork.MapNetworkDrive "W:", "\\THOR\Apps", True
```

Discussion

The MapNetworkDrive method connects a drive to a network share. The syntax for this method is as follows:

```
objectNetwork.MapNetworkDrive strDrive, strShare, [bUpdateProfile], [strUserID],
[strPassword]
```

Table 4-2 lists the parameters for the MapNetworkDrive method.

Table 4-2. MapNetworkDrive *Parameters*

PARAMETER	DESCRIPTION
strDrive	Local drive letter to map the network share to.
strShare	Name of share in UNC format (e.g., \\server\sharename).
bUpdateProfile	Optional Boolean parameter that indicates if drive connection is remembered for next session.
strUserID	Optional user ID to use when connecting to network share.
strPassword	Optional password specified to use when connecting to network share. This is used together with the strUserID parameter.

An error will occur if you try to connect to a drive that is already connected to a share or if the specified share does not exist. Use the On Error Resume Next statement to trap any errors when connecting to network resources.

If you want to connect a share to a drive letter that is already connected to another share, you must first remove the existing connection using the WScript.Network object's RemoveNetworkDrive method. The syntax for the method is as follows:

```
objNetwork.RemoveNetworkDrive strDrive, [bForce], [bUpdateProfile]
```

Table 4-3 lists the parameters for the RemoveNetworkDrive method.

Table 4-3. RemoveNetworkDrive *Parameters*

PARAMETER	DESCRIPTION
strDrive	Local drive letter to remove
bForce	Optional Boolean parameter that if True will attempt to forcefully disconnect share, even if resources are in use on the share
bUpdateProfile	Optional Boolean parameter that indicates if drive removal is remembered for next session

The following (forcefully) removes the T: drive connection and updates the user's profile so the removal is remembered at the next logon:

```
objNetwork.RemoveNetworkDrive "T:", True, True
```

For user home directories, there is no comparable command like the command-line `net use /h`, which maps a user to his or her home directory defined under the NT User Manager. This is not as much a problem with Windows NT/2000/XP/2003 workstations and servers that map these drives automatically, but Windows 9*x* and ME clients don't.

Using the `Network` object's `Username` property to return the name of the current user can solve this problem. You can use this name to connect to the home directory. This assumes that you follow a naming convention that uses the user name in the naming of the network shares. This is a common naming convention for home shares.

```
Set objNetwork = CreateObject("Wscript.Network")
objNetwork.MapNetworkDrive "H:", _
        "\\odin\" & objNetwork.UserName & "$" , True
```

The last parameter in the `MapNetworkDrive` method is an optional Boolean value that determines if the user's profile is to be updated or not. It is important to set this to `True` so the connection is remembered the next time the user logs on.

4.4 Migrating File Services from One Server to Another Server

Problem

You have migrated file services from one NT server (ODIN) to a new server (THOR). ODIN contained all user home directories, as well as a number of application file shares and miscellaneous shares that were created for users. Because ODIN will remain in place performing other operations, all of the existing shares must be remapped from ODIN to THOR.

The standard network connections, such as home drives, will connect to THOR in the logon script, but there is no set standard as to where users may map other drives. Some users may have any combination of mapped drives to the old server. To minimize support calls, you want to automatically remap any drives from ODIN to THOR.

Solution

The following code is run during the logon script for each client. The THOR server is the new file server, while the ODIN server is the old server.

```
'migrate.vbs
Dim objWshNetwork, nF
Dim sShare, sDrive, objEnumNetwork

Set objWshNetwork = CreateObject("WScript.Network")

Set objEnumNetwork = objWshNetwork.EnumNetworkDrives

For nF = 0 To objEnumNetwork.Count - 1 Step 2

    'get the drive letter and share name for the current share
    sShare = objEnumNetwork(nF)
    sDrive = objEnumNetwork(nF + 1)

    'check if the current share is connected to ODIN.
    If StrComp(Left(sShare, 7), "\\ODIN\", vbTextCompare) = 0 Then
        'remove the existing share
        objWshNetwork.RemoveNetworkDrive sDrive, True, True

        'remap the drive to the new server
        objWshNetwork.MapNetworkDrive sDrive, _
                                        "\\THOR\" & Mid(sShare, 8), True

    End If
Next
```

Discussion

In order for this to work, the shares on ODIN must not actually be deleted until the migration is complete. The contents of the shares should be moved to THOR, but the shares themselves shouldn't be removed until all the users have logged on and have been connected to the new server.

You can enumerate the collection using a `For Each` statement, but it is more practical to access the collection as an array.

The collection/array starts at element 0:

```
'display the drive letter of the first connection
Wscript.Echo objWshNetwork.EnumNetworkDrives.Item(0)
'display the share name of the first connection
Wscript.Echo objWshNetwork.EnumNetworkDrives.Item(1)
```

When a drive is disconnected, the `EnumNetworkDrives` collection is automatically resized to reflect the change. Two items are removed from the collection: the local drive letter and the corresponding share.

So, if you have three network connections and you remove the second connection, the collection is resized and the third connection becomes the second connection.

If you assign the `EnumNetworkDrives` collection to a variable, the variable makes a copy of the collection. If a drive is added or disconnected, the variable, which is a copy of the collection, is not updated. In the following example, an `EnumNetworkDrives` collection is assigned to a variable before a drive is connected to a share:

```
Dim objEnumNetwork, objNetwork

Set objNetwork = CreateObject("WScript.Network")

Set objEnumNetwork = objNetwork.EnumNetworkDrives
'display the count of items in collection
WScript.Echo objEnumNetwork.Count
'connect to share
objNetwork.MapNetworkDrive "T:", "\\odin\data"
'display count of
WScript.Echo objEnumNetwork.Count
WScript.Echo objNetwork.EnumNetworkDrives.Count
```

After the share is connected, the count of items in the `EnumNetworkDrives` collection and the variable is displayed. The count will be different because the `EnumNetworkDrives` collection is bigger as a result of connecting to the new drive.

When the remote share is disconnected, the user's profile must be updated. This ensures that when the drive is reconnected at the next logon time, the user's profile will have reflected the change. Note that the second parameter, forceful disconnect, is set to guarantee that the network connection is disconnected:

```
objNetwork.RemoveNetworkDrive sDrive, True, True
```

The same applies when you want to add the new share. You must set the update profile flag to `True` to ensure the share is reconnected at the next logon.

4.5 Connecting to a Network Printer

Problem

You want to connect to a networked printer.

Solution

You can use the `WScript.Network` object's `AddWindowsPrinterConnection` method to connect to a networked Windows printer:

```
Dim objNetwork

Set objNetwork = CreateObject("WScript.Network")
objNetwork.AddWindowsPrinterConnection  "\\odin\Brother HL-730"
```

Discussion

The `AddWindowsPrinterConnection` method adds a networked printer to the local machine and was introduced in WSH 2.0. The syntax for the method is as follows:

```
objNetwork.AddWindowsPrinterConnectionstrPrinterPath, [strDriverName] [,strPort]
```

Table 4-4 lists the parameters for the `AddWindowsPrinterConnection` method.

Table 4-4. `AddWindowsPrinterConnection` *Parameters*

PARAMETER	DESCRIPTION
`strPrinterPath`	Path to the printer in UNC format (e.g., `\\server\printername`).
`strDriverName`	Name of the driver to use. Required on Windows 95/98/ME; ignored if used on Windows NT/2000/2003 or XP platform.
`strPort`	Optional. Specifies the port to attach the printer to on Windows 95/98/ME. Default is LPT1. Ignored if used on Windows NT/2000/2003 or XP platform.

Using this method is the same as using the Control Panel Printers applet to add a printer connection. In Windows 95/98/ME, the printer driver must already be installed on the machine in order for the `AddWindowsPrinterConnection` method to work, which reduces the usefulness of this method on these platforms.

Windows NT/2000/2003 will download the driver if the driver is not installed on the local computer the printer is being installed on. An error will occur if the driver does not successfully install.

Once you have added a printer, you may want to make it, or an existing printer, the default printer for your Windows applications. A default printer is automatically selected when you attempt to print from a Windows application. The syntax for the method is as follows:

```
objNetwork.SetDefaultPrinter(strPrinterPath)
```

The `strPrinterPath` parameter specifies the UNC path of the printer you want to make the default printer. The printer must be installed as a Windows printer appearing under the Control Panel Printer applet. The following code snippet sets the default printer to the network printer `\\odin\brother`:

```
Dim objNetwork
Set objNetwork = CreateObject("WScript.Network")
objNetwork.SetDefaultPrinter "\\odin\brother"
```

WSH has supported the addition of printers since the initial release using the `AddPrinterConnection` method. This method is useful only if you need to connect to printers from the command-line environment; the method is the equivalent of using the `net use` command. Printers that are connected using this method are not available from Windows applications.

The syntax for this method is as follows:

```
objNetwork. AddPrinterConnection strPort, strPrinterPath,[bUpdateProfile],
[strUser], [strPassword]
```

Table 4-5 lists the parameters for the `AddPrinterConnection` method.

Table 4-5. `AddPrinterConnection` *Parameters*

PARAMETER	DESCRIPTION
`strPrinterPort`	The local printer port to connect the network printer to (e.g., LTP1:).
`strPrinterPath`	Path to the printer in UNC format (e.g., `\\server\printername`).
`bUpdateProfile`	Optional Boolean parameter that determines if printer connection is stored in user profile and reconnected in future sessions.
`strUserID`	Optional user ID for connecting to remote printer with.
`strPassword`	Optional password for connecting to remote printer. This is used in combination with the `strUserID` parameter.

The following code snippet connects the LPT2 port to the remote printer laserjet on computer Odin:

```
Set objNetwork = CreateObject("Wscript.Network")
objNetwork.AddPrinterConnection "LPT2", "\\odin\laserjet"
```

4.6 Listing Connected Network Printers

Problem

You want to list all the connected networked printers.

Solution

You can use the `WScript.Network` object's `EnumPrinterConnections` property to loop through connected printers:

```
'lstprinters.vbs
Set objNetwork = CreateObject("Wscript.Network")
Set objPrinters = objNetwork.EnumPrinterConnections

'loop through and display all connected printers..
For nF = 0 To objPrinters.Count - 1 Step 2
    Wscript.Echo  objPrinters(nF) & _
            " is connected to " & objPrinters(nF + 1)
    objNetwork.RemovePrinterConnection objPrinters(nF + 1)
Next
Set objNetwork = Nothing
```

Discussion

The `EnumPrinterConnections` method returns a special WSH collection, which is similar to the collection that is returned by the `EnumNetworkDrives` property (as described in Solution 4.2). The collection is represented as an array.

Each connected printer stores two elements to the array: the first being the printer port and the second being the UNC path to the printer. The collection returns twice as many elements as there are connected printers.

The number of elements in the collection can be determined by the EnumPrinterConnections collection's Count property. This returns the double the number of actual connected printers, so to determine the number of connected printers, divide this value by two.

The EnumPrinterConnections collection returns Windows as well as MS-DOS connected network printers, such as those added using net use on the command prompt or the WScript.Network object's AddPrinterConnection method.

4.7 Disconnecting Network Printers

Problem

You want to disconnect a networked printer.

Solution

You can use the WScript.Network object's RemovePrinterConnection method to remove a connection to a shared network printer:

```
Set objNetwork = CreateObject("Wscript.Network")
  objNetwork. RemovePrinterConnection "LPT1:", True
```

Discussion

The RemovePrinterConnection method disconnects connected network printers. The syntax for the method is as follows:

```
objNetwork.RemovePrinterConnection strPort, [bForceDisconnect], [bUpdateProfile]
```

Parameters for the RemovePrinterConnection method are listed in Table 4-6.

Table 4-6. `RemovePrinterConnection` *Parameters*

PARAMETER	DESCRIPTION
`strPort`	Local printer port for the printer to remove
`strForce`	Optional Boolean parameter that if `True` will attempt to forcefully disconnect the shared printer, even if the printer is in use
`bUpdateProfile`	Optional Boolean parameter that indicates if printer share removal is remembered for next session

Prior to WSH version 5.6, the `RemovePrinterConnection` method could only remove MS-DOS networked printers added using `net use` from a command prompt or the `WScript.Network` object's `AddPrinterConnection` method. This is fixed in WSH 5.6, so any networked printer can be removed.

CHAPTER 5

File Operations

THE DEFAULT WINDOWS SCRIPT HOST (WSH) scripting languages (VBScript and JScript) do not have any built-in file manipulation capabilities, nor does WSH itself. This functionality is provided by the COM File System Object (FSO) that is part of the Microsoft Scripting Runtime Library.

The FSO exposes a number of separate objects that provide the ability to perform file-related operations. Table 5-1 lists the objects exposed by the FSO component.

Table 5-1. FileSystemObject Objects

OBJECT	DESCRIPTION
Folders	A collection that contains a list of folders in a specified folder
Folder	Exposes folder information such as size, attributes, and date information, and methods to move, delete, and copy
Files	A collection that contains a list of files in a specified folder
File	Exposes file information such as size, attributes, and date information, and methods to move, delete, and copy
Drives	Collection object that contains a list of available drives on the local machine
Drive	Exposes drive information, such as size and type
TextStream	Supports text file creation and manipulation

The FSO exposes methods and properties that perform file manipulation operations. Before you can use any of the objects listed in Table 5-1 you must create an instance of the FSO:

```
'create an instance of an FSO object
Set objFSO = CreateObject("Scripting.FileSystemObject")
```

See Also

The Scripting Run-Time Reference and File System Object Tutorial, which is part of the VBScript or JScript documentation, is available for download at `http://msdn.microsoft.com/scripting`.

5.1 Determining the Readiness of a Floppy Drive

Problem

You want to check if a floppy drive is usable.

Solution

Use the `IsReady` property to determine if a given drive is available for operations:

```
Dim objFSO, objDrive
Set objFSO = CreateObject("Scripting.FileSystemObject")
Set objDrive = objFSO.GetDrive("A")
'check if drive is ready,
If objDrive.IsReady Then
 'drive is ready, do something..
End If
```

Discussion

The `Drive` object provides information on system drives. These may be fixed, CD-ROM, removable, or network drives. To get a reference to a `Drive` object, use the FSO object's `GetDrive` method. Its syntax is as follows:

```
Set objDrive = objFSO.GetDrive(strDriveSpec)
```

The `strDriveSpec` parameter identifies which drive to reference. You can represent the parameter as a single drive letter or a network UNC path; it is not case-sensitive. If you pass a drive letter, you can specify the drive letter followed by a colon or a colon and backslash.

If you specify a drive using a UNC path, you don't need to connect the network share as a drive. The following code snippet demonstrates different methods of identifying a drive:

```
Dim objFSO, objDrive
Set objFSO = CreateObject("Scripting.FileSystemObject")
'the following will return a drive object for the D: drive
Set objDrive = objFSO.GetDrive("D")
Set objDrive = objFSO.GetDrive("d:\")
'return the drive object for a network share
Set objDrive = objFSO.GetDrive("\\thor\d$")
```

Table 5-2 contains `Drive` object properties. All properties are read-only unless otherwise specified.

Table 5-2. `Drive` *Object Properties*

PROPERTY	DESCRIPTION
`AvailableSpace`, `FreeSpace`	Free space on the drive in bytes. These properties return the same information.
`DriveLetter`	Drive letter associated with the drive.
`DriveType`	Type of drive. Unknown=0, Removable=1, Fixed=2, Remote=3, CD-ROM=4, and RamDisk=5.
`FileSystem`	File system that the drive uses (e.g., FAT, NTFS, or CDFS).
`IsReady`	Returns `True` if the drive is ready for access; otherwise it returns `False`. A removable media drive (such as a CD-ROM drive) will be "not ready" if there is no disc in the drive. A network drive will be "not ready" if it is disconnected.
`Path`	Returns the drive path.
`RootFolder`	Returns the root folder for the drive as a `Folder` object.
`SerialNumber`	Serial number uniquely identifying the drive.
`ShareName`	Displays the share name in the case of a network drive. Returns a blank string for a local drive.
`TotalSize`	Total size of the drive in bytes.
`VolumeName`	Name of the drive. This is read/write, so you can set a drive's volume name.

5.2 Listing the Drives on a System

Problem

You want to list information on system drives.

Solution

You can use the FSO's Drives collection to enumerate system drives:

```
Dim objFSO, objDrive
Set objFSO = CreateObject("Scripting.FileSystemObject")
For Each objDrive In objFSO.Drives
   'check if drive is ready,
   If objDrive.IsReady Then
      Wscript.Echo objDrive.DriveLetter & " is " & _
      Fix(((objDrive.TotalSize - objDrive.FreeSpace) _
            / objDrive.TotalSize) * 100) & "% used"
   Else
      Wscript.Echo objDrive.DriveLetter & " is not ready"
   End If
Next
```

Discussion

The Drives collection contains a list of drives available to the local machine. This includes any drive visible to the system, including fixed hard, removable floppy, CD-ROM, or network drives. This collection is returned from the FileScriptingObject. The information for each object in the collection is exposed as a Drive object.

You can reference drives from the collection by specifying a drive letter. The drive letter is not case-sensitive and may be followed by a colon or a colon and backslash, as demonstrated by the following code snippet:

```
Set objFSO = CreateObject("Scripting.FileSystemObject")

'the following two statements return a reference to the C drive
Set objDrive = objFSO.Drives("C:\") 'get a reference to the C drive
Set objDrive = objFSO.Drives("C") 'get a reference to the C drive
```

If you reference a drive in the collection that does not exist, an error occurs. If you need to check for the existence of a drive, use the FSO DriveExists method. The syntax is as follows:

```
bResult = objFSO.DriveExists(strDrive)
```

The strDrive parameter identifies which drive to check. It is not case-sensitive and may be followed by a colon or a colon and backslash. If the drive exists, it returns True; otherwise, it returns False. The following example checks if the drive F: exists:

```
Set objFSO = CreateObject("Scripting.FileSystemObject")
If objFSO.DriveExists("F:") Then
    Wscript.Echo "Drive f: exists"
End If
```

5.3 Finding the Size of a User Directory

Problem

You want to list the size of user directories.

Solution

You can use the GetFolder method to retrieve a reference to the user root Folder object, and then iterate through each subfolder of the object's SubFolders collection:

```
Dim objFSO, objFolder, objSub, nTotal
Set objFSO = CreateObject("Scripting.FileSystemObject")
Set objFolder = objFSO.GetFolder("D:\Users")

nTotal = 0
'loop through each subfolder, displaying its size
For each objSub In objFolder.SubFolders
   Wscript.Echo "Folder " & objSub.Name & " is " & objSub.Size _
   & " bytes"
    nTotal = nTotal + objSub.Size
Next

Wscript.Echo "Total for all folders:" & nTotal & " bytes"
```

Discussion

Folders (also referred to as directories) are used by Windows to organize files and folders. To obtain a reference to a Folder object, use the FSO's GetFolder method. The syntax is as follows:

```
Set objFolder = objFSO.GetFolder(strFolderPath)
```

The strFolderPath parameter identifies the folder to return. This can be the path to either a local folder or a network UNC, and it is not case-sensitive:

```
Dim objFSO, objFolder, objFolder2
Set objFSO = CreateObject("Scripting.FileSystemObject")

Set objFolder2 = objFSO.GetFolder("e:\data")
Set objFolder = objFSO.GetFolder("\\thor\e$\data")
```

Table 5-3 lists Folder object's properties. Properties are read-only unless otherwise indicated.

Table 5-3. Folder *Properties*

PROPERTY	DESCRIPTION
Attributes	Folder attributes
DateCreated, DateLastAccessed, or DateLastModified	Returns the folder created, last accessed, and last modified dates
Drive	The Drive object where the folder resides
Files	Collection containing all files in the folder
IsRootFolder	Boolean value; returns True if Folder is a root folder
Name	Name of folder
ParentFolder	Folder object for parent folder
Path	Full path to the file
Size	Size of the folder
ShortName/ShortPath	MS-DOS short name (8.3 format) for the folder
SubFolders	Folders collection containing all Folder objects in a folder
Type	Type description, returns File Folder

5.4 Determining the Size of a File

Problem

You need to determine the size of a file.

Solution

You can use the `File` object's `Size` property to return the file size:

```
Dim objFSO, objFile, nSize

'create an instance of an FSO object
Set objFSO = CreateObject("Scripting.FileSystemObject")

'get a reference to a specified file
Set objFile = objFSO.GetFile("d:\data\report.doc")

nSize = objFile.Size 'get the size of the file
```

Discussion

You obtain the `File` object for an individual file by using the FSO's `GetFile` method. The syntax is as follows:

```
Set objFile = objFSO.GetFile(strFilePath)
```

The `strFilePath` is the path to the file. This can either be the path to a local file or a network UNC, and it is not case-sensitive.

Once you have obtained a `File` object, you can inspect a number of file-related properties in addition to the file's size. Table 5-4 lists the `File` object's properties. All properties are read-only unless otherwise specified.

Table 5-4. `File` *Object Properties*

PROPERTIES	DESCRIPTION
`Attributes`	Read/Write. File attributes. Numeric value comprised of one or more file attribute types. The attribute values are added together to form the read-write Attributes property. The individual attribute values are Normal=0, Hidden=2, System=4, Volume=8, Archive=32, and Compressed=2048.
`DateCreated`, `DateLastAccessed`, or `DateLastModified`	Returns the file's created, last accessed, and last modified dates.
`Drive`	The Drive object on which a file resides.
`Name`	Read/Write. Name of file.
`ParentFolder`	Folder object that contains the file's parent folder.
`Path`	Full path to the file.
`ShortName/ShortPath`	MS-DOS short name (i.e., in 8.3 format) for the file.
`Size`	Size of the file in bytes.
`Type`	File type description (e.g., Text Document).

5.5 Reading and Changing File Attributes

Problem

You want to change a file's read-only and/or hidden attributes.

Solution

You can use the `File` object's `Attributes` property to read and set a file's attributes:

```
'set read-only and toggle hidden attribute for a file
Const ReadOnly = 1
Const Hidden = 2

Dim objFSO, objFile

Set objFSO = CreateObject("Scripting.FileSystemObject")
```

```
'get a reference to a file
Set objFile = objFSO.GetFile("e:\data\report.doc")

'set the Readonly attribute
objFile.Attributes = objFile.Attributes Or ReadOnly

'toggle the Hidden attribute
objFile.Attributes = objFile.Attributes Xor Hidden
```

Discussion

A file attribute is a combination of any of the values listed in Table 5-5.

Table 5-5. File Attribute Values

CONSTANT	VALUE	DESCRIPTION
Normal	0	No attributes are set.
ReadOnly	1	Read-only access.
Hidden	2	Hidden file.
System	4	System attribute.
Archive	32	Used by backup programs to determine if the file has been changed since the last operation. File is always turned on when any modification is made to a file.
Compressed	2048	Compressed files.

To check if an attribute is set, use the And operator to perform a bitwise comparison of a file attribute with the value of the attribute you are checking for. The following example checks if the archive attribute is set:

```
Const Archive= 32
Set objFSO = CreateObject("Scripting.FileSystemObject")
Set objFile = objFSO.GetFile("e:\data\report.doc")

If objFile.Attributes And Archive Then
  Wscript.Echo "Archive bit is set"
End If
```

If you And the binary value against another value and the bit you are checking for is set, the bitwise operation returns the value you are checking for. In the previous example, And-ing the file attribute against 32 (the value for the archive attribute) returns 32 if the archive bit is set.

To set an attribute, use the bitwise Or operator to set the bit. The following example sets the archive bit:

```
objFile.Attributes = objFile.Attributes Or Archive
```

To turn off an attribute, perform the Not And bitwise operation against the value you want to change together with the attribute value you want to reset. The following example turns off the archive bit:

```
objFile.Attributes = objFile.Attributes Not And Archive
```

To "toggle" an attribute (in other words, to turn the attribute "off" if it is "on" or "on" if it is "off"), perform the Xor bitwise operation with the value you want to change against the bit value you want to change. The following example toggles the archive bit for a file:

```
objFile.Attributes = objFile.Attributes Xor Archive
```

You can turn the archive, readonly, system, and hidden attributes for all files except certain system files. You can read but not modify the compressed attribute. See Chapter 10 for methods of compressing and uncompressing files and folders using WMI.

The archive attribute can be useful for scripts where you only want to process files that have not been manipulated since the last execution of the script. Whenever a file is created or modified, the file system turns the archive bit on.

In the following example, all the files in a document folder are copied to a network backup folder if the archive attribute is not set.

```
Const Archive= 32
Dim objFSO, objFile, objFolder

 Set objFSO = CreateObject("Scripting.FileSystemObject")

Set objFolder = objFSO.GetFolder("d:\data\documents")

For Each objFile In objFolder.files
```

```
 'check if the archive attribute is set
 If objFile.Attributes And Archive Then
    'copy to backup location
    objFile.Copy "h:\backup\documents"
    'turn the archive bit off
    objFile.Attributes = objFile.Attributes And Not Archive
 End If
Next
```

Turning the archive bit off does not have any adverse effects on a file. Note that some backup software and certain MS-DOS commands such as XCOPY may use this attribute to determine if a file has been created or modified since the last operation.

See Also

Solution 10.11.

5.6 Determining the Existence of a File or Folder

Problem

You need to check if a file exists.

Solution

You can call the FSO's `FileExist` method:

```
Dim objFSO
'create an instance of an FSO object
Set objFSO = CreateObject("Scripting.FileSystemObject")

'check if the specified file exists
    If objFSO.FileExists("d:\data\report.doc") Then
        WScript.Echo "File exists"
    End If
```

Discussion

The FSO object's `FileExists` method returns `True` if the specified file exists and `False` otherwise. Its syntax is as follows:

```
bExists = objFSO.FileExists(strPath)
```

The `strPath` parameter represents the path and name of the file, and it can be either a local file path or UNC format (e.g., `\\thor\data\report.doc`).

To determine if a folder exists, use the FSO object's `FolderExists` method. Its syntax is as follows:

```
bFlag = objFSO.FolderExists(strPath)
```

The `strPath` parameter identifies the folder path you want to check. It can be a local path or a network path that is specified by using the UNC. The path may be followed by a backslash. The function returns `True` if the path exists and `False` if the path is not found. The following code snippet tests for the existence of the folder `H:\data`:

```
Set objFSO = CreateObject("Scripting.FileSystemObject")
bFlag = objFSO.FolderExists("H:\Data")
```

5.7 Renaming a File or Folder

Problem

You want to rename a file or folder.

Solution

You can modify the file or folder object's `Name` property:

```
Set objFSO = CreateObject("Scripting.FileSystemObject")
Set objFile = objFSO.GetFile("d:\data\report.doc")
objFile.Name = "newreport.doc"
```

Discussion

To rename a file or folder, change the Name property to the new name of the file or folder.

If you are renaming a file that is currently opened by another application, the operation may fail and an error will occur. If you attempt to rename a folder that has open files in it, the operation fails and an error occurs.

5.8 Comparing Files by Version Number

Problem

You want to compare files from two different folders and list any files that have different version numbers.

Solution

The following script uses the FSO's GetFileVersion method to compare the version of each file that is found in two specified folders that have different version numbers:

```
'compvers.vbs
Dim objFSO, strFolder1, strFolder2, objFolder
Dim objFile, strVer1

'check if correct number of arguments passed
 If WScript.Arguments.Count <> 2 Then
   WScript.Echo _
     WScript.ScriptName & _
     " compares versions of files in two folders." & vbCrLf & _
     "Output is all files which exist in both folders but " & vbCrLf & _
     "have different version stamps." & vbCrLf & _
     "Syntax:" &  vbCrLf & _
     WScript.ScriptName & " folder1 folder2" &  vbCrLf  & vbCrLf
      WScript.Quit -1
  End If

  strFolder1 = WScript.Arguments(0)
  strFolder2 = WScript.Arguments(1)
```

```
  Set objFSO = CreateObject("Scripting.FileSystemObject")
  EnsureFolder strFolder1
  EnsureFolder strFolder2

  Set objFolder = objFSO.GetFolder(strFolder1)

 'loop through each file in folder and compare with second folder
 For Each objFile In objFolder.Files
   strPath2 = strFolder2 & objFile.Name
   If objFSO.FileExists(strPath2) Then
      CompareFiles objFile, objFSO.GetFile(strPath2)
   End If
 Next

'check if folder exists
Sub EnsureFolder(strFolder)
    If Not objFSO.FolderExists(strFolder) Then
        WScript.Echo strFolder & " is not a valid folder." & vbCrLf
        WScript.Quit -1
    End If

  'append backslash to folder if does not exist
  If Right(strFolder, 1) <> "\" Then strFolder = strFolder & "\"
End Sub

'compare versions of two passed file objects and display version info
'if different
Sub CompareFiles(objFile1, objFile2)

    If  objFSO.GetFileVersion(objFile1.Path) = _
          objFSO.GetFileVersion(objFile2.Path) Then Exit Sub

     WScript.Echo objFile1.Path & " has version [" & _
                  strVer1 & "] and " & _
                 objFile2.Path & " has version [" & _
                  strVer2 & "]"
End Sub
```

Discussion

The FSO object's `GetFileVersion` method returns the version of a specified file. It was introduced in WSH version 2.0. Its syntax is as follows:

```
strVersion = objFSO.GetFileVersion(strPath)
```

The strPath parameter represents the path to the file, and it can be either a local or UNC file path.

GetFileVersion returns a file version as a string for any file that has a file version associated with it. It is mainly for application-related files, such as DLL and EXE files. If the file has no version, it returns an empty string.

5.9 Creating a Folder

Problem

You want to create a folder.

Solution

You can use the FSO's CreateFolder method or a Folders object's Add method to create a new folder. The following script demonstrates both methods:

```
Set objFSO = CreateObject("Scripting.FileSystemObject")
 Set objFolder1 = objFSO.CreateFolder("c:\data")
'create a folder below the new data folder using the Folders object's Add method
Set objFolder2 = objFolder1.SubFolders.Add("Word")
```

Discussion

You can create file folders by using the FSO object's CreateFolder method. Its syntax is as follows:

```
Set objFolder = objFSO.CreateFolder (strPath)
```

The strPath parameter identifies the folder path that you want to create. It can be a local path or a network path that you specify by using a UNC. The path can be followed by a backslash. If the path does not exist, an error occurs. If successful, the method returns a Folder object for the newly created folder.

Alternatively, you can use the Folder object's Add method:

```
Set objFolder = objFolder.Add(strPath)
```

This method creates a folder that is relative to its parent folder, which means you can only create a folder. The path specified by the strPath parameter is relative to the Folder object's parent folder.

```
Set objFolder1 = objFSO.CreateFolder("c:\data")
'create a folder below the new data folder using the Folders object's Add method
Set objFolder2 = objFolder1.SubFolders.Add("Word")
```

If successful, the method returns a Folder object for the newly created folder. These methods can only create one folder at a time. If you want to create a folder structure in which one or more folders in the path do not exist, you must first create the parent folder:

```
'create the folder H:\Data\Word\Reports
Set objFSO = CreateObject("Scripting.FileSystemObject")Set objFolder =
objFSO.CreateFolder("H:\Data")
Set objFolder = objFSO.CreateFolder("H:\Data\Word")
Set objFolder = objFSO.CreateFolder("H:\Data\Word\Reports")
```

The following subroutine, CreatePath, provides a more flexible method of creating a folder:

```
Sub CreatePath(strPath)
 Dim nSlashpos, objFSO
 Set objFSO = CreateObject("Scripting.FileSystemObject")

 ' strip any trailing backslash
  If Right(strPath, 1) = "\" Then
   strPath = Left(strPath, Len(strPath) - 1)
  End If

   'if path already exists, exit
   If objFSO.FolderExists(strPath) Then Exit Sub
    'get position of last backslash in path
    nSlashpos = InStrRev(strPath, "\")
     If nSlashpos <> 0 Then
              If Not objFSO.FolderExists(Left(strPath, nSlashpos)) Then
                     CreatePath Left(strPath, nSlashpos - 1)
     End If
   End If

  objFSO.CreateFolder strPath
End Sub
```

This routine creates a specified folder hierarchy. If any folders in the path do not exist, they are created. The syntax is as follows:

```
CreatePath strFolderPath
```

The `strFolderPath` parameter identifies the path you want to create. The `CreatePath` routine uses the FSO object's `FolderExists` method to check if a folder exists.

5.10 Finding and Deleting Temporary Files

Problem

You want to list files from a directory structure that meet certain criteria.

Solution

The following code contains the logic for the Windows Script component `ENTWSH.RecurseDir`, which recursively searches a specified directory and subdirectories for files that meet certain criteria:

```
<?xml version="1.0"?>
<component>
<registration
  description="RecurseDir"
  progid="ENTWSH.RecurseDir"
  version="1.00"
classid="{4402a970-43d3-11d3-bbf7-00104b164591}"
>
</registration>
 <public>
  <property name="Path"><put/>
 </property>
  <property name="Filter"><put/>
 </property>
  <method name="Process"></method>
 <event name="FoundFile">
  <parameter name="filepath"/>
 </event>

</public>
```

```
<script language="VBScript">
<![CDATA[

Dim objFSO, objRegExp, Filter, Path

Function put_Path(newValue)
  Path = newValue
End Function

Function put_Filter(newValue)
  Filter = newValue
End Function

Function Process()
Dim objFolder

 Set objFSO = CreateObject("Scripting.FileSystemObject")
 Set objRegExp = New RegExp

 objRegExp.Pattern = Filter  objRegExp.IgnoreCase = True
 Set objFolder = objFSO.GetFolder(Path)
RecurseDirs objFolder

Set objFSO = Nothing
Set objRegExp = Nothing End Function

'recurse through specified folder
Sub RecurseDirs(objFolder)

Dim objFile, objSub
 'go through each file in folder and compare filename against
 'regular expression pattern
 For Each objFile In objFolder.Files
    If objRegExp.Test(objFile.Name) Then
     fireEvent "FoundFile", objFile.Path
    End If
Next

  For Each objSub In objFolder.SubFolders
   RecurseDirs objSub
  Next
End Sub
```

```
]]>
</script>
</component>
```

The ENTWSH.RecurseDir scripting component is used to recurse a directory structure and then process all files that meet a certain condition. When a file meets the condition, an event is fired, which allows you to perform a user-defined operation against the file.

The following script example creates an instance of the ENTWSH.RecurseDir component. It searches for all files under a specified path (d:\data) with the extension .tmp and deletes them:

```
'deltemp.vbs
Dim objDelTempFiles , objFSO

'create an instance of the ENTWSH.RecurseDir object.
'any sinked events will be prefixed with ev_
Set objDelTempFiles = Wscript.CreateObject ("ENTWSH.RecurseDir","ev_")

Set objFSO = CreateObject("Scripting.FileSystemObject")

objDelTempFiles.Path = "d:\data" 'set the path to search
'set the filter for files to find. This will find all files with tmp extension
objDelTempFiles.Filter = "\.tmp$"

objDelTempFilesEvent.Process
Sub ev_FoundFile(strPath)
    objFSO.DeleteFile strPath
End Sub
```

Discussion

The ENTWSH.RecurseDir object searches the path, including all subfolders, for files that meet the specified filter pattern. When a file is found that matches the pattern, the FoundFile event is fired.

To use the object, register the ENTWSH.RecurseDir script.

The calling script is responsible for providing an event handler. The path of the file that is found is passed to the event handler as a parameter; the resulting event can perform any required processing. Table 5-6 lists the properties of the RecurseDir object.

Table 5-6. `ENTWSH.RecurseDir` *Object Properties*

ATTRIBUTES	DESCRIPTION
Path	Path you want to search (e.g., `d:\data`).

Filter	Optional. Specifies filter for files you want to process. This filter is a regular expression pattern. If this property is not set, all files will be processed. Examples:
	`\.tmp$`
	Return all tmp files, same as `*.tmp`.
	`\.tmp$\|\.bat$`
	Return all tmp files and bat files.

Once the properties have been set in the calling script, you can call the `RecurseDir` component's `Process` method. The `Process` method recursively goes through all folders under the specified path.

When a file is found that matches the pattern specified by the `Filter` property, the `FoundFile` event is fired. The event parameters are the path and name of this file. The event handler can then determine what action to take with the file.

5.11 Finding Files That Meet Criteria

Problem

You want to list files from a folder structure that meet certain criteria.

Solution

You can use the `Edir.vbs` solution script:

```
'edir.vbs
  'enhanced directory utility. Lists all files that meet criteria from
  'specified directories
  Dim strCriteria, objFile, objFSO, objArgs

  Set objArgs = Wscript.Arguments

  'check if less than 2 arguments are being passed
  If objArgs.Count < 2 Then
```

```
    ShowUsage
    Wscript.Quit -1
 End If

  Set objFSO = CreateObject("Scripting.FileSystemObject")

 If Not objFSO.FolderExists(objArgs(0)) Then
    Wscript.Echo "Path '" & objArgs(0) & "' not found "
   Wscript.Quit -1
 End If

   Set objEvent = Wscript.CreateObject ("ENTWSH.RecurseDir","ev_")

   objEvent.Path = objArgs(0)
   strCriteria = objArgs(1)

    strCriteria = Replace(strCriteria, "Size","objFile.Size",1,-1,1)

    strCriteria = Replace(strCriteria, "Modified", _
                "objFile.DateLastModified",1,-1,1)

    strCriteria = Replace(strCriteria, "Accessed", _
                   "objFile.DateLastAccessed",1,-1,1)

    strCriteria = Replace(strCriteria, "Created", _
                  "objFile.DateCreated",1,-1,1)

    strCriteria = Replace(strCriteria, "Attributes", _
              "objFile.Attributes",1,-1,1)

  'check if third argument passed - this is regular expression file filter
  If objArgs.Count = 3 Then
   objEvent.Filter = objArgs(2)
  End If

  Set objFSO = CreateObject("Scripting.FileSystemObject")
  objEvent.Process
Sub ShowUsage
   WScript.Echo "edir. Enhanced directory." & vbCrLf & _
       "Syntax:" &  vbCrLf & _
      "edir.vbs path criteria [filter] [/s]" &  vbCrLf & _
      "path      path to folder to search " & vbCrLf & _
      "criteria criteria to filter files on " & vbCrLf & _
```

```
      "filter   option regular expression filter "
End Sub

Sub ev_FoundFile(strPath)
   Set objFile = objFSO.GetFile(strPath)

  If Eval(strCriteria) Then
    Wscript.StdOut.WriteLine strPath
  End If
End Sub
```

Discussion

There are no built-in commands in the command-line environment to list files that meet certain criteria, apart from using the DIR wildcards to return filenames that match a certain pattern.

The `Edir.vbs` solution script provides the functionality to execute relatively complex search expressions. It recursively searches a specified folder path for all files that meet the criteria. The script uses the `ENTWSH.RecurseDir` Windows Script component to perform the directory recursion.

The following command-line statement lists all files under the `d:\users` directory that are greater than 500,000 bytes in size and have been modified before January 1, 1999:

```
edir "Size > 500000 And modified<#1/1/99# " "d:\users"
```

The expression that is executed can contain any number of conditional logic operators (such as And, Or, Not, and so on). Table 5-7 lists the filename properties that you can filter.

Table 5-7. Filename Properties

FILE	DESCRIPTION
Size	Size of file
Modified	Last modified date and time
Created	Creation date and time
Attributes	File attributes
Accessed	Last accessed date and time

The script can take an optional parameter to filter filenames. This parameter is passed as a regular expression. This regular expression is evaluated against each file as well as the file properties criteria. The following command-line statement lists all files with a .doc extension that are over 500,000 bytes:

```
edir "Size > 500000" "d:\users" "\.doc$"
```

The script uses the VBScript Eval function to evaluate the expressions. The Eval function is a recent addition to VBScript. The syntax is as follows:

```
result = Eval(strExpression)
```

The `strExpression` parameter is any valid expression. If successful, Eval returns the evaluated expression.

The following example creates a simple command-line calculator:

```
'calc.vbs
Dim objArgs

Set objArgs = Wscript.Arguments

If objArgs.Count=1 Then
 Wscript.StdOut.WriteLine Eval(objArgs(0))
Else
 Wscript.StdErr.WriteLine "calc.vbs. Performs mathematical operations" & _
                           vbCrLf & "Syntax: " & vbCrLf & _
                          "calc.vbs expression " & vbCrLf & _
                          "expression   mathematical expression"
End If
```

To use `calc.vbs`, you can pass an expression to the command-line script, which is demonstrated in the following example:

```
calc "5*10+10/5-(5+6*3)"
```

Eval can access all global script variables from the current executing script. The search keywords (size, modified, and so on) are replaced with a string representing the file in the script.

5.12 Deleting a Folder

Problem

You want to delete a folder.

Solution

You can use the FSO's DeleteFolder or the Folder object's Delete method to delete a folder:

```
Dim objFSO, objFolder
Set objFSO = CreateObject("Scripting.FileSystemObject")
'delete the folder e:\data\word
objFSO .DeleteFolder "e:\data\word"

'get and delete the folder e:\data\excel
Set objFolder = objFSO.GetFolder("e:\data\Excel")
objFolder.Delete
```

Discussion

You can delete folders by invoking the FSO object's DeleteFolder method. Its syntax is as follows:

```
objFSO.DeleteFolder strPath [,bForce]
```

The strPath parameter is the path to the folder to delete. The path can be in UNC format and it can contain wildcards. The DeleteFolder method deletes the folder and any content below the folder.

The optional bForce parameter is a Boolean value that, when True, indicates if any item in the folder being deleted is flagged as read-only locked. If this is the case, it attempts to force the deletion if required. The default is False.

If the bForce parameter is False (the default) and the DeleteFolder method encounters a read-only folder or file while executing, an error occurs and the method terminates. The directory being deleted is left in an incomplete state because some folders and files in the structure may have been deleted before the operation terminated.

You can also remove folders by invoking the Delete method for a Folder object. Its syntax is as follows:

```
objFolder.DeleteFolder [bForce]
```

The bForce parameter is the same as the bForce parameter for the DeleteFolder method.

No files or folders removed using DeleteFolder or Folder object's Delete method are put in the Recycle Bin. You should be careful when using these methods because they could cause a great deal of irreversible damage if the wrong folder, such as the root of your C: drive, is removed.

5.13 Copying a File

Problem

You need to copy a file.

Solution

You can use the File object's Copy method to copy a file:

```
Dim objFSO, objFile
Set objFSO = CreateObject("Scripting.FileSystemObject")
Set objFile = objFSO.GetFile("C:\Data\report.doc")
'copy items from folder to network folder
objFile.Copy "H:\Data\"
```

Discussion

The File object's Copy and Move methods copy or move the specified file to a specified destination. Their respective syntaxes are as follows:

```
objFile.Copy strDestination [,bOverwriteFiles]
objFile.Move strDestination
```

Both methods require a destination parameter. The destination may be a folder or a new filename.

When you specify a folder, make sure the path ends with a backslash (\). If you do not do so, the method assumes that you are trying to copy or move the file to a new file with the name of the folder, and the operation generates an error. The Copy and Move methods do not attempt to create folders if they do not exist.

The Copy method has an optional parameter. This parameter is set to True by default, but if it is set to False, the copy operation generates an error if a file already exists in the destination folder. If the destination file has the same name as the source and the destination is flagged as read-only and/or hidden, a copy fails, even if the bOverWriteFiles flag is set.

You can also use two other methods for copying and moving files—namely, the FSO's CopyFile and MoveFile methods. The File object's Copy and Move methods only perform the operations on the individual File objects. The CopyFile and MoveFile methods allow you to copy individual files as well as process multiple files using wildcards. Their respective syntaxes are as follows:

```
objFSO.CopyFile strSource, strDestination [,bOverwriteFiles]
objFSO.MoveFile strSource, strDestination
```

The strSource parameter identifies one or more files that you want to process. You can use the wildcards * and ? to filter the files you want to process.

The strSource and strDestination parameters are the same as the parameters of the File object's Copy and Move methods. They identify the destination folder or file to copy or move the source file(s) to. If the destination directory does not exist, an error occurs. You cannot use wildcards in the destination path.

The CopyFile method's optional bOverwriteFiles parameter overwrites a file(s) in the destination directory that has the same name as a file(s) from the source directory. By default the parameter is set to True. If it is set to False, an error occurs if there is an attempt to copy a file from the source directory that has the same name as a file in the destination directory. If this happens, the CopyFile operation does not attempt to "roll back" any file copy operations that have already been completed successfully.

```
Set objFSO = CreateObject("Scripting.FileSystemObject")

'copy all VBS files from wsh to backup directory
objFSO.CopyFile "d:\data\wsh\*.vbs", "d:\data\backup\"

'try copying again to the backup folder, an error will occur
'since the overwrite flag is set to False
objFSO.CopyFile "d:\*.vbs", "d:\data\backup", False

'an error would occur here since cannot use wildcards in destination name
objFSO.MoveFile "d:\*.vbs", "d:\data\backup\*.vbs"
```

5.14 Copying and Moving a Folder

Problem

You want to copy data from a local folder to a network folder.

Solution

You can use the Folder object's Copy method:

```
Dim objFSO, objFolder
Set objFSO = Wscript.CreateObject("Scripting.FileSystemObject")
Set objFolder = objFSO.GetFolder("C:\Data")
'copy items from folder to network folder
objFolder.Copy "H:\Data"
```

Discussion

The Copy and Move methods copy or move the contents of a specified folder to a specified destination folder. Their respective syntaxes are as follows:

```
objFolder.Copy strDestination, [,bOverwriteFiles]
objFolder.Move strDestination
```

Both methods require a strDestination destination folder parameter. The Copy method has an optional bOverWriteFiles parameter. These parameters are the same as those used in the File object's corresponding Copy and Move methods. This parameter is set to True by default. If it is set to False, the copy operation generates an error if a file already exists in the destination folder.

The contents of all files and folders in the strDestination folder are either be copied or moved to the specified destination.

Two other methods for copying and moving folders are the FSO's CopyFolder and MoveFolder methods. Their syntaxes are as follows:

```
objFSO.CopyFolder strSource, strDestination [,bOverWriteFiles]
objFSO.MoveFolder strSource, strDestination
```

The strSource and strDestination parameters are the same as those of the Folder object's Copy and Move methods. The CopyFolder and MoveFolder methods do not require that you first get a reference to a Folder object.

If you use bOverwriteFiles with Copy/CopyFolder or use the Move/MoveFolder methods, an error occurs if any file or folder exists in the destination path, including the root folder of the destination path itself.

You should take care when moving whole directories because the source directory may contain files that other applications are dependent on and these applications may not function correctly if any dependent files are moved to another location.

5.15 Deleting a File

Problem

You want to delete a file.

Solution

You can call the FSO's DeleteFile or the File object's Delete method:

```
Dim objFSO, objFile

Set objFSO = CreateObject("Scripting.FileSystemObject")
 objFSO.DeleteFile "d:\data\report.doc"

Set objFile = objFSO.GetFile("d:\data\payroll.xls")
objFile.Delete
```

Discussion

The FSO object's DeleteFile method deletes a specified file. Its syntax is as follows:

```
objFSO.DeleteFile strPath [,bForce]
```

The strPath parameter is the path to the file(s) to delete. The directory path can be a standard file path or it can use UNC format. You can use the wildcards * and ? to specify multiple files to delete. You must provide file criteria, either by specifying a single file or by using a wildcard.

Providing the path to a directory (as you can do using the DELETE command) does not delete the contents of the directory—you must use wildcards (*.*) after the directory path to delete the contents. If you specify a wildcard for a specific file (e.g., `*.DOC`) and no files that meet the criteria are found, an error occurs. This doesn't happen if you use the *.* wildcards and no files are found.

```
Set objFSO = CreateObject("Scripting.FileSystemObject")

'attempt to delete the contents of the data directory
'this won't do anything - no error will occur
objFSO.DeleteFile "d:\data"
'this will delete the contents of the data directory
objFSO.DeleteFile "d:\data\*.*"
```

The optional `bForce` parameter is a Boolean value and, if set to `True`, it attempts to force the deletion of read-only files. The default is `False`. If the file that is specified for deletion does not exist, an error occurs. If you attempt to delete multiple files, the `DeleteFile` operation terminates when the error is encountered.

The `File` object's `Delete` method deletes a specified file. Its syntax is as follows:

```
objFile.Delete [,bForce]
```

The `File` object's `Delete` method can also take an optional `bForce` parameter (like the `DeleteFile` method) that attempts to force the deletion of a read-only file. The default is `False`.

Files deleted using either the `DeleteFile` or `Delete` method are not moved to the Recycle Bin.

5.16 Creating and Writing to a Text File

Problem

You want to create a text file and add some text to it.

Solution

You can use the FSO's `CreateTextFile` method to create a new `TextStream` object, and then add text using either the `Write` or `WriteLine` methods:

```
Dim objFSO, objTextFile

Set objFSO = CreateObject("Scripting.FileSystemObject")
Set objTextFile = objFSO.CreateTextFile("D:\data.txt")
objTextFile.WriteLine "Write a line to a file with end of line character"
```

```
objTextFile.Write "Write string without new line character"
objTextFile.Close
```

Discussion

The TextStream object provides powerful text file creation and manipulation abilities. To create a new TextStream object, invoke the FSO object's CreateTextFile method. Its syntax is as follows:

```
Set objText = objFSO.CreateTextFile(strFileName, [bOverwrite],[ intTriState])
```

The strFileName parameter identifies the new filename. The optional bOverwite parameter overwrites an existing file with the same name if True. The default value is True. If the bOverwite parameter is set to False and the file that is specified by strFileName exists, an error occurs. The optional intTriState parameter creates a Unicode file if set to –1; it creates an ASCII file if set to 0. A value of –2 uses system settings. The default is 0.The following example creates a new text file:

```
Set objFSO = CreateObject("Scripting.FileSystemObject")
Set objTextFile = objFSO.CreateTextFile("C:\Data\data.txt")
```

Once you have created a TextStream object, you are ready to write data to it. The Write or WriteLine methods write data to the file. Their syntax is as follows:

```
objTextStream.Write|WriteLine strText
```

The strText parameter is the text that is written to the file. The difference between the Write and WriteLine methods is that the WriteLine method writes an end-of-line character (represented by the VBScript intrinsic constant vbCrLf) at the end of the line.

You can add blank lines to a text file using the WriteBlankLines method:

```
objTextStream.WriteBlankLines nLinesCount
```

A blank line represents a carriage return/linefeed combination.

Whenever you are done performing operations on a TextStream object, call its Close method. The Close method closes the object and writes any updates to the file to disk.

5.17 Opening and Reading a File

Problem

You want to read a text file.

Solution

You can use the FSO's `OpenTextFile` method to open a file, and you can use the `Read` or `ReadLine` methods to read individual lines. The following sample contains a function that searches a specified .ini file for a key and then returns the associated value:

```
'readini.vbs
Dim dAccess

dAccess = ReadINI("e:\data.ini", "DateLastAccessed")

Function ReadINI(strINIFile, strKey)
 Dim objFSO, objTextFile, strLine

 Set objFSO = CreateObject("Scripting.FileSystemObject")
 Set objTextFile = objFSO.OpenTextFile(strINIFile)

 'loop through each line of file and check for key value
 Do While Not objTextFile.AtEndOfStream
    strLine = objTextFile.ReadLine
    If Left(strLine, Len(strKey) + 1) = strKey & "=" Then
        ReadINI = Mid(strLine, InStr(strLine, "=") + 1)
    End If
 Loop

 objTextFile.Close

End Function
```

Discussion

To open an existing text file, call the FSO's `OpenTextFile` method. Its syntax is as follows:

```
Set objText =
  objFSO.OpenTextFile(strFileName, [intIOMode],[ bCreat],[ intTriState])
```

Table 5-8 lists the `OpenTextFile` method parameters.

Table 5-8. `OpenTextFile` *Method Parameters*

PARAMETER	DESCRIPTION
`strFileName`	Name of file to open.
`intIOMode`	Optional. Specifies whether file is to be opened for Reading =1, Writing=2, or Appending=8. The default is Reading.
`bCreate`	Optional. If set to `True`, a new text file will be created if it is not found. The default is `False`.
`TriState`	Optional. If –2, it opens the file using file system settings; –1 uses Unicode; and 0 uses ASCII. The default is 0.

An alternative is to invoke the `OpenAsTextStream` method on an existing `File` object:

```
Set objText = objFile.OpenAsTextStream([intIOMode],[ intTriState])
```

The `intIOMode` and `intTriState` parameters correspond to the parameters in the `OpenTextFile` method. Also like the `OpenTextFile` method, `OpenAsTextStream` returns a `TextStream` object.

If you have opened the file for read access, you can read parts of the file or the whole file. There are three methods for reading data. The `ReadAll` method returns the whole text file as a string. `ReadLine` reads the line up to the end-of-line character sequence. The `Read` method reads a specified number of characters.

```
strData = objTextFile.ReadLine  'read a single line
strData = objTextFile.Read(10)    'read 10 characters
strData = objTextFile.ReadAll   'read the whole file
```

If you are reading the file either character by character using the `Read` method or line by line using the `ReadLine` method, you need to be able to determine when you hit the end of the file. You do this by retrieving the value of the `AtEndOfStream` property. `AtEndOfStream` is `True` if the file pointer is at the end of the file; otherwise, it is `False`.

You should also check the `AtEndOfStream` property when using the `ReadAll` method—attempting to read an empty file using `ReadAll` generates an error.

If you want to jump a number of characters or lines when processing a text file, you can use the `SkipLine` or `Skip` method. Their syntaxes are as follows:

```
objTextFile.Skip nChars
objTextFile.SkipLine
```

SkipLine moves to the next line, which is the position after the next carriage return/linefeed combination. The Skip method skips nChars characters. The Skip method can only move forward in a file; you cannot move backward by specifying a negative value.

5.18 Updating a Text File

Problem

You want to update a text file.

Solution

The following script contains a routine to update a key in an .ini file:

```
'iniwrite.vbs
'updates an INI file entry
Const ForWriting = 2
Const ForAppending = 8

UpdateINI "e:\settings.ini", "DateLastAccessed", Now

Sub UpdateINI(strINIFile, strKey, strValue)
 Dim objFSO, objTextFile, strFileText, aDataFile, nF, bFound

 Set objNetwork = CreateObject("WScript.Network")

 Set objFSO = CreateObject("Scripting.FileSystemObject")

 'open the user file
 Set objTextFile = objFSO.OpenTextFile(strINIFile)

 'read the whole file
 If Not objTextFile.AtEndOfStream Then
   strFileText = objTextFile.ReadAll

   'split the file into an array.
   aDataFile = Split(strFileText, vbCrLf)
```

```
    'loop through each item in the array
    For nF = 0 to Ubound(aDataFile)
       If Left(aDataFile(nF), Len(strKey)+1)=strKey & "=" Then
         aDataFile(nF) = strKey & "=" & strValue
         bFound = True
         Exit For
     End If
    Next

  End If

  objTextFile.Close

  'if entry was found then write back contents
  If bFound Then
    strFileText = Join(aDataFile, vbCrLf)
    Set objTextFile = _
            objFSO.OpenTextFile(strINIFile, ForWriting )
    objTextFile.Write strFileText
  Else
    'entry not found, add new entry to end of file
    Set objTextFile = _
            objFSO.OpenTextFile(strINIFile, ForAppending )
    objTextFile.WriteLine strKey & "=" & strValue
  End If

  objTextFile.Close
 End Sub
```

Discussion

The TextStreamObject's file manipulation methods have a number of limitations. You cannot open a file for reading and writing at the same time. You must first read the contents of a file, close the file, manipulate the contents, and write the contents out again.

The Solution script uses the Split function to break the lines of a text file into an array that is based on the carriage return/newline character. Each element of the array is checked for a matching key value and, if found, is changed to a specified value. If the value is not found, it is appended to the end of the file.

Next, the array is converted back to a string using the Join function and written back to the source text file.

This method is useful for small files but it is less practical for larger ones because of the memory issues that are involved with reading the file, converting to an array, and writing to the source file.

A solution is to create a secondary temporary work file in which any change is written. This file is renamed to the source file upon completion of the operation and then deleted. In the following sample, the file `bigfile.txt` is converted to uppercase using a temporary work file:

```
Const TemporaryFolder = 2
Dim objFSO, strFilePath, objFolder, objSrcFile, objDestFile
Dim strLine, strSourceFile

Set objFSO = CreateObject("Scripting.FileSystemObject")

strSourceFile = "d:\data\bigfile.txt"

'get a reference to the temporary file folder
Set objFolder = objFSO.GetSpecialFolder(TemporaryFolder)

'create the path to the temporary file
strFilePath = objFolder.Path & "\" & objFSO.GetTempName
'create a temporary file and open the source file for processing
Set objDestFile = objFSO.CreateTextFile(strFilePath)
Set objSrcFile = objFSO.OpenTextFile(strSourceFile)

strLine = objSrcFile.ReadLine
'loop through each line of source file and write to temp file
Do While Not objSrcFile.AtEndOfStream
  'read line from source and write to temp file - convert line to uppercase
  strLine = objSrcFile.ReadLine
  objDestFile.WriteLine UCase(strLine)
Loop

objSrcFile.Close
objDestFile.Close

'copy temporary work file to source and delete temp file
objFSO.CopyFile strFilePath, strSourceFile
objFSO.DeleteFile strFilePath
```

The script uses the FSO's `GetTempName` method to return a randomly generated unique file name. Its syntax is as follows:

```
strTempName = objFSO.GetTempName
```

The example uses the FSO's `GetSpecialFolder` method to reference the temporary folder. It returns a `Folder` object for a specified systems folder. Its syntax is as follows:

```
Set objFolder = objFSO.GetSpecialFolder(nSpecialFolder)
```

The `nSpecialFolder` parameter determines the folder object to return. Valid values, along with constants that you can declare in your own code, are listed in Table 5-9.

Table 5-9. `GetSpecialFolder` *Constants*

CONSTANT	VALUE	DESCRIPTION
`WindowsFolder`	0	Windows directory
`SystemFolder`	1	Windows system directory (e.g., C:\Winnt\System32)
`TemporaryFolder`	2	Windows temporary directory (e.g., C:\Temp)

CHAPTER 6

Input/Output Streams

EVEN WITH THE GRAPHICAL user interface, command-line console applications are still important, especially when mass repetitive changes are required that would take a great amount of time to perform through the graphical user interface or when scripts are designed to perform operations that do not require user interaction.

Windows Script Host (WSH) 1.0 allowed the processing of command-line parameters. WSH version 2.0 introduces the ability to process standard input and output streams (`StdIn` and `StdOut`). This new feature is of great importance for the creation of flexible console applications.

The command-line environment has always supported the capability of "piping" streams from one console application to another, but it has never provided a great number of built-in commands to use this ability, apart from the `MORE` and `SORT` commands.

This capability has always been an important feature in the UNIX environment, and most native UNIX shell commands allow (or require) input to be provided via standard input, allowing complex sequences of operations to be executed within a single command line.

> **NOTE** *You can download* `StdIn`, `StdOut`, *and* `StdErr` *property documentation and WSH documentation from* `http://msdn.microsoft.com/scripting`.

6.1 Using Regular Expressions to Filter the Contents of an Input Stream

Problem

You require a routine that filters supplied information and then outputs any results that meet the criteria to the standard output (`StdOut`). The resulting output can be used by other console applications.

Solution

The following script reads input from standard input using the WScript.StdIn object, and then it filters the line against a regular expression. Only lines that match the expression are written to standard output:

```
<?xml version="1.0" ?>
<job>
<!--comment
Script:wshgrep.wsf
performs regular expression filtering against standard input
-->
 <script language="VBScript" src="fsolib.vbs">
<![CDATA[

 Option Explicit

 Dim nF, objFSO, strLine
 Dim objRegExp, strFilter
 On Error Resume Next

If Not IsCscript Then ExitScript _
    "This script must be run from command line using cscript.exe", True


 If WScript.Arguments.Count <> 1 Then
  ShowUsage
  WScript.Quit
End If
  strFilter= WScript.Arguments(0)
  Set objRegExp = New RegExp
  objRegExp.Pattern = strFilter   objRegExp.IgnoreCase = True


  Do While Not WScript.StdIn.AtEndOfStream
    strLine = WScript.StdIn.ReadLine

    If objRegExp.Test(strLine) Then
WScript.StdOut.WriteLine(strLine)
   End If
 Loop
```

```
Sub ShowUsage()
 WScript.Echo _
     WScript.ScriptName & " filters standard input against a regular
expression." _
    & vbCrLf & "Syntax:" &  vbCrLf & _
    WScript.ScriptName & "  regexp" &  vbCrLf & _
    "regexp  regular expression"
 End Sub
  ]]>
  </script>
</job>
```

Discussion

WSH version 2.0 provides access to the standard input and outputs (StdIn and StdOut) from the Windows console. This allows scripts to "pipe" information between console applications.

Piping allows for information to be passed from one console application to another. Using the vertical bar (|) pipes information between one or more console applications. For example:

```
dir /b | sort | more
```

To access the StdIn or StdOut stream, use the StdIn and StdOut property of the WScript object. These properties return TextStream objects that can be read and written to as if they were text files. For example, the following WSH script reads a line from the standard input and writes its uppercase equivalent to the standard output by using the StdIn and StdOut properties:

```
'ucasein.vbs
'converts standard Input stream to uppercase
'and redirects to stdout
Dim strText
strText = WScript.StdIn.ReadAll
WScript.StdOut.Write Ucase(strText)
```

To use the ucasein script, pipe output to it from other applications. The following command-line snippet pipes the file users.txt to the script:

```
cscript ucasein.vbs < users.txt > ucusers.txt
```

The contents of the input stream (in this case, `users.txt`) is converted to uppercase and written to standard output. The standard output in this case is redirected to a new file: `ucusers.txt`. Information can be piped to a WSH script from any existing console application or other scripts that write information to the `StdOut` stream.

If you execute a console script that reads `StdIn` but does not have information piped from another application or from a file, the application will take input from the user's standard input device, the keyboard. In this case, the script will pause to accept keyboard input. The following command line starts the `ucasein` script and accepts input from the keyboard because no other source is redirected/piped to the script:

```
cscript ucasein.vbs
```

Press Ctrl-Z to end the processing of keyboard input from `StdIn`. This keystroke combination sends an end of file (EOF) sequence to the stream. Pressing Ctrl-Break when reading keyboard input from `StdIn` will force an EOF.

To pipe information to a WSH script, execute a console application and pipe the output to the WSH script. The following script pipes the contents of a `dir` command to the `ucasein` script:

```
dir | cscript ucasein.vbs | more
```

The output of the `dir` command is converted to uppercase. This result is then piped to the `more` command, which displays one screen of text at a time.

When you chain commands together on non–Windows 2000/XP/2003 machines, the script must be prefixed by `Cscript` or `Wscript`. The following command line is the equivalent of the previous sample:

```
dir | ucasein.vbs | more
```

This generates an error when run on Windows NT 4.0/9*x*/ME computers. On Windows 2000/XP/2003, it will use the default script host, either `Cscript` or `Wscript`. If a script writes to `StdOut`, you should use `Cscript` because if the result of the output is not piped to another process, an error will occur. The following example will not work:

```
dir | wscript ucasein.vbs
```

The preceding example doesn't work because the results are not piped to another process and the `Wscript` script host does use the results. Replacing `Cscript` with `Wscript` in the example would result in the output being displayed in the console. The earlier example in which the results were piped to the `more` command would work using `Wscript`.

Even though you can use `Wscript` to execute scripts that use `StdIn`, you should avoid using it to write to `StdOut`.

The Solution script evaluates each line on the `StdIn` against a regular expression. Any resulting matches are written to `StdOut`. For example, say you want to output the routing tables to a file without any of the additional headings:

```
route print | cscript //NoLogo wshgrep.wsf (\d+\.\d+\.\d+\.\d.+){4} > rt.txt
```

The `Route Print` command pipes the routing information to the `wshgrep.wsf` script. `WshGrep` filters out all lines that meet the criteria and outputs them to `StdOut`. This output is redirected to the file `rt.txt`.

The `//Nologo` switch ensures that no "logo" information from the execution of the script appears with the output. This includes the Microsoft WSH version and copyright information.

If you want to prevent the display of the Microsoft logo and copyright information by default, use the `//S` switch to save the command-line settings as the default:

```
wscript //NoLogo //S
```

This saves the `//NoLogo` switch as a default switch.

The `wshgrep.wsf` script and other scripts in this section include an `fsolib.vbs` script library to implement repetitive functions. The `fsolib.vbs` script library is shown here:

```
'fsolib.vbs
'Description: Contains routines used by FSO scripts

'check if script is being run interactively
'Returns:True if run from command line, otherwise false
Function IsCscript()
  IsCScript = (StrComp(Right(WScript.Fullname,11),"cscript.exe",1) = 0)
End Function

'display an error message and exist script
'Parameters:
'strMsg          Message to display
'strUseWscript Use Wscript.Echo to display message.
'    By default StdErr is used, but this cannot be used in
'    interactive (wscript) mode unless redirected to somewhere else.
Sub ExitScript(strMsg, bUseWscript)
```

```
 If bUseWscript Then
  WScript.Echo strMsg
 Else
  'get the standard error stream
   WScript.StdErr.WriteLine strMsg
 End If
 WScript.Quit -1
End Sub

'returns contents of specified file. If file doesn't exist
'terminates script and displays error message
'Parameters:
'strFile Path to file to return
'Returns
'contents of specified file
Function GetFile(strFile)
    On Error Resume Next
    Dim objFSO, objFile
    Set objFSO = CreateObject("Scripting.FileSystemObject")
    Set objFile = objFSO.OpenTextFile(strFile)
    If Err Then ExitScript _
        "Error " & Err.Description & " opening file " & _
        strFile, False
    GetFile = objFile.ReadAll
    objFile.Close
End Function

'terminates script with message if script not run using cscript.ext
'Parameters:None
Sub CheckCScript()
    If Not IsCscript Then ExitScript _
        "This script must be run from command line using cscript.exe", True
End Sub

'checks if specified number of arguments have been passed and exits script
'displaying usage information if not
'Parameters:
'nCount  Number of arguments expected
Sub CheckArguments(nCount)
    If WScript.Arguments.Count <> nCount Then
        WScript.Arguments.ShowUsage
        WScript.Quit
    End If
End Sub
```

See Also

Solution 3.1 and Solution 8.1.

6.2 Reading Keyboard Input

Problem

You want to create a simple text-based menu.

Solution

You can read a character from standard input using the Read method:

```
<?xml version="1.0" ?>
<job>
<!--comment
Script:menu.wsf
demonstrate a simple text-based menu
-->
 <script language="VBScript" src=""fsolib.vbs">
 <![CDATA[
'menu.wsf
Dim strOption

CheckCScript

WScript.Echo "-------Menu Options-------------"
WScript.Echo "1 - Copy Information"
WScript.Echo "2 - Move Information"
WScript.Echo "3 - Quit"
WScript.Echo "Select option and press the Enter key to continue"

'read the standard input
strOption = WScript.StdIn.Read(1)

Select Case strOption
 Case "1"
    WScript.Echo "option 1 selected"
Case "2"
    WScript.Echo "option 2 selected"
```

```
Case "3"
    WScript.Quit -1
Case Else
    WScript.Echo "Invalid option selected"
End Select

WScript.StdIn.Close
 ]]>
  </script>
</job>
```

Discussion

Even though Windows provides an advanced graphical user interface, it can still be useful to provide text-based menus for console applications. `StdIn` provides a method of reading input from the console.

If no stream is redirected to `StdIn`, the keyboard is used to read `StdIn`. `StdIn` returns a `TextStream` object and supports the methods provided through this object to read input (`Read`, `ReadLine`, and `ReadAll` methods).

Using the `Read` method, you can specify the number of characters you want to read. The method does not terminate once the number of characters specified has been entered; you must press the Enter key or the EOF key combination (Ctrl-Z). Only the number of characters specified by the `Read` method is actually returned.

See Also

Solution 3.2.

6.3 Generating Template-Based Data

Problem

You want to be able to search and replace values from standard input.

Solution

You can read the standard input stream using `WScript.StdIn` and then use the results to populate templates that are provided through a command-line parameter or external file:

```
<?xml version="1.0" ?>
<job>
<runtime>
    <description>
<![CDATA[
This script demonstrates use of WScript.StdIn/Out/Err by
doing some template processing.  A comma-separated list
of replacement strings is read in from stdin, merged into
a template file and the result is dumped out to stdout.
The process is repeated for each line of replacement strings.
]]>
    </description>
    <unnamed name="TemplateFile" many="false" required="true"
    helpstring="File containing template text." />
    <example>
<![CDATA[
CScript sar.wsf Template.txt < Replacements.txt > Out.txt

Suppose Replacements.txt contained

Bob,*.doc
Sue,*.txt

and Template.txt contained

net use \\odin\</1/> /user:admin /password:bigsecret
copy \\odin\</1/>\backmeup\</2/> \\loki\backups\</1/>\
net use /d \\odin\</1/>

then Out.txt would contain

net use \\odin\bob /user:admin /password:bigsecret
copy \\odin\bob\backmeup\*.doc \\loki\backups\bob\
net use /d \\odin\bob
net use \\odin\sue /user:admin /password:bigsecret
copy \\odin\sue\backmeup\*.txt \\loki\backups\sue\
net use /d \\odin\sue
]]>
    </example>
</runtime>
<script language="VBScript" src="fsolib.vbs">
<![CDATA[
   Dim strTemplate
```

```
 Sub ReplaceText
  Dim strRepls, aRepls, strOut, objRegExp
  Set objRegExp = New RegExp
  objRegExp.Pattern = "<\/\d+\/>"

   'loop through each line of standard input
  Do While Not WScript.StdIn.AtEndOfStream
   strRepls = WScript.StdIn.ReadLine
   aRepls = Split(strRepls, ",")
   strOut = strTemplate
    'replace each element in template
    For nF = 0 To Ubound(aRepls)
      strOut = Replace(strOut , "</" & nF+1 & "/>" , aRepls(nF))
    Next
   'check if all elements were replaced
   If objRegExp.Test(strOut) Then _
      ExitScript "Replacement file has too few values.", False
    WScript.StdOut.Write strOut
   Loop
End Sub

CheckCScript
CheckArguments 1
strTemplate = GetFile(WScript.Arguments(0))
ReplaceText
]]>
</script>
</job>
```

Discussion

The search and replace script creates output in which tags in a template string are replaced by elements from standard input.

Each line of the standard input must consist of data elements delimited by a comma. These elements are identified by their ordinal position in the line, so the first element is 1, the second element is 2, and so on.

The following users.txt text file contains information that can be piped to the script. In this example, there are three elements for each line:

```
Freds,Fred Smith,Accounting Manager
Joeb,Joe Blow,Computer Operator
```

The template string can either be a text file or a command-line parameter. In the template, any instance of an element number surrounded by **</** and **/>** is replaced with the corresponding element from standard input.

In the following example, `</1/>` is replaced by the first element from standard input, `</2/>` with the second, and so on:

```
net user password </1/> /ADD /FULLNAME:"</2/>" /COMMENT:"</3/>"
```

Using first line of `users.txt` as input, the following output is generated:

```
net user password Freds /ADD /FULLNAME:"Fred Smith" /COMMENT:"Accounting Manager"
net user password Joeb /ADD /FULLNAME:"Joe Blow" /COMMENT:"Computer Operator"
```

To run the `users.txt` file against a layout string and redirect the output to a batch file called `newusers.bat`, use the following:

```
cscript sar.wsf template.txt  < users.txt  > newusers.bat
```

The `sar` script processes each line of the standard input for data. You can use this ability to use the search and replace script to fill in a template with data as a very flexible tool for creating formatted output. For example, suppose that you want to take the list of users from a text file and generate an HTML file containing the user list in a table. The following layout file, `details.txt`, contains the template table details for each user:

```
<tr><td></1/></td><td></2/></td><td></3/></td></tr>
```

With this template, you can generate the HTML table details using the `users.txt` file:

```
cscript sar.wsf details.txt < users.txt
```

However, to create a complete HTML document, you need to include the appropriate HTML `<html>`, `<body>`, and `<table>` elements to surround the detail lines. You can't use the `sar.wsf` script to insert the details into the body because it processes line by line and would generate an unusable HTML document. You require results of the table generation to be inserted into the body of an HTML document.

To do this, create a modified version of the `sar.wsf` script called `sarw.wsf` to treat the standard input as one element to be replaced in a template:

```
<?xml version="1.0" ?>
<job>
```

```
<runtime>
    <description>
<![CDATA[
This script demonstrates use of WScript.StdIn/Out/Err by
doing some template processing.  The whole StdIn is read and
merged into a template file and the result is dumped out to stdout.
]]>
    </description>
    <unnamed name="TemplateFile" many="false" required="true"
    helpstring="File containing template text." />
    <example>
<![CDATA[
CScript sarw.wsf Template.txt < Replacement.txt > Out.txt

Suppose Replacements.txt contained
Fred Smith  555-1234
Joe Blow    555-2432

and Template.txt contained
     Phone List
Name         Phone
</1/>

then Out.txt would contain:
     Phone List
Name         Phone
Fred Smith  555-1234
Joe Blow    555-2432
]]>
    </example>
</runtime>
<script language="VBScript" src="fsolib.vbs">
<![CDATA[
   Dim strTemplate
   Sub ReplaceText
    Dim strRepls, strOut

    'check if replacement element exists
     If Instr(strTemplate,"</1/>") = 0 Then _
         ExitScript "Template file missing replacement element ", False

     'read the body from standard input and replace template layout
     strRepls = WScript.StdIn.ReadAll
```

```
    strOut = Replace(strTemplate , "</1/>" , strRepls)

  WScript.StdOut.Write strOut
  End Sub

  CheckCScript
  CheckArguments 1
  strTemplate = GetFile(WScript.Arguments(0))
  ReplaceText
  ]]>
 </script>
</job>
```

The `sarw.wsf` script replaces the element `</1/>` in a template file with the `StdIn` contents and writes the results to `StdOut`. The following template file, `body.txt`, is used to generate the body of the HTML file:

```
<html>
<head></head>
<body>
<table border="1" width="100%">
  </1/>
</table>
</body>
</html>
```

The following command sequence generates the HTML file `usrs.htm` using the `details.txt` and `body.txt` templates:

```
cscript sar.wsf details.txt < users.txt | cscript sarw.wsf body.txt > usrs.htm
```

The resulting output is similar to this:

```
<html>
<head></head>
<body>
<table border="1" width="100%">
  <tr><td>Freds</td><td>Fred Smith</td><td> Accounting Manager</td></tr>
  <tr><td>Joeb</td><td>Joe Blow</td><td>Computer Operator</td></tr>
</table>
</body>
</html>
```

The first step redirects the `users.txt` file to `sar.wsf`, which generates the HTML table details. The result of this operation is piped to `sarw.wsf`, which inserts it into the `body.txt` template. The result of this operation is redirected to the `usrs.htm` file.

6.4 Creating Multiple-User Prompts

Problem

Existing data files usually provide the standard input that scripts read. This is useful when processing multiple items, but it can be a bit impractical for single pieces of information. You want to be able to query the user with one or more predefined prompts and then take the results and send them to the standard output.

Solution

You can use the `StdErr` output stream to prompt users for information, which is then piped to standard output for further processing. Using `StdErr` instead of `StdOut` to output information ensures that the user prompts do not get piped with the user input results.

```
<?xml version="1.0" ?>
<job>
<runtime>
    <description>
<![CDATA[
This script demonstrates use of WScript.StdIn/Out/Err by
prompting the user with a set of prompts read from a file
and then dumping the results of those prompts as a comma-
separated list to stdout.
]]>
    </description>
    <unnamed name="PromptFile" many="false" required="true"
    helpstring="File containing prompts." />
    <example>
<![CDATA[
CScript prompt.wsf Prompts.txt

Suppose Prompts.txt contained

What is the user's name?
```

```
What files should be backed up? (eg, *.doc)

Then this program would ask the user for the values and
output

Bob,*.txt
]]>
    </example>
</runtime>
<script language="VBScript" src="fsolib.vbs">
<![CDATA[

Dim strPromptFile, strPrompts

Sub AskUser
    Dim aPrompts, strPrompt, fComma
    aPrompts = Split(strPrompts, vbCrLf)
        fComma = False
    For Each strPrompt In aPrompts
        ' The file may contain blank lines.
        If Trim(strPrompt) <> "" Then
            If fComma Then WScript.StdOut.Write ","
            WScript.StdErr.Write strPrompt
            WScript.StdOut.Write WScript.StdIn.ReadLine
             fComma = True
        End If
    Next
End Sub

 CheckCScript
 CheckArguments 1
 strPrompts = GetFile(WScript.Arguments(0))
 AskUser
]]>
  </script>
</job>
```

Discussion

The `prompt.wsf` script queries the user for input with prompts that are defined by a template file. This allows the script to prompt the user for information that is piped or redirected to another process, and it provides an alternative to building data files to redirect to scripts.

You use the script to create a solution that builds a batch file to create a new NT user by prompting for user details. The following `nusr.txt` file contains the prompts to create a new user:

```
Enter user id:
Enter user full name
Enter comment:
```

Each prompt appears on its own line in the file. You now need a template file to fill in the user details. Use the `sar.wsf` script from Solution 6.3 to insert the prompts into a template. The following text file contains the layout for the `nuser.txt` template:

```
rem nuser.txt
Rem create user
net user </1/> /ADD

Rem create a user directoryMd d:\users\</1/>

rem Create the share
net share </1/>$=d:\users\</1/>

rem Grant </1/> and Domain Admins full access to the share
rem shrperm is part of Backoffice resource kit
shrperm \\Odin\</1/>$ </1/>:F "Domain Admins":F

rem Grant user </1/> full access to his or her directory
cacls d:\users\</1/> /T /E /G </1/>:F

rem Remove Everyone access from directory
cacls d:\users\</1/> /T /E /R Everyone

remPermit Domain Admins to have full access in directory.
cacls d:\users\</1/> /T /E /P "Domain admins":F

rem set the home directory setting for user </1/>

net user </1/> /HOMEDIR:\\Odin\</1/>$
net user </1/> /FULLNAME:"</2/>"
net user </1/> /COMMENT:"</3/>"
```

The following command line uses prompt.wsf to prompt for a user ID, description, and comment:

```
cscript prompt.wsf inp.txt | cscript sar.wsf nuser.txt > nuser.bat
```

Next, this information is piped to the sar.wsf script, which builds the nuser.bat batch file using the nuser.txt template file.

The prompt.wsf script generates user prompts from a file. These prompts are displayed using the StdErr stream. The standard error (StdErr) output stream is used to display the prompts. Functionally, StdErr appears similar to StdOut. It returns a TextStream object and any output written to it appears on the console.

The difference is that anything written to the StdErr stream is not available to be read by the StdIn stream. The purpose of the StdErr stream is to display error messages in console scripts that perform StdIn/StdOut operations. This behavior is used by prompt.wsf to display the prompts. If StdOut or WScript.Echo had been used, the prompts would be piped with the results of user prompts.

See Also

Solution 3.8 and Solution 3.9.

CHAPTER 7

Registry Operations

WINDOWS STORES ALL underlying application and system configuration information in the registry.

The registry information is stored in a hierarchical tree structure that contains keys. Each key can contain values as well as additional keys.

The ability to manipulate the registry enables you to change virtually any system setting. This might involve changing desktop settings, colors or fonts, application settings (such as the location of documents), or system configuration (such as network settings).

While all of these settings can be accessed manually through a configuration utility such as a Control Panel applet, the ability to make mass changes to consistently set multiple settings at once programmatically can save you a great deal of time and effort.

There are a number of alternatives available to perform registry manipulation with Windows Script Host (WSH). One is the `WScript.Shell` object, which is included with all versions of WSH and provides basic registry functionality.

Another is Windows Management Instrumentation (WMI) version 1.5 or later. WMI is included with Windows 2000, 2003, and XP, and it is available as a separate installation for Windows 9*x*/ME and NT 4.0.

If your registry manipulation requirements are limited to string and basic numeric values, especially if you are working with a large installed base of Windows 9*x*, ME, and NT 4.0 systems, the `WScript.Shell` object is sufficient. If you need to read or write large binary values, enumerate the registry, or access remote computer registry values, WMI is the way to go.

One problem you might encounter is determining what registry keys contain the values for the setting you are attempting to change. There are literally thousands of keys.

An excellent free utility called Regmon is available from Sysinternals (`http://www.sysinternals.com/`) that shows modifications made to the registry in real time.

Another option is the `sysdiff.exe` utility available on the Windows NT 4.0 CD or in the NT Resource Kit. Sysdiff creates a "snapshot" of Windows NT configuration, including the registry, and it can perform a comparison to show the differences between the snapshot and the current settings.

There is also a large amount of registry setting information available on Microsoft's Web site (`http://www.microsoft.com/`), as well as third-party Web sites such as `http://www.regedit.com/`.

Also be aware of other alternatives to managing system settings, such as the Windows NT System Policy Editor or Windows 2000 and 2003 Group Policies. These tools can provide a more robust solution, and they are easier to manage through a graphical interface.

7.1 Reading a Value from the Registry

Problem

You want to read a value from the registry.

Solution

Use the `WScript.Shell` object's `RegRead` method to read a specified registry value:

```
Dim objShell
Set objShell = CreateObject("WScript.Shell")
WScript.Echo "Your wallpaper Is " & _
    objshell.RegRead("HKCU \Control Panel\Desktop\Wallpaper")
```

Discussion

WSH supports reading of values from the registry using the `WScript.Shell` object's `RegRead` method. The syntax is as follows:

```
strVal = objShell.RegRead(strKeyPath)
```

`strKeyPath` is a path to the registry value you want to read. The path consists of the registry root key name followed by the path to the registry key you want to read. Each element of the path is separated by a backslash (\).

The registry root key is always the first part of the path to the registry key you are trying to read. Table 7-1 lists the registry root key names. Some registry root keys can be listed in short or long form.

Table 7-1. Registry Root Key Names

SHORT	LONG
HKCU	HKEY_CURRENT_USER
HKLM	HKEY_LOCAL_MACHINE
HKCR	HKEY_CLASSES_ROOT
None	HKEY_USERS
None	HKEY_CURRENT_CONFIG
None	HKEY_DYN_DATA

For example, the path to the Windows 98 version number can be represented as `HKLM\Software\Microsoft\Windows\CurrentVersion\VersionNumber` or `HKEY_LOCAL_MACHINE\Software\Microsoft\Windows\CurrentVersion\VersionNumber`.

One way to get the path for registry values is to use the RegEdit application to search for registry information and copy the key path to the clipboard using Edit > Copy Key Name. Then paste the registry path into the script where required.

A registry key can store different data types, such a string, DWORD (which is an integer), binary, and multistring values. If the value is a string or integer value, it is returned when the `RegRead` method is called.

```
Set objShell = CreateObject("WScript.Shell")
WScript.Echo "Your Windows 98 Version Number is " & _
objshell.RegRead("HKLM\Software\Microsoft\Windows\CurrentVersion\VersionNumber")
```

Binary values are returned as an array of byte values.

```
Set objShell = CreateObject("WScript.Shell")

'read a binary value
aBinary = _
  objshell.RegRead("HKEY_CURRENT_USER\Software\MyApp\Config\coords")

'loop through and display each value
For Each val In aBinary
  WScript.Echo val
Next
```

Multistring values are returned as an array of strings and can be read using the same method as binary values.

If the registry value does not exist or you do not have appropriate security access to the key, a runtime error will occur.

The most recent versions (1.5 or later) of WMI include a registry services provider that allows you to create, read, write, and enumerate registry values.

The Shell object's registry methods are capable of reading and writing some registry information. The WMI provider offers additional features. For instance, the Shell object cannot read or write the "default" registry value.

WMI is included with Windows 2000/2003 and XP and can be installed separately on Windows NT and Windows 9x/ME. See Chapter 10 for more information on how to use WMI.

To use the provider, connect to the root\default namespace. Create an instance of the StdRegProv provider class. This class exposes a number of static methods that perform registry operations.

To read a value, you need to call the appropriate Get method for the registry value data type you want to read. The generic syntax for these methods is as follows:

```
nReturn= objRegistry.GetTypeValue([nRootKey], strKey, strValueName, vValue)
```

The optional nRootKey parameter represents the root key value for the root key. If the nRootKey parameter is not specified, the local machine (HKEY_LOCAL_MACHINE) root key is used. Table 7-2 lists valid root key values.

Table 7-2. Valid Root Key Values

DOCUMENT TITLE	VALUE
HKEY_LOCAL_MACHINE	&H80000002
HKEY_CURRENT_USER	&H80000001
HKEY_CLASSES_ROOT	&H80000000
HKEY_USERS	&H80000003
HKEY_CURRENT_CONFIG	&H80000005
HKEY_DYN_DATA	&H80000006

strKey represents the path to the key where the value is located. Each key in the path is separated by a backslash (\).

strValueName is the name of the value to read. If strValueName is an empty string, the "default" registry value will be set.

The value read is returned through the vValue parameter. The data type returned depends upon the method being used to read the data. Table 7-3 lists the methods that are available to read registry values.

Table 7-3. WMI Registry Read *Methods*

METHOD	VALUE RETURNED
GetStringValue	String value
GetMultiStringValue	Array of string values
GetExpandedStringValue	String value
GetBinaryValue	Array of byte values
GetDWORDValue	Integer

If the read is successful these methods return 0.

The following sample reads the registry value Identifier under the key path HARDWARE\DESCRIPTION\System from the HKEY_LOCAL_MACHINE root key:

```
Const WMICONST = "winmgmts:{impersonationLevel=impersonate}!root\default:"

Const HKEY_CURRENT_USER = &H80000001
Dim objRegistry, nRet, strValue

'create an instance of the StdRegProv registry provider
Set objRegistry = GetObject(WMICONST & "StdRegProv")

'read the value Identifier under key HARDWARE\DESCRIPTION\System
'since the local machine root key is the default, the first parameter is omitted
nRet = objRegistry.GetStringValue(, "HARDWARE\DESCRIPTION\System", _
                                    "Identifier", strValue)

If nRet = 0 Then
    WScript.Echo "The system type is " & strValue
Else
    WScript.Echo "Error reading the HARDWARE\DESCRIPTION\System key"
End If
```

See Also

For more information about GetStringValue, search for the terms "WMI GetStringValue" at http://msdn.microsoft.com. Information about RegRead is available by searching for "RegRead" at http://msdn.microsoft.com.

7.2 Writing a Value to the Registry

Problem

You want to write a value to the registry.

Solution

You can use the Shell object's RegWrite method to write to a specified registry value:

```
'change the default document directory for Word 97
Set objShell = CreateObject("WScript.Shell")
objShell.RegWrite _
" HKEY_CURRENT_USER\Software\MyApp\Config\username" _
, "H:\Data\Word"
'create new registry key
objShell.RegWrite _
     "HKEY_CURRENT_USER\Software\MyApp\Config\NewKey\" , ""
```

Discussion

The Shell object's RegWrite method writes a value to a specified key value or creates a new key. The syntax is as follows:

```
objShell.RegWrite strPath, anyValue [,strType]
```

The strPath parameter is the path to the key to write. If the registry path ends with a backslash, RegWrite will attempt to create a new key.

Table 7-4 lists possible values for the optional strType parameter.

Table 7-4. Registry Data Types

REGISTRY TYPE	VALUE	DESCRIPTION
REG_SZ	String value	This is the default value.
REG_EXPAND_SZ	Expandable string	
REG_DWORD	Integer value	
REG_BINARY	Binary value	

Registry values of type REG_EXPAND_SZ appear to be functionally the same as REG_SZ string values. But applications that read entries of type REG_EXPAND_SZ expand any elements surrounded by percent signs (%) to their corresponding environment variable values.

```
Dim objShell
Set objShell = CreateObject("WScript.Shell")
strPath = "HKCU\Software\MyApp\Config\coordinates"

objshell.RegWrite strPath, "%SystemRoot%\heh", "REG_EXPAND_SZ"
```

RegWrite creates a registry path if it does not already exist.

Under regedit, the registry entry appears to be the same as a string. Using Windows NT/2000/2003/XP RegEdt32, you can see the data type shown in Figure 7-1.

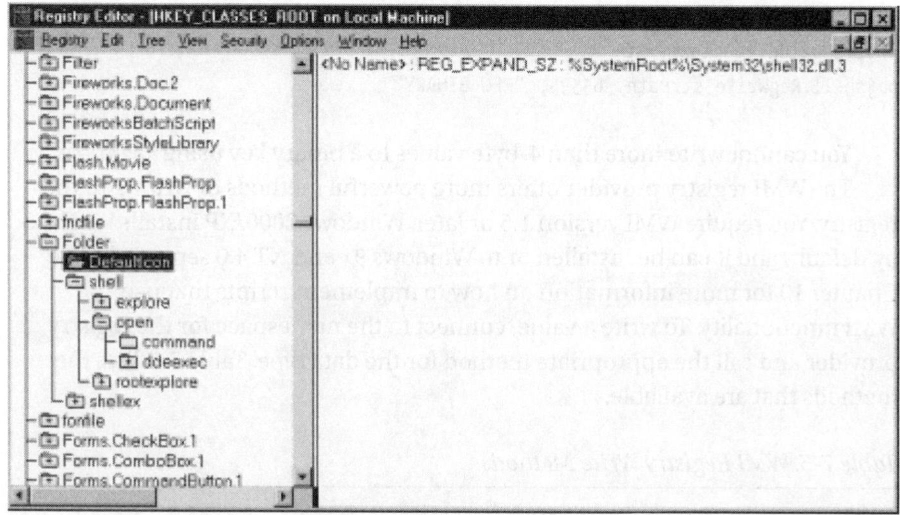

Figure 7-1. Regedt32.exe registry value types

Reading the REG_EXPAND_SZ value back using RegRead does not expand the environment variables in the string. You must manually expand any environment variables by using the Shell object's ExpandEnvironmentStrings method.

Binary values cannot be written in the same method they can be read. RegRead returns an array of byte values. RegWrite does not allow this array to be written back to the binary key. The following code sample attempts to write a binary value to the same registry value from which it was read:

```
Dim objShell, aVal, strPath
Set objShell = CreateObject("WScript.Shell")
strPath = "HKCU\Software\MyApp\Config\coordinates"

'read the value
aVal =objshell.RegRead(strPath)
'attempt to write the value back to the same string - this will not work
'an error will occur
objshell.RegWrite strPath, aVal, "REG_BINARY"
```

You can only write an integer (4 byte) value to a binary key using `RegWrite`. Each byte of the value represents one byte entry under `regedit`.

```
Dim objShell, strPath
Set objShell = CreateObject("WScript.Shell")
strPath = "HKCU\Software\MyApp\Config\coordinates"

'write value to binary key
objshell.RegWrite strPath, 65535, "REG_BINARY"
```

You cannot write more than 4-byte values to a binary key using `RegWrite`.

The WMI registry provider offers more powerful methods of writing to the registry. You require WMI version 1.5 or later. Windows 2000/XP installs WMI 1.5 by default, and it can be installed onto Windows 9*x* and NT 4.0 separately. See Chapter 10 for more information on how to implement scripts that use WMI functionality. To write a value, connect to the namespace for the registry provider and call the appropriate method for the data type. Table 7-5 lists the methods that are available.

Table 7-5. WMI Registry Write Methods

METHOD	VALUE
`SetStringValue`	String value
`SetMultiStringValue`	Array of string values
`SetExpandedStringValue`	String value
`SetBinaryValue`	Array of byte values
`SetDWORDValue`	Integer

The generic syntax for these methods is as follows:

```
nReturn= objRegistry.SetTypeValue([nRootKey], strKey, strValueName, vValue)
```

The optional nRootKey parameter represents the root key value. These values are listed in Table 7-2. If the nRootKey parameter is not specified, the local machine HKEY_LOCAL_MACHINE root key is used:

> strKey represents the path to the key where the value is located. Each key in the path is separated by a backslash (\). If a level of the path does not exist, it will not be created and the Set method will return an error value.
>
> strValueName is the name of the value to set. If the value does not exist, it will be created. If strValueName is an empty string, the "default" registry value will be set.
>
> vValue represents the value to set, and it depends upon the method being used to write the data.

If the path that is specified by strKey does not exist, it is not created and an error will occur. If you require a key to be created, use the StdRegProv provider's CreateKey method. The syntax is as follows:

```
nReturn= objRegistry.CreateKey ([nRootKey], strKeyPath)
```

The optional nRootKey parameter represents the root key value. These values are listed in Table 7-2. If the nRootKey parameter is not specified, the local machine HKEY_LOCAL_MACHINE root key is used.

The strKeyPath parameter specifies the path to be created. Each subkey in the path is separated by a backslash (\). Any subkeys that do not exist are created.

The following code sample creates a registry key with the path software\test and writes a string, multistring, binary, and expanded string registry value:

```
Const WMICONST = "winmgmts:{impersonationLevel=impersonate}!root\default:"
Const HKEY_LOCAL_MACHINE = &H80000002

Dim strPath, nRet, objRegistry, strKeyPath

'set the key path to write the values to.
strKeyPath = "software\test"

'create an instance of the registry provider
Set objRegistry = GetObject(WMICONST & "StdRegProv")

'write a binary value
nRet = objRegistry.CreateKey(HKEY_LOCAL_MACHINE, strKeyPath)
```

```
'write a binary value
nRet = objRegistry.SetBinaryValue(HKEY_LOCAL_MACHINE, _
                                   strKeyPath, "binary", Array(1, 2, 3, 4))
'write expanded registry string
nRet = objRegistry.SetExpandedStringValue(HKEY_LOCAL_MACHINE, _
                                   strKeyPath, "expanded", "%path%")
'write expanded string
nRet = objRegistry.SetStringValue(HKEY_LOCAL_MACHINE, _
                                   strKeyPath, "string", "heh")
'write multistring value
nRet = objRegistry.SetMultiStringValue(HKEY_LOCAL_MACHINE, strKeyPath, _
                                   "multistring", Array("1", "2", "3", "4"))
```

See Also

For more information about `SetBinaryValue`, search for the terms "WMI SetBinaryValue" at `http://msdn.microsoft.com`. Information about `RegWrite` is available by searching for "RegWrite" at `http://msdn.microsoft.com`.

7.3 Deleting a Registry Entry

Problem

You want to delete a value from the registry.

Solution

Use the `Shell` object's `RegDelete` method to delete a value or key:

```
Set objShell = CreateObject("WScript.Shell")

'delete a registry value
objShell.RegDelete "HKEY_CURRENT_USER\Software\MyApp\Config\coords"
```

Discussion

The `Shell` object's `RegDelete` method deletes an existing registry key or value. The syntax follows:

```
objShell.RegDelete strPath
```

The strPath parameter is the path to the value or key you want to delete. If the registry path ends with a backslash, RegDelete attempts to delete the specified key.

RegDelete functions differently depending on the operating system it is executed under. Under Windows 9*x*/ME, executing RegDelete deletes all child values and keys. Under Windows NT, you must delete all child keys and values before deleting a key that contains values and subkeys.

The WMI registry provider has separate methods for deleting registry keys and values: DeleteKey and DeleteValue.

```
nRet = objRegistry.DeleteKey([nRootKey], strKey)
nRet = objRegistry.DeleteValue([nRootKey], strKey, strValueName)
```

The optional nRootKey parameter represents the root key value. These values are listed in Table 7-2. If the nRootKey parameter is not specified, the local machine HKEY_LOCAL_MACHINE root key is used.

strKey represents the key path. Each key in the path is separated by a backslash (\). This is the registry key that gets deleted by the DeleteKey method.

strValueName is the name of the registry value to delete by the DeleteValue method.

The DeleteKey method will not delete a key if it contains any subkeys, even if the subkeys are empty. The method will delete a key if it contains registry values. The following sample deletes a key called subkey from the HKEY_CURRENT_USER registry root:

```
Const WMICONST = "winmgmts:{impersonationLevel=impersonate}!root\default:"
Const HKEY_CURRENT_USER = &H80000001
Dim strPath, nRet, objRegistry, strKeyPath

'set the key path
strKeyPath = "software\test"

'create an instance of the registry provider
Set objRegistry = GetObject(WMICONST & "StdRegProv")
'delete a key called 'subkey'
nRet = objRegistry.DeleteKey(HKEY_CURRENT_USER, "testkey\subkey")
```

See Also

Information about the DeleteValue method is available by searching for the terms "DeleteValue WMI" at http://msdn.microsoft.com. For information about the CreateKey method, search for the terms "CreateKey WMI" at http://msdn.microsoft.com. You can find information about the RegDelete method by searching for the terms "WMI RegDelete" at http://msdn.microsoft.com.

7.4 Listing the Registry Key Values

Problem

You want to list all of the values under a registry key.

Solution

The following script lists all the values in a specified key using the WMI provider:

```
'enumwmi.vbs
Const WMICONST = "winmgmts:{impersonationLevel=impersonate}!root\default:"
Const HKEY_LOCAL_MACHINE  = &H80000002

Dim strPath, nRet, objRegistry, strKeyPath, aNames
Dim strValue, aValues, nF, nRoot, aRet

strKeyPath = "software\test"
nRoot = HKEY_LOCAL_MACHINE
'create an instance of the registry provider
Set objRegistry = GetObject(WMICONST & "StdRegProv")

'enumerate all values
nRet = objRegistry.EnumValues(nRoot, strKeyPath, aNames, aValues)

'if enumeration successful, loop through returned values and display values
If nRet = 0 Then
 For nF = LBound(aValues) To UBound(aValues)

  strValue = ""
  Select Case aValues(nF)
   Case 1 'String
    nRet = objRegistry.GetStringValue(nRoot, strKeyPath, _
                                       aNames(nF), strValue)
   Case 2 'Expanded String
    nRet = objRegistry.GetExpandedStringValue(nRoot, strKeyPath, _
                                       aNames(nF), strValue)
```

```
   Case 3 'Binary values
    nRet = objRegistry.GetBinaryValue(nRoot, strKeyPath, _
                                   aNames(nF), aRet)
    strValue = Join(aRet)

   Case 4 'DWORD
    nRet = objRegistry.GetDWORDValue(nRoot, strKeyPath, _
                                  , aNames(nF), strValue)

   Case 7 'Multi string values
    nRet = objRegistry.GetMultiStringValue(nRoot, strKeyPath, _
                                   aNames(nF), aRet)
    strValue = Join(aRet)
   End Select

    WScript.Echo "Value " & aNames(nF) & " has value " & strValue
 Next
End If
```

Discussion

The `WScript.Shell` does not provide any methods to enumerate registry values and keys. Registry values and keys can be enumerated using the WMI registry provider, which exposes two methods: `EnumKey` and `EnumValues`.

`EnumKey` enumerates any subkeys below a specified key, while `EnumValues` enumerates all values within a key.

The WMI registry provider has a separate method for deleting registry keys and values:

```
nRet = objRegistry.EnumKey ([nRootKey], strKey, aNames)
nRet = objRegistry.EnumValues([nRootKey], strKey, aNames, aTypes)
```

The optional `nRootKey` parameter represents the root key value. These values are listed in Table 7-2. If the `nRootKey` parameter is not specified, the local machine `HKEY_LOCAL_MACHINE` root key is used.

> `strKey` represents the path to the registry key to enumerate. Each key in the path is separated by a backslash (`\`).

> `strValueName` is the name of the registry value to delete by the `DeleteValue` method.

`aNames` returns an array of keys for the `EnumKey` method and an array of values for the `EnumValues` method. If the key contains no subkeys when calling `EnumKey` or no values for the `EnumValues` method, an empty array is returned.

The `EnumValues` method returns an array of value types through the `aTypes` parameter. This array contains the data type for the corresponding value name returned in the `aNames` array. The values for each data type are listed in Table 7-6.

Table 7-6. Registry Data Type Values

REGISTRY TYPE	VALUE
String	1
Expanded string	2
Binary	3
DWORD	4
Multistring	7

See Also

Solution 11.1. Information about the `EnumValues` method is available by searching for the terms "WMI EnumValues" at `http://msdn.microsoft.com`.

7.5 Searching and Replacing Registry Values

Problem

You want to search and optionally replace registry values.

Solution

The following command-line script searches a specified registry path and all subkeys in the path for any string value that matches a search string and optionally replaces the value:

```
'regsrch.vbs
'searches for specified registry values and optionally replaces them
Const WMICONST = "winmgmts:{impersonationLevel=impersonate}!root\default:"

Dim strRoot, nPos
Dim strFind, strPath, strReplace, bReplace, objRegistry, nRoot

'check the argument count
If WScript.Arguments.Count < 2 Or WScript.Arguments.Count > 3 Then
    ShowUsage
End If

strPath = WScript.Arguments(0)
strFind = WScript.Arguments(1)

nPos = InStr(strPath, "\")

If nPos > 0 Then
    strRoot = Mid(strPath, 1, InStr(strPath, "\") - 1)
    strPath = Mid(strPath, nPos + 1)
Else

End If

'get the registry root key
Select Case strRoot
    Case "HKEY_LOCAL_MACHINE", "HKLM"
      nRoot = &H80000002
    Case "HKEY_CURRENT_USER", "HKCU"
      nRoot = &H80000001
    Case "HKEY_CLASSES_ROOT"
      nRoot = &H80000000
    Case "HKEY_USERS"
      nRoot = &H80000003
    Case "HKEY_CURRENT_CONFIG"
      nRoot = &H80000005
    Case "HKEY_DYN_DATA"
      nRoot = &H80000006
    Case Else
     WScript.Echo "Invalid registry root key: " & strRoot
     WScript.Quit
End Select
```

```
'create an instance of the registry provider
Set objRegistry = GetObject(WMICONST & "StdRegProv")

'check if replace parameter is passed
 If WScript.Arguments.Count = 3 Then
   strReplace = WScript.Arguments(2)
   bReplace = True
End If

RecurseReg strPath

Sub ShowUsage
WScript.Echo "regsrch search and optional replace registry values." & vbLf & _
    "Syntax:" &  vbLf & _
    "regsrch.vbs key findvalue [replacevalue] " &  vbCrLf & _
    "key            key to search. Will search child keys." & vbCrLf & _
    "findvalue     value to search for" & vbCrLf & _
    "replacevalue optional. Value to replace"
    WScript.Quit -1
End Sub

Sub RecurseReg(strRegPath)
Dim nRet, aNames, bFound
Dim strValue, aValues, nF, aRet

nRet = objRegistry.EnumKey(nRoot, strRegPath, aNames)

'loop through and enumerate any sub-keys
If nRet = 0 Then
 For nF = LBound(aNames) To UBound(aNames)
    RecurseReg strRegPath & "\" & aNames(nF)

 Next
End If

'enumerate all values
nRet = objRegistry.EnumValues(nRoot, strRegPath, aNames, aValues)

If nRet = 0 Then
 For nF = LBound(aValues) To UBound(aValues)

  strValue = ""
```

```
    'check values, only interested in string or expand string values
    Select Case aValues(nF)
     Case 1 'String
      nRet = objRegistry.GetStringValue(nRoot, strRegPath, _
                                        aNames(nF), strValue)

     Case 2 'Expanded String
      nRet = objRegistry.GetExpandedStringValue(nRoot, strRegPath, _
                                        aNames(nF), strValue)
     End Select

    If strValue = strFind And (aValues(nF) = 1 Or aValues(nF) = 2) Then
      WScript.Echo "Value '" & strValue & "' found in " _
                          & strRegPath & "\" & aNames(nF)

     'replace the registry value?
     If bReplace Then
      'check what type and call appropriate method
      Select Case aValues(nF)
       Case 1 'write registry string
          nRet = objRegistry.SetStringValue(nRoot, _
                                  strRegPath, aNames(nF), strReplace)

       Case 2 'write expanded registry string
          nRet = objRegistry.SetExpandedStringValue(nRoot, _
                                  strRegPath, aNames(nF), strReplace)
       End Select

       'was replace successful?
       If nRet = 0 Then
        WScript.Echo "Value '" & strValue & "' change to '" _
               & strReplace & "' in " & strRegPath & "\" & aNames(nF)
       Else
        WScript.Echo "Value '" & strValue & "' not replaced '" _
               & strReplace & "' in " & strRegPath & "\" & aNames(nF)
       End If
      End If
     End If

    Next
  End If
  End Sub
```

Discussion

Neither `WScript.Shell` nor WMI provides any built-in methods to search a key and all registry subkeys below it. The Solution script implements a command-line program to search and optionally replace a registry value. It searches all values, including subkeys, below the start key.

The script uses the WMI `StdRegProv` provider to recursively search a specified key path.

7.6 Accessing the Remote Registry

Problem

You want to manipulate remote registry values.

Solution

You can connect to a remote computer using WMI and perform the required registry operation using `StdRegProv`. The following script connects to the remote computer Odin and reads a registry value:

```
Const WMICONST = "winmgmts:{impersonationLevel=impersonate}!\\odin\root\default:"

Const HKEY_CURRENT_USER = &H80000001
Dim objRegistry, nRet, strValue

'create an instance of the StdRegProv registry provider
Set objRegistry = GetObject(WMICONST & "StdRegProv")

'read the value Identifier under key HARDWARE\DESCRIPTION\System
'since the local machine root key is the default, the first parameter is omitted
nRet = objRegistry.GetStringValue(, "HARDWARE\DESCRIPTION\System", _
                                    "Identifier", strValue)

If nRet = 0 Then
    WScript.Echo "The system type is " & strValue
Else
    WScript.Echo "Error reading the HARDWARE\DESCRIPTION\System key"
End If
```

Discussion

The `WScript.Shell` object registry methods do not provide access to the registries of remote machines.

By default, WMI supports a connection to remote computers. All WMI `StdRegProv` provider registry operations that are detailed in this chapter can be performed on a remote computer. A version of WMI must exist on the local computer as well as a remote computer that can perform the registry operations.

No changes are required to registry manipulation code using WMI apart from the connection string. You must have appropriate security rights to access the remote computer, and the appropriate version of WMI must be installed on the local and remote computers.

> **NOTE** *See Chapter 10 for more information about connecting WMI to remote computers.*

See Also

Solution 7.4.

CHAPTER 8

Regular Expressions

A *REGULAR EXPRESSION* IS A powerful pattern-matching facility that enables you to compare patterns against target strings to find pattern matches.

So what *exactly* is a regular expression? Let's say that you want to evaluate a simple North American phone number (999) 999 9999 using VBScript string functions:

```
Function IsPhone(strPhone)
 If Len(strPhone) = 13 And Left(strPhone, 1) = "(" And _
    IsNumeric(Mid(strPhone, 2, 3)) And Mid(strPhone, 5, 1) = ")" And _
    IsNumeric(Mid(strPhone, 6, 3)) And IsNumeric(Mid(strPhone, 9, 4)) Then
  IsPhone = True
 Else
  IsPhone = False
 End If
End Function
```

The IsPhone function will return True if the argument that is passed matches a phone number in the format (999) 999 9999. It would return True if the number (123) 456 7890 was passed, but not 456 7890 or 555-124 3445.

The following code performs phone-number matching using a regular expression:

```
Function IsPhone(strPhone)
 Set objRegExp = New RegExp
 objRegExp.Pattern = " ^(\(?\d{3}\)?)?[ -]?\d{3}[ -]?\d{4}$"
   IsPhone = objRegExp.Test(strPhone)
End Function
```

This function matches phone numbers with or without area codes. It also matches phone numbers with spaces or hyphens as separators. It returns True if any of the following phone numbers are tested: (123) 456 789, 123456 7890, 555-1234, 6663434, or 604-434-2343.

To provide the same functionality, it is possible to use VBScript, but the code would quickly become unwieldy and difficult to manage and maintain. The regular expression version could be easily extended to check for overseas phone numbers by simply modifying the string pattern—no additional code would be required.

Regular expression patterns can perform sophisticated text matching, extracting, and search and replace operations.

This chapter gives a general introduction to building regular expression patterns and how to use them to match as well as search for and replace items in strings of text. For a much more detailed immersion in the art of regular expressions, get the book *Mastering Regular Expressions*, by Jeffrey Friedl.

> **NOTE** *For more information on regular expressions, refer to the MSDN Library article "What's New in Windows Script 5.5"* (`http://msdn.microsoft.com/workshop/languages/clinic/scripting121399.asp`). *You can also review the article "Microsoft Beefs Up VBScript with Regular Expressions"* (`http://msdn.microsoft.com/workshop/languages/clinic/scripting051099.asp`).

8.1 Validating a String

Problem

You want to validate a string.

Solution

You can create an instance of the `RegExp` object and set the `Pattern` property with the expression you want to validate against. Invoke the `Test` method against the string you want to test. The following snippet validates e-mail strings:

```
Dim objRegExp, strAddress

 'create a new instance of the regexp object
 Set objRegExp = New RegExp
 'set case matching off
 objRegExp.IgnoreCase = True
 'set pattern
 objRegExp.Pattern = "\w+(\.\w+)?@\w+(\.\w+)+"

 strAddress= InputBox("Enter an E-mail address")
 'check if address is valid
```

```
 If Not objRegExp.Test(strAddress) Then
   MsgBox "Not a valid E-mail address"
 End If
```

Discussion

Regular expression operations are exposed through the RegExp object in VBScript version 5.0 and later. This object is actually a built-in native VBScript object. Unlike other components such as file manipulation (which is exposed through external objects), new instances of the RegExp object can be created by invoking the New operator:

```
Dim objRegExp
'create a new instance of a RegExp object
Set objRegExp = New RegExp
```

Once an instance of the object has been created, you can set a number of properties before evaluating the expression.

By default, regular expressions tests are case-sensitive. To turn case testing off, set the IgnoreCase property to True.

The Pattern property contains the actual expression pattern you are going to test.

If the pattern is a string of characters, the pattern searches for that string against a target string for any occurrences. Use the Test method to test a target string against a regular expression. The syntax is as follows:

```
bResult = objRegExp.Test(strTarget)
```

strTarget represents the target string being tested. The Test method returns True if the pattern finds a match anywhere in the target string.

In the following sample, a string is checked for an occurrence of "fred":

```
Dim objRegExp, strName

Set objRegExp = New RegExp
 objRegExp.IgnoreCase = True
 objRegExp.Pattern = "fred"
strName = InputBox("Enter your name")

 If objRegExp.Test(strName) Then
    MsgBox "The name matched"
 Else
```

```
    MsgBox "The name didn't match"
End If
```

Regular expressions use *metacharacters* to perform more complex operations than matching simple string patterns. On the simplest level, metacharacters can provide operations somewhat similar to wildcards used in command-line operations. These metacharacters are called *quantifiers*.

Quantifiers match the preceding subexpression in the regular expression a certain number of times, depending on the metacharacter.

A subexpression may represent a single character or a group of characters and metacharacters. Table 8-1 lists metacharacter quantifiers.

Table 8-1. Metacharacter Quantifiers

MODIFIER	DESCRIPTION
*	Matches preceding subexpression zero or more times. The pattern fred* would match fred, freddy, and french.
+	Matches one or more (but not zero) times. The pattern fred+ would match fred and freddy, but not french.
?	Matches preceding subexpression zero or one time. The pattern fred+ would match fred and freddy, but not french.

In the previous examples, the metacharacter affected the previous single character subexpression. You may want to group characters and modifiers into strings. Any expression surrounded by parentheses "`()`" is treated as a single subexpression.

For the regular expression `(Fred)+(Bob)?` Fred and Bob are subexpressions because they are surrounded by parentheses. The first plus sign (+) metacharacter applies to subexpression Fred, and the question mark (?) metacharacter applies to subexpression Bob.

Without the brackets, the plus sign (+) metacharacter in the regular expression `Fred+Bob?` would only apply to the preceding *d* character and the question mark (?) would apply to the preceding *b*.

If you want to treat a metacharacter as a normal character in a regular expression, precede it with a backslash. The expression `\(\*\*\)` would match the string `(**)` because each of the characters is preceded by a backslash (\).

The dollar sign ($) metacharacter matches the end of a string. The caret (^) metacharacter matches the beginning of a string. Table 8-2 lists examples using these metacharacters.

Table 8-2. The Dollar Sign ($) and Caret (^) Metacharacters

REGULAR EXPRESSION	DESCRIPTION
end$	Matches the string “the end” but not “end of the world”
^beginning	Matches the string “beginning of line” but not “in the beginning”

To match one or another pattern, use the vertical bar (|) alternate metacharacter to separate alternate choices. Table 8-3 lists alternate metacharacter samples.

Table 8-3. Alternate Metacharacters

<table>
<tr><th>REGULAR EXPRESSION</th><th>DESCRIPTION</th></tr>
<tr><td>^(mon|tues|wednes|thurs|fri)day</td><td>Will match any string that starts with a weekday (e.g., Monday or Wednesday, but not Saturday or Sunday)</td></tr>
<tr><td>january|jan</td><td>Matches a string that contains either january or jan</td></tr>
<tr><td>^(http|ftp):</td><td>Matches a string that starts with http: or ftp:</td></tr>
<tr><td>(403|404)$</td><td>Matches any string that ends with 403 or 404</td></tr>
</table>

Use the period (.) metacharacter to test for one occurrence of any character except the newline character. Table 8-4 lists period metacharacter samples.

Table 8-4. Period Metacharacters

REGULAR EXPRESSION	DESCRIPTION
<title>.+</title>	Matches any string that contains text surrounded by <title> and </title> tags

The pattern ^Mr .+ .+ would match any string starting with Mr and containing a first and last name of any length.

To test for a range or set of characters in a pattern, surround the range with square brackets. The pattern ^Mr [A-Z]+ [A-Z]+$ would test for Mr firstname lastname, where the names must contain valid alphabetic characters. While the range specified only lists uppercase letters, if the IgnoreCase property is set to True, the case will be ignored when testing.

Prefixing the range with a carat (^) indicates that you want to match all characters except those in the specified range. The pattern H[^A-F] would match H1 and HG, but not HA.

To match a string with the salutation Mr. (with a period), the pattern `^Mr. .+ .+$` wouldn't work. This is because the period (.) is a pattern metacharacter, so instead of matching the period in the salutation, it allows any character.

If you test for a character that also represents a metacharacter operator, prefix it with a backslash (\).

The pattern used to match the salutation with a period would look like this: `^Mr\. .+ .+$`.

Certain characters prefixed by the backslash represent special characters, such as the newline and form-feed characters, or sequences and ranges of other metacharacters. Table 8-5 lists additional metacharacters.

Table 8-5. Additional Metacharacters

METACHARACTER ASSERTIONS	MATCHES
\d	Digit character. Same as `[0-9]`.
\D	Nondigit character. Same as `[^0-9]`.
\f	Form-feed character.
\n	Newline character.
\r	Carriage return character.
\s	White space characters. This includes space, newline, tab, and form feed. Same as `[ \t\n\r\f\v]`.
\S	Non–white space characters. Same as `[^ \t\n\r\f\v]`.
\t	Tab character.
\v	Vertical tab character.
\w	Any alphanumeric character. Same as `"[A-Za-z0-9_]"`.
\W	Nonword character. Same as `"[^A-Za-z0-9_]"`.
\b	Word boundary. Matches the space between word (\w) and nonword (\W) characters.
\B	Nonword boundary.

Let's look at the pattern used in the Solution script to check e-mail addresses: `\w+(\.\w+)?@\w+(\.\w+)+`. The first part, `\w+`, checks for one or more occurrences of alphanumeric characters. The second part, `(\.\w+)?`, checks for zero or more occurrences of a string sequence starting with a period followed by any number of alphanumeric characters. The at sign (@) indicates it must exist in the string.

After the at sign, you see `\w+`, which would match one or more occurrences of alphanumeric characters. The last bit of the pattern, `(\.\w+)+`, would match one or more string combinations starting with a period followed by any number of alphanumeric characters.

You've seen how you can use the +,*, and ? quantifiers to perform repetitive matches. They can be used to represent none, one, or any number of matches. But what if you want to perform a set number of matches?

Use the brace brackets ({}) to perform a set number of matches. The quantifier `{5}` would match the preceding subexpression exactly 5 times, `{5,}` would match at least 5 times, and `{2,5}` would match a minimum of 2 and a maximum of 5 times. Table 8-6 lists regular expression samples.

Table 8-6. Regular Expressions

REGULAR EXPRESSION	MATCH DESCRIPTION
`\d{4}`	Matches exactly four numbers.
`\d{2,}`	Matches at least two numbers.
`^\d{5}(-\d{4})?$`	A 5- or 9-digit ZIP code.
`^(\d+(\.|\b)){4}$`	IP address, such as 192.168.1.1.
`^\d{1,2}\/\d{1,2}\/\d{2,4}$`	Date in mm/dd/yyyy format. The year can be either two or four digits.
`^(ftp|http)://(\w+(\.|\b)){2,}\b$`	Web or FTP server address. Must contain at least two elements of a fully qualified domain name, so `http://odin` is not valid, but `http://acme.com` is.
`^(\(?\d{3}\)?)?[ -]?\d{3}[ -]?\d{4}$`	North American phone number. Would validate 555-1234, (123)555-1234, and 124-545234. Would not validate international area codes.

The metacharacters can be used with a number of range operators to only check for a range of values. Any character surrounded by square brackets is considered a range. Table 8-7 lists regular expression range samples.

Table 8-7. Regular Expression Ranges

REGULAR EXPRESSION	DESCRIPTION
[1-9][1-9]	A number between 11 and 99.
[^B-K][1-9]	Matches a string that starts with any character outside of the range of B to K and ends with a number between 1 and 9. A3 and y5 are valid, but E4 and S0 are not.
^([a-zA-Z0-9_-]\.?)+@([a-zA-Z0-9_-])+(\.[a-zA-Z0-9_-])+	Checks for valid e-mail address (e.g., fred@acme.com).
^([1-9]|1[0-2]):[0-5][0-9]$	Matches time (e.g., 12:30 but not 44:30).
[0-9a-fA-F]{1,2}	A 1- or 2-digit hexadecimal value.

You can reference subexpressions elsewhere in the regular expression by a backslash followed by the number of the subexpression you want to reference, starting from 0. This is known as *back-referencing.*

For example, to match any valid HTML tag sequence, use <(.*)>.*<\/\1>. The <(.*)> expression matches any HTML tag, such as <centre>. The parentheses surrounding the expression (.*) indicate the text that it matches will be stored as a subexpression.

The \1 expression back-references the first subexpression match, which in this case is the first HTML tag.

A backslash followed by an x character and then a one- or two-digit hexadecimal value, such as \x22, will match the character with the corresponding ASCII value.

A backslash followed by an x character and then a two- or three-digit octal number value, such as \x22, will match the character with the corresponding ASCII value.

Regular expressions are more of an integral part of JScript. Unlike VBScript, JScript allows literal regular expressions similar to literal strings. Forward slashes (/) are used to surround these literal regular expressions:

```
objRegExp = /strPattern/[strSwitch];
```

JScript can also create a regular expression using the new operator and built-in RegExp object:

```
var objRegExp = new RegExp(strPattern,[strSwitch]);
```

strPattern is the regular expression pattern you want to use. The strSwitch parameter represents one or more optional switches. The switches that are available are i, which ignores case when matching text, and g, which performs a global search.

```
//the following statements create two Instances of a regexp object
//with the same pattern
var objRegExp = new RegExp("Mr .+ .+", "i");

objRegExp2 = /Mr .+ .+/i;
```

If you want to use the regular expression functions in a scripting language or development environment that supports COM objects (such as Visual Basic), you can create an instance of the regular expression object using the `Vbscript.RegExp` program ID:

```
'the following statement can be used to create an instance of the
'regular expression object in other VB dialects
Set objRegExp= CreateObject("vbscript.RegExp")
```

> **NOTE** *For more information, read the MSDN Library article "Microsoft Beefs Up VBScript with Regular Expressions," which is available at* `http://msdn.microsoft.com/workshop/languages/clinic/scripting051099.asp`.

See Also

Search for "Regular expression syntax" in the VBScript documentation Help file. Solution 5.10, Solution 6.1, and Solution 9.2.

8.2 Matching Multiple Patterns

Problem

You want all the expressions in a string that match a pattern.

Solution

You can create a `RegExp` object, setting the `Pattern` property to the pattern you want to match and setting the Global property to `True`. Any matches are stored in the Matches collection. The following sample returns a list of all numeric values from a comma-delimited string:

```
Set objRegExp = New RegExp
'set pattern to extract all numeric values from string
objRegExp.Pattern = "\d+\.?\d*|\.\d+" objRegExp.IgnoreCase = True
objRegExp.Global = True
Set objMatches = objRegExp.Execute("111.13,1232,ABC,444,55")

For Each objMatch In objMatches
  Wscript.Echo "Found match:" & objMatch.Value & " at position " & _
                objMatch.FirstIndex
Next
```

Discussion

Repetitive patterns can be extracted from a string using regular expressions.

The Regular expression object contains a Global property. Setting this property to True indicates that the input will be checked for multiple occurrences of the pattern.

To return a list of any matches from the expression, invoke the Execute method:

```
Set objMatches = objRegExp.Execute(strString)
```

objRegExp represents a regular expression object, while the strString parameter is the string to test.

Any matches returned from the string are stored in the Matches collection. This collection contains all matches from the input string represented as Match objects.

Each Match object contains a Value and FirstIndex property. The Value property returns the value extracted from the string, while the FirstIndex property returns the offset in the string where the match was made.

The following generic function extracts items from a comma-delimited string. The elements are stored in an array, which is returned by the function:

```
Function ExtractCSV(strCSV)

 Dim objRegExp, objMatch, aRet, objMatches, nF
 Set objRegExp = New RegExp
```

```
 ' matches digits, digits followed by a
 ' point and then more digits, a point followed by digits, or anything
 ' enclosed by double-quotes
   objRegExp.Pattern = "\d+\.?\d*|\.\d+|\x22[^""]+\x22"

objRegExp.IgnoreCase = True
objRegExp.Global = True
  Set objMatches = objRegExp.Execute(strCSV)
  If objMatches.Count > 0 Then

    ReDim aRet(objMatches.Count)
    For nF = 0 To objMatches.Count - 1  ' iterate Matches collection.
     Set objMatch = objMatches.item(nF)
    ' check if the string is surrounded by quotes, if so remove them
     If Left(objMatch.Value, 1) = """" And _
          Right(objMatch.Value, 1) = """" Then
      aRet(nF) = Mid(objMatch.Value, 2, Len(objMatch.Value) - 2)
     Else
      aRet(nF) = objMatch.Value
     End If
    Next

    ExtractCSV = aRet
  Else
    ExtractCSV = Empty
  End If

End Function
```

The string elements can be numeric or text values. Any text values must be surrounded by double quotes and can contain any character, including commas.

```
aValues = ExtractCSV("10.50,10,""Fred Smith"",20")
```

See Also

For more information, search for the terms "Visual Basic Scripting Global Property" at `http://msdn.microsoft.com`.

8.3 Matching Subexpressions

Problem

You want to extract all regular expression subexpression matches from a target string.

Solution

Use the Matches collection's SubMatches property to list all matched subexpressions:

```
Set objRegExp = New RegExp
' match "digits slash digits slash digits"
objRegExp.Pattern = "(\d+)\/(\d+)\/(\d+)"
objRegExp.IgnoreCase = True

Set objMatches = objRegExp.Execute("5/13/2000")

'list all subexpressions [
For nF = 0 To objMatches(0).SubMatches.Count - 1
  Wscript.Echo objMatches(0).SubMatches(nF)
Next
```

Discussion

The Regular expression object's Matches collection returns a list of matches by executing a single expression against a string. This is useful when matching multiple matches of a single pattern, as demonstrated by Solution 8.2.

If you need to match multiple different expressions or a set number of expressions in a certain order, you need to use subexpressions. For example, the following regular expression matches two subexpressions:

```
(.+):(.+)
```

If this regular expression was executed against the string "10:30", it would return two subexpressions: 10 and 30. VBScript did not support subexpression matching until VBScript version 5.5. Documentation provided with earlier VBScript versions states that it can process subexpressions using the Matches collection, but this is not the case.

VBScript 5.5 introduces a SubMatches property to the Match object, which provides access to any subexpressions returned from the execution of a regular expression against a string.

The first Match element of the Matches collection contains the string matches, which can be accessed through the SubMatches property. The SubMatches property exposes a Count property that returns the number of submatches.

Each submatch can be accessed through this collection as an array element. The following sample extracts the month, day, and year from a date string and displays each element from the SubMatches collection:

```
Dim objRegExp, objMatches, objSubMatches
'Set objRegExp = New RegExp
Set objRegExp = CreateObject("VBScript.RegExp")
' match "digits slash digits slash digits"
objRegExp.Pattern = "(\d+)\/(\d+)\/(\d+)"
Set objMatches = objRegExp.Execute("5/13/2000")
'the first element of the matches collection contains the submatches
Set objSubMatches = objMatches(0).SubMatches
'list the number of sub expression matches and matches
Wscript.Echo "Subexpression count " & objSubMatches.Count
Wscript.Echo "Subexpression 1 " & objSubMatches (0)
Wscript.Echo "Subexpression 2 " & objSubMatches (1)
Wscript.Echo "Subexpression 3 " & objSubMatches (2)
```

The following script, regflt.vbs, is a generic command-line program that executes a regular expression pattern against standard input, outputting any extracted subexpressions to standard output delimited by a comma:

```
'regflt.vbs
'command line regular expression filter
Dim nF, strDelim, strLine
 If WScript.Arguments.Count < 1 Or WScript.Arguments.Count > 2 Then
   ShowUsage
 End If

 strDelim = "," 'set delimiter
 strPattern = WScript.Arguments(0)

 'check if alternate output delimiter specified
 If WScript.Arguments.Count = 2 Then strDelim = WScript.Arguments(1)

 'create regular expression object and set properties
 Set objRegExp = New RegExp
```

```
objRegExp.Pattern = strPattern
objRegExp.IgnoreCase = True
objRegExp.Global = True

 'loop until the end of the text stream has been encountered
 Do While Not WScript.StdIn.AtEndOfStream

 'read line from standard input
  strLine = WScript.StdIn.ReadLine

 'execute regular expression match
 Set objMatches = objRegExp.Execute(strLine)
 strOut = ""
 'if matches are made, loop through each match and append to output
 If objMatches.Count > 0 Then
    For nF = 0 To objMatches(0).SubMatches.Count - 2
      Wscript.Stdout.Write objMatches(0).Submatches(nF) & strDelim
    Next
   Wscript.Stdout.WriteLine objMatches(0).Submatches(nF)
 End If
Loop

Sub ShowUsage()
WScript.Echo "regflt filters standard input against " & _
    "a regular expression." & vbLf & _
    "Syntax:" & vbLf & _
   "regflt.vbs regexp [delimiter]" & vbLf & _
   "regexp     regular expression" & vbLf & _
    "delimiter  optional. Character to delimiter output columns"
   WScript.Quit -1
End Sub
```

Only one parameter is required for the script, which is the regular expression that is being executed against each line of the standard input. An optional second parameter can be passed to change the output delimiter, which by default is a comma.

The script can be useful for extracting values from existing files and building delimited files based on the output.

In the following sample, a price list is stored in a text file called `prices.txt`:

```
Bakery Price List Page 1
White bread         $1.20
```

```
Brown bread         $1.25
Whole wheat         $1.30
Buns                  0.30ea
```

To extract the descriptions and prices to an output file called prices.csv, use this code:

```
cscript regflt.vbs "^(\w+ \w*).+(\d+\.\d+)" < prices.txt
```

The results are stored in the prices.csv file:

```
White bread,1.20
Brown bread,1.25
Whole wheat,1.30
Buns,0.30
```

Values can be piped from any other application that outputs information to standard output. The following currency exchange page is stored on a remote Web server:

```
<html><head>
<title>Exchange Rates</title>
</head><body>
<p>Exchange Rates for date:1/12/2000</p>
<table border="1" width="529">
   <tr><td>Canadian Dollar</td><td>CAN</td><td>.67</td></tr>
   <tr><td>Australian Dollar</td><td>AUS</td><td>.64</td></tr>
   <tr><td>German Mark</td><td>GDR</td><td>.7</td></tr>
   <tr><td>British Pound</td><td>PND</td><td>1.5</td></tr>
   <tr><td>Japanese Yen</td><td>YEN</td><td>.9</td></tr>
 </table>
</body></html>
```

Using the httpget script from Chapter 11, the page is retrieved and piped to the regflt script:

```
cscript httpget.wsf "http://acme.com/xchange.htm" | cscript regflt.
vbs "<tr><td>(.+)</td><td>(.+)</td><td>(.+)</td></tr>" > exchange.csv
```

The exchange values are extracted and redirected to a file called exchange.csv:

```
Canadian Dollar,CAN,.67
Australian Dollar,AUS,.64
```

```
German Mark,GDR,.7
British Pound,PND,1.5
Japanese Yen,YEN,.9
```

JScript has always provided access to subexpressions. Use the RegExp class to access subexpressions. JScript's way of accessing subexpressions is different than VBScript's as a result of language standard considerations.

To access a subexpression, either reference the RegExp class match property for the match number you want to return or the array of matches returned from the execution of the regular expression.

The numeric match properties are identified by a dollar sign ($) followed by the match number:

```
  var objRegExp = new RegExp("(.+):(.+)","ig");
  var aMatches = objRegExp.exec("hello:there");

//output the first and second subexpression match
  WScript.Echo (RegExp.$1);
  WScript.Echo (RegExp.$2);

//do the same as above, except reference the matches array
  WScript.Echo (aMatches[1]);
  WScript.Echo (aMatches[2]);
```

If you are processing an unknown number or more than nine subexpressions, you can access them through the Matches collection. The following JScript code sample implements a command-line regular expression filter similar to the Solution script:

```
//regflt.js
//filters regular expression elements from strings
var nF, rst, strLine, strOut;

if(WScript.Arguments.length< 1 || WScript.Arguments.length>1)
  WScript.Quit(-1);

// get the regular expression string
  rst = WScript.Arguments.Item(0);

   //loop until the end of the text stream has been encountered
   while(!WScript.StdIn.AtEndOfStream)
```

```
{
 strLine = WScript.StdIn.ReadLine();

 arg = strLine.match(rst);

 arg = strLine.match(rst);
 if (arg)
 {
    for(nF=1;nF<arg.length;nF++)
         WScript.StdOut.Write(arg[nF] + (nF<arg.length-1 ? "," : ""));
     WScript.StdOut.WriteLine();
   }
}
```

See Also

For more information, search `http://msdn.microsoft.com` for the article "What's New in Windows Script 5.5."

8.4 Replacing Values

Problem

You want to replace all occurrences of a pattern with something else.

Solution

In the following example, a match is made against a date string and the first date element is swapped with the second:

```
Dim objRegExp, strName

Set objRegExp = New RegExp
 objRegExp.IgnoreCase = True
 objRegExp.Pattern = "^(\d{1,2})\/(\d{1,2})\/(\d{2,4})$"

 Wscript.Echo objRegExp.Replace("5/3/2000","$2/$1/$3")
```

The result of this script is 3/5/2000.

Discussion

Regular expressions provide powerful search and replace capabilities.

A replace operation can replace a string that matches a regular expression with another string or with a subexpression result. It can also call a separate function to perform the replace operation.

```
objRegExp.Replace(strInput, strReplaceText)
```

The `Replace` method arguments are listed in Table 8-8.

Table 8-8. `Replace` *Method Arguments*

PARAMETER	DESCRIPTION
`objRegExp`	Regular expression object. The criteria to be used to search for the expression to replace are specified in the `Pattern` property of the regular expression.
`strInput`	String to search.
`strReplaceText`	Replacement text or reference to replacement function.

The `Replace` method returns the results of the replace operation(s). If no matches and replacements were made, the method returns the original input string.

A simple search and replace can be made by passing a string value as the replacement text.

The replace operation can also perform operations using subexpression matches. To reference subexpressions in the replacement string, insert dollar signs ($) followed by the subexpression number—for example, $1, $2, and so on.

As of version 5.5 of VBScript and JScript, replacement operations can call a function to perform the replacement.

To pass a function, use the `GetRef` function to pass a reference to the name of the replacement function. The function must take three parameters: the match string, position, and source.

The result returned by the function is used as the replacement value. The following example illustrates how to call a replace function to perform a "proper" case conversion (the first letter is uppercase and the rest are lowercase) on a string:

```
Dim objRegExp

Set objRegExp = New RegExp
objRegExp.IgnoreCase = True
objRegExp.Pattern = "\w+\b"
objRegExp.Global = True

Wscript.Echo _
   objRegExp.Replace("FRED MCTAVISH", GetRef("Proper"))

Function Proper(strMatch, nPos, strSource)
 'check if the match starts with MC
 If StrComp(Left(strMatch,2), "Mc", vbTextCompare)=0 Then
  Proper= "Mc" & Ucase(Mid(strMatch,3,1)) & Lcase(mid(strMatch,4))
 Else
  Proper= Ucase(Left(strMatch,1)) & Lcase(mid(strMatch,2))
 End If
End Function
```

The Proper function is passed to the Replace method. On each string match, the function is called and the string is converted to "proper" case. The capability to call a function allows for additional logic and calculations to be executed against the matched strings.

JScript implements the replace functionality through the Replace method of the string class:

```
strResult = objString.Replace(objRegExp, strReplaceText)
```

Instead of invoking a Replace method on the regular expression object, a regular expression object is passed to the string class Replace method. The objRegExp parameter represents the regular expression object, while strReplaceText is the replacement text.

```
//swap day/month in date
  var strResult, objRegexp;
  var strDate = "5/3/2000";
  //create regular expression object
  objRegExp = /^(\d{1,2})\/(\d{1,2})\/(\d{2,4})$/i;
  //replace first value with second
  strResult = strDate.replace(objRegExp, "$2/$1/$3");

  WScript.Echo(strResult);
```

See Also

Solution 9.2. For more information, search `http://msdn.microsoft.com` for the article "Microsoft Beefs Up VBScript with Regular Expressions."

CHAPTER 9

Application Automation

SPECIFIC OPERATIONS ARE generally accessed in Windows Script Host (WSH) through a certain COM object for the related operation, such as CDO for e-mail operations or ADO for database functionality. Many of today's major desktop applications, such as Microsoft Office and Corel Office, expose rich object models that can be manipulated by WSH.

Program automation allows WSH to use features from applications to automate operations, using the best features and capabilities of each application.

Many of these applications include features that allow for diverse data sources to be imported and manipulated, allowing WSH to automate building complex documents, which is not possible with the standard application import facilities.

Any Microsoft Office examples will run under Office 97, 2000, XP, and 2003.

> **NOTE** *For more information, search* `http://msdn.microsoft.com` *for the articles "Office Objects and Object Models," "Microsoft Developer Object Model Guide," and "Working with Office Applications."*

9.1 Creating Formatted Word Documents

Problem

You want to create a formatted Word document.

Solution

The following script builds a document by automating Word:

```
On Error Resume Next
 'attempt to get an existing running copy of Word
 Set objWord = GetObject(, "Word.Application")
 'if error occurred, then couldn't find Word, create new instance
 If Err Then
    Err.Clear
    Set objWord = CreateObject("Word.Application")
 End If
 objWord.Documents.Add
 objWord.Selection.TypeText "Hello World!"
```

Discussion

You can build Office documents by automating Office applications.

Before you even attempt to manipulate an application, try and identify features in the application that you want to use that can simplify the creation of the document. For both Word and Excel, these features include the following:

- *Templates:* Predefined, reusable document layouts
- *Styles:* Predefined character formatting
- *Bookmarks (Word) or range names (Excel)*

A template is simply a document that contains a predefined layout. To create a template, create a new document by selecting File > New, but instead of creating a document, select the Template option, as shown in Figure 9-1.

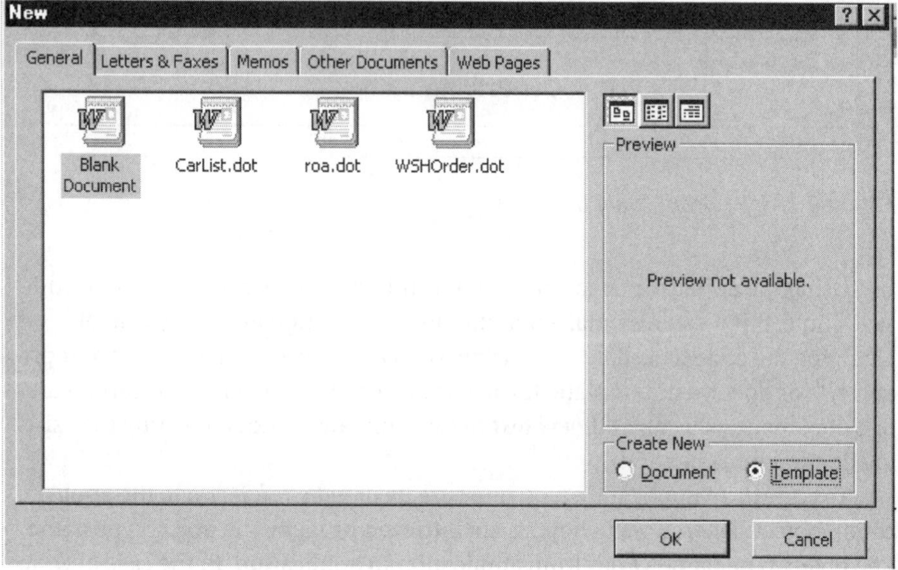

Figure 9-1. New document dialog box

Build the general layout of the document, but don't populate any areas with information.

Use bookmarks to identify areas in the document you want to quickly and easily navigate to, such as a data entry field. This is a better alternative than programming navigation keystrokes, because if any changes to the document are made, recorded keystrokes may move to the wrong location.

Document styles allow predefined formatting to be applied to a paragraph or selected text area. This might be a combination of various formatting elements, such as fonts and visual formatting (e.g., bold, italic, and so on). Excel supports styles, but it is not as obvious as Word (you must add the Style button to the Excel toolbar).

Both Excel and Word support creating styles by example. To create a style by example, format a paragraph with the formatting attributes you want to apply (fonts, colors, and borders). Then click in the Style box on the toolbar, as shown in Figure 9-2, and type in the name of the style.

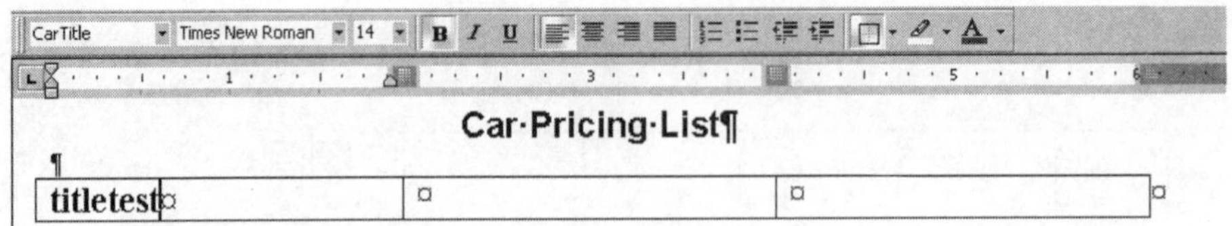

Figure 9-2. Style drop-down box

Using the application features not only minimizes programming code and saves time, but it can also make maintaining the solution easier. Instead of changing the code to update formatting, you can make changes to the appropriate style or document template. If you use bookmarks to navigate to certain areas of a document, you can add new text to the template without affecting the existing document navigation.

To control an application, you must create or get a reference to the application object. References to objects are retrieved by using the object type name. The object type name varies from application to application. In the case of Office applications, it's the application name followed by a period and the term "application," so the Word ProgID name is `Word.Application`.

You can make references to Office applications that are already running by using the `GetObject` method:

```
Set objApplication = GetObject([strFile][,strApp])
```

`strFile` allows the creation of a document object based on the application associated with the file. If you were to specify a valid filename ending with a `.doc` extension, a reference to a Word document object would most likely be returned (assuming Word is installed and associated with the `.doc` extension):

```
'get a reference to the Word file report.doc
Set objDocument = GetObject("d:\data\report.doc")
```

Specifying the `strApp` parameter together with `strFile` will attempt to open the file with the specified application ProgID. This is useful if more than one application is associated with the file extension.

```
'get a reference to the Word file report.doc
Set objDocument = GetObject("d:\data\report.doc", "Word.Application")
```

If `strApp` is specified on its own, a reference to an existing running copy of the application is returned. If no copy is found, an error is generated. You can use this code to use an existing copy of an application instead of creating a new instance:

```
On Error Resume Next
 'attempt to get an existing running copy of Word
 Set objWord = GetObject(, "Word.Application")
 'if error occurred, then couldn't find Word, create new instance
 If Err Then
    Err.Clear
    Set objWord = CreateObject("Word.Application")
 End If
```

Now that you got a reference to the application, you can start constructing the document. When it comes to the actual Office application code, don't try to manually build the code. Word, Excel, and the latest version of PowerPoint support recording macros. These macros are VBA code, which can be converted to work in a WSH script with a few minor changes. Create the macro and perform a "dry run," simulating the steps required to create the document, as well as performing any operations that will be used in your script, such as creating, saving, and closing the document. The following Word macro jumps to the bookmark called TableStart, fills in a few table cells of data, and selects and merges a table cell:

```
Selection.GoTo What:=wdGoToBookmark, Name:="TableStart"
Selection.TypeText Text:="name"
Selection.MoveRight Unit:=wdCell
Selection.TypeText Text:="type"
Selection.MoveRight Unit:=wdCell
Selection.TypeText Text:="price"
Selection.MoveRight Unit:=wdCell
Selection.SelectRow
Selection.Cells.Merge
```

Using the macro recorder, you can easily build the logic for 90 percent of the solution and simply cut and paste the results into your script. VBA code generated by the macro recorder requires some changes.

VBScript doesn't support the method of parameter passing used by VBA, where the parameter name is passed with an assignment operator followed by the value. The following VBA statement:

```
Selection.MoveRight Unit:=wdCell
```

would be changed to this:

```
Selection.MoveRight wdCell
```

Another issue that you will encounter is constants. Macros include the application-specific constants. You can manually add these constants to your scripts or you can use the `<reference>` element provided by WSF script files to add them:

```
<reference object="Word.Document"/>
```

You would assume that the `Word.Application` application ProgID would be used to get a reference to the type library for Word, but this doesn't work. This is because the type library for Word is not associated with `Word.Application`. It is, however, associated with `Word.Document` under Word 97, so using this ProgID instead will provide access to all constants exposed through the application.

The `Word.Application` ProgID does not work on later versions of Word. For Word 2000 onwards reference a GUID :

```
<reference guid="{00020905-0000-0000-C000-000000000046}"/>
```

The recorded script methods are part of the `Application` object. Use the `With` statement together with the `Application` object followed by the application methods:

```
<?xml version="1.0" ?>
<job>
<reference guid="{00020905-0000-0000-C000-000000000046}"/>
<!--comment
Build a simple table -->
 <script language="VBScript">
 <![CDATA[
 Dim nF, nI, objWord, objWordDoc
 Set objWord = CreateObject("Word.Application")
 objWord.Visible = True
   With objWord
   'create a new document
   .Documents.Add
   .ActiveDocument.Tables.Add .Selection.Range, 2, 3
  End With
  ]]>
  </script>
</job>
```

All Office applications (except Access) expose the active documents through a collection. These collections are named `Documents` for Word, `Worksheets` for Excel, and `Presentations` for PowerPoint.

```
'list active Word documents
Set objWord = GetObject(, "Word.Application")
 'loop through each Word document
 For Each objDoc In objWord.Documents
  Wscript.Echo objDoc.Path, objDoc.Name
 Next
```

The Documents collection allows for any active documents to be referenced by either document name or number. The document numbers start at the offset 1.

```
'get a reference to an existing copy of Word
 Set objWord = GetObject(, "Word.Application")
'get a reference to the first document
Set objDocument = objWord.Documents(1)
'get a reference to the document Data.doc
Set objDocument = objWord.Documents("Data.doc")
```

The following example gets a reference to an existing running copy of Word and closes any open documents:

```
'quitword.vbs
'Finds a running copy of Word, saves and closes all files
Dim objWord, objDoc
'get an instance to an existing copy of Word
 Set objWord = GetObject(, "Word.Application")
  For Each objDoc In objWord.Documents
  'check if the filename is empty
  If objDoc.Path = "" Then
     objDoc.SaveAs objDoc.Name
     objDoc.Close
  Else
     objDoc.Close True
  End If
 Next

objWord.Quit
```

While recording macros provides an easy way to build script logic, you may want to fine-tune your application by manipulating the generated code.

One way of investigating what commands and operations are available to you (other than Help references) is to use an object browser. All recent Microsoft Office application releases (Word, Excel, Access, and PowerPoint) provide access to the object browser through the VBA development environment.

Use the Office object browser to view the properties and methods the applications expose. The object browser is available by starting the Visual Basic Editor from the Tools > Macro menu in Word, Excel, or PowerPoint. In Access, create a new or edit an existing code module.

Once you are in the Visual Basic environment, press F2 to display the object browser, as shown in Figure 9-3.

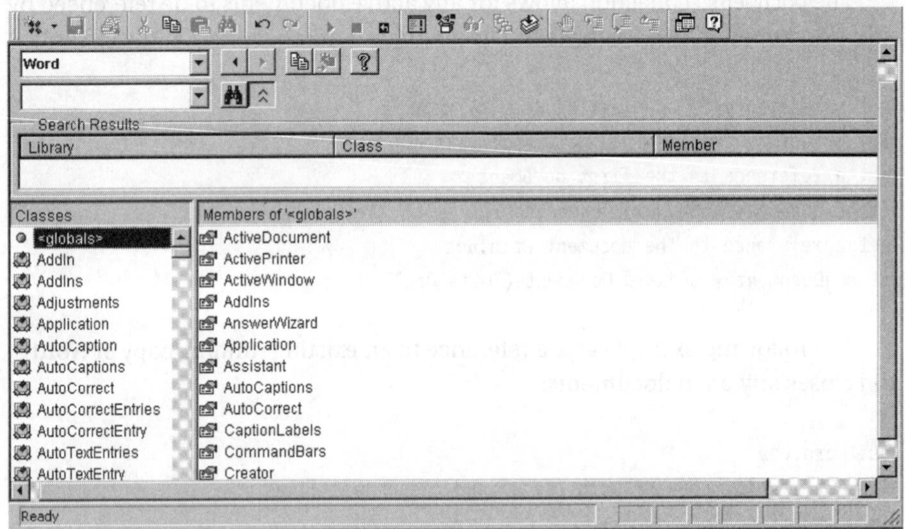

Figure 9-3. Object browser

You can use the object browser to view any method or property. The browser will show the syntax for any given method as well as parameter and return value data types.

By default, you are able to view the object model for the application you are currently in. You may want to view the object model for another application or automation object, such as the ADO, CDO, or FSO object models.

To add object references, select Tools > References. The dialog box shown in Figure 9-4 appears.

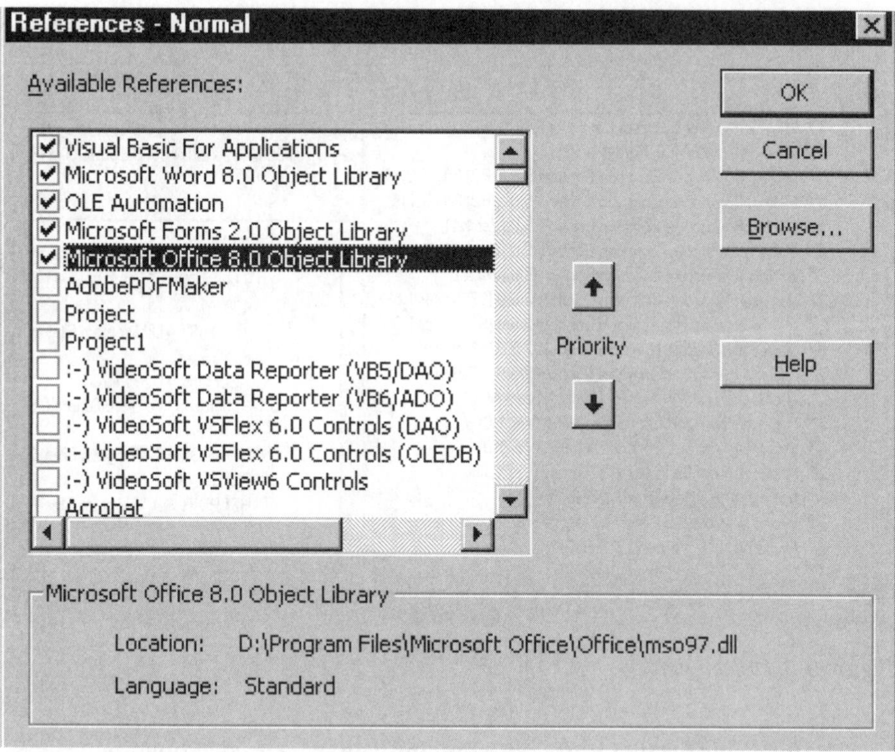

Figure 9-4. References dialog box

The References dialog box lists all available object references. To select or deselect a given reference, click the check box beside the object you want to browse.

If you do not have an Office or Visual Basic application installed, an alternative is to use the freely available automation object browser from Microsoft, the OLE/COM Object Viewer. It is available for download from `http://www.microsoft.com/Com/resources/oleview.asp`, and it is also included in NT Resource Kits and MSDN subscriptions.

The OLE/COM Object Viewer is a less friendly version of the object browser included with the VB/VBA environment, but it does allow viewing of object properties, methods, and constants, as well as easy retrieval of an object's class ID (CLSID), which is useful for referencing objects when a ProgID is unavailable or unknown. Figure 9-5 shows the CLSID for the Word object library.

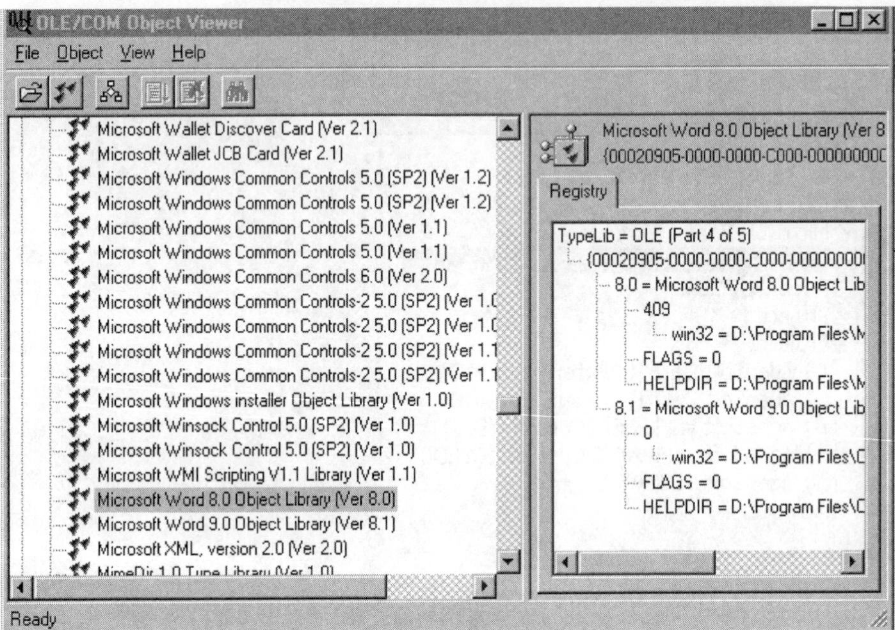

Figure 9-5. Object viewer

The following text file, `cars.txt`, contains data to be used in building a formatted Word document:

```
"BMW","Z3","Sports",50000
"GM","Grand Am","Sedan",25000
"GM","Yukon","Truck",40000
"Ford","Mondeo","Sedan",23000
"Ford","Festiva","Compact",12000
"Ford","Explorer","Truck",35000
"Hyundai","Excel","Compact",17000
```

The `cars.txt` file is used by the following script to build a Word document:

```
<?xml version="1.0" ?>
<job>
<reference guid="{00020905-0000-0000-C000-000000000046}"/>
<!--comment
Script:bword.wsf
builds Word document from text file
Includes regarr.vbs, which is the ExtractCSV function defined in Solution 8.2
-->
 <script language="VBScript" src="regarr.vbs">
```

```
<![CDATA[
Option Explicit
Dim nF, nI, objWord
Dim objFSO, objTxtStrm, strLine
Dim aVar, strLast
'create a FSO object and open data file
Set objFSO = CreateObject("Scripting.FileSystemObject")
Set objTxtStrm = objFSO.OpenTextFile("d:\data\cars.txt")
On Error Resume Next
'attempt to get an existing running copy of Word
Set objWord = GetObject(, "Word.Application")
'if error occurred, then couldn't find Word, create new instance
If Err Then
   Err.Clear
   Set objWord = CreateObject("Word.Application")
End If
objWord.Visible = True
On Error GoTo 0
  With objWord
'create a new document based on the carlist template
.Documents.add("carlist.dot")
'move to the beginning of the table using a bookmark
.Selection.Goto wdGoToBookmark, , , "TableStart"
strLast = ""
 'loop through each line in the source document
 Do While Not objTxtStrm.AtEndOfStream
    'read line and extract values into an array
   strLine = objTxtStrm.ReadLine
   aVar = ExtractCSV(strLine)
    'if new car maker then make heading in table
    If strLast <> aVar(0) Then
     .Selection.SelectRow
     .Selection.Cells.Merge
     .Selection.Style = "CarTitle"
     .Selection.TypeText aVar(0)
     .Selection.MoveRight wdCell
     .Selection.Style = "Normal"
     .Selection.Cells.Split 1, 3, False
     strLast = aVar(0)
    End If

   'build row of data
   .Selection.TypeText aVar(1)
```

```
    .Selection.MoveRight wdCell
    .Selection.TypeText aVar(2)
    .Selection.MoveRight wdCell
    .Selection.TypeText aVar(3)
    .Selection.MoveRight wdCell
  Loop
 .Selection.SelectRow
 .Selection.Rows.Delete
 End With
  ]]>
  </script>
</job>
```

The script opens the `cars.txt` file and gets a reference to an instance of Word. A new document is created using the template `carlist.dot`. The script uses the `ExtractCSV` function from Solution 8.2 to extract CSV values from a string into an array.

> **NOTE** *For more information, search* `http://msdn.microsoft.com` *for the articles "Using the Object Browser," "Microsoft Word Object Model," "Working with Microsoft Word Objects," "Using the OLE/COM Object Viewer,"" and "OLE/COM Object Viewer."*

See Also

Solution 8.2.

9.2 Identifying Office Documents by Their Properties

Problem

You want to identify all Office documents that have certain properties.

Solution

To list the properties stored in a document, iterate through the `BuiltinDocumentProperties` collection and display the value for each property object:

```
'get a reference to a document
Set objDoc = GetObject("d:\data\word\report.doc")

On Error Resume Next
For Each objProp In objDoc.BuiltinDocumentProperties
  Wscript.Echo objProp.Name, objProp.Value
Next
```

Discussion

All Office documents allow you to set document properties. These properties can be used to store document information—for example, author, keyword description, and creation information. To set these properties, choose File > Properties. The Document Properties dialog box appears, as shown in Figure 9-6.

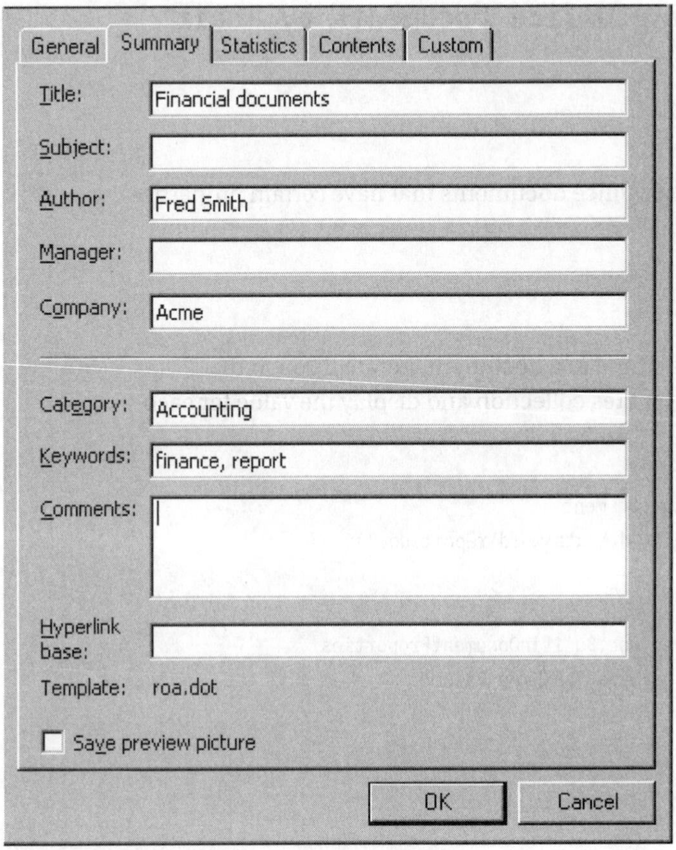

Figure 9-6. Document Properties dialog box

Information is exposed through the `BuiltinDocumentProperties` property of a Word Document, Excel Worksheet, or PowerPoint Presentation object. This property is a collection that stores each value set in the file's properties page. Each property in the collection is stored as a property object, with a `Name`, `Value`, and `Type` property.

Most single-word property names that appear in the file property dialog box have the equivalent property name in the `BuiltinDocumentProperties` collection. These include Title, Subject, Author, and Keywords. To reference a particular document property, use the following code:

```
'get a reference to a document
Set objDoc = GetObject("d:\data\word\report.doc")
Wscript.Echo "The author is:" & objDoc.BuiltinDocumentProperties("Author")
```

Table 9-1 lists additional properties with longer names. The data type is string unless otherwise noted.

Table 9-1. Document Properties

PROPERTY	DESCRIPTION
Revision number	Document revision number.
Last print date	Date last printed. Date type.
Creation date	Document creation date. Date type.
Last save time	Date document last saved. Date type.

The following command-line script, `offprops.vbs`, allows for queries to be executed against all Office documents in a specified path:

```
'offprops.vbs
'lists office documents that contain document properties that
'meet certain criteria
Dim strCriteria,  bSubDirs
Dim objRegExp, objEvent
bSubDirs = False
'check that two arguments are being passed
If Wscript.Arguments.Count <> 2 Then
  ShowDetails
    Wscript.Quit
End If
  'create a FSO and recursedir object (see Chatper 5)
  Set objEvent = Wscript.CreateObject ("WSH.RecurseDir","ev_")
  'set the path to search and get criteria
  objEvent.Path = Wscript.Arguments(0)
  strCriteria = Wscript.Arguments(1)
  'filter only on DOC, XLS and PPT documents
  objEvent.Filter = "^\w+\.(doc|xls|ppt)$"
  'replace ` (ASCII 96) characters with double quotes
  strCriteria = Replace(strCriteria, "`", chr(34),1,-1,1)
  'replace all instances of document criteria doc.property with
  'objDoc.BuiltinDocumentProperties(property)
  Set objRegExp = New RegExp
  objRegExp.Pattern = "\[\w+\]"
  objRegExp.IgnoreCase = True
  objRegExp.Global = True
  strCriteria = objRegExp.Replace(strCriteria, GetRef("Repl"))
  strCriteria = Replace(strCriteria, "_", " ",1,-1,1)
  Call objEvent.Process()
```

```
Sub ShowDetails
    WScript.Echo "offprops Queries office document properties." & vbCrLf & _
     "Syntax:" &  vbCrLf & _
    "offprops.vbs path criteria" &  vbCrLf & _
    "path      path to search" & vbCrLf & _
    "criteria  office property criteria " & vbCrLf & _
    "Example: List all documents authored by Fred Smith " & vbCrLf & -
    " offprops.vbs d:\data\word ""[Author]= `Fred Smith`"""
End Sub
'
Function Repl(strMatch, nPos, strSource)
  Repl = "objDoc.BuiltinDocumentProperties" & _
         "(""" & Mid(strMatch,2, len(strMatch)-2) & """)"
End Function

Sub ev_FoundFile(strPath)
   Dim objDoc, bResult
   On Error Resume Next
   'get reference to document found
   Set objDoc = GetObject(strPath)
   bResult = Eval(strCriteria)
   If  bResult And Not Err Then
      If Not Err Then
       Wscript.StdOut.WriteLine strPath
      Else
       Wscript.StdErr.WriteLine "Error opening file " & strPath _
                  & vbCrLf & "Error:" & Err.Description
      End If
   End If
End Sub
```

The command-line syntax for `offprops.vbs` is as follows:

```
offprops.vbs DocPath Query
```

`DocPath` represents the directory path to start the search. The script recursively searches the directory and all subdirectories for files that meet the criteria. Any files that meet the criteria are piped to the standard output.

The second parameter, `Query`, contains the query to execute against each file. It can contain any valid VBScript function and logical Boolean operators, such as AND, OR, and NOT.

Document property names must be surrounded by square brackets, so the `Creation date` property would be represented as `[Creation date]`.

Any double quotes used in the criteria must be represented by the grave accent (`) character (ASCII value 96). This character is replaced with double quotes by the script.

The following examples demonstrate the script. To list all Word documents created by Fred Smith:

```
offprops.vbs "d:\data\word" "[Author]= `Fred Smith`"
```

To list all files that contain the keyword "Finance":

```
offprops.vbs "d:\data\word" "Instr([keywords], `Finance`)>0"
```

The script uses the `WSH.RecurseDir` scripting component from Chapter 5 to recursively search the subdirectories.

> **NOTE** *For more information, search* `http://msdn.microsoft.com` *for the article "BuiltInDocumentProperties Property."*

See Also

Solution 5.10.

9.3 Importing Data into Excel

Problem

You want to import data into Excel.

Solution

The following script, `xlimport.wsf`, imports comma-delimited input from standard input in an Excel spreadsheet:

```
<?xml version="1.0" ?>
<job>
<reference guid="{00020813-0000-0000-C000-000000000046}"/>
```

```
<!--comment
Script:xlimport.wsf
inserts text from delimited input streams
-->
 <script language="VBScript">
 <![CDATA[
 Option Explicit
Dim nF, objFSO, strLine
 Dim objExcel, nRcount, nCcount, nRowStart, nColStart
 Dim bAdd, strRange, strFile, objWorkBook, strPath
 Dim aVals
On Error Resume Next
If Wscript.Arguments.Count <> 2 Then
   ShowUsage
 End If

  strPath = Wscript.Arguments(0)
  strRange = Wscript.Arguments(1)
  'attempt to get reference to running copy of Excel
  Set objExcel = GetObject(,"Excel.Application")
  'if no running copies of Excel, start a new one
  If Err Then Set objExcel = CreateObject("Excel.Application")
  With objExcel
    .Visible = True
    'check if specified workbook is already loaded
    Set objWorkbook= .Workbooks(Mid(strPath, InstrRev(strPath,"\")+1))
    'if not, then load workbook
    If Err Then
     Err.Clear
      Set objWorkBook =  .Workbooks.Open(strPath)
    End If

    If Err Then
      ExitScript _
         "Unable to open file " & strPath & vbCrLf & _
         "Error: " & Err.Description , True
    End If
    objWorkBook.Activate
   .Goto strRange

   'did range name not exist?
   If Err Then
    'move to 'last cell' of spreadsheet
```

```
  .ActiveCell.SpecialCells(xlLastCell).Select
  'select range at end of spreadsheet
  .Range(.Cells(.ActiveCell.Row + 1, 1), _
            .Cells(.ActiveCell.Row + 1, 1)).Select
  'add range name
  .ActiveWorkbook.Names.Add strRange, "=" & .ActiveSheet.Name _
                      & "!" & .Application.Selection.Address
   nRcount = 0 'set row count to nothing
 Else
   nRcount = .Selection.Rows.Count
 End If
'get the dimensions of the range
 nCcount = .Selection.Columns.Count
 nRowStart = .Selection.Row
 nColStart = .Selection.Column

'loop through all lines in the input stream
  Do While Not Wscript.StdIn.AtEndOfStream
  'insert a blank row below the range if adding to range
   If nRcount>0 Then
    .Range(.Cells(nRowStart + nRcount, nColStart), _
                      .Cells(nRowStart + nRcount, _
                      nColStart + nCcount - 1)).Insert xlDown
   'move to the bottom of the data range to insert new data
   .Range(.Cells(nRowStart + nRcount, nColStart), _
                 .Cells(nRowStart + nRcount,  nColStart)).Select
  End If
  'read data from input stream and parse into array
  strLine = Wscript.StdIn.ReadLine
   aVals = Split(strLine, ",")
  'insert values into spreadsheet
   For nF = 0 To Ubound(aVals)
    .Activecell.Value =aVals(nF)
    .Activecell.Offset (0,1).Select
   Next
   If Ubound(aVals)>= nCcount Then nCcount = Ubound(aVals) + 1
  nRcount = nRcount + 1
 Loop
 'resize the range name for the range
 .Range(strRange).Resize (nRcount,nCcount).Select
 .ActiveWorkbook.Names.Add strRange, "=" & .ActiveSheet.Name _
                       & "!" & .Application.Selection.Address
End With
```

```
Sub ShowUsage()
WScript.Echo _
   "xlimport.wsf imports data into Excel from comma delimited input stream." _
    & vbCrLf & "Syntax:" &  vbCrLf & _
   "xlimport.wsf FilePath RangeName" &  vbCrLf & _
   "FilePath   path to Excel file to update" &  vbCrLf & _
   "RangeName  Excel range to add data to" & vbCrLf & _
   "Example:Import data from file data.txt into range dat2 in file book.xls" _
    & vbCrLf & "cscript xlimport.wsf e:\book.xls dat2 < data.txt"
   WScript.Quit -1
 End Sub
  ]]>
  </script>
</job>
```

Discussion

Much of an Excel script solution can be implemented by recording an Excel macro and inserting the results into a script, much the same as demonstrated with Word in Solution 9.1.

More complex manipulation of a spreadsheet requires mastering the Range object. All navigation, selection, and manipulation of a spreadsheet are performed using the Range object.

A range in a spreadsheet represents an area of one or more cells. Use Excel named ranges to identify specific areas of the spreadsheet. Named ranges can be defined by selecting a range of cells in a spreadsheet and entering a valid range name in the Range Name box.

Creating named ranges is useful for defining an area that you might need to navigate to. The advantage of using named ranges over fixed cell references (e.g., A10) is if areas of the spreadsheet are moved, appended, or deleted in the range's vicinity, the range reference updates accordingly.

The following example inventories the specified computer using WMI:

```
'create an instance of the ENTWSH.SysInfo object. This object
'is created In Solution 10.1
Set objSysInfo = CreateObject("ENTWSH.SysInfo ")
'attempt to get reference to running copy of Excel
Set objExcel = GetObject(,"Excel.Application")
'if no running copies of Excel, start a new one
If Err Then Set objExcel = CreateObject("Excel.Application")
With objExcel
```

```
 'create a Excel workbook based on the inventory template
 .Workbooks.Add "D:\Program Files\Microsoft Office\Templates\inventory.xlt"
.Application.Goto "BIOS"
 .ActiveCell.FormulaR1C1 = objSysInfo.BIOSVersion
.Application.Goto "ComputerName"
 .ActiveCell.FormulaR1C1 = "computername"
 .Application.Goto "OSSerial"
 .ActiveCell.FormulaR1C1 = objSysInfo.SerialNumber
.Application.Goto "VirtualMemory"
 .ActiveCell.FormulaR1C1 = objSysInfo.VirtualMemory
.Application.Goto "CPU"
 .ActiveCell.FormulaR1C1 = objSysInfo.CPU
.Application.Goto "Memory"
 .ActiveCell.FormulaR1C1 = objSysInfo.Memory
.Application.Goto "OSVersion"
 .ActiveCell.FormulaR1C1 = objSysInfo.OS
.Application.Goto "OSUser"
 .ActiveCell.FormulaR1C1 = objSysInfo.RegisteredUser
End With
```

The previous sample uses an Excel template called `inventory.xlt` to build a new document. Cells used to store system information are defined by range names. The `Goto` method is used to jump to the cells in order to populate them with the appropriate information. The script uses the `ENTWSH.SysInfo` Windows Script Component from Solution 10.1.

To create a range, call the `Name` collection's `Add` method:

```
Set objExcel = CreateObject("Excel.Application")
With objExcel
   .Visible = True
   'create a new Excel workbook
   .Workbooks.Add
   'create a range called SourceData that references the range B2 to F10
   .ActiveWorkbook.Names.Add "SourceData", "=$B$2:$F$10"
End With
```

In the preceding example, the spreadsheet area that is specified for the named range is displayed in absolute format, in which each row/column that is referenced is prefixed by a dollar sign ($). If the range was specified in relative format (i.e., no dollar signs), the range name would be added relative to the active cell.

Using range names makes it easy to identify the location, size, and amount of information stored in the range.

A range is composed of one or more cells. You can reference individual cells by using an absolute spreadsheet reference (letter and column combination—for example, A1) or a named range:

```
'display value from cell A1 from the current active worksheet
Wscript.Echo objExcel.Range("A1")

'display value from named range UserName from the active workbook
Wscript.Echo objExcel.Range("UserName")

'display value from named range UserName from the first workbook
Wscript.Echo objExcel.WorkSheet(1).("UserName")

'display value from named range Computer Name from the first worksheet from
'the inventory2 workbook
Wscript.Echo objExcel.Workbooks("inventory2").Worksheets (1).range("ComputerName")
```

You can also apply formatting such as fonts, colors, and shading to a Range object:

```
'xlformat.vbs
Const xlSolid = 1
Const Red = 3
Const Yellow = 6
'create new instance of Excel application
Set objExcel = CreateObject("Excel.Application")
With objExcel
  .Visible = True
  'create a new Excel workbook
  .Workbooks.Add
  'set the font color for range A4:F8 to red
  .Range("A4:F8").Font.ColorIndex = Red
  'set the fill of current selected cells to solid yellow
  With .Selection.Interior
    .ColorIndex = Yellow
    .Pattern = xlSolid   End With
End With
```

Formatting is applied to all cells in the specified range. The Borders, Font, Interior, and Style properties allow for formatting to be set on a Range object.

While you can use online Help to find out property values for formatting, the easiest way to determine what to set is to record a macro and apply the formatting you want to use. The resulting recorded macro will contain all the appropriate constants.

Individual cells within a range are represented as Range objects. A Range object is a collection of these individual cells and it can be enumerated. This allows for the processing of each cell in the range:

```
'xlupd.vbs
'updates values in specific range based on criteria
'create new instance of Excel application
Set objExcel = CreateObject("Excel.Application")

With objExcel
 .Visible = True
 'load an existing spreadsheet
 .Workbooks.Open "C:\data.xls"
  Set objRange = .Range("Prices")
  'go through each cell in the range
  For Each objCell In objRange
   'update cell value according to current value
   If objCell.Value<100 Then
    objCell.Value = objCell.Value * 1.04
   ElseIf objCell.Value< 200 Then
    objCell.Value = objCell.Value * 1.05
   Else
    objCell.Value = objCell.Value * 1.07
   End If
  Next
End With
```

Referencing cells using spreadsheet row/column (e.g., A5) can be tedious if you want to access a cell's content using a numeric column reference. The Cells property returns a reference to a range specified by a numeric row/column combination:

```
Set objExcel = CreateObject("Excel.Application")
With objExcel
  .Visible = True
  'create a new Excel workbook
  .Workbooks.Add
  For nCol = 1 to 20
    For nRow = 1 to 20
      .Cells(nRow, nCol) = (nRow - 1) * 20 + nCol
    Next
```

```
  Next
End With
```

Both row and column offsets start at 1, so `Cells(2,3)` returns a reference to the contents of cell C3.

Excel doesn't provide any simple navigation methods that provide movement in any direction of a spreadsheet (such as move left, right, up, or down). The `Range` object's `Offset` property returns a range offset by a specified number of rows and columns from a range.

Use the `Offset` property together with the `Select` method to navigate a spreadsheet:

```
Set objExcel = CreateObject("Excel.Application")
With objExcel
  .Visible = True
  'create a new Excel workbook
  .Workbooks.Add
  For nCol = 1 to 20
    For nRow = 1 to 20
      'insert a value into the current cell
      .Selection = (nRow - 1) * 20 + nCol
      'move one column to the right
      .Selection.Offset(0,1).Select
    Next
     'move one row down and 20 cells to the left
     .Selection.Offset(1,-20).Select
  Next
End With
```

Specifying a negative offset moves the selection by either a negative number of rows or a column offset.

Note the class GUID was used to reference the Excel type library:

```
<reference guid="{00020813-0000-0000-C000-000000000046}"/>
```

Using the `Excel.Application` reference to access the type library wouldn't work. Word uses a reference to the `Word.Document` class ID (CLSID), which returns a reference to the required type library.

Excel can't make a reference to a type library in a similar way using `Excel.Worksheet`, so the object's CLSID must be passed instead. Application CLSIDs can be referenced using Microsoft's class OLE/COM Object Viewer, as shown in Figure 9-7.

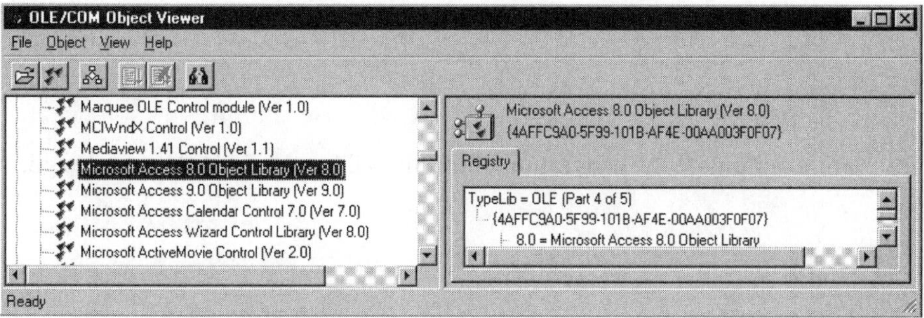

Figure 9-7. OLE/COM Object Viewer

The Solution script, `xlimport.wsf`, allows for comma-delimited standard input to be imported into an existing spreadsheet. The script appends the data to a named range specified in the command line.

If the specified range name doesn't exist, it is created. The new range is created starting in the first column, below the last row of existing data. The syntax for the script is as follows:

```
xlimport.wsf FilePath RangeName
```

`FilePath` specifies the path to Excel file to update. `RangeName` is the name of the range to update or create. The following command-line sample redirects the text file `dat.txt` into the `xlimport` script, which will append the contents to the range `dat2`:

```
cscript xlimport.wsf d:\book1.xls dat2 < dat.txt
```

> **NOTE** *For more information, search* `http://msdn.microsoft.com` *for the articles "Working with Microsoft Excel Objects" and "Microsoft Excel Object Model."*

See Also

Solution 10.2.

9.4 Generating Thumbnail Images for Web Pages

Problem

You want to automate the generation of thumbnail images for Web page design.

Solution

Corel PHOTO-PAINT exposes a COM automation interface that can be accessed from any environment that can manipulate COM objects. The following command-line script, `thumbnail.vbs`, converts images from a specified directory into thumbnails using CorelDRAW version 8:

```
'thumbnail.vbs
Const Height= 18
Const JPEG = 774
Dim aMenus, nF, strPath, objCorel
Dim objFSO , objFolder, objFile, strNew
Dim strDestination, strSource
If WScript.Arguments.Count <> 2 Then
        ShowUsage
        WScript.Quit
End If

  'get destination path and menu names
  strSource =  Wscript.Arguments(0)
  strDestination =  Trim(Wscript.Arguments(1))
'make sure destination path ends in a backslash
 If Not Right(strDestination,1) = "\" Then _
              strDestination = strDestination & "\"
Set objCorel = CreateObject("CorelPhotoPaint.Automation.8")
'get a reference to the source folder to read
 Set objFSO = CreateObject("Scripting.FileSystemObject")
 Set objFolder = objFSO.GetFolder(strSource)
  For Each objFile In objFolder.files
   strNew = objFile.Name
   strNew = Left(strNew, InStr(strNew, ".") - 1) & "tm.jpg"
  CreateThumbnail objFile.Path, strDestination & strNew
 Next

Sub ShowUsage()
WScript.Echo _
```

```
    "thumbnail.vbs creates jpg. image thumbnails ." _
     & vbCrLf & "Syntax:" &  vbCrLf & _
    "thumbnail.vbs Source Destination" &  vbCrLf & _
    "Source       path to source directory with images" &  vbCrLf & _
    "Destination destination directory to store thumbnails" &  vbCrLf & _
     "Example:" & vbCrLf & " thumbnail.vbs d:\pictures d:\pictures\thumbs\"
End Sub

Sub CreateThumbnail(strSource, strDestination)

 With objCorel
    'arguments 2 to 5 represent left, top, right, bottom coordinates '
    'of image. Argument 6 represents load type, 7 and 8 are used
     'if movie file is being loaded and represents start and end frame.
    .FileOpen strSource, 0, 0, 0, 0, 0, 1, 1
    'check if width is greater than height and resize accordingly
    If objCorel.GetDocumentWidth < objCorel.GetDocumentHeight Then
       'arguments 1 and 2 repesent width and height. 3 and 4 are
       'horizontal and vertical resolution in dots per inch and
       'argument 5 is anti-aliasing flag, which if True sets
       'anti-aliasing on
        .ImageResample 107, 143, 144, 144, True
    Else
        .ImageResample 144, 108, 144, 144, True
    End If
    'save resized. Second argument represents image format and third
     'is compression format used
    .FileSave strDestination, JPEG, 0
    .FileClose
 End With
End Sub
```

Discussion

Creating thumbnails for browsing images on Web pages is an effective way of navigating pictures. Creating thumbnails can be a time-consuming exercise because it involves manually resizing images to the appropriate size.

Corel PHOTO-PAINT implements a scripting language that can be used to automate tasks. The scripting language accesses PHOTO-PAINT operations through a COM interface, which can also be manipulated through WSH.

> **NOTE** *The following steps are implemented using Corel PHOTO-PAINT version 10. Older versions may not support these operations, and the steps may vary in more recent implementations. Script versions for PHOTO-PAINT version 8 is available for download on the source code file at* `http://www.apress.com`.

PHOTO-PAINT includes a script recorder that you can use to record the steps you want to automate, as you would use the Word or Excel macro recorder.

To record a script, select the Record Script icon from the Recorder roll-up. Figure 9-8 shows the Recorder roll-up after a few operations have been recorded.

Figure 9-8. Recorder roll-up

Perform the operations you want to automate. Each recorded step will appear in the Recorder window.

When script recording is finished, save the script to a file. The script format is saved as a text ASCII file. Open the script file with a text editor or the Corel script editor:

```
WITHOBJECT "CorelPhotoPaint.Automation.8"
     .SetDocumentInfo 640, 480
     .ImageResample 145, 109, 144, 144, TRUE
     .FileSave "C:\PhotoWise Images\Jun10\Image02sm.jpg", 774, 0
END WITHOBJECT
```

The recorded script can be easily converted to WSH by replacing the `With` statement and adding a line to create the PHOTO-PAINT object:

```
Set objPaint = CreateObject("CorelPhotoPaint.Automation.8")
With objPaint
     .SetDocumentInfo 640, 480
     .ImageResample 145, 109, 144, 144, TRUE
     .FileSave "C:\PhotoWise Images\Jun10\Image02sm.jpg", 774, 0
End With
```

The Solution script, `thumbnail.vbs`, is a command-line script that creates a JPEG thumbnail file from all graphics files found in the directory specified in the command line:

```
thumbnail.vbs Source Destination
```

The `Source` parameter is the name of the directory to find images in. The `Destination` parameter points to the directory path to store the thumbnails. The source and destination directories must be different. The following command line creates thumbnails of all images in `d:\data\pictures` and saves them to `d:\data\pictures\thumbnails`:

```
thumbnail.vbs "d:\data\pictures" " d:\data\pictures\thumbnails\"
```

The image is resized to a thumbnail and saved to the destination directory specified by the destination parameter. The filename is padded with `tn` to identify it as a thumbnail.

See Also

Search the Corel Script reference (`scedit.hlp`) installed with Corel PHOTO-PAINT.

9.5 Building Web Page Rollover Images

Problem

You want to create rollover images for Web page menus.

Solution

The following script creates rollover images by automating Corel PHOTO-PAINT version 10:

```
'buildmenus.vbs
Const Height = 18
Dim aMenus, nF, strPath, objCorel

 If Wscript.Arguments.Count <> 2 Then
   ShowUsage
   Wscript.Quit
 End If

  'get destination path and menu names
  strPath = Wscript.Arguments(0)
  aMenus = Split(Wscript.Arguments(1),";")

  Set objCorel = CreateObject("CorelPhotoPaint.Automation.10")

  'loop through and build menu elements
  For nF = 0 To UBound(aMenus)
  'build
   BuildElements CStr(aMenus(nF)), strPath  _
                 & aMenus(nF) & "ON.jpg", 0, 0, 0
   BuildElements CStr(aMenus(nF)), strPath  _
                 & aMenus(nF) & ".jpg", 255, 255, 255
  Next

Sub ShowUsage()
WScript.Echo _
    "buildmenus.vbs builds on/off images for Web rollovers ." _
     & vbCrLf & "Syntax:" &  vbCrLf & _
    "buildmenus.vbs Path Menus" &  vbCrLf & _
    "Path       path where images are stored" &  vbCrLf & _
    "Destination Titles for each button, separated by semicolon" &  vbCrLf & _
    "Example:" & vbCrLf & " buildmenus.vbs d:\images Home;Shop;Help"
End Sub
```

```
Sub BuildElements(strText, strFileName, nRed, nGreen, nBlue)
 Dim nWidth, nHeight
 'calculate width of box
 nWidth = Int(7 * Len(strText))
With objCorel
   'create a new file with white background
  .FileNew nWidth + 2, HEIGHT, 1, 72, 72, False, _
            False, 1, 0, 0, 0, 0, 255, 255, 255, 0, False
  'draw a blue rectangle
  .RectangleTool 0, 0, 0, 0, True, False, True
  .FillSolid 5, 32, 102, 176, 0
  .Rectangle 0, 0, nWidth, HEIGHT
  'add centred text box
  .TextTool nWidth / 2, 2, strText
  .SetPaintColor 5, nRed, nGreen, nBlue, 0
  .TextSettings 400, False, False, 1, "Arial", 14, True, 0, 100, 0, False
  'save file and close
  .FileSave strFileName, 774, 0
  .FileClose
 End With
End Sub
```

Discussion

All image and text manipulation facilities implemented in PHOTO-PAINT can be scripted.

While creating the script to create these images can initially be time-consuming and tedious, once the logic is in place a lot of effort can be saved producing images that contain a set format.

Web page "rollover" menus are one such example. Rollovers are the effect where the mouse moves over an image the image changes to highlight the action. This requires at least two images for each menu.

The `buildmenus` script creates two sets of images based on parameters passed through the command line. The first image is a white-on-blue menu button, while the second is the highlighted button with a black-on-blue text button:

```
buildmenus DestinationPath Menus
```

The `DestinationPath` parameter identifies the location where the images will be stored. It can be a local or UNC path and must end with a backslash (`\`).

The `Menus` parameter contains the name of the menus separated by semicolons.

The following command line generates eight images and stores them in the `d:\wwwroot\images` directory:

```
buildmenus "d:\wwwroot\images\" "Products;Information;Support;Purchase"
```

For each menu there would be a standard button saved as a JPEG file using the name of the menu, such as `products.jpg`, `information.jpg`, and so on, as well as a corresponding image for the highlighted menu.

Highlighted images take the name of the menu with "ON" appended to it—for example, `ProductsON.jpg`, `InformationON.jpg`, and so on.

See Also

Search the Corel Script reference (`scedit.hlp`) included with the CorelDRAW installation.

9.6 Generating Electronic Copies of Access Reports

Problem

You want to generate electronic copies of Access reports.

Solution

Microsoft Access can generate electronic "snapshots" of reports. The following script generates a snapshot using the Northwind sample database:

```
<?xml version="1.0" ?>
<job>
<reference guid="{4AFFC9A0-5F99-101B-AF4E-00AA003F0F07}"/>
<!--comment
snpcreate.wsf
Build a snapshot from the Sales by Year Dialog report in
the Northwind database
-->
 <script language="VBScript">
```

```
 <![CDATA[
Option Explicit
Dim objAccess, objForm
Set objAccess = CreateObject("Access.Application")
objAccess.OpenCurrentDatabase "d:\northwind.mdb"
objAccess.DoCmd.OpenForm "Sales by Year Dialog"
Set objForm = objAccess.Forms("Sales by Year Dialog")
objForm.Controls("BeginningDate").Value = "1/1/95"
objForm.Controls("EndingDate").Value = "12/31/95"

'build the report
objAccess.DoCmd.OutputTo acOutputReport, "Sales by Year", _
                        "Snapshot Format", "d:\SalesByYear.snp"
objAccess.Quit
  ]]>
  </script>
</job>
```

Discussion

Access 97 with Service Release 2 (SR2) and Access 2000 onwards allow you to generate report "snapshots." A snapshot is an electronic copy of the report that you can view in a separate viewer application.

You do not need the Access application installed on your computer to view snapshots; you just need the Snapshot Viewer, which is available as a download from the Microsoft Web site (`http://www.microsoft.com/`).

To output an Access report to an external file, use the `DoCmd.OutputTo` procedure to build the file using a specified output format. Reports can be output to HTML, Active Server Pages (ASP), plain text, and Excel, as well as the Snapshot format.

For a simple report that doesn't require any parameters, specify the report name, type, and destination:

```
<?xml version="1.0" ?>
<job>
<reference guid="{4AFFC9A0-5F99-101B-AF4E-00AA003F0F07}"/>
<!--comment
Build a snapshot from the Sales by Year Dialog report in
the Northwind database
-->
 <script language="VBScript">
 <![CDATA[
```

```
  Dim objAccess
  Set objAccess = CreateObject("Access.Application")
  objAccess.OpenCurrentDatabase "d:\northwind.mdb"
  objAccess.DoCmd.OutputTo acOutputReport, "Sales Totals by Amount", _
                             acFormatHTML, "d:\rep.snp"
  objAccess.Quit
  ]]>
  </script>
</job>
```

Reports that require parameter values entered in a form are a bit trickier because the parameter cannot be passed to the report. Open the form using the `DoCmd.OpenForm` method and get a reference to the appropriate form through the `Forms` collection.

Set the parameters required by referencing the required fields through the form's `Controls` collection.

This Solution uses the Northwind sample database that is supplied with Access.

> **NOTE** *For more information, search* `http://msdn.microsoft.com` *for the articles "About Report Snapshots and Snapshot Viewer" and "Working with Microsoft Access Objects."*

See Also

Search for "OutputTo method" in Microsoft Access online Help.

CHAPTER 10

Network Administration/WMI

GATHERING SYSTEM INFORMATION is a never-ending task for today's IT professionals.

The traditional method of querying Windows system-related information is calling a Windows API routine. This method is inconsistent and may not work over all Windows platforms, and an API for Windows 2000/2003/XP may have a different interface than one for Windows 9*x* or NT. In addition, such APIs are not directly callable through scripting languages such as WSH, so a wrapper object must be written to encapsulate the logic.

An effort has been made to address the problem of adhering to a consistent standard to query system information that is known as Web-Based Enterprise Management (WBEM). WBEM is an attempt to provide a standard way of representing and accessing enterprise system information. WBEM is an industry standard that was implemented by the Desktop Management Task Force (DMTF), an industry standards organization.

Windows Management Instrumentation (WMI) is Microsoft's implementation of WBEM. WMI is an extensible architecture, which allows for additional functionality to be implemented within the WMI framework. Functionality is implemented through providers, and additional providers can be developed to interface new software. For example, Exchange 2000 and 2003 include WMI providers that allow for monitoring and administering Exchange services.

Using WMI you can query a wide variety of system information, such as computer memory, BIOS, network adapters, drive controllers, video, and printer configurations. It also provides the ability to query Event Viewer, SNMP, registry, and performance counter information.

WMI exposes system information through object *classes.* A class can represent a system element, such as a hard drive or network adapter. Information is exposed through properties, while operations can be performed against classes by executing methods. Methods perform class-related operations, which might be to set an IP address for a network adapter object or clear an event log for an event log object. The default installation of WMI contains hundreds of classes.

Classes are organized in *namespaces.* A namespace represents a collection of logically grouped classes. By default, there is a root namespace and additional namespaces reside below the root, similar to a directory structure.

To use a WMI object you need to know the object's path. The path consists of a combination of the computer name, namespace, and object class:

```
\\Computer\Namespace:Class
```

The computer name must be prefixed by two backslashes (`\\`) and followed by a single backslash (`\`) as separator between the namespace and computer name. The ability to specify a remote computer name is one of the most exciting aspects of WMI, because it allows operations to be performed against remote computers. If the computer name is omitted from the path, the local computer is assumed.

The namespace is where to find the WMI object class you want to use. Namespaces can have multiple levels and start from a root level, which contains additional namespace levels. The namespace levels are separated using the backslash character (`\`). One of the most used namespaces is the Common Information Model Version 2 (CIMV2) namespace, which resides below the root level. The path to this namespace is `root\cimv2`.

The final part of the path is the class object. The class object is appended to the end of the path and separated from the namespace by a colon (:).

The full path to the `Win32_ComputerSystem` object that resides in the `Cimv2` namespace under `Root` is `Root\Cimv2:Win32_ComputerSystem`. If you attempt to create an instance of this object on the remote computer Thor, you prefix the path with the computer name: `\\Thor\Root\Cimv2:Win32_ComputerSystem`.

Most important, WMI is accessible through a COM interface, allowing all information and operations to be accessed from WSH. WMI comes installed with Windows 2000/2003/XP and can be installed on Windows NT and Windows 9*x*.

This chapter concentrates on how to access information and perform operations through WMI classes, but it also covers how to use available tools to navigate the WMI classes and namespaces.

> **NOTE** *For more information, search* `http://msdn.microsoft.com` *for the articles "WMI: A Simple, Powerful Tool for Scripting Windows Management," "Managing Windows with WMI," "WMI: Administering Windows and Applications across Your Enterprise," "Microsoft Windows Management Instrumentation Scripting," "Administrating Windows through WSH," "WMI Scripting Primer," and "WMI SDK."*

10.1 Accessing Information about a Computer

Problem

You want to access general computer information such as operating system (OS) details and system information.

Solution

Create an instance of the `Win32_ComputerSystem` WMI class to get computer details:

```
Dim objService, objWMIObject, objWMIObjects

'create an instance of a Services object for namespace root\cimv2
Set objServices = _
    GetObject("winmgmts:{impersonationLevel=impersonate}!root\cimv2")

'create a collection of Win32_ComputerSystem class objects
Set objWMIObjects = objServices.InstancesOf("Win32_ComputerSystem")

'enumerate collection.. there will only be one object, the local computer
For Each objWMIObject In objWMIObjects
    'display some information from the class
    WScript.Echo "Computer description:" & objWMIObject.Description
    WScript.Echo "Physical memory:" & objWMIObject.TotalPhysicalMemory
    WScript.Echo "Manufacturer:" & objWMIObject.Manufacturer
Next
```

Discussion

To get references to WMI objects, you must create a WMI `Services` object for the namespace you want to query for information and/or perform operations against.

There are two ways to create a WMI `Services` object. One way is to create a `SwbemLocator` object and connect to a local or remote server:

```
Set objLocator = CreateObject("WbemScripting.SWbemLocator")
```

Once you have an instance of the SwbemLocator object, use its ConnectServer method to connect to a WMI service for a specified computer. The syntax is as follows:

```
Set objSrv = objLoc.ConnectServer([strSrvr], [strNameSpace], [strUser],
[strPass])
```

Table 10-1 lists the ConnectServer method's arguments.

Table 10-1. ConnectServer *Method Arguments*

PARAMETER	DESCRIPTION
strSrvr	Name of the computer to connect to. If not specified, the local computer that code is executed on is assumed. Even though the name implies a server, it can be any computer with WMI installed.
strNameSpace	WMI namespace to access. If omitted, the default namespace configured on the machine is used, which is generally root \CIMV2. The default namespace is determined by the HKEY_LOCAL_MACHINE\Software\Microsoft\WBEM\Scripting\Default Namespace registry key.
strUser	Account name to use to authenticate against the service. Use only if a level of authentication is required that is not provided by the current logged-on user. The user name can be specified as username or domain\username. If omitted, the security credentials of the current logged-on user are used.
strPass	Password required to authenticate the strUser account.

All parameters for the ConnectServer method are optional. If you omit all parameters, the Locator object will attempt to connect to the default namespace on the local machine using the authentication of the logged-on user:

```
'connect to local computer
Set objLocator = CreateObject("WbemScripting.SWbemLocator")

  Set objServices = objLocator.ConnectServer()
```

An error will occur if the locator is unable to connect to the specified computer.

Before you perform any operations, it is important to make sure the level of security provided by the Service object is sufficient. Access to WMI objects is determined by the security level of the caller. This is determined by the *impersonation level.*

The impersonation level is determined by the ImpersonationLevel property of the Services object's .Security_ property, and it can have any of the values listed in Table 10-2.

Table 10-2. Impersonation Security Levels

IMPERSONATION LEVEL	VALUE	MEANING
Anonymous	1	Hides information about the caller
Identify	2	Allows objects to query the identification of the caller
Impersonate	3	Uses the security credentials of the caller
Delegate	4	Allows objects to use the security access of the caller

Using an impersonation level that is too low (Anonymous or Identify) might prevent access to WMI objects. Using the Delegate level allows objects created by the user to create instances of other objects using the security level of the caller and should not be used unless there's a specific need for it. The Impersonate level is the recommended level.

```
'connect to WMI services for the default namespace on the local computer
Set objLocator = CreateObject("WbemScripting.SWbemLocator")

Set objService = objLocator.ConnectServer()

'set security level for service object to 3, impersonate
objService.Security_.ImpersonationLevel = 3
```

If the impersonation level is not specified, it is set to the default value, which is determined by the registry value stored under `HKEY_LOCAL_MACHINE\Software\Microsoft\WBEM\Scripting\ Default Impersonation Level`. This value is set to 3, Impersonate, during the WMI installation.

Another way to create a WMI `Services` object is to use the `GetObject` function to bind to a `Service` object. `GetObject` requires that you pass a *moniker*. A moniker is a connection string that contains the path to the WMI namespace you want to access together with optional security information.

The following snippet returns a reference to a `Services` object for the WMI namespace `root\cimv2` using `GetObject`:

```
'get a reference to a WMI service object
Dim objServices
Set objServices = GetObject("winmgmts:root\cimv2")
```

Note the path to the service namespace is prefixed by `winmgmts` (Windows Management). Any references to WMI objects using `GetObject` must be prefixed by `winmgmts` so Windows can determine how to create the object. The moniker string is not case-sensitive.

If the namespace is omitted in the moniker, the default namespace is used, similar to the `ConnectServer` method. As a result, the following code statement is equivalent to the previous example, assuming `root\cimv2` is the default namespace:

```
'get a reference to a WMI services object for the default namespace
Set objService = GetObject("winmgmts:")
```

To specify security within the moniker, include the setting(s) enclosed within braces ({}). An exclamation point (!) separates the security settings and object path:

```
Set objService = _
    GetObject("winmgmts:{impersonationLevel=impersonate}!root\cimv2")
```

In this example, `impersonationLevel` is set to `impersonate`. The impersonation level can be set to any of the levels listed earlier in this section. If the impersonation level is omitted, the default impersonation level for the computer is used.

> **NOTE** *WMI provides additional connection information to be set when connecting to a namespace, such as system locale and connection privileges. Coverage of this information is beyond the scope of this chapter.*

You can now use the WMI `Services` object to create instances of specific WMI classes. Use the `Services` object's `InstancesOf` method to create a set of one or more instances of a class:

```
Set objWMIObjects = objServices.InstancesOf(strClassName)
```

The `strClassName` parameter is the name of the WMI class to create an instance of.

The `InstancesOf` method returns a collection of one or more WMI objects. The Solution script creates an instance of a `Win32_OperatingSystem` class and displays a number of associated OS properties for each object in the collection.

You can reference individual WMI objects from the collection by providing an index value. The index is a key associated with the object class.

Unlike collections found in other object models, you cannot reference instances of a class by an index number.

In the Solution script, an instance of the Win32_ComputerSystem class is created and enumerated. The Win32_ComputerSystem class exposes information related to a specific computer, so it will never return more than one instance.

The Win32_ComputerSystem class is keyed on a Name property, which is the name assigned to the computer. To get a reference to the Win32_ComputerSystem object on the computer Odin where the script is running, use the following code:

```
Set objService = _
    GetObject("winmgmts:{impersonationLevel=impersonate}!root\cimv2")

'create an instance of the Win32_ComputerSystem class
Set objWMIObjects = objService.InstancesOf("Win32_ComputerSystem")
'get a reference to the local computer Odin
Set objWMIObject = objWMIObjects("Win32_ComputerSystem.Name=" _
                   & "'Odin'")
```

Even though you are getting a reference to the local computer called Odin, you must specify the name of the computer because it is the key property for the class. Specifying a remote computer name will result in an error.

If you want to get a reference to the Win32_ComputerSystem class on the remote machine Thor (a remote call) you have to specify the name of the remote computer you are trying to reference as part of the namespace path when creating a Services object:

```
'get a reference to a WMI service on remote computer Thor
Set objService = _
  GetObject("winmgmts:{impersonationLevel=impersonate}!\\Thor\root\cimv2")

'create an instance of the Win32_ComputerSystem class
Set objWMIObjects = objService.InstancesOf("Win32_ComputerSystem")
'get a reference to the computer object Thor
Set objWMIObject = objWMIObjects("Win32_ComputerSystem.Name=" _
                   & "'Thor'")
```

Prefixing the WMI path with the computer name attempts to connect to the remote computer Thor. Any remote computer you are connecting to using WMI must also have a copy of WMI installed. You must also have appropriate security access to the computer you are accessing.

Individual instances of WMI object classes can be created using GetObject. This results in less code than first creating a Services object and enumerating individual instances.

To create a specific instance of a class, append a colon (:) followed by the key to the object you want to reference:

```
Set objWMIObject = GetObject( _
        "winmgmts:{impersonationLevel=impersonate}!root\cimv2:" & _
        "Win32_ComputerSystem.Name='Odin'")
```

In the previous sample an instance of the `Win32_ComputerSystem` class is created for the computer Odin.

While the method of referring to individual instances of WMI objects results in less code, it is better to create a single instance of a `Services` object if you intend to create more than one instance of any given class within a namespace.

Not all properties exposed through `Win32_ComputerSystem` will return values. This depends upon the underlying operating system. Some operating systems expose more information through the providers than others.

To determine information about WMI classes, such as property and index values, you can use the WBEM CIM Studio that comes with the WBEM/WMI SDK. The WMI CIM Studio only runs under Windows NT/2000/2003/XP.

To start the WMI CIM Studio, perform the following steps:

1. Select Start menu > WMI SDK > WMI CIM Studio.

2. The "Connect to namespace" dialog box appears, as shown in Figure 10-1.

Figure 10-1. Connect to namespace

Clicking the button enables you to connect to a remote computer or use alternative user authentication.

Once you have selected a namespace and optionally a remote computer, you can connect to the WMI service. The WMI CIM Studio will enumerate all classes within the namespace. Figure 10-2 shows the WMI CIM Studio when it's connected to the `root\CIMV2` namespace.

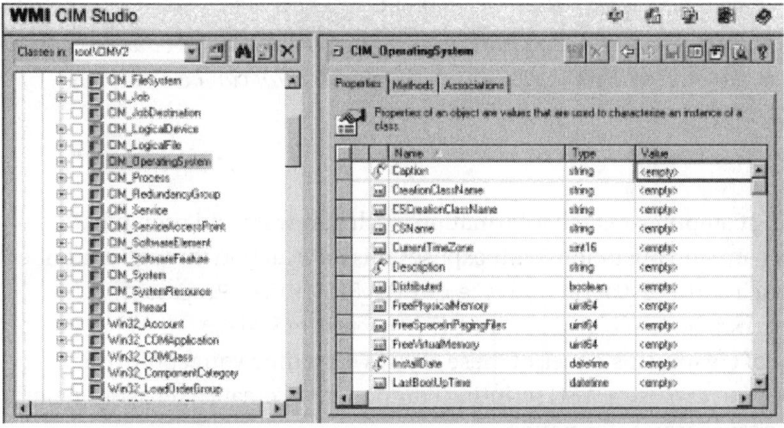

Figure 10-2. WMI CIM Studio

You can now browse the classes within the namespace and inspect the properties exposed by any given class.

A useful feature of the WMI CIM Studio is the capability to create instances of any given class. This allows for the properties of the created objects to be browsed.

To create instance(s) of a class, select the class from the WMI CIM Studio and select the Instances button.

Figure 10-3 shows the results of creating an instance of the `Win32_ComputerSystem` class from the WMI CIM Studio.

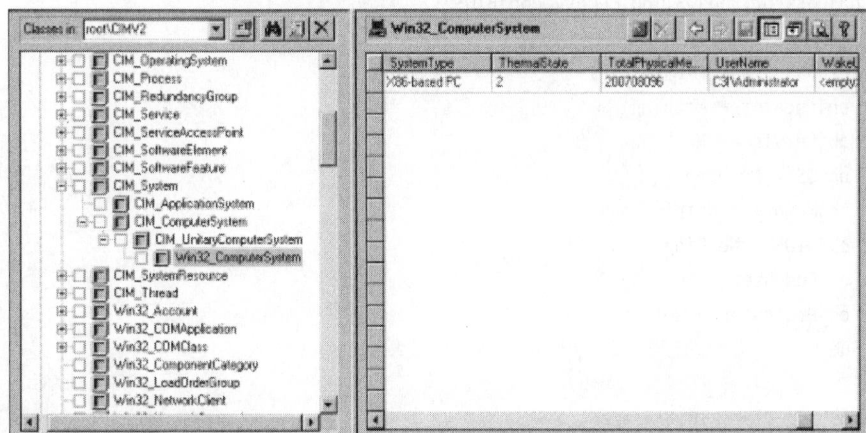

Figure 10-3. `Win32_ComputerSystem` *class*

> **NOTE** *Some classes cannot be instantiated from the WMI CIM Studio. Other classes may return more instances of objects than can be displayed in the WMI CIM Studio.*

Querying computer-related information, such hardware and user information, is a common operation. WMI exposes this information through a number of classes, such as `Win32_OperatingSystem`, `Win32_BIOS`, `Win32_Processor`, `Win32_LogicalMemoryConfiguration`, and `Win32_ComputerSystem`.

Instead of creating instances of these classes each time you require this information, you can use a WSC scripting component to create a reusable generic object that exposes this information.

The following two code listings show the code for such an object. The first segment contains the code for a `SysInfo` class. This contains the logic to create instances of WMI objects.

The second segment contains the code for the actual WSC object. The object uses the code from the `SysInfo` class to generate the system information, which is then encapsulated and exposed in the component.

```
'Sysinfo class
Option Explicit
Const Impersonate = 3
Class SysInfo

Dim objService, objComputer, objProcessor
Dim objLocator, objOS, objMemory, objBIOS

Private Sub Class_Terminate()
 Set objLocator = Nothing
 Set objService = Nothing
 Set objOS = Nothing
 Set objMemory = Nothing
 Set objBIOS = Nothing
 Set objComputer = Nothing
 Set objProcessor = Nothing
End Sub

Private Sub Class_Initialize()

  Set objLocator = CreateObject("WbemScripting.SWbemLocator")
```

```
  'connect to specified machine
  Set objService = objLocator.ConnectServer()
  objService.Security_.ImpersonationLevel =  Impersonate

  Set objOS = GetReference("Win32_OperatingSystem")
  Set objMemory = GetReference("Win32_LogicalMemoryConfiguration")
  Set objBIOS = GetReference("Win32_BIOS")
  Set objComputer = GetReference("Win32_ComputerSystem")
  Set objProcessor = GetReference("Win32_Processor")
 End Sub

Private Function GetReference(strObjectName)
 Dim objInstance, objObjectSet

 'get reference to object
 Set objObjectSet = objService.InstancesOf(strObjectName)
 'loop through and get reference to specified
 For Each objInstance In objObjectSet
    Set GetReference = objInstance
 Next

End Function

Public Property Get BIOSObject()
  Set BIOSObject = objBIOS
End Property

Public Property Get ProcessorObject()
  Set ProcessorObject = objProcessor
End Property

Public Property Get MemoryObject()
  Set MemoryObject = objMemory
End Property

Public Property Get OSObject()
  Set OSObject = objOS
End Property

End Class

<?xml version="1.0"?>
<component>
```

```
<registration
    description="SysInfo"
    progid="ENTWSH.SysInfo"
    version="1.00"
    classid="{91e4c710-9a6c-11d3-bc4a-00104b164591}"
>
</registration>
<public>
    <property name="BIOSVersion">
        <get/>
    </property>
    <property name="CPU">
        <get/>
    </property>
    <property name="Memory">
        <get/>
    </property>
    <property name="OS">
        <get/>
    </property>
    <property name="RegisteredUser">
        <get/>
    </property>
    <property name="SerialNumber">
        <get/>
    </property>
    <property name="VirtualMemory">
        <get/>
    </property>
</public>
<script language="VBScript" src="sysinfo.vbs"></script>
<script language="VBScript">
<![CDATA[
Dim BIOSVersion,CPU, Memory, OS, RegisteredUser, SerialNumber
Dim VirtualMemory
Dim objSysInfo
'create a new instance of the SysInfo class
Set objSysInfo = New SysInfo

'return BIOS version
Function get_BIOSVersion()
    get_BIOSVersion = objSysInfo.BIOSObject.Version
End Function
```

```
'return CPU information
Function get_CPU()
    get_CPU = objSysInfo.ProcessorObject.CurrentClockSpeed & "Mhz " & _
            objSysInfo.ProcessorObject.Name & _
            ", " & objSysInfo.ProcessorObject.Description
End Function

'return total physical memory
Function get_Memory()
    get_Memory = objSysInfo.MemoryObject.TotalPhysicalMemory
End Function

'return OS information
Function get_OS()
     Dim strOS

 strOS = objSysInfo.OSObject.Caption & ", Ver:" & _
        objSysInfo.OSObject.Version

  If Not IsNull(objSysInfo.OSObject.BuildNumber) Then _
        strOS = strOS & ", Build:" & objSysInfo.OSObject.BuildNumber
  If Not IsNull(objSysInfo.OSObject.BuildType) Then strOS = _
         strOS & ", Build Type:" & objSysInfo.OSObject.BuildType
  If Not IsNull(objSysInfo.OSObject.CSDVersion) Then strOS =_
        strOS & ", SP:" & objSysInfo.OSObject.CSDVersion
  get_OS = strOS
End Function

'return who software is registered to
Function get_RegisteredUser()
    get_RegisteredUser = objSysInfo.OSObject.RegisteredUser
End Function

'return OS serial #
Function get_SerialNumber()
    get_SerialNumber = objSysInfo.OSObject.SerialNumber
End Function

'return virtual memory
Function get_VirtualMemory()
    get_VirtualMemory = objSysInfo.MemoryObject.TotalVirtualMemory
End Function
```

```
]]>
</script>
</component>
```

The advantage of using a class object is the `Class_Initialize` and `Class_Terminate` subroutines. The `Class_Initialize` routine is executed upon creation of the class, while the `Class_Terminate` method executes upon termination of the class. This ensures that a cleanup of object resources is performed and no separate methods need to be called to initialize the objects before performing operations.

To use the object, register the `SysInfo.wsc` scripting component file by either right-clicking the file from Explorer and selecting register or by using the `regsvr32.exe` program from the command line:

```
regsvr32.exe SysInfo.wsc
```

The object is demonstrated in the following snippet:

```
Dim objSysInfo
Set objSysInfo = CreateObject("ENTWSH.SysInfo")
WScript.Echo "BIOS Version:" & objSysInfo.BIOSVersion
 WScript.Echo "CPU:" & objSysInfo.CPU
 WScript.Echo "Memory:" & objSysInfo.Memory
 WScript.Echo "O/S Version:" & objSysInfo.OS
 WScript.Echo "O/S Registered User:" & objSysInfo.RegisteredUser
 WScript.Echo "O/S Serial #:" & objSysInfo.SerialNumber
 WScript.Echo "Virtual Memory:" & objSysInfo.VirtualMemory
```

See Also

See the following topics from the WMI SDK: "Object Creation and Monikers" and "Connecting To WMI." For more information, search `http://msdn.microsoft.com` for the articles "Win32_OperatingSystem," "Win32_ComputerSystem," "Win32_LogicalMemoryConfiguration," "Win32_Processor," "Windows Management Instrumentation: Administering Windows and Applications across Your Enterprise," and "Win32_BIOS."

10.2 Determining the Role of a Computer

Problem

You want to determine if a computer is a network primary domain controller.

Solution

The Win32_ComputerSystem class contains computer-related information properties, such as make and model. It also exposes a Roles property, which is an array of values listing what roles a computer performs. Roles include the OS type as well as services the computer may run, such as PDC, BDC, SQL, and browse master.

The ispdc.vbs script creates an instance of the Win32_ComputerSystem class for the local computer and checks if the Roles property contains Primary_Domain_Controller.

```
'ISPDC.VBS
'checks if computer is a Primary Domain Controller (PDC)
Dim objWMIObject, objServices, objNetwork, nF, bFound, objRole
Set objNetwork = CreateObject("WScript.Network")
'get an instance of the Win32_ComputerSystem for the local computer
Set objWMIObject = _
            GetObject("winmgmts:{impersonationLevel=impersonate}" & _
            "!Win32_ComputerSystem='" & objNetwork.ComputerName & "'")
bFound = False

'check if Roles property is Empty array
If Not IsNull(objWMIObject.roles) Then
  'loop through roles array and check if it contains any occurrence
'of Primary_Domain_Controller
For nF = LBound(objWMIObject.roles) To UBound(objWMIObject.roles)
   For Each objRole In objWMIObject.Roles
    If objRole = "Primary_Domain_Controller" Then
        bFound = True
        Exit For
    End If
  Next
End If

'if PDC then return -1, otherwise 0
If bFound Then WScript.Quit -1
WScript.Quit 0
```

The script can be used from a batch file to determine if the computer the script is executing on is a PDC. The `WScript.Quit` method sets the ERRORLEVEL environment variable to –1 within the script if a PDC is detected and 0 if it is not a PDC. This can be

```
Rem Execute the ispdc.vbs script
cscript ispdc.vbs
Rem Check if ERRORLEVEL was set to -1, which indicates a PDC
If ERRORLEVEL = -1 Goto Exit
Echo This is not a PDC
:Exit
```

Discussion

To create an instance of the `Win32_ComputerSystem` class for your local computer, reference the class using the key property. The key for the `Win32_ComputerSystem` class is the computer name. The following code gets a reference to the computer Thor:

```
Const WMIConnect = "winmgmts:{impersonationLevel=impersonate}!:"
Dim objWMIObject
Set objWMIObject = _
GetObject("WMIConnect & Win32_ComputerSystem.Name='Thor'")
```

If you intend to perform multiple WMI operations against a local or remote computer, it is more efficient to first get a reference to the WMI service and then create instances of the WMI class from that service:

```
Dim objWMIObject, objServices

'get an instance to the Services object for the default namespace on '
'remote computer Odin
Set objServices = _
 GetObject("winmgmts:{impersonationLevel=impersonate}!\\odin")
'get an instance of the WMI class Win32_ComputerSystem for computer Odin
  Set objWMIObject = _
    objServices.Get("Win32_ComputerSystem='odin'")

'output  some info about the computer
WScript.Echo "Owner: " & objWMIObject.PrimaryOwnerName
WScript.Echo "Startup delay: " & objWMIObject.SystemStartupDelay
```

The Win32_ComputerSystem object's Roles property is an array of values that identify what operations the computer can perform. Examples of roles for Windows NT and 2000 computers are LM_Workstation, LM_Server, SQLServer, Primary_Domain_Controller, Print, Master_Browser, and Backup_Browser.

WMI array properties can contain one or more items. If empty, they contain a Null value. The Lbound and Ubound functions are used to determine the upper and lower index of the array, because it's not guaranteed the provider will return an array starting with 0 or 1 subscript:

```
'get a reference to local computer Odin
Set objWMIObject = _
        GetObject("winmgmts:{impersonationLevel=impersonate}" & _
        "!Win32_ComputerSystem='Odin'")

'check if empty array and then print each role
If Not IsNull(objWMIObject.roles) Then
  For nF = Lbound(objWMIObject.roles) To Ubound(objWMIObject.roles)
     WScript.Echo objWMIObject.roles(nF)
  Next
End If
```

See Also

See the following topics from the WMI SDK: "Object Creation and Monikers" and "Connecting To WMI." For more information, search http://msdn.microsoft.com for the article "Win32_ComputerSystem."

10.3 Obtaining IP Information

Problem

You want to determine IP information for the active network cards that are installed on your computer.

Solution

Use the ExecQuery method of the WMI service object to execute a WQL query against the Win32_NetworkAdapterConfiguration class, specifying criteria so only IP-enabled network adapters are returned.

The following sample script lists the physical MAC address and IP address(es) for each IP-enabled device:

```
'IPMacInfo.vbs
'list IP and MAC information for local computer
Const wbemFlagReturnImmediately =16
Const wbemFlagForwardOnly = 32
Dim objServices, objWMIObjects, objWMIObject, nF

'create Services object for default namespace on local computer
Set objServices = GetObject("winmgmts:{impersonationLevel=impersonate}")
'get all instances of IP enabled devices for
'Win32_NetworkAdapterConfiguration class
Set objWMIObjects = _
                         objServices.ExecQuery( _
                         "Select * From Win32_NetworkAdapterConfiguration" _
                          & " Where IPEnabled = True",, wbemFlagReturnImmediately _
                              + wbemFlagForwardOnly)
'enumerate each Win32_NetworkAdapterConfiguration instance
For Each objWMIObject In objWMIObjects
   WScript.Echo objWMIObject.Caption & " has the MAC address " _
                                  & objWMIObject.MACAddress
    'make sure array is not empty
    If Not IsNull(objWMIObject.IPAddress) Then
     'list all associated IP addresses with adapter
     For nF = 0 To UBound(objWMIObject.IPAddress)
        WScript.Echo "     " & objWMIObject.IPAddress(nF)
     Next
    End If
Next
```

Discussion

The `Win32_NetworkAdapterConfiguration` class contains information related to network adapters installed on your computer. A network adapter refers to any device that is bound to an address, and it may be a physical device, such as a network card, or a virtual device, such as an RAS service or proxy agent.

You may have other network devices that are not IP-enabled. An instance of the `Win32_NetworkAdapterConfiguration` class has an `IPEnabled` Boolean property that if set to `True` is bound to an IP address.

You could enumerate all instances of the Win32_NetworkAdapterConfiguration class to filter out any IP-enabled instances, or alternatively you could execute a query against the WMI service provider to return only the instances that meet the criteria.

WMI allows for SQL-like queries to be executed against the WMI Service provider. These queries return information limited by the criteria in the query:

```
Set objWMIObjectSet = objService.ExecQuery(strQuery[, strLanguage][,nFlags])
```

The strQuery parameter represents the query to be executed. The query is defined using WQL, which resembles SQL. The query starts with a SELECT statement followed by properties to return and criteria:

```
SELECT fieldcriteria FROM WMIClass WHERE Criteria
```

WQL queries cannot contain ORDER BY statements like SQL dialects, nor can it contain any functions.

The strLanguage parameter is the language to be interpreted by the ExecQuery method. The strLanguage parameter defaults to WQL and should not be changed.

The nFlags parameter is a combination of numeric values that determines the behavior of the ExecQuery method. This value defaults to 16, which causes ExecQuery to return immediately with results. Adding the value 32 to the flag makes query results forward-only. This provides faster query performance.

A successfully executed query returns the results in the form of a collection of instances of the object. This is the same type of collection returned by the InstancesOf method except it only returns instances that meet any criteria in the query.

Table 10-3 lists commonly referenced network device properties.

Table 10-3. Win32_NetworkAdapterConfiguration *Properties*

PROPERTY	TYPE	DESCRIPTION
IPAddress	Array of strings	IP addresses associated with the device.
DefaultIPGateway	Array of strings	Computer gateways associated with the computer. The default gateway is the first element of the array.
DHCPEnabled	Boolean	If True, DHCP is enabled; otherwise, False.
MACAddress	String	Physical MAC address.

continues

Table 10-3. Win32_NetworkAdapterConfiguration *Properties (continued)*

PROPERTY	TYPE	DESCRIPTION
WINSPrimaryServer	String	Address of primary WINS server.
WINSSecondaryServer	String	Address of secondary WINS server.
DNSEnabledForWinsResolution	Boolean	If True, DNS for Windows name resolution is enabled.
DNSDomain	String	Name of DNS domain.
DNSHostName	String	Name of DNS host.

This information can be queried using the following command-line script, ipinfo.wsf:

```
<?xml version="1.0" ?>
<job>
<!--comment
Script:ipinfo.wsf
Description:lists ip information
-->
 <script language="VBScript" src="wmiinc.vbs">
 <![CDATA[
 Option Explicit
 Const wbemFlagReturnImmediately  =16
 Const wbemFlagForwardOnly = 32
  Dim objWMIObject, nF, objWMIObjects, objService, bFirst
  On Error Resume Next
    'check if command line argument specified, if so then connect to
  'remote computer
  If WScript.Arguments.Count = 1 Then
    Set objService = GetObject( _
                  "winmgmts:{impersonationLevel=impersonate}!" _
                  & "\\" & WScript.Arguments(0))
  Else
    Set objService = GetObject( _
                  "winmgmts:{impersonationLevel=impersonate}")
  End If

 If Err Then _
      ExitScript("Error getting reference to WMI service")
```

```
 Set objWMIObjects = _
                objService.ExecQuery( _
                "Select * From Win32_NetworkAdapterConfiguration" _
              & " Where IPEnabled = True",, wbemFlagReturnImmediately  _
                + wbemFlagForwardOnly)

If Err Then _
     ExitScript("Error getting reference to network adapter information")

  bFirst = False
 'loop through each IP enabled device
 For Each objWMIObject In objWMIObjects
   'is it the first adapter -print IP info that applies to all adapters
   If Not bFirst Then

     If Not objWMIObject.DNSDomain = "" Then
         WScript.Echo "DNS Domain:" & objWMIObject.DNSDomain
     End If

     If Not objWMIObject.DNSHostName = "" Then
         WScript.Echo "DNS Host:" & objWMIObject.DNSHostName
     End If

      If Not objWMIObject.WINSScopeID = "" Then _
                WScript.Echo "NETBIOS Scope ID: "& _
                              objWBEMObject.WINSScopeID
     WScript.Echo "DNS Enabled for WINS resolution:"_
                 & Cbool(objWMIObject.DNSEnabledForWinsResolution)
          bFirst = True
      WScript.Echo
   End If

   ShowInfo(objWMIObject)
   WScript.Echo
 Next

 'Procedure: showinfo
 'lists IP related information for specified network device
 'Parameters:
 'objWBEMObject Object representing network device
 Sub ShowInfo(objWBEMObject)
  WScript.Echo "Device#:" & objWBEMObject.Index
  WScript.Echo objWBEMObject.Description
```

```
      'loop through each IP address for the adapter
       For nF = Lbound(objWBEMObject.IPAddress) To _
                                          Ubound(objWBEMObject.IPAddress)
           WScript.Echo "IP Address:" & objWBEMObject.IPAddress(nF) _
                   & " Subnet Mask:" & objWBEMObject.IPSubnet(nF)
       Next

     'check if IP gateway addresses assigned
     If Not IsNull(objWBEMObject.DefaultIPGateway) Then
     'list all ip gateways
      For nF = Lbound(objWBEMObject.DefaultIPGateway) _
                 To Ubound(objWBEMObject.DefaultIPGateway)
       WScript.Echo "IP Gateway:" & objWBEMObject.DefaultIPGateway(nF)
      Next
     End If

    'list DHCP related info
      WScript.Echo "DHCP Enabled:" & objWBEMObject.DHCPEnabled
      If objWBEMObject.DHCPEnabled Then
           WScript.Echo "DHCP Lease Obtained:" _
              & DMTFDate2String(objWBEMObject.DHCPLeaseObtained)

         WScript.Echo "DHCP Lease Expires:" _
              & DMTFDate2String(objWBEMObject.DHCPLeaseExpires)
      End If

     'list MAC address and WINS server information
      WScript.Echo "MAC Address :" & objWBEMObject.MACAddress

      WScript.Echo "WINS primary server  :" _
       & objWBEMObject.WINSPrimaryServer

      WScript.Echo "WINS secondary server:" & _
                         objWBEMObject.WINSSecondaryServer

      Set objWBEMObject = Nothing
     End Sub
     ]]>
     </script>
    </job>
```

The ipinfo.wsf script displays information for any IP-enabled network device it finds. It functions similarly to the Windows NT ipconfig utility, listing the device description, IP address, MAC address, and DHCP and WINS settings for each device.

The script must be run from the DOS command. It requires no parameters, but it can take an optional computer name as a parameter. If a computer name is specified, the script attempts to connect to the computer using WMI and list the IP information for that computer.

The ipinfo.wsf script uses functions from the wmiinc.vbs support code file. The wmiinc.vbs file contains a number of WMI-related routines for performing date conversion, error handling, and connection to WMI services, and it is used in other scripts in this chapter.

```
'wmiinc.vbs
'contains reusable WMI support code
Option Explicit
Const WMIConst = "winmgmts:{impersonationLevel=impersonate}!"
Const wbemCimtypeDatetime =101
Const wbemCimtypeString = 8
Const wbemCimtypeChar16 = 103
Const Impersonate = 3
'ExitScript
'Displays message and terminates script
'Parameters:
'strMessage    Message to display
'bStdOut       Boolean value. If true then writes to StdErr
Sub ExitScript(strMessage, bStdOut)

If bStdOut Then
    'get a reference to the StdErr object stream
    WScript.StdErr.WriteLine strMessage
Else
    WScript.Echo strMessage
End If
    WScript.Quit
End Sub

Function Convert2DMTFDate(dDate, nTimeZone)
Dim sTemp, sTimeZone

sTimeZone = nTimeZone
If nTimeZone>=0 Then sTimeZone = "+" & sTimeZone
sTemp = Year(Now) & Pad(Month(dDate), 2, "0") & Pad(Day(dDate), 2, "0")
```

```
sTemp = sTemp & Pad(Hour(dDate), 2, "0") & Pad(Minute(dDate), 2, "0")
sTemp = sTemp & Pad(Second(dDate), 2, "0") & ".000000" & sTimeZone
Convert2DMTFDate = sTemp
End Function

Function Pad(sPadString, nWidth, sPadChar)
    If Len(sPadString) < nWidth Then
        Pad = String(nWidth - Len(sPadString), sPadChar) & sPadString
    Else
        Pad = sPadString
    End If

End Function

'DMTFDate2String
'Converts WMI DMTF dates to a readable string
'Parameters:
'strDate    Date in DMTF format
'Returns
'formatted date string
Function DMTFDate2String(strDate)
 strDate = Cstr(strDate)
 DMTFDate2String = Mid(strDate, 5, 2) & "/" & Mid(strDate, 7, 2) _
          & "/" & Mid(strDate, 1, 4) & " " & Mid(strDate, 9, 2) _
          & ":" & Mid(strDate, 11, 2) & ":" & Mid(strDate, 13, 2)
End Function

'check if script is being run interactively
'Returns:True if run from command line, otherwise false
Function IsCscript()
  If StrComp(Right(WScript.Fullname,11),"cscript.exe", vbTextCompare)=0 Then
    IsCscript = True
  Else
    IsCscript = False
  End If
End Function

'GetBinarySID
'Returns user's SID as array of integer values
'Parameters:
'strAccount User account in Domain\username or username format
'Returns
```

```
'array of integer values if successful, otherwise Null
Function GetBinarySID(strAccount)
Dim objAccounts, objAccount, bDomain, bFound, objSIDAccount

bDomain = False
bFound = False
'check if a backslash exists in the account name. if so search for
'domainname\accountname
If InStr(strAccount, "\") > 0 Then bDomain = False

'get an instance of the Win32_Account object
Set objAccounts = GetObject( WMICONST & "root\cimv2") _
                    .InstancesOf("Win32_Account")

'loop through each account
For Each objAccount In objAccounts
    'if domain name specified, search against account caption
    If bDomain Then
        'check if name is found
        If StrComp(objAccount.Caption, strAccount, vbTextCompare) = 0 Then
            bFound = True
            Exit For
        End If
    Else 'check against just user name
        If StrComp(objAccount.Name, strAccount, vbTextCompare) = 0 Then
        'check if name is found
            bFound = True
            Exit For
        End If
    End If
    Next

'if found then retrieve SID binary array
If bFound Then
Set objSIDAccount=GetObject(WMICONST & "Win32_SID.SID=" _
                & """ & objAccount.sid & """)
    GetBinarySID = objSIDAccount.BinaryRepresentation
Else
    GetBinarySID = Null
End If
End Function
```

```
Class WMISupport
 Dim objLocator, strErrorMsg, objService
 Dim strServer, strNameSpace, strUserName, strPassword


'creates WMI session and returns WMI service object
 Function Connect()
    On Error Resume Next
    'set the default return value
    Connect = Null
    'create locator object
    Set objLocator = CreateObject("WbemScripting.SWbemLocator")

   If Err Then
    strErrorMsg =  "Error getting reference to WBEM locator object"
    Exit Function
   End If
   'connect to specified machine
   Set objService = objLocator.ConnectServer(strServer, _
                             strNameSpace, strUserName, _
                             strPassword)

   If Err Then
    strErrorMsg =  "Error connecting to " & strServer
    Exit Function
   End If
    'set impersonation level to Impersonate
    objService.Security_.ImpersonationLevel = Impersonate

   If Err Then
    strErrorMsg =  "Error setting security level"
    Exit Function
   End If
    Set Connect = objService
 End Function

 Public Property Let Computer (strComputerName)
    strServer = strComputerName
 End Property

 Public Property Let UserName (strUser)
    strUserName =strUser
 End Property
```

```
 Public Property Let Password (strPass)
    strPassword = strPass
 End Property

 Public Property Let NameSpace (strNameSpc)
    strNameSpace = strNameSpc
 End Property

 Public Property Get ErrorMessage()
  Set ErrorMessage = strErrorMsg
 End Property
End Class
```

See Also

See the following topics from the WMI SDK: "WMI Query Language" and "SWbemServices." For more information, search `http://msdn.microsoft.com` for the article "Win32_NetworkAdapterConfiguration."

10.4 Changing the Location of an NT Dump File

Problem

You want to change the location of the memory dump file for Windows NT.

Solution

You can create an instance of the `Win32_OSRecoveryConfiguration` class and set the `DebugFilePath` property:

```
'osrecover.vbs
Dim objServices
Dim objWMIObject, objWMIObjects
'create an instance of a Services object for the local machine
Set objServices = _
    GetObject("winmgmts:{impersonationLevel=impersonate}!root\cimv2")

'create an instance of the Win32_OSRecoveryOption class
Set objWMIObjects = objServices.InstancesOf _
                        ("Win32_OSRecoveryConfiguration")
```

```
'loop through each object (there will be only one)
For Each objWMIObject In objWMIObjects
    'set the DebugFilePath property
    objWMIObject.DebugFilePath = "d:\MEMORY.DMP"
    'update the settings
    Call objWMIObject.Put_
Next
```

Discussion

Windows NT/2000/2003/XP recovery information is exposed through the `Win32_OSRecoveryConfiguration` class. Properties that are available through this class include location of the dump file, notification, and reboot information should Windows NT/2000/2003 encounter a crash (i.e., Blue Screen Of Death, or BSOD).

Table 10-4 lists some the properties that can be modified.

Table 10-4. `Win32_OSRecoveryConfiguration` *Properties*

PROPERTY	TYPE	DESCRIPTION
AutoReboot	Boolean	Automatically reboot at BSOD
DebugFilePath	String	File to write debug information in event of BSOD
SendAdminAlert	Boolean	Determines if alert is sent to administrators in event of BSOD
WriteToSystemLogFile	Boolean	Determines if message should be written to Event Viewer system log in event of BSOD
WriteDebugInfo	Boolean	Determines if debug information should be written to file specified by DebugFilePath property

To change a property, update it with the new value you want to assign to it and invoke the object's `Put_` method. Object properties are not updated until this method is invoked.

If the properties are successfully updated, the `Put_` method returns a WMI `Path` object. This object contains information about the path to the updated object. If the `Put_` method is unsuccessful, it returns an `Empty` object and generates an error.

To determine if a property can be written to, use the WMI CIM Studio included with the WMI SDK or the WMI SDK documentation at `http://msdn.microsoft.com/library`.

WMI CIM Studio provides a visual method of inspecting class properties and determining how the can be manipulated. Figure 10-4 shows the `Win32_OSRecoveryOption` class viewed by the WMI CIM Studio.

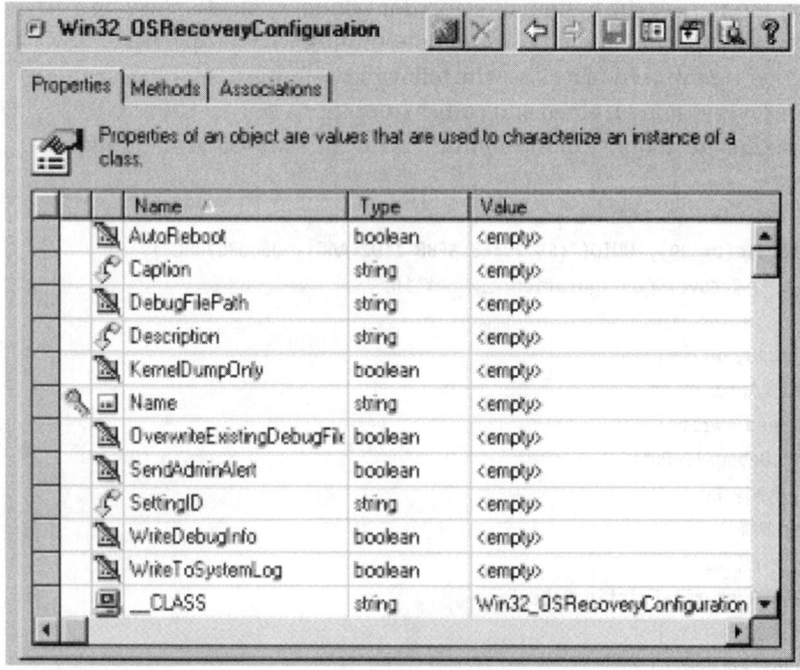

Figure 10-4. `Win32_OSRecoveryOption` *class details*

Table 10-5 describes the class property icons.

Table 10-5. Class Property Icons

ICON	DESCRIPTION
	Property can be written to.
	System property.
	Property inherited from another class.
	Local property.
	Key property. This is the property used to create instances of the class.

If you do not have the SDK, as a last resort you can read the Managed Object Format (MOF) files. A MOF file contains the definition for WMI classes and is used to define the interface between the provider and WMI.

MOF files are stored under the System32 directory for Windows NT/2000/2003/XP computers or the System directory for Windows 9*x*/ME. Viewing MOF files is a simple but effective way of determining what properties and methods are exposed in a class. The following definition is for the `Win32_OSRecoveryConfiguration` and comes from the `CIMWIN32.MOF` file, which contains the majority of the definitions for the `root\cimv2` namespace:

```
[Dynamic, Provider ("CIMWin32") ,
        Locale(0x409), UUID("{8502C4E8-5FBB-11D2-AAC1-006008C78BC7}") ]
class Win32_OSRecoveryConfiguration:CIM_Setting
{
        [read, write]
    boolean AutoReboot ;
        [read, write]
    string DebugFilePath ;
        [read, key]
    string Name ;
        [read, write]
    boolean OverwriteExistingDebugFile ;
        [read, write]
    boolean SendAdminAlert ;
        [read, write]
    boolean WriteDebugInfo ;
        [read, write]
    boolean WriteToSystemLog ;
};
```

> **NOTE** *The MOF file structure has been changed in the latest versions of WMI, but it can still be used to determine class information.*

See Also

For more information, search `http://msdn.microsoft.com` for the article "Win32_OSRecoveryConfiguration."

10.5 Setting TCP/IP Information

Problem

You want to set network adapter TCP/IP settings.

Solution

You can create an instance of the `Win32_NetworkAdapterConfiguration` class for a network adapter. The following code sample gets the first network adapter and sets a static IP address:

```
Const WMICConst = "winmgmts:{impersonationLevel=impersonate}!"
Dim objWMINetConfig, nResult

'get the instance for the first adapter
Set objWMINetConfig = _
    GetObject(WMICConst & "Win32_NetworkAdapterConfiguration.Index=1")

'assign two static IP addresses to the adapter
nResult=objWMINetConfig.EnableStatic(Array("192.168.1.2","192.168.1.3"), _
                                     Array("255.255.255.0", "255.255.255.0"))
```

Discussion

Network configuration information is exposed through properties of the `Win32_NetworkAdapterConfiguration` class. All of the properties are read-only.

A number of methods are exposed through the class that provides the ability to configure network adapters. This includes the ability to set IP addresses, and configure WINS and DHCP.

To set a setting for a specific adapter, get a reference to the adapter you want to access. Each adapter is identified by a number, starting sequentially from either 0 or 1. There is no specific logic as to the order of the adapters, but generally the default network adapter appears as the first device.

Once you have a `Win32_NetworkAdapterConfiguration` instance, you can invoke a method to modify an IP-related setting. The following sample renews the DHCP address associated with the network adapter with ID 1:

```
Const WMIConst = "winmgmts:{impersonationLevel=impersonate}!"
Dim objWMINetConfig
'get the instance for the adapter with ID 1
```

```
Set objWMINetConfig = _
    GetObject(WMIConst & " Win32_NetworkAdapterConfiguration.Index=1")

'renew the DHCP address for the adapter
objWMINetConfig.RenewDHCPLease
```

A number of DHCP-related operations can be executed by calling any of the methods listed in Table 10-6 from an instance of the `Win32_NetworkAdapterConfiguration` class.

Table 10-6. `Win32_NetworkAdapterConfiguration` *Class Methods*

METHOD	DESCRIPTION
EnableDHCP	Enables DHCP addresses for the adapter. Any static IP addresses associated with the adapter are lost.
RenewDHCPLease	Renews the DHCP lease for the adapter.
ReleaseDHCPLease	Releases the DHCP lease for the adapter.

These methods return 0 if they are successful. If a nonzero value is returned, an error occurred while performing the operation. Runtime errors generally do not occur if the execution of the method fails.

To set a static IP address for an adapter, use the `EnableStatic` method. The syntax is as follows:

```
nResult = objWMIObject.EnableStatic(aIpAddress,aSubnetMask)
```

`aIpAddress` is an array of IP addresses and `aSubnetMask` is an array of corresponding subnet mask addresses. The earlier Solution script assigns two IP addresses to an adapter. Setting a static IP address overrides the existing DHCP settings, while enabling DHCP disables any static IP addresses.

Network gateways and WINS servers can also be set. The `SetWINSServer` method sets an IP address for the primary and optionally the secondary server:

```
nResult = objWMINetConfig.SetWINSServer(strPrimaryServer[, strSecondaryServer])
```

`strPrimaryServer` is the IP address for the primary WINS server. The optional `strSecondaryServer` argument sets the secondary WINS server.

```
nResult = objWMINetConfig. SetGateways (aGateWays)
```

The SetGateways method takes an array of strings as a parameter. Each element of the array can contain an IP address representing a WINS gateway.

These methods return 0 if they are successful. If a nonzero value is returned, an error occurred during the execution of the method.

```
Const WMICONST = "winmgmts:{impersonationLevel=impersonate}!"
Dim objWMINetConfig, nResult

'get the instance for the first adapter
Set objWMINetConfig = _
    GetObject(WMICONST & "Win32_NetworkAdapterConfiguration.Index=1")

'set the primary WINS server
nResult = objWMINetConfig.SetWINSServer("192.161.1.1")
'set WINS gateway
nResult = objWMINetConfig.SetGateways(Array("192.161.1.1"))
```

The SetWINSServer method in the previous sample only set the first parameter, PrimaryWINSServer. While this is valid, any value in the secondary WINS server will be overwritten, even though the parameter wasn't specified.

When you set multiple gateway addresses, the first array element represents the default gateway.

NOTE *The OS you are executing these methods under may impose limitations on the functionality of the method. For example, Windows 9x does not support multiple IP addresses per adapter.*

There are network settings that apply to all IP-enabled adapters as a whole and are not set per adapter. Methods that can only be invoked on class objects and not instances of a class are known as *static* methods.

For example, the RenewDHCPLeaseAll and ReleaseDHCPLeaseAll methods affect the DHCP settings for all adapters.

To determine if a method is static, use the WMI CIM Studio to view the qualifiers for the method. To view method qualifiers, find the method for the appropriate class you are querying and double-click the class. Figure 10-5 shows the qualifiers for the EnableWINS method.

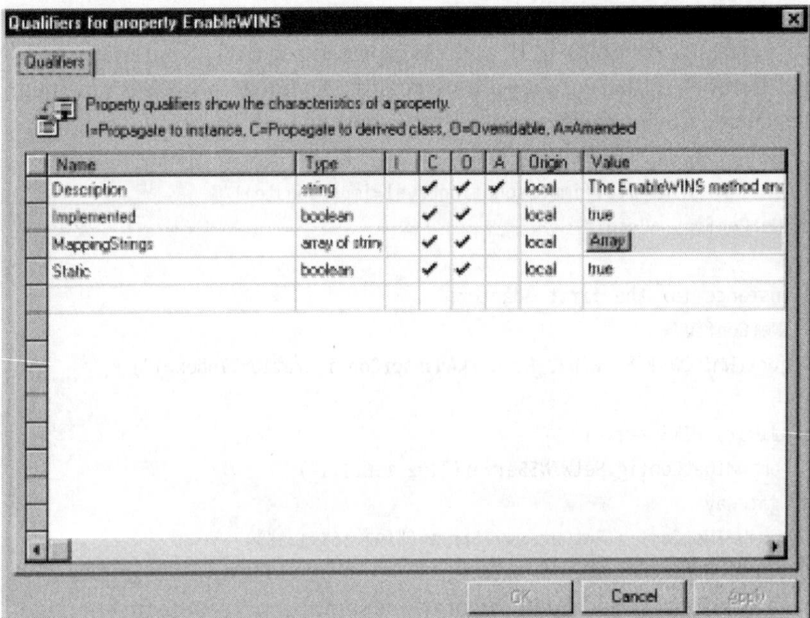

Figure 10-5. `EnableWINS` *qualifiers*

The `Static` qualifier indicates the method can only be invoked on the class object.

The following sample renews the DHCP leases for all adapters:

```
Const WMICONST = "winmgmts:{impersonationLevel=impersonate}!"

Dim objWMINetConfig, nResult

'get an instance of the Win32_NetworkAdapterConfiguration class
Set objWMINetConfig = _
    GetObject(WMICONST & "Win32_NetworkAdapterConfiguration")

'set the primary WINS server
nResult = objWMINetConfig.RenewDHCPLeaseAll
```

Table 10-7 lists static methods.

Table 10-7. `Win32_NetworkAdapterConfiguration` *Static Methods*

METHOD	DESCRIPTION
`RenewDHCPLeaseAll`	Renews all DHCP addresses for all adapters
`ReleaseDHCPLeaseAll`	Releases the DHCP lease for the adapter

The following script, ipmaint.wsf, provides general-purpose IP maintenance facilities. It allows network settings for static IP, DHCP, WINS, and DNS settings to be manipulated.

```
<?xml version="1.0" ?>
<job>
<!--comment
Script:ipmaint.wsf
Description:
Performs IP adapter maintenance
-->
 <script language="VBScript" src="wmiinc.vbs">
 <![CDATA[
 Dim objWMINetAdapter, objWMINetConfig, nF
 Dim nDevice, strAddress, strAction, strGatewayAddress, strDHCPAction
 Dim strWINSPrimary, strWINSSecondary, bWINSAddress, strDHCPAllAction
 Dim bLMHostsLookup, bDNSForWinsRes, strWINSScopeID, bEnableWins
 Dim aAddress, strDNSDomain, nResult
  strDHCPAction = ""
 strAddress = ""
 nDevice = 1
 strDNSDomain = ""

 'check if script is being run from command prompt
 If Not IsCscript Then
  ExitScript "This script must be run from command line using cscript.exe",False
 End If

 'check the argument count
 If WScript.Arguments.Count = 0 Then
   ShowUsage
   WScript.Quit
 End If

   'get an instance of the Win32_NetworkAdapterConfiguration class
   Set objWMINetConfig = _
    GetObject(WMICONST & "Win32_NetworkAdapterConfiguration")

   If Err Then _
       ExitScript "Unable to get a reference to IP information", True

   'retrieve current default settings for IP global settings..
   bLMHostsLookup = objWMINetConfig.WINSEnableLMHostsLookup
```

```
bDNSForWinsRes = objWMINetConfig.DNSEnabledForWINSResolution
strWINSScopeID = objWMINetConfig.WINSScopeID
bEnableWins = False

strWINSPrimary = objWMINetConfig.WINSPrimaryServer
strWINSSecondary = objWMINetConfig.WINSSecondaryServer
bWINSAddress = False
GetArguments
'check if WINS enabling is specified
If bEnableWins Then
 'enable WINS settings
    nResult = objWMINetConfig.EnableWINS(bDNSForWinsRes, bLMHostsLookup _
              , Null, strWINSScopeID)

 If Err  Then ExitScript "Error enabling WINS settings", True
 WScript.Echo "Successfully set WINS settings"
End If

'check if DHCP operation for all devices is specified
If Not strDHCPAllAction = "" Then
 'release ALL DHCP addresses?
    If strDHCPAction = "RELEASEDHCP" Then
     nResult = objWMINetConfig.ReleaseDHCPLeaseAll

     If Err Or Not nResult = 0 Then _
        ExitScript "Error releasing DHCP leases", True

     WScript.Echo "Successfully released all DHCP leases"
 Else
     nResult = objWMINetConfig.RenewDHCPLeaseAll
     If Err Or Not nResult = 0 Then _
        ExitScript "Error renewing DHCP leases", True
     WScript.Echo "Successfully renewed DHCP leases"
 End If

End If

'check if network card information is to be set
If bWINSAddress Or Not strGatewayAddress = "" Or Not strAddress = "" _
       Or Not strDHCPAction = "" Or Not strWINSPrimary = "" _
     Or Not strWINSSecondary = "" Or Not strDNSDomain = "" Then
```

```
'get the network adapter to set
Set objWMINetAdapter = GetObject(WMICONST & _
                       "Win32_NetworkAdapterConfiguration.Index=" _
                       & nDevice)

If Err Then _
     ExitScript "Error getting reference to network adapter" _
                & nDevice, True

'set WINS server addresses for adapter
  If bWINSAddress Then
    nResult = objWMINetAdapter.SetWINSServer(strWINSPrimary _
                                        , strWINSSecondary)
    If Err Or Not nResult = 0 Then _
         ExitScript "Error enabling WINS settings", True
    WScript.Echo "Successfully set WINS server addresses"
  End If

If strDHCPAction = "ENABLEDHCP" Then
      nResult = objWMINetAdapter.EnableDHCP
      WScript.Echo nResult
    If Err Or Not nResult = 0 Then _
         ExitScript "Error enabling DHCP", True
    WScript.Echo "Successfully enabled DHCP"

End If

If Not strDNSDomain = "" Then
  nResult = objWMINetAdapter.SetDNSDomain(strDNSDomain)
  If Err Or Not nResult = 0 Then _
      ExitScript "Error setting DNS domain", True
  WScript.Echo "Successfully DNS domain"
End If

'set default gateway address
If Not strGatewayAddress = "" Then
      nResult = objWMINetAdapter.SetGateways(Array(strGatewayAddress))
    If Err Or Not nResult = 0 Then _
            ExitScript "Error setting default gateway", True
    WScript.Echo "Successfully set default gateway address"
End If

'check if static IP address is specified for adapter
If Not strAddress = "" Then
```

```
      aAddress = Split(strAddress,":")
       If Ubound(aAddress)<>1 Then
          ExitScript "Must specify IP address and subnet separated " _
                        & "by a colon e.g. 192.168.1.1:255.255.255.0" _
                        , True
       Else
          nResult = objWMINetAdapter.EnableStatic(Array(aAddress(0)) _
                                              ,Array(aAddress(1)))
          WScript.Echo nResult, aAddress(0),aAddress(1)
         If Err Or Not nResult = 0 Then _
               ExitScript "Error setting static IP address " _
                        & strAddress, True
           WScript.Echo "Successfully set static IP addresses"
         End If
     End If
   End If

   Sub ShowUsage
   WScript.Echo "ipmaint provides IP network settings admin" & vbCrLf & _
   "Syntax:"  &  vbCrLf & _
   "ipmaint.wsf [optional parameters]" &  vbCrLf & _
   "IPmaint assumes default network card when setting IP settings" & vbCrLf & _
   "unless otherwise specified" &  vbCrLf & _
   "/DEVICE Device Specifies a device number to set, default is 1" & vbCrLf & _
   "/STATIC address:subnet sets static IP address" & vbCrLf & _
   "/RELEASEDHCP releases the DHCP address for current adapter" & vbCrLf & _
   "/ENABLEDHCP  enables DHCP address resolution for current device" & vbCrLf & _
   "/RENEWDHCP   renews IP address for current adapter" & vbCrLf & _
   "/RELEASEALLDHCP releases all DHCP addresses" & vbCrLf & _
   "/RENEWALLDHCP  renews all DHCP addresses" & vbCrLf & _
   "/GATEWAY        specifies default gateway IP address" & vbCrLf & _
   "/WINSPRIMARY   sets primary wins server IP address" & vbCrLf & _
   "/WINSSECONDARY sets secondary wins server IP address" & vbCrLf & _
   "/DNSFORWINSRES boolean parameter - set DNS for WINS resolution" & vbCrLf & _
   "/DNSDOMAIN      sets DNS domain" & vbCrLf & _
   "/WINSSCOPEID    sets WINS scope ID" & vbCrLf & _
   "" & vbCrLf & _
   "Example: set DNS for WINS resoultion and default gateway:" & vbCrLf & _
   "ipmaint /DNSFORWINSRES True /GATEWAY 10.0.0.1 " & vbCrLf & _
   "Example: set static IP for second card:" & vbCrLf & _
   "ipmaint /STATIC 10.0.0.2:255.255.255.0 /DEVICE 2"
  End Sub
```

```
'Reads command line arguments and sets appropriate flags
Sub GetArguments
Dim nF, strArg
'loop through command line parameters
For nF = 0 to WScript.Arguments.Count - 1

 Select Case Ucase(WScript.Arguments(nF))
   Case "/DEVICE" 'get device number
        nDevice = GetParameter(nF)

   Case "/STATIC" 'set static ip addresses
      strAddress = GetParameter(nF)

   Case "/RELEASEDHCP"
      strDHCPAction = "RELEASEDHCP"

   Case "/ENABLEDHCP"
      strDHCPAction = "ENABLEDHCP"

   Case "/RENEWDHCP" 'delimiter
      strDHCPAction = "RENEWDHCP"

   Case "/RELEASEALLDHCP"
      strDHCPAllAction = "RELEASEDHCP"

   Case "/RENEWALLDHCP" 'delimiter
      strDHCPAllAction = "RENEWDHCP"

   Case "/GATEWAY" 'set default gateway
      strGatewayAddress = GetParameter(nF)

   Case "/WINSPRIMARY" 'set primary WINS server
      strWINSPrimary = GetParameter(nF)
      bWINSAddress = True

   Case "/WINSSECONDARY" 'set secondary WINS server
      strWINSSecondary = GetParameter(nF)
      bWINSAddress = True

   Case "/DNSFORWINSRES" 'set DNS for Windows resolutions
      bDNSForWinsRes = Cbool(GetParameter(nF))
      bEnableWins = True
```

```
        Case "/LMHOSTSLOOKUP" 'enable LMHOSTS lookup
           bLMHostsLookup = Cbool(GetParameter(nF))
           bEnableWins = True

        Case "/WINSSCOPEID" 'set WINS scope ID
           strWINSScopeID = Cbool(GetParameter(nF))
           bEnableWins = True

        Case "/DNSDOMAIN" 'set DNS domain
           strDNSDomain = GetParameter(nF)
       End Select
     Next
   End Sub

 'gets next command line argument
 'Parameters nIndex command line argument number to process
 Function GetParameter(nIndex)
   If nIndex+1> WScript.Arguments.Count-1 Then _
                  ExitScript "Not enough arguments", True
   GetParameter = WScript.Arguments(nIndex+1)

 End Function
  ]]>
 </script>
</job>
```

To get the command-line syntax, run the `ipmaint.wsf` script from a command line with no parameters.

See Also

For more information, search `http://msdn.microsoft.com` for the article "Win32_NetworkAdapterConfiguration."

10.6 Inventorying Computer Components

Problem

You want to inventory the main components of a computer.

Solution

You can use the following command-line script to inventory computer components such as BIOS, CPU, memory, OS, hard drive, video, network adapter, modem, and SCSI controllers. The script uses the `ENTWSH.SysInfo` component from Solution 10.1 to get some of the information.

```
<?xml version="1.0" ?>
<job>
<!--comment
Script:inventory.wsf
Description:displays system inventory for local machine
-->
 <script language="VBScript" src="wmiinc.vbs">
 <![CDATA[
  Const wbemFlagReturnImmediately  =16
  Const wbemFlagForwardOnly = 32
 Dim objWMI, objService, objWBEMObject, objWBEMObjects, nF
  Set objService = _
       GetObject("winmgmts:{impersonationLevel=impersonate}!root\cimv2")

  Set objSysInfo = CreateObject("SysInfo.WSC")
  WScript.Echo "BIOS Version:" & objSysInfo.BIOSVersion
  WScript.Echo "CPU:" & objSysInfo.CPU
  WScript.Echo "Memory:" & objSysInfo.Memory
  WScript.Echo "O/S Version:" & objSysInfo.OS
  WScript.Echo "O/S Registered User:" & objSysInfo.RegisteredUser
  WScript.Echo "O/S Serial #:" & objSysInfo.SerialNumber
  WScript.Echo "Virtual Memory:" & objSysInfo.VirtualMemory

  WScript.Echo "Disk Drives:"
  WScript.Echo WMIInfo("Select Description, InterfaceType," & _
                  "Manufacturer, Model, Size From Win32_DiskDrive" _
             , Array("Description", "InterfaceType", "Manufacturer" _
            ,"Model", "Size") _
             , Array( "Description", 25, "Interface", 10, _
             "Manufacturer" , 20, "Model", 15, "Size", 10)) & vbCrLf

  WScript.Echo "Video Configuration:"
  WScript.Stdout.WriteLine WMIInfo("Select AdapterType, AdapterRAM From " & _
               "Win32_VideoConfiguration"  _
              ,Array("AdapterType", "AdapterRAM") _
               , Array("Description", 50, "Video Memory", 30)) & vbCrLf
```

```
    WScript.Echo "Network Card:"
    WScript.Echo WMIInfo("Select Description, MacAddress From " & _
                "Win32_NetworkAdapterConfiguration Where IPEnabled = True"_
                  , Array("Description", "MacAddress") _
                  , Array("Description", 60, "MAC Address", 30)) & vbCrLf

    WScript.Echo "Modems:"
    WScript.Echo WMIInfo("Select Model, ProviderName From " & _
                 "Win32_POTSModem", Array("Model", "ProviderName") _
                 , Array("Model", 50, "Manufacturer", 30)) & vbCrLf

    WScript.Echo "Controllers:"
    WScript.Echo WMIInfo("Select Description, Manufacturer From " & _
                   "Win32_SCSIController" , Array("Description", _
                   "Manufacturer") , Array("Description", 60, _
                   "Manufacturer", 40)) & vbCrLf

'WMIInfo
'returns specified information from WMI query
'Parameters:
'strQuery     SQL query to execute against WMI service
'aFields      Array of fields to output
'aLayout      Two dimensional array that determines the layout of the
'              query results. First element is the heading and second is
'              the width to output. There must be one formatting array for
'              each WMI field specified by aFields
'Returns:
'Formatted string with results
Function WMIInfo(strQuery, aFields, aLayout)
Dim objInstance, objEnumerator, objProp
Dim strLine,nC ,nF, st
Dim strReturn, strText
Set objEnumerator = objService.ExecQuery(strQuery,, _
                         wbemFlagReturnImmediately +  wbemFlagForwardOnly)
On Error Resume Next
'loop through layout and build headers
For nF = LBound(aLayout) To UBound(aLayout) Step 2
   strReturn = strReturn & Left(aLayout(nF) & _
               Space(aLayout(nF + 1)), aLayout(nF + 1))
Next
```

```
'loop through each instance and build the output lines
For Each objInstance In objEnumerator
strLine = ""
'loop through each property
For nF = LBound(aFields) To UBound(aFields)
    strText = ""
    Set objProp = objInstance.Properties_(aFields(nF))
        'if property is date then format accordingly
    If objProp.CIMType = wbemCimtypeDatetime And _
          Not IsNull(objProp.Value) Then
            strText = DMTFDate2String(objProp.Value)
        Else 'check if array, output each element
         If objProp.IsArray Then
          If Not IsNull(objProp) Then                For Each st In objProp.Value
                strLine = strLine & st & ","
            Next
          End If
         Else
           strText = objProp.Value
         End If
        End If
       'build output lines
       strLine = strLine & Left(strText & _
            Space(aLayout(nF * 2 + 1)), aLayout(nF * 2 + 1))
     Next
     strReturn = strReturn & vbCrLf & strLine
  Next
  WMIInfo = strReturnEnd Function
  ]]>
  </script>
</job>
```

Discussion

WMI services expose a number of classes that can be used to query computer configuration. Table 10-8 lists a number of WMI classes that expose commonly queried system properties.

Table 10-8. WMI Computer Information Classes

CLASS	DESCRIPTION
Win32_NetworkAdapter	Network adapter information, such as IP information, model information, and the physical MAC address.
Win32_DiskDrive	Disk drive information. Includes model, capacity, adapter, manufacturer, and size.
Win32_VideoConfiguration	Video adapter configuration, such as adapter type and current resolution settings.
Win32_SCSIController	SCSI controller information.
Win32_POTSModem	Modem information and configuration.

Use the WMI CIM Studio (see Solution 10.2) included with the SDK to browse the available classes and their associated properties exposed through WMI.

All properties might not be available for all classes listed. Some properties may be available on some OSs but not others, even if they are running on the same machine. This is generally related to features supported under a given OS, so Windows 2000 might return more properties for a given device than Windows NT 4.0 as a result of plug-and-play support.

The `inventory.wsf` script inventories the local computer's main components.

See Also

For more information, search `http://msdn.microsoft.com` for the article "Computer System Hardware Classes."

10.7 Executing Generic WMI Queries

Problem

You want a command-line script to execute WMI queries and then pipe the output to standard output.

Solution

The following command-line script executes a WQL query and sends output to standard output:

```
<?xml version="1.0" ?>
<job>
<!--comment
Script:wmiexec.wsf
Description:executes WMI query and sends output to StdOut
-->
 <script language="VBScript" src="wmiinc.vbs">
 <![CDATA[
  Const wbemFlagReturnImmediately  =16
  Const wbemFlagForwardOnly = 32
 Dim objWMI, objService, objWBEMObject, objWBEMObjects, nF
 Dim objProp, bFirst, st, strProv, objTextStream
 Dim strLine, strHeader, strDelim, strQry, bShowFields
 Dim strUser, strPassword, strComputer, strNameSpace, strStringChar
 bShowFields = False
 bFirst = False
 strStringChar = chr(34)

 If Not IsCscript Then
  ExitScript "This script must be run from command line using cscript.exe", True
  WScript.Quit
 End If

 'check the argument count
 If WScript.Arguments.Count = 0 Then
    ShowUsage
 End If

  strQry = WScript.Arguments(0)
  strDelim = ","
  GetArguments
  Set objWMI = New WMISupport

  objWMI.Computer = strComputer
  objWMI.UserName = strUser
  objWMI.Password = strPassword
  objWMI.NameSpace = strNameSpace
  Set objService = objWMI.Connect()
  If IsNull(objService) Then ExitScript objService.ErrorMessage, True
    strQry = ExpandStr(strQry)
     Set objWBEMObjects = objService.ExecQuery( _
  StrQry,,  wbemFlagReturnImmediately + wbemFlagForwardOnly)
```

```
strHeader = ""
For Each objWBEMObject In objWBEMObjects
 If Not bFirst And bShowFields Then
     For Each objProp In objWBEMObject.Properties_
         strHeader = strHeader & objProp.Name & strDelim
     Next
     WScript.StdOut.WriteLine Left(strHeader, Len(strHeader)-1)
     bFirst = True
  End If
     strLine = ""

 'loop through each property
 For Each objProp In objWBEMObject.Properties_
   'check if the property is a date type, then convert date to text
   If objProp.CIMType = wbemCimtypeDatetime And Not _
     IsNull(objProp.Value) Then
      strLine = strLine & DMTFDate2String(objProp.Value) _
               & strDelim
     Else
      If objProp.IsArray Then
       If Not IsNull(objProp) Then
         For Each st In objProp.Value
           strLine = strLine & st & ":"
         Next
       End If
     Else
       'if it's a string then surround with string delimiters
        If objProp.CIMType = wbemCimtypeString _
             Or objProp.CIMType = wbemCimtypeChar16 Then
             strLine = strLine & strStringChar & objProp.Value _
             & strStringChar  & strDelim
       Else
               strLine = strLine & objProp.Value & strDelim
       End If
     End If
    End If
 Next
  WScript.StdOut.WriteLine Left(strLine, Len(strLine)-Len(strDelim))
 Next

Sub ShowUsage
     WScript.Echo "wmiexec executes WMI and outputs results to" & _
 "StdOut" & vbCrLf & _
 "Syntax:"  &  vbCrLf & _
```

```
    "wmiexec.wsf query [/H] [/U user] [/P pasword] [/N namespace] " & _
    "[/C computer] [/D:delimiter] [/Q:quote]" &  vbCrLf & _
    "wmiexec executes the query against local computer" & vbCrLf & _
    "unless otherwise specified" &  vbCrLf & _
    "query query to execute  " & vbCrLf & _
    "/H     shows headers for each field name" & vbCrLf & _
    "/U     user name" & vbCrLf & _
    "/P     password" & vbCrLf & _
    "/N     WMI namespace. Default is root\CIMV2" & vbCrLf & _
    "/C     name of computer to query" & vbCrLf & _
    "/D:    delimiter for output. Default is comma" & vbCrLf & _
    "/Q:    quote characters to surround character strings" & vbCrLf & _
    "Example: list shares on remote computer thor" & vbCrLf & _
    "wmiexec.wsf ""Select * From Win32_Share"" /C thor /H"
     Wscript.Quit
End Sub

  'Reads command line arguments and sets appropriate flags
  Sub GetArguments
  Dim nF, strArg

  'loop through command line parameters
  For nF = 1 to WScript.Arguments.Count - 1

   Select Case Ucase(Left(WScript.Arguments(nF),3))
     Case "/H"
          bShowFields= True
     Case "/U" 'user name
        strUser = GetParameter(nF)
     Case "/P" 'password
        strPassword = GetParameter(nF)
     Case "/C" 'computer
         strComputer = GetParameter(nF)
     Case "/D:" 'delimiter
          strDelim = Mid(WScript.Arguments(nF),4)
     Case "/N" 'name space
        strNameSpace = GetParameter(nF)
     Case "/Q:" 'string character
          strStringChar = Mid(WScript.Arguments(nF),4)
    End Select
   Next
  End Sub
```

```
'gets next command line argument
'Parameters nIndex command line argument number to process
Function GetParameter(nIndex)
 If nIndex+1> WScript.Arguments.Count-1 Then _
       ExitScript "Not enough arguments", True
 GetParameter = WScript.Arguments(nIndex+1)
End Function

'ExpandStr
'Evaluates all subexpressions in string surrounded by </ and />
'Parameters:
'strProcess  String to check for expressions
'Returns: String with evaluate subexpressions
'
Function ExpandStr(strProcess)
 Dim nLoc, nNext, strEval, strResult

 strProcess = Replace(strProcess, "`" , chr(34))

 nLoc = Instr(strProcess,"</")

 Do While nLoc>0

  nNext = Instr(strProcess,"/>")

  If nNext > 0 Then
       strEval = Mid(strProcess, nLoc+2, (nNext - nLoc)-2)
    strResult = Eval(strEval)

    If Not Err Then
        strProcess = Replace(strProcess, "</" & strEval & "/>", strResult)
    Else
       ExpandStr = ""
       Exit Function
    End If
  Else
    Exit Do
  End If

 nLoc = Instr(strProcess,"</")
Loop
ExpandStr = strProcess
End Function
```

```
'ComputerName
'Returns the name of the local computer
Function ComputerName
Dim objNetwork
Set objNetwork = CreateObject("WScript.Network")
 ComputerName = objNetwork.ComputerName
End Function
 ]]>
</script>
</job>
```

Discussion

The command-line `wmiexec` script executes a WQL query and outputs the results the standard output.

The following command line outputs disk drive information for the local machine:

```
wmiexec "Select Description, InterfaceType,  Model, Size From Win32_DiskDrive" /H
```

Output is delimited by commas. Any string values are surrounded by double quotes. Field names are not output unless specified by using the `/H` switch.

You may want to execute a query that requires calculated criteria, such as the current date or time. WQL queries passed to the `wmiexec` script can contain VBScript functions to perform calculations. Any statement surrounded by </ and /> will be evaluated.

The ability to pass evaluate statements in the command line allows generic queries to be executed where the appropriate criteria is filled in. In the following example, all properties are queried for the `Win32_ComputerSystem` class where the computer name matches the local computer name:

```
wmiexec.wsf "Select * From Win32_ComputerSystem Where Name='</ComputerName/>'"
```

The `ComputerName` function is evaluated between </ and /> and returns the local computer name.

The following example returns all items from the Applications event log within the last 48 hours:

```
wmiexec.wsf "Select Category, ComputerName, EventIdentifier, Message, SourceName
, TimeGenerated FROM Win32_NTLogEvent WHERE LogFile='Application' AND
TimeWritten > '</Convert2DMTFDate(DateAdd(`H`, -48, Now), 630 )/>'"
```

The result of the statement executed between </ and /> is inserted into the query. It uses the `Convert2DMTFDate` function included in the `wmiinc.vbs` support code file to return the time from 2 hours ago to DMTF format (see Solution 10.14 for details on Event Viewer access).

Double quotes cannot be used in a command-line parameter, so use the grave accent (`) character (ASCII value 96) instead. This character is usually located above the Tab key on a keyboard. It is replaced in the command-line string with double quotes before the query is executed.

Queries can be executed against WMI providers on a remote computer by providing the `/C` switch together with the name of the remote computer. The following command line lists all running processes on the remote computer Odin:

```
wmiexec "Select Caption, ExecutablePath From Win32_Process" /h /c odin
```

Table 10-9 lists available optional switches.

Table 10-9. `WMIExec` *Command-Line Switches*

SWITCH	DESCRIPTION
/H	Shows headers for each field name.
/U	User name to connect with.
/P	Password for specified user.
/N	WMI namespace. Default is `root\CIMV2`.
/C	Name of remote computer to query. Default is local.
/D:	Delimiter for output. Default is comma.
/Q:	Quote character for string values. Default is double quotes.

10.8 Changing Environment Variables

Problem

You want to change environment variables for all users on a computer.

Solution

You can enumerate all instances of the `Win32_Environment` class and then modify any instances in which the environment variable name is TMP or TEMP:

```
'envtmpchng.vbs
'changes the location of temporary file environment
'variables Tmp and Temp
Dim objServices
Dim objWMIObject, objWMIObjects

'get a reference to a WMI service
Set objServices = _
    GetObject("winmgmts:{impersonationLevel=impersonate}")
Set objWMIObjects = objServices.InstancesOf("Win32_Environment")
On Error Resume Next
'loop through each environment variable for temp
For Each objWMIObject In objWMIObjects
'check if environment variable is TEMP or TMP
If objWMIObject.Name = "TEMP" Or objWMIObject.Name = "TMP" Then
    objWMIObject.VariableValue = "d:\temp"

    'update the settings
    Call objWMIObject.Put_
 End If
Next
```

Discussion

Under Windows NT, environment variables can be modified for the current logged-on user. A profile is created for each user that uses the NT machine. The profile stores a copy of the user's local environment variables.

The `Shell` object's `Environment` object can change a variable for the current user, but not for any other profiles stored on the local system. The WMI object exposes environment variables through the `Win32_Environment` class.

If the user is logged on with administrative rights, he or she can access the environment variables of all profiles on the local machine.

The `Win32_Environment` class key is a combination of the environment variable name and user name. The user name and environment variable name are exposed through the `Win32_Environment` class as the `UserName` and `Name` properties, respectively. The user name can optionally have a domain name and backslash prefixed to it to distinguish it from a local or domain account.

To reference an instance of a WMI object with a multivalue key, specify the criteria for each field separated by a comma.

The following example gets an instance of the environment variable Temp for user Fred and sets the value to `d:\temp`:

```
Dim objServices, objWMIObject
'get a reference to a WMI service
Set objServices = _
    GetObject("winmgmts:{impersonationLevel=impersonate}")

'gets a reference to the environment variable TEMP for user Administrator
Set objWMIObject = objServices.Get _
            ("Win32_Environment.Name='TEMP',UserName='C3I\Administrator'")

objWMIObject.VariableValue = "d:\temp"
Call objWMIObject.Put_
```

Windows 9*x*/ME machines can list environment variables but cannot modify the values.

See Also

Solution 2.3. For more information, search `http://msdn.microsoft.com` for the article "Win32_Environment."

10.9 Terminating a System Process

Problem

You want to terminate a system process.

Solution

You can get a reference to the system process you want to terminate by querying `Win32_Process` for the handle (process ID) for the process you want to terminate. You can invoke the `Terminate` method on the process object in this way:

```
Dim objServices, objWMIObject, nResult
 Set objServices = GetObject("winmgmts:{impersonationLevel=impersonate}")
Set objWMIObject = objServices.Get("Win32_Process.Handle=326")
nResult = objProcess.Terminate(0)
```

Discussion

System processes are exposed through the WMI Win32_Process class. Access to process information is available to Windows NT/2000/2003/XP/9*x*/ME.

Each process is identified by a handle/process ID (PID). The PID is a numeric identifier assigned to the process when the process is created. The process handle is unique for each instance of the process. The following script lists all running processes with their handle and executable name:

```
Dim objWMIObjects, objWMIObject, objServices
Set objServices = _
    GetObject("winmgmts:{impersonationLevel=impersonate}!root\cimv2")
'create an instance of the Win32_Process class
Set objWMIObjects = objServices.InstancesOf("Win32_Process")

'loop through each process and list the handle and executable
For Each objWMIObject In objWMIObjects
    WScript.Echo objWMIObject.Handle & " " & objWMIObject.ExecutablePath
Next
```

The PID is exposed through the Handle property. The path to executable represented by the process can be retrieved through the ExecutablePath property, while the Description, Name, and Caption properties return the executable name.

To terminate an existing process, get a reference to the process you want to terminate and invoke the Terminate method. The syntax is as follows:

```
nResult = objProcess.Terminate(nReason)
```

The nReason parameter is a process-specific reason code. Unless you know of any specific values to pass to a process, this value is 0. The Terminate method returns 0 if successful—any other value indicates that an error occurred.

The following script, procmaint.wsf, allows for processes to be listed and terminated for local or remote computers:

```
<?xml version="1.0" ?>
<job>
<!--comment
Script:procmaint.wsf
Description:
Performs process operations
-->
 <script language="VBScript" src="wmiinc.vbs">
 <![CDATA[
Const wbemFlagReturnImmediately  =16
```

```
Const wbemFlagForwardOnly = 32
 Dim avar, objDescriptor
 Dim objInstance, strMachine, strPermission
 Dim objService, nProcID, bList, objProcess, nResult
 strMachine = Null
 nProcID = Null
 On Error Resume Next
 'check if script is being run from command prompt
 If Not IsCscript Then
  ExitScript _
      "This script must be run from command line using cscript.exe",False
 End If

If WScript.Arguments.Count = 0 Then
   ShowUsage
 End If
  GetArguments
  If strMachine<> "" Then
   Set objService = _
             GetObject("winmgmts:{impersonationLevel=impersonate}!\\" _
                        & strMachine)
  Else
   Set objService = _
             GetObject("winmgmts:{impersonationLevel=impersonate}")
  End If

  'check if list flag is set..
  If bList Then
   'get list of processes
   Set objInstance = _
        objService.ExecQuery("Select Handle, Description From Win32_Process",, _
                                                  wbemFlagReturnImmediately + _
                                                   wbemFlagForwardOnly )


    For Each objProcess In objInstance
        WScript.Echo objProcess.Handle, objProcess.Description
    Next

  ElseIf Not IsNull(nProcID) Then
   'get a reference to specified process specified by the PID
    Set objProcess = objService.Get("Win32_Process.Handle=" _
                        & chr(34) & nProcID & chr(34))
```

```
    If Err Then  ExitScript _
             "Unable to get reference to process:" & nProcID,False

    'terminate process
     nResult = objProcess.Terminate(0)
            If nResult Then
        WScript.Echo "Successfully terminated process# " & nProcID
    Else
        WScript.Echo "Unable to terminate process# " & nProcID
    End If
    End If

  'Reads command line arguments
  Sub GetArguments
  Dim nF, strArg
  'loop through command line parameters
  For nF = 0 to WScript.Arguments.Count - 1
   Select Case Ucase(WScript.Arguments(nF))
     Case "/KILL" 'stop specified process
          nProcID = GetParameter(nF)
    Case "/LIST" 'lists specified processes
          bList = True
     Case "/MACHINE" 'gets machine name
          strMachine = GetParameter(nF)
   End Select
   Next
  End Sub

 'gets next command line argument
 'Parameters nIndex command line argument number to process
 Function GetParameter(nIndex)
  If nIndex+1> WScript.Arguments.Count-1 Then
     ExitScript "Not enough arguments", True
  End If
  GetParameter = WScript.Arguments(nIndex+1)
 End Function

 Sub ShowUsage
WScript.Echo "procmaint performs process operations" & vbCrLf & _
  "Syntax:"  &  vbCrLf & _
  "procmaint.wsf [/LIST] [/MACHINE name] [/KILL procid]" & vbCrLf & _
  "/LIST    optional. Lists active process information " & vbCrLf & _
  "/MACHINE optional. Name of machine to perform operations" & vbCrLf & _
```

```
  "/KILL    optional. Terminates process for specified procid" & vbCrLf & _
  "Example: list processes on machine thor:" & vbCrLf & _
  "procmaint.wsf /MACHINE thor /list" & vbCrLf & _
  "Example: terminate process with id 100:" & vbCrLf & _
  "procmaint.wsf /kill 100"
 End Sub
  ]]>
 </script>
</job>
```

Execute the `procmaint.wsf` script from the command line without any parameters to retrieve the syntax.

See Also

For more information, search `http://msdn.microsoft.com` for the article "Managing Windows with WMI."

10.10 Starting an Application on a Remote Computer

Problem

You want to start an application on a remote computer.

Solution

You can create an instance of the `Win32_Process` class, specifying the remote computer on which you want to start the application. Use the `Win32_Process` object's `Create` method to start the application on the remote machine.

```
'get a reference to the Win32Process class object on specified machine
Set objProcess=GetObject("winmgmts:{impersonationLevel=impersonate}!" & _
             "\\Odin\root\cimv2:Win32_Process" )
   'create process on remote machine
 nResult = objProcess.Create("notepad.exe", , ,nProcID)
 WScript.Echo "The PID for the new instance of notepad is " & nProcID
```

Discussion

Applications can be started locally using the `Shell` object's `Run` method, but this method cannot start remote instances of an application. Applications can be executed on a remote machine using the Create method of the Win32_Process class. The syntax is as follows:

```
nResult = objProcess.Create(strApp,strCurrentDir,objProcessStartInfo,nProcID)
```

strApp represents the name of the application to start. If no explicit path to the application is specified, the directories specified in the PATH environment variable are searched.

strCurrentDir is an optional parameter that identifies the path to the start-up directory for the application.

The optional objProcessStartInfo parameter is an instance of the Win32_ProcessStartup class that contains start-up information, such as application title, environment variables, and application appearance.

The nProcID parameter is the numeric process ID assigned to the new process. This is set by the Create method—you cannot assign your own process IDs.

The Create method returns 0 if the process was successfully created. A nonzero value is returned if an error occurred while attempting to start the remote application, and a runtime error is not generated if the remote application is not successfully started. You must have appropriate administrative rights to create processes on remote machines.

The Win32_Process object's Create method cannot create interactive applications under NT 4.0 SP6, Windows 2003, Windows 2000 SP3, and Windows XP. A process will be created, but no Windows interface will appear. This is for security purposes, so no malicous remote applications can be executed. However, there may be valid occasions where you require the execution of remote interactive applications.

The WMI Win32_ScheduledJob object can be used to execute an interactive application under Windows 2003, XP, and 2000 with recent service packs. The Win32_ScheduledJob object is used to create scheduled jobs and is the equivalent of using the AT command. It cannot create Scheduled Tasks.

To schedule an application, use the Create method of the Win32_ScheduledJob class. The syntax is as follows:

```
nResult = objSchedule.Create(strAppPath,strDateTime,bRunRepeat, _
                                        nWeekDay,nMonthDay,bInteract)
```

strAppPath is the path of the application to schedule.

strDateTime represents the date and time in DMTF format. See Solution 10-14 for more information on DMTF format.

bRunRepeat is a Boolean parameter that determines if the scheduled job runs repeatedly.

nWeekDay is 2 to the power of the day of the week where Monday is 1, Tuesday is 2, Wednesday is 4, and so on. Jobs can be scheduled on multiple days by adding values together. For example, the value 9 would schedule the job on Monday and Thursday (1 + 8).

nMonthDay is the day of the month minus one to the power of 2, where day one is 1, day two is 2, day three is 4, and so on. Jobs can be scheduled on multiple days of the month by adding values together. For example, the value 130 would schedule the job on the second day (2^0) and the eigth day (2^7).

The following script will schedule the file backup.bat to be executed on Wednesday and Friday at 10:00 p.m.:

```
Const Friday = 16
Const Wednesday = 4
strComputer = "Thor"

Set objService = GetObject("winmgmts:\\" & strComputer & "\root\CIMV2")

'get computer object and determine timezone
Set objComputer = objService.Get("Win32_ComputerSystem='" & strComputer & "'")
nTimeZone = objComputer.Currenttimezone

If nTimeZone >= 0 Then
  strTimeZone = "+" & nTimeZone
Else
  strTimeZone = "-" & nTimeZone
End If

Set objNewJob = objService.Get("Win32_ScheduledJob")
'schedule job to repeatedly run on Wednesday and Friday at 10PM
 errJobCreated = objNewJob.Create _
    ("e:\data\backup.bat", "********220000.000000" & strTimeZone, _
    False, Friday + Wednesday , , True, JobID)
```

The following script will execute Notepad interactively on the remote computer Loki:

```
strComputer = "Loki"
Set objService = GetObject("winmgmts:\\" & strComputer & "\root\CIMV2")
'get computer object and determine timezone
Set objComputer = objService.Get("Win32_ComputerSystem='" & strComputer & "'")
nTimeZone = objComputer.Currenttimezone

If nTimeZone >= 0 Then
  strTimeZone = "+" & nTimeZone
Else
  strTimeZone = "-" & nTimeZone
End If
```

```
'get local time on remote computer
Set objTime = objService.Get("Win32_LocalTime=@")

'add 30 seconds to the current time on remote computer
dTm = TimeSerial (objTime.Hour,objTime.Minute,objTime.Second + 30)

strTime = Right("0" & Hour(dTm),2) & _
          Right("0" & Minute(dTm),2) & _
          Right("0" & Second(dTm),2)

nDay = 2 ^ (Day(Date) -1)

Set objNewJob = objService.Get("Win32_ScheduledJob")
'create a one off scheduled job that will run 30 seconds in future
 errJobCreated = objNewJob.Create _
    ("notepad.exe", "********" & strTime  & ".000000" & strTimeZone, _
    False, ,nDay True, JobID)
```

This preceding script will run only under Windows XP and Windows 2003, because it uses the `Win32_LocalTime` class to determine local time on remote computer. See Solution 10-18 for more information on the `Win32_LocalTime` class.

The following `rmtexecute.wsf` command-line script allows for the execution of applications on remote computers:

```
<?xml version="1.0" ?>
<job>
<!--comment
Script:rmtexecute.wsf
Description:
Executes applications on remote machine
-->
 <script language="VBScript" src="wmiinc.vbs">
 <![CDATA[
 Option Explicit
 Dim avar, strMachine, strApp
 Dim nProcID, objProcess, nResult
 strMachine = Null
 nProcID = Null

 On Error Resume Next
 'check if script is being run from command prompt
 If Not IsCscript Then
  ExitScript _
      "This script must be run from command line using cscript.exe",False
```

```
 End If
 'check the argument count
 If WScript.Arguments.Count <> 2 Then
  ShowUsage
  WScript.Quit
 End If

  'get machine and application name
  strMachine = WScript.Arguments(0)
  strApp = WScript.Arguments(1)
    'get a reference to the Win32Process class object on specified machine
  Set objProcess = GetObject("winmgmts:{impersonationLevel=impersonate}!" & _
                  "\\" & strMachine & "\root\cimv2:Win32_Process" )

  If Err Then
      ExitScript "Unable to get reference to machine" & strMachine, False
 End If
  'create process on remote machine
  nResult = objProcess.Create(strApp,Null,Null,nProcID)

  If nResult = 0 Then
   WScript.Echo "Application " & strApp & _
                    " started with process id: " & nProcId
  Else
   WScript.Echo "Unable to start application '" & strApp & _
                    "' on computer " & strMachine
  End If

Sub ShowUsage
  WScript.Echo "rmtexecute executes programs on remote computers" & vbCrLf & _
  "Syntax:"  &  vbCrLf & _
  "rmtexecute.wsf computer application" & vbCrLf & _
  "computer    name of computer to start application" & vbCrLf & _
  "application name of application to start" & vbCrLf & _
  "Example: start notepad on computer thor:" & vbCrLf & _
  "rmtexecute.wsf thor notepad.exe"
End Sub
 ]]>
 </script>
</job>
```

Execute the script from the command line, passing the computer name and the name of the application to execute:

```
rmtexecute.wsf thor notepad.exe
```

If you do not specify the full path, the directories specified in PATH environment variable search for the application.

See Also

For more information, search `http://msdn.microsoft.com` for the articles "Win32_Process" and "Create Method in Class Win32_Process."

10.11 Compressing Folders and Files

Problem

You need to compress all folders over a certain size.

Solution

The following script applies the compressed attribute to all user folders that are over 25MB:

```
'compress.vbs
Option Explicit
Dim objFSO, strWMIPath, objService, objFolders, objFolder, objWMIObject
Set objFSO = CreateObject("Scripting.FileSystemObject")
'get a reference to a WMI service on the local machine
Set objService = _
    GetObject("winmgmts:{impersonationLevel=impersonate}!root\cimv2")

'get the folder to search
Set objFolders = objFSO.GetFolder("D:\Users")

For Each objFolder In objFolders.SubFolders
    'if folder over certain size, then compress
    If objFolder.Size > 25000000 Then
```

```
    'get a reference to the directory to compress
    Set objWMIObject = _
      objService.Get("Win32_Directory.Name=" & chr(34) & _
          Replace(objFolder.Path,"\","\\") & chr(34))

    objWMIObject.Compress
      WScript.Echo "Compressed folder " & objFolder.Path
      End If
Next
```

Discussion

Windows NT and Windows 2000/2003/XP enable you to compress files and folders.

The Compress method is exposed through the CIM_LogicalFile class. Instances of files and directories are exposed through the Win32_Directory and CIM_DataFile classes respectively, which inherit the Compress method from the CIM_LogicalFile class.

The following sample compresses a local directory and file:

```
Dim objService, objWMIObject, nResult
'get a reference to a WMI service
Set objService = GetObject("winmgmts:{impersonationLevel=impersonate}")

'get a reference to the directory D:\Data\Reports and compress it
Set objWMIObject = _
            objService.Get("Win32_Directory.Name=""D:\\Data\\Reports""")
nResult = objWMIObject.Compress

'get a reference to the file D:\Data\data.mdb and compress it
Set objWMIObject = _
            objService.Get("CIM_DataFile.Name=""D:\\Data\\data.mdb""")
nResult = objWMIObject.Compress
```

Paths to directories and files cannot be in UNC format. Backslashes in the path must be prefixed with another backslash. The Compress method returns 0 if successful.

The WMI provider allows for decompression in version 1.5 and later. Windows 2000/2003/XP includes version 1.5 as standard, but if you are running Windows NT 4.0 you might have an older version of WMI. The version 1.5 provider exposes an Uncompress method that can decompress files or folders:

```
Dim objService, objWMIObject, nResult
'get a reference to a WMI service
Set objService = GetObject("winmgmts:{impersonationLevel=impersonate}")

'get a reference to a directory
Set objWMIObject = _
              objService.Get("Win32_Directory.Name=""D:\\Data\\Reports""")
'decompress directory
nResult = objWMIObject.Uncompress
```

The `Uncompress` method returns 0 if successful.

Queries can be executed against the `CIM_DataFile` class to return files that meet certain criteria. The following sample uncompresses all ZIP files on the `D:` drive on the local machine. Because ZIP files are already compressed, unnecessary CPU time is used when accessing them.

```
Dim objService, objWMIFiles, nResult, objFile

On Error Resume Next

'get a reference to a WMI service
Set objService = GetObject("winmgmts:{impersonationLevel=impersonate}")

'return all zip files from the D: drive that are compressed
Set objWMIFiles = _
      objService.ExecQuery("Select * From CIM_DataFILE Where Drive='D:'" & _
                                      " And Extension='zip' And Compressed=True")
'loop through any compressed files and uncompress them
For Each objFile In objWMIFiles
    WScript.Echo "Uncompressing file " & objFile.Name
    objFile.Uncompress
Next
```

See Also

For more information, search `http://msdn.microsoft.com` for the articles "Win32_Directory" and "Win32_NTEventlogFile."

10.12 Copying Files on a Remote Computer

Problem

You want to copy a file on a remote computer.

Solution

File manipulation can be easily performed using the File System Object (FSO). But FSO methods assume that a path exists to the files you are manipulating, by either a physical or UNC path.

The WMI `CIM_DataFile` class allows for files to be manipulated on remote machines that have not shared directories.

The following code gets a reference to the file `report.doc` on the remote computer Odin and copies it to a backup directory:

```
Dim objServices, nResult, objFile
'connect to remote computer Odin
Set objServices = GetObject("winmgmts:{impersonationLevel=impersonate}!\\Odin")
'get a reference to file reports.doc
Set objFile = _
          objServices.Get("CIM_DataFile.Name='d:\\data\\reports.doc'")
'copy file to backup reports directory
nResult = objFile.Copy("d:\\backup\\reports\reports.doc")
```

Discussion

WMI provides methods for copying, deleting, and renaming files. These operations can be performed more easily using the File System Object (FSO), but WMI has some advantages when performing operations on remote machines.

- *A network path to the file or directory does not need to exist.* The FSO requires a connection to a network share. File operations can be performed on computers that have no shared resources.

- *Network traffic.* Copying and moving local files on a remote computer are executed by the remote WMI provider, and no traffic is sent back to the calling machine. Any copy or move operation performed by FSO methods, Explorer, or existing command-line utilities like copy transfer data between the calling and remote computer. This is useful over slow links when working with large files.

Files are referenced through the CIM_DataFile class. When referencing a file, any path separators (backslashes) must be prefixed by a second backslash.

Once you have a reference to a file, you can copy or rename it. The syntax is as follows:

```
nResult = objFile.Copy| Rename(strDestination)
```

The strDestination parameter identifies the path name of the file you are copying or moving the source file to. It must point to a local path on the machine you are copying the file to; a UNC network path cannot be used. You must specify the full path, including the name of the file. Specifying only the destination directory will not automatically copy or move the file to that directory.

The methods return 0 if the operation was successful. If the destination path is invalid, an empty value is returned. If the destination file already exists, it is not overwritten and an error value is returned.

Wildcards cannot be specified using these methods—however, a query can be executed against the provider and the results processed. In the following sample, all temporary files from the C: drive are deleted:

```
Const wbemFlagReturnImmediately  =16
Const wbemFlagForwardOnly = 32
Dim objService, objWMIFiles, nResult, objFile
'get a reference to a WMI service
Set objService = GetObject("winmgmts:{impersonationLevel=impersonate}")

'get all files with .tmp extenstion on the C: drive
Set objWMIFiles = _
objService.ExecQuery ("Select Name From CIM_DataFILE Where " & _
"Drive='C:' And Extension='tmp'"),, _
  wbemFlagReturnImmediately + wbemFlagForwardOnly )
'loop through all files and attempt to delete them
For Each objFile In objWMIFiles
    nResult = objFile.Delete
    If nResult <> 0 Then
      WScript.Echo "*Unable to delete " & objFile.Name
    Else
      WScript.Echo "Successfully deleted file:" & objFile.Name
    End If
Next
```

The Delete method returns 0 if successful. Deleted files are not moved to the Recycle Bin.

Directories can be copied, renamed, and deleted using the same method as the CIM_DataFile class. To perform these operations on a directory, get a reference to the directory through the Win32_Directory class.

Once you have a reference to a directory, you can invoke the `Copy`, `Rename`, or `Delete` method. The following example makes a copy of the directory `D:\data` to `D:\data` backup on the remote computer Odin:

```
Dim objServices, nResult, objDir

'connect to remote computer Odin
Set objServices = _
        GetObject("winmgmts:{impersonationLevel=impersonate}!\\Odin")

'get a reference to directory
Set objDir = objServices.Get("Win32_Directory.Name='d:\\data'")

'copy to directory to data backup
nResult = objDir.Copy("d:\\backup\\data")
```

These methods return 0 if successful. The `Copy` method copies an existing directory structure, including all files and subdirectories. If the directory already exists, nothing is copied.

The `Delete` method deletes the whole directory structure if there are files and subdirectories in the directory you are trying to delete.

Appropriate security access is required to perform any file operations on a remote computer.

The following `rmtcopy.wsf` script copies individual files on a remote computer using WMI:

```
<?xml version="1.0" ?>
<job>
<!--comment
Script:rmtcopy.wsf
Description:
Copies file on remote computer
-->
 <script language="VBScript" src="wmiinc.vbs">
 <![CDATA[
 Dim strComputer, strSource, strDest, avar
 Dim objFile, nResult
 On Error Resume Next
 'check if script is being run from command prompt
 If Not IsCscript Then
  ExitScript _
      "This script must be run from command line using cscript.exe",False
 End If
```

```
 'check the argument count
 If WScript.Arguments.Count <> 3 Then
    ShowUsage
    WScript.Quit
 End If

  'get comptuer and source and destination file
  strComputer = WScript.Arguments(0)
  strSource = WScript.Arguments(1)
  strDest = WScript.Arguments(2)

  'get a reference to the file to copy
  Set objFile = GetObject("winmgmts:{impersonationLevel=impersonate}!" & _
               "\\" & strComputer & "\root\cimv2:CIM_DataFile.Name='" & _
               Replace(strSource,"\","\\") & "'")

  If Err Then  ExitScript _
             "Unable to get reference to file " & strSource & _
           " on computer:" & strMachine, False

  'create process on remote machine
  nResult = objFile.Copy(strDest)

If IsEmpty(nResult) Then nResult = 0
  If nResult = 0 And Not Err Then
   WScript.Echo "File " & strSource & _
                    " Successfully copied to: " & strDest
  Else
   WScript.Echo "Unable to copy file " & strSource & _
                    " to " & strDest
  End If

Sub ShowUsage
  WScript.Echo "rmtcopy copies files on remote computers" & vbCrLf & _
  "Syntax:"  &  vbCrLf & _
  "rmtcopy.wsf computer source destination" & vbCrLf & _
  "computer    name of computer where source file is located" & vbCrLf & _
  "source      file to copy" & vbCrLf & _
  "destination destination file to copy to"
End Sub
]]>
 </script>
</job>
```

The script requires the name of the remote computer followed by the path to the source and destination files:

```
rmtcopy.wsf d:\data\report.doc d:\backup\report.doc
```

See Also

For more information, search `http://msdn.microsoft.com` for the articles "Win32_Directory" and "Win32_NTEventlogFile."

10.13 Rebooting a Computer

Problem

You want to reboot a computer.

Solution

You can get the active "primary" OS for the computer you want to reboot by executing a query against the `Win32_OperatingSystem` class. Then you call the `Reboot` method.

The following example reboots the remote computer Thor:

```
Dim nStatus, objService, objWMIObject, objWMIObjects
'create process on remote machine
Set objService = _
 GetObject("winmgmts:{impersonationLevel=impersonate,(Shutdown)}!\\thor")
'get the active OS
Set objWMIObjects = objService.ExecQuery _
          ("Select * From Win32_OperatingSystem Where Primary = True")

For Each objOS In objWMIObjects
    Set objWMIObject = objOS
Next
nStatus = objWMIObject.Reboot
```

Discussion

A computer can be shut down or rebooted by using the `ShutDown` or `Reboot` methods exposed through the `Win32_OperatingSystem` class. First, get a reference to the computer you want to shut down/reboot—this may be a local or remote machine. If the machine is remote, you must be logged on with appropriate administrative access or supply the appropriate credentials.

You must also specify the `Shutdown` *privilege* in the connection string to perform shutdowns or reboots for local computers. A privilege is setting that is required to be specified for certain operations. Even if you have the appropriate level of security access to perform the operation, you must still specify the privilege.

Privileges can be passed with the connection string moniker when you create a `Services` object:

```
Set objService = _
 GetObject("winmgmts:{impersonationLevel=impersonate,(Shutdown)}")
```

All methods invoked using this `Services` object will inherit the privilege. To determine if a method requires privileges or not, use WMI CIM Studio to inspect the method you need to use—in this case, the `Reboot` method. Figure 10-6 shows the `Reboot` method under WMI CIM Studio.

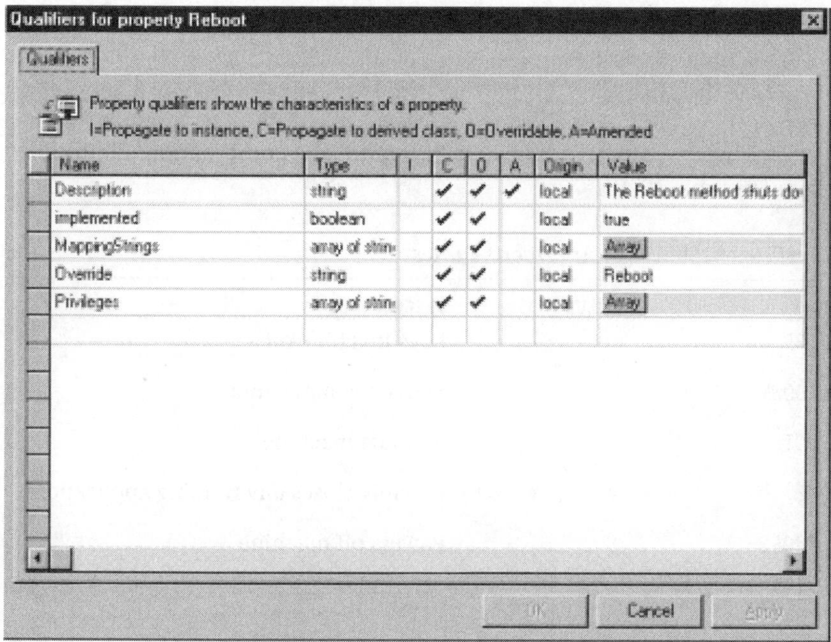

Figure 10-6. The `Reboot` method in WMI CIM Studio

If you see a Privileges qualifier in the list, this indicates that a privilege is needed to call the method on a local machine. Click the Array button to list the privilege(s) required for the method. This will list the privileges in the format SePRIVILEGEPNAMEPrivilege, where PRIVILEGEPNAME represents the name of the privilege to be used in the connection string. The Reboot method will show the SeShutdownPrivilege qualifier under WIM CIM Studio, and it will use Shutdown in the connection string.

Get a reference to an instance of the active OS for the machine you want to shut down. You can retrieve the reference by querying the Primary property of the Win32_OperatingSystem class. The instance where the Primary property is True is the active OS.

Then invoke the Shutdown or Reboot method. The syntax is as follows:

```
nStatus = objWMIInstance.ShutDown | Reboot
```

Both the Reboot and Shutdown methods forcibly terminate any running applications. If you have an application with unsaved data, the information will be lost if these methods are used.

The methods return 0 if the operation completed successfully.

The Win32_OperatingSystem class also exposes a Win32Shutdown method that provides additional functionality over the Reboot and Shutdown methods on Windows NT and Windows 2000/2003 computers. The syntax is as follows:

```
nStatus = objWMIInstance.Win32ShutDown(nConstant)
```

The nConstant parameter represents one value or a combination of multiple values listed in Table 10-10.

Table 10-10. Win32ShutDown *Argument Values*

CONSTANT	VALUE	DESCRIPTION
EWX_LOGOFF	0	Logs machine off
EWX_SHUTDOWN	1	Shuts down machine
EWX_REBOOT	2	Reboots machine
EWX_FORCE	4	Forcibly closes any running applications
EWX_POWEROFF	8	Powers off machine

When you attempt to shut down, log off, or reboot a computer, Win32ShutDown will check if there are unsaved documents open and the applications will prompt accordingly.

For example, if you have an unsaved Office document and you attempt to shut down the computer using Win32ShutDown, you will be prompted to save the document. If the prompt is cancelled, the shutdown procedure is terminated.

Adding the EWX_FORCE constant to any of the other values forcibly terminates any applications that are running in a manner similar to the Reboot and Shutdown methods.

To force a logoff, pass the value of 5, which is a combination of EWX_SHUTDOWN (1) and EWX_FORCE (4).

Windows NT 4.0 does not support being powered off. Attempting to power off an NT 4.0 machine will have the same effect as rebooting the machine.

The following script performs reboots on remote computers:

```
'reboot.vbs
'reboots local or remote computer
 Dim objOS, nStatus, objService, objWMIObject, objWMIObjects, strMachine
On Error Resume Next
 strMachine = ""
 'check if argument passed, if so assume remote computer
 'to reboot
 If WScript.Arguments.Count = 1 Then
     strMachine =  "!\\" & WScript.Arguments(0)
 End If

 'create instance of WMI service with Shutdown privilege
 Set objService = GetObject( _
                "winmgmts:{impersonationLevel=impersonate,(Shutdown)}" _
                 & strMachine )

 If Err Then
   WScript.Echo "Error getting reference to computer " & strMachine
 End If

 'get the primary O/S to reboot
 Set objWMIObjects = objService.ExecQuery( _
            "Select * From Win32_OperatingSystem Where Primary = True")

 'get the instance of the O/S to reboot  For Each objOS In objWMIObjects
    Set objWMIInstance = objOS
 Next

 nStatus = objWMIInstance.Reboot()
 If nStatus = 0 Then
   WScript.Echo "Computer successfully rebooted"
```

```
Else
  WScript.Echo "Error rebooting computer: Status returned by Reboot:"  & nStatus
End If
```

The command-line script requires a computer name to be passed. The script attempts to reboot the specified computer.

See Also

Read the following topics in the WMI SDK documentation: "Setting Privileges for the Scripting API," "Calling the Method," and "Security Issues When Writing WMI." For more information, search `http://msdn.microsoft.com` for the article "Win32_OperatingSystem."

10.14 Checking the Event Viewer for Unauthorized Access

Problem

You want to check the Event Viewer for any file audit events in order to determine unauthorized file access.

Solution

You can execute a query against the `Win32_NTLogEvent` class to return all records for event identifiers that meet certain criteria. In the case of unauthorized file access (trapped via file auditing), this is event 560:

```
<?xml version="1.0" ?>
<job>
<!--comment
Script:fileaccess.wsf
Description:
Shows all Event log security events on audited files within last 48 hours
-->
 <script language="VBScript" src="wmiinc.vbs">
 <![CDATA[
 Option Explicit
Const wbemFlagReturnImmediately  =16
Const wbemFlagForwardOnly = 32
 Dim objService
```

```
Dim objWMI,objWMISet, objInstance
  'get an WMI Service object. Privilege is set as Security to access
 'security Event logs
 Set objService =GetObject("winmgmts:{impersonationLevel=impersonate," & _
               "(Security)}!root\cimv2")

'execute query, filtering on event # 560 (object access)
'from Security logs. Only retrieve entries within the last two days
 Set objWMISet = objService.ExecQuery("SELECT InsertionStrings, " & _
    "TimeWritten, Type  FROM Win32_NTLogEvent WHERE " & _
    "LogFile='Security' AND EventIdentifier=560 AND  TimeWritten > '" & _
    Convert2DMTFDate(DateAdd("h", -48, Now), 630) & "'' ",, _
    wbemFlagReturnImmediately  + Const wbemFlagForwardOnly)

  'loop through each instance
  For Each objInstance In objWMISet

  'check if there are insertion strings
   If Not IsNull(objInstance.InsertionStrings) Then
    If UBound(objInstance.InsertionStrings) > 0 Then
        'if it's file access, then print details.
        If objInstance.InsertionStrings(1) = "File" Then

         WScript.Echo objInstance.InsertionStrings(2) _
                  & " accessed by " & _
               objInstance.InsertionStrings(7) & " at " & _
               DMTFDate2String(objInstance.TimeWritten)

        End If
    End If
   End If
  Next
  ]]>
 </script>
</job>
```

Discussion

Event log information is exposed through the Win32_NTLogEvent class. Using the ExecQuery statement, queries can be executed against the WMI provider to return event log information that meets certain criteria.

Windows NT 4.0 exposes security, application, and system logs. Windows 2000/2003/XP includes these logs as well as service-specific logs, such as DNS and directory services.

If you are uncertain of the names of available logs, use the following code sample to list the available log files. You can use these log file names when you query the Win32_NTLogEvent class:

```
'list event logs
Dim objWMIObjects, objWMIObject

Set objService = GetObject("winmgmts:{impersonationLevel=impersonate}")
Set objWMIObjects = objService.InstancesOf("Win32_NTEventLogFile")

'loop through and list all available event logs
For Each objWMIObject In objWMIObjects
    WScript.Echo objWMIObject.LogFileName
Next
```

Each log exposes events related to the log type.

Table 10-11 lists the Win32_NTLogEvent object's properties.

Table 10-11. Win32_NTLogEvent *Object Properties*

PROPERTY	DESCRIPTION
EventIdentifier	Application-specific event identifier.
TimeWritten	Time event was written to the log in DMTF format.
TimeGenerated	Time event was generated in DMTF format. Same as TimeWritten.
Type	Event type. Can be error, information, warning, audit failure, or audit success.
User	User name. If not available, returns Null value.
SourceName	Source application or service that generated the event.
Category	Numeric value representing category. Represents the descriptive category displayed in Event Viewer and is application specific. There is no method of mapping the numeric value returned by this property to the descriptive category that appears in Event Viewer via WMI.
Message	The event message.
Data	Array of byte values representing any additional data stored in event.
InsertionStrings	Array of strings inserted into event message.

The TimeWritten property is in DMTF date format, which is returned as a string in the following format:

```
yyyymmddHHMMSS.mmmmmmsUUU
```

where yyyy is a four-digit year, mm is two-digit month (01–12), dd is a two-digit day, HH is the hour in 24-hour clock format, MM is minutes, SS is seconds, and mmmmmm is microseconds.

The last four characters (sUUU) represent the time zone stored in Universal Time Coordinates(UTC), also known as Greenwich Mean Time (GMT). UTC is represented by the number of minutes from GMT. So for the West Coast of the United States, which is 8 hours behind GMT, the UTC time code is –480.

This number doesn't take into consideration issues such as daylight saving time. To get the current time zone settings, get a reference to the CurrentTimeZone property for the Win32_ComputerSystem class.

The following code snippet gets the time zone for the local computer Odin:

```
Dim objWMI, nTimeZone
'get a reference to instance of Win32_ComputerSystem class for computer Odin
Set objWMI = GetObject("winmgmts:{impersonationLevel=impersonate}" & _
            "!Win32_ComputerSystem='Odin'")

nTimeZone = objWMI.Currenttimezone
```

The Convert2DMTFDate function from the wmiinc.vbs support file provides the conversion of dates to the DMTF data format. The syntax is as follows:

```
strResult = Convert2DMTFDate(dDate, nTimeZone)
```

The dDate parameter is the date and optional time you want to convert and the strTimeZone parameter represents the time zone as a numeric value.

Also included in the wmiinc.vbs file is the DMTFDate2String function, which converts DMTF dates stored in WMI date/time properties to a "readable" date format. The syntax is as follows:

```
strDate = DMTFDate2String (strDMTFDate)
```

The strDMTFDate parameter contains the DMTF date to convert.

If you are querying event records from the Security event log, the Security privilege must be assigned to the user. Assigning the Security privilege to a user doesn't affect the querying of other logs, but it is required for the Security log.

Event log records expose an InsertionStrings property. This property is an array of values that are inserted into the event message.

Insertion string order is event specific. In the Solution script, the InsertionStrings are checked if the audit event was for file access.

The following code sample returns all of the Security log events with event ID 529 or 539, which are logon failures. This is useful for identifying locked-out accounts and potential security breaches:

```
<?xml version="1.0" ?>
<job>
<!--comment
Script:logonoffchk.wsf
lists all event log events for events 529 and 539, which are logon/off failures
-->
 <script language="VBScript" src="wmiinc.vbs">
 <![CDATA[
Const wbemFlagReturnImmediately  =16
Const wbemFlagForwardOnly = 32
Dim objService, objWMI, nTimeZone, objWMISet, objEvent, objOut, strComputer

If WScript.Arguments.Count = 0 Then
  WScript.Echo "You must specify a computer"
  WScript.Quit
End If
strComputer = WScript.Arguments(0)

'bind to the WMI service, note the Security privilege is specified, this
'is required to access the Security log
Set objService = GetObject("winmgmts:{impersonationLevel=impersonate," & _
                           "(Security)}!\\" & strComputer)


'get time zone
Set objWMI = objService.Get("Win32_ComputerSystem='" & strComputer & "'")
nTimeZone = objWMI.Currenttimezone
'execute query, filtering on event # 529 or 539 (Logon/Logoff access
'from Security logs
'only retrieve entries within the last two days
 Set objWMISet = objService.ExecQuery("SELECT InsertionStrings, " & _
   "TimeWritten FROM Win32_NTLogEvent WHERE " & _
   " (EventIdentifier=529  Or EventIdentifier=539) And LogFile='Security'" & _
   " AND Type='audit failure'  AND  TimeWritten > '" & _
   Convert2DMTFDate(DateAdd("h", -1, Now), nTimeZone) & "' ",, _
        wbemFlagReturnImmediately + wbemFlagForwardOnly)

 Set objOut = WScript.Stdout
 'loop through each event
```

```
 For Each objEvent In objWMISet
    'make sure there are insertion strings to write
    If UBound(objEvent.InsertionStrings) > 0 Then
      objOut.WriteLine objEvent.InsertionStrings(0) & " for user:" & _
                              objEvent.InsertionStrings(1)
     objOut.WriteLine "Time: " & DMTFDate2String(objEvent.TimeWritten)
     objOut.WriteLine "Workstation: " & objEvent.InsertionStrings(6)
 End If
 Next
 ]]>
 </script>
</job>
```

The script requires a computer name to be passed as a parameter to the script from the command prompt. This allows multiple sources to be checked.

The following batch file outputs all logon problems to a text file called `logprob.txt` for the computers Thor, Odin, and Loki:

```
cscript logonoffchk.wsf thor > logprob.txt
cscript logonoffchk.wsf odin > logprob.txt
cscript logonoffchk.wsf loki > logprob.txt
```

> **NOTE** *Accessing large event logs, especially on remote computers, can be time-consuming. The WMI provider can also consume a large number of CPU cycles when initially executing a query, so test for any performance issues with other applications in your environment.*

The NT event log is a powerful tool, but it can be time-consuming to filter through the logged information, especially across multiple computers. The following script outputs the details for all warning, error, and audit failure events for the last 24 hours for the computer specified by the command-line parameter:

```
<?xml version="1.0" ?>
<job>
<!--comment
Script:checkbadevents.wsf
lists all warning, audit failures and errors events for the last 24 hours
-->
 <script language="VBScript" src="wmiinc.vbs">
 <![CDATA[
Const wbemFlagReturnImmediately  =16
```

```
Const wbemFlagForwardOnly = 32
Dim objService, objWMI, nTimeZone, objWMISet, objEvent, strComputer

If WScript.Arguments.Count <> 1 Then
  WScript.Echo "You must specify a computer"
  WScript.Quit
End If

strComputer = WScript.Arguments(0)
'bind to the WMI service, note the Security privilege is specified, this
'is required to access the Security log
Set objService = GetObject("winmgmts:{impersonationLevel=impersonate," _
                          & "(Security)}!\\" & strComputer)

'get time zone
Set objWMI = objService.Get("Win32_ComputerSystem='" & strComputer & "'")

nTimeZone = objWMI.Currenttimezone
'only retrieve entries within the last two days
 Set objWMISet = objService.ExecQuery("SELECT Message, " & _
   "TimeWritten, User,Type, SourceName FROM Win32_NTLogEvent WHERE " & _
   " (Type='audit failure' Or Type='error' Or Type='warning' ) And " & _
   "TimeWritten> '" & Convert2DMTFDate(DateAdd("h", -24, Now), _
    nTimeZone) & "'",, wbemFlagReturnImmediately + wbemFlagForwardOnly)

 'loop through each event
 For Each objEvent In objWMISet
     WScript.Stdout.WriteLine "Time: " & DMTFDate2String(objEvent.TimeWritten)
     WScript.Stdout.WriteLine "Source: " & objEvent.SourceName & " User: " & _
                                  objEvent.User & " Type:" & objEvent.Type

     If Not IsNull(objEvent.Message) Then
             WScript.Stdout.WriteLine _
                               Replace(objEvent.Message,chr(13) & chr(10), chr(13))

     End If
     WScript.Stdout.WriteLine
 Next
 ]]>
 </script>
</job>
```

Event messages stored in the Message property of the event object store a carriage return and linefeed (ASCII characters 13 and 10) for each new line.

When the message is outputted it appears with an additional line between each line of the message, so strip out the line feed character using the Replace function, as in the previous example.

See Also

Read the following WMI SDK documentation topics: "Setting Privileges for the Scripting API," "Object Creation and Monikers," "Calling the Method," "Security Issues When Writing WMI," and "Date and Time Format." For more information, search `http://msdn.microsoft.com` for the articles "Win32_NTEventLogFile" and "Managing Windows with WMI."

10.15 Backing Up Event Viewer Events

Problem

You want to back up event logs exceeding a certain record count.

Solution

You can reference an instance of the `Win32_NTEventLogFile` class for the event log that you want to back up and then invoke the `BackupEventlog` method.

The Solution script checks all event logs on the local machine, and if there are more than 10,000 events in the log, the events are backed up. The backed up logs are named `log month-date-year hh-mm.evt`. For example, an Application log backed up at 9:35 PM on February 4 would be stored as `Application 2-4-2000 21-35.evt`:

```
'clrevent.vbs
'backs up and clears local event log if number of records is
'more than 5000 records
Dim objWMISet, objInstance, nResult, strFile, objServices
'get an instance of a WMI Service object
Set objServices = _
  GetObject("winmgmts:{impersonationLevel=impersonate,(Backup,Security)}")

'get the instances of the Win32_NTEventLogFile class
Set objWMISet = objServices.InstancesOf("Win32_NTEventLogFile")
 For Each objInstance In objWMISet
 'check if number of event records is more than 5000, clear log
   If objInstance.NumberOfRecords > 5000 Then
```

```
    strFile = "d:\eventlogs\backup" & objInstance.LogFileName _
                                      & " " & MonthName(Month(Date)) & _
                                      "-" & Day(Date) & "-" & Year(Date) & _
                                      " " & Hour(Now) & "-" & _
                                      Minute(Now) & ".evt"

    'backup and clear log
    nResult = objInstance.BackupEventlog(strFile)
       'check if operation successful
    If nResult<> 0 Then
      WScript.Echo objInstance.LogFileName & " backed up to " & strFile
   Else
     WScript.Echo "Error ocurred backing up event log " _
                                & objInstance.LogFileName & " to " & strFile
    End If
    End If
  Next
```

Discussion

When you use the Windows NT Event Viewer, you can set event logs to be cleared at certain events automatically, such as when the event log reaches a certain size or a certain number of records. However, there is no option to automatically back up the events that are being deleted. The script backs up the event log after a specified number of events are accumulated.

NT events are exposed through the `Win32_NTEventLogFile` class. Creating an instance of this class returns a collection of all event logs. On Windows NT 4.0 machines this can be Application, Security, and System. Windows 2000/2003/XP provides these logs as well as additional logs for specific services, such as DNS Server server and Directory service.

If you are backing up the Security event log, you must set the `Security` privilege when connecting to the namespace.

The `NumberOfRecords` property returns the number of event log records that exist in the specific event log, while the `LogFileName` property returns the name of the log (Application, Security, or System).

The event log can be backed up by the `BackupEventLog` method. The syntax is as follows:

```
nResult = objInstance.BackupEventlog(strFile)
```

The strFile parameter specifies the path to the file to back up the event log. The path can be a local path but not a UNC path. The local path is relative to the machine where the event log resides. The method returns 0 if successful.

If a backup file with the same name already exists, it is not replaced and an error value is returned.

The Win32_NTEventLogFile class exposes a ClearEventlog method that clears the event log. The ClearEvent log method can back up the data before clearing any events. The syntax is as follows:

```
nResult = objInstance.ClearEventlog([strFile])
```

The optional strFile parameter specifies the path to the file to back up. It operates in the same way as the BackupEventLog method. The method returns 0 if successful. If the file already exists, it is not overwritten. If the optional backup file name is specified, the method will not clear the events unless the data is successfully backed up.

The following code sample gets a reference to the application event log and backs up and clears the events:

```
Dim objEvt
'get a reference to the Application event log. The key for the
'Win32_NTEventLogFile class is the Name property, which represents the
'path to the event log.
Set objEvt = _
  GetObject("winmgmts:{impersonationLevel=impersonate,(Backup,Security)}" & _
  "!Win32_NTEventLogFile.Name='C:\WINNT40\System32\config\AppEvent.Evt'")
 objEvt.ClearEventlog ("D:\Data\EvenBackup\AppBackup.evt")
```

See Also

For more information, search http://msdn.microsoft.com for the articles “Win32_NTEventLogFile” and “Managing Windows with WMI.”

10.16 Processing Event Viewer Events

Problem

You want to process Event Viewer events when an event is generated.

Solution

You can invoke the ExecNotificationQuery method against the WMI namespace you want to process events:

```
'connect to Services object for local computer
Set objServices = GetObject("winmgmts:{impersonationLevel=impersonate,(Security)}")

'execute an event notification query to generate events when a new
'event record is created
Set objEvents = objServices.ExecNotificationQuery _
                    ("select * from __instancecreationevent " & _
                     "where targetinstance isa 'Win32_NTLogEvent'")

'check if error occurred during execution of
if Err <> 0 then
   WScript.Echo Err.Description, Err.Number, Err.Source
End If

'wait forever..
WScript.Echo "Waiting for NT objEvents. . ."
Do
   Set NTEvent = objEvents.nextevent
   'check if error occurred
   If Err <> 0 Then
      WScript.Echo Err.Number, Err.Description, Err.Source
      Exit Do
   Else
      WScript.Echo NTEvent.TargetInstance.Message
   End if
Loop
```

Discussion

The WMI CIM Manager can consume events from WMI providers by executing a notification query against them. A notification query is different than a normal query in that it returns data from events as they occur.

The ExecNotificationQuery method is used to execute a notification query against a WMI provider. The syntax is as follows:

```
set objEvents = objService.ExecNotificationQuery(strEventQuery)
```

strEventQuery contains the query to execute and specifies what conditions an event will fire. The query is constructed using WQL statements.

The source for the queries can be the creation of a new instance of a WMI class or the modification of an existing instance. Use the _instancecreationevent statement to specify the creation of a WMI class or _instancemodificationevent to specify the modification of an existing instance of a class.

The following sample executes an event notification query that generates an event whenever a new instance of the Win32_NTLogEvent class is generated. This occurs whenever a new event log item is generated:

```
Set objService = GetObject("winmgmts:{impersonationLevel=impersonate,(Security)")

Set objEvents = objService.ExecNotificationQuery _
("select * from __instancecreationevent where targetinstance isa  " & _
        "'Win32_NTLogEvent'")
```

If the query executed through the ExecNotificationQuery method is successful, it returns an EventSource object. The EventSource object exposes a NextEvent method, which is used to retrieve events returned from the query. The syntax is as follows:

```
set objEvents = objService.NextEvent([nDelay])
```

The optional nDelay parameter specifies how long to wait (in milliseconds) for an event before quitting. If the parameter is omitted, the NextEvent method will wait indefinitely for an event to be generated. The following script executes a notification query that fires events when new event log items are created:

```
Set objService = GetObject("winmgmts:{impersonationLevel=impersonate,(Security)")
Set objEvents = objService.ExecNotificationQuery _
("select * from __instancecreationevent where targetinstance isa " & _
        "'Win32_NTLogEvent'")

Set objEvent = objEvents.NextEvent()
```

The Win32_NTEventLog provider is known as an event provider. This means that it can "call back" to the originating program when an event is generated.

Providers that do not generate events require a WITHIN clause in the WQL statement. The WITHIN clause specifies a time delay for when the query is refreshed. The CIMV2 provider, which includes most of the informational Win32 and CIM classes discussed in this chapter, does not generate events and requires the WITHIN clause.

In the following script, an event fires whenever a new process starts on the remote machine Odin:

```
<?xml version="1.0" ?>
<job>
<!--comment
Script:newproc.wsf
Description:monitors the creation of new processes
-->
 <script language="VBScript" src="wmiinc.vbs">
 <![CDATA[
  Dim objService, objEvent, objEvents
  Set objService = _
     GetObject("winmgmts:{impersonationLevel=impersonate}!\\Odin")
  'check for the creation of any new programs/processes every 60 seconds
  Set objEvents = objService.ExecNotificationQuery _
      ("select * from __instancecreationevent within 60 " & _
        "where targetinstance isa 'Win32_Process'")

 ' Note this next call will wait indefinitely - a timeout can be specified
  WScript.Echo "Waiting for process creation. . ."
  Do
   Set objEvent = objEvents.Nextevent
   WScript.Echo objEvent.TargetInstance.ExecutablePath & " started at " & _
                DMTFDate2String(objEvent.TargetInstance.CreationDate)
  Loop
  ]]>
 </script>
</job>
```

The following sample checks if the status of any NT service changes and displays the status of the service and the time a change occurred:

```
'svcstatus.vbs
'Description:monitors changes in service status
 Option Explicit
 Dim objService, objEvent, objEvents

 Set objService = GetObject("winmgmts:{impersonationLevel=impersonate}")
```

```
'query for any changes in services every 60 seconds
Set objEvents = objService.ExecNotificationQuery _
     ("select * from __instancemodificationevent within 60 " & _
       "where targetinstance isa 'Win32_Service'")

WScript.Echo "Waiting for service change. . ."
Do
 Set objEvent = objEvents.Nextevent
 WScript.Echo objEvent.TargetInstance.Description & " state changed to " & _
              objEvent.TargetInstance.State & " at " & Now
Loop
```

See Also

Read the following WMI SDK documentation topics: "Object Creation and Monikers" and "SwbemServices and SWbemServices.ExecNotificationQuery Examples." For more information, search `http://msdn.microsoft.com` for the article "Managing Windows with WMI."

10.17 Changing NT Service Account Information

Problem

You want to change the user ID and password for an NT service.

Solution

You can invoke the `Change` method for an instance of the `Win32_Service` class. This enables you to set the service for which you want to change the password.

```
'servicechng.vbs
'changes the password for all services with specific user ID
Dim objWMIObjects, objWMIObject, objServices, nResult
'get a reference to local WMI service
Set objServices = _
    GetObject("winmgmts:{impersonationLevel=impersonate}")
```

```
'get all services that use the Administrator account
Set objWMIObjects = objServices.ExecQuery( _
                                          "Select * From Win32_Service " & _
                                          Where StartName='Acme\\Administrator'")

'loop through each service and change the password
For Each objWMIObject In objWMIObjects
    nResult = objWMIObject.Change(, , , , , , , "newpassword")
    If nResult = 0 Then
         WScript.Echo "Password successfully set for " & _
                        objWMIObject.DisplayName
    Else
        WScript.Echo "Error setting password set for service " _
                        &  objWMIObject.DisplayName
    End If
Next
```

Discussion

Windows NT services can have either an NT service account or an NT account associated with them. If a user account is associated with the service, a password is required to be stored for the service.

When the passwords for an account are changed, they must be changed for the service to function properly. This can be a time-consuming process, especially if the account is used in services across multiple computers.

The WMI `Win32_Service` class exposes NT service information. The `Change` method can be used to change any service parameters. The syntax is as follows:

```
nResult = objWMIService.Change([Name],[DisplayName],[PathName] ,
[ServiceType],[StartMode],[DesktopInteract],[StartName],[StartPassword,]
[LoadOrderGroup],[LoadOrderGroupDependencies], [ServiceDependencies])
```

Table 10-12 lists the `Change` method's parameters.

Table 10-12. Change *Method Parameters*

PARAMETER	DESCRIPTION
Name	Internal service name used to reference service by WMI and ADSI.
DisplayName	Display name as it appears in service manager.
PathName	Path to service executable.
ServiceType	Integer value. 0 = Kernel, 1 = File System driver, 2 = Adapter, 3 = Recognizer driver, 4 = Process, and 5 = Win32 share process.
ErrorControl	Integer value. Indicates action taken by service manager if service fails to start. 0 = Ignore, 1 = Normal, 2 = Server, and 3 = Critical.
StartMode	Service start mode. Valid values are Boot, System, Automatic, Manual, or Disabled.
DesktopInteract	Boolean. If `True`, service can interact with desktop.
StartName	Account service runs under a `Domain\Username` format. If the service is logged on as `LocalSystem`, this value is set to `Null`.
StartPassword	Password for account.
LoadOrderGroup	Group name that service is associated with.
LoadOrderGroupDependencies	Array of service groups that service is dependent upon. These groups must start before the service starts.
ServiceDependencies	Array of services that service is dependent upon. These services must start before the service starts.

All parameters are optional. If you do not supply a specific parameter, the current setting is used. The method returns 0 if successful.

> **TIP** *Do not make changes to service parameters unless you are absolutely sure of the effect of the change.*

You can make individual references to services by querying the service with the `Win32_Service` value, which is the internal service's name:

```
Dim objService
'get a reference to the SQL Server service
Set objService = _
   GetObject("winmgmts:{impersonationLevel=impersonate}" & _
             "!Win32_Service.Name='MSSQLServer'")
'change the user ID and password for the service
 nResult = objWMIObject.Change(, , , , , , "Acme\SQLAdmin", "newpassword")
```

See Also

For more information, search `http://msdn.microsoft.com` for the article "Win32_Service."

10.18 Changing System Time

Problem

You want to change the system time.

Solution

Windows XP and 2003 allow you to set the system date and time by calling the SetDateTime method of the Win32_OperatingSystem class:

```
'synchronize time on remote computer against local computer
strComputer = "w2k3-01"

Set objService = _
  GetObject("winmgmts:{impersonationLevel=impersonate,(SystemTime)}!\\" _
                        & strComputer)

Set objOS = objService.Get("Win32_OperatingSystem")

Set objComputer = objService.Get("Win32_ComputerSystem='" & strComputer & "'")
nTimeZone = objComputer.Currenttimezone

'get the active OS
```

```
Set objOSColl = objService.ExecQuery _
          ("Select * From Win32_OperatingSystem Where Primary = True")

'set the time on the remote computer using the local systems current time
For Each objOS In objOSColl
    nSuccess = objOS.SetDateTime(Convert2DMTFDate(Now, nTimeZone))
Next
```

Discussion

Windows XP and 2003 provide the ability to read and set time on local and remote computers using WMI.

Date and time information can be read through the `Win32_LocalTime` class. The `Win32_LocalTime` class exposes properties listed in Table 10-13.

Table 10-13. `Win32_LocalTime` *Properties*

PROPERTY	DESCRIPTION
Day	Day of month between 1 and 31.
DayOfWeek	Day of week between 0 and 6. The value 0 represents Sunday.
Hour	Current hour between 0 and 23.
Milliseconds	Not implemented.
Minute	Current minute between 0 and 59.
Month	Current month between 1 and 12.
Quarter	Current quarter between 1 and 4.
Second	Current second between 0 and 59.
WeekInMonth	Current week between 1 and 6.
Year	Year in four-digit value.

The following script shows the current local time:

```
'get WMI service for local computer and Win32_LocalTime class instance
Set objService = _
  GetObject("winmgmts:{impersonationLevel=impersonate}")

Set objDateTime = objService.Get("Win32_LocalTime=@")

Wscript.Echo "The current time is " & objDateTime.Hour & ":" & objDateTime.Minute
```

To change the date and time, use the Win32_OperatingSystem class's SetDateTime method. The syntax is as follows:

```
nError = objOS.SetDateTime(strDateTime)
```

strDateTime represents the WMI DMTF date and time format. The Solution script uses the Convert2DMTFDate function from wmiinc.vbs. See Solution 10.14 for more information on the WMI DMTF date format.

See Also

For more information, search http://msdn.microsoft.com for the terms "Win32_OperatingSystem SetDateTime."

10.19 Defragging a Drive

Problem

You want to defrag all drives that are overfragmented.

Solution

Windows 2003 provides the Defrag method through the Win32_Volume class. The following script will defrag all local drives:

```
Dim objWMIService, objVolumes, objVolume, bDefragRecommended
Dim strComputer, nError, objDefragAnalysis

strComputer = "."
Set objWMIService = GetObject("winmgmts:\\" & strComputer & "\root\cimv2")

'get all local fixed drives
Set objVolumes = objWMIService.ExecQuery _
    ("Select * from Win32_Volume Where DriveType=3")

'loop through each drive volume and only
For Each objVolume In objVolumes
    'check if drive needs to be defragged
```

```
    nError = objVolume.DefragAnalysis(bDefragRecommended _
            , objDefragAnalysis)

    'if defrag recommended then defrag drive
    If bDefragRecommended Then
        Wscript.Echo "Attempting to defrag " & objVolume.DriveLetter
        nError = objVolume.Defrag(True, objDefragAnalysis)

        'if no error then report success
        If Not nError Then
            Wscript.Echo "Error " & nError & " defragging " &
objVolume.DriveLetter
        End If

    Else
        Wscript.Echo "Drive " & objVolume.DriveLetter & " not defragmented"
    End If
Next
```

Discussion

Windows versions from Windows 2000 onward included the Disk Defragmenter utility. Disk Defragmenter is very useful, but no mechanism was provided to automate the defragmentation process. Windows 2003 provides new WMI classes that interface with the Disk Defragmenter program.

The Win32_Volume class represents local storage, such as hard drives, removable storage, network and RAM drives.

The defragmentation process is accessed through the `Win32_Volume` class. The `Win32_Volume` class provides two methods, `DefragAnalysis` and `Defrag`. The `DefragAnalysis` method returns fragmentation information and a recommendation flag for a specified volume. The syntax is as follows:

nError = *objVolume*.`DefragAnalysis`(*bDefragRecommended*, *objDefragAnalysis*)

The `bDefragRecommended` and `objDefragAnalysis` parameters are returned when the method is executed successfully. The `bDefragRecommended` parameter is set to `True` if defragmention is recommended; otherwise, it is set to `False`. The `objDefragAnalysis` parameter is a `WMI Win32_DefragAnalysis` object that contains information about the fragmentation analysis. Table 10-14 lists `Win32_DefragAnalysis` properties.

Table 10-14. `Win32_DefragAnalysis` *Object Properties*

PROPERTY	DESCRIPTION
AverageFileSize	Average size of file in bytes.
AverageFragmentsPerFile	Average number of fragments per file.
ClusterSize	Cluster size in bytes.
ExcessFolderFragments	Number of excess folder fragments.
FilePercentFragmentation	Percentage of files that are fragmented.
FragmentedFolders	Number of fragmented folders.
FreeSpace	Number of bytes free.
FreeSpacePercent	Drive free space in bytes.
FreeSpacePercentFragmentation	Percentage of drive free space that is fragmented.
MFTPercentInUse	Percentage of Master File Table that is in use.
MFTRecordCount	Number of records in Master File Table.
PageFileSize	Size of page file in bytes. If no page file is on the drive, the value is `Null`.
TotalExcessFragments	Total excess fragments on drive.
TotalFiles	Total number of files on drive.
TotalFolders	Total number of folders on drive.
TotalFragmentedFiles	Total number of fragmented files.
TotalMFTFragments	Total number of Master File Table fragments.
TotalMFTSize	Size of Master File Table in bytes.
TotalPageFileFragments	Total number of fragments in page file.
TotalPercentFragmentation	Percentage of drive fragmented.
UsedSpace	Total used space in bytes.
VolumeName	Volume name.
VolumeSize	Total size of drive in bytes.

In the following script, the file fragmentation percentage and defragmentation reccomendation are shown for the C: drive on the local computer:

```
Dim objService, objVolumes, objVolume, nError, bDefragRecommended, objDA

'get the defrag status on the C: for the local computer
Set objService = GetObject("winmgmts:root\cimv2")

'get a reference to the C: drive
Set objVolumes = objService.ExecQuery( _
                                "Select * from Win32_Volume Where Name = 'C:\\'")

'loop through the collection and process the single returned drive
For Each objVolume In objVolumes
    nError = objVolume.DefragAnalysis(bDefragRecommended, objDA)
    If Not nError Then
          Wscript.Echo objDA.FilePercentFragmentation & "% of files are
fragmented."
        If bDefragRecommended Then
            Wscript.Echo "This volume should be defragged."
        Else
            Wscript.Echo "This volume does not need to be defragged."
        End If
    End If
Next
```

See Also

For more information, search `http://msdn.microsoft.com` for the term "Win32_DefragAnalysis."

10.20 Listing DNS Resources

Problem

You want to list Domain Name Server (DNS) addresses.

Solution

DNS operations can be performed through the WMI DNS provider. The following solution will list all A type addresses for the DNS zone acme.com:

```
strDNSServer = "dnsserver.acme.com"
Set objService = GetObject("winmgmts:\\" & strDNSServer & "\root\MicrosoftDNS")

Set objNames = objService.ExecQuery( _
              "Select * FROM MicrosoftDNS_AType Where DomainName='acme.com'")

For Each objName In objNames
    Wscript.Echo objName.OwnerName & " " & objName.IPAddress
Next
```

Discussion

The WMI DNS provider allows for manipulation of Windows 2000 and 2003 DNS servers. The WMI DNS provider is installed by default under Windows 2003.

The Windows 2000 WMI DNS provider was introduced after Windows 2000 was released and is available as a separate download from ftp://ftp.microsoft.com/reskit/win2000/dnsprov.zip. Once you have downloaded the ZIP file, extract the contents to any directory.

1. Copy dnsschema.mof to the %systemroot%\system32\wbem\mof directory.

2. Copy dnsprov.dll to the %systemroot%\system32\wbem directory.

3. Go to the command prompt and change the directory to %systemroot%\system32\wbem.

4. Enter **regsvr32 dnsprov.dll**.

The WMI DNS provider is located under the MicrosoftDNS namespace. The following script gets a reference to the DNS service on computer dnsserver.acme.com:

```
strDNSServer = "dnsserver.acme.com"
Set objService = GetObject("winmgmts:\\" & strDNSServer & "\root\MicrosoftDNS")
```

DNS servers are used to resolve "friendly" names to IP addresses and locate computers and resources on TCP/IP networks. These resources include computers, and mail and Web servers.

DNS servers organize resources into *zones*. Zones manage information about one or more domains. For example, a zone might exist to store information about `acme.com`.

Resource information is stored as *resource records* (RRs). There are different RRs used to represent different resources. An RR may map a fully qualified domain name (FQDN) to an IP address, domain name, or e-mail server.

The Windows DNS server can contain almost 30 different RR types, as shown in Table 10-15.

Table 10-15. WMI Resource Record Objects

RESOURCE RECORD	DESCRIPTION
`MicrosoftDNS_AType`	Maps an FQDN to an IP address (A)
`MicrosoftDNS_AAAAType`	Maps an FQDN to an IPv6 address
`MicrosoftDNS_AFSDBType`	Andrew File System Database Server record
`MicrosoftDNS_ATMAType`	ATM address-to-name record
`MicrosoftDNS_CNAMEType`	Maps an alias FQDN to another FQDN
`MicrosoftDNS_HINFOType`	Stores host CPU and operating system information
`MicrosoftDNS_ISDNType`	ISDN (ISDN) record
`MicrosoftDNS_KEYType`	Encryption key (KEY) record
`MicrosoftDNS_MBType`	Mailbox (MB) record
`MicrosoftDNS_MDType`	Mail agent for domain (MD) record
`MicrosoftDNS_MFType`	Mail forwarding (MF) record
`MicrosoftDNS_MGType`	Mail group (MG) record
`MicrosoftDNS_MINFOType`	Mail information (MINFO) record
`MicrosoftDNS_MRType`	Mailbox rename (MR) record
`MicrosoftDNS_MXType`	Mail exchanger (MX) record
`MicrosoftDNS_NSType`	Name server (NS) record
`MicrosoftDNS_NXTType`	Next (NXT) record
`MicrosoftDNS_PTRType`	Pointer (PTR) record
`MicrosoftDNS_RPType`	Responsible person (RP) record
`MicrosoftDNS_RTType`	Route through (RT) record
`MicrosoftDNS_SIGType`	Signature (SIG) record

continues

Table 10-15. WMI Resource Record Objects (continued)

RESOURCE RECORD	DESCRIPTION
MicrosoftDNS_SOAType	Start of authority (SOA) record
MicrosoftDNS_SRVType	Service (SRV) record
MicrosoftDNS_TXTType	Text (TXT) record
MicrosoftDNS_WINSType	WINS server (WINS) record
MicrosoftDNS_WINSRType	WINS reverse-lookup (WINSRT) record
MicrosoftDNS_WKSType	Well-known services (WKS) record
MicrosoftDNS_X25Type	X.25 record

Table 10-16 lists the common WMI properties shared by these records.

Table 10-16. Resource Record Common Properties

PROPERTY	DESCRIPTION
DomainName	Name of the domain the resource is stored under
DNSServerName	Name of DNS server where resource record is stored
OwnerName	Represents the address
TTL	Time record can be cached in seconds

The most common RR is the `A` (address or host) record. When you enter an FQDN in a Web browser, a DNS server will use A type records to resolve the IP address for the browser to go to. The Solution script lists all A type records for the domain `acme.com`. The `AType` record object exposes the `IPAddress` property, which represents the FQDN IP address.

See Also

For more information, search `http://msdn.microsoft.com` for the terms "Win32_DefragAnalysis," "DNS WMI Classes," or "Managing DNS Resource Records."

10.21 Creating a DNS Zone

Problem

You want to create a DNS zone.

Solution

The following script creates the primary zone acme.com:

```
'create basic non-ADSI primary zone on a Windows 2003 server
strNewZoneName = "acme.com"
strDNSServer = "dnsserver.acme.com"

'connect to DNS server and create DNS zone object
Set objService = GetObject("winmgmts:\\" & strDNSServer & "\root\MicrosoftDNS")
Set objZone = objService.Get("MicrosoftDNS_Zone")

objZone.CreateZone strNewZoneName, 0
```

Discussion

The WMI DNS provider allows for manipulation of DNS servers under Windows 2000 and 2003.

> **NOTE** *You should not make DNS changes unless you have good working knowledge of your DNS infrastructure. Back up all files from the* windows\system32\dns *directory before making any mass changes to a production DNS server.*

A DNS zone organizes one or more domains. For example, the acme.com zone will contain all addresses that end with acme.com. To create a DNS zone using the WMI provider, you must first get a reference to a MicrosoftDNS_Zone object for the DNS server you want to create the zone in. The following script gets a reference to the DNS service on the computer dnsserver.acme.com:

```
strDNSServer = "dnsserver.acme.com"
Set objService = GetObject("winmgmts:\\" & strDNSServer & "\root\MicrosoftDNS")
```

Once you have a `MicrosoftDNS_Zone` object, call the `CreateZone` method. The `CreateZone` method creates a new DNS zone. The Windows 2000 DNS provider has a different syntax than Windows 2003. The Windows 2003 syntax is as follows:

```
objZone.CreateZone NewZoneName, ZoneType, _
DSIntegrated,IPAdresses,DataFileName,AdminEmailName
```

The Windows 2000 syntax is as follows:

```
objZone.CreateZone NewZoneName, ZoneType, IPAdresses,DataFileName,AdminEmailName
```

Table 10-17 lists the `CreateZone` parameters.

Table 10-17. `CreateZone` *Parameters*

PARAMETER	DESCRIPTION
`ZoneName`	Name of the zone.
`ZoneType`	For Windows 2003 ZoneType values are 0 Primary 1 Secondary 2 Stub. For Windows 2000 ZoneType values are 0 DS integrated 1 Primary 2 Secondary.
`DSIntegrated` (optional)	Windows 2003 only; Boolean flag. If `True`, it creates Active Directory integrated domain. The default value is `False`.
`IpAddresses` (optional)	Array of addresses for the master DNS server. This is required only when you are creating a secondary zone.
`DataFileName` (optional)	Name of file the zone information is stored in.
`AdminEmailName` (optional)	E-mail address of the administrator responsible for the zone.

The following script creates an Active Directory primary domain on a Windows 2003 DNS server:

```
'create basic non-AD primary zone for domain on a Windows 2003 server
'connect to DNS server and create DNS zone object
Set objService = GetObject("winmgmts:\\dnsserver.acme.com\root\MicrosoftDNS")
Set objZone = objService.Get("MicrosoftDNS_Zone")

objZone.CreateZone strNewZoneName, 0, True, , , "admin@adomain.com"
```

The following script creates a primary domain on a Windows 2000 DNS server:

```
'create basic non-ADSI primary zone for domain on a Windows 2000 server
'connect to DNS server and create DNS zone object
Set objService = GetObject("winmgmts:\\w2k-01\root\MicrosoftDNS")
Set objZone = objService.Get("MicrosoftDNS_Zone")

objZone.CreateZone"adomainW2K.com", 1
```

DNS servers can contain forward and reverse lookup zones. Forward lookup zones store domain name information (i.e., `acme.com`) and map FQDNs to IP addresses. The solution script creates a primary zone for `acme.com`.

Reverse lookup zones map IP addresses to FQDNs. Reverse lookup zones are not used in day-to-day name resolution by Internet applications such as Web browsers or e-mail, but are useful in network diagnostics.

The steps for creating a reverse lookup zone are the same as for a forward lookup zone. The only difference is the zone name. The zone name must follow the format `o3.o2.o1.in-addr.arpa`, where o1, o2, and o3 represent octet 1, 2, and 3 of an IP address. The zone name `1.168.192.in-addr.arpa` would represent the IP range 192.168.1.0 to 192.168.1.255.

The following script creates a reverse lookup zone on a Windows 2003 DNS server:

```
'create basic non-ADSI reverse lookup zone on a Windows 2003 server
strDNSServer = "dnsserver.acme.com"

'connect to DNS server and create DNS reverse zone
Set objService = GetObject("winmgmts:\\" & strDNSServer & "\root\MicrosoftDNS")
Set objZone = objService.Get("MicrosoftDNS_Zone")

objZone.CreateZone "1.168.192.in-addr.arpa", 0
```

DNS zones can be configured to replicate to a secondary DNS server. This provides redundancy if the primary DNS server goes down. To create a secondary DNS zone using the WMI, first create the primary DNS zone.

The primary DNS zone requires security to be configured for the secondary zone. This security determines what secondary servers can access the primary zone. This access is set by the `ResetSecondaries` method under Windows 2003 and `ResetSecondaryIpArray` under Windows 2000. The Windows 2003 syntax is as follows:

```
objZone. ResetSecondaries SecondaryServers, SecureSecondaries, _
      NotifyServers, Notify, AdminEmailName
```

The Windows 2000 syntax is as follows:

```
objZone. ResetSecondaryIpArray SecondaryServers, SecureSecondaries, _
    NotifyServers, Notify, AdminEmailName
```

Table 10-18 lists `ResetSecondaries` and `ResetSecondaryIpArray` method parameters.

Table 10-18. `ResetSecondaries` *and* `ResetSecondaryIpArray` *Method Parameters*

PARAMETER	DESCRIPTION
`SecondaryServers` (optional)	Array of IP addresses that specify what secondary DNS servers can update from primary zone.
`SecureSecondaries` (optional)	Determines level of security. 0 = No security, and secondary server can update. 1, 2 = Only servers specified by `SecondaryServers` property.
`NotifyServers` (optional)	Array of servers to notify when resources are changed.
`Notify` (optional)	Determines notification level 0 No notify 1 Servers listed in servers tab 2 Only transfer to servers specified in NotifyServers
`AdminEmailName` (optional)	E-mail address of the administrator responsible for the zone.

The following script creates a primary zone and secondary zone for the domain `acme.com` on a Windows 2003 DNS server:

```
'create a primary and secondary zone
strNewZoneName = "acme.com"
strPrimaryServer = "dnsserver.acme.com"
strSecondaryServer = "dnsserver2.acme.com"
strSecondaryIP = "192.168.0.226"

'get DNS service for primary service
Set objService = GetObject("winmgmts:\\" & strPrimaryServer & "\root\MicrosoftDNS")

'create a new zone
Set objZone = objService.Get("MicrosoftDNS_Zone")
objZone.CreateZone strNewZoneName, 0

'get a reference to the newly create zone
Set objZone = objService.Get("MicrosoftDNS_Zone.ContainerName=""" & _
                          strNewZoneName &  """,DnsServerName=""" & _
                           strPrimaryServer & """,Name=""" & strNewZoneName & """")

'set secondary server address
objZone.ResetSecondaries Array(strSecondaryIP), 2

'get WMI service for secondary DNS server and create DNS object
Set objService = GetObject("winmgmts:\\" & _
                              strSecondaryServer & "\root\MicrosoftDNS")
Set objZone = objService.Get("MicrosoftDNS_Zone")

aMasterIP = Array(strSecondaryIP)
'create secondary zone pointing to the primary zone
objZone.CreateZone strNewZoneName, 1, strNewZoneName & ".dns", aMasterIP
```

See Also

For more information, search `http://msdn.microsoft.com` for the terms "MicrosoftDNS_Zone CreateZone."

10.22 Modifying DNS Zone Properties

Problem

You want to modify DNS zone properties.

Solution

Get a reference to a zone and set the properties you wish to modify:

```
Set obj = GetObject ("winmgmts:\\W2K3-01\root\MicrosoftDNS:MicrosoftDNS_Zone" _
            & ".ContainerName=""acme.com"",DnsServerName=""dnsserver.acme.com""" _
            & ",Name=""acme.com""")

objZone.DataFile = "acemcomzone.dns"
objZone.NoRefreshInterval = 34
objZone.RefreshInterval = 75
obj.Put_
```

Discussion

WMI zone objects expose a large number of properties, of which only a few can be modified through the WMI DNS provider. Table 10-19 lists writeable WMI zone properties.

Table 10-19. Writeable DNS Zone Properties

PROPERTY	DESCRIPTION
DataFile	DNS zone data file
ForwarderTimeout	Time in seconds the DNS server waits for resolution before it resolves the address itself
NoRefreshInterval	Time in hours between a record's timestamp update and the next time the timestamp can be refreshed
RefreshInterval	Interval in hours between the most recent timestamp refresh and the moment the timestamp may be refreshed again

10.23 Creating DNS Address

Problem

You want to create a DNS address.

Solution

To create a DNS address, create an instance of the Microsoft DNS record type class and call the `CreateInstance FromPropertyData` method. The following script creates an A type DNS record:

```
strDNSServer = "dnsserver.acme.com"
strContainer = "acme.com"
strOwnerAddress = "shop1.acme.com"
intRecordClass = 1
nTTL = 600
strIPAddress = "192.168.1.101"

Set objService = GetObject("winmgmts:\\" & strDNSServer & "\root\MicrosoftDNS")
Set objAType = objService.Get("MicrosoftDNS_AType")
objAType.CreateInstance FromPropertyData  strDNSServer, strContainer, _
            strOwnerAddress, intRecordClass, nTTL, strIPAddress
```

Discussion

Resource records store information in the DNS server that can be used to process client queries. There are different types of resource records that contain different types of information that can be stored in a DNS database.

The DNS WMI Provider currently supports the resource record types shown in Table 10-15.

To create an address, get a reference to the appropriate WMI RR object and use the `CreateInstanceFromPropertyData` method. Table 10-20 lists common parameters used by all `CreateInstanceFromPropertyData` methods. Each RR has one or more additional parameters that are unique to the RR type.

Table 10-20. `CreateInstanceFromPropertyData` *Common Properties*

PROPERTY	DESCRIPTION
DnsServerName	FQDN or IP address of the DNS server that contains this RR.
ContainerName	Name of the container for the Zone, Cache, or RootHints instance that contains this RR.
OwnerName	Resource record owner. This varies depending on RR type.
RecordClass (optional)	RR record class. The default value is 1.
TTL	Time to live in seconds.

The A type record is a commonly used record. To create an A type record, use the `CreateInstanceFromPropertyData` method of the `MicrosoftDNS_AType` object. The syntax is as follows:

```
objAType.CreateInstanceFromPropertyData DNSServer, Container, OwnerAddress, _
RecordClass, TTL, IPAddress
```

The first five parameters are listed in Table 10-20.The `IPAddress` parameter resolves an IP address to the `OwnerAddress`. The method returns 0 if successful. The Solution script creates an A type record.

Canonical Names (CNAME) type records create address "aliases." CNAME records translate an FQDN to another FQDN.

To create a CNAME record, use the `CreateInstanceFromPropertyData` method of the `MicrosoftDNS_CNAMEType` object. The syntax is as follows:

```
objAType.CreateInstanceFromPropertyData (DNSServer, Container, _
      OwnerAddress, RecordClass, TTL, PrimaryName)
```

The first five parameters are listed in Table 10-20. The `PrimaryName` parameter represents the alias address. The following script creates a CNAME address that redirects the address `www.acme.com` to `eshop.acme.com`:

```
strDNSServer = "dnsserver.acme.com"
strContainer = "acme.com"
strAddress = "www.acme.com"
intRecordClass = 1
nTTL = 600
strPrimaryName = "eshop.acme.com"

Set objService = GetObject("winmgmts:\\" & strDNSServer & "\root\MicrosoftDNS")
Set objItem = objService.Get("MicrosoftDNS_CNAMEType")
```

```
objItem.CreateInstanceFromPropertyData _
    strDNSServer, strContainer, strAddress, intRecordClass, nTTL, strPrimaryName
```

Mail Exchange (MX) records are used by SMTP mail services to deliver e-mail.

To create a CNAME record, use the CreateInstanceFromPropertyData of the MicrosoftDNS_CNAMEType object. The syntax is as follows:

```
objMXType.CreateInstanceFromPropertyData DNSServer, Container, OwnerAddress, _
              RecordClass, TTL, Preference,FQDN
```

The first five parameters are listed in Table 10-20. The Preference parameter is a numeric value that represents a mail server preference. If there is more than one MX record for a given domain, a mail service will attempt to contact the server with the lowest preference number and work its way up. The FQDN parameter represents the FQDN of the mail server.

The following script creates two MX addresses for acme.com with different preference levels:

```
strDNSServer = "dnsserver.acme.com"
strContainer = "acme.com"
strOwnerAddress = "acme.com"
intRecordClass = 1
nTTL = 600

Set objService = GetObject("winmgmts:\\" & strDNSServer & "\root\MicrosoftDNS")
Set objItem = objService.Get("MicrosoftDNS_MXType")

'create two MX records
objItem.CreateInstanceFromPropertyData _
    strDNSServer, strContainer, strOwnerAddress, intRecordClass, _
        nTTL, 10, "mail1.acme.com"

objItem.CreateInstanceFromPropertyData _
    strDNSServer, strContainer, strOwnerAddress, intRecordClass, _
                        nTTL, 20, "mail2.acme.com"
```

Pointer (PTR) records are used in reverse lookup domains to map an IP address to an FQDN. To create a PTR record, use the CreateInstanceFromPropertyData method of the MicrosoftDNS_PTRType object. The syntax is as follows:

```
objPTRType.CreateInstanceFromPropertyData DNSServer, Container, OwnerAddress _
                              , RecordClass, TTL, FQDN
```

The first five parameters are listed in Table 10-20. The `FQDN` parameter maps an FQDN to the IP address specified by the `OwnerAddress` parameter. The `OwnerAddress` parameter is the IP address in reverse format followed by `in-addr-arpa`.

The following script creates a PTR that resolves the IP address 192.168.1.101 to `www.acme.com`:

```
strDNSServer = "dnsserver.acme.com"
strContainer = "1.168.192.in-addr.arpa"
strIPAddress = "101.1.168.192.in-addr.arpa"

intRecordClass = 1
nTTL = 600

Set objService = GetObject("winmgmts:\\" & strDNSServer & "\root\MicrosoftDNS")
Set objItem = objService.Get("MicrosoftDNS_PTRType")

objItem.CreateInstanceFromPropertyData _
    strDNSServer, strContainer, strIPAddress, intRecordClass, nTTL, "www.acme.com"
```

The following script creates 100 A type and corresponding PTR records in the domain `acme.com`. Each address is prefixed with `wkst` and a number (`wkst1`, `wkst2`, and so on). The addresses are assigned the range 192.168.1.1 to 192.168.1.100. The script assumes that `acme.com` and reverse lookup zones already exist.

```
'create 100 addresses in the domain Acme.com
strDNSServer = "dnsserver.acme.com"
strContainer = "acme.com"
'strPTRContainer ="168.192.in-addr.arpa"
intRecordClass = 1
nTTL = 600

Set objService = GetObject("winmgmts:\\" & strDNSServer & "\root\MicrosoftDNS")
Set objItem = objService.Get("MicrosoftDNS_AType")
Set objPTRItem = objService.Get("MicrosoftDNS_PTRType")

For nF = 1 To 100
    strOwner = "wkst" & nF & ".acme.com"
    objItem.CreateInstanceFromPropertyData _
    strDNSServer, strContainer, strOwner, intRecordClass, _
    nTTL, "192.168.1." & nF

    'create corresponding PTR record
    objPTRItem.CreateInstanceFromPropertyData _
```

```
    strDNSServer, "1.168.192.in-addr.arpa", nF & ".1.168.192.in-addr.arpa", _
    intRecordClass, nTTL, strOwner
Next
```

See Also

For more information, search http://msdn.microsoft.com for the term "CreateInstanceFromPropertyData MicrosoftDNS_AType."

10.24 Deleting DNS Resources

Problem

You want to delete a DNS record.

Solution

To delete a DNS record, get a reference to the DNS record and call the Delete_ method. The following script deletes the A type record for the address wkst1.acme.com:

```
strDNSServer = "dnsserver.acme.com"
Set objService = GetObject("winmgmts:\\" & strDNSServer & "\root\MicrosoftDNS")

Set objNames = objService.ExecQuery( _
        "Select * FROM MicrosoftDNS_AType Where OwnerName='wkst1.acme.com'")

For Each objName In objNames
    objName.Delete_
Next
```

Discussion

To delete a DNS object, call the Delete_ method. The syntax is as follows:

```
objDNSObject.Delete_
```

Deleting a forward lookup resource record will delete any corresponding reverse lookup resource records. The Solution script deletes the A type resource record for the address `wkst1.acme.com`. If there is a corresponding reverse lookup record, it will also be deleted.

Deleting a zone object will delete all records contained in the zone. It will not delete any reverse lookup records for resource records contained in the zone.

The following script deletes all A type records in the `acme.com` zone and then deletes the zone itself:

```
strDNSServer = "dnsserver.acme.com"
strDomain = "acme.com"
Set objService = GetObject("winmgmts:\\" & strDNSServer & "\root\MicrosoftDNS")

Set objRecords = objService.ExecQuery( _
      "Select * FROM MicrosoftDNS_AType Where DomainName='" & strDomain & "'")

'loop through and delete all A type records in domain Acme.com
For Each objRecord In objRecords
    Wscript.Echo "Deleting record " & objRecord.OwnerName
    objRecord.Delete_
Next

'delete the zone Acme.com on server dnsserver.acme.com
Set objZone = objService.Get("MicrosoftDNS_Zone.ContainerName=""" & strDomain & _
        """,DnsServerName=""" & strDNSServer & """,Name=""" & strDomain & """")
objZone.Delete_
```

See Also

For more information, search `http://msdn.microsoft.com` for the term "MicrosoftDNS_AType Delete_."

10.25 Modifying DNS Addresses

Problem

You want to modify a DNS address.

Solution

Get a reference to a DNS resource record and call the `Modify` method. The following script modifies the CNAME record for `www.acme.com` to point to `estore1.acme.com`:

```
strDNSServer = "dnsserver.acme.com"
Set objService = GetObject("winmgmts:\\" & strDNSServer & "\root\MicrosoftDNS")

Set objNames = objService.ExecQuery( _
        "Select * FROM MicrosoftDNS_CNAMEType Where OwnerName='www.acme.com'")

For Each objName In objNames
    Wscript.Echo objName.OwnerName & " " & objName.DomainName
    objName.Modify 600, "estore1.acme.com"
Next
```

Discussion

Each WMI resource record object has a `Modify` method that can be used to modify the record settings. These settings vary according to record type. The syntax is as follows:

```
objRR.Modify(TTL, setting1[,setting2])
```

`TTL` is time to live in seconds. The additional parameters vary depending on the record object. Table 10-21 lists the parameters for commonly used record objects.

Table 10-21. Resource Record `Modify` *Parameters*

RECORD TYPE	PARAMETERS
A type	An IP address that maps to the record's FQDN
CNAME	An alias FQDN address that maps to the record's FQDN
PTR	An FQDN that maps to the record's IP address

The Solution script modifies a CNAME record.

The following script changes the subnet for all A type records in the acme.com domain. New PTR records are created for each A record:

```
strDNSServer = "dnsserver.acme.com"
strNewSubnet = "172.30.1."
strPTRContainer = "1.30.172.in-addr.arpa"

Set objService = GetObject("winmgmts:\\" & strDNSServer & "\root\MicrosoftDNS")

Set objPTRItem = objService.Get("MicrosoftDNS_PTRType")
Set objARecords = objService.ExecQuery( _
        "Select * FROM MicrosoftDNS_AType Where DomainName='acme.com'")

For Each objARecord In objARecords

    If Left(objARecord.OwnerName, 4) = "wkst" Then
        Wscript.Echo objARecord.OwnerName & " " & objARecord.IPAddress _
                                & " " & objARecord.DomainName
        'get the last octet from the current record
        strOctet = Mid(objARecord.IPAddress, 11)
        strNewIP = strNewSubnet & strOctet

        'modify the IP address to 172 subnet
        objARecord.Modify 600, strNewIP

        'create corresponding PTR record
        objPTRItem.CreateInstanceFromPropertyData _
            strDNSServer, strPTRContainer, strOctet & "." & strPTRContainer, _
            intRecordClass, nTTL, objARecord.OwnerName

    End If
Next
```

See Also

For more information, search http://msdn.microsoft.com for the terms "MicrosoftDNS_AType Modify."

CHAPTER 11

Internet Applications

COMMUNICATION AND APPLICATION protocols form the foundation of Internet applications, which have also been implemented in other applications and operating systems that we use every day. Two of these protocols are HTTP and FTP.

Web page serving is provided using the HTTP protocol, while the pages that are presented use the HTML markup language, which allows for a rich graphical interface. The latest Internet Explorer (IE) browser implements dynamic HTML (DHTML) and the Document Object Model (DOM), which exposes Web page elements through a structured object model. The properties of these elements, such as color and content, can be manipulated through this model dynamically.

The IE application itself is a container for a browser control object, which provides the functionality of rendering HTML pages and facilitating communications between remote computers. This browser control exposes the functionality for any application that can manipulate COM objects, such as Windows Script Host (WSH).

Using the objects that are exposed by IE, you can perform HTTP operations, such as PUTting and GETting information. Scripts can use IE to integrate graphical interfaces into scripts, thus providing a more attractive and flexible alternative to the limited graphical Windows commands that are included with VBScript, such as `Popup` and `InputLine`. Because the whole DHTML object model is accessible through the browser component, forms can be manipulated by scripts. This enables powerful, event-driven data entry applications to be implemented, providing the WSH scripting environment with a much-needed graphical user interface (GUI) capability.

In addition to the functionality that is exposed through the IE objects, file transfer using the FTP protocol and IP diagnostics utilities such as address resolving (DNS) and pinging are also covered in this chapter.

11.1 Retrieving HTML Data

Problem

You want to download data from a Web site.

Solution

Internet Explorer 5.0 and later incorporate an XMLHTTP component that performs transfer data operations using the HTTP (Web server) protocol. Using this component, you can get information from a Web server.

The following sample retrieves the fictitious page data.htm from http://www.acme.com/:

```
Dim objXMLHTTP
  Set objXMLHTTP = CreateObject("Microsoft.XMLHTTP")
  'get the data.htm page from www.acme.com
  objXMLHTTP.Open "GET", "http://www.acme.com/data.htm", False
  objXMLHTTP.send
  'check if retrieval was successful
  If objXMLHTTP.statusText = "OK" Then
      WScript.Echo objXMLHTTP.responseText
  Else
      WScript.Echo "Error getting page:" & objXMLHTTP.statusText
  End If
```

Discussion

Internet Explorer 5.0 exposes a number of components that provide data transfer capabilities.

The XMLHTTP component was designed for referencing remote XML sources, but it can be used to perform HTTP requests against Web servers. The ProgID for the XMLHTTP component is Microsoft.XMLHTTP.

Documents can be retrieved by sending an HTTP request to a server by calling the Open method. The syntax is as follows:

```
objXMLHTTP.open Request, URL [, Async] [, User] [, Password]
```

The Open method arguments are listed in Table 11-1.

Table 11-1. `Open` *Method Arguments*

PARAMETER	DESCRIPTION
`Request`	HTTP request method, such as GET or PUT. To retrieve a page use GET.
`URL`	URL of page to retrieve. Must be in fully qualified format—for example, `http://www.acme.com/data.htm` instead of `www.acme.com/data.htm`.
`Async`	Optional Boolean value. Determines if request will be executed asynchronously. If executed synchronously, execution of script will continue and an event will fire when page is retrieved.
`User`	Optional. User ID to access password-secured Web resources.
`Password`	Optional. Password for user specified by `User` property.

Once a request has been made using the `open` method, invoke the `XMLHTTP` object's `send` method to process the request.

If the `send` method is unable to communicate with the server specified by the URL, a runtime error will occur.

Problems may occur when retrieving the page—for example, the page does not exist on the specified server or access is denied as a result of security access limitations. To determine if the request was successful, query the `statusText` property.

The `statusText` property returns the status of the last operation performed by the `XMLHTTP` object's `open`/`send` methods. If the retrieval of the specified page was successful, it will return OK. If there were problems finding or accessing the page, the `statusText` property will return the message sent by the Web server.

If the execution of the `send` method completes successfully, the contents of the request can be read from the `responseText` property.

The following generic command-line script retrieves the contents of a Web page specified in the command line and writes the contents to the standard output:

```
<?xml version="1.0" ?>
<job>
<!--comment
Script:httpget.wsf
Description:
Retrieve the contents of a URL
-->
 <script language="VBScript" src="fsolib.vbs">
 <![CDATA[
```

```
Option Explicit
Dim objXMLHTTP, strURL, nf, nResult
'check if script is being run from command prompt
If Not IsCscript Then
 ExitScript _
    "This script must be run from command line using cscript.exe",True
End If

'check the argument count
If Not WScript.Arguments.Count = 1 Then
  ShowUsage
  WScript.Quit
End If
 Set objXMLHTTP = CreateObject("Microsoft.XMLHTTP")
 strURL = WScript.Arguments(0)
 objXMLHTTP.Open "GET", strURL, False
 objXMLHTTP.Send
  'check if error occurred resolving page or sending request
 If Err Then _
    ExitScript "Error sending request for page " & strURL, True
 'check if page not found..
If Not objXMLHTTP.statusText = "OK" Then
ExitScript "Error retrieving page " & strURL & vbCrLf & _
              "Error status:" & objXMLHTTP.statusText & vbCrLf & _
              "Error message:" & objXMLHTTP.responseText, True
 Else
    WScript.Stdout.Write objXMLHTTP.responseText
 End If

Sub ShowUsage
 WScript.Echo "httpget retrieves specified URL" & vbCrLf & _
 "Syntax:"  &  vbCrLf & _
 "httpget.wsf URL" & vbCrLf & _
 "URL        URL of requested page to be downloaded" & vbCrLf & _
 "            .Must be in absolute format e.g http://site/page"
End Sub
]]>
</script>
</job>
```

The syntax for the command-line script is as follows:

```
httpget URL
```

The URL parameter represents a fully qualified URL.

The result is output to the standard output and can be piped to a file or another script or application for further processing. The following command-line snippet retrieves the data.htm page and writes the contents to the data.txt file:

```
cscript httpget http://www.acme.com/data.htm > data.txt
```

Binary sources, such as pictures, can be retrieved using the XMLHTTP component. You cannot use the responseText property to retrieve the content's binary files because it only stores text values.

Data retrieved from a source URL can also be referenced through the responseBody property, which represents the data in an array of byte values. This property can be used to reference binary values.

The File Scripting Object (FSO) file operations do not provide any binary read/write capabilities. To overcome this, you use the ActiveX Data Object's (ADO) capability to write to binary streams and save the results to a local file. This capability requires ADO 2.5 or later. See Chapter 13 for more information on how stream manipulation works.

The following sample function reads a picture from a remote site and saves it to a local file using the ADO Stream object:

```
'getimage.vbs
Const adSaveCreateOverWrite = 2
Const adTypeBinary = 1
Function GetImage(strPath, strDest)
  Dim objXMLHTTP, nF, arr, objFSO, objFile
  Dim objRec, objStream
  'create XMLHTTP component
  Set objXMLHTTP = CreateObject("Microsoft.XMLHTTP")
  'get the image specified by strPath
  objXMLHTTP.Open "GET", strPath, False
  objXMLHTTP.Send

  'check if retrieval was successful
  If objXMLHTTP.statusText = "OK" Then
    'create binary stream to write image output
    Set objStream = CreateObject("ADODB.Stream")
     objStream.Type = adTypeBinary
     objStream.Open
     objStream.Write objXMLHTTP.ResponseBody
     objStream.SavetoFile strDest, adSaveCreateOverwrite
     objStream.Close
     GetImage = "OK"
```

```
    Else
       GetImage = objXMLHTTP.statusText
    End If
End Function
```

To use the function, pass the URL to the picture you want to download and the path locally where you want to save the file:

```
strResult = GetImage("http://www.acme.com/picture.jpg","d:\picture.jpg")
If Not strResult = "OK" Then
   WScript.Echo "Error getting page:" & strResult
End If
```

The function will return the text string OK if it is successful. If the function is not successful, the error code is returned.

11.2 Displaying HTML

Problem

You want to use Internet Explorer (IE) to display information.

Solution

To use IE to display information, create an instance of IE using the ProgID InternetExplorer.Application and reference the Document object.

The following script starts IE and displays the message "hello world":

```
Dim objIE
Set objIE = CreateObject("InternetExplorer.Application")
objIE.Navigate "about:blank"
objIE.Visible = True
objIE.Document.Write "<b>hello world</b>"
```

Discussion

WSH does not provide native GUI interface capabilities, apart from limited text input and display using the MsgBox and InputLine functions.

Internet Explorer (IE) provides a flexible GUI interface for WSH to output information. Any content sent to the browser can be formatted using existing HTML elements.

The `Document` object exposes the `writeln` and `write` methods, which can be used to output information to the browser. Their syntax is as follows:

```
objDocument.writeln | write strOutput
```

The difference between the `writeln` and `write` methods is that `writeln` adds a linefeed at the end of each line.

In the Solution script, the `Navigate` method is used to start a page. A page must first be navigated to before any document output can be generated.

The `Navigate` method requires a URL as the parameter. The URL can be in HTTP format (`http://www.acme.com/default.htm`) or file path format (`D:\data\default.htm`).

Manually building HTML formatting statements can be repetitive and time-consuming, and it can also generate large scripts. The following component, `HTMLGen`, simplifies the generation of HTML by encapsulating the core generation logic in a Windows Script Component:

```
<?xml version="1.0"?>
<component>
<registration
    description="HTMLGen"
    progid="ENTWSH.HTMLGen"
    version="1.00"
    classid="{b653fb70-9425-11d3-bc98-00104b164591}"
>
</registration>
<public>
    <property name="HTML">
        <get/>
    </property>
    <property name="Object">
        <get/>
    </property>
    <method name="WriteLine">
        <PARAMETER name="strLine"/>
    </method>
    <method name="WritePara">
        <PARAMETER name="strLine"/>
    </method>
    <method name="StartDOC">
```

```
            <PARAMETER name="strTitle"/>
            <PARAMETER name="bCreateDoc"/>
        </method>
        <method name="EndDOC">
        </method>
        <method name="StartTable">
            <PARAMETER name="aTableWidth"/>
            <PARAMETER name="strBorderWidth"/>
        </method>
        <method name="EndTable">
        </method>
        <method name="WriteRow">
            <PARAMETER name="aVals"/>
            <PARAMETER name="strAttributes"/>
        </method>
    </public>
    <script language="VBScript">
    <![CDATA[

     Dim objIE , objDoc, bFirstRow
     Dim aWidth, bC, strLine, strDoc
     strDoc = ""

     'writes a line to the HTML document
     Public Sub WriteLine(strLine)
      strDoc = strDoc & strLine & vbCrLf
     End Sub

     'writes a paragraph to HTML document
     Public Sub WritePara(strLine)
      strDoc = strDoc & "<p>" & strLine & "</p>" & vbCrLf
     End Sub

     'writes a paragraph to HTML document
     Public Sub StartDOC(strTitle, bCreateDoc)
       bC = bCreateDoc
      strDoc = "<html><head><title>" & strTitle & "</title></head>" & vbCrLf
        If bCreateDoc Then
       Set objIE = CreateObject("InternetExplorer.Application")
       objIE.Navigate "about:blank"
         While objIE.Busy
       Wend
           objIE.Visible = True
```

```
    End If
  End Sub

  Public Sub EndDOC()
   strDoc = strDoc & "</body></html>" & vbCrLf
   If bC Then
     Set objDoc = objIE.Document
    objDoc.WriteLn (strdoc)
   End If
  End Sub

  Public Sub StartTable(aTableWidth, strBorderWidth)
   aWidth = aTableWidth
   strDoc = strDoc & "<table border = """ & strBorderWidth & """>" & vbCrLf
  End Sub

  Public Sub EndTable()
   strDoc = strDoc & "</table>" & vbCrLf
  End Sub

  Public Sub WriteRow(aVals, strAttributes)
   Dim nF
   strDoc = strDoc & "<tr " & strAttributes & ">" & vbCrLf
    For nF = 0 To UBound(aVals)
      strDoc = strDoc & "<td width=" & aWidth(nF) & ">" & aVals(nF) _
             & "</td>" & vbCrLf
    Next
    strDoc = strDoc & "</tr>" & vbCrLf
  End Sub

  Function get_Object()
   Set get_Object = objIE
  End Function

  Function get_HTML()
   get_HTML = strDoc
  End Function
]]>
</script>
</component>
```

To use the component, create an instance of the object using the ENTWSH.HTMLGen ProgID.

The StartDoc function starts building the HTML document. The first parameter specifies the title for the document, while the second is a Boolean parameter that if True will create an instance of IE.

Data can be added to the document by using the WritePara or WriteLine functions. Each of these functions requires a parameter that specifies the information you want to add to the document. The WritePara function adds an HTML paragraph tag (<p>) to the parameter, while WriteLine adds the line to the document without any additional formatting.

The following sample creates an instance of the HTMLGen component and outputs some text to the browser:

```
Set objIE = CreateObject("ENTWSH.HTMLGen")
  objIE.StartDOC "Hello World", True
  objIE.WriteLine "<b><center>Hello World</center></b>"
  objIE.WritePara "The quick brown dog. etc.. etc.."
  objIE.EndDOC
```

HTMLGen simplifies the creation of tables through the StartTable, WriteRow, and EndTable functions.

To create a table, call the StartTable function. It requires two parameters: the first is an array of values identifying the width of each cell, and the second is a value specifying the width of the table border.

Rows are added to the table using the WriteRow function. WriteRow takes two parameters: The first is an array of values for each cell in the row, and the second is a string of formatting characters that is applied to the whole row.

Once the table is built, use the EndTable function to complete the table.

```
Set objIE = CreateObject("ENTWSH.HTMLGen")
  objIE.StartDOC "Phone List", True

 'start a table with 3 columns and border width 0.
  objIE.StartTable (Array(100, 300)), "0"
  objIE.WriteRow (Array("<b>Folder Name", "<b>Size")), "bgcolor=""#FFFF00"""
  objIE.EndDOC
  objIE.WriteLine "<b><center>Phone List</center></b>"
  objIE.WritePara "The quick brown dog.. etc.. etc.."
  objIE.EndDOC
```

The following script uses the WSHCB.HTMLGen component to build a list of all directories over a certain size:

```
'dirinfo.vbs
 Dim objIE, objFSO
```

```
Dim objFolder, objSrcFolder
Set objIE = CreateObject("ENTWSH.HTMLGen")
Set objFSO = CreateObject("Scripting.FileSystemObject")
On Error Resume Next
  objIE.StartDOC "Folder Size", True
objIE.WriteLine "<c><b><h2>User Folder Size, over 5 megs</c></b></h2>"
objIE.StartTable Array(100, 300), "0"
objIE.WriteRow Array("<b>Folder Name","<b>Size"), "bgcolor=""#FFFF00"""

 For Each objFolder In objFSO.GetFolder("d:\").SubFolders
   If objFolder.Size > 5000000 Then
     objIE.WriteRow Array(objFolder.Name, objFolder.Size), "
   End If
 Next

 objIE.EndTable
 objIE.EndDOC
   strHTML = objIE.HTML
```

11.3 Displaying an HTML Logon Message

Problem

You want to display an HTML message at logon.

Solution

You can create an instance of IE and *sink* IE events by specifying the second parameter to the `WScript.CreateObject` method. This will allow the script to process actions performed by IE, such as when IE is exited. This allows scripts to process events generated by other applications—in this case, determining when IE is exited.

The Solution script displays the following `welcome.htm` HTML page:

```
<html>
<head>
<title>Welcome To Acme</title>
</head><body>
<p align="center">
<b><font face="Arial Black">Welcome To Acme's Home Page</font></p>
<p align="center">
```

```
<input type="button" value="Continue" name="cmdContinue"></p>
</body>
</html>
```

The script creates an instance of Internet Explorer and customizes the appearance by removing the application menu and toolbar, as well as setting a custom window width and height. This hides the identity of the browser application from the users. The `welcome.htm` Web page is then displayed, and the script will not exit until the window is closed or the Continue button is clicked in the page:

```
'logon.vbs
 Option Explicit
 Dim objIE, bDone, objDoc
'create an instance of the IE browser. Allow IE events to be caught
'by specifying the second parameter, ie_
 Set objIE = WScript.CreateObject("InternetExplorer.Application","ie_")
 'turn off all on screen 'clutter'
 objIE.MenuBar = False
 objIE.ToolBar = 0
 objIE.Height = 350 'resize browser form
 objIE.Width = 550
 'select the page to display
 objIE.Navigate "d:\data\wsh\ie\welome.htm" 'wait to load page
 While objIE.Busy
  WScript.Sleep 100
 Wend
 objIE.Visible = True
 bDone = False
  'link to the browser document
 Set objDoc = objIE.Document
 'assign the onclick event of the HTML pages cmdContinue button to the
 'cmdContinue_OnClick sub routine in this script
 Set objDOC.All("cmdContinue").onclick = GetRef("cmdContinue_OnClick")
 'loop until done
 While Not bDone
   wscript.sleep 100
 Wend

 'this event is fired when IE is exited
 Sub ie_OnQuit
  bDone = True
 End Sub
```

```
Sub cmdContinue_OnClick
 objIE.Quit
 bDone = True
End Sub
```

Discussion

Internet Explorer (IE) exposes a number of events that can be accessed through WSH.

In order to attach to IE events, known as *sinking*, specify the second parameter for the `WScript.CreateObject` method. Specifying this parameter makes the script an *event sink*. The script will "listen" to events generated by the object, and it can optionally trap the events in subroutines. This parameter identifies what will be prefixed to the name of the event subroutines. The subroutines are associated with events fired from the object, in this case IE.

In the following sample an instance of IE is started and events are sinked to subroutines prefixed with `ie_`:

```
'create an instance of the IE browser. Allow IE events to be caught
'by specifying the second parameter, ie_
 Set objIE = WSscript.CreateObject("InternetExplorer.Application","ie_")
```

When an event in IE is fired, the WSH script looks for a subroutine with the name of the event prefixed with `ie_`. When IE is shut down, it fires an `OnQuit` event. If you wanted to trap it in the script, you would create a subroutine called `ie_OnQuit`. This subroutine would execute in the script when IE was closed down.

The script starts by opening a "welcome" Web page through the `Navigate` method. This operation is asynchronous, which means the script will not wait until the page is loaded, so a loop is added to wait until the page is successfully loaded.

If this loop was not added and a reference was made to the `Document` property of IE before the requested page was generated, an error would occur. Note that even with this loop, IE can indicate the page is loaded before it has actually completed, thus generating an error, so additional logic may have to be added to trap any errors generated. In the previous example, a `WSscript.Sleep` statement is used to prevent this.

Once the page is displayed, the script will stop in a loop and not continue until the `bDone` variable is `True`. This is set when Internet Explorer is closed, which occurs when the `OnQuit` event fires, which will call the `ie_OnQuit` subroutine in the script.

Table 11-2 lists a number of events that IE exposes.

Table 11-2. IE Events

EVENT	DESCRIPTION
`DocumentComplete`	Fires when a document has completed and displayed in browser
`DownloadBegin`	Fires when a document has been requested for download
`DownloadComplete`	Fires when a download is complete but has not been displayed yet
`OnQuit`	Fires when IE application is terminated

Table 11-3 lists a few of the methods that IE exposes.

Table 11-3. IE Methods

METHOD	DESCRIPTION
`Stop`	Stops the current IE operation
`Quit`	Exits IE

Table 11-4 lists a few of the properties that IE exposes.

Table 11-4. IE Properties

PROPERTY	DESCRIPTION
`AddressBar`, `MenuBar`, `ToolBar`	Boolean values. If `True`, the browser element the property represents is displayed. If `False`, the element is not shown.
`Height`, `Width`	Height and width of the browser in pixels.
`Top`, `Left`	Location of the browser in pixels.

The preceding tables do not list all methods, events, and properties exposed by the IE object. The best way to determine all available object attributes is to use the object browser integrated into Microsoft Office applications or Visual Basic, or the separate object browser available from Microsoft (see Solution 9.1). The script also traps the events from the HTML Continue button. Solution 11.4 covers capturing events from HTML elements.

See Also

For more information, search http://msdn.microsoft.com for the article "Reusing the WebBrowser Control."

11.4 Creating an HTML Form

Problem

You want to create a data entry form using Internet Explorer (IE).

Solution

The code for this HTML page is used as the source for the Solution script. Save it as calcage.htm:

```
<html><head>
<title>Calculate Age</title>
</head><body>
First Name: <input type="text" name="txtFirstName" size="20"><br>
Last Name: <input type="text" name="txtLastName" size="20"><br>
Date of birth: <input type="text" name="txtBirthDate" size="19"><br>
Age  <input type="text" name="txtAge" size="6"></p>
<p align="center"><input  type="button" value="Calculate Age" name="cmdCalculate">
<input type="button" value="Quit" name="cmdQuit"></p>
</body></html>
```

The following sample displays the calcage.htm HTML page. The page queries for the user's name and birth date and calculates the user's age based on his or her birth date. Events from HTML elements such as buttons and fields are trapped by the script, allowing the script to execute subroutines when certain events occur on the page, such as buttons being clicked, the mouse moving in and out of fields, and on the change of values in a field:

```
'calcage.vbs
Dim objIE, objDoc, bDone
'create an instance of the IE browser
Set objIE = WScript.CreateObject("InternetExplorer.Application","ie_")
'turn off all menus/toolbars and set window size
```

```
objIE.AddressBar= False
objIE.MenuBar= False
objIE.ToolBar= 0
objIE.Width = 400
objIE.Height = 250

'go to the page
objIE.Navigate "e:\data\wsh\wsh\chapter 11\calcage.htm"
 'wait to load page
 While objIE.Busy
 Wend
 objIE.Visible = True  'display page
 Set objDoc = objIE.Document.All
 'assign HTML form buttons to subroutines
 Set objDOC("cmdQuit").onclick = GetRef("cmdQuit_OnQuit")
 Set objDOC("cmdCalculate").onclick = GetRef("cmdCalculate_OnClick")
 Set objDOC("txtBirthDate").OnChange = GetRef("txtBirthDate_OnChange")
 Set objDOC("txtBirthDate").OnMouseOver = GetRef("txtStatus_Change")
 Set objDOC("txtBirthDate").OnMouseDown = GetRef("txtStatus_Change")
 Set objDOC("txtBirthDate").OnMouseUp = GetRef("txtStatus_Change")

  bDone = False
  While Not bDone
    WScript.Sleep 100
  Wend

Sub txtStatus_Change
 objDOC("txtBirthDate").value = Date
End Sub

'event fires when IE is exited.
 Sub cmdQuit_OnQuit
  objIE.Quit
  bDone = True
 End Sub

 'event fires when value in birth date field is changed
 Sub txtBirthDate_OnChange
   Call CalculateAge()
 End Sub

 'event fires when value in Full Name field is changed
 Sub cmdCalculate_OnClick
```

```
  If CalculateAge() Then
   WScript.Echo  objDOC("txtFirstName").value & " " & _
                 objDOC("txtLastName").value & " is " & _
                 objDOC("txtAge").value
  End If
End Sub

'validates date field and calculates age
Function CalculateAge
 Dim strDate
 'get the birthdate entered on the form
 strDate = objDoc("txtBirthDate").value
   'validate date and calulate age
 If Not IsDate(strDate) Then
  MsgBox "You must enter a valid date"
  CalculateAge = False
 Else
  objDoc("txtAge").value = DateDiff("yyyy",CDate(strDate), Date)
  CalculateAge = True
 End If
End Function
```

Discussion

Using Internet Explorer and standard HTML forms, WSH can perform sophisticated data entry operations, allowing for an event-driven forms environment similar to that provided by Microsoft Visual Basic or Access.

Internet Explorer (IE) provides the ability to host complex HTML forms. These forms can be composed of any number of fields and other form objects, such as drop-down lists, radio buttons, and check boxes.

Create an HTML form using a standard HTML editor such as FrontPage or Dreamweaver, or even Notepad. Make note of the names given to any fields, buttons, or other HTML interface elements you want to reference from your script.

Open the page in the script using the `Navigate` method and get a reference to the HTML page. The URL for the page can be a remote Web server or a local file.

All elements in an IE form—actually, all elements in any HTML document—are exposed through an object model called the Document Object Model (DOM). This model exposes the structure of an HTML document, allowing elements to be enumerated and manipulated.

The ability to access DOM elements is particularly useful for HTML forms, because the values of form fields can be updated or read as required:

```
'create an instance of the IE browser
Set objIE = CreateObject("InternetExplorer.Application")

'build a page containing a text field prompting for a date
objIE.Navigate "aboutblank"

'wait to load page

objIE.Document.body.innerHTML = _
          "<html>Date <input type=""text"" name=""txtDate"" size=""10""</html>"

While objIE.Busy : Wend'display page
objIE.Visible = True

Set objDoc = objIE.Document.All
'set the value for the field txtDate to today's date
objDoc("txtDate").Value = Date
```

A field is displayed in the browser prompting for a date value. The script sets the value of the field by setting the DOM object's `Value` property to today's date.

The names used to reference the HTML DOM elements are the ones associated with the elements when creating the HTML document. A consistent naming convention for the elements can be useful when building the HTML forms, allowing the type of elements to be easily identified in the script. In the examples in this section, text fields are prefixed with `txt`. For example, Figure 11-1 shows the Microsoft FrontPage Text Box Properties dialog box, which displays the name that has been assigned to an HTML text box field.

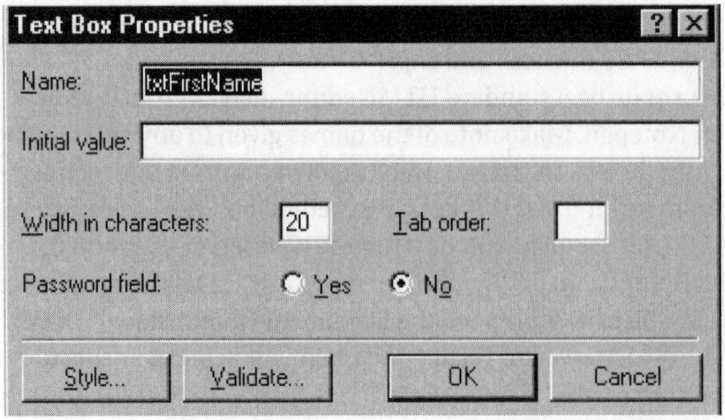

Figure 11-1. Microsoft FrontPage text box name assignment

DOM elements also expose events. When a form button is clicked or form fields are modified, an event is generated. Unfortunately, you cannot sink DOM events using the `WSscript.Create` method in the same way as the IE object. Because you cannot create instances of HTML `Document` objects, you cannot specify an event prefix to bind document events to, as you can with IE events.

You can use the `GetRef` function to get the reference to the function in the script to which you want to bind. The syntax is as follows:

```
Set objDOMElement.event = GetRef(strFunction)
```

The `objDOMElement` object represents an HTML Document Object Model (DOM) element object to bind the subroutine to. This may be a button, a text field, or any other HTML object on a Web page. `event` identifies the DOM object event, while `strFunction` identifies the name of the VBScript subroutine the event is to bind to.

DOM events can be bound to any input element (buttons, text boxes, and so on) on an HTML page. The following sample binds the HTML element `txtDescription's onchange` event to the `txtDescription_OnChange` subroutine:

```
Set objDOC.All("txtDescription").onchange = _
                                   GetRef("txtDescription_OnChange")
```

When the value of the HTML field `txtDescription` changes, the subroutine `txtDescription_OnChange` in the script is executed.

Multiple events can be bound to the same subroutine. Table 11-5 lists commonly used events.

Table 11-5. HTML Events

EVENT	DESCRIPTION
`onclick`, `ondblclick`	Fires when an element is clicked or double-clicked
`onchange`	Fires when a change is made to an element, such as a text or check box
`onmouseover`, `onmouseout`	Fires when the mouse moves over or out of an element
`onmousedown`, `onmouseup`	Fires when the mouse button is clicked and depressed

`GetRef` is specific to VBScript and the functionality provided by it may be implemented differently in other scripting languages. JScript can reference function pointers by directly referencing the function name. The following VBScript and JScript statements provide the equivalent functionality of assigning a subroutine for the `onclick` event of a DHTML element.

VBScript:

```
'VBScript
Set objDOC("cmdQuit").onclick = GetRef("cmdQuit_OnQuit")
```

JScript:

```
//JScript
objDOC("cmdQuit").onclick = cmdQuit_OnQuit;
```

See Also

For more information, search http://msdn.microsoft.com for the article "Reusing the WebBrowser Control."

11.5 Enumerating HTML Elements

Problem

You want to download a Web page, including any images in the page.

Solution

You can get a reference to the Document object for the page you want to download and then list the images collection for each image in the page. Use the GetImage function created in Solution 11.1 to download the images:

```
<?xml version="1.0" ?>
<job>
<!--comment
Script:getpage.wsf
Description:creates local copy of web page. Downloads
all images if required.
-->
 <script language="VBScript" src="getimage.vbs">
 <![CDATA[
  Const ForWriting = 2
  Dim objIE, objImg, strSrc, strDest, strResult
```

```
  'create an instance of the IE browser
  Set objIE = CreateObject("InternetExplorer.Application")
  strDstPath = "e:\Data\LocalCopy\"

  'go to the page
  objIE.Navigate "http://www.microsoft.com/windows/default.asp"
  'wait to load page
  While objIE.Busy: Wend
  'loop through all elements in the HTML document
  For Each objImg In objIE.Document.images
    'get the source URL for the image
    strSrc = objImg.src
    'build a local path for the image
    strDest = strDstPath & Mid(strSrc, InStrRev(strSrc, "/") + 1)
    'get the image
     On Error Resume Next
    strResult = GetImage(strSrc, strDest)
    'modify the path of the image to point to the local image
    objImg.src = strDest

    If strResult <> "OK" Then
      WScript.Echo "Error:'" & strResult & "' retrieving image " & _
                   strSrc
     End If
  Next
  'write the modified page to a local file
  Set objFSO = CreateObject("Scripting.FileSystemObject")
  Set objFile = objFSO.OpenTextFile(strDstPath & "page.htm", _
                ForWriting, True)
  objFile.Write objIE.Document.documentelement.innerhtml
  objFile.Close
  ]]>
  </script>
</job>
```

Discussion

All elements in HTML documents can be accessed through automation. This allows for specific parts of an HTML document to be listed.

The Document object exposes a number of collections that store elements associated with the page, such as the images and links collections. The images collection stores all images stored in the document, while the links collection stores any links to other pages. The Solution script uses the images collection to list all images for a specified page.

As well as specific collections, the whole DHTML structure of a document can be enumerated. The Document object's All property is a collection of all elements within a page.

The following sample command-line script, htmlelem.vbs, opens the HTML document specified in the command line and outputs all DHTML elements in the document:

```
'htmlelem.vbs
 'lists all elements in document specified by command line argument
 Dim objIE, objDoc
 If WScript.Arguments.Count <> 1 Then
   WScript.StdErr.WriteLine "You must specify a URL to process"
   WScript.Quit
 End If

 'create an instance of the IE browser
 Set objIE = CreateObject("InternetExplorer.Application")

 'go to the page
 objIE.Navigate Wscript.Arguments(0)
 'wait to load page
 While objIE.Busy : Wend
 Set objDoc = objIE.Document.All
 'loop through all elements in the HTML document
 For Each objItem In objDOC
 'check if the element is an input element (input box, check box etc.)
  If TypeName(objItem) = "HTMLInputElement" Then
    Wscript.Echo objItem.value, objItem.name, objItem.type
  Else
    Wscript.Echo TypeName(objItem) 'just output the HTML object type
  End If
 Next
```

The htmlelem.vbs script requires a URL to the page you want to enumerate. The URL can point to a page on a Web server or a local path. The script uses the TypeName function to determine the name of the object being referenced.

Many of the properties exposed through the HTML object can be modified. In the Solution script, the source for each image in the HTML page, identified by the src property, is modified to point to a local path for the downloaded image.

Each DHTML element can expose a number of properties, methods, and events, which vary from element to element. To determine the functionality exposed by any given event, use the object browser included with Microsoft Office 97 and later applications or Visual Basic.

To browse DHTML elements from an Office 97 or later application, follow these steps:

1. Start an Office application, such as Word or Excel.

2. Choose Tools > Macro > Visual Basic Editor.

3. Select Tools > References. From the list of available objects, find the Microsoft HTML Object Library and click the check box.

4. Click OK.

5. At any time within the Visual Basic Editor, press the F2 key. This will display the object browser.

6. From the Project/Library drop-down in the upper-left corner, select MSHTML Library.

You will now see a list of HTML objects. Associated events, methods, and properties appear in the left pane and all properties, methods, and events appear in the right pane, as shown in Figure 11-2.

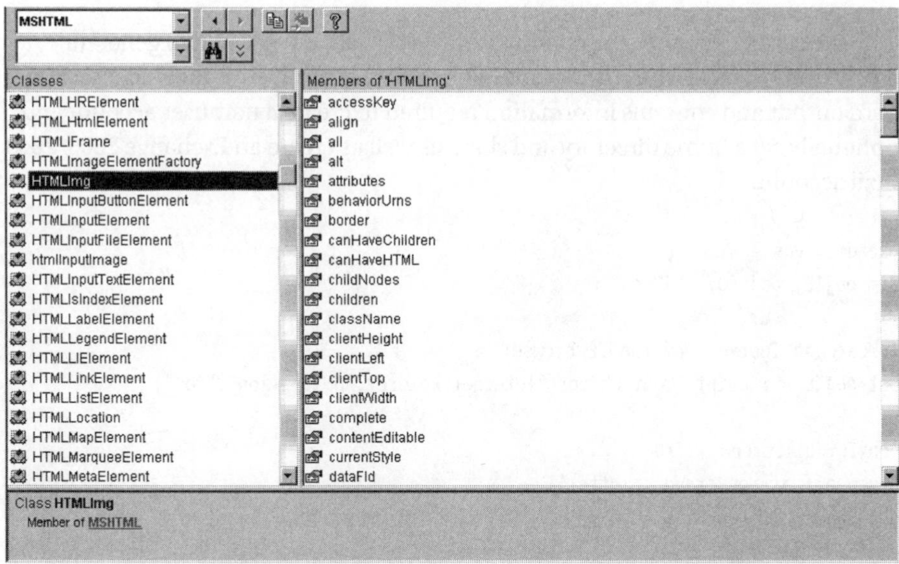

Figure 11-2. MSHTML Library Object Browser

The next script, `ieadmin.vbs`, uses an administrative HTML form, `adminform.htm`, to build a batch file to create a new user. Figure 11-3 shows the completed form.

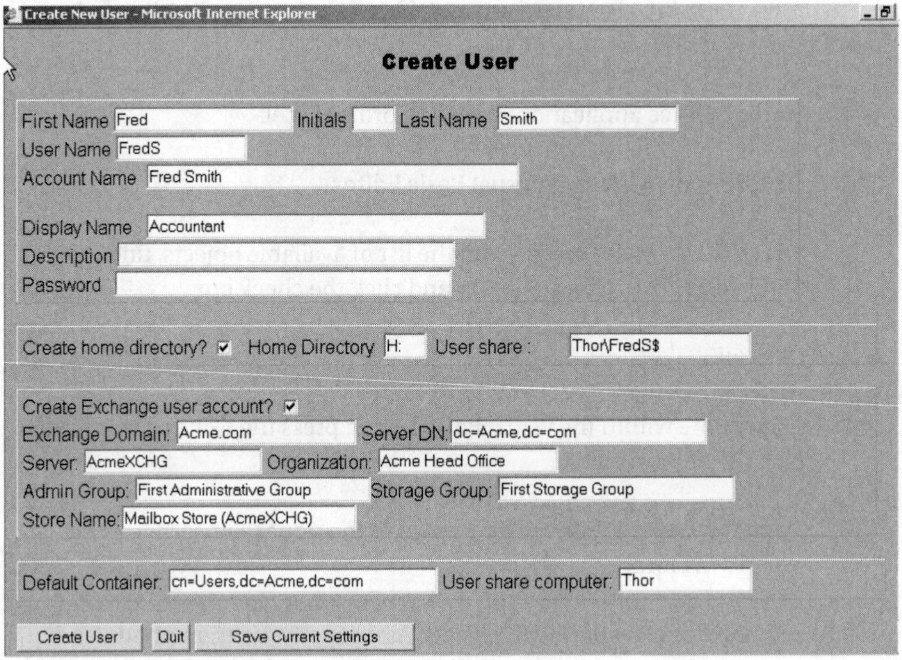

Figure 11-3. IE Create User form

The script generates the command-line commands required to generate a new user based on the criteria entered into the form. The output is sent to standard output and contains information required to create a new user account and optionally set a home directory and share as well as create an Exchange 2000/2003 mail account.

```
'ieadmin.vbs
Dim objIE, objFSO, objDoc

'create an instance of the IE browser
Set objIE = Wscript.CreateObject("InternetExplorer.Application","ie_")

'objIE.FullScreen = True
'turn off all onscreen 'clutter'
objIE.AddressBar= False
objIE.MenuBar= False
objIE.ToolBar= 0
objIE.Navigate "D:\Code Download\chapter 11\adminform.htm" '

 'wait to load page
 While objIE.Busy
```

```
 WScript.Sleep 100
Wend

Set objDoc = objIE.Document
Set objFSO = CreateObject("Scripting.FileSystemObject")
Set objTS = objFSO.OpenTextFile("settings.ini",1)

Do While Not objTS.AtEndOfStream
  strLine = objTS.ReadLine
  nPos = Instr(strLine,"=")
  If nPos > 0 Then
    Set objItem = objDoc.all(Trim(Left(strLine,nPos-1)))
wscript.echo Trim(Left(strLine,nPos-1))
     If objItem.type = "checkbox" Then
       objItem.checked = Cbool(Mid(strLine,nPos+1))
     Else
     'objDoc.all(Trim(Left(strLine,nPos-1))).value = Mid(strLine,nPos+1)
      objItem.value = Mid(strLine,nPos+1)
    End If

  End If
Loop

Set objDOC.All("cmdCreateUser").onclick = GetRef("cmdCreateUser_OnClick")
Set objDOC.All("cmdQuit").onclick = GetRef("Quit_OnQuit")
Set objDOC.All("cmdSaveSettings").onclick = _
                                      GetRef("cmdSaveSettings_OnChange")

Set objDOC.All("txtUserName").OnChange = GetRef("txtUserName_OnChange")
Set objDOC.All("txtLastName").OnChange = GetRef("txtName_OnChange")
Set objDOC.All("txtFirstName").OnChange = GetRef("txtName_OnChange")

Set objDOC.All("txtDescription").OnChange = GetRef("txtDescription_OnChange")

objIE.Visible = True

bDone = False
 While Not bDone
  wscript.sleep 100
 Wend

Sub Quit_OnQuit
 objIE.Quit
 bDone = True
End Sub
```

```
'event fires when value in Full Name field is changed
Sub txtUserName_OnChange

objDoc.all("txtUserShare").value = objDoc.all("txtShareComputer").value _
                                   & "\" & objDoc.all("txtUserName").value & "$"

End Sub

'event fires when value in last or first Name fields is changed
Sub txtName_OnChange
 objDoc.all("txtAccountName").value = objDoc.all("txtFirstName").value & " " _
                                      & objDoc.all("txtLastName").value
 objDoc.all("txtUserName").value = objDoc.all("txtFirstName").value

 If Len(objDoc.all("txtLastName").value)> 1 Then
          objDoc.all("txtUserName").value = objDoc.all("txtUserName").value _
                   & Left(objDoc.all("txtLastName").value,1)
 End If

 txtUserName_OnChange
End Sub



'event fires when value of Description field changes
Sub txtDescription_OnChange
 'set Exchange Title field to value of account description
 objDoc.all("txtTitle").value = objDoc.all("txtDescription").value
End Sub

'event fires when Create User button is clicked
Sub cmdSaveSettings_OnChange

 'open settings file
 Set objFSO = CreateObject("Scripting.FileSystemObject")
 Set objTS = objFSO.OpenTextFile("settings.ini",2,True)

 'loop through all elements in the HTML document
 For Each objItem In objDOC.All

 'check if the element is an input element (input box, check box, etc.)
 'and contains a value
 If TypeName(objItem) = "HTMLInputElement" Then
   If (objItem.type = "text") _
        And objItem.value<>"" Then
    'write the value to the settings file
```

```
    objTS.WriteLine objItem.name & "=" & objItem.value
   ElseIf  objItem.type = "checkbox" Then
    objTS.WriteLine objItem.name & "=" & objItem.checked
    End If
  End If
 Next
  objTS.Close
End Sub

 Sub cmdCreateUser_OnClick()
  Dim strLine, objD, objTS
  Dim strServer, strDomain, strOrganization, strAdminGroup
  Dim strStorageGroup, strStoreName
  Dim objPerson, objMailbox

  Set objD = objDOC.All
  Set objContainer = GetObject("LDAP://" & objD("txtContainer").value)
  Set objUser = objContainer.Create("User", "cn=" &  objD("txtAccountName").value)
  objUser.Put "samAccountName", objD("txtUserName").value

  objUser.SetInfo

  objUser.pwdLastSet = -1

  objUser.GivenName =  objD("txtFirstName").value
  objUser.sn =  objD("txtLastName").value

  If objD("txtDisplayName").value<>"" Then
    objUser.DisplayName =  objD("txtDisplayName").value
  End If

  objUser.AccountDisabled = False

  If objD("txtDescription").value<>"" Then
   objUser.Description = objD("txtDescription").value
  End If

'set home directory?
If objD("chkHomeDirectory").checked Then
 objUser.HomeDrive = objD("txtHomeDirectory").value
 objUser.HomeDirectory = objD("txtUserShare").value
End If

 objUser.SetInfo
```

```
        objUser.SetPassword objD("txtPassword").value

        If objDOC.All("chkCreateExchangeAccount").checked Then

          strServer = objD("txtExchangeServer").value
          strDomain = objD("txtExchangeDomain").value
          strOrganization = objD("txtExchangeOrganization").value
          strAdminGroup = objD("txtAdminGroup").value

          strStorageGroup =  objD("txtStorageGroup").value
          strStoreName =  objD("txtStoreName").value

          strServer = objD("txtExchangeServer").value
          strDomain = objD("txtExchangeDomain").value
          strOrganization = objD("txtExchangeOrganization").value
          strAdminGroup = objD("txtAdminGroup").value


          Wscript.Echo objD("txtExchangeServer").value
          Wscript.Echo objD("txtExchangeDomain").value
          Wscript.Echo objD("txtExchangeOrganization").value
          Wscript.Echo objD("txtAdminGroup").value

          Wscript.Echo strStorageGroup
          Wscript.Echo strStoreName

          'create mailbox for specified server
           objUser.CreateMailbox "LDAP://" & _
                         strServer & _
                         "/CN=" & _
                         strStoreName & _
                         ",CN=" & _
                         strStorageGroup & ",CN=InformationStore,CN=" & _
                         strServer & _
                         ",CN=Servers,CN=" & _
                          strAdminGroup & "," & _
                         "CN=Administrative Groups,CN=" & _
                          strOrganization & "," & _
                         "CN=Microsoft Exchange,CN=Services," & _
                         "CN=Configuration," & objD("txtServerDN").value


          objUser.SetInfo
       End If
     End Sub
```

Default settings are saved by selecting the Save Current Settings button on the HTML form. The values are stored in the file `settings.ini`. These values are loaded into the page when the script is started. Each element in the HTML document is checked to see if it is an input element (text or check box), and if it contains a value it is written to the settings file.

See Also

Solution 11.4.

11.6 Creating a GUI Menu

Problem

You want to create a generic GUI menu that displays a list of selections and then passes the result to a batch file or another WSH script.

Solution

You can use the following script, `guimenu.vbs`, to display a graphical menu:

```
'guimenu.vbs
 'build menu in IE based on command line parameter
 Option Explicit
 Dim objIE, objDoc, aMenuItems, nReturnValue
 Dim nReturn, nF, bDone
 If WScript.Arguments.Count <> 1 Then
  WScript.StdErr.WriteLine _
         "You must specify a list of menu items seperated by semicolons"
  Wscript.Quit -1
 End If

 'create an instance of the IE browser
 Set objIE = WScript.CreateObject("InternetExplorer.Application", "ie_")
   'get the menu items
 aMenuItems = Split(WScript.Arguments(0),";")
 'turn off all on screen elements
 objIE.AddressBar= False
 objIE.MenuBar= False
 objIE.ToolBar= 0
```

```
 objIE.Navigate "about:blank"
 'wait to load page
 While objIE.Busy : Wend
 Set objDoc = objIE.Document

'build HTML page based on menu items
For nF = 0 To Ubound(aMenuItems)
 objDoc.Write  "<center><input type=""button"" value=""" & _
          aMenuItems(nF) & """ name=""" & nF & """></p></center>"

 Set objDOC.All(Cstr(nF)).onclick = GetRef("OnButton_Click")
Next

objIE.Height = 60 * nF + 35
objIE.Width = 300
objIE.Visible=True
bDone = False
 While Not bDone
  WScript.Sleep 100
 Wend
 Wscript.Stdout.WriteLine nReturnValue
 nReturn = nReturnValue
 'check if menu button selected, exit IE
 If nReturnValue <> -1 Then objIE.Quit
  WScript.Quit nReturn

'event fires when IE is exited
 Sub ie_OnQuit
  nReturnValue = -1
  bDone = True
 End Sub

'this subroutine is called when a menu button is clicked
 Sub OnButton_Click
  nReturnValue = objdoc.activeelement.name
  bDone = True
 End Sub
```

Discussion

Traditionally, command-line scripts have implemented simple text menus. The GUI menu script provides similar functionality, but instead opens an Internet Explorer (IE) window and displays a list of options specified on the command line.

The Solution script builds a menu using IE based on command-line options. The syntax is as follows:

```
guimenu.vbs menuoptions
```

The `menuoptions` parameter contains the menu items to be displayed. The items are separated by semicolons.

Menu items are represented as HTML buttons. When a menu item is clicked, it outputs the value to standard output as well as setting the DOS errorlevel value, which allows menus to return values to DOS batch files. The item selected is identified as a number, starting sequentially from 0.

If IE is terminated before a menu item is selected, the value –1 is returned.

The following batch file displays two menu options and performs an operation based on which menu item was selected:

```
Rem Display menu and perform appropriate action
Rem based on selected option
@echo off
guimenu "Create User;List Process"
Rem check errorlevel
If errorlevel -1 goto quit
If errorlevel 0 goto option1
If errorlevel 1 goto option2

:option0
Echo Option 0 selected
goto quit

:option1
Echo Option 1 selected
goto quit
:quit
```

To use `guimenu` with another WSH script, pipe the results of `guimenu` to the script you are using to check the selected menu items. In the following sample, two menu items are displayed and the results are piped to the `opt.vbs` script:

```
cscript guimenu.vbs "Create User;List Process" | cscript opt.vbs
```

The opt.vbs script reads the menu selection from the standard input:

```
'opt.vbs
'performs operation based on selected menu item
Dim strOption
strOption = WScript.Stdin.ReadLine

Select Case strOption
 Case "0"
  Wscript.Echo "Option 0 was selected. . ."
 Case "1"
  Wscript.Echo "Option 1 was selected. . ."
End Select
```

11.7 Transferring Files Using FTP

Problem

You want to transfer a directory from an FTP server to your local machine.

Solution

WSH does not include any FTP component, nor are there any flexible FTP freeware components available. Mabry Software (http://www.mabry.com/) sells an FTP COM (FTP/X) object that provides FTP file transfer functionality.

The Solution code uses the Mabry FTP component to transfer files from an FTP server to a local directory:

```
'ftpget.vbs
'copies files from FTP directory to local directory
Const SynchronousMode = 1
Dim objFTP, nF, strName
 Set objFTP = CreateObject("Mabry.FtpXObj")
'connect to FTP server Thor
 objFTP.Blocking =  SynchronousMode
 objFTP.LogonName = "administrator"
objFTP.LogonPassword = "downunder"
 objFTP.host = "thor" 'hostname
 objFTP.Connect

 If Err Then
```

```
  WScript.Echo "Error connecting to FTP host"
End If

 'get a directory listing for remote machine
 objFTP.GetDirList "/"
 For nF = 0 To objFTP.DirItems - 1
   'get item from array
   strName = objFTP.DirItem(nf)
       'check if item is not a directory
   If Not InStr(strName, "<dir>") > 0 Then
    'get the name of the file, which for IIS starts at position 40
    strName = Mid(strName, 40)
    'strip off carriage return/line feed from end of string
    strName = Left(strName, Len(strName) - 2)
    'get file, store in local drive
    objFTP.GetFile strSrcDir & strName, "d:\data\" & strName
   End If
 Next
 objFTP.Disconnect
```

Discussion

The Mabry FTP object performs standard FTP operations, such as file upload and download, in addition to file and directory maintenance operations (directory creation and file/directory deletion operations).

To use the object, create an instance using the ProgID `Mabry.FtpXObj`. Before you can perform any operations, you must first connect to an FTP server.

To connect to a server, identify the server you want to use by setting the `Host` property. This can be either a fully qualified domain name (e.g., `ftp.acme.com`) or an IP address.

Call the `Connect` method to open a connection to the server. The `Connect` method can take the `LogonName`, `LogonPassword`, and `Account` parameters.

The `LogonName` and `LogonPassword` parameters identify the logon user ID and optional password. The `Account` parameter is also optional and is specific to certain FTP servers.

Parameters for the `Connect` method are optional and can be set using the corresponding `LogonName` and `LogonPassword` properties, as demonstrated in the Solution.

Once connected, you can send and receive files using the `GetFile` and `PutFile` methods. Both methods require a source and destination path for the file to be specified.

For the GetFile method, the source is the file on the remote FTP server and the destination is a local file path. When using the PutFile method, this is reversed: The source is a local file and the destination is the path to the remote FTP server. You must specify the exact path for both source and destination files and you cannot use wildcards in the file paths to specify multiple files.

The following sample implements a command-line script that copies the contents of a local directory, including all subdirectories and files, to an FTP server:

```
'ftpxcopy.vbs
'copies directory and all sub directories to FTP server
Const SynchronousMode = 1
Dim objFile, objFSO, objFTP, strUser
Dim strSrcRoot, nStart, strDstRoot

If Not WScript.Arguments.Count = 5 Then
    ShowUsage
    Wscript.Quit
End If
'get user id, host, password and source/destination directories
strSrcRoot = Wscript.Arguments(3)
strDstRoot = Wscript.Arguments(4)
If Not Right(strSrcRoot,1) = "\" Then strSrcRoot = strSrcRoot & "\"
If strDstRoot = "/" Then strDstRoot = ""

nStart = Len(strSrcRoot)
Set objFSO = CreateObject("Scripting.FileSystemObject")
Set objEvent = Wscript.CreateObject ("ENTWSH.RecurseDir","ev_")
Set objFTP = CreateObject("Mabry.FtpXObj")
 objFTP.Blocking = SynchronousMode
objFTP.host = Wscript.Arguments(0)
objFTP.Connect Wscript.Arguments(1), Wscript.Arguments(2)
objEvent.Path = strSrcRoot
Set objFSO = CreateObject("Scripting.FileSystemObject")
Call objEvent.Process()
objFTP.Disconnect

Sub ShowUsage
WScript.Echo "ftpxcopy.vbs copies local directory to FTP server" _
    & vbLf & "Syntax:" &  vbCrLf & _
   "ftpxcopy host user password source destination " & vbCrLf & _
   "host         FTP server to copy to" & vbCrLf & _
   "user         user name to log on to FTP server" & vbCrLf & _
   "password     password to logon onto FTP server" & vbCrLf & _
```

```
   "source       local path to source directory" & vbCrLf & _
   "destination path to FTP directory" & vbCrLf & _
   "Example: ftpxcopy acme freds sderf d:\data\website\acme /webroot/acme"
 End Sub

 Sub ev_FoundFile(strPath)
   On Error Resume Next
   'get a reference to specifed file
   Set objFile = objFSO.GetFile(strPath)

   'convert file path to corresponding FTP directory
   strFTPDir = Mid(objFile.ParentFolder, nStart)
   strFTPDir = strDstRoot & Replace(strFTPDir, "\","/")

   If Not Right(strFTPDir,1) = "/" Then strFTPDir =  strFTPDir & "/"
   objFTP.PutFile strPath, strFTPDir & objFile.Name

   If Not objFTP.LastError = 0 Then
     MakeDirPath (Left(strFTPDir,Len(strFTPDir)-1))
    objFTP.PutFile strPath, strFTPDir & "/" &  objFile.Name
   End If
End Sub

'Procedure MakeDirPath
'Description
'Creates a directory path on remote FTP server
'Parameters
'strPath FTP directory path to create
Sub MakeDirPath(strPath)
Dim nF, strRest, strNextPath
On Error Resume Next
bDone = False
strNextPath = strPath

 Do While Not bDone
 'check if directory exists
  objFTP.ChangeDir strNextPath ', strRest
 'if directory doesn't exist, then parse next level in path
  If Not objFTP.LastError = 0 Then
   nF = InStrRev(strNextPath, "/")
     strRest = Mid(strNextPath, nF) & strRest
     strNextPath = Left(strNextPath, nF - 1)
   Else
```

```
    'directory found, create path below it
    strRest = Mid(strRest,2) & "/"
     nF = 0
     Do While True
        nF = Instr(strRest,"/")
       strNextPath = strNextPath & "/" & Left(strRest, nF - 1)
       objFTP.CreateDir strNextPath
                    WScript.Echo "Creating directory " & strNextPath
        If nF = Len(strRest) Then Exit Do
       strRest = Mid(strRest, nF + 1)
     Loop
    bDone = True
   End If
 Loop
End Sub
```

The ftpxcopy script copies all files and subdirectories over. If the subdirectory does not exist on the FTP server, it is created. The FTP protocol does not provide the ability to copy directories, so the directory structure is recursively copied using the ENTWSH.RecurseDir component created in Solution 5.10.

Directories that don't exist on the FTP server are built using the MakeDirPath subroutine using the FTP component's CreateDir method.

No method exists to determine if a directory already exists, so the FTP component's ChangeDir method is used to change the directory. If the directory does not exist, an error will occur, which is checked using LastError. The directory is then created.

The syntax for the command-line script is as follows:

```
ftpxcopy host user password source destination
```

The host parameter specifies the FTP server to connect to, by either fully qualified domain name or IP address. FTP Logon credentials are specified by the user and password parameters. The local source and remote destination directories are identified by the source and destination parameters, respectively.

The following command line copies the local directory from d:\data\website\acme to the FTP directory /webroot/acme on server ftp.acme.com:

```
ftpxcopy ftp.acme.com freds sderf d:\data\website\acme /webroot/acme
```

Note that the FTP server you are connecting to must be configured for write access and allow for the creation of directories.

If you just require the ability to send and receive individual files, you can use the free ASPInet FTP control that you can download from http://www.serverobjects.com/. The control must be registered using the regsvr32.exe program on each computer you want to use it. This control allows for sending and receiving individual files:

```
Const FTP_TRANSFER_TYPE_ASCII = 1
Const FTP_TRANSFER_TYPE_BINARY = 2
Dim objFTP
Set objFTP = CreateObject("AspInet.FTP")
If objFTP.FTPGetFile("ftp.acme.com", "userid", "password", _
      "/data.txt", "d:\data\data.txt", True, FTP_TRANSFER_TYPE_ASCII) Then
     WScript.Echo "File download succeeded"
End If

If objFTP.FTPPutFile("ftp.acme.com", "userid", "password", _
      "/data.txt", "d:\data\data.txt", FTP_TRANSFER_TYPE_ASCII) Then
     Wscript.Echo "File download succeeded"
End If
```

The ASPInet object exposes two methods: FTPGetFile and FTPPutFile. FTPGetFile retrieves a file from a FTP server, while FTPPutFile downloads a text file to an FTP server.

```
result=objFTP.FTPGetFile(Host,Userid,Password,Remotefile,Localfile,Overwrite,Type)
result = objFTP.FTPPutFile(Host, Userid, Password, Remotefile, Localfile, Type)
```

Both methods share the first five parameters: Host, Userid, Password, Remotefile, and Localfile. The Host parameter is the address of the FTP server, and Userid and Password are the FTP logon user ID and password associated with the account, respectively. Remotefile is the path to the file on the FTP server and Localfile is the path to the local file.

FTPGetFile provides a Boolean Overwrite parameter. If True, the local destination file is overwritten if it already exists. The Type parameter identifies the data type of the file being transferred—if the value is 1, the file is ASCII, if the value is 2, the file is binary.

See Also

For more information on the FTP/X COM component, visit http://www.mabry.com, and for information on the ASPInet component, visit http://www.serverobjects.com.

11.8 Domain Name Resolution

Problem

You want to translate an IP address to a domain name.

Solution

WSH doesn't provide any IP lookup capabilities. A third-party freeware component, the System Scripting Runtime object from Netal (`http://www.netal.com/`), provides this functionality:

```
Dim objIP, strAddress
'create an instance of the scripting host object
Set objIP = CreateObject("SScripting.IPNetwork")
'lookup the domain name for a IP address
strAddress = objIP.DNSLookup("207.46.230.219")
WScript.Echo "The FQDN for the address is " & strAddress
```

Discussion

Reverse lookup is the process of translating an IP address to a domain name and vice versa. There is no support for reverse lookups supplied by the standard WSH objects.

Netal (`http://www.netal.com/`) provides a freeware component library, System Scripting Runtime, which is an element of their commercial System Script Host scripting environment product. The component must be registered using the `regsvr32.exe` program on each computer you want use it. Once registered, an instance of the object can be created using the `SScripting.IPNetwork` ProgID.

System Scripting Runtime provides a number of IP- and system-related operations. Address lookups are provided by the `DNSLookup` method. The syntax is as follows:

```
strAddress = objSSIP.DNSLookup(strHost)
```

`strHost` represents the address to look up. It can be either an IP address (for example, 192.168.1.100) or a domain name (e.g., `http://www.acme.com`). The method returns a resolved address if successful. If not successful, it returns an empty string. No error is generated if the host address cannot be resolved.

The following script opens an IIS log file and performs a reverse lookup on each IP address in the file. A count is maintained for each valid address that is referenced, providing a simple page hit counter mechanism.

```
Dim objFSO, objTxtStrm, strLine
 Dim objRegExp, objIP, objDict
 Dim strResolve, strKey
   'create dictionary, FSO and IPnetwork objects..
 Set objDict = CreateObject("Scripting.Dictionary")
 Set objIP = CreateObject("SScripting.IPNetwork")
 Set objFSO = CreateObject("Scripting.FileSystemObject")
 'create Regular expression
 Set objRegExp = CreateObject("Vbscript.RegExp")
'set pattern to validate ip address.. x.x.x.x
 objRegExp.Pattern = "(\d+(\.|\b)){4}"

 'open log file
 Set objTxtStrm = _
    objFSO.OpenTextFile("d:\winnt\system32\logfiles\w3svc1\ex990611.log")
  'loop through and process each line
 Do While Not objTxtStrm.AtEndOfStream
   strLine = objTxtStrm.ReadLine
   'test line against regular expression
   If objRegExp.test(strLine) Then
     'reverse lookup IP address in line
     strResolve = _
           objIP.DNSLookup(Mid(strLine, 10, InStr(10, strLine, " ") - 10))
    'if resolved to valid domain address add to dictionary
    If Not strResolve = "" Then
      'if already exists, increase count
      If objDict.Exists(strResolve) Then
        objDict(strResolve) = objDict(strResolve) + 1
      Else
        objDict.add strResolve, 1
      End If
    End If
     End If
 Loop

 'loop through and list domain name hit counts
 For Each strKey In objDict.Keys
    WScript.Echo strKey & "  " & objDict.item(strKey)
 Next
```

See Also

The System Scripting Runtime download, documentation, and examples are available at `http://www.netal.com/ssr.htm`.

11.9 Pinging a Computer

Problem

You want to ping a computer.

Solution

WSH doesn't provide any ping capabilities through its object model. There are a number of freeware COM controls, however, that provide this functionality. One example is the System Scripting Runtime object from Netal:

```
Dim objIP

 'create IPnetwork object
 Set objIP = CreateObject("SScripting.IPNetwork")
 'check if machine 'elvis' is
 If objIP.Ping("elvis") = 0 Then
    WScript.Echo "Elvis is alive!"
 End If
```

Discussion

Ping functionality is available through the freeware System Scripting Runtime component available from `http://www.netal.com/`. The syntax is as follows:

```
nResult = objIP.Ping(Address, [Response,] [Source,] [Timeout,] [TTL,]
[BufferSize])
```

Table 11-6 lists `Ping` method arguments.

Table 11-6. `Ping` *Method Arguments*

PARAMETER	DESCRIPTION
`Address`	Machine to ping. Can be either a fully qualified domain name or an IP address.
`Response`	Response time in milliseconds.
`Source`	IP address from which response was sent.
`Timeout`	Response timeout in milliseconds. Default is 1,000.
`TTL`	Time-to-live of the request packet. Uses system default value.
`BufferSize`	Number of bytes to send in each echo request packet. Size in bytes. Default is 32.

All parameters except `Address` are optional.

Windows XP and 2003 expose the `Win32_PingStatus` class through Windows Management Instrumentation (WMI). This class provides a ping capability to these operating systems. The following script pings a specified target address:

```
strTarget = "216.239.51.104"

Set objPings = GetObject("winmgmts:{impersonationLevel=impersonate}" & _
        "root/cimv2").ExecQuery("SELECT * FROM Win32_PingStatus " & _
        "WHERE Address = '" & strTarget & "' ")

For Each objPing In objPings
    If objPing.StatusCode = 0 Then
        Wscript.Echo strTarget & " is alive "
        Wscript.Echo "Response time  = " & objPing.ResponseTime
        Wscript.Echo "TTL  = " & objPing.ResponseTimeToLive
    Else
        Wscript.Echo strTarget & " is not responding"
        Wscript.Echo "Status code is " & objPing.StatusCode
    End If
Next
```

Table 11-7 lists the `Win32_PingStatus` properties.

Table 11-7. `Win32_PingStatus` *Properties*

PROPERTY	DESCRIPTION
Address	Machine to ping. This can be either a fully qualified domain name or an IP address.
ResponseTime	Response time in milliseconds. This property is read-only.
ResponseTimeToLive	Time-to-live from the moment the request is received.
Timeout	Response timeout in milliseconds. The default value is 1,000.
TimeToLive	Time-to-live of the request packet. The default value is 128.
BufferSize	Number of bytes to send in each echo request packet; size in bytes. The default is 32.

Properties can be set through the executed WQL statement. The following sample pings the address `www.ibm.com` and sets different `Timeout`, `TimeToLive`, and `BufferSize` properties:

```
strTarget = "www.ibm.com"

Set objPings = GetObject("winmgmts:{impersonationLevel=impersonate}" & _
        "root/cimv2").ExecQuery("SELECT * FROM Win32_PingStatus " & _
        "WHERE Address = '" & strTarget & _
          "' AND Timeout=4000 AND TimeToLive =90 And Buffersize=64 ")

For Each objPing In objPings
    If objPing.StatusCode = 0 Then
        Wscript.Echo strTarget & " is alive "
    Else
        Wscript.Echo strTarget & " is not responding"
        Wscript.Echo "Status code is " & objPing.StatusCode
    End If
Next
```

See Chapter 10 for more information on WMI.

If the control is not available, the good old command ping included with all versions of Windows will do. The results of a ping can be piped to a WSH script, which can then interpret the results.

The following script processes the results of a Windows NT ping:

```
'pingit.vbs
Dim strLine, nCount, objTextStream, strComp, bBad
nCount = 0
'loop until the end of the text stream has been encountered
```

```
Do While Not WScript.StdIn.AtEndOfStream
  strLine = Wscript.StdIn.ReadLine
  'check if bad IP address encountered
  If Left(strLine, 14) = "Bad IP address" Then
    bBad = True
    Exit Do
  End If

  If Left(strLine, 10) = "Reply from" Then
    nCount = nCount + 1
  End If
  If Left(strLine, 7) = "Pinging" Then
    strComp = Mid(strLine, 9, Instr(strLine, "]") - 8)
  End If
Loop
'check if bad IP address encountered
If bBad Then
  WScript.Echo "Bad IP address:" & Mid(strLine,15)
Else
  Wscript.Echo nCount & " replies received from " & strComp
End If
```

To use the script, pipe the results of ping to the script:

```
ping www.acme.com | cscript pingit.vbs
```

The script checks each line piped from the ping command. Each successful reply is accumulated.

See Also

The System Scripting Runtime download, documentation, and examples are available from `http://www.netal.com/ssr.htm`.

CHAPTER 12

Messaging Operations

THIS CHAPTER COVERS GENERAL e-mail-related tasks, such as logging into, sending, receiving, and processing e-mail, as well as more complicated processing of e-mail messages, filtering, maintenance, and address book management.

In Windows 95, Microsoft included a mail client called Exchange. It was a general-purpose mail client. After Exchange Server 4.0 was introduced, Microsoft informally changed the name to Windows Messaging to avoid confusion. This client has now evolved into the mother of all e-mail clients (and a pile of other capabilities): Outlook.

However, regardless of what the underlying application is called, Windows Messaging strives to serve a noble cause: the Universal Inbox.

Before Windows 95 and Windows Messaging, you generally required one e-mail client for each mailbox you used. So if you had MS Mail you'd need the MS Mail client. If you had a separate Internet mail account, you'd need an Internet mail client such as Eudora. And if you had a CompuServe mail account, you'd need to have yet another client—all with different interfaces and access mechanisms.

Windows 95 introduced the concepts of Messaging Services and the Universal Inbox. You would have one mail client, such as the Windows Messaging/Exchange or Outlook client, and a number of mail services installed. Each mail service would provide support for a certain mail type—for example, MS Mail server, Internet mail, and CompuServe mail.

Each service configuration and underlying functionality would generally be different. An Internet mail account has different setup values than, say, an MS Mail account, but they perform the same options: They deliver e-mail to and receive e-mail from one inbox.

So when you access your mail inbox, you may be processing messages received from a variety of different mail systems. The beauty is that there is no additional programming required to process messages from different mail platforms.

The concept of the Universal Inbox is not limited to only mail messages—fax and even voice mail services can be integrated into it.

Messaging API (MAPI) has long been the foundation of messaging standards for Microsoft. Usually they were only accessible by directly calling the MAPI DLL's libraries from a programming language such as C or C++.

The advent of Windows Messaging changed the way these services were accessed. The messaging services became implemented as a COM object, making it easier to access from any environment that could host COM objects, such as WSH.

You can use this technology to perform e-mail–related operations, such as logging onto a mail system, creating and sending e-mail messages, processing e-mail messages and attachments, and manipulating recipient addresses and distribution lists.

There are a number of different versions of the messaging library. Initially it was called OLE Messaging, then Active Messaging, and now Collaborative Data Objects (CDO). The versions were introduced in different client versions, as listed in Table 12-1.

Table 12-1. MAPI Library Versions

VERSION	APPLICATIONS
OLE Messaging 1.0	Exchange 4.0 client, Exchange Server 4.0, Outlook 97 client installed with Office 97 (version 8.0)
CDO 1.1/Active Messaging 1.1	Exchange Server 5.0, Exchange Server 5.0, Outlook client Outlook 97 (version 8.*x*)
CDO 1.*x*	Exchange Server 5.5, 2000 and 2003, Outlook 98, Outlook 2000, Outlook 2002 (XP), and Outlook 2003

Apart from the naming differences, there are functional differences between the versions. These differences are covered in this chapter where required.

You do not need to rush out and install new mail clients if you don't have the latest versions, because even the original OLE Messaging contained a functional set of routines to send and receive mail. The more recent libraries include methods to access new features, such as appointment information in Outlook. In addition, more recent versions of the libraries can be installed on the older e-mail clients.

NOTE *Many of the topics covered in this chapter may be limited due to the Outlook security patch. This applies to Outlook 98, 2000, 2002, and 2003. Operations that are related to sending messages or accessing address book information will result in dialog boxes that appear to prompt the user to accept or reject the operations. Operations that are related to extracting files from attachments may fail for certain attachments.*

> **NOTE** *For more information, search* `http://msdn.microsoft.com` *for the articles "Where to Acquire the CDO Libraries," "Active Messaging and Collaboration Data Objects (1.x)," "Information About the CDO E-mail Security Update," and "Developer Information About the CDO E-mail Security Update."*

12.1 Logging On

Problem

You need to log onto a mail session to send mail.

Solution

You can create a `Session` object and invoke the `Logon` method:

```
Dim objSession ' Session object
' create a MAPI session, then log on
Set objSession = CreateObject("MAPI.Session")
'attempt to logon. Since parameters are omitted, you will be prompted
'for a valid mail profile
objSession.Logon
```

Discussion

Before you can even think about sending or receiving messages, you need to log onto your mail system. To do this, you need a valid Windows Messaging profile.

First, create a MAPI `Session` object using the ProgID `MAPI.Session`. Once the `Session` object is created, you can log on and perform messaging operations, such as sending mail.

Windows Messaging stores mail services configuration information in *mail profiles.* A profile can contain one or more mail services. Each mail service provides the support for transport of different mail types, such as an Exchange server or Internet mail connection. While the mail service (e.g., Internet, Exchange mail server, CompuServe) processing a message is transparent when you receive the message, you need to know what addressing method your service will employ when sending a message, because the format does vary.

You can see what profiles are available on your system by selecting the Control Panel's Mail (or Mail and Fax) applet and clicking the Show Profiles button, as shown in Figure 12-1. You may have as many profiles as you want—Figure 12-1 shows a system with multiple mail profiles. If there are multiple users on the same machine, there may be one profile for each user. A valid profile is required to use CDO.

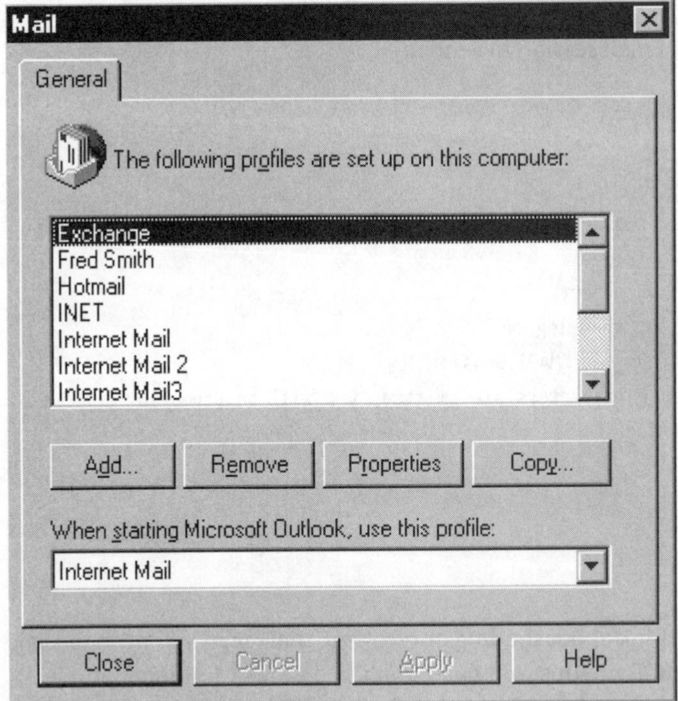

Figure 12-1. Profile configuration

You log on using the `Logon` method of the `Session` object. Its syntax is as follows:

```
objSession.Logon [ProfileName], [Password], [ShowDialog], [NewSession], _
                 [ParentWindow], [NoMail], [ProfileInfo]
```

The `Logon` method can take a number of optional parameters. If you omit the parameters, you will be prompted to select a valid profile, as in the sample Solution. If you know what profile you are using, you can specify it. You can optionally supply a password if required.

> **NOTE** *The password supplied in the* `Logon` *method is not guaranteed to apply to all providers.*

Table 12-2 lists the parameters available for the `Logon` method.

Table 12-2. `Logon` *Method Parameters*

NAME	TYPE	DESCRIPTION
`ProfileName`	String	Name of a valid profile. For example, if present, `ProfileName` must correspond exactly to the name of a profile on the current system. If this parameter refers to a nonexistent profile or is left empty, you will be prompted to select from an existing profile. If the `ProfileInfo` parameter is also included, the `ProfileName` parameter is ignored.
`Password`	String	Password for the profile (if any). If a password is set for the profile and you want to be prompted for the password, omit this parameter.
`ShowDialog`	Boolean	If `True`, displays a Choose Profile dialog box. The default value is `False`.
`NewSession`	Boolean	If `True`, a new MAPI session is started. If there is an existing MAPI session in progress and this property is set to `False`, the existing MAPI session is used. Its default value is `False`.
`ParentWindow`	Long	Does not apply under WSH.
`NoMail`	Boolean	If set to `True`, messages cannot be sent or received. Its default is `False`.

Table 12-2. `Logon` *Method Parameters (continued)*

NAME	TYPE	DESCRIPTION
ProfileInfo	String	Provides a method of logging onto a session without specifying a profile. This method only works for Microsoft Exchange Server–based mail sessions. When using ProfileInfo, you specify the mail server and user ID you want to connect to. The user ID is not the display name or mail name of the user—it is the *mail alias*. The mail alias is usually the same as your NT logon ID, but it can be different; it is the alias configured under the Exchange administrator program. You do not need to supply a password; you are validated against your current network logon. When you connect using ProfileInfo, a temporary profile that is discarded after use is created. Also, you cannot access any local mail-related files, such as Personal Address Books or Personal Mail folders—you can only access information stored on the server. The ProfileInfo parameter is specified in the format Exchange Server + Linefeed + Alias. The linefeed character is ASCII character 10. To log on Fred Smith, whose alias is freds, to the server ODIN: `objSession.Logon , , , , , , "Odin" & chr(10) & "freds"` The ProfileName parameter is ignored if ProfileInfo is supplied.

Logon functionality might be determined by the different mail services stored in the profile. For example, you might have an Exchange profile configured for a remote NT service that requires NT authentication credentials that cannot be set through the CDO/MAPI interface. Workarounds here include storing the appropriate authentication credentials or other required information under the service as required.

Once you have completed your mail operations, you can log off. To log off from a mail session, use the Logoff method. The following example attempts to log onto a MAPI session, lists information for the session, and logs off:

```
Dim objSession
Dim sMsg
' create a session then log on, supplying username and password
Set objSession = CreateObject("MAPI.Session")
' change the parameters to valid values for your configuration
objSession.Logon
'retrieve some Session properties available after a valid logon
sMsg = "OS: " & objSession.OperatingSystem & vbCr ' use vbCr
sMsg =  sMsg & "User Name:" & objSession.CurrentUser & vbCr
sMsg = sMsg & "MAPI Version:" & objSession.Version & vbCr
sMsg = sMsg  & "Profile Name:" &  objSession.Name
Wscript.Echo sMsg
objSession.Logoff
```

See Also

For more information, search `http://msdn.microsoft.com` for the articles "Starting a CDO Session" and "Using the Logon Method."

12.2 Determining the Default Profile

Problem

You want to add code to a logon script to log on automatically and then send a message for the current client.

Solution

You can use the MAPI `Session` object's `OperatingSystem` property to determine the client operating system and read the default profile from the registry depending on the version of the OS:

```
Dim objSession, objShell, strProf
Set objShell = CreateObject("WScript.Shell")
' create a MAPI session
Set objSession = CreateObject("MAPI.Session")
```

```
If InStr(objSession.OperatingSystem, "NT") > 0 Then
  strProf = "HKCU\Software\Microsoft\Windows NT\CurrentVersion\" & _
         "Windows Messaging Subsystem\Profiles\DefaultProfile"
Else
  strProf = "HKCU\Software\Microsoft\Windows Messaging Subsystem" & _
        "\Profiles\DefaultProfile"
End If
'logon using the default profile name
objSession.Logon objShell.RegRead(strProf)
```

Discussion

Automating the logon process is straightforward enough if you know the name of the profile you need to use. But what if you don't know the profile name?

If the Messaging service is installed on a machine and has been configured, there will be a default profile for the user. Profile information is stored in the registry, along with information on the default profile for the current user.

To make things a bit more difficult, Windows 9*x*/ME and Windows NT/2000/2003/XP store profiles in slightly different locations, so you must first determine what version of Windows you are running before you can retrieve the default profile. Use the CDO `Session` object's `OperatingSystem` property to determine what the current operating system is and then read the profile name from the appropriate registry setting. Windows NT/2000/2003/XP stores the default profile name in the `DefaultProfile` value of the `HKCU\Software\Microsoft\Windows NT\CurrentVersion\Windows Messaging Subsystem\Profiles\DefaultProfile` key, while Windows 9*x*/ME stores it in the `DefaultProfile` value of `HKCU\Software\Microsoft\Windows Messaging Subsystem\Profiles`.

See Also

For more information, search `http://support.microsoft.com` for the article "Q171422 Logging on CDO (1.x) to Active Messaging Session with Default Profile."

12.3 Sending Anonymous Mail

Problem

You want to be able to send mail from clients using an anonymous account, regardless of if they have any profiles configured (although they must have Windows Messaging).

Solution

You can create an Anonymous group on your Exchange server that authenticates all users:

```
' create a session then log on
Set objSession = CreateObject("MAPI.Session")
' logon using the Anonymous account on server Odin
objSession.Logon , , , , , , "Odin" & vbLF & "Anonymous"
```

Discussion

Another way of sending a message for a user without necessarily knowing the user profile for the current machine is using an Anonymous account. The Anonymous account is an account anyone can send a message from. This method, however, only works for clients using an Exchange e-mail server.

To create an anonymous user under Exchange Server 5.5, follow these steps:

1. On your Exchange Server 5.5, add a new mail user.
2. Call the user Anonymous, or whatever makes the most sense for you (see Figure 12-2). The most important piece of information is the account alias that is used when logging on.
3. Set the Primary Windows NT Account to Domain Users. This will allow any logged-on user in the domain to send mail via this account. If you want to limit it to a smaller group of users, select or create another NT group.

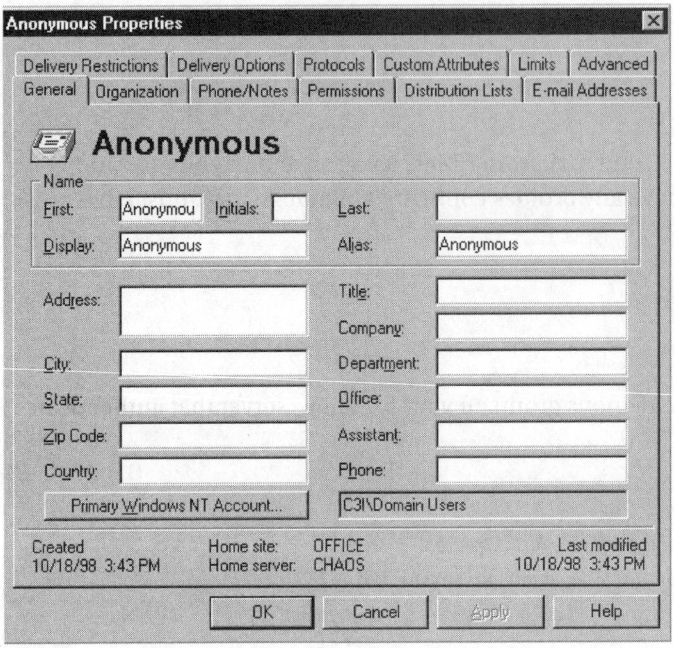

Figure 12-2. Exchange Server 5.5 anonymous user configuration

To create an anonymous mailbox under Exchange Server 2000 or 2003, follow these steps:

1. On your Exchange Server 2000 or 2003, mail-enable a user account.

2. Display the Exchange Advanced property sheet for the user. Click the Mailbox Rights button.

3. Assign mailbox rights to the user or group you wish to provide anonymous access to. Figure 12-3 shows the Windows group Domain Users assigned full access to the Anonymous user mailbox.

When logging on, you need to specify the Exchange server name, followed by a linefeed and then the name of the account:

```
objSession.Logon , , , , , , "Servername" vbLF & "Accountname"
```

There are limitations on using this type of logon: You can only access server-based mail, and you cannot access any local messages files or address books, such as Personal Message Stores (PST) or Personal Address Book (PAB) files.

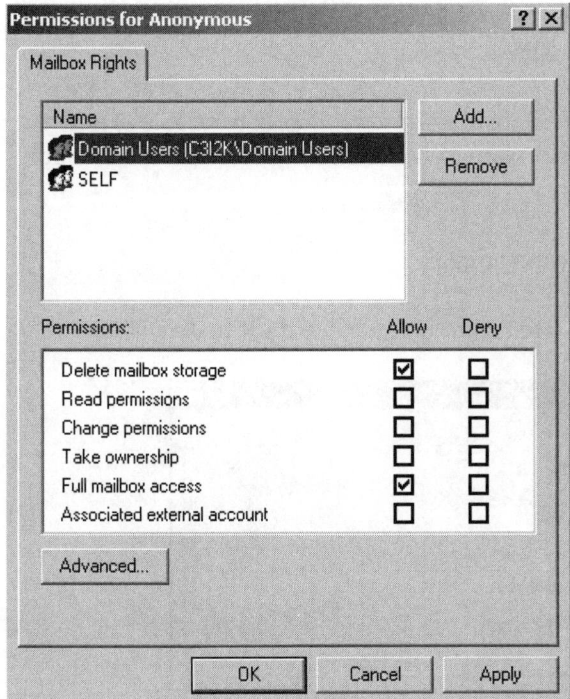

Figure 12-3. Exchange 2000/2003 anonymous user configuration

See Also

For more information, read "Configure an Exchange Mailbox for Anonymous Access" (`http://support.microsoft.com/support/kb/articles/Q195/6/81.ASP`).

12.4 Running Message Scripts Using NT Scheduler Service

Problem

You want to schedule a script to run while logged off (noninteractive).

Solution

Because CDO configuration is stored in user profiles, the scheduled task must log on as a user that has a valid Windows Messaging profile. If you are worried about security, you may want to create a user that has limited access to resources. The steps needed to do this are as follows:

1. Log on as the user and create the Windows Messaging profile (if not already created). You may want to create a special low-security account for this purpose.

2. Create all scripts to use the profile.

3. Under Task Scheduler (see Figure 12-4), create the scheduled item.

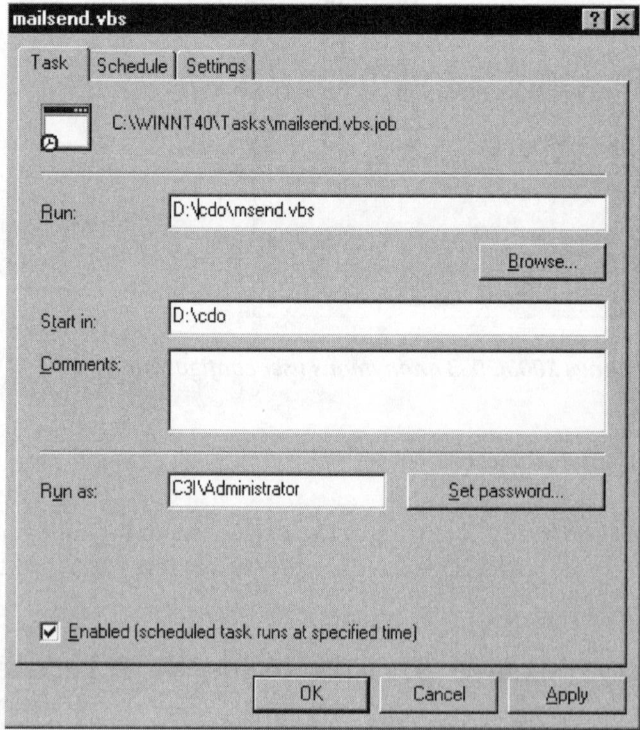

Figure 12-4. Scheduled task

4. In the "Run as" field, enter the account under which the messaging profiles were created.

5. Click the "Set password" button. The Set Password dialog box appears, as shown in Figure 12-5.

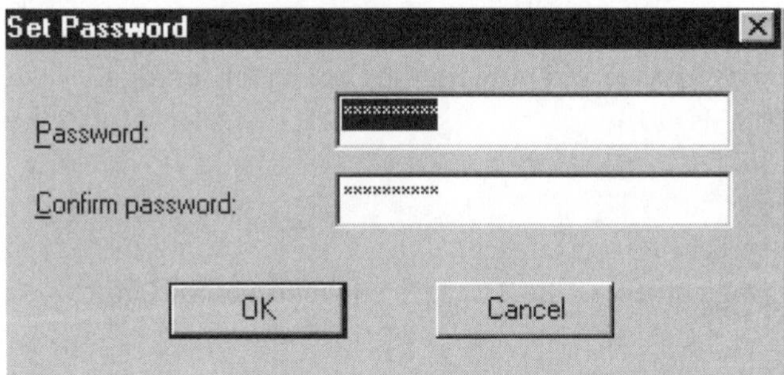

Figure 12-5. Scheduled task run as user password

6. Enter the password and click OK.

When the scheduled script is executed, it will log on as the specified user.

Discussion

Messaging scripts run as noninteractive scheduled items under NT. Scripts should not perform any UI actions such as displaying a message box before sending. Even the `DeliverNow` method, which displays the animated mail sequence when delivering and sending mail, should not be used.

This limits the types of mail services you can use. Any mail service that requires forcing the delivery of messages cannot be used to send and receive messages noninteractively. This includes Internet mail services that you would use to connect to your ISP (it doesn't affect Internet mail sent through an Exchange server).

Messaging profiles depend upon a user's logon. So when running under NT scheduler services, make sure the service has access to a user account or is permitted to connect anonymously to an Exchange server.

The other option for running scheduled scripts is creating an Anonymous user. The advantage of doing so is that no profile is required to access messaging services. The disadvantage is that you are limited to Exchange server–based resources, so any locally configured services such as PSTs and PABs are not available.

See Also

Solution 3.2.

12.5 Creating a Mail Message

Problem

You want to create a message and put it in the Outbox for sending.

Solution

You can add a Message object to the Messages collection of the Outbox folder object:

```
Dim objMessage
Dim objSession Set objSession = CreateObject("MAPI.Session")
objSession.Logon
'create a new message, setting the subject to Hello There
Set objMessage = objSession.Outbox.Messages.Add("Hello There")
objMessage.Text = "this is the body of the message"
' perform operations and log off. . .
```

Discussion

Creating a message is a relatively straightforward process. The Message object is added to the Outbox folder of the current MAPI session. Properties for the message, such as recipients, subject, and message body are then set.

In addition to the normal message properties, such as message body and subject, one or more file attachments can be included with the message.

The Message object contains all information that can be stored in a message from an e-mail package, such as the message subject, recipients, and body.

The Message object allows the inspection of existing messages in a folder and is required when creating a new message. You will see later how to process existing messages using the Message object.

To create a new message to send, you need to add a Message object to the Messages collection of the Outbox folder. Outbox is a Folder object and is where new mail items are created and sent. The Messages collection and Folder object are discussed in more detail later in this chapter.

When a new message has been successfully added to the Messages collection, a reference to the Message object is returned. The syntax is as follows:

```
Set objMessage = objMsgCollection.Add( [Subject, Text, Type, Importance] )
```

Table 12-3 lists the `Add` method's parameters.

Table 12-3. `Messages` *Collection* `Add` *Method Parameters*

NAME	TYPE	DESCRIPTION
`Subject`	String	Sets the subject for the message.
`Importance`		Long `MsgLow` 0 Low importance. `MsgNormal` 1 Normal importance (default). `MsgHigh` 2 High importance.
`Text`	String	The actual body of the message.
`Type`	String	Identifies the message class. This can be used in a custom application to identify the message. Changing the message type will not affect how the message is processed or handled at the destination, unless it is being processed by a custom application. The default is `IPM.Note`.

Each property for `Add` is optional but can be set using the `dot` method and setting the property against the `Message` object returned by the `Add` method.

See Also

For more information, search `http://msdn.microsoft.com` for the article "Add Method CDO (Messages Collection)."

12.6 Setting Message Properties

Problem

You want to determine if the message was transmitted successfully and read by the recipient, as you would using an Outlook mail client.

Solution

You can set the ReadReceipt and DeliveryReceipt properties of the Message object before sending the message:

```
Const MsgHigh = 2

Dim objSession, objMessage Set objSession = CreateObject("MAPI.Session")
objSession.Logon
Set objMessage = objSession.Outbox.Messages.Add

objMessage.Subject = "Test message"
objMessage.Importance = MsgHighobjMessage.Sensitivity =  True
objMessage.ReadReceipt = True
objMessage.DeliveryReceipt = True objMessage.Type = "IPM.SCBSpecialMessage"
objMessage.Text= "Testing"
```

Discussion

Once you have created a Message object to manipulate, you can set or get a number of properties for the message.

Table 12-4 lists properties that are available when sending a new message.

Table 12-4. Message Properties

NAME	TYPE	DESCRIPTION
ReadReceipt	Boolean	Set the ReadReceipt property to True to obtain a notification message when the recipient(s) has read your message. The default setting for the CDO is False.
Sensitivity	Long	This property is only available in CDO 1.2 and greater. It sets the sensitivity level of the message. NoSensitivity 0 Personal 1 Private 2 Confidential 3 Setting the Sensitivity property does not prevent anyone from reading the message—it is merely intended to identify the sensitivity of the message. Setting the property to Confidential doesn't make it any easier to access. The default setting is 0, NoSensitivity.

Table 12-4. Message Properties (continued)

NAME	TYPE	DESCRIPTION
`DeliveryReceipt`	Boolean	Set the `DeliveryReceipt` property to `True` to obtain a notification message when the recipient(s) receives your message. The default setting for the CDO is `False`.

See Also

For more information, search `http://msdn.microsoft.com` for the article "Viewing MAPI Properties."

12.7 Creating Message Recipients

Problem

You want to send a message to Fred Smith and a carbon copy to Joe Blow. Fred Smith is set up in your e-mail application's address book, while Joe Blow isn't, but you know Joe Blow's e-mail address.

Solution

You can create new recipients by invoking the `Recipients` object's `Add` method:

```
Const MsgTo = 1
Const MsgCC = 2
Const MsgBCC = 3
Dim objSession, objMessage, objRecipient
Set objSession = CreateObject("MAPI.Session")
objSession.Logon  "Valid Profile"
Set objMessage = objSession.Outbox.Messages.Add

objMessage.Subject = "Test message"
objMessage.Text= "This is the body of the message"
Set objRecipient = objMessage.Recipients.Add("Fred Smith",, MsgTo)
objRecipient.Resolve
'carbon copy Joe Blow
Set objRecipient =objMessage.Recipients.Add("Joe B","SMTP:joeb@abc.com", MsgCC)
objRecipient.Resolve objMessage.Send
objSession.Logoff
```

Discussion

The Message object contains a reference to the Recipients collection. The Recipients collection for each message represents one or more recipients of the message.

The Recipient object contains details relating to a specific recipient in the mail message.

To add a new recipient to a message, invoke the Add method for the Recipients collection on the Message object you want to add a new recipient to. The Add method can take a number of optional parameters, but these can be set after the recipient has been added to the message. The syntax is as follows:

```
Set objOneRecip = objMessage.Recipients.Add([Name,Address,Type])
```

Table 12-5 lists the parameters for the Recipients collection's Add method.

Table 12-5. Add *Method Parameters*

NAME	DESCRIPTION
Name	The Name property identifies the display name for the recipient—this would be the "proper" name of the recipient (e.g., Fred Smith). This can also be the name of a distribution list.
Address	Sets the value of the Recipient object's Address property to specify a custom address. The recipient address uses the following syntax: AddressType:AddressValue. The AddressType and Value are discussed in the following section.
Type	The recipient type is either To, Carbon Copy (CC), or Blind Carbon Copy (BCC). The following are valid values for the Type property: To 1 The recipient(s) on the To line (default). Cc 2 The recipient(s) on the Cc line. Bcc 3 The recipient(s) on the Bcc line.

When you create a new message to be sent, the recipient can be identified in one of two ways: either by his or her display name (Name property) or by his or her address (Address property). The display name would be the name listed in the address book when using the e-mail application. This would be the recipient's "real" name (e.g., Fred Smith).

Note that when using the display name, you need to enter the *exact* match of the name as it appears in your address book.

Once the Name property is set, you must invoke the Resolve method to set the Recipient's e-mail address:

```
Set objRecipient = objMessage.Recipients.Add("Fred Smith")
objRecipient.Resolve
```

If there is an entry for Fred Smith in your address book, the e-mail address is assigned to the Address property. This assumes that there is an address entry for a Fred Smith in your address book.

If there isn't an entry for Fred Smith in your address book, or there are multiple entries for Fred Smith, a Check Names dialog box appears (see Figure 12-6) that attempts to list names closest to the one that you specified.

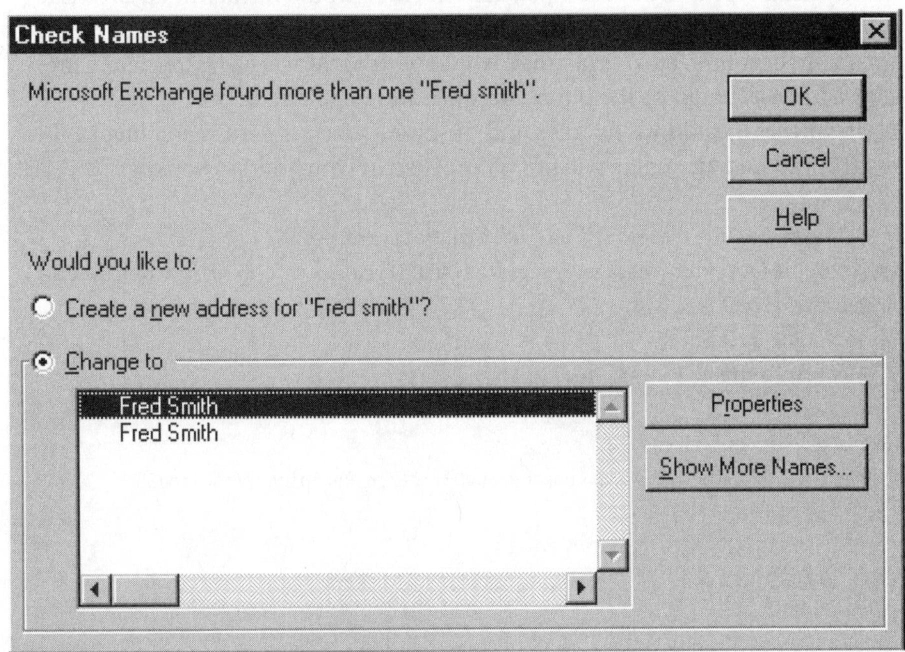

Figure 12-6. Check Names dialog box

The appearance of a dialog box is not desirable during the execution of a noninteractive script. The Resolve method supports an additional ShowDialog parameter, which takes a Boolean argument value. If set to False, a dialog box will not appear to resolve ambiguous names. The default is True.

```
On Error Resume Next
Set objRecipient = objMessage.Recipients.Add("Fred Smith")
' attempt to resolve name from Address book- don't display dialog box
```

```
'if name doesn't resolve
objRecipient.Resolve False
If Err Then ' check if Recipient was successfully resolved
   ' Perform error checking...
End If
```

The other option for addressing is to use the full e-mail address—that is, the address used by the mail system to determine where to deliver the message. This address is split into two parts: the Type and Address properties.

The Type property identifies what messaging type the address is associated with. Because the underlying transport mechanisms used for your mail system might be MS Mail, Internet, CompuServe, or even your fax modem, you need to specify what type it is. For example, Internet mail would be identified as SMTP.

The Address part is the actual address used by the particular transport mechanism. An example for Internet mail would be fsmith@acompany.com, while for a fax address it could be the phone number and recipient name.

If you set the address Address and the name Name properties and invoke the Resolve method, the name will not be checked in your address book.

```
'set the recipient address to an Internet Mail address
Set objRecipient = objMessage.Recipients.Add("Fred Smith","fsmith@acompany.com")
objRecipient.Resolve
'Windows Fax message
objOneRecip.Address = "FAX:Fred Smith@555-1234"

'Exchange Server address
objOneRecip.Address = "EX:/o=Company/ou=Office/cn=Recipients/cn=FredS"
```

See Also

For more information, search http://msdn.microsoft.com for the articles "Using Addresses" and "Add Method (Recipients Collection)."

12.8 Sending the Message

Problem

You want to send the message that has been created.

Solution

You can create a message and set the appropriate properties to call the Send method:

```
Const MsgTo = 1
Dim objSession, objSession, objRecipient

Set objSession = CreateObject("MAPI.Session")
objSession.Logon  "Valid Profile"

Set objMessage = objSession.Outbox.Messages.Add
objMessage.Subject = "Test message"
objMessage.Text= "This is the body of the message"
'add Fred Smith as a recipient - resolve e-mail address from Address book
Set objRecipient = objMessage.Recipients.Add("Fred Smith",, MsgTo)
objRecipient.Resolve
objMessage.Send
objSession.Logoff
```

Discussion

Once the Recipients and Message properties have been set, you can send the message. This simply involves invoking the Send method for the Message object. The syntax is as follows:

```
objMessage.Send([SaveCopy, ShowDialog, ParentWindow])
```

The Send method can take any of the parameters listed in Table 12-6.

Table 12-6. Send Method Parameters

NAME	TYPE	DESCRIPTION
SaveCopy	Boolean	If True, saves a copy of the message in a user-specified folder, which is defined by the e-mail application. This folder is usually the Sent Items folder. The default value is True.
ShowDialog	Boolean	If True, displays a Send Message dialog box where the user can change the message contents or recipients. The default value is False.
ParentWindow	Long	The parent window handle for the Send Message dialog box. Does not apply to WSH.

If you are sending and receiving mail in a server-based environment such as Exchange server, your mail will be delivered and sent automatically during your sessions.

If you are using a machine that stores mail locally and does not have a dedicated connection to an e-mail server, such as an Internet POP3 mail account, you may have to manually force the transmission of messages. If you create and send an e-mail message in this type of environment, the message will not automatically be sent.

The `Session` object has a method called `DeliverNow` that forces the delivery and retrieval of mail messages. If your mail client is configured to send and receive mail on demand, invoking the `DeliverNow` method will connect and send any messages in the Outbox and retrieve any new messages.

To use, simply add the `DeliverNow` method when you have sent a message or want to retrieve new messages. `DeliverNow` has no optional parameters.

```
objSession.DeliverNow
```

NOTE *Some providers may require additional authentication or connection steps that cannot be controlled through the MAPI interface.*

Windows 2000 and later include the CDOSYS mail component. The CDOSYS component can send e-mail without the need for a Outlook client profile or Exchange server. The component can send mail using an IIS or third-party SMTP server.

To send an e-mail using CDOSYS and an IIS 5 or 6 SMTP server, create an instance of the `CDO.Message` object and set the recipient and sender information.

NOTE *Information on configuring an IIS SMTP server is beyond the scope of this book.*

The following example creates an instance of the `CDO.Send` object and sends a message using the local IIS server:

```
Set objMessage = CreateObject("CDO.Message")
objMessage.Subject = "administrator@acme.com"
objMessage.From = "joeb@acme.com"
objMessage.To = "test@acme.com"
```

```
objMessage.CC = "test@acme.com"
objMessage.BCC = "test@acme.com"
objMessage.TextBody = "This is some sample message text."
objMessage.Send
```

The `CDO.Message` object's `From`, `To`, `CC`, and `BCC` properties represent the from, to, carbon copy (CC), and blind carbon copy (BCC) e-mail addresses, respectively. Multiple e-mail addresses can be specified by separating the addresses with a comma. The `Subject` and `TextBody` properties store the message subject and body, respectively.

The flexibility of the CDOSYS component is its ability to use any local or remote SMTP service. The SMTP service can be an IIS, Exchange, or non-Windows SMTP server. To set the SMTP service, create an instance of the `CDO.Configuration` object and set the SMTP server properties.

The following example sends an e-mail to a remote SMTP service on the server `exchange.acme.com`:

```
Const cdoSendUsingPort = 2
Const schema = "http://schemas.microsoft.com/cdo/configuration/"
strSmartHost = "exchange.acme.com"

Set objMsg = CreateObject("CDO.Message")
Set objConf = CreateObject("CDO.Configuration")

Set objFlds = objConf.Fields
'set the CDOSYS configuration fields to use port 25 on the SMTP server
'and use
With objFlds
  .Item(schema & "sendusing") = cdoSendUsingPort
  .Item(schema & "smtpserver") = strSmartHost
  .Item(schema & "smtpserverport") = 25
  .Update
End With

' apply the settings to the message
With objMsg
Set .Configuration = objConf
  .To = "administrator@acme.com"
  .From = "freds@acme.com"
  .Subject = "Set message subjects"
  .TextBody = "Set body of text"
  .Send
End With
```

The `CDOSYS.Configuration` object exposes properties that configure which SMTP service to use. The object properties are accessed through the `Items` collection. The properties are stored as *uniform resource identifiers* (URIs). A URI looks similar to a Web URL and is composed of a namespace and a local identifier. The namespace for CDOSYS server configuration is `http://schemas.microsoft.com/cdo/configuration`.

The `smtpserver` name represents the SMTP server used to send e-mail. The `sendusing` name represents how the e-mail messages are sent. If it is set to 2, the remote server is used; if it is set to 1, then the IIS local server drop directory is used. The `smtpserverport` name sets the SMTP port to use. By default, this is 25.

See Also

For more information, search `http://msdn.microsoft.com` for the article "Send Method (Message Object)."

12.9 Using a Command-Line Script to Send E-mail

Problem

You require a command-line script to send e-mail messages.

Solution

You can use the following script:

```
'Script: MailSend.VBS
'Description
'Sends a mail message to specified recipient
Option Explicit
Dim sExchangeProfile 'exchange profile
Dim sRecipient, sSubject, sMessage, objOneRecip, objShell
Dim objSession, objMessage

If WScript.Arguments.Count <> 4 Then ShowUsage
     sExchangeProfile = WScript.Arguments(0)
     sRecipient = WScript.Arguments(1)
     sSubject = WScript.Arguments(2)
     sMessage = WScript.Arguments(3)
    On Error Resume Next
    Set objSession = CreateObject("MAPI.Session")
    CheckError Err,"Unable to create mail session"

    ' logon using specified profile.
```

```
    objSession.Logon sExchangeProfile, , False
    CheckError Err,"Unable to logon using profile: " & sExchangeProfile
    ' create a message and fill in its properties
    Set objMessage = objSession.Outbox.Messages.Add
    objMessage.Subject = sSubject
    objMessage.Text = sMessage

    ' create the recipient
    Set objOneRecip = objMessage.Recipients.Add(,sRecipient)
    objOneRecip.Resolve
    CheckError Err,"Unable to add recipient: " & sRecipient

    ' send the message and log off
    objMessage.Send
    CheckError Err,"Unable to send message " 'check for error
    objSession.DeliverNow
    objSession.Logoff

Sub ShowUsage()
WScript.Echo "Syntax of this script is:" &  vbCrLf & _
  "mailsend exchangeprofile, recipient, subject, message " & vbCrLf & _
  "Mailsend sends a message to a specified recipient."  & vbCrLf & _
  "exchangeprofile  Valid messaging profile" &  vbCrLf & _
  "recipient        Address of recipient in format AddressType:Address. " _
  &  vbCrLf & _
  "subject          Message subject. " &  vbCrLf & _
  "text             Message text. " &  vbCrLf & vbCrLf & _
  "Example:" & vbCrLf & _
  "mailsend ""My Profile"" ""SMTP:fred@x.com"" ""message subject"" " & _
  """message text """
  WScript.Quit -1
End Sub

'Procedure: CheckError
'Description
'Checks if error has occurred and if so, displays error information
'and quits.
'Parameters objErr Err object
'             sMsg   Message to display if error occurs
Sub CheckError(objErr, sMsg)
 If objErr Then
   WScript.Echo  "A fatal error has occurred: " & vbLf & sMsg & _
            vbCrLf & "Err #:" & Err _
          & vbCrLf & "Description: " & Err.Description & vbCrLf
   WScript.Quit
 End If
End Sub
```

Discussion

Execute `mailsend.vbs` with four parameters: mail profile, recipient address, subject, and message.

The recipient address must be in `Type:Address` format—that is, the e-mail type (SMTP, X400, EX, or FAX) followed by a valid address for the format. For example:

```
Mailsend "My Profile" "SMTP:freds@x.com" "subject" "message body"
```

The following solution is a reusable COM script component that provides send mail functionality. It's used in other examples to send messages.

```
<?xml version="1.0"?>
<component>
<registration
    description="CDO.Send"
    progid="CDO.Send"
    version="1.00"
    classid="{1e99aa40-19ad-11d3-bbec-00104b164591}"
>
</registration>
<public>
    <property name="Profile"><put/>
    </property>
    <property name="Subject"><put/>
    </property>
    <property name="Message"><put/>
    </property>
    <property name="Session"><get/>
    </property>
    <method name="Send"></method>
    <method name="NewMessage"></method>
    <method name="AddRecipient">
        <PARAMETER name="Address"/>
    </method>
    <method name="LogOn"></method>
    <method name="LogOff"></method>
</public>

<script language="VBScript">
<![CDATA[

Dim objOneRecip,objSession,objMessage
Dim Profile, ErrorString
```

```
Function put_Profile(newValue)
    Profile = newValue
End Function

Function put_Subject(newValue)
    objMessage.Subject = newValue
End Function

Function put_Message(newValue)
    objMessage.Text = newValue
End Function

Function get_Error()
    get_Error = ErrorString
End Function

Function get_Session()
    get_Session = objSession
End Function

Function Send()
    ' sEnd the message
    objMessage.SEnd
End Function

Function NewMessage()
    On Error Resume Next
    ' create a message and fill in its properties
    Set objMessage = objSession.Outbox.Messages.Add

    If Err Then
        ErrorString = CreateErrMsg (Err, _
            "Error occured attempting to create new message")
        NewMessage = False
        Exit Function
    Else
        NewMessage = True
    End If
End Function

Function AddRecipient(Address)
    ' create the recipient
    On Error Resume Next
    Set objOneRecip = objMessage.Recipients.Add
    objOneRecip.Address = Address
    objOneRecip.Resolve
```

```
        If Err Then
            ErrorString = CreateErrMsg (Err, _
                "Error occured after adding recipient" & Address)
            AddRecipient = False
            Exit Function
        Else
            AddRecipient = True
        End If
End Function

Function LogOn()

        On Error Resume Next
        'check if MAPI session exists.
        If Not IsObject(objSession) Then
            Set objSession = CreateObject("MAPI.Session")
        End If

        ' logon using a valid profile
        objSession.Logon Profile
        If Err Then
            ErrorString = CreateErrMsg (Err, _
            "Error occured attempting to log on with profile:" & Profile)
            LogOn = False
            Exit Function
        Else
            LogOn = True
        End If
End Function

Function LogOff()
        objSession.Logoff
        Set objSession = Nothing
End Function

Function  CreateErrMsg(objErr,sMsg)
Dim sTemp
 sTemp = "Error# [" & Err & "] " & Err.Description
 If Not sMsg = "" Then sTemp = sTemp & vbCrLf & sMsg
 CreateErrMsg = sTemp
End Function
]]>
</script>
</component>
```

The CDO.Send object provides the ability to create and send messages. Table 12-7 lists the CDO.Send object's properties.

Table 12-7. CDO.Send *Object Properties*

PROPERTY	DESCRIPTION
Profile	Profile string used to log on
Message	Message to send
Subject	Message subject
Session	Returns the Session object of current MAPI session
Error	Returns a string describing the last error that occurred

Table 12-8 lists the CDO.Send object's methods.

Table 12-8. CDO.Send *Object Methods*

METHOD	DESCRIPTION
Logon	Attempts to create a MAPI session and log on using the profile specified by the Profile property. Returns True if the logon was successful; otherwise, it returns False.
NewMessage	Creates a new message to send.
AddRecipient	Attempts to add a new recipient to the current message. Requires a recipient address parameter. The recipient address must be in Type:Address format—that is, the e-mail type (SMTP, X400, EX, or FAX) followed by a valid address for the format. Returns True if successful; otherwise, it returns False. For example: `objMail.AddRecipient ("SMTP:fred@abc.com")` You can add as many recipients as required.
Send	Attempts to send the current message. Returns True if successful; otherwise, it returns False.
LogOff	Logs off the current MAPI session.

The following example creates an instance of the CDO.Send object and sends a message:

```
Dim objMail
Set objMail = CreateObject("CDO.Send")
objMail.Profile = "My Profile" 'set the profile you want to use
```

```
If objMail.Logon() Then
 objMail.NewMessage
 objMail.AddRecipient ("SMTP:fred@abc.com")
  objMail.Message = "Hello Fred"
 objMail.Subject = "Message to Fred"
 objMail.Send objMail.Logoff
End If
```

12.10 Checking the Event Log

Problem

You want to check the event log on the current machine for the last hour for any failed logon attempts.

Solution

You can use the following script:

```
Dim objWebems, objWeb, objWebem, sMsg, st, objMail
Set objWebem = GetObject("winmgmts:\\")
Set objWebems = objWebem.ExecQuery("SELECT TimeWritten, EventIdentifier " & _
    ", Message  FROM Win32_NTLogEvent WHERE EventIdentifier=529 " & _
    "AND SourceName='Security' AND TimeWritten > '" & _
    Convert2DMTFDate(Date - 1, "630") & "' ")

sMsg=""
For Each objWeb In objWebems
    st = objWeb.Properties_("TimeWritten")

    st = Mid(st, 5, 2) & "/" & Mid(st, 7, 2) & "/" & Mid(st, 1, 4) & _
        "  " & Mid(st, 9, 2) & ":" & Mid(st, 11, 2) & ":" & Mid(st, 13, 2)

sMsg = sMsg & "Time Logged " & st & vbCrLf
sMsg = sMsg & Replace(objWeb.Properties_("Message"),_
        vbCrLf & vbCrLf, vbCrLf)
Next

If Not sMsg=""
Set objMail = CreateObject("CDO.Send")
  objMail.Profile = "My Profile"
```

```
 objMail.NewMessage
 objMail.AddRecipient ("SMTP:administrator@abc.com")
 objMail.Message = sMsg
  objMail.Subject = "Logon failures detected"
 objMail.Send  objMail.Logoff
End If

'convert date to DMTF date required by WMI
Function Convert2DMTFDate(dDate, sTimeZone)
Dim sTemp
sTemp = Year(Now) & Pad(Month(dDate), 2, "0") & Pad(Day(dDate), 2, "0")
sTemp = sTemp & Pad(Hour(dDate), 2, "0") & Pad(Minute(dDate), 2, "0")
sTemp = sTemp & "00.000000+" & sTimeZone
Convert2DMTFDate = sTemp
End Function

'pad a string
Function Pad(sPadString, nWidth, sPadChar)
    If Len(sPadString) < nWidth Then
        Pad = String(nWidth - Len(sPadString), sPadChar) & sPadString
    Else
        Pad = sPadString
    End If
End Function
```

Discussion

You must have Windows NT/2000/2003 auditing set to log Logon and Logoff failures in order for the event log to record logon attempts. A recent version of WMI must be installed to access the events.

See Also

Solution 10.14.

12.11 Getting Computer Status Notification

Problem

You want to be notified if a machine becomes unavailable on your network.

Solution

Using the System Scripting Runtime component discussed in Chapter 11, you can ping machines. If you get no response from a machine, there might be a problem, so notify a specified user via e-mail.

This example e-mails a digital mobile phone using a mobile phone connectivity service. You could alternatively get a page e-mail service and have a message sent to your pager. Check your local communications provider for service details.

```
'Script: ISAlive.VBS
'Description
'Checks if machines are unavailable and e-mails a specified user
'if can't reach machines (machines might be down)
Dim objPing, strResult, objMail
Set objPing = CreateObject("SScripting.IPNetwork")
strResult = ""
Ping "Mars", strResult
Ping "Jupiter", strResult
Ping "Thor", strResult

'check if the return result is not empty - if not empty, then unable to ping
'one or more machines
If strResult <> "" Then
 sResult = "Unable to contact following machines:" & vbCrLf & sResult
 Set objMail = CreateObject("CDO.Send")
 objMail.Profile = "SCB"
 objMail.Logon
 objMail.NewMessage
 objMail.AddRecipient "SMTP:administrator@c3i.com"
 objMail.Message = "Machine(s) Not Available "
 objMail.Subject = strResult
 objMail.Send
 objMail.Logoff
End If

Sub Ping(strHost, ByRef strMsg)
  If Not objPing.Ping(strHost) = 0 Then strMsg = strMsg & strHost & vbCrLf
End Sub
```

12.12 Using the Performance Monitor Event

Problem

You are using Windows NT's Performance Monitor program to monitor for problems on a machine. You want to be notified if a monitored threshold is exceeded.

Solution

Performance Monitor can have alerts set when a certain threshold is exceeded. A program can be run at this time. To do so, follow these steps:

1. Start Performance Monitor.
2. Click the View the Alerts icon.
3. Under Windows NT 4.0, select the Add to Alert icon to add a new Alert. Under Windows 2000 and later, select New Alert Settings from the Actions menu. The Add to Alert dialog box appears, as shown in Figure 12-7.

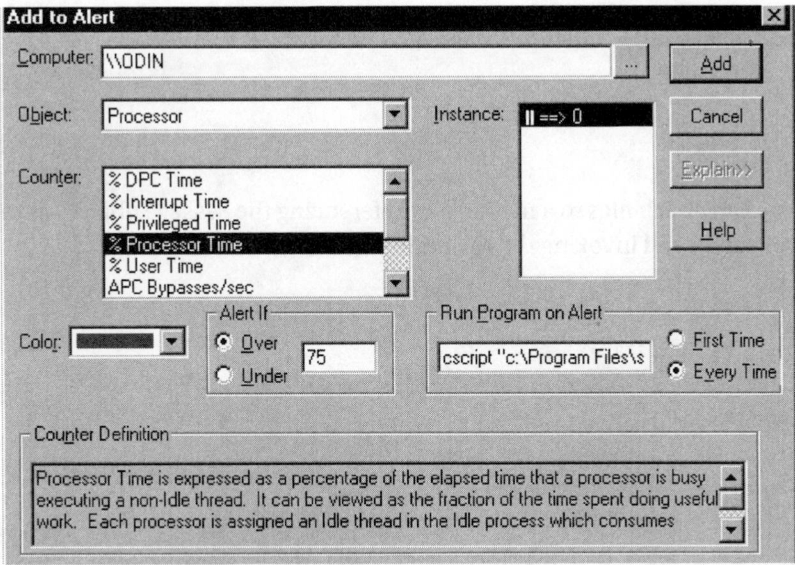

Figure 12-7. Windows NT 4.0 Add to Alert dialog box

4. Now set the counter and threshold you want to monitor.

5. In the Run Program on Alert box, enter the path of the program you want to run. For WSH scripts, you cannot just enter the path of the script (e.g., `c:\scripts\script.vbs`). You must execute the script with cscript or wscript (cscript is the logical choice).

Any parameters you want to pass that contain spaces must be surrounded in quotes. For example, the following command line would execute the `MailSend` script, passing the profile, e-mail address, subject, and mail message:

```
cscript d:\scripts\MailSend.vbs  "Profile" "SMTP:freds@x.com" "Subject" "message"
```

> **NOTE** *Under Windows NT 4.0, you have the option to run the script only once with the First Time option button, and this may be desirable if you only want to be notified of the first instance; otherwise, you might be overwhelmed by messages.*

12.13 Attaching Files to a Message

Problem

You need to attach files to a message.

Solution

You can attach files to a message by referencing the `Message` object's `Attachment` collection and invoking the `Add` method:

```
'sendattach.vbs
Const MsgFileData =1
Const MsgFileLink = 2
Const MsgOLE = 3
Dim objSession, objMessage, objRecipient '
Set objSession = CreateObject("MAPI.Session")
objSession.Logon "SCB"
Set objMessage = objSession.Outbox.Messages.Add("Attachment Test")
```

```
objMessage.Text= "This is the body of the message"
Set objRecipient = _
                    objMessage.Recipients.Add("Joe Blow ",
"SMTP:administrator@acme.com")
objRecipient.Resolve
Set objAttachment = objMessage.Attachments.Add("Attached File", , _
                    MsgFileData,"c:\data\Weekly.xls")

Set objAttachment = objMessage.Attachments.Add("Linked File", , _
                    MsgFileLink, "\\odin\xldata\Weekly.xls")

Set objAttachment = objMessage.Attachments.Add("Embedded File", , _
                    MsgOLE, "c:\data\Weekly.xls")
objMessage.Update
objMessage.Send
objSession.Logoff
```

Discussion

Messages can also include file attachments. Sending file attachments embeds a specified file in the message, which can then be extracted at the destination. Mail messages can contain one or more file attachments.

Attachments can be included by calling the Add method for the Attachments collection for the current message. The syntax is as follows:

```
Set objAttachment = objAttachColl.Add( [Name, Position, Type, Source] )
```

Upon successful execution, it returns a new Attachment object.

The Add method can take any of the parameters listed in Table 12-9.

Table 12-9. Attachment *Collection* Add *Method Parameters*

NAME	TYPE	DESCRIPTION
Name	String	Descriptive name that appears in the actual message. This is not the file path.
Position	Long	Determines the order in which the attachment will appear in the message.

continues

Table 12-9. `Attachment` *Collection* `Add` *Method Parameters (continued)*

NAME	TYPE	DESCRIPTION
`Type`	Long	The type of attachment: `MsgFileData`, `MsgFileLink`, `MsgOLE`, or `MsgEmbeddedMessage`. The default value is `MsgFileData`.
`Source`	String	Specifies the source of the attachment. This varies depending on the attachment type. See the Table 12-10 to determine the source format.

The attachment types listed in Table 12-10 determine how the attachment is included in the message.

Table 12-10. Message Attachment Types

VALUE	DESCRIPTION
`MsgFileData` = 1	Specifies that the full contents of a file are included in the message.
`MsgFileLink` = 2	A file link only sends a pointer to the file. This pointer is the location of the file on disk. This is only practical on internal networks where the recipient(s) has access to the specified disk location. The file link should be specified using the Universal Naming Convention (UNC) format—for example, `\\Server\Share\FileName.DOC`. No file data is actually included in the message—only a reference to the file location.
`MsgOLE` = 3	Specifies the contents of the document are embedded in the message as an OLE document. The contents of the document appear inside the message, so if an Excel file is included, you actually see the whole spreadsheet or part of the spreadsheet in the message. Specify the full path and file name to a valid OLE document file—for example, `C:\DOCUMENT\SALES.XLS`.
`MsgEmbeddedMessage` = 4	Indicates an existing e-mail message is to be included as the attachment. The attachment source is identified using the message ID property of the message you want to attach.

The attachment is saved in the message when you call the update or send method on the parent Message object.

See Also

For more information, search http://msdn.microsoft.com for the article "Adding Attachments to a Message."

12.14 Processing Messages

Problem

You want to list the subject of each message in the Inbox.

Solution

You can reference the InBox Folder object and iterate through the object's Messages collection:

```
Dim objSession, objMessage
Set objSession = CreateObject("MAPI.Session")
objSession.Logon "Profile Name"
' loop through all messages in the InBox folder, displaying the subject
For Each objMessage In objSession.Inbox.Messages
    WScript.Echo objMessage.Subject
Next
objSession.Logoff
```

Discussion

To get messages, you first need to get a Folder object for the folder that contains the messages. Start with the Inbox folder—the default folder where messages are received.

Each MAPI Session keeps track of the InBox as well as the OutBox. While you may have a profile that contains several InBox folders, there is only one that is considered to be your default InBox. This InBox is the default folder for message delivery where all new messages are delivered.

To get access to the InBox, simply reference the InBox property of the Session object. This returns a reference to the InBox Folder object.

The Folder object doesn't contain a huge selection of properties or methods. The main information you get from it is a reference to a Messages collection—the reference to all of the messages contained in the folder.

```
Dim objFolder, objSession, objMessage, objMessages
Set objSession = CreateObject("MAPI.Session")
objSession.Logon "Profile Name"
Set objFolder = Session.InBox 'get the Messages collection for the InBox
Set objMessages = objFolder.Messages
```

Apart from the obvious reason that the InBox is where you are likely to find new messages to process, it is very easy to get a reference to the InBox using the Session object's InBox property. As you'll see later, getting references to any other folder apart from the InBox requires a bit more work.

Now that you have a reference to a folder, you can start processing the messages in it. The logic that applies to the InBox folder also applies to any other folder.

The Messages collection contains references to a set of messages for a specific folder. Once the Messages collection for a folder has been retrieved, all messages in the folder can be iterated through and processed.

While you can process all Message objects within a Messages collection using the usual For - Each sequence, the Messages collection provides Get methods that can offer you more control over what messages are processed. These methods are listed in Table 12-11.

Table 12-11. Message Get *Methods*

METHOD	DESCRIPTION
GetFirst	Gets the first message in the Messages collection. An optional Type parameter can be passed, which will filter on that message type.
GetLast	Gets the last message in the Messages collection. An optional Type parameter can be passed, which will filter on that message type.
GetNext	Gets the next message to be processed. If there are no more messages to process, a reference to Nothing is returned.
GetPrevious	Gets the previous message to be processed. If there are no more messages to process, a reference to Nothing is returned.

The following script example displays the subject of each message in the Inbox:

```
Dim objFolder, objSession, objMessage, objMessages
Set objSession = CreateObject("MAPI.Session")
```

```
objSession.Logon " Profile Name "
Set objFolder = objSession.InBox ' get a reference to the InBox Folder object
' return the Messages collection for the InBox
Set objMessages = objFolder.Messages
'get the first message in the folder that is of message type IPM.Note.
Set objMessage = objMessages.GetFirst("IPM.Note")
' loop through all messages in the InBox folder, displaying the subject
Do While Not objMessage Is Nothing
    WScript.Echo objMessage.Subject 'display the subject of the message
    'get the next message
     Set objMessage = objMessages.GetNext
Loop
objSession.Logoff
```

See Also

For more information, search `http://msdn.microsoft.com` for the article "Reading a Message from the Inbox."

12.15 Filtering Mail

Problem

You want to filter out all unread messages of type `IPM.NOTE` that are less than 6 months old.

Solution

You can set the `Messages` collection's `Filter` object's properties:

```
'filter.vbs
Set objSession = CreateObject("MAPI.Session")
objSession.Logon "SCB"
Set objMsgColl = objSession.InBox.Messages
Set objFilter = objMsgColl.Filter

'set the filter properties to filter all messages that are unread, of
'type IPM.Note and were received over 6 months a go
objFilter.Type = "IPM.Note"
objFilter.Unread = True
objFilter.TimeLast = DateAdd("d", -180, Date)
```

```
' loop through the Messages collection and display the subject
' for any messages that meet the filter criteria
Set objMessage = objMsgColl.GetFirst()
Do While Not objMessage Is Nothing
 'display the subject for the current message..
 WScript.Echo objMessage.Subject
'get the next message
 Set objMessage = objMsgColl.GetNext()
Loop
objSession.Logoff
```

Discussion

You have seen how you can traverse each message in the InBox folder. If you want to process messages that meet a certain criteria, you can use `If Then` conditional statements to check the properties of each message. Using the `GetFirst`/`GetNext` method combination in a `Messages` collection, you can specify that only certain message types be processed.

What if your folder contains hundreds, or even thousands, of messages and you only want to process the latest unread messages, or maybe only messages since a certain date?

You can apply a `Filter` object to the `Messages` collection for a particular folder to drill down on more specific data. The `Filter` object is only available in Active Messaging 1.1 and later.

To set a filter, simply reference the `Filter` object for the `Messages` collection you want to `Filter` on:

```
Set objMsgFilter = objSession.Inbox.Messages.Filter
```

Table 12-12 lists the `Filter` object properties that can be used to query messages.

Table 12-12. `Filter` *Object Properties*

NAME	TYPE	DESCRIPTION
`Recipients`	String	Returns any messages where any part of the message recipient's name matches part of the string (e.g., if Fred was specified, filter out messages with recipients named Fred Smith and Fred Jones).

continued

Table 12-12. Filter *Object Properties (continued)*

NAME	TYPE	DESCRIPTION
Sender	String	Returns any messages where any part of the message recipient's name matches part of the string (e.g., if Fred was specified, filter out messages with recipients named Fred Smith and Fred Jones).
Size	Long	Returns only messages where the message size is greater than the value of Size. The Size property represents the sum of all the message's properties, including Subject, Text, Attachments, and Recipients.
Subject	String	Returns any messages where any of the message Subject matches part of the string.
Text	String	Returns any messages where any of the message Text body matches part of the string.
TimeFirst	Variant	If the TimeFirst property is not set, the message filter passes all messages received at or before the date and time in the TimeLast property. If neither property is set, the filter passes messages regardless of their date and time of reception. The TimeFirst and TimeLast properties represent local time. The TimeFirst property corresponds to the MAPI property PR_MESSAGE_DELIVERY_TIME.
TimeLast	Variant	If the TimeLast property is not set, the message filter passes all messages received at or since the date and time in the TimeFirst property. If neither property is set, the filter passes messages regardless of their date and time of reception. The TimeFirst and TimeLast properties represent local time.
Type	String	Filters on messages of specified type.
Not	Boolean	Read/write.
Or	Boolean	Read/write.
Unread	Boolean	If set to True, filters all messages that are unread; if False, filters all read messages.

Once the filter is set, you can iterate through the Messages collection.

You can use either the Messages GetFirst/GetLast and GetNext/GetPrevious combination or a For - Next combination to reference each element in the filtered Messages collection.

To reset the filter, set the Filter property to Nothing.

See Also

For more information, search http://msdn.microsoft.com for the article "Filtering Messages in a Folder."

12.16 Extracting Attachments

Problem

You want to extract the file attachments from all unread messages.

Solution

You can filter all unread messages and enumerate each attachment, extracting the files by using the Attachment collection's WriteToFile method:

```
'extract.vbs
Dim objSession, objMsgColl, objMessage, strFile
Set objSession = CreateObject("MAPI.Session")
' supply a valid profile
objSession.Logon "Valid Profile"

'get a reference to the InBox messages
Set objMsgColl = objSession.InBox.Messages
'filter all unread messages
objMsgColl.Filter.Unread = True

'loop through the Messages collection and extract attachment for any messages
'that meet the filter criteria
Set objMessage = objMsgColl.GetFirst()
```

```
Do While Not objMessage Is Nothing
 WScript.Echo objMessage.Subject, objMessage.Attachments.Count
   For Each objAttachment In objMessage.Attachments
    strFile = objAttachment.Source
      If strFile <> "" Then
      strFile = Mid(strFile,InstrRev(strFile,"\") + 1)
      objAttachment.WriteToFile "d:\data\" & strFile
     End If
   Next
   objMessage.Unread = False ' flag message as read
   objMessage.Update 'update message
  'get the next message
  Set objMessage = objMsgColl.GetNext()
Loop
objSession.Logoff
```

Discussion

Adding attachments manually or automatically through code in the e-mail application can be extracted to a file on disk.

To extract file attachments from a `Message` object, invoke the `WriteToFile` method for the `Attachment` object you want to extract the file from. The syntax is as follows:

```
objAttachment.WriteToFile(FileName)
```

The `FileName` parameter specifies the full file path the attachment should be written to (e.g., `c:\Data\DataFile.Doc`). If a file already exists with the same name it will be overwritten.

See Also

For more information, search `http://msdn.microsoft.com` for the article "Write toFile Method (Attachment Object)."

12.17 Using a WSH Script Mail Agent

Problem

Users' machines require new files to perform basic maintenance. While this could be automated through logon scripts in a small environment with no remote clients, it is more difficult when some clients are remotely based and do not log into the system on a frequent basis. You could use e-mail to distribute files and automate processes, but you don't want any end-user intervention.

Solution

The following script uses a Microsoft launch agent together with an Exchange or Outlook client to execute the following script, which processes the contents of the message:

```
'extractor.vbs
Dim objMessage, objSession, objMessages, objFilter
Dim objFolder, sline, sBody
Dim nLast, nPos, nF

Set objSession = CreateObject("MAPI.Session")

'logon using an existing session..
objSession.Logon , , False, False
Set objShell = CreateObject("WScript.Shell")
'get the command line arguments
On Error Resume Next
nLast = 1
'get the message..
If WScript.Arguments.Count = 0 Then
  WScript.Echo "Requires MAPI message ID"
  WScript.Quit
End If

Set objMessage = objSession.GetMessage(WScript.Arguments(0))

'check if valid message
If objMessage Is Nothing Then WScript.Quit

 'get the body of the message
 sBody = objMessage.Text
```

```
'check body is not empty..
If Len(sBody)=0 Then WScript.Quit
 'loop through and process each line of the message
 Do
  'get the end of the current line
   nPos = InStr(nLast, sBody, vbCrLf)
    If nPos = 0 Then nPos = Len(sBody)
     sline = Trim(Mid(sBody, nLast, nPos - nLast))
    'check the first 4 characters of each line
    Select Case UCase(Left(sline, 4))

    Case "XTR:" 'extract command
     'get the position of a comma in the line -
     ' the text after the comma is the directory to extract to
     nF = InStr(sline, ",")
     If Not nF Then
       ProcessAttachments objMessage, "XTR", _
                  Trim(Mid(sline, 5, nF - 5)), Trim(Mid(sline, nF + 1))
     End If

    Case "EXE:" 'execute command
    ProcessAttachments objMessage, "EXE", Trim(Mid(sline, 5)), ""

    Case "DEL:" 'delete command
     ProcessAttachments objMessage, "DEL", Mid(sline, 5), ""

    End Select
    nLast = nPos + 2
  Loop While nLast < Len(sBody)
objSession.Logoff

Function ProcessAttachments(objMessage, sType, sFile, sPath)
Dim objAttachment, objFS, objFolder, objShell, sTemp
    For Each objAttachment In objMessage.Attachments
     'check if the current attachment name is equal to the one you
     'want to process
     If StrComp(objAttachment.Name, sFile, vbTextCompare) = 0 Then
                 Select Case sType
            Case "EXE"
             Set objShell =CreateObject("WScript.Shell")
             sTemp = objShell.ExpandEnvironmentStrings("%TEMP%")
             objAttachment.WriteToFile sTemp & "\" & sFile
               objShell.Run sTemp & "\" & sFile, 1, True
```

```
            Set objFS = CreateObject("Scripting.FileSystemObject")
        Set objFile = objFS.GetFile(sTemp & "\" & sFile)
        objFile.Delete
         Case "XTR"
            'create a file system object
            Set objFS = CreateObject("Scripting.FileSystemObject")
            Set objShell =CreateObject("WScript.Shell")
          sPath = objShell.ExpandEnvironmentStrings(sPath)

            'if folder doesn't exist, exit function
            If Not objFS.FolderExists(sPath)Then
              Exit Function
            End If
            'if folder exists, then extract attachment into folder
             objAttachment.WriteToFile sPath & "\" & sFile

          Case "DEL"
             Set objShell = CreateObject("WScript.Shell")
            sPath = objShell.ExpandEnvironmentStrings(sPath)
            'create a file system object
            Set objFS = CreateObject("Scripting.FileSystemObject")
       Set objFile = objFS.GetFile(sPath)
       objFile.Delete
      End Select
        Exit For
    End If
    Next
End Function
```

Discussion

Microsoft has created a simple launcher extension for Exchange client and Outlook users. This program is a custom Rules Wizard/InBox Assistant extension. It allows the execution of a specified program based on Rules Wizard/InBox Assistant rules.

> **NOTE** *To get the launcher and install it, visit* `http://support.microsoft.com/support/kb/articles/q173/9/15.asp`. *The ability to run custom rules has been disabled in Outlook 2002 (XP) and 2003. This is an acknowledged bug and hopefully will be addressed in future Office service packs.*

Once the launcher is installed, you need to create a rule to launch the scripts when a message arrives. The rule needs to be unambiguous so that unintended messages do not fire the rule.

Figure 12-8 shows an Outlook Rules Wizard that launches the extractor script if a message contains the phrase "WSHEXTRACTOR."

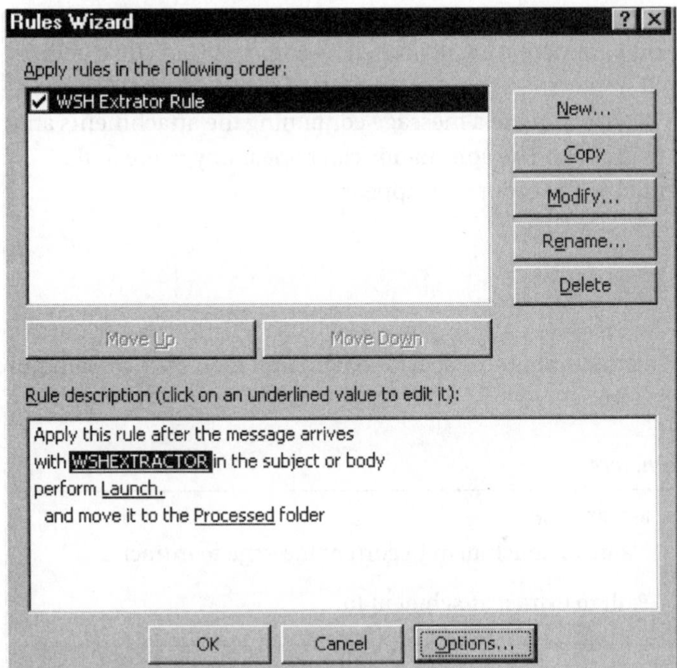

Figure 12-8. Outlook Rules Wizard

Figure 12-9 shows the setting for the Rules Wizard custom action.

Figure 12-9. Rules Wizard Select Custom Action dialog box

The launcher will launch the extractor script when the criteria are met on a message. Then it will process the message and its attachments.

The script will process "commands" in the text body of the message. These commands allow for the extraction of attachments, execution of message attachments, or deletion of a specified file.

The command statement starts with a three-letter instruction followed by a colon (:). The instruction can be `xtr` (extract), `exe` (execute), or `del` (delete).

After the instruction parameters are delimited by commas. Each instruction has a different set of parameters.

To use the extractor script, create a message containing the attachments and commands you want to process. The commands can appear anywhere in the message and are executed in the order they appear.

XTR

XTR extracts a specified attachment to a specified path and requires two parameters, which are listed in Table 12-13.

Table 12-13. XTR Parameters

PROPERTY	DESCRIPTION
`Attachment Name`	Name of attachment in current message to extract
`Path`	Path to extract attachment to

The following example extracts the `hello.vbs` attachment from the message into the `c:\scripts` directory:

```
xtr:hello.vbs,c:\scripts
```

EXE

EXE executes the specified attachment. You cannot execute a file on the local system, but you could create a script that executed local programs. The EXE command requires the name of an attachment you want to execute.

The following example executes the `hello.vbs` script attachment:

```
exe:hello.vbs
```

DEL

DEL deletes a specified system file.

The following example extracts the `newocx.ocx` attachment from the current message into `c:\windows\system directory` and then executes the `registerocx.vbs` script, which registers the OCX.

```
xtr:newocx.ocx,c:\windows\system
exe:registerocx.vbs
```

> **NOTE** *The use of such a mail processing agent can be extremely dangerous because malicious code could be executed upon arrival in the Inbox. Caution should be taken upon implementing any such script and the appropriate security procedures should be implemented to ensure rogue code is not executed inadvertently.*

12.18 Retrieving a Folder

Problem

You want a function that will return the `Folder` object reference to a folder specified by a full path. The function recursively processes the folder path until the end of the path is found.

Solution

The following `GetFolderObj` function returns a `Folder` object based on a specified folder path. The function traverses a folder path until the destination folder is retrieved.

```
'Procedure GetFolderObj
'Description
'Returns a reference to a Folder object for the specified folder path
'the folder path is specified with the full Exchange folder path
'delimited with backslashes.
'Parameters  objSession reference to MAPI session object
'             sFolderSearch Folder path delimited with backslashes
'Returns     reference to Folder object if folder found. If folder not
'             found, returns Nothing
```

```
Function GetFolderObj(objSession, sFolderSearch )
Dim objFolder, objInfoStore
On Error Resume Next
'get a reference to the Infostore object for the path
Set objInfoStore = objSession.InfoStores.Item(StripPath(sFolderSearch))

'check if problem getting reference Infostore.
If Err Then
    Set GetFolderObj = Nothing
    Exit Function
End If

'get a reference to the root folder for the Infostore
Set objFolder = objInfoStore.RootFolder
'loop through path searching for the specified folder
Do While Len(sFolderSearch) > 0
        'get next folder in hierarchy
    Set objFolder = objFolder.Folders.Item(StripPath(sFolderSearch))

    'check if error - folder not found
    If Err Then
        Set GetFolderObj = Nothing
        Exit Function
    Exit Function
End If
Loop
'return reference to folder
Set GetFolderObj = objFolder
End Function

'Procedure: StripPath
'Description
'Returns the next level from a folder path
'Parameters  sPath Folder path delimited with backslashes
'Returns     next level in path.
Function StripPath(sPath)
Dim nF
'look for the next level
nF = InStr(sPath, "\")
'if more levels in path, return name of level
If nF > 0 Then
    StripPath = Left(sPath, nF - 1)
    sPath = Trim(Mid(sPath & " ", nF + 1))
Else
```

```
    StripPath = Trim(sPath)
    sPath = ""

End If
End Function
```

Discussion

There is no quick method to find a folder, other than the InBox or OutBox. You have to traverse the folder structure until the folder you are looking for is found.

But before you can traverse the folder structure, you must find the Infostore for that folder structure.

The InfoStore object provides access to the folder hierarchy of a message store. In your mail application, Infostores are represented by the different root objects. For example, under Exchange server, your personal messages would be considered an Infostore, as would the Public Folders.

Each PST file you use is also considered to be an Infostore.

In Figure 12-10, Mailbox – Fred Smith, Personal Mail, and Public Folders are separate Infostores.

Figure 12-10. Infostore structure

You can reference InfoStore objects from the InfoStores collection of the Session object. You can iterate through the InfoStores collection or reference via the Item method:

```
Set objSession = CreateObject("MAPI.Session")
objSession.Logon
'loop through an
For Each objInfoStore In objSession.Infostores
   WScript.Echo objInfoStore.Name
Next
```

```
'reference the Personal Folder Infostore by name..
Set objInfoStore = objSession.InfoStores.Item("Personal Folder")

'reference the first Infostore object in the InfoStores collection
Set objInfoStore = objSession.InfoStores.Item(1)
```

Once you have retrieved the InfoStore object, you can reference the RootFolder object. From the RootFolder you can reference all of the folders. You can now work your way to the folder you want to use.

The RootFolder object contains a reference to a Folders collection of folders contained in it. From this, you can find a folder on the next level.

If you need to find a folder further down, you repeat the process: Get the Folders collection of the folder and then find the Folder in the collection for the next level.

The following example gets a reference to the Junk Mail folder under the Misc. folder in the Personal Mail Infostore:

```
'reference the Personal Folder Infostore by name..
Set objInfoStore = objSession.InfoStores.Item("Personal Mail")
'get the Misc folder
Set objFolder = objInfoStore.Folders.Item("Misc.")

'get the Junk Mail folder..
Set objFolder = objInfoStore.Folders.Item("Junk Mail")
```

Another way of accessing a specific Infostore is using the InfoStore property of an existing Message or Folder object.

Getting references to mail folders can require a lot of repetitive coding. The Solution code's GetFolderObj function returns a reference to a folder object based on its mail path.

```
Set objFolder = GetFolderObj (objSession, "Personal Folder\Archive\Junk Mail")
```

The full folder path is specified by the name of the Infostore, followed by the folder path. Each folder in the path is separated by backslashes (\).

The GetFolderObj function is used in the following example to get a reference to the folder Mail Storage under the Personal Mail Infostore:

```
Set objFolder = GetFolderObj(objSession,"Personal Mail\Mail Storage")
```

The GetFolderObj function is used in later problems and is part of a maillib.vbs file of commonly used mail routines.

If you use Outlook, you can use the CDO `GetDefaultFolder` method to return a `Folder` object for specific folders. Along with the InBox and OutBox, you can get references to the default Deleted Items, Journal, Calendar, Notes, Tasks, and Sent Items folders.

The `GetDefaultFolder` method is executed via a valid `Session` object:

```
Set objFolder = objSession.GetDefaultFolder(FolderType)
```

Call the method and specify what folder you want to reference with the `FolderType` parameter. The method will return a `Folder` object with a reference to the specified folder. Table 12-14 contains valid constant values for `FolderType`.

Table 12-14. `GetDefaultFolder` *Folder Types*

FOLDERTYPE	VALUE	DEFAULT FOLDER RETRIEVED
CdoDefaultFolderCalendar	0	Calendar
CdoDefaultFolderContacts	5	Contacts
CdoDefaultFolderDeletedItems	4	Deleted Items
CdoDefaultFolderInbox	1	Inbox
CdoDefaultFolderJournal	6	Journal
CdoDefaultFolderNotes	7	Notes
CdoDefaultFolderOutbox	2	Outbox
CdoDefaultFolderSentItems	3	Sent Items
CdoDefaultFolderTasks	8	Tasks

The following example gets a reference to the Calendar folder:

```
Const CdoDefaultFolderCalendar = 0

' create a MAPI session,then log on
Set objSession = CreateObject("MAPI.Session")
objSession.Logon "My profile"
'get a reference to the Calendar folder
Set objFolder = objSession.GetDefaultFolder(CdoDefaultFolderCalendar )
```

The `GetDefaultMethod` only works with CDO 1.2 or greater.

See Also

For more information, search http://msdn.microsoft.com for the article "Accessing Folders."

12.19 Posting Messages to an Exchange Server Public Folder

Problem

You want to post a message to an Exchanger server folder.

Solution

You can add a message to an Exchange server public folder, set the appropriate properties, and update the message. The message does not get sent.

```
<?xml version="1.0" ?>
<job>
<!--comment
Script:postpublic.wsf
-->
 <script language="VBScript" src="maillib.vbs">
 <![CDATA[
 ' create a MAPI session,then log on
  Set objSession = CreateObject("MAPI.Session")
  ' supply a valid profile
  objSession.Logon "Valid Profile"
  'get a Reference to the Public Folders folder Public Posting
  Set objFolder = GetFolderObj(objSession, _
        "Public Folders\All Public Folders\Public Posting")

  'add a new message to the Public Folder. Note that no recipient is 'required.
  Set objMessage = objFolder.Messages.Add("New Post", "Testing Posting")
  objMessage.TimeReceived = Now
  objMessage.TimeSent = Now
  objMessage.Unread = True
  objMessage.Sent = True
  objMessage.Submitted = False
  'set type as a posted message - not required, but message will appear
  'with a small 'posted' icon
```

```
    objMessage.Type = "IPM.Post"
    objMessage.Update
    objSession.Logoff
    ]]>
    </script>
</job>
```

Discussion

To post a message to a public folder, create a message within the public folder by adding it to the folder's Messages collection. Then add your subject and message text as you would for other messages.

Note that for messages in public folders, you must also set a few more message properties than you would when sending a message to a recipient. When you post a message to a public folder, the components of the MAPI architecture that usually handle a message and set its properties do not manage the message. Your application must set the Sent and Unread properties to True, the Submitted property to False, and the TimeReceived and TimeSent properties to the current time.

When you are ready to make the message available, call the Update method. The message is not accessible by any other messaging user until you call Update method.

See Also

For more information, search http://msdn.microsoft.com for the article "Posting Messages to a Public Folder."

12.20 Creating Folders

Problem

You need a function to create folders for a specified folder path. You can't assume the parent folders for the folder you are creating exist, so the routine must create any folders in the path that are missing.

Solution

The following CreateFolder function creates a folder for the specified folder path and any parent folders if they do not already exist:

```
'Procedure: CreateFolder
'Description
'Creates a new message folder.
'Parameters  objSession reference to MAPI session object
'             sFolderSearch Folder path for new folder, delimited with
'             backslashes
'Returns     Reference to folder object if successful, otherwise Nothing.
Function CreateFolder(objSession, ByVal sFolderSearch)

Dim objfolder, objInfoStore, objfldr, sFindFolder
On Error Resume Next
'get a reference to the Infostore object for the path
Set objInfoStore = objSession.InfoStores.Item(StripPath(sFolderSearch))
'check if problem getting reference Infostore.
If Err Then
    Set CreateFolder = Nothing
    Exit Function
End If

'get a reference to the root folder for the Infostore
Set objfolder = objInfoStore.RootFolder
'loop through path searching for the specified folder
Do While Len(sFolderSearch) > 0
    sFindFolder = StripPath(sFolderSearch)
    For Each objfldr In objfolder.Folders
        If UCase(objfldr.Name) = UCase(sFindFolder) Then
           Exit For
        End If
    Next

    If objfldr Is Nothing Then
        Set objfolder = objfolder.Folders.Add(sFindFolder)
    Else
        Set objfolder = objfldr
    End If
Loop
Set CreateFolder = objfolder
End Function
```

Discussion

To create additional folders, invoke the Add method for the Folders collection where you want to add the new folder.

If you want to create a folder under the root of the current InfoStore, invoke the Add method for the Folders collection of the RootFolder.

To create a new folder called "Old Messages" under the root folder, use the following code:

```
'get the RootFolder reference the Personal Folder Infostore by name..
Set  objRootFolder = objSession.InfoStores.Item("Personal Folder").RootObject
'add a new folder under the root folder
Set  objFolder = objFolder.Folders.Add("Old Messages")
```

CreateFolder requires you specify a messaging Session object followed by the path you want to create. The full folder path is specified by the name of the InfoStore followed by the folder path. Each folder in the path is separated by backslashes (\).

```
Set objFolder = CreateFolder(objSession,"Personal Mail\Archive\FredS")
```

The previous sample returns a reference to the newly created Folder object if successful; otherwise, it returns Nothing. It will create multiple folders in a folder path if required.

CreateFolder uses the StripPath function from the GetFolderObj function from Solution 12.18, which is included in the maillib.vbs mail function library.

See Also

For more information, search http://msdn.microsoft.com for the article "Add Method (Folders Collection)."

12.21 Copying or Moving Messages

Problem

You want to copy or move a message.

Solution

For any operation that requires folder references, such as copy and moving folders or messages, the folder ID of the Folder objects(s) involved must be retrieved.

The folder ID uniquely identifies a folder and doesn't change from one session to another. It is hexadecimal string value and is referenced using the ID property of the Folder object.

The Folder object has two ID properties: FolderID and ID. The ID property identifies the Folder, and FolderID is the ID property for the Parent folder. Therefore, when performing a Folder-related operation, make sure you use the correct property. Call the CopyTo or MoveTo method of the message you want to move, specifying the destination Folder object and optionally the InfoStore ID of the destination Folder.

The following example copies and then moves a message from the Inbox to a public folder:

```
<?xml version="1.0" ?>
<job>
<!--comment
Script:copymove.wsf
-->
 <script language="VBScript" src="maillib.vbs">
 <![CDATA[
Dim objSession, objDestFolder, objSourceFolder, objCopiedMessage
Dim objSourceMessage
' create a MAPI session,then log on
Set objSession = CreateObject("MAPI.Session")
' supply a valid profile
objSession.Logon "Valid Profile"

Set objDestFolder = GetFolderObj(objSession, _
                    "Public Folders\All Public Folders\Public Posting")
'get a reference to the InBox Folder
Set objSourceFolder = objSession.Inbox

' get a reference to the first message in the InBox Messages collection
Set objSourceMessage = objSourceFolder.Messages(1)
'copy the message to the Public Folder - Freds Mail. The StoreID is passed
'since the destination folder is in a difference InfoStore than the original
'source message
Set objCopiedMessage = objSourceMessage.CopyTo(objDestFolder.ID, _
 objDestFolder.StoreID)
'update the copied message. The message will not be available until it is
```

```
'updated
objCopiedMessage.Update

'now move the message to the destination folder. The message will automatically
'be moved do not need to invoke the Update method for the moved message to
'become available.
Set objCopiedMessage = objSourceMessage.MoveTo(objDestFolder.ID, _
                          objDestFolder.StoreID)
  ]]>
  </script>
</job>
```

Discussion

To copy a message, invoke the CopyTo method on the Message object you want to copy. You need to specify the Folder ID for the destination folder, and if the destination Folder object resides in a different Infostore, you must also supply the InfoStore ID.

The CopyTo method returns a reference to the new Message copy. You must invoke the Update method on this Folder object in order to access the new copy. If the Update method is not invoked on the new copy, it will not appear.

If the destination folder resides in a different Infostore, a reference to the InfoStore ID for the destination Infostore must be passed.

The steps required to move a message are almost the same as those to copy a message. Invoke the MoveTo method on the message you want to move. The MoveTo method returns a reference to the moved message object. However, unlike the CopyTo method, you do not have to invoke the Update method on the moved message.

```
Set objCopiedMessage = objMessage.CopyTo(FolderID [, StoreID] )
Set objMovedMessage = objMessage.MoveTo(FolderID [, StoreID] )
```

Table 12-15 lists the arguments for the MoveTo and CopyTo methods.

Table 12-15. CopyTo *and* MoveTo *Methods' Arguments*

NAME	TYPE	DESCRIPTION
FolderID	String	Unique identifier of the destination Folder object.
StoreID	String	Optional parameter. Unique InfoStore identifier. If the destination folder resides in a different InfoStore than the source, the InfoStore ID must be provided.

See Also

For more information, search http://msdn.microsoft.com for the article "Copying a Message to Another Folder."

12.22 Copying and Moving Folders

Problem

You want to copy an existing folder to a new folder.

Solution

The following example uses the GetFolderObj function from Solution 12.18 to get a reference to the source and destination Folder objects for folders Store Mail\Processed and Personal Mail\Backup. The Processed folder is copied by calling the CopyTo method on the Folder object:

```
<?xml version="1.0" ?>
<job>
<!--comment
Script:copymovefld.wsf
-->
 <script language="VBScript" src="maillib.vbs">
 <![CDATA[
  Dim objSession, objDestFolder, objSourceFolder, objCopiedMessage
  Dim objSourceMessage
  Set objSession = CreateObject("MAPI.Session")
  ' supply a valid profile
  objSession.Logon "Valid Profile"

  'get a reference to a destination folder, using the GetFolderObj
  'function listed earlier in  this section
  Set objDestFolder = GetFolderObj(objSession, "Personal Mail\Backup")

  'get a reference to source folder to be copied..
  Set objSourceFolder = GetFolderObj(objSession, "Store Mail\Processed")

  'copy the source folder to the destination folder. The StoreID is passed
  'since the destination folder is in a difference InfoStore than the
  'original source message
```

```
  Set objNewCopiedFolder=objSourceFolder.CopyTo(objDestFolder.ID, _
                         objDestFolder.StoreID, , True)
  objSession.Logoff
  ]]>
  </script>
</job>
```

Discussion

To copy a folder, invoke the CopyTo method on the Folder object you want to copy. You need to specify the Folder ID for the destination folder, and if the destination Folder object resides in a different InfoStore, you must also supply the InfoStore ID.

All messages stored in the source folder are also copied to the destination folder. The CopyTo method returns a reference to the new folder copy.

There is also the option of renaming the folder in the destination folder and copying all subfolders.

If the destination folder resides in a different InfoStore, a reference to the InfoStore ID for the InfoStore must be passed. The syntax for the CopyTo method is as follows:

```
Set objFolder = objFolder.CopyTo(FolderID [,StoreID] [, Name] [,CopySubfolders ])
```

Table 12-16 lists the CopyTo method's parameters.

Table 12-16. CopyTo *Method Parameters*

NAME	TYPE	DESCRIPTION
FolderID	String	Unique identifier of the destination Folder object.
StoreID	String	Optional parameter. Unique InfoStore identifier. If the destination folder resides in a different InfoStore than the source, the InfoStore ID must be provided.
Name	String	Optional parameter. Name of the destination folder.
CopySubfolders	Boolean	If True, copies all subfolders from source folder to destination.

Upon the successful completion of the folder copy, a reference to the copied folder is returned.

Use the `MoveTo` method to move the contents of a folder:

```
Set objMovedMessage = objMessage.MoveTo(folderID [, storeID ] )
```

The two parameters applicable to the `MoveTo` method are the same as those provided to the `CopyTo` method. All messages and subfolders stored in the source `Folder` are also copied to the destination folder.

The `MoveTo` method returns a reference to the new moved `Folder`.

If the destination folder resides in a different InfoStore, a reference to the InfoStore ID for the InfoStore must be passed.

See Also

For more information, search `http://msdn.microsoft.com` for the article "MoveTo Method (Folder Object)."

12.23 Deleting Messages and Folders

Problem

You want to delete a message or folder.

Solution

You can reference the `Folder` or `Message` object that you want to delete and then invoke the `Delete` method:

```
<?xml version="1.0" ?>
<job>
<!--comment
Script:delfolder.wsf
-->
 <script language="VBScript" src="maillib.vbs">
 <![CDATA[
  Dim objSession, objFolder
  Set objSession = CreateObject("MAPI.Session")
  ' supply a valid profile
  objSession.Logon "Valid Profile"
```

```
  'get a reference to the folder to be deleted and delete it
  Set objFolder = GetFolderObj(objSession, "Personal Mail\Backup")
  objFolder.Delete
  objSession.Logoff
  ]]>
  </script>
</job>
```

Discussion

To delete a folder or message, simply execute the `Delete` method on the `Folder` or `Message` object you want to remove. Deleting a folder removes the folder and all messages and subfolders within that folder.

`Folder` and `Message` object deletion cannot be undone—the contents are not put into the Undeleted folder.

12.24 Creating New Message Fields

Problem

You want to display the values for all fields in a message.

Solution

You can reference the `Message` object's `Fields` collection and then count all the fields in the collection:

```
'get the Fields collection from a message
Set objFields = objMessage.Fields
'continue if error occurs - certain field types cannot be outputted and will
'generate an error if attempted  to display
On Error Resume Next
'loop through all of the fields in the objFields collection
For Each objField In objFields
'display the Field value and ID.
    WScript.Echo objField.Values & " " & objField.ID
Next
```

Discussion

Messages often have data fields containing information supplied via the e-mail application. This might be information such as message and formatting types. Custom Forms created in Outlook and Exchange also store fields in the message.

These fields are not directly visible in the message itself, except in the case of forms where they are displayed in the form. They can be referenced programmatically via the `Message` object's `Fields` collection.

If you look at the properties of other objects, such as `Attachments`, `Folders`, `Recipients`, and `Infostores`, you will notice they also contain a `Fields` collection.

These collections contain references to specific fields associated with the object—for example, the `Attachment` object contains fields identifying the original path name and the long filename for the attachment.

While there may be a constant for a particular property, the property may not actually be set for the object.

The `Field` object contains a reference to a specific field in a `Fields` collection.

Each `Field` has a unique numeric ID property that is associated with it; a field can be directly referenced using the ID.

The `Field` object can store different types of data, which are identified by using the `Type` property. Table 12-17 lists the different `Type` data type values.

Table 12-17. Field Data Types

DESCRIPTION	FIELD TYPE DESCRIPTION	DECIMAL VALUE
`VbEmpty`	Not initialized	0
`VbNull`	Null (no valid data)	1
`VbInteger`	2-byte integer	2
`VbLong`	4-byte integer	3
`VbSingle`	4-byte real (floating point)	4
`VbDouble`	8-byte real (floating point)	5
`VbCurrency`	8-byte integer (scaled by 10000)	6
`VbDate`	8-byte real (date in integer, time in fraction)	7
`VbString`	String	8
`VbBoolean`	Boolean	11
`VbDataObject`	Data object	13
`VbBlob`	Binary (unknown format)	65
`VbArray`	Multivalued type	8192

The Value property returns the value stored in the Field object.

You can add your own custom fields to messages. Additional fields can be added to an application, sent, and then processed at the destination. Setting message fields for extraction can be an alternative to storing values as text in the body of the message, which saves having to parse the message.

To add a new field to a message, invoke the Add method on the Fields collection for the Message object you want to add the field to. The following code sample adds two fields, SCBWeeklySales and SCBWeeklyWages, to a message:

```
Const vbSingle = 4
objSession.Logon "Valid Profile"
Set objMessage = objSession.Outbox.Messages.Add 'create a new message

objMessage.Subject = "Weekly Sales"
objMessage.Text = "Weekly Sales Message"
objMessage.Type = "IPM.Note.SCBWeeklySales" 'set the message type
Set objField = objMessage.Fields.Add("SCBWeeklySales", vbSingle,143545.50)
Set objField = objMessage.Fields.Add("SCBWeeklyWages", vbSingle, 2333.50)
```

Processing the message fields requires access to the Fields collection for the message object you are manipulating.

Reference the field using the property ID for the property. If the property is not set for the message, an error will occur, so make sure you have error trapping enabled when attempting to reference any fields.

If you have added your own fields to a message, the field may be referenced by its actual field name:

```
'get all messages that contain sales data and extract custom sales fields
'create a MAPI session,then log on
Set objSession = CreateObject("MAPI.Session")
' supply a valid profile
objSession.Logon "Valid Profile"
'get a reference to the InBox messages
Set objMsgColl = objSession.InBox.Messages
'get a reference to the filter for the InBox messages
Set objFilter = objMsgColl.Filter
'set the filter properties to filter all messages that are unread, of type
'IPM.Note.SCBWeeklySales
objFilter.Type = " IPM.Note.SCBWeeklySales"
objFilter.Unread = True '  filter only messages that haven't been read
objFilter.Subject = "Weekly Sales"
```

```
'loop through the Messages collection and display the SCBWeeklySales
'and SCBWeeklyWages for any 'messages that meet the filter criteria
Set objMessage = objMsgColl.GetFirst()

Do While Not objMessage Is Nothing
'display the subject for the current message
 WScript.Echo objMessage.Fields("SCBWeeklySales")
 WScript.Echo objMessage.Fields("SCBWeeklyWages")
 'get the next message
 Set objMessage = objMsgColl.GetNext()
Loop
objSession.Logoff
```

See Also

For more information, search http://msdn.microsoft.com for the article "Fields Property (Message Object)."

12.25 Retrieving an Address Book Recipient

Problem

You want to get a reference to an AddressEntry by specifying the recipient name.

Solution

The following Solution returns a reference to the specified AddressEntry object if found; otherwise, it returns Nothing:

```
'Procedure GetAddressObj
'Description
'Returns a reference to an AddressEntry object for the specified
'recipient display name
'Parameters  objSession reference to MAPI session object
'             sAddressList Address list to search. E.g. Recipients
'             sAddress display name of recipient you are searching for
'Returns     reference to AddressEntry object if recipient is found.
 If recipient not found, returns Nothing
Function GetAddressObj(objSession, sAddressList, sAddress)
Dim objAddressList, objAddressEntry
```

```
On Error Resume Next
'get a reference to the specified address list
Set objAddressList = objSession.AddressLists(sAddressList)
'if error, then unable to get specified address list
If Err Then
    Set GetAddressObj = Nothing
    Exit Function
End If
Set GetAddressObj = Nothing
'loop through all addresses and search for name
For Each objAddressEntry In objAddressList.AddressEntries
  If UCase(sAddress) = Ucase(objAddressEntry.Name) Then
    Set GetAddressObj = objAddressEntry
    Exit For
  End If
Next
End Function
```

Pass a valid MAPI `Session` object, address list, and recipient display name:

```
Set objAddressEntry = GetAddressObj(objSession, "Recipients", "Fred Smith")
```

Discussion

The MAPI application provides the maintenance of the address book(s), and new recipients and related data can be entered through the application.

Depending on your configuration, there may be one or many address book entries. If you are using the Exchange/Windows Message client and you're not connected to an Exchange server, you probably only have one copy of addresses in a Personal Address Book (PAB). A PAB is a file that stores recipient details.

If you are using Outlook as your client, you also have a Contacts folder. The Outlook Contacts folder is a general contact-management application that provides storage of recipient details and a number of other pieces of information.

If you are using Exchange server, you have access to the Global Address List (GAL), which is a list of all recipients on the server and individual recipient "containers." Containers are created on the Exchange server and are used to logically segment groups of recipients. The GAL contains a list of all recipients from all containers.

To CDO, however, it is transparent as to what version or application you are using—you can access all of the address lists. Address lists may vary in the information they provide—for example, Outlook Contacts provides detailed contact information, such address, phone number, and personal information, while Personal Address Books store a more limited set of data.

Application address lists are exposed through the `Session` object's `AddressLists` collection object and provides access to all address books available for the current session.

```
Set objAddressLists = objSession.AdressLists
```

References to `AddressList` objects can be retrieved from the `AddressLists` collection by specifying the `AddressList` name or element index you want to reference:

```
'get a reference to the Recipients address list
Set objAddressList = objSession.AddressLists("Recipients")

'get a reference to the first address list.
Set objAddressList = objSession.AddressLists(1)
```

Address list names are case-sensitive. As a result, `objSession.AddressLists("RECIPIENTS")` would not return a reference to the `Recipients AddressList` object.

The following code snippet lists the names of available `AddressList` objects in the current session:

```
'get a reference to the Session's AddressLists collection
Set objAddressLists = objSession.AddressLists
'go through each AddressList and display the name for each of the
'individual
' AddressList objects also identify if the AddressList can be modified.
For Each objAddressList In objAddressLists
    WScript.Echo objAddressList.Name & " " & objAddressList.IsReadOnly
Next

'get a reference to the Personal Address Book Address List object
Set objAddressList = objAddressLists.Item("Personal Address Book")
```

You cannot create new `AddressList` objects from CDO/Active Messaging code. They must be created from your e-mail application, such as Outlook or Exchange client.

Once you have a reference to the `AddressList` you want to use, you can access the individual address stored in it. The addresses are stored in the `AddressEntries` collection.

The `AddressEntry` object contains the actual recipient data.

The object contains the bare minimum of properties to describe a mail recipient: the e-mail address, type of recipient (distribution list, single recipient), and display name. Other details, such as mailing address, phone numbers, and professional information are stored in the `Fields` collection.

Table 12-18 lists some `AddressEntry` object properties.

Table 12-18. `AddressEntry` *Object Properties*

NAME	TYPE	DESCRIPTION
`Address`	String	The mail system address, such as `fred@company.com`.
`DisplayType`	Long	Type of address. See Table 12-19 for a description of the address types.
`Name`	String	Display name of recipient (e.g., Fred Smith).
`Type`	String	Identifies the messaging type for the address (e.g., SMTP for Internet mail, EX for Exchange server, or FAX for fax number).

Table 12-19 lists address types.

Table 12-19. Address Types

NAME	VALUE	DESCRIPTION
`User`	0	A local messaging user
`DistList`	1	A public distribution list
`Forum`	2	A forum, such as a bulletin board or a public folder
`Agent`	3	An automated agent
`Organization`	4	A special address entry defined for large groups
`PrivateDistList`	5	A private administered distribution list
`RemoteUser`	6	A user in a remote messaging system

The following example displays the AddressEntry Type and Address of a resolved address for a new message:

```
'add a new recipient to the message
Set objRecipient = objMessage.Recipients.Add

'set the display name to resolve from the Address book
objRecipient.Name = "Fred Smith"
objRecipient.Resolve ' resolve the name
'show the AddressEntry type of the resolved address.
WScript.Echo objRecipient.AddressEntry.Type & vbCrLf & objRecipient.Address
```

To get access to a specific AddressEntry object, you must traverse the AddressEntries collection until you find the specified AddressEntry object, or specify the index value for the AddressEntry object you want to access from the AddressEntries collection. You cannot directly get an AddressEntry by specifying the address display name or address.

```
'this will work, returns a reference to the first AddressEntry in
'the AddressEntries collection
Set objAddressEntry = objAddressList.AddressEntries(1)
'this WILL NOT work, you cannot reference an AddressEntry object
'using the display name
Set objAddressEntry = objAddressList.AddressEntries("Fred Smith")
```

The functionality to reference address book information has been available since CDO/Active Messaging 1.0.

See Also

For more information, search http://msdn.microsoft.com for the article "Selecting Recipients from the Address Book."

12.26 Creating Recipient Entries

Problem

You want to add a new recipient to your address book.

Solution

You can reference the `AddressEntries` collection for the address list to which you want to add a new recipient and then call the `Add` method:

```
' create a session then log on
Set objSession = CreateObject("MAPI.Session")
' change the parameters to valid values for your configuration
objSession.Logon "Valid Profile"

'get a reference to the Recipient
Set objList = objSession.AddressLists("Personal Address Book")
Set objAddressEntries = objList.AddressEntries

'add an Internet mail address
   Set objAddressEntry = objAddressEntries.Add("SMTP", "Fred Smith", "freds@x.com")
objAddressEntry.Update
```

Discussion

You cannot add new `AddressEntries` to certain `AddressLists` objects. Server-based `AddressLists`, such as the Global Address List (GAL) and recipient containers stored on Exchange servers, cannot have new addresses added to them via CDO.

Local `AddressLists`, such as Personal Address Books (PAB) and Outlook Contacts folders, can have new `AddressEntries` added to them.

To add a new `AddressEntry`, invoke the `Add` method for the `AddressEntries` collection of the `AddressList` you want to add the entry to. The syntax is as follows:

```
Set objAddressEntry = objAddrEntriesColl.Add(EmailType [, Name] ,Address] )
```

The parameters are listed in Table 12-20. They are all string values.

Table 12-20. `AddressEntry Add` *Method Parameters*

NAME	DESCRIPTION
`EmailType`	The address type. This may be SMTP for an Internet type address, FAX for a fax number, or EX for an Exchange address.
`Name`	Optional. Display name for the e-mail address.
`Address`	The actual e-mail address (e.g., `freds@x.com`).

The Add method returns the new AddressEntry object upon the successful addition of a new address. You must call the AddressEntry object's Update method to save the settings to the address book.

See Also

For more information, search http://msdn.microsoft.com for the article "Creating a New Address Book Entry."

12.27 Adding a Distribution List

Problem

You want to add a new distribution list.

Solution

You can reference the AddressEntries collection for the address list for which you want to create a distribution list and then add an AddressEntry entry of type MAPIPDL. Add members to the Members property of the newly created AddressEntry object. The following example creates a new distribution list called New List and adds three recipients to it:

```
Set objAddresslist = objSession.AddressLists("Personal Address Book")
Set objAddressEntries = objAddresslist.AddressEntries
'add a new address entry called New List. Make it a distribution list
Set objAddressDLEntry = objAddressEntries.Add("MAPIPDL", "New List", _
"dist@x.com")
objAddressDLEntry.Update 'update AddressEntry so changes are saved

'add user Fred Smith to distribution list
Set objAddressEntry = objAddressDLEntry.Members.Add("SMTP", "Fred Smith", _
"freds@x.com")
objAddressEntry.Update 'update AddressEntry so changes are saved

'add user Joe Blow to distribution list
Set objAddressEntry = objAddressDLEntry.Members.Add("SMTP", "Joe Blow", _
"joeb@x.com")
objAddressEntry.Update 'update AddressEntry so changes are saved
```

```
'add user Sally Jones to distribution list
Set objAddressEntry = objAddressDLEntry.Members.Add("SMTP", "Sally Jones", _
"sallyj@x.com")
objAddressEntry.Update 'update AddressEntry so changes are saved
```

Discussion

A *distribution list* is a collection of multiple recipients represented as a single address entry.

Distribution lists appear as normal AddressEntry objects. They contain the same properties as a single recipient, such as Name and Address.

The multiple recipients are represented by the Members property. The Members property is an AddressEntries collection that contains AddressEntry objects for all recipients listed in the distribution list.

The following example gets a reference to the distribution list Project Group from the Personal Address Book and lists all of the recipients:

```
Set objAddressDistEntry = GetAddressObj(objSession, _
                              "Personal Address Book", "Project Group")

For Each objAdress In objAddressDistEntry.AddressEntries
    WScript.Echo objAddress.Name
Next
```

To create a new distribution list, add a new AddressEntry and set the type to MAPIPDL (MAPI Personal Distribution List). You can *only* create a distribution list in your local address books (e.g., PAB files). You cannot create or modify distribution lists on Exchange servers. See Chapter 16 for information on manipulating Exchange server distribution lists.

See Also

For more information, search http://msdn.microsoft.com for the article "Add Method (AddressEntries Collection)."

CHAPTER 13

Data Access

WINDOWS SCRIPT HOST (WSH) doesn't provide any built-in database access. It relies on parts of a database strategy that Microsoft refers to as Universal Data Access (UDA). This strategy consists of three elements: Open Database Connectivity (ODBC), Object Linking and Embedding Database (OLE DB), and ActiveX Data Objects (ADO).

ODBC

Open Database Connectivity (ODBC) provides database access to any database source that has a driver available for it. It has been available since versions of Windows 3.*x*.

ODBC is considered to be a "standard," and there are hundreds of drivers available that allow access to data sources from ASCII text files to high-end database servers that run on mini and mainframe computers. However, there is no way to use ODBC drivers directly in WSH.

OLE DB

Microsoft has changed the way data is accessed via the new Object Linking and Embedding Database (OLE DB). OLE DB will provide access to data sources in a similar way to ODBC: A client will connect to a data source via a driver.

OLE DB goes beyond the capabilities of what is possible with ODBC. OLE DB provides access to traditional database sources, such as SQL Server, Oracle, Access, and FoxPro, as well as nondatabase-type applications. These nondatabase data sources include any application or environment that can represent data in a tabular format. This could include graphical applications, spreadsheet data, and traditional relational databases.

It's with regard to nondatabase-type data access where OLE DB provides more capabilities than ODBC. Examples of nonrelational data providers that exist today are the IIS Index Server, Internet Provider, and ADSI interfaces.

Another way that OLE DB differs from ODBC is that OLE DB is implemented as a COM interface. Any environment that can interface with COM objects can use OLE DB.

The following terminology is used to describe the various components of the OLE DB architecture:

- *Data consumer:* A data consumer is a client environment that "consumes" or uses the data. This can be any application that is able to create COM objects, such as VB, C++, Delphi, Office applications or, in our case, WSH.
- *Data provider:* An OLE data provider is a provider that exposes its data in a tabular form by using its native data format. A data provider such as ADSI exposes an OLE DB interface to a data consumer. Examples of data providers include relational DBMSs, spreadsheets, and e-mail systems.
- *Service provider:* A service provider is both a data consumer and a data provider. A service provider doesn't own its data, but rather it encapsulates some service by producing and consuming data through OLE DB interfaces. For example, a query processor might serve to join two tables in two different data sources. The query processor retrieves data from the base tables and then returns the resultant join of the tables to the data consumer.

SQL Server 2000 is an example of a service provider. It provides transparent linking of diverse data sources using its linked server capability.

OLE DB will not replace ODBC anytime in the near future, mainly due to the huge existing base of ODBC drivers and the fact that ODBC still works.

There is an OLE DB provider that provides access to ODBC drivers, so existing investments in ODBC drivers and applications are not lost.

Using ADO

You don't natively access OLE DB through WSH. A COM interface, ActiveX Data Objects (ADO), provides access and interfaces to data providers. OLE DB is the framework for Universal Data Access in Microsoft environments. How do you get at that data? ADO is the interface that provides access to the data. As the name implies, ADO is implemented as a COM object.

History of ADO

ADO has been in use since late 1996 in Microsoft's Internet Information Server (IIS) 3.0 and later versions. IIS uses ADO 1.0 in Active Server Pages (ASP) to provide data manipulation capabilities to Web pages. With ADO and IIS 3.0, ASP Web pages could query, update, delete, and manipulate data from any ODBC data source.

ADO 1.5 is available in Internet Explorer 4.0 and IIS 4.0, and it is also available as a stand-alone download known as Microsoft Data Access Components.

Table 13-1 lists the various ADO versions and the differences among them.

Table 13-1. ADO Versions

VERSION	HOW TO INSTALL	FEATURES
1.0	IIS 3.0/Active Server Pages	General data access features: query, update, delete
1.5	IIS 4.0, Internet Explorer 4.0, Windows 98	
2.0	Downloadable installation, Visual Studio 6.0	Hierarchical Recordsets—data shaping
2.1	Downloadable installation, Microsoft Explorer 5.0/Office 2000	ADO Extensions (ADOX)
2.5	Windows 2000	Provides access to data streams
2.6	Included with SQL Server 2000	
2.7	Windows XP	
2.8	Windows 2003	

If clients on your network are using Internet Explorer and/or Windows 98, they have ADO installed. Windows 2000 and later have ADO installed. You can get the latest ADO version from the Microsoft Data Access Components (MDAC) download at `http://msdn.microsoft.com/data`.

Unless otherwise specified, this chapter concentrates on core database access capabilities that are available in all versions of ADO.

NOTE *Extensive documentation is included with the ADO 2.x installation. It's located in* `\Program Files\Common Files\System\ADO`. *This Help file includes a general ADO reference as well as a number of examples. You can find other ADO-related information on Microsoft's Universal Data Access (UDA) site (*`http://www.microsoft.com/data`*). This site contains the latest information on ADO, OLE DB, and ODBC, as well as articles and reference information.*

Identifying Your Data

Before you can start working with some data, you need to know how to identify to ADO what data source you want to work with. This is accomplished with a *connection string*. The connection string identifies the data source and can supply optional parameters such as a user ID and a password. These optional parameters depend upon the data source—for example, some data sources may not support a user ID and password.

There are two types of (similar) connection strings: a data source name (DSN) connection and a DSN-less connection.

13.1 Data Source Name Connection Strings

ADO can access ODBC data sources through an ODBC OLE DB interface. This means that any database that can be accessed through an ODBC driver can be accessed through ADO, so you don't lose any investment in existing ODBC driver software and configurations.

The disadvantage of using a data source name (DSN) to specify a data source is that the DSN must exist either on the local machine or alternatively reference a file DSN. A file DSN consists of a file containing data source connection information and provides a more centralized way of managing connections because you do not require configuration of the DSN on each machine (see Solution 13.3).

A DSN connection specifies an existing defined ODBC data source. The data source can be defined using the Control Panel's ODBC Data Source Administrator (under Windows NT 4.0/ME/9*x*) or Data Sources (Windows 2000/XP) applet, which allows the creation of data sources via a user interface.

To create an ODBC data source, follow these steps:

1. Select Start menu > Control Panel.

2. For Windows NT/9*x*/ME, double-click the ODBC Data Sources icon. For Windows 2000 and later, double-click Data Sources (ODBC) under the Control Panel's Administrative Tools entry.

   A dialog box similar to the one shown in Figure 13-1 appears.

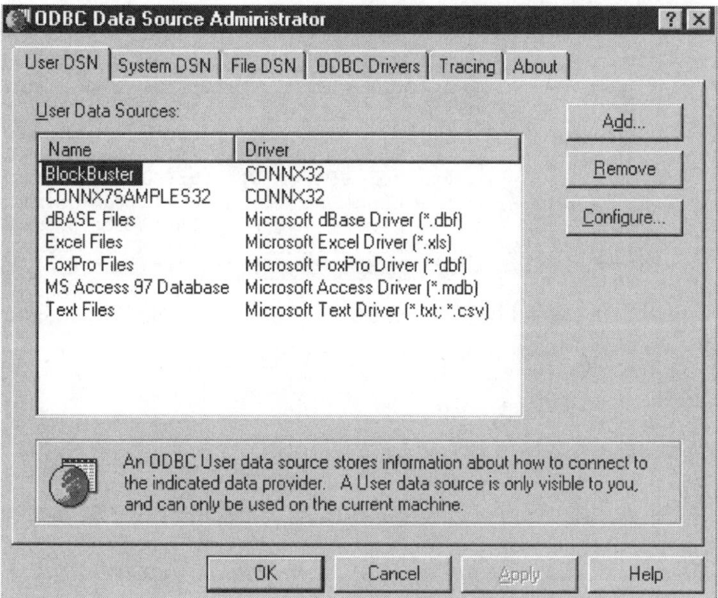

Figure 13-1. ODBC Data Source Administrator dialog box

The ODBC Drivers tab lists the available driver and version information. Looking at this tab is a good way of determining what ODBC drivers are installed on your system.

3. Select either the User DSN or System DSN tab. The System DSN tab only applies to Windows NT and later. Under Windows NT and later, a System DSN is available to all logons, including services, while a User DSN is available to the user currently logged on.

4. Click the Add button.

   You are now presented with a list of drivers, as shown in Figure 13-2. If a particular driver does not appear in the list, it's not installed on your system.

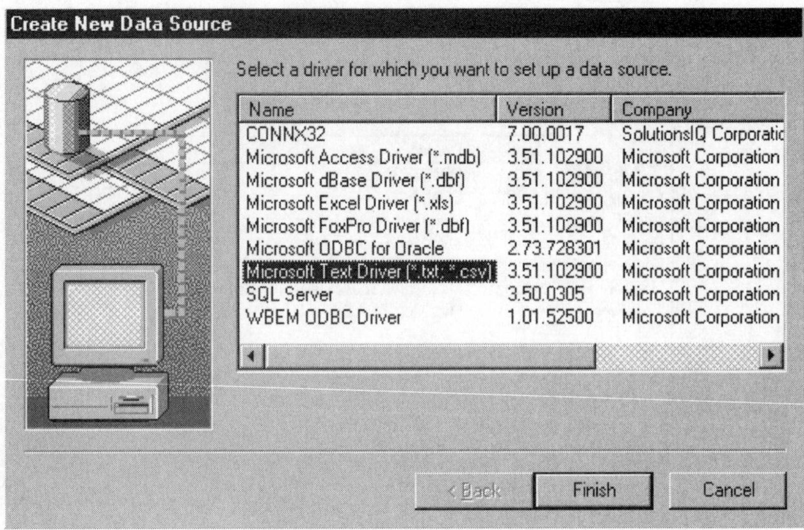

Figure 13-2. The Create New Data Source dialog box lists drivers.

5. Select the driver you want to use and click the Finish button.

A dialog box appears for the driver you specified. Figure 13-3 shows the setup dialog box for a text file.

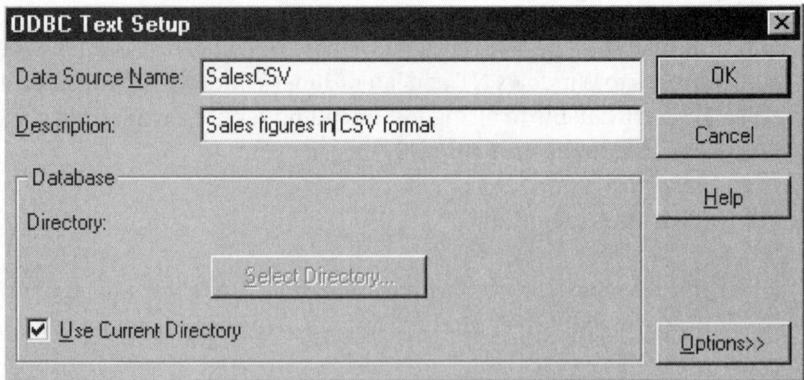

Figure 13-3. ODBC Text Setup dialog box

Settings will vary between drivers, but all drivers use the Data Source Name and Description fields. The Data Source Name field is used to identify the data source and is what is used when connecting to the data source via ADO.

Once you have created a data source, you can connect to it in a script. To perform a connection to a data source you need a `Connection` object.

The `Connection` object represents the physical connection to the data provider. It is required in order to perform data access operations. While all ADO objects can be created independently of each other, they all need one thing in order to function (or at least in order to do anything useful): a connection to data provider.

The connection process can be implemented in a couple of ways. You can first create a `Connection` object that you can reuse among other ADO objects, or you can create an ADO object such as a Recordset, which handles the process of creating a `Connection` object and opening a connection to the data source.

To connect to a data source, supply the connection string for the data source to the `Open` method of a `Connection` object. Its syntax is as follows:

```
connection.Open [ConnectionString][, UserID][, Password]
```

Table 13-2 lists the `Open` method's arguments.

Table 13-2. `Open` *Method Arguments*

PARAMETER	DESCRIPTION
`ConnectionString`	String. Contains connection information. See Table 13-3 for a list of connection string syntax.
`UserID`	Optional string. Specifies the user name to use when establishing the connection.
`Password`	Optional string. Specifies the user password to use when establishing the connection.

The format of the connection string is as follows:

```
strConn = "[Provider=providername;] { DSN=name | FileDSN=filename } ;
          [DATABASE=database;] UID=user; PWD=password"
```

Table 13-3 lists the connection string syntax.

Table 13-3. Connection String Syntax

PARAMETER	DESCRIPTION
`Provider`	Identifies the data provider. The default provider is MSDASQL, which specifies that the data source you are using is an ODBC data source. Therefore, its use is optional when specifying ODBC data sources. See the DSN connection section for its use.
`DSN`	The name of the ODBC definition. This is the name defined in the Control Panel ODBC Data Source Administrator. If you're just specifying the data source name, you do not need to specify the `DSN=` keyword. Therefore, the connection strings `StrConnect = "Northwind"` and `strConnect = "DSN=Northwind"` are the same.
`FileDSN`	Specifies a file that contains the connection information. See Solution 13.2 for more information.
`DATABASE`	Specifies the database to access. For database servers such as SQL Server, you are required to specify the database name you want to work with.
`UID`	User ID.
`PWD`	Password. Due to the low level of WSH security (WSH scripts can be read in normal text editors), it is wise to avoid storing passwords in the actual WSH files. It might be prudent to create low-security access user IDs that provide the minimal required access to the data source in question.

13.2 File DSN Connection

File-based DSNs can ease the distribution and centralize the maintenance of data sources, because they can be maintained in a central location, such as a network file server.

File DSNs can be created from the ODBC Data Source Administrator (under the File DSN tab). The following steps demonstrate the creation of a file DSN used in the Solution:

1. Select Start menu > Control Panel.

2. For Windows NT/9*x*/ME, double-click the ODBC Data Sources icon. For Windows 2000 and later, double-click Data Sources (ODBC) under the Control Panel's Administrative Tools entry.

3. Select the File DSN tab.

   A dialog box appears, as shown in Figure 13-4.

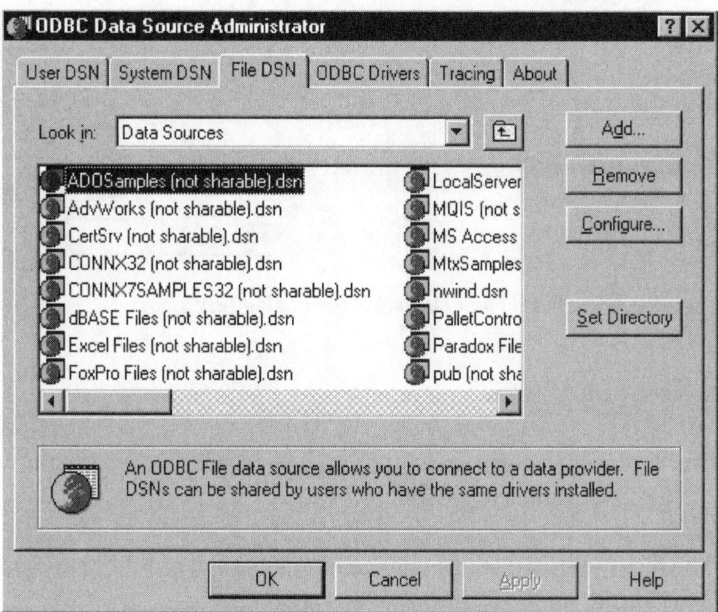

Figure 13-4. File DSN tab

From the File DSN tab you can add new file DSNs and configure the location of the files.

4. Click the Add button.

   You are now presented with a list of drivers. If a particular driver does not appear in the list, it's not installed on your system.

5. Select the driver you want to use and click the Next button.

   A dialog box similar to the one shown in Figure 13-5 appears, prompting you to type a filename. This filename represents the name of the file where the connection settings will be stored. The filename is also used to identify the data source in the connection string.

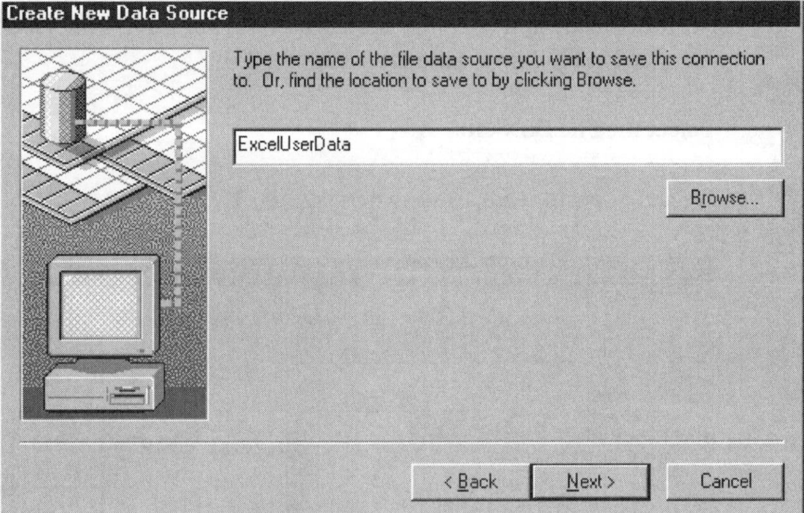

Figure 13-5. Create New Data Source dialog box

6. Click the Next button.

   The dialog box shown in Figure 13-6 appears, listing information about the file DSN you have created.

   The files are stored in a locally defined location, but they can be moved to a central, shared location such as a file server.

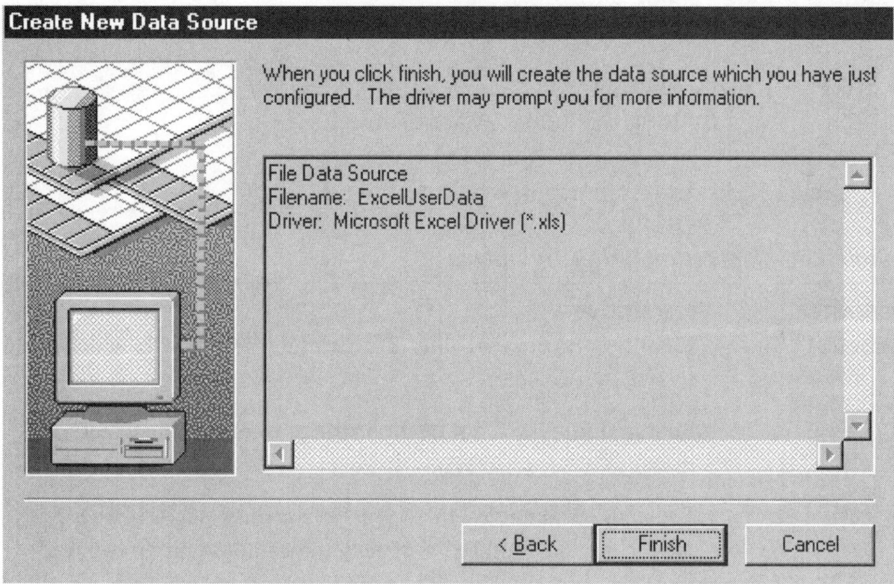

Figure 13-6. File DSN information

13.3 DSN-Less Connection Strings

OLE DB data providers allow access to a wide variety of sources. Some of these OLE DB data providers are shown in Table 13-4. The string in the Provider Name column is supplied as an argument to the `Provider=` parameter of the connection string.

Table 13-4. Data Interfaces

DATA SOURCE	PROVIDER NAME
ODBC	MSDASQL
Access	Microsoft.Jet.OLEDB.3.51 Microsoft.Jet.OLEDB.4.0 (Office 2000/IE 5.0)
Oracle	MSDAORA
MS Index Server	MSIDXS
SQL Server	SQLOLEDB
ADSI	AdsDSOObject
Microsoft IIS Index Server	MSIDXS

DSN-less connections also allow for connections without having a pre-existing ODBC connection or file-based DSN.

The syntax of a DSN-less connection string is as follows:

```
strConn = "[Provider=MSDASQL;] DRIVER=driver; SERVER=server;
          DATABASE=database; UID=user;PWD=password"
```

Table 13-5 lists the connection string arguments.

Table 13-5. Connection String Arguments

PARAMETER	DESCRIPTION
Provider	Identifies the data provider. The default is MSDASQL, which is the ODBC provider.
Driver	Required for ODBC connection strings. Specifies the ODBC driver to use (e.g., DRIVER={Microsoft Access Driver (*.mdb)}).
Database	Specifies the database to access. For database servers like SQL Server, you are required to specify the database name you want to work with.
UID	User ID.
PWD	Password.

Because you can omit the Provider= parameter when building connection strings for the ODBC provider, you can compose a connection string that is identical to an ODBC connection string for the same data source, using the same parameter names (DRIVER=, DATABASE=, DSN=, and so on) as well as the same values and syntax you would when composing an ODBC connection string. You can connect with or without a predefined data source name (DSN) or file DSN.

```
strConn = "driver={SQL Server};server=Odin;" & _
          "database=pubs;uid=pubreado;pwd=pubpass"
```

OLE DB providers can support a great number of parameters to fine-tune the connection to a database provider. The only problem with these parameters is that it can be hard to remember the possible syntax and variations. It can be hard enough to remember the provider name, let alone any additional parameters. What would be helpful is an interface similar to ODBC Data Source configuration option under the Control Panel that provides a visual interface to set connection parameters.

To address this limitation, Microsoft introduced Microsoft Data Link files (files with an extension of .udl) in ADO version 2.0. These files contain OLE DB connection information.

To create a UDL file to connect to an OLE DB data source, follow these steps:

1. Right-click within an Explorer window or from your desktop and select Microsoft Data Link from the New menu.

   This method of creating a UDL was removed from ADO version 2.5 and later. To create a UDL under ADO 2.5 and later, create a text file and change the file extension from `.txt` to `.udl`.

2. Give the new UDL file a descriptive name.

3. Right-click the file and select Properties from the menu. Alternatively, double-click the file.

4. A tabbed dialog box like the one shown in Figure 13-7 appears. You can now set the properties of the UDL file.

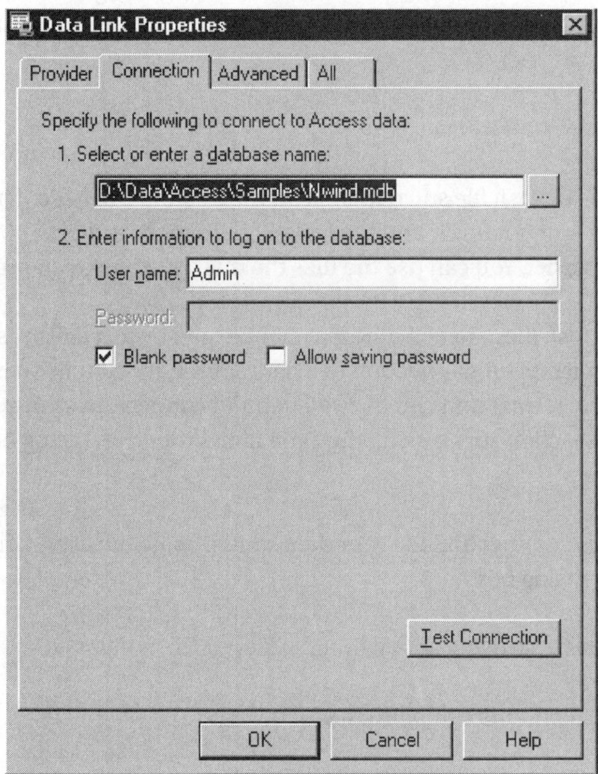

Figure 13-7. The Data Link Properties dialog box

The Provider tab enables you to select the provider type. Looking at this tab is a good way of determining what OLE DB providers are installed on your system. If a particular provider does not appear on the list, it's not installed.

The Connection and Advanced tabs enable you to set provider-specific information. The parameters you can set here vary from provider to provider. For example, Figure 13-7 shows a Connection tab that has been customized for the Microsoft Jet OLE DB provider.

The All tab alphabetically lists all property settings from the Advanced and Connection dialog boxes.

5. Once you are finished configuring your data link, click the OK button.

You can modify the UDL file at any time by double-clicking it from Explorer.

To use a UDL file, reference it in the connection string using the `File Name` parameter. For example, you would reference a `.udl` file named `Northwind.udl` with the following statement:

```
strConn = "File Name=d:\Northwind.udl"
```

Using a `.udl` file or `.dsn` file still depends on the existence of a file. The ODBC Data Source Administrator and the Data Link Properties dialog box makes creating these files easier. You can use the files the interfaces create to build connection strings.

Both `.udl` and `.dsn` files are text files that can be read by text editors such as Notepad. The parameters for connecting to a data source are contained in the files in user-readable format and can be used to build connection strings.

To create a connection string using the Data Link Properties dialog box, follow these steps:

1. Create a `.udl` connection for your data source using the Data Link Properties dialog box.

2. Open the `.udl` file using an ASCII text editor such as Notepad.

   You will see contents similar to the following:

```
[oledb]
; Everything after this line is an OLE DB initstring
Provider=Microsoft.Jet.OLEDB.4.0;Data Source=D:\inventory.mdb;
Persist Security Info=False
```

The connection strings will vary depending on the provider you specified in the `.udl` file.

3. Copy the string from the second line onward. You can paste this string directly into your script as a connection string.

To create a connection string using the ODBC Data Source Administrator to create a file DSN, do the following:

1. Create a file DSN connection using the ODBC Data Source Administrator.

2. Open the `.dsn` file using an ASCII text editor, such as Notepad.

   The contents of the following DSN file contain connection information for an Excel file:

```
[ODBC]
DRIVER=Microsoft Excel Driver (*.xls)
UID=admin
UserCommitSync=Yes
Threads=3
SafeTransactions=0
ReadOnly=1
PageTimeout=5
MaxScanRows=8
MaxBufferSize=512
ImplicitCommitSync=Yes
FIL=excel 5.0
DriverId=790
DefaultDir=H:\
DBQ=H:\xldata.xls
```

3. Combine all lines after the `[ODBC]` entry in the file into one line. Separate each entry with a semicolon (;).

```
DRIVER=Microsoft Excel Driver (*.xls);UID=admin;UserCommitSync=Yes;Threads=3;
SafeTransactions=0;ReadOnly=1;PageTimeout=5;MaxScanRows=8;MaxBufferSize=512;
ImplicitCommitSync=Yes;FIL=excel 5.0;DriverId=790;DefaultDir=d:\;DBQ=d:\xldata.xls
```

This creates quite a long connection string. You will notice that a large number of parameters are being set. To shorten the connection string, remove all items that you have not explicitly set in the ODBC Data Source Administrator. The following connection string is a shortened version of the previous sample:

```
DRIVER=Microsoft Excel Driver (*.xls);DBQ=d:\xldata.xls
```

The following code snippets provide examples of connection strings.

For example, the following code creates a connection to the Northwind database using the Jet 4.0 provider:

```
'Opens a Access MDB using the Access 4.0 data provider
Set objConn = CreateObject("ADODB.Connection")
objConn.Provider = "Microsoft.Jet.OLEDB.4.0"
```

The following example opens a connection to SQL Server and sets the default database to Pubs:

```
Set objConn = CreateObject("ADODB.Connection")
objConn.ConnectionString = "Provider=SQLOLEDB;User ID=sa;Data Source=Odin"
objConn.Open
objConn.DefaultDatabase = "pubs"
```

The following code fragment opens an Access MDB using ODBC:

```
objConn.ConnectionString = "DBQ=D:\Data\Samples\Northwind.MDB;" & _
"DRIVER={Microsoft Access Driver (*.mdb)};" & _
"UID=admin;PWD=;"
objConn.Open
```

> **NOTE** *For more information, read "How to Use Data Link Files with ADO"* (`http://support.microsoft.com/?kbid=189680`) *and "Connection String Syntax"* (`http://msdn.microsoft.com/library/en-us/oledb/htm/oledbconnectionstringsyntax.asp`).

13.4 Opening a Secure Database

Problem

You want to open a secure database.

Solution

You can use the following script:

```
Dim objConn, objRst
Set objConn = CreateObject("ADODB.Connection")
'open a connection and provide a user id and password
objConn.Open "Provider=SQLOLEDB.1;Initial Catalog=pubs;Data Source=ODIN" _
    , "freds", "sderf"

'execute a query
Set objRst = objConn.Execute("Select Sum(ytd_sales) As TotalSales From titles")
'display the value
Wscript.Echo objRst("TotalSales").Value
objRst.Close
objConn.Close
```

Discussion

Many databases, especially server-based ones such as SQL Server, provide sophisticated security mechanisms to limit access to data. They can require authentication before access to the data is possible.

The problem with scripts is that they are plain text and easily readable. There are a couple of ways to eliminate passwords from being sent. The security mechanisms will vary from provider to provider.

The level of security required should be determined by the sensitivity of the data being accessed.

SQL Server provides different levels of security. SQL Server can provide an internal user database that is maintained using SQL Enterprise Manager, or NT authentication, where access to the database is determined by the user's NT ID. The advantage of using NT authentication is it requires no passwords to be stored in the script file. These security mechanisms are determined by how your SQL Server is configured: You may have a user database, NT security, or both.

For any user's account that requires a password, try to limit the access the user has to the database to the absolute minimum for the operations required.

Microsoft Access also provides database security. Users are stored in a systems database and can be assigned different levels of access to a database. By default, when a user connects to an Access database, he or she is automatically assigned the admin user, who by default has a blank password.

The security database information is stored in a workgroup security (MDW) file. The workgroup file included at installation is called `system.mdw`. This file contains user and group security information. You can change or create new security files using a Microsoft Access Workgroup Administrator file. If you are connecting to an Access database that was secured locally, you do not need to specify what MDW file to use. Figure 13-8 shows a dialog box from the Workgroup Administrator application.

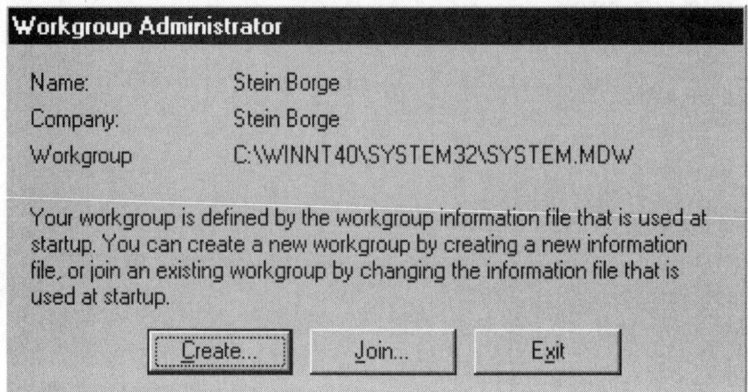

Figure 13-8. Microsoft Access Workgroup Administrator

If you have secured a database and want to provide remote access to it, you must make the .mdw file available to the users and specify it in the connection string. This is identified with the Jet OLEDB:System Database keyword:

```
'open a Access MDB file using a different system.mdw file specifying
'a user name and password
objConn.Open "Provider=Microsoft.Jet.OLEDB.4.0;Data Source=\\odin\data\" & _
      " system.mdw:\data.mdb;Jet OLEDB:System Database=\\odin\data\system.mdw", _
      "freds", "sderf"
```

An alternative is to encrypt the script file. The Microsoft Script Encoder provides a method of securing script files so they cannot be read. The Script Encoder encrypts the file and makes it appear unreadable to a user.

To encrypt a script, download and install the Script Encoder from http://msdn.microsoft.com/scripting/vbscript/download/x86/sce10en.exe. The Script Encoder is a command-line application and no Windows user interface is provided.

The syntax of the Script Encoder is as follows:

```
screnc source destination
```

The `source` parameter is the source file you are encoding, while the `destination` parameter is the name of the encrypted file.

```
Example: screnc swpwd.vbs swpwd.vbe
```

The file extensions for the encrypted files are `.vbe` and `.jse` for VBScript and JScript, respectively. Once the files are encrypted, they are executed in the same way as normal script files—from Explorer or the command prompt using `cscript.exe`. No special command is required to execute them. Another reason to encode scripts is to protect intellectual property—you might not want the contents of your scripts to be read.

You do not need to install the Microsoft Script Encoder on the machine you are running the encrypted file on. You need at least version 5.0 of the JScript or VBScript scripting engine.

If you are distributing scripts that you do not want read for professional reasons, the Script Encoder provides a means of protecting the scripts.

The Script Encoder has no built-in method of reverse encrypting.

> **NOTE** *The Script Encoder provides security against casual access, but it can be cracked by a determined user using publicly available tools.*

See Also

For more information, search `http://msdn.microsoft.com` for the article "Microsoft Jet 4.0 OLE DB Properties Reference."

13.5 Compacting Access Databases

Problem

You want to compact an Access database.

Solution

You can use the Jet Replication Objects (JRO) object that is included with the ADO installation to compact a database. The JRO object exposes a `JetEngine` object with which you can compact a database using the `CompactDatabase` method:

```
'compact.vbs
'compacts a database
Dim objJRO, objFSO,strSource, strTemp
strSource = "D:\test.mdb"
strTemp = "D:\temp.mdb"
Set objFSO = CreateObject("Scripting.FileSystemObject")

'check if temporary file exists from previous operation, if so delete it
If objFSO.FileExists(strTemp) Then objFSO.DeleteFile strTemp

'create Jet Replication Object..
Set objJRO = CreateObject("JRO.JetEngine")
On Error Resume Next
'compact data
objJRO.CompactDatabase "Provider=Microsoft.Jet.OLEDB.4.0;" & _
"Data Source=" & strSource & ";Jet OLEDB:Engine Type=4", _
        "Provider=Microsoft.Jet.OLEDB.4.0;Data Source=" & strTemp &  -
         ";Jet OLEDB:Engine Type=5"

'check if error occurred. . .
If Not Err Then
    'double check the file was compacted
    If objFSO.FileExists(strTemp) Then
        'copy compacted temporary file to original
        objFSO.CopyFile strTemp, strSource, True
        objFSO.DeleteFile strTemp
    End If
Else
End If
```

Discussion

Space used by deleted Access data is not freed up, so an Access database can grow quickly in size. This has the obvious disadvantage of using excess disk space, but it also increases the chances of database corruption.

The JRO object is primarily used for managing Access database replicas, but the `JetEngine` object exposed through this object exposes the useful `CompactDatabase` object. The syntax is as follows:

```
objJRO.CompactDatabase strSource, strDestination
```

The database being compacted is represented by the `strSource` parameter. The compacted file is copied to the `strDestination` table. Compacting a database does not result in the source database file automatically being compacted—the temporary strDestination database must be renamed or copied to the original filename.

Because the routine requires a temporary file, you need at most (worst-case scenario) twice the disk space as the original file. Whenever an Access table is opened, the space that would be freed by a compact procedure is calculated. This information can be retrieved through the Connection object's Jet OLEDB:Compact Reclaimed Space Amount property:

```
Set objConn = CreateObject("ADODB.Connection")
'open an Access database
objConn.Open "Provider=Microsoft.Jet.OLEDB.4.0;Data Source=D:\utl.mdb "

Wscript.Echo "Space that would be freed up after compact:" & _
    objConn.Properties("Jet OLEDB:Compact Reclaimed Space Amount")
```

The value returned is the freed space in bytes. This number is an approximation, but it is usually accurate within a few thousand bytes.

The source and destination files specified through the strSource and strDestination parameters are OLE DB connection strings (see Solution 13.3 for more information).

The minimum requirement for the connection strings is the Data Source property, which specifies the path to the files. If the Provider is not specified, it assumes the MS Jet 4.0 provider.

If your source database implements any security features, such as user IDs and passwords, you must set the additional connection string properties listed in Table 13-6.

Table 13-6. Connection String Security Properties

PROPERTY	DESCRIPTION
User ID	Valid Access user ID
Password	Password for the user ID specified by the User ID property
Jet OLEDB:System Database	Path to Access security file
Jet OLEDB:Database Password	Access database password

The User ID, Password, and Jet OLEDB:System Database properties only apply to the source database. The destination database inherits the security settings of the original. You can set or change the database password for the destination database using the Jet OLEDB:Database Password property.

The following snippet compacts a database, specifies a different system.mdw security file, and uses the admin user ID:

```
objJRO.CompactDatabase "Provider=Microsoft.Jet.OLEDB.4.0;" & _
    "Data Source=d:\test.mdb" & _
   & ";Jet OLEDB:System Database=d:\system.mdw;User " & _
   & "ID=admin;Password=admin", "Provider=Microsoft.Jet.OLEDB.4.0;" & _
    & "Data Source=d:\temp.mdb"
```

When you compact a database, the destination database is converted to the database engine version that is distributed with the ADO release, which for ADO 2.5 is Jet 4.0, which is the underlying database engine for Access 2000.

So if the source database was created by an older Access/Jet engine version, and you want to keep it that way, you need to specify the `Jet OLEDB:Engine Type` property in the destination or source connection string. Table 13-7 lists valid Jet OLEDB:Engine Type values and the associated Jet engine version.

Table 13-7. Jet Engine Version Values

VALUE	DESCRIPTION
1	Jet version 1.0
2	Jet version 1.1
3	Jet version 2.*x*
4	Jet version 3.*x*
5	Jet version 4.*x*

You cannot specify a Jet engine version less than the version of the current source database, so it cannot be used to convert to an older version.

An Access database cannot be compacted when other users have it open. It can be difficult to determine who is currently accessing an Access database. Access creates an LDB file that tracks the current access to the database, but this can be tricky to read.

The Jet OLE DB provider exposes properties that can be read through the `Properties` collection available through a number of ADO objects, such as `Connection` and Recordset. However, some provider-specific information is not accessible through these collections, such as the `JET_SCHEMA_USERROSTER` property, which contains a list of connected users.

This information is accessible through the `Connection` object's `OpenSchema` method. `OpenSchema` is a general method to enumerate information about a database provider and its underlying structure. It allows database information to be enumerated, but it cannot be used to modify the database structure.

`OpenSchema` requires a `QueryType` parameter and can take optional `Criteria` and `SchemaID` parameters. `QueryType` determines what provider information is to be returned, `Criteria` provides constraints for the `QueryType`, and `SchemaID` is a unique GUID identifier for provider properties that are not accessible through the OLE DB provider.

OpenSchema returns a RecordSet object containing provider information related to the query specified. The Jet database engine tracks the current active users, and this information can be returned by querying the Jet database engine–specific property using OpenSchema:

```
'list all connected users to an Access database
Const JET_SCHEMA_USERROSTER = _
                                        "{947bb102-5d43-11d1-bdbf-00c04fb92675}"
Const adSchemaProviderSpecific = -1
Dim objConn,objRst,objField, nValue
Set objRst = CreateObject("ADODB.Recordset")
Set objConn = CreateObject("ADODB.Connection")

objConn.Open "Provider=Microsoft.Jet.OLEDB.4.0;Data Source=D:\data.mdb "
'create a RecordSet using OpenSchema, returning the connected users.
'OpenSchema queries the JET specfic property JET_SCHEMA_USERROSTER,
'which returns a list of connected users
Set objRst = objConn.OpenSchema(adSchemaProviderSpecific, , _
                                   JET_SCHEMA_USERROSTER)

Do While Not objRst.EOF
 Wscript.Echo  objRst("COMPUTER_NAME") & " " & objRst("LOGIN_NAME")
 objRst.MoveNext
Loop
objRst.Close
objConn.Close
```

The preceding routine will always return at least one connected user, which is whoever is running the script, because that opens the database. Querying the JET_SCHEMA_USERROSTER property returns a RecordSet containing all connected users. The RecordSet contains a COMPUTER_NAME field, which identifies the connected computer; LOGIN_NAME, which is the Access user ID; and CONNECTED, which is a Boolean value that if True indicates the user has a lock on the file.

See Also

For more information, read "Compact Microsoft Access Database via ADO" (http://support.microsoft.com/?kbid=230501).

13.6 Querying a Table

Problem

You want to return all records from a table.

Solution

You can create an ADO `Connection` object and open the data source to query. Execute a query against the open connection and iterate through the returned results:

```
<?xml version="1.0" ?>
<job>
<reference object="ADODB.Recordset"/>  <!--comment
Script:enumtbl.wsf
enumerate all records from a table
-->
 <script language="VBScript">
   Option Explicit
   Dim objRst, objConn
   'create a ADO connection and open a Access database
   Set objConn = CreateObject("ADODB.Connection")
   objConn.Open "Provider=Microsoft.Jet.OLEDB.4.0;" & _
               "Data Source=D:\northwind.mdb"

  'check if script is run using Wscript or Cscript
   If Not StrComp(Right(Wscript.Fullname,11),"cscript.exe",vbTextCompare)=0 Then
       Wscript.Echo "This script is best run using Cscript.exe"
    Wscript.Quit
   End If

   'execute the query against the provider
   Set objRst = objConn.Execute("Select * From Customers",, adCmdText)
   'loop through each record in the recordset and ouput the Companyname
   While Not objRst.Eof
    Wscript.Echo objRst.Fields("CompanyName")
    objRst.MoveNext
   Wend

  objRst.Close
  objConn.Close
```

```
    </script>
</job>
```

Discussion

The Connection object provides the Execute method for executing requests against the data provider In the case of relational database providers, this is in the form of SQL statements. While the Execute method is mostly used for updating, deleting, and adding data (as you will see later on), it can also be used to return data from a provider. Its syntax is as follows:

```
Set objRecordset = connection.Execute (CommandText, [RecordsAffected], [Options])
```

The Execute method's arguments are listed in Table 13-8.

Table 13-8. Execute *Method Arguments*

PARAMETER	TYPE	DESCRIPTION
CommandText	String	Contains the provider-specific command to execute. This may be in the form of a SQL statement, a table, a stored procedure, or special command text.

RecordsAffected	Long	Optional. Returns the number of records affected.
		
		For example: `'return the number of items deleted from customers.`
		
		`Set rst = objconn.Execute ("Delete * from Customers", _ NumDel)`
		
		`Wscript.Echo NumDel & " items were deleted"`
		
		You may find that certain providers do not provide an accurate count of records processed.

Options	Long	Optional. Identifies what type of command the CommandText parameter contains. Table 13-9 lists the possible values. Providing this parameter speeds up the initial processing, because the provider does not have to determine what CommandText represents.

The recordset created using the Execute method is limited in the operations that can be performed on it. It is a read-only, forward-scrolling cursor. With this type of recordset, you can only start at the beginning of the data and move forward. You cannot move backward to previous records. The advantage of this type of recordset is that it's the "cheapest" in terms of resources and provides the best performance. Table 13-9 lists the possible values.

Table 13-9. Values of the Execute *Method's* Option *Parameter*

CONSTANT	VALUE	DESCRIPTION
adCmdText	1	Identifies the command text as a raw command string, such as a SQL statement.
adCmdTable	2	Identifies the command text as referencing a table in the provider.
adCmdStoredProc	4	Identifies the command text as referencing a stored procedure in the provider.
adCmdUnknown	8	Default. Identifies the command text as unknown. The provider attempts to identify what the source string is.
adCmdFile	256	Opens data from a persistent file-based recordset.

The most common way of processing a recordset is looping through and processing each record encountered until the end of the recordset is reached. Navigation of a recordset is provided by a number of Move methods, which are shown in Table 13-10. Not all Recordset types support all navigation methods. For example, the read-only, forward-scrolling cursor created by the Connection object's Execute method does not allow for the MovePrevious method. The general syntax of the Move methods is as follows:

```
recordset.MoveFirst | MoveLast | MoveNext | MovePrevious
```

Table 13-10. Recordset Move *Methods*

METHOD	DESCRIPTION
MoveFirst	Attempts to move to the first record in the Recordset
MoveLast	Attempts to move to the last record in the Recordset
MoveNext	Attempts to move to the next record in the Recordset
MovePrevious	Attempts to move to the previous record in the Recordset

To determine the current position in a recordset, you can use the BOF (beginning of file) and EOF (end of file) properties. These properties return True if the current position in the recordset is at the beginning or the end, respectively. If the Recordset is empty (i.e., it contains no records), both BOF and EOF properties are set to True.

The end of file occurs when the current record is the last record and the MoveNext method is invoked, or there are no records in the recordset. (The end of file is not the last record in the Recordset.) If you invoke the MoveNext method when at the end of the file, an error will occur.

The beginning of file is similar to the end of file: It is reached when the current record is the first record and the MovePrevious method is invoked. The beginning of the file is not the first record in the recordset. If you invoke the MovePrevious method when at the beginning of file, an error will occur.

Recordset objects contain a Fields collection that contains references to each field in the recordset. You can reference field values by either specifying the field name or number. For example:

```
Wscript.Echo objRecordSet.Fields("Field Name").Value 'any field name
'reference the field by index - faster but not very
'practical to use.
Wscript.Echo objRecordSet.Fields(1).Value
```

The Fields collection is the default member property of the recordset, so you can omit a specific reference to the Fields collection when referencing a field. The following code snippet is equivalent to the previous statements:

```
Wscript.Echo objRecordSet("Field Name")
Wscript.Echo objRecordSet(1)
```

The Solution script uses the Northwind.mdb sample database that's included with Access. It's implemented using a WSF file to take advantage of the WSF file to reference object type libraries—in this case, ADODB.Recordset. This saves the redeclaration of constants used by the ADO functions.

See Also

For more information, search http://msdn.microsoft.com for the articles "ADO Using the Connection Object" and "MoveFirst, MoveLast, MoveNext, and MovePrevious Methods."

13.7 Opening a Table for Writing

Problem

You want to open a table for reading and writing.

Solution

The following script creates a Recordset from the Northwind sample database that can be read and written:

```
Dim objRst
Const adOpenDynamic = 2
Const adLockPessimistic = 2
Const adCmdText = 1
Set objRst = CreateObject("ADODB.Recordset")
'get all products
objRst.Open "Select UnitPrice From Products", _
"Provider=Microsoft.Jet.OLEDB.4.0; Data Source=d:\data\nwind\northwind.mdb", _
  adOpenDynamic, adLockPessimistic, adCmdText
'loop through and update all product prices by 2%
Do While Not objRst.EOF
    objRst("UnitPrice") = objRst("UnitPrice") * 1.02
    objRst.MoveNext
Loop
objRst.Close
```

Discussion

The Connection object's Execute method provides a quick way of creating a recordset. But the recordset it creates is limited in scope, because it only allows forward movement and doesn't allow additions, updates, or deletions. The Recordset object's Open method provides the ability to create recordsets with more functionality. Its syntax is as follows:

```
recordset.Open [Source], [ActiveConnection], [CursorType], [LockType], [Options]
```

Table 13-11 lists the optional parameters available for the Open method. Each of these parameters, except for Options, can be set as an individual property of a Recordset object before invoking the Open method, as illustrated in the Solution.

Table 13-11. `Open` *Method Optional Parameters*

NAME	TYPE	DESCRIPTION
`Source`	Variant	Provider-specific text, such as a SQL statement, a table name, a stored procedure name, special command text, or a `Command` object.
`ActiveConnection`	Variant	Either a valid `Connection` object or a connection string.
`CursorType`	Integer	Optional. The cursor type. See Table 13-12 for a list of available cursor types. The default is forward-only.
`LockType`	Integer	Optional. The lock type. See Table 13-14 for list of available lock types. The default is read-only.
`Options`	Integer	Optional. Identifies the `Source` type. Table 13-9 lists the different options. Specifying the `Source` type helps speed the opening of the recordset, because the provider doesn't have to figure out what the `Source` text represents.

Recordsets support four different cursor types: forward-only, keyset, static, and dynamic. Table 13-12 describes different cursors and their capabilities.

Table 13-12. Different ADO Recordset Cursors

TYPE	VALUE	DESCRIPTION
`adOpenForwardOnly`	0	Allows only forward movement through records (the `MoveNext` method). Does not allow the `MoveFirst`, `MovePrevious`, or `MoveLast` methods, and doesn't provide a record count. Any additions, deletions, or updates made by other users to the data are not reflected in the recordset.
`adOpenKeyset`	1	Allows all navigation methods (all `Move` methods and bookmarks). Deletions and additions made by other users are not reflected in the cursor, so if another user adds a new record it will not be visible in the recordset. Changes made by other users to records in the recordset are visible.
`adOpenDynamic`	2	Allows you to view additions, changes, and deletions by other users, and allows all types of movement through the recordset. Does not support a record count.

Table 13-12. Different ADO Recordset Cursors (continued)

TYPE	VALUE	DESCRIPTION
`adOpenStatic`	3	Makes a local copy of requested data. Allows all navigation methods (all `Move` methods and bookmarks). Deletions and additions made by other users are not reflected in the cursor, so if another user adds a new record, it will not be visible in the recordset.

Recordset cursor types and their pros and cons are listed in Table 13-13.

Table 13-13. Recordset Cursor Pros and Cons

CURSOR	PROS	CONS
Forward	Least expensive in terms of memory and performance.	Limited navigation abilities: can only perform `MoveNext` operations.
Keyset	Provides full navigational functionality: all `Move` methods. More economical than a dynamic cursor.	Additions and deletions made by other users are not automatically reflected in the recordset. This is most important for deleted records, because an error will occur if a record deleted by another user is referenced.
Dynamic	All navigation	Most expensive in terms of memory and performance. Any changes made by other users are reflected in the recordset.
Static	Good performance on small sets of data that are continuously traversed, because a temporary local copy is made that does not require additional fetches from the data source.	Lower performance on larger sets of data.

If you want to add or modify data, you need to specify what type of *record locking* is to be used when modifying the data. Record locking is required to prevent problems when more than one user is working with the same data. For example, you may want to prevent any user editing the same data that you are working on to prevent any conflicts. You might have just modified a record and then updated it, only to have another user who was editing it simultaneously wipe out your modifications.

Table 13-14 lists the recordset lock types available with the Recordset object's Open method. If you want to guarantee that nobody else modifies the record while you are working on it, use *pessimistic* locking. Otherwise, use *optimistic* locking. And if you don't want to do any modifications at all, make it read-only.

Table 13-14. Recordset Lock Types

CONSTANT	VALUE	DESCRIPTION
adLockReadOnly	1	Read-only is the default value. You cannot delete or modify data.
adLockPessimistic	2	Pessimistic locking locks the record for the duration of the edit, until the Update method is called or the current record is moved. No other users can make changes to the record while it is locked.
adLockOptimistic	3	Optimistic locking only locks a record for the time required to perform the updates on a record.
adLockBatchOptimistic	4	Optimistic batch updates. Required for batch update mode, as opposed to immediate update mode.

Recordsets can be created independently of a Connection object by passing the connection string as a parameter to the Open method, as in the following code fragment:

```
Const adOpenDynamic =2
Const adLockPessimistic = 2
Const adCmdText = 1
Set objRst = CreateObject("ADODB.Recordset")

'create a recordset from a SQL statement against the Northwind database.
objRst.Open "Select * From Customers", _
"Provider=Microsoft.Jet.OLEDB.4.0; Data Source=C:\data\northwind.mdb", _
  adOpenDynamic, adLockPessimistic, adCmdText
```

It is also possible to open a recordset by using an already established connection, as the following code fragment illustrates:

```
Const adOpenDynamic =2
Const adLockPessimistic = 2
Const adCmdTable = 2
objConn.Open "Provider=SQLOLEDB;User ID=sa;Data Source=Odin"
objConn.DefaultDatabase = "pubs"
objRst.Open "publishers", objConn, adOpenDynamic, adLockPessimistic, _
            adCmdTable
```

See Also

For more information, search http://msdn.microsoft.com for the article "ADO Using the Connection Object."

13.8 Manipulating a Text File

Problem

You want to open a text file and perform calculations on the values.

Solution

The following example opens a comma-delimited text file with the following format and totals the SalesTotal column:

```
Products,SalesTotal
"Dairy",4543.45
"Meat",2344.34
"Produce",1347.54
```

The ODBC Text file driver is used to access ASCII delimited text file tables:

```
Dim objConn, objRst, nTotal
Set objConn = CreateObject("ADODB.Connection")
'open a connection to a text file using a DSN
objConn.Open "SalesCSV"
'select all data from the text file Orders data.txt
Set objRst = objConn.Execute("Select * From [Orders data.txt]")

'loop through and total the contents
```

```
While Not objRst.EOF
    nTotal = nTotal + objRst("SalesTotal").Value
    objRst.MoveNext
Wend

Wscript.Echo "Total sales is:" & nTotal
'close the connection and recordset object
objRst.Close
objConn.Close
```

Discussion

You can find the Microsoft Text driver used in this Solution in the Microsoft ODBC installation. The driver provides read-only access to text files; you cannot modify the data in the data source. To configure the driver, specify in the data source definition what directory the text files will reside in. You can open as many text files from this directory as required.

The Text driver by default assumes that the data file is in comma-delimited format and that the first row contains the field names. If you need to import different text file formats, such as tab-delimited text, or you need more exact descriptions of the data types in the file, you require a `schema.ini` file. A `schema.ini` file is a text file that describes the layout of a delimited text file. A single `schema.ini` file can contain layout details on as many files as you want. The `schema.ini` file resides in the same directory as the data files. An entry is made in the schema file for each text file you need to describe. For example, the following `schema.ini` file contains the layout of two text files: `datatab.txt` is tab delimited and `datafixed.txt` is a fixed-length text file.

```
[DATATAB.TXT]
ColNameHeader = False
Format = TabDelimited
CharacterSet = ANSI
Col1=ProductName char width 40
Col2=UnitPrice currency
Col3=SupplierId long
Col4=QuantityPerUnit char width 20
Col5=Discontinued bit

[DATAFIXED.TXT]
ColNameHeader = False
Format = FixedLength
CharacterSet = ANSI
```

```
Col1=ProductName char width 40
Col2=UnitPrice currency width 10
Col3=SupplierId long width 10
Col4=QuantityPerUnit char width 20
```

For each entry, you specify the file type (TabDelimited, CSVDelimited, Delimited(*), or FixedLength) and define each column. For each column, you define the data type and optionally its width. The width is required for FixedLength text files where the driver needs to know the position of the data.

See Also

For more information, read "Use RDO and ODBC Text Driver to Open a Delimited Text" (http://support.microsoft.com/?kbid=187670).

13.9 Accessing Excel Data

Problem

You want to connect to an Excel data file.

Solution

The following Solution is executed at logon. It connects to an Excel spreadsheet using an ODBC Excel driver and checks if the user has logged on for the current day. If not, it updates the spreadsheet with the current logon time. This spreadsheet can be used to determine the initial logon time of the user.

```
Dim objConn, objRst, objNetwork, strDay
'get the current name of day e.g. Monday
strDay = WeekDayName(Weekday(Date))
Set objNetwork = CreateObject("WScript.Network")
Set objConn = CreateObject("ADODB.Connection")

'open a connection using the ExcelUserData file DSN
objConn.Open "FileDSN=\\Thor\FileDSN$\ExcelUserData.dsn"
```

```
'get the record for todays date for the current user
    Set objRst = objConn.Execute("Select " & strDay & _
       " From UserList Where UserID='" & objNetwork.UserName & "'")
    'check if the time column for the current day. If it is empty, then
    'update the time.
    If IsNull(objRst(strDay).Value) Then
        objConn.Execute "UPDATE UserList Set " & strDay & "='" & Time & _
           "' Where UserID='" & objNetwork.UserName & "'"
    End If
objRst.Close
objConn.Close
```

Discussion

The Excel data ODBC driver provides access to Microsoft Excel spreadsheets. The data is defined within the spreadsheets as named ranges, so you can have as many data areas as required defined in named ranges.

To create a spreadsheet named range for use as a data source, follow these steps:

1. In an Excel spreadsheet, create the table structure you want to use. The top row in the structure should contain the field names you want to use. Figure 13-9 shows the spreadsheet layout used by the Solution script.

UserID	Monday	Tuesday	Wednesday	Thursday	Friday	Saturday	Sunday
Administrator					9:23:15 AM		
FredS							

Figure 13-9. Excel data source

2. Select the range.

3. Choose Insert > Name >Define. The Define Name dialog box appears, as shown in Figure 13-10.

Figure 13-10. The Define Name dialog box

4. Enter a name for the range and click the OK button.

The range name is the source for your queries. The data areas can have mixed table structures in the spreadsheet. Spreadsheet ranges in the format *worksheetname$range* can also be used to identify data, but only for spreadsheet files created with Excel 5.0 and later.

All data within the ranges except formulas can be modified. Data can be added to a range, but not deleted. If data is added to a named range, the named range will automatically expand accordingly to take advantage of the new row.

By default, the driver assumes the first row of a range contains headers, and these headers can be used when referencing fields. The following code fragment adds a row of data to the spreadsheet range LogData:

```
Const adOpenForwardOnly = 0
Const adLockOptimistic = 3
Dim objConn,objRst
Set objConn = CreateObject("ADODB.Connection")
Set objRst = CreateObject("ADODB.Recordset")
'open the datasource
objConn.Open "FileDSN=ExcelData.dsn"
'open the named range LogData
objRst.Open "LogData", objConn, adOpenForwardOnly, adLockOptimistic

'add a new row to the range
objRst.AddNew
objRst("LogTime") = Now
objRst("UserID") = "Fred Smith"
```

```
objRst("Description") = "An event has occurred"
'update and close data source
objRst.Update
objRst.Close
objConn.Close
```

See Also

For more information, read "Use ADO with Excel Data from Visual Basic or VBA" (http://support.microsoft.com/?kbid=257819).

13.10 Querying the Index Server

Problem

You want to search for files using the IIS Index Server engine.

Solution

You can use the Index server ODBC driver to execute queries against the IIS Index server:

```
Dim objRst, strQuery, strContents, strKeyWord, strCriteria
Set objRst = CreateObject("ADODB.Recordset")
'check if there is either one or two parameters passed
If WScript.Arguments.Count = 0 Or WScript.Arguments.Count >2 Then
  ShowUsage
  Wscript.Quit
End If

'if only one argument has been passed, then set the search type to 'contents
If WScript.Arguments.Count = 1 Then
 strKeyWord = "Contents"
 strCriteria = WScript.Arguments(0)
Else
 strKeyWord = WScript.Arguments(0)
 strCriteria = WScript.Arguments(1)
End If

'build the query for the search engine. Replace all single quotes in the
```

```
'command line parameter with double quotes since the Index server wants
'double quotes.
 strQuery = "SELECT Path, DocLastSavedTm FROM Scope() WHERE CONTAINS("_
                & strKeyWord & ",'" & Replace(strCriteria, "'", chr(34)) &
"')>0"
'build the query for the search engine
  objRst.Open strQuery, "PROVIDER=MSIDXS"

'display each item
  While Not objRst.EOF
   Wscript.StdOut.WriteLine objRst(0)
    objRst.MoveNext
  Wend
   objRst.Close
   objRst.ActiveConnection.Close

Sub ShowUsage
 WScript.Echo "Idxsrv executes a query against Microsoft Index Server"  _
     & vbCrLf & "Syntax:" &  vbCrLf & _
    "idxsrv [Type] IndexQuery" & vbCrLf & _
    "Type (optional) Server propery to search against. Default is Contents" & _
vbCrLf & "IndexQuery  query to execute"
End Sub
```

Discussion

The Solution uses the IIS Index Service provider to execute queries against a Microsoft Index Server. The Microsoft Index Server provides indexing capabilities for many types of document formats, such as text, HTML, and Microsoft Office. Directories that are indexed are configured using the IIS Internet Service Manager interface. The directories you index do not have to be Web folders, so you can index document directories and use the Index Service provider to quickly query documents based on their content.

The Index Server provider allows a query to be executed against the indexed document database. The queries are constructed using a SQL query syntax. A limitation of the MSIDXS provider is that it can only be executed on the machine the Index Server resides on—it does not allow for remote querying.

The Solution is a command-line script that outputs the path of all documents that meet specified search criteria.

The following is the syntax for the command line:

```
idxsrv [Type] IndexQuery
```

The query Type is an optional parameter that specifies what Index Server property to search against. The default is Contents, which indicates the body of the documents will be searched. The following example returns all Microsoft Office documents where the document's author property has been set to Fred Smith:

```
cscript idxsrv.vbs DocAuthor "'Fred Smith'"
```

IndexQuery is the criteria executed against the provider. This criteria is passed as a Boolean expression.

The following sample returns all documents that contain the words "data" and "office":

```
cscript idxsrv.vbs "data AND office"
```

If any of the criteria contains spaces, surround them with single quotes:

```
cscript idxsrv.vbs "'sales figures' OR  'northern region'"
```

The results are output to the console standard output. The results can be piped to other applications that can process the standard input stream. Because it uses the standard input/output, WSH version 2.0 or later is required and the script must be run using the command-line interpreter cscript.exe.

See Also

For more details on the Index provider, read "Idxadovb.exe: Using Index Server OLE DB Provider and ADO in Visual Basic" (http://support.microsoft.com/?kbid=179326).

13.11 Adding Data

Problem

You want to add a new record to a database.

Solution

There are two ways of adding data. Each has advantages and disadvantages.

- You can use the Recordset object's AddNew method. The advantage of AddNew is that it produces relatively simple code. The disadvantage is a performance hit. This performance penalty is provider dependent, and it is negligible for a few additions, but if you're attempting a large number of additions, it will become noticeable.

- The alternative is executing the appropriate command statement against a data source using the Command object's Execute method. In the case of a relational database source, this would be via the SQL INSERT statement. The advantage is better performance over the AddNew method, while its disadvantage is that more code is required to build the appropriate statements.

Also note that not all providers allow for the addition of data:

```
Const adCmdTable = 2
Const adLockPessimistic = 2
Const adOpenForwardOnly = 1
Set objRst = CreateObject("ADODB.Recordset")
'open the data source
objRst.Open "Customers", _
 "Provider=Microsoft.Jet.OLEDB.3.51; Data Source=C:\data\northwind.mdb", _
  adOpenForwardOnly, adLockPessimistic, adCmdTable
objRst.AddNew
objRst("CompanyName") = "Fred's Food Company"
objRst("CustomerID") = "MNOPQ"
objRst.Update
objRst.Close
```

Discussion

The AddNew method provides a straightforward way of adding new records to a data source. To use the AddNew method, follow these steps:

1. Create a Recordset object that is not read-only (its LockType property is not adLockReadOnly) and invoke the AddNew method.

2. Assign the new values to the record.

3. Invoke the Recordset object's Update method.

Note that if you execute any Move methods after adding new items, the new data is automatically updated. It is a good programming habit to explicitly invoke the Update method.

If you are using ADO version 1.5 or greater, you can specify the fields and values you want to add via optional parameter arrays. The syntax of the AddNew method is as follows:

```
objRst.AddNew Fields, Values
```

Table 13-15 lists the AddNew method's arguments.

Table 13-15. AddNew *Method Arguments*

PARAMETER	DESCRIPTION
Fields	Either a single string value for an individual field or an array of field names for the fields you want to add
Values	Either a single variant value for an individual field or an array of values for multiple fields

For example, the following code fragment makes use of arrays to add information to four fields of a new record of a Customers table:

```
'adds a new value to the Customers table
objRst.AddNew( _
        Array("CustomerID","CompanyName","ContactName","ContactTitle"), _
        Array("ABCDE", "Fred's Food", "Fred", "President")
```

The alternative to the AddNew method is to use the provider's native method for inserting data, which in most cases is the SQL INSERT INTO statement. In the following example, a record is added to the SQL Server's Pubs sample database using a SQL statement:

```
Const adCmdText = 1
'create a connection
objConn.Open "Provider=SQLOLEDB;User ID=sa;Initial Catalog=pubs;Data Source=Odin"
objConn.Execute "INSERT INTO authors (au_id, au_lname, au_fname, phone, contract) _
VALUES ('323-43-4333', 'Smith', 'Fred','604-555-1234',1)", , adCmdText
objConn.Close
```

The advantage to using the SQL statement over the AddNew method is performance. The native statement is generally faster, so if you need to add a lot of data to a database, you should use it rather than AddNew.

The Solution code uses the Access Northwind sample database to add a new record.

See Also

For more information, search http://msdn.microsoft.com for the article "AddNew Method ADO."

13.12 Updating Data

Problem

You want to update records.

Solution

There are a couple of different ways to update data. The easiest way is to create a Recordset object and open a data source with any lock type except read-only. Once the data source is opened, you can proceed to modify the data. Invoke the Update method after modifying each record. The other option is to build a SQL query statement and execute it with the Command object's Execute method.

In the following code snippet the price of all nondiscontinued items in the Products table is increased by 7 percent:

```
Const adCmdTable = 2
Const adLockOptimistic = 3
Const adOpenForwardOnly = 1
Dim objConn, objRst
Set objConn = CreateObject("ADODB.Connection")
objConn.Open "Provider=Microsoft.Jet.OLEDB.4.0; Data Source=e:\Nwind.mdb"
Set objRst = CreateObject("ADODB.Recordset")
'open the recordset
    objRst.Open "Products", objConn, _
    adOpenForwardOnly, adLockOptimistic, adCmdTable

'loop through all records
Do While Not objRst.EOF
```

```
    'only update if item is not discontinued
    If Not objRst("Discontinued")  Then
       objRst("UnitPrice") = objRst("UnitPrice") * 1.07
       objRst.Update
    End If
    objRst.MoveNext
Loop
```

Discussion

To update data in a recordset, create a Recordset object that is not read-only (its LockType property is not adLockReadOnly). That's it. As long as you've opened the recordset as not read-only, and no one else has locked the record, you can modify the underlying data.

However, the data provider must allow for the modification of data. Some providers, such as the Index server and Active Directory OLE DB interfaces, do not allow delete/update/create operations. Even if the provider allows for updates, such as SQL Server or Oracle, the underlying data source might implement security that prevents you from updating it.

After you've updated a value, you can invoke the Update method to save the changes. If you do not invoke the Update method and move from the current record, any changes made to the record are automatically saved.

If you want to cancel any changes you have made to the record, you can invoke the CancelUpdate method, which undoes any changes made to the current record. CancelUpdate does not work after you've invoked the Update method or moved to another record.

You can also update data using the provider's native method for updating data, which in most cases is the SQL UPDATE statement. Apart from being faster than the Update method, you can easily modify large quantities of data with a single statement. The following example updates the prices of all business titles from the Pubs database by 5 percent and shows the number of records affected:

```
Const adCmdText = 1
Set objConn = CreateObject("ADODB.Connection")
objConn.Open "Provider=SQLOLEDB;User ID=sa;Initial Catalog=pubs;Data Source=Odin"

objConn.Execute _
  "Update titles Set price = price * 1.05 where type='business'" _
   , nCount, adCmdText
Wscript.Echo nCount & " records were updated"
objConn.Close
```

The `CancelUpdate` method does not work with the SQL `Update` statement. You can, however, use transaction processing to "roll back" any update transaction if your provider supports it. See Solution 13.23 for a transaction sample.

See Also

For more information, search `http://msdn.microsoft.com` for the article "Update Method ADO."

13.13 Accessing HTML Data

Problem

You want to open a remote HTML table as a recordset.

Solution

The following code sample opens an HTML table stored in the following HTML listing and compares each product with the items stored in the Northwind sample database Products table. If the product does not exist in the local table, it is added, and if it does exist, the price is updated. The script uses the HTML ODBC driver to open the table.

The following table is the source HTML table used in the script:

```
<html>
<head>
<title>Product List</title>
</head>
<body>
<table>
  <caption>Atable</caption>
  <tr>
    <td>ProductName</td>
    <td>UnitPrice</td>
    <td>QuantityPerUnit</td>
  </tr>
  <tr>
    <td>Konbu</td>
    <td>6.5</td>
    <td>2 kg box</td>
```

```
  </tr>
  <tr>
    <td>Tofu</td>
    <td>25.20</td>
    <td>40 - 100 g pkgs.</td>
  </tr>
  <tr>
    <td>Wasabi</td>
    <td>34.</td>
    <td>50 - 500 g pkgs.</td>
  </tr>
</table>
</body>
</html>
```

```
<?xml version="1.0" ?>
<job>
<reference object="ADODB.Recordset"/>
<!--comment
Script:ADOHTML.wsf
Updates a local Access table from remote HTML data source
-->
 <script language="VBScript">
 Option Explicit

 Dim objHTMLRst , objProductsRst, objRST
Set objHTMLRst = CreateObject("ADODB.Recordset")
 Set objProductsRst = CreateObject("ADODB.Recordset")

 'open a connection to an HTML file
 objHTMLRst.Open "Atable", _
      "Provider=Microsoft.Jet.OLEDB.4.0" & _
       ";Data Source=http://www.acme.com/products.htm;" & _
        "Extended Properties='HTML Import;HDR=YES'",_
         adOpenForwardOnly, adLockReadOnly

'open the products table
 objProductsRst.Source = "Products"
 objProductsRst.ActiveConnection = "Provider=Microsoft.Jet.OLEDB.4.0;" & _
                        "Data Source=d:\data\access\Samples\Nwind.mdb;"

 objProductsRst.CursorType = adOpenDynamic
 objProductsRst.LockType = adLockPessimistic
```

```
 objProductsRst.Open
'loop through and total the contents
 While Not objHTMLRst.EOF
    objProductsRst.MoveFirst
    objProductsRst.Find "ProductName='" & objHTMLRst(0) & "'"

'if the item is not found in the local table then add record
    If objProductsRst.EOF Then
        objProductsRst.AddNew
        objProductsRst("ProductName") = objHTMLRst("ProductName")
        objProductsRst("QuantityPerUnit") = objHTMLRst("QuantityPerUnit")
        objProductsRst("UnitPrice") = objHTMLRst("UnitPrice")
        objProductsRst("SupplierID") = 6
        objProductsRst.Update
    Else
        objProductsRst("UnitPrice") = objHTMLRst("UnitPrice")
        objProductsRst.Update
    End If
    objHTMLRst.MoveNext
  Wend
'close the Recordset objects
 objProductsRst.Close
 objHTMLRst.Close
  </script>
</job>
```

Discussion

The Solution script uses an HTML ODBC driver to open an HTML file for reading. The data in the HTML file is stored in a table format. This table is constructed using the standard HTML table definition tags: `<TD>` and `</TD>`.

You can have multiple data tables in the HTML source. The tables can be identified in a number of ways. An HTML caption can be used as the table source identifier. If there is no table caption and only one table in the file, the filename is used as the data source identifier. If there are multiple tables in the file and no captions, the tables are identified using the sequential table number (e.g., table1, table2, and so on).

The HTML driver is similar to the Text and Excel drivers in that it depends upon the Access Jet database engine. In order to connect to an HTML table, you must create a connection string using the Jet provider and specify an `Extended Properties` parameter. The Extended Properties keyword is used to specify additional extended properties of a given provider.

The HTML import driver has an HDR parameter that specifies if the table(s) being accessed has headers or not. If it is set to Yes, the first row of HTML will be read as field names. By default, this value is No and it assumes that the first row of HTML does not include field names.

```
objHTMLRst.Open "Atable", _
   "Provider=Microsoft.Jet.OLEDB.4.0" & _
   ";Data Source=http://www.acme.com/data/products.htm;" & _
   "Extended Properties='HTML Import;HDR=YES'", _
      adOpenForwardOnly, adLockReadOnly
```

The Solution also uses the Find method, which provides a search ability with an open Recordset object. The Find method provides the ability to search a recordset in any direction without having to re-execute a query. Its syntax is as follows:

```
objRst.Find (criteria, [skiprows,] [searchdirection] [, start])
```

Table 13-16 lists the Find method's arguments.

Table 13-16. Find *Method Arguments*

PARAMETER	TYPE	DESCRIPTION
criteria	String	Search expression criteria composed of the field name followed by comparison operator and comparison value (e.g., Name = 'Fred').
skiprows	Long	Specifies the number of rows from the current row to start searching. Default value is 0, which will start from the current row.
searchdirection	Integer	Direction the search will go. Possible parameters are as follows: adSearchForward = 1 adSearchBackward =-1 If searching in a forward direction and the criteria is not found, the search will end at the end of the file. If searching in a backward direction and the criteria is not found, the search will end at the beginning of the file.
start	Variant	Bookmark to start the search from.

The comparison operator for the criteria string can be any mathematical comparison operator such as =, <, >, <=, >=, and <>. You can use a Like operator to perform comparisons using the * wildcard operator.

The Find method starts the search from the current record. If the item you are searching for is not found, the current record is set to end of file (EOF). If you attempt to find a record that occurs before the current record, the record will not be found. If you are doing repeated Find operations, you must move to the beginning of the table before each Find operation is executed.

String values must be surrounded by single quote (') delimiters, while dates must use the number sign (#) delimiter.

See Also

For more information, search http://msdn.microsoft.com for the article "Using the Connection Object ADO."

13.14 Deleting Data

Problem

You need to delete a record.

Solution

To delete a record from a table, simply invoke the Delete method on the record you want to delete:

```
Set objConn = CreateObject("ADODB.Connection")
objConn.Open "Provider=Microsoft.Jet.OLEDB.4.0;
Data Source=D:\data\Access\Samples\Northwind.mdb"
Set objRst = CreateObject("ADODB.Recordset")
'open the Products table and delete a record
    objRst.Open "Products", objConn, adOpenForwardOnly, adLockOptimistic
objRst.Delete
objRst.Close
```

The alternative to the `Delete` method is to use the provider's native method, which is usually the SQL DELETE statement. The following example attempts to delete all business titles from the Titles table in the Pubs database:

```
Const adCmdText = 1
Set objConn = CreateObject("ADODB.Connection")
objConn.Open "Provider=SQLOLEDB;User ID=sa;Initial Catalog=pubs;Data Source=Odin"
objConn.Execute "Delete From titles where type='business'" _
, nCount, adCmdText
Wscript.Echo nCount & " records were deleted"
objConn.Close
```

Discussion

Records can be deleted by either calling the `Delete` method on the current record of an open Recordset or executing a SQL DELETE statement against the data source.

See Also

For more information, search `http://msdn.microsoft.com` for the article "Delete Method ADO."

13.15 Accessing Internet Resources

Problem

You want to download an image from a Web site.

Solution

You can use the `Stream` object to open and save the resource. The following script writes the contents of a remote Web file to a local file:

```
Const adSaveCreateOverWrite = 2
Const adModeRead = 1
Const adTypeBinary = 1
Dim objRec, objStream
Set objStream = CreateObject("ADODB.Stream")
```

```
objStream.Open "URL=http://www.microsoft.com/library/toolbar/images/mslogo.gif" _
        , adModeRead
'set stream type to Binary and save file
objStream.Type = adTypeBinary
objStream.SaveToFile "e:\data\mslogo.gif", adSaveCreateOverWrite
objStream.Close
```

Discussion

The Microsoft OLE DB Provider for Internet Publishing is an OLE DB provider that provides access to Web server file resources. It is included as part of Internet Explorer 5.0 and Office 2000 and later.

The OLE DB Provider for Internet Publishing requires the Web Distributed Authoring and Publishing (WebDAV) protocol to be enabled on the host server that is being accessed. The Internet Publishing provider can also use the FrontPage Web Extender Client (WEC), which allows Web authoring on older IIS Web servers that don't support WebDAV.

WebDAV is a standard protocol that allows clients to access resources on remote servers and perform administrative tasks, such as creating, copying, moving, and deleting files.

Because WebDAV is a standard, you are not dependent on Microsoft IIS servers to provide WebDAV access. Other popular Web servers such as Apache are capable of providing WebDAV services.

WebDAV is enabled on Microsoft IIS 5.0, which comes with Windows 2000. Under Windows 2003 you must install and configure FrontPage extensions.

The connection string requires that a valid URL path is specified as the source, together with an optional access mode, user ID, and password. Table 13-17 details the elements of a connection string for the Internet Publishing provider.

Table 13-17. OLE DB Provider for Internet Publishing Connection String Parameters

PARAMETER	DESCRIPTION
`Source`	URL to reference.
`Mode`	Determines the level of access to be available. Combination of Read, ReadWrite, Share Deny None, Share Deny Read, Share Deny Write, Share Exclusive, and Write.
`User ID`	Required if read/write operations are to be performed.
`Password`	Password for the specified user.

Once a connection has been made, you can iterate the records and perform deletion operations. Table 13-18 lists a number of provider field names that are available to Web objects.

Table 13-18. Internet Publishing Provider Fields

FIELD NAME	DESCRIPTION
RESOURCE_STREAMSIZE	Size of file. If a folder, returns `Null`.
RESOURCE_LASTWRITETIME	Last time the file was written to/updated.
RESOURCE_DISPLAYNAME	Filename.
RESOURCE_ABSOLUTEPARSENAME	Full URL for the file.

Although ADO 2.0 and 2.1 can be used to enumerate and delete Web files, to take full advantage of WebDAV features you need ADO 2.5 or later. ADO 2.5 provides an additional object, the `Record` object, which allows for additional resource manipulation.

The RecordSet object can be used to return results in a fixed table format from a wide variety of sources, such as databases, text files, and Excel spreadsheet data. What the Recordset can't do is represent unstructured data. A Web site is an example of unstructured data, where there is no fixed format.

The `Record` object allows ADO to access "unstructured" data, such as a directory hierarchy from a Web server or file system, or a mailbox structure from an e-mail service. A `Record` object can represent an individual Web resource, such as a file, or a resource collection, which represents a directory under a Web server.

To access a `Record` object, use the `Record` object's `Open` method to reference the remote resource:

```
objRecord.Open Source, Connection [, nConnectMode] [,nCreateOptions]
```

The `Open` method requires at least a `Source` and `Connection` parameter. `Source` represents a file object within the directory specified by the `Connection` parameter. The `Connection` parameter can be either a connection string or an existing ADO `Connection` object that points to the Web resource you want to access.

The following two code snippets open the page `http://www.acme.com\default.htm`:

```
'method one
Set objRecord = CreateObject("ADODB.Record")
objRecord.Open "default.htm", "URL=http://www.acme.com"
'method two, use existing Connection object
```

```
Set objConn = CreateObject("ADODB.Connection")
Set objRecord = CreateObject("ADODB.Record")

'open a connection to a Web server using Internet Publishing
'OLE DB provider
 objConn.Open "Provider=MSDAIPP.DSO;Data " & _
        "Source=http://www.acme.com;Mode=Read|Write"
objRecord.Open "default.htm", objConnection
```

The nConnectMode parameter identifies how the file is to be accessed, such as adModeRead (1), adModewrite (2), and adModeReadWrite (3).

If you want to open a directory, pass an empty string as the Source parameter to the Open method:

```
Set objRecord = CreateObject("ADODB.Record")
'open the data directory under the www.acme.com site
objRecord.Open "", "URL=http://www.acme.com/data"
```

If you attempt to open a nonexistent resource, an error will occur.

The Open method can also be used to create a file or directory. By default, when you open a URL the URL assumes you are attempting to access an existing directory or file. Use the nCreateOptions parameter to indicate you want to create a new file or directory.

If you specify adCreateCollection (8192) as the nCreateOptions parameter, a new directory will be created, and adCreateNonCollection (0) will create a new file. Adding adCreateOverwrite (67108864) to either of these values will overwrite the existing file or directory if it already exists.

```
'create a new file
Const adCreateNonCollection =0
Const adCreateOverwrite = &H4000000
Set objRecord = CreateObject("ADODB.Record")
'create a new data.txt file, overwriting the any file with the same name
objRecord.Open "data.txt", "URL=http://www.acme.com/" _
                  , , adCreateNonCollection + adCreateOverwrite
```

Once you have a reference to a Web resource, you can perform a number of operations on it, such as deleting it. To delete an object, simply call the Delete method:

```
Set objRecord = CreateObject("ADODB.Record")
'open the data directory under the www.acme.com site
objRecord.Open "", "URL=http://www.acme.com/data"
```

Deleting resources cannot be undone. If you delete a directory, all files and directories below it will be deleted.

The following script uses the Internet Publishing provider to delete any files that are older than 30 days on a Web server:

```
Dim objRst, objConn
Set objConn = CreateObject("ADODB.Connection")
Set objRst = CreateObject("ADODB.Recordset")
'open a connection to a Web server using Internet Publishing
'OLE DB provider
 objConn.Open "Provider=MSDAIPP.DSO;Data " & _
        "Source=http://odin/data;Mode=Read|Write;" & _
        "User ID=Administrator;Password=we56oi90"

'list all files from the folder
objRst.Open "*", objConn
'loop through all files
While Not objRst.EOF
'check if the size of file is a numeric value - indicates
'a file
If Not IsNull(objRst("RESOURCE_STREAMSIZE")) Then
'checks if file is older than 30 days and if it is a htm file
If DateDiff("d", objRst("RESOURCE_LASTWRITETIME"), Date) < 30 _
   And Right(objRst("RESOURCE_DISPLAYNAME"), 3) = "htm" Then
         objRst.Delete
       End If

    End If
    objRst.MoveNext
Wend
objRst.Close
objConn.Close
```

Web resources can be copied or moved. The `Record` object exposes the `CopyRecord` and `MoveRecord` methods, which can be used to copy and move resources. The syntax is as follows:

```
objRecord.CopyRecord | MoveRecord strSource, strDest,[ strUser,][ strPassword,]
[nOptions]
```

The `strSource` and `strDest` parameters represent the URL to the source and the destination of the object you want to copy or move. If the `Record` object is a Web directory, the URL for strSource can represent the relative path to an object in this directory.

```
'create ADO record object
Set objRecord = CreateObject("ADODB.Record")
'open a Record object to the root of Acme.com
objRecord.Open "", "URL=http://www.acme.com"
'copy data.htm from www.acme.com root to backup.htm
objRecord.CopyRecord "data.htm", "URL=http://www.acme.com/backup.htm"

'move history.htm from www.acme.com root to data directory
objRecord.MoveRecord "history.htm", "http://www.acme.com/data/history.htm"
'move data.htm from www.acme.com root to dataold.htm in same directory,
'this is the same as a rename
objRecord.MoveRecord "data.htm", " dataold.htm"
```

If the strSource parameter is blank, the operation applies to the Record object, either copying or moving it to the specified strDestination:

```
'create ADO record object
Set objRecord = CreateObject("ADODB.Record")
'open a Record object to the root of Acme.com
objRecord.Open "data.htm", "URL=http://www.acme.com"
'copy data.htm from www.acme.com root to backup.htm
objRecord.CopyRecord "", "URL=http://www.acme.com/backup.htm"
```

The strUser and strPassword parameters represent an optional user name and password for the destination location, if the security requirement is different from the source.

If a file or directory exists with the same name of the destination file you are attempting to copy or move, an error will occur. The optional nCopyOptions parameter can take an adCopyOverWrite value that overwrites the destination if it already exists:

```
Const adCopyOverWrite = 1
'create ADO record object
Set objRecord = CreateObject("ADODB.Record")
'open a Record object for the file data.htm in the root of Acme.com
objRecord.Open "", "URL=http://www.acme.com"
'copy data.htm from www.acme.com root to backup.htm and overwrite if
'file already exists
objRecord.CopyRecord "data.htm", "backup.htm", , , adCopyOverWrite
```

Where a Record object is different from a RecordSet is that it can represent an individual item, such as a file, or a collection of items, such as a directory. The Record object's RecordTypeEnum property identifies the type of Record object. Table 13-19 lists RecordTypeEnum's values.

Table 13-19. RecordTypeEnum *Property Values*

VALUE	DESCRIPTION
adSimpleRecord	Simple record, no child nodes. In the case of the OLE DB Internet provider, this would be a file.
adCollectionRecord	Collection record, contains child nodes. In the case of the OLE DB Internet provider, this would be a directory.
adStructDoc	Structured document record. No Record objects of this type are exposed through the Internet OLE DB provider.

If the Record object is a collection you may want to enumerate the contents. Use the GetChildren method, which returns a RecordSet containing the contents of the container. In the case of a Web server directory, this would contain a list of all files and directories the next level under the directory represented by the Record object.

Perhaps one of the most interesting new features of ADO 2.5 is the introduction of the Stream object. Streams provide access to the contents of Record objects, which in the case of the Internet provider are the files on the Web server.

To use streams, create a Stream object and invoke the Open method:

```
objStream.Open [strSource,][nConnectMode,] [nType]
```

The strSource parameter represents the path to the source, which is a URL to the file to access. If no strSource parameter is specified, any operations are stored in memory.

nConnectMode determines if the file is to be opened for read and/or write access. Valid values for the connect mode are adModeRead (1), adModewrite (2), and adModeReadWrite (3). Use a WSF file and the element to reference the type libraries for the Stream object.

```
<?xml version="1.0" ?>
<job>
<reference object="ADODB.Stream"/>
<!--comment
Script:openstream.wsf
Creates and opens a Stream object
```

```
-->
 <script language="VBScript">
  Dim objStream
  Set objStream = CreateObject("ADODB.Stream")
  objStream.Open "URL=http://thor/visitors.txt", adModeReadWrite
  objStream.Close
  </script>
</job>
```

You can pass an existing open Record object as the strSource parameter when opening a Stream, but if you do you must specify the nType parameter as adOpenStreamFromRecord (4).

If you are going to manipulate the Stream, you should set the object's Type property. This defaults to adTypeText (2), but if you are working with a binary type file, such as an image or executable, you should change it to adTypeBinary (1).

The Stream object exposes the LoadFromFile and SaveToFile methods, which allow easy transfer of files from a Web server to local storage.

LoadFromFile allows for local files to be loaded into a Stream object. The syntax is as follows:

```
objStream.LoadFromFile strPath
```

strPath represents the local path or UNC to the file you want to load into the Stream.

SaveToFile allows the contents of a Stream to be saved to a local file:

```
objStream.SaveToFile strPath [,nSaveOptions]
```

strPath represents the local path or UNC to the file you want to save the stream to. If the destination file you are attempting to save to already exists, an error will occur. Setting the nSaveOptions to adSaveCreateOverWrite (2) will overwrite the existing file with the contents of the Stream object.

The following code sample copies a local file to a Web server:

```
'copy a local file to a Web server
Option Explicit
Const adTypeBinary = 1
Const adCreateNonCollection = 0
Const adCreateOverwrite = &H4000000
Const adModeReadWrite = 3
Const adOpenStreamFromRecord=4

Dim objRst, objConn, objRecord, objRec, objStream
```

```
Set objStream = CreateObject("ADODB.Stream")
Set objRecord = CreateObject("ADODB.Record")

'create a new data.dat file, overwriting the any file with the same name
objRecord.Open "data.zip", "URL=http://www.acme.com/" _
               , adModeReadWrite, adCreateNonCollection + adCreateOverwrite

'open the Stream object using the objRecord object
objStream.Open objRecord, adModeReadWrite, adOpenStreamFromRecord
objStream.Type = adTypeBinary \
'load local file in Stream object
objStream.LoadFromFile "d:\data\data.dat"
objStream.Close
objRecord.Close
```

Streams can be written to and read from in a similar fashion to the File Scripting Object.

Data can be read by using either the `Read` or `ReadText` method. Both methods can take an optional `nChars` parameter that returns only the number of bytes specified. If this parameter is omitted, all data from the stream is returned. The `ReadText` method can pass a special `nChars`, `adReadLine`, that will read a single line of text up to an end-of-line character sequence controlled by the `LineSeperator` property. By default, the `LineSeperator` property is carriage return/linefeed combination.

When you work with text it can be important to change the character set being used to read and write the files. By default, the character set type is set to Unicode, which is not appropriate for a lot of Web operations that only understand 8-bit ASCII text. To change the character set, set the `charset` property to the appropriate value. These values are determined by the entries under the `HKEY_CLASSES_ROOT\MIME\Database\Charset` entry in the Windows registry.

To determine if the end of the stream has been reached, check the `Stream`'s EOS property. If it is `True`, the end of the stream has been reached; otherwise, it is `False`.

The following code snippet reads a text file on a Web server and outputs the contents to the screen:

```
Const adReadLine = -2
Const adTypeText = 2
'read the contents of a Web file
Set objStream = CreateObject("ADODB.Stream")
'open to log.txt file on www.acme.com site
objStream.Open "URL=http://www.acme.com/log.txt"
'set type to text and character set to Ascii
```

```
objStream.Type = adTypeText
objStream.charset = "ascii"

'read contents of file and output
Do While Not objStream.EOS
 'read the next line of text
  strLine = objStream.ReadText(adReadLine)
  Wscript.Echo strLine
Loop
objStream.Close
```

To write to a Stream, use either the Write or WriteText method. The Write method requires a variant array of bytes to write and is used for writing binary data.

WriteText requires a string parameter that is the text that will be written to the Stream. It can also take an optional parameter that determines if an end-of-line character is added to the data. By default, no end-of-line character is added, but if the parameter is adWriteLine (1) it is.

You may want to append to the stream or start at the beginning of the stream. To change the location of where the data will be written to, set the Position property. The Position property returns the current location in the stream and determines where the next data will be written.

To append data, set the Position property to the Size property of the Stream object, which will set it at the end of the stream:

```
<?xml version="1.0" ?>
<job>
<reference object="ADODB.Stream"/>
<!--comment
Script:write2stream.wsf
Writes to a text stream
-->
 <script language="VBScript">
  Option Explicit
  Dim objStream
  Set objStream = CreateObject("ADODB.Stream")
  'open Stream object and set character type to text and ASCII
  objStream.Open "URL=http://thor/log.txt", adModeReadWrite
  objStream.Type = adTypeText
  objStream.charset = "ascii"
  'set position to end of stream
  objStream.Position = objStream.Size
  'write to Stream and close it
  objStream.WriteText "Operation successful", adWriteLine
```

```
  objStream.Close
  </script>
</job>
```

See Also

For more information, search http://msdn.microsoft.com for the articles "Platforms Supported by the OLE DB Provider for Internet Publishing," "Internet Publishing Scenario," "ADO Stream Object," "ADO Record Object," and "Microsoft OLE DB Provider for Internet Publishing."

13.16 Exporting Data

Problem

You want to be able to export a recordset to a CSV text file.

Solution

You can open a Recordset and use the Fields collection to enumerate all fields for each record, outputting the results to a text file:

```
Const adVarWChar = 202
Const adWchar = 130
Dim objConn, strDestinationFile
Dim objRst
Set objConn = CreateObject("ADODB.Connection")
objConn.Open "Provider=Microsoft.Jet.OLEDB.4.0;" & _
        "Data Source=d:\data\access\Samples\Northwind.mdb;"
    Set objRst = objConn.Execute("Select * From Products")
     CreateCSVFile "d:\output.txt", objRst, ","
    objRst.Close
    objConn.Close
Sub CreateCSVFile(strDestinationFile, objRst, strDelimiter)
Dim objField, strLine , objFileSystem, objTextFile
'create a file scripting object
Set objFileSystem = CreateObject("Scripting.FileSystemObject")
'create the output file..
Set objTextFile = objFileSystem.CreateTextFile(strDestinationFile, True)
```

```
    'loop through each record in the recordset
    Do While Not objRst.EOF
    strLine = ""
    'loop through each field in the record, building the output string.
    For Each objField In objRst.Fields
            Select Case objField.Type
            Case adVarWChar, adWchar
             strLine = strLine & """" & objField.Value & """" & ","
             Case Else
                    strLine = strLine & objField.Value & ","
            End Select
    Next
            'write the line to the file
            objTextFile.WriteLine Left(strLine, Len(strLine) - 1)
    objRst.MoveNext
    Loop
    objTextFile.Close
End Sub
```

Discussion

When a recordset is created it exposes a `Fields` collection. This collection contains all fields in the recordset.

The full syntax for referencing a field value by name is as follows:

```
Wscript.Echo objRst.Fields(strFieldName).Value
```

The following code displays the value of the `Description` field for the `objRst` recordset:

```
Wscript.Echo objRst.Fields("Description").Value
```

The `Fields` collection is the default property of a Recordset object, so you are not required to specify the `Fields` keyword in a statement:

```
Wscript.Echo objRst("Description").Value
```

The `Field` object's default property is the `Value` property, so it is not required when referencing a value. The following statement is the same as the previous statement:

```
Wscript.Echo objRst("Description")
```

Wscript.Echo and other methods used to display values such as MsgBox know how to display a value even if the Value property is not specified. This is because they can only display a nonobject value, so when the object is specified as a parameter its default property is referenced instead.

The Name property identifies the name of the field. These properties can be used to process all the fields in a recordset where the field names are not known or explicitly specified.

The following code snippet lists each field and its field type in a recordset:

```
Dim objField, objRst
objRst.Open "Select CompanyName From Companies", "Northwind"
'display the name and type of each field
For Each objField In objRst.Fields
   Wscript.Echo objField.Value, objField.Type
Next
objRst.Close
Set objRst.Close
```

The CreateCSVFile subroutine in the Solution script accepts a recordset as a parameter. It loops through each Field and checks its Type property. If the Type property is a string data type, the output value is surrounded in double quotes, otherwise it assumes it's a numeric value.

See Also

For more information, search http://msdn.microsoft.com for the article "Fields Collection."

13.17 Importing Data

Problem

You want to import the data from a comma-delimited text file (such as the one that follows) into a table:

```
ProductName,UnitPrice,SupplierId,QuantityPerUnit, Discontinued
"Swiss Chocolate Bunny",$10.00,22,"Case of 20", 0
"White Chocolate Bar",$10.00,22,"Case of 20", 0
```

Solution

The following `WSHENT.CopyTable` WSC component uses the ODBC Text import driver to process text files and builds SQL statements to insert the information into a database:

```
<?xml version="1.0"?>
<component>
<registration
     description="CopyTable"
     progid=" WSHENT.CopyTable"
     version="1.00"
     classid="{f8329d80-0b7e-11d3-bbe1-00104b164591}"
>
</registration>
<public>
     <property name="Source">
          <put/>
     </property>
     <property name="Destination">
          <put/>
     </property>
     <property name="Table">
          <put/>
     </property>
     <property name="Readit">
          <get/>
     </property>
     <method name="CopyTable">
     </method>
</public>

<script language="VBScript">

Const adVarWChar = 202
Const adWchar = 130
Const adVarChar = 200
Const adCmdText = 1

Dim objRst, objConnDestination, strTargetTable

Function put_Source(newValue)
     Set objRst = newValue
End Function
```

```
Function put_Destination(newValue)
      Set objConnDestination = newValue
End Function

function put_Table(newValue)
      strTargetTable = newValue
end function

Function CopyTable()
Dim strInsertQuery, strValues
Dim objField

'make sure not empty file..
If Not objRst.EOF Then

     'build the initial insert query..
     strInsertQuery = "INSERT INTO " & strTargetTable & " ("

     For Each objField In objRst.Fields
         strInsertQuery = strInsertQuery & objField.Name & ","
     Next

     'remove the last comma and append a bracket
     strInsertQuery=Left(strInsertQuery, Len(strInsertQuery) - 1) & _
                  ") VALUES ("

     Do While Not objRst.EOF

         strValues = ""
         For Each objField In objRst.Fields
            Select Case objField.Type
               'check if it's a character string..
               Case adVarWChar, adWchar, adVarChar
                  If IsNull(objField.Value) Then
                      strValues = strValues &  "Null,"
                  Else
                     strValues = strValues & Chr(34) & objField.Value _
                               & Chr(34) & ","
                 End If
                 'otherwise non-character string
               Case Else
                  strValues = strValues & objField.Value & ","
```

```
            End Select
        Next
objConnDestination.Execute strInsertQuery & Left(strValues, _
                                                        Len(strValues) - 1) & ")"
        objRst.MoveNext
        Loop

End If
End function
</script>
</component>
```

Discussion

While more sophisticated mechanisms for portable data exchange, such as XML, are being introduced, importing data using a delimited text file is still commonplace. With the use of data warehousing on the increase, scheduled bulk data imports from various enterprise platforms is common. WSH and ADO can be a practical way of integrating this data into one source.

The `WSHENT.CopyTable` WSC component copies data from a source Recordset to a specified destination table recordset. It's useful for copying data from different data sources.

The properties for the `CopyTable` object are listed in Table 13-20.

Table 13-20. `CopyTable` *Object Properties*

PROPERTY	DESCRIPTION
`Destination`	ADO `Connection` object for the destination data source to copy data to
`Source`	ADO Recordset representing the source to copy data from
`Table`	Name of table to copy data to

Once you have set the properties, invoke the `CopyTable` method. This will add the data from the source recordset to the table in the `Destination` connection. The routine does not provide any mechanism for trapping errors in the case of duplicate data that violates key integrity or referential integrity constraints.

The following example copies data from a text file recordset to an Access table:

```
Const adCmdText = 1
Dim objConn, objRst
Dim objConnDestination, objCopyData
Set objConnDestination = CreateObject("ADODB.Connection")
Set objConn = CreateObject("ADODB.Connection")
Set objRst = CreateObject("ADODB.Recordset")
'open the destination data file
objConnDestination.Open _
      "Provider=Microsoft.Jet.OLEDB.4.0;Data Source=d:\data\ \Nwind.mdb;"

objConn.Open _
  "DRIVER={Microsoft Text Driver (*.txt; *.csv)};DBQ=D:\data\wsh\ado;"

Set objRst = objConn.Execute("Select * From [Products.csv]")
Set objCopyData = CreateObject("WSHENT.CopyTable")
objCopyData.Source = objRst
'set the destination connection
objCopyData.Destination = objConnDestination objCopyData.Table = _
                                             "Products" 'set the destination

table
Call objCopyData.CopyTable

objRst.Close
objConn.Close
```

For large quantities of data, WSH/ADO might not be able to provide sufficient performance and reliability. An option is to use Data Transaction Services (DTS), which ships with SQL Server 7.0 and later. DTS provides a powerful mechanism to transfer data between different data sources.

DTS allows for the importing and exporting of data between various data sources using a DTS package, which is a set of rules governing what information is to be copied or moved. Even though DTS is a part of SQL Server 7.0 and 2000, neither the source nor the destination have to be SQL Server tables—you can import/export between any ODBC or OLE DB data source. You could even purchase SQL Server just for the DTS capability.

DTS also provides detailed logging of package execution, as well as transaction support, which allows unsuccessful transfers to be "rolled back," ensuring the data is returned to its original state before the execution of the package.

DTS also provides mechanisms to "massage" the data on import, so you can add VBScript or JScript code to manipulate the data as it's being imported.

DTS is also exposed as a COM object, so any packages you create can be invoked from WSH.

The following example creates a DTS package that imports a delimited text file into the SQL Server Northwind sample database's Products table. It demonstrates how to manipulate DTS packages from WSH.

The DTS solution will be used to import a delimited text file containing a product description, package size, and price:

```
Nigiri Sushi,250G, 4.50
Tempura Batter,Package 500g,3.95
Soya Sauce,500ml,2.95
Green Tea,500g, 3.25
```

To create a DTS package, follow these steps:

1. Start SQL Server 2000 Enterprise Manager and connect to the SQL Server you want to create the package on. Right-click any database on the server and select All Tasks > Import Data. The DTS Import Wizard dialog box appears, as shown in Figure 13-11. This starts the Import Wizard, which guides you through the steps of creating a DTS import package.

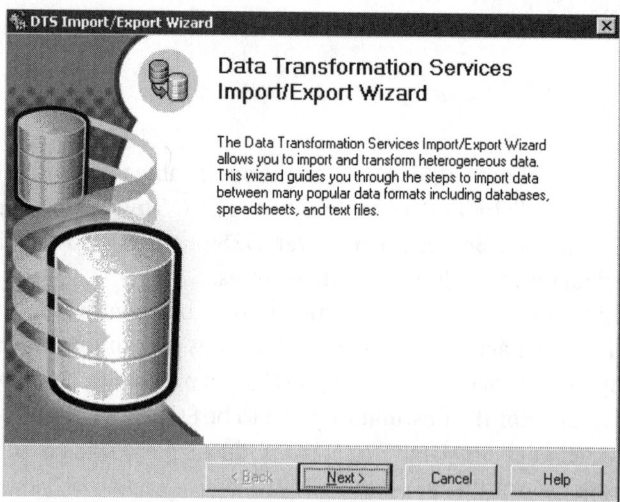

Figure 13-11. DTS Import Wizard

2. Select Text File as the source. Use `importproducts.txt` as a sample file, as shown in Figure 13-12.

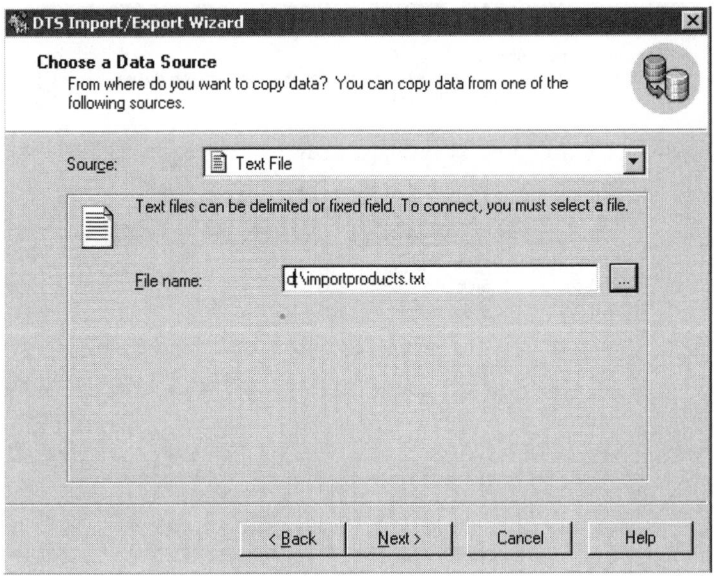

Figure 13-12. Choose a data source.

3. Accept the defaults selected by the Wizard: delimited text file and comma delimiters (shown in Figure 13-13 and Figure 13-14).

DTS Import/Export Wizard

Select file format

To import the data, confirm the source file format. Confirm that the file properties are correctly detected before proceeding.

Delimited. The columns are separated by any character(s).

Fixed field. Information is aligned into columns of equal width.

File type: ANSI — Skip rows: 0

Row delimiter: {CR}{LF} — First row has column names

Text qualifier: Double Quote {"}

Preview of file: h:\importproducts.txt

```
Nigiri Sushi,250G, 4.50
Tempura Batter, Package 500g, 3.95
Soya Sauce, 500ml, 2.95
Green Tea, 500g, 3.25
```

< Back | Next > | Cancel | Help

Figure 13-13. Select a file format.

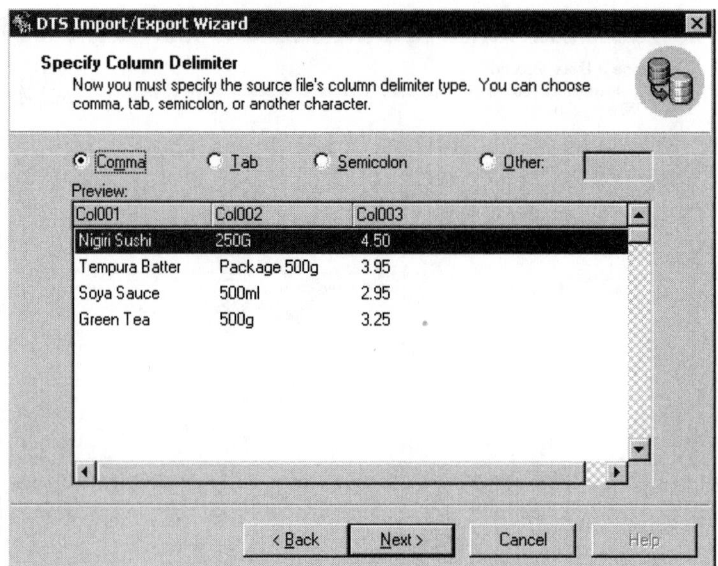

Figure 13-14. Specify a column delimiter.

4. Select the Northwind database as the destination database, as shown in Figure 13-15.

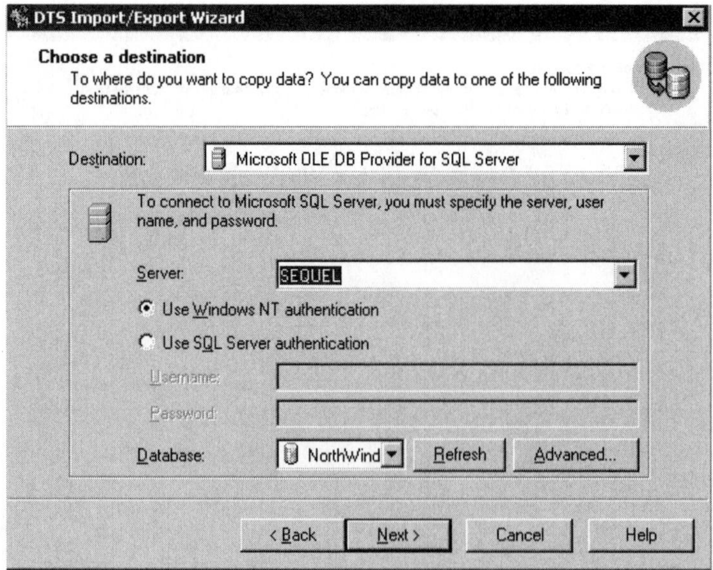

Figure 13-15. Choose a destination.

5. Select the Products table as the destination and select the Transform ... button to map the columns, as shown in Figure 13-16.

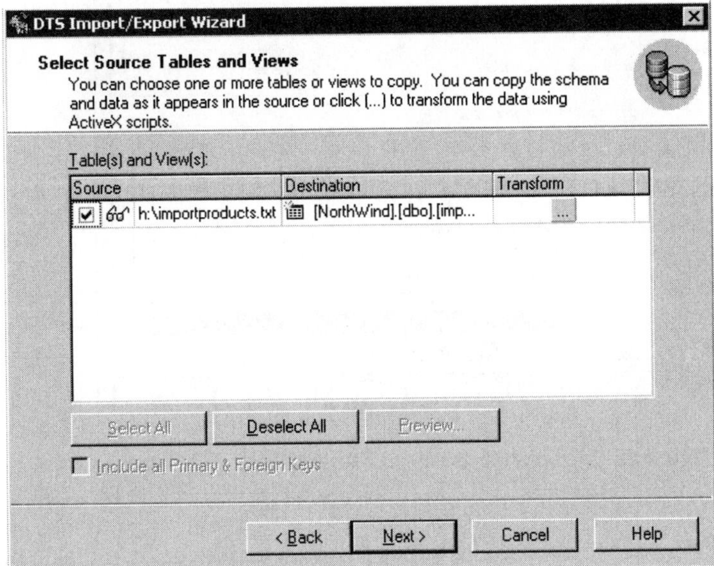

Figure 13-16. Select a destination table.

6. Map the columns as shown in the Figure 13-17, and select the "Append rows to destination table" radio button.

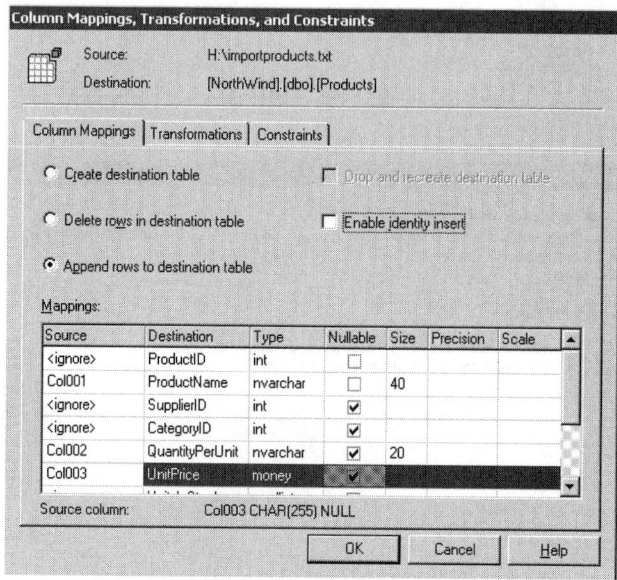

Figure 13-17. Control the column mappings.

7. Click the "Enable identity insert" option to deselect it. A dialog box similar to the one shown in Figure 13-18 appears.

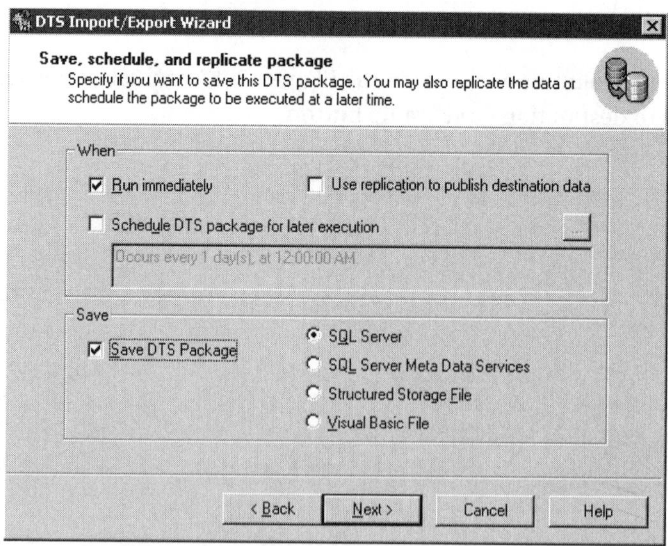

Figure 13-18. Save and schedule

8. In the bottom portion of the dialog box, click the Save DTS Package option to select it, but don't run the package immediately.

9. Type **ProductsImport** in the Name field as shown in Figure 13-19. Don't set any passwords.

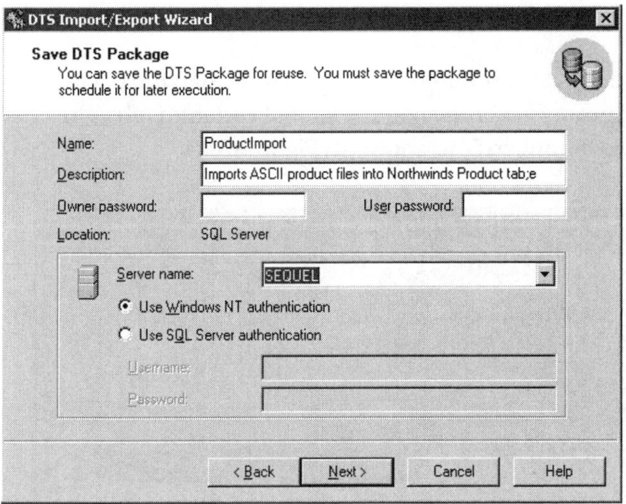

Figure 13-19. Save DTS package

10. The package is now complete. Click the Finish button. A dialog box similar to the one shown in Figure 13-20 appears.

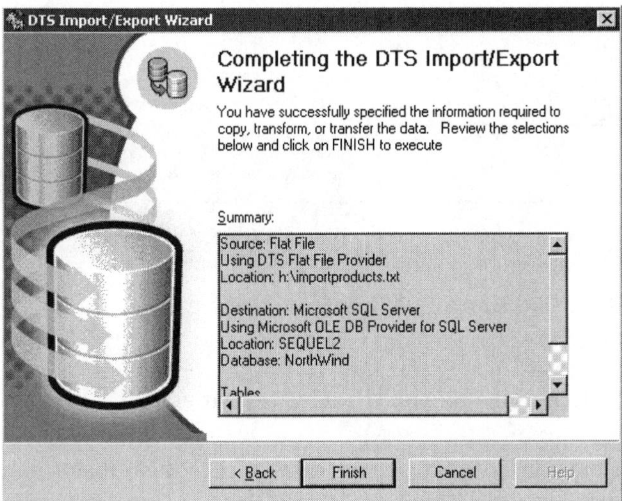

Figure 13-20. DTS Wizard completion dialog box

The finished package can be used to import the `importproducts.txt` text file, but you are going to modify the package to add some additional functionality to it. These features will be manipulated from the WSH scripting. To modify the package, follow these steps:

1. From the SQL Server Enterprise Manager, design the package. View the package properties, and go to the Global Variables tab. Add a new variable called SupplierID, as shown in Figure 13-21.

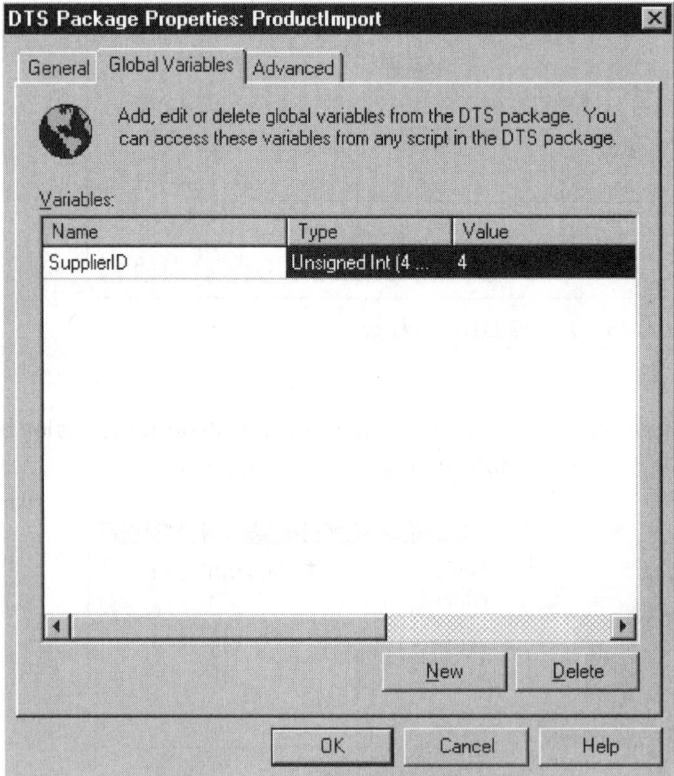

Figure 13-21. DTS Package Properties dialog box

2. Click the OK button after you've added the variable.

3. From the main DTS design screen, double-click the transformation arrow between Connection 1 and Connection 2. This displays the Data Transformation properties.

4. Select the Transformations tab.

5. Select the Supplier ID field from the Destination table column.

6. Select an empty column from the Source table column on the left. Do not select any of the source fields (Col1, Col2, or Col3) from the Source table column.

7. From the New transformations drop-down box, select ActiveX Script. Select the New button to create a new ActiveX transformation script. The ActiveX Script Transformation Properties dialog box appears, as shown in Figure 13-22.

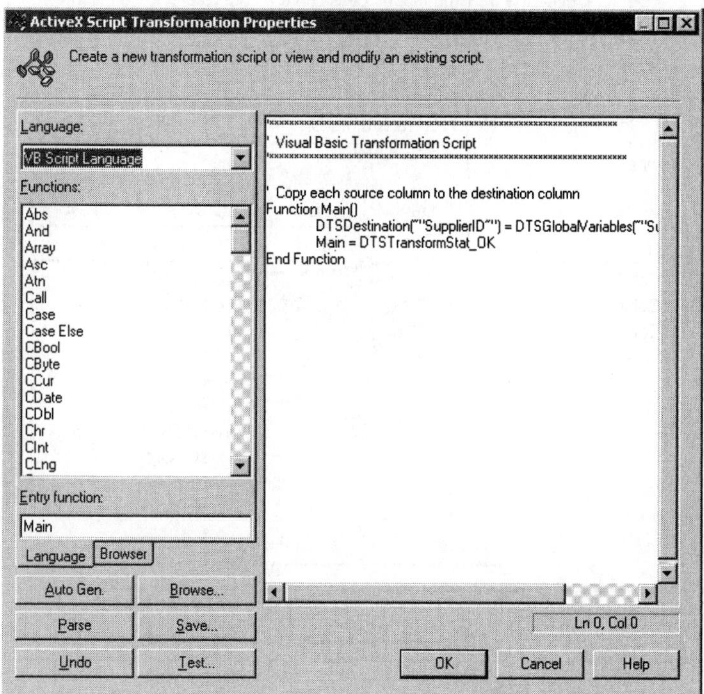

Figure 13-22. ActiveX Script Transformation Properties dialog box

8. Add the following line:

```
DTSDestination("SupplierID") = DTSGlobalVariables("SupplierID").Value
```

Figure 13-22 shows the location of this statement.

This code passes the value stored in the DTS Global variable Supplier ID to the SupplierID field. This value will be set from the WSH script before execution of the package.

9. Click OK to exit the ActiveX Script Transformation Properties dialog box. The Data Transformation Properties dialog box should now display an arrow that is connected to the SupplierID field but not linked to a Source table field, as shown in Figure 13-23.

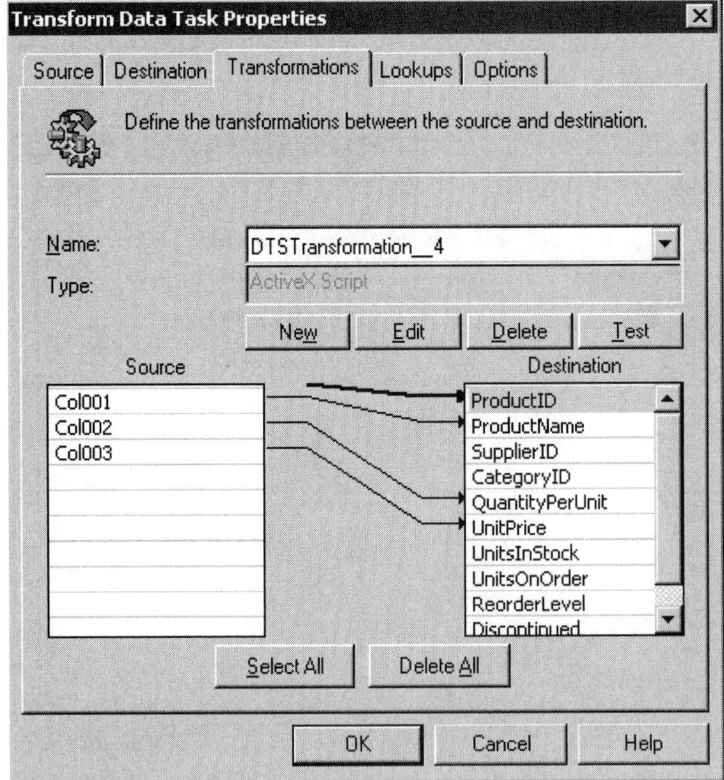

Figure 13-23. Data Transformation Properties dialog box

10. Click OK to exit the Data Transformation Properties dialog box.

11. Save and exit from the package designer screen.

To access the package from WSH, you require DTS COM objects, which are installed with SQL Server. You do not require the SQL Server engine to reside on the machine you are executing the script from. The easiest way to ensure the

COM components are installed is to install the SQL Server Enterprise Manager on the computer you want to execute the script from.

A DTS Package object can be created using the DTS.Package ID. The Package object exposes a number of DTS-related collection properties, such as Connections, Tasks, and Steps.

To load a DTS package, use the Package object's LoadFromSQLServer method. The syntax is as follows:

```
objDTS.LoadFromSQLServer strServer, [strUserID], [strPassword], _
       [nFlag], [strPackagePassword], [strPackageGUID],
        [strVersionGUID],[strPackageName]
```

The parameters for the LoadFromSQLServer method are listed in Table 13-21.

Table 13-21. LoadFromServer *Method Parameters*

PARAMETER	DESCRIPTION
strServer	SQL Server the DTS package resides on.
strUserID	SQL user ID.
strPassword	Password to use for user specified by the SQL user ID.
nFlag	Determines if security access is to be provided by SQL Server–defined user ID and password (the default) or if NT authentication is used. Specify UseTrustedConnection, which has a value of 256, to use NT authentication.
strPackagePassword	Package password.
strPackageGUID	Package identifier—not required if package name is passed.
strVersionGUID	Version identifier if not using the most recent package version.
strPackageName	Name of the package.

The following code snippet shows how to load and execute a DTS. The DTS package is opened and the data source for the text connection is set to the file you want to import. The DTS global variable SupplierID is set to the value for the Tokyo Traders supplier, which is determined from the Northwind Supplier table:

```
Const DTSSQLStgFlag_UseTrustedConnection = 256
Dim objDTS
Set objDTS = CreateObject("DTS.Package")
'open the ProductImport package from the Odin server using NT
```

```
'authentication
objDTS.LoadFromSQLServer "Odin", , , _
            DTSSQLStgFlag_UseTrustedConnection, , , , "ProductImport"

'set the data source for the text connection.
objDTS.Connections("Connection 1").DataSource = "d:\importproducts.txt"

'enable writing of the completion status to event logs
objDTS.WriteCompletionStatusToNTEventLog = True

'set the supplier ID global variable to 4, which is the Tokyo Traders 'supplier
objDTS.GlobalVariables("SupplierID") = 4

objDTS.Execute
```

See Also

Solution 13.1. For more information, read "DTS Package Development, Deployment and Performance" (`http://support.microsoft.com/support/kb/articles/Q242/3/91.ASP`).

13.18 Executing a Stored Procedure

Problem

You want to execute a SQL Server stored procedure and return the result(s) as a Recordset.

Solution

You can create an ADO `Command` object and specify an open `Connection` object to the server you want to execute the stored procedure on. Call the `Execute` method and specify any parameters you want to pass to the procedure.

The following code sample executes the byroyalty stored procedure from the SQL Server Pubs sample database, passing the parameter value of 50:

```
Const adCmdStoredProc = 4
Set objCmd = CreateObject("ADODB.Command")
Set objConn = CreateObject("ADODB.Connection")
' open the pubs data source
```

```
objConn.Open "Provider=SQLOLEDB.1;User ID=sa;Initial Catalog=pubs;Data Source=Odin"

'set the active connection
Set objCmd.ActiveConnection = objConn
'set the stored procedure to execute
objCmd.CommandText = "byroyalty"

'execute the stored procedure, passing parameters to it.
Set objRst = objCmd.Execute(,Array(50), adCmdStoredProc)

'loop through and display the results
While Not objRst.Eof
  Wscript.Echo objRst(0)
  objRst.MoveNext
Wend

objConn.Close
```

Discussion

You can execute a query in Access or a stored procedure in SQL Server to return data. The advantage of using stored procedures or prebuilt queries is performance: They have already been optimized and "compiled," which saves time when they execute.

In addition to performance advantages, database servers may implement security that prevents queries from executing directly against a database's underlying tables, so you may find that performing certain operations against your database server might not be possible. Instead, all access is provided by stored procedures. A number of the advantages of using stored procedures are listed in Table 13-22.

Table 13-22. Advantages of Using Stored Procedures

ADVANTAGE	DESCRIPTION
Security	A database server may be configured to allow no or minimal direct access to the database data.
Performance	Precompiled and optimized stored procedures.
Integrity	Stored procedures can contain logic that performs parameter checking and prevents incorrect data from being added to tables.

A stored procedure can perform anything from simple queries to sophisticated data manipulation. But what if you want to execute a stored procedure on SQL Server that requires a parameter? To pass parameters to the data source, you need to use a Command object.

The Command object allows the execution of commands against your data source. If you don't pass any parameters, it functions much like the Connection object's Execute method.

Before you can execute a Command object, you must first set the ActiveConnection and CommandText properties. Then you can invoke the Command object's Execute method. Unlike the Recordset object's Open method, you cannot pass the connection and query information as parameters to the Execute method. Its syntax is as follows:

```
Set objRecordset = cmd.Execute ([RecordsAffected,] [Parameters,] [Options])
```

The results of the stored procedure are returned as a recordset. When executing action queries and stored procedures that do not return any data, you do not need to return a Recordset:

```
cmd.Execute [RecordsAffectfed,] [Parameters,] [Options]
```

The optional parameters for the Execute method are listed in Table 13-23.

Table 13-23. Execute *Method Parameters*

PARAMETER	TYPE	DESCRIPTION
RecordsAffected	Long	Returns the number of records that the operation affected. This value is returned when delete/update/create operations are performed, but not with SELECT operations.
Parameters	Variant array	An array of parameter values to be used for the CommandText operation.
Options	Long	Specifies how the CommandText property should be evaluated. This is the same as the Command object's Execute method's Options property. See Table 13-9 for parameter values.

The ActiveConnection property defines what data source the Command object is to use. You can pass either an existing Connection object or a valid connection string. The following example uses a Connection object:

```
' open the pubs data source
objConn.Open "Provider=SQLOLEDB.1;User ID=sa;Initial Catalog=pubs;Data Source=Odin"
objConn.ActiveConnection = objConn
```

This example passes a connection string:

```
objConn.ActiveConnection = _
"Provider=SQLOLEDB.1;User ID=sa;Initial Catalog=pubs;Data Source=Odin"
```

The CommandText property defines the command text used to query the data source. This may be a query or a database stored procedure, as illustrated by the following code fragments that assign a value to the CommandText property:

```
objConn.CommandText = "Select * From Suppliers"
objConn.CommandText = "byroyalty" ' SQL Server stored procedure, from Pubs database
objCmd.CommandText = "Select * From Suppliers Where CompanyName = ?"

' Access query from Northwind - note the square brackets,
'this is because of spaces in the query name
objConn.CommandText = "[Ten Most Expensive Products]"
```

You can execute a query or stored procedure that may not return values, such as delete/update/create operations. To return data from a Command object, assign the results of the Execute method to a Recordset object. The Recordset created by the Command object's Execute method is a forward-only, read-only cursor. For example, the following code fragment creates a forward-only, read-only Recordset:

```
objCmd.CommandText = "Select * From Suppliers Where CompanyName = ?"
Set objRst = objCmd.Execute(, Array("Grandma Kelly's Homestead"))
```

See Also

For more information, search http://msdn.microsoft.com for the article "Calling a Stored Procedure with a Command."

13.19 Executing an Access Parameter Query

Problem

You want to execute an Access parameter query and return the results as a Recordset.

Solution

You can create an ADO Command object and set CommandText to the name of the Access query. The name of the query must be in square brackets:

```
Set objCmd = CreateObject("ADODB.Command")
'check if script is run using Wscript or Cscript
   If StrComp(Right(Wscript.Fullname,11),"cscript.exe", vbTextCompare) <>0 Then
Wscript.Echo "This script is best run using Cscript.exe"
    Wscript.Quit
   End If

objCmd.ActiveConnection = "Provider=Microsoft.Jet.OLEDB.4.0;" & _
            "Data Source=D:\data\Access\Samples\Northwind.mdb"
objCmd.CommandText = "[Employee Sales by Country]" 'set the query
'execute the command, passing an array of parameters to it.
Set objRst = objCmd.Execute(, Array(#1/1/1996#, #12/12/1996#))

While Not objRst.EOF
Wscript.Echo objRst("ShippedDate") & " " & objRst("SaleAmount")
objRst.MoveNext
Wend

objRst.Close
```

Discussion

While a great deal of emphasis is put on dedicated database servers and stored procedures, Access is fully capable of using parameter queries. Access queries provide the same performance enhancements as stored procedures: The query is precompiled and optimized in the Access database. It's also a good habit to build parameter queries in the event the database is upsized to a dedicated database server, because the client logic can remain intact while the queries are converted to stored procedures on the database server.

If the query name contains spaces, surround the query in square brackets ([]) or the grave accent character (`), which is ASCII character 96.

To add a parameter to an Access query, create the query in Access and insert the name of the parameter you want to query in square brackets.

Note that ADO 2.0 and Jet 3.51 OLE DB provider do not provide the ability to execute parameter queries. You can do this from either Access ODBC drivers with ADO 2.1 and later and the Jet 4.0 OLE DB provider. The following example creates a parameter query.

1. In the Access Northwind sample database, create the following query, qryListProducts:

```
PARAMETERS category Text, company Text;
SELECT Products.*
FROM Suppliers INNER JOIN (Categories INNER JOIN Products
 ON Categories.CategoryID = Products.CategoryID)
ON Suppliers.SupplierID = Products.SupplierID
WHERE (((Categories.CategoryName)=[category])
AND ((Suppliers.CompanyName)=[company]));
```

2. Save the query as qryListProducts.

The following script will execute the query and return the results to a Recordset:

```
objCmd.ActiveConnection = "Provider=Microsoft.Jet.OLEDB.4.0;" & _
                "Data Source=D:\data\Access\Samples\Northwind.mdb"

objCmd.CommandText = "qryListProducts" 'set the query
'execute the command, passing an array of parameters to it.
Set objRst = objCmd.Execute(, Array("Beverages", "Exotic Liquids"))

While Not objRst.EOF
Wscript.Echo objRst("ProductName") & " " & objRst("Unitprice")
objRst.MoveNext
Wend
objRst.Close
```

See Also

For more information, read "How to Use Parameters with ActiveX Data Objects (ADO) and Jet" (http://support.microsoft.com/?kbid=225897).

13.20 Processing Multiple Recordsets

Problem

You need to access all of the results from a SQL Server query that returns multiple recordsets.

Solution

You can execute the stored procedure against the server and use the `NextRecordset` method to process each Recordset returned.

The following sample uses the reptq3 stored procedure that comes with the SQL Server Pubs sample database:

```
Const adCmdStoredProc = 4
Const adStateClosed = 0
Dim objCmd, objConn, objRst
Set objCmd = CreateObject("ADODB.Command")
Set objConn = CreateObject("ADODB.Connection")

' open the pubs data source
objConn.Open "Provider=SQLOLEDB.1;User ID=sa;Initial
Catalog=pubs;Data Source=Odin"
objCmd.CommandText = "reptq3"

Set objCmd.ActiveConnection = objConn
Set objRst = objCmd.Execute(,Array(0, 1000, "business"), adCmdStoredProc)

'loop through each Recordset
Do While objRst.State <> adStateClosed
 Do While Not objRst.Eof
  Wscript.Echo objRst(0)
  objRst.MoveNext
 Loop
```

```
Set objRst = objRst.NextRecordset
Loop
objConn.Close
```

Discussion

Database server stored procedures offer a great deal of flexibility and power. In the preceding Solution, the reptq3 stored procedure from the Pubs database is executed and returns all titles within a certain price range that are of a certain type. It also returns the number of books for each book type that meets the criteria. This represents two recordsets: One shows all the books for each category that meet the criteria, and the other subtotals the count of the books.

In order to process multiple Recordsets, invoke the `NextRecordset` method to get the next Recordset in the set. Use the Recordset's `State` property to determine when no more Recordsets are available.

See Also

For more information, search `http://msdn.microsoft.com` for the article "Generating Multiple Recordsets."

13.21 Modifying Command Results

Problem

You want to be able to modify the results of a query that is executed through the `Command` object.

Solution

You can use a `Command` object as the source parameter to a RecordSet's `Open` method. Specify an updateable Recordset type when opening the Recordset.

The Solution uses the Ten Most Expensive Products query from the Access Northwind sample database as the source for the `Command` object and updates the price of each record returned by the query by 5 percent:

```
<?xml version="1.0" ?>
<job>
```

```
<reference object="ADODB.Recordset"/>
<!--comment
Script:modifycmd.wsf
modifies the contents of a Command object
-->
 <script language="VBScript">
 Option Explicit
   Dim objCmd, objConn, objRst
    Set objCmd = CreateObject("ADODB.Command")
    Set objConn = CreateObject("ADODB.Connection")
    Set objRst = CreateObject("ADODB.RecordSet")
        'open the Northwind database
    objConn.Open "Provider=Microsoft.Jet.OLEDB.4.0;" & _
                 "Data Source=D:\data\Access\Samples\Northwind.mdb"

    Set objCmd.ActiveConnection = objConn

    objCmd.CommandText = "[Ten Most Expensive Products]"
    objRst.Open objCmd, , adOpenKeyset, adLockOptimistic
        Do While Not objRst.EOF
        objRst("UnitPrice") = objRst("UnitPrice") * 1.05
        objRst.MoveNext
    Loop
    objRst.Close
    objConn.Close
   </script>
</job>
```

Discussion

A Recordset created by the Command object's Execute method is a forward-only, read-only cursor. This is a "cheap" recordset: It offers good performance using low resources, but it doesn't provide much navigational functionality or any ability to modify the data.

To create a more functional recordset, create a Command object and set the appropriate properties, including ActiveConnection and CommandText. Create a Recordset object and invoke its Open method, passing it the Command object as an argument to the Source parameter.

You do not have to set the Connection object for the Recordset object. It will inherit the Connection object from the Command object. Make sure you specify cursor and lock options that allow for adding or updating information in the resulting Recordset.

See Also

For more information, search `http://msdn.microsoft.com` for the article "Open Method (ADO Recordset)."

13.22 Returning a Parameter Value from a Stored Procedure

Problem

You need to execute a stored procedure that returns a value.

Solution

In SQL Server, create a stored procedure under the Pubs database and call it AddNewStore. This procedure will add a new store record to the Stores table in the Pubs database and return the new store ID:

```
CREATE PROCEDURE AddNewStore @StoreName varChar(40), @Address varChar(40),
@City varChar(20),@StoreID integer OUTPUT
AS

DECLARE @newid int
Select @newid=max(stor_ID) from stores
Set @newid = @newid + 1

Insert into stores (stor_id,stor_name,stor_address,city)
Values(@newid,@StoreName,@Address,@city)

Select @StoreID =@newid
```

Executing the following script will create a `Command` object and add parameters to it that will be passed to the stored procedure upon execution. One parameter is created as an output parameter to store a return value from the stored procedure:

```
<?xml version="1.0" ?>
<job>
<reference object="ADODB.Recordset"/>
```

```
<!--comment
Script:retparamvals.wsf
returns parameter values from
-->
 <script language="VBScript">
  Option Explicit
  Dim objCmd, objConn, objRst
  Set objCmd = CreateObject("ADODB.Command")
  Set objConn = CreateObject("ADODB.Connection")
' open the pubs data source
 objConn.Open _
  "Provider=SQLOLEDB.1;User ID=fred;Initial Catalog=pubs;Data Source=Odin"
Set objCmd.ActiveConnection = objConn
    'set the stored procedure name
    objCmd.CommandText = "AddNewStore"
     'add parameters
    objCmd.Parameters.Append objCmd.CreateParameter("@StoreName", _
     adVarChar, , 40, "Store")

    objCmd.Parameters.Append objCmd.CreateParameter("@Address", _
     adVarChar, , 40, "Address")

    objCmd.Parameters.Append objCmd.CreateParameter("@City", _
     adVarChar, , 20, "City")

   ' add the @StoreID parameter as output.
     objCmd.Parameters.Append objCmd.CreateParameter("@StoreID", _
     adInteger, adParamOutput)

   'execute the stored procedure
   objCmd.Execute , , adCmdStoredProc

   ' get the new store ID
   StoreID = objCmd.Parameters("@StoreID")

   objConn.Close
  </script>
</job>
```

Discussion

Parameters can be passed to a stored procedure by calling the Command object's Execute method and passing an array containing parameter values. There are a few drawbacks to calling stored procedures using this method.

- When passing parameters via arrays, the provider has to figure out what data type the parameter being passed is. This is really only a problem where you're executing the Command object multiple times (hundreds or thousands of times) with varying parameter sets.
- Stored procedures can return values, and to get access to returned parameters you must use a Command object. But you cannot return values when using an array to pass parameters.
- When using the Command object as the source for a Recordset object's Open method, you can't pass parameters when opening the recordset.

The Command object has a Parameters collection. This collection contains all parameters passed to the Command object. When you pass an array of parameters to the Command object's Execute method, the Parameter objects are automatically created and added to the Command object's Parameters collection.

To return a value from a stored procedure, declare one of the stored procedure parameters as an output parameter. You can add the parameters to the Parameters collection by calling the Command object's CreateParameter method to create a separate Parameter object and then append it to the Parameters collection. The syntax of the CreateParameter method is as follows:

```
Set objParam =objCmd.CreateParameter([Name],[ Type], [Direction], [Size], [Value])
```

The CreateParameter method returns a Parameter object and takes the optional arguments listed in Table 13-24. The parameter direction types and data types are listed in Table 13-25 and Table 13-26, respectively.

Table 13-24. `Parameter` *Object Arguments*

NAME	STRING	PARAMETER NAME
Type	Long	Data type for the parameter being passed. See Table 13-26 for a list of available types and their corresponding numeric values.
Direction	Long	Parameter "direction." A parameter may be input-only, a return output value, or both. The default is input-only, `adParamInput`. Table 13-25 lists the direction types.
Size	Long	Length of the parameter. This only applies to variable-length data types, such as string values. For fixed-length types, such as numbers and dates, it is not required.
Value	Variant	Value of the parameter.

Table 13-25. Parameter Direction Types

CONSTANT	VALUE	DESCRIPTION
adParamInput	1	Default
adParamOutput	2	Output parameter—return value
adParamInputOutput	3	Can be both an input and output parameter
adParamReturnValue	4	Only returns a value, not used as input

Table 13-26. Parameter Data Types

CONSTANT	VALUE
adBigInt	20
adBinary	128
adBoolean	11
adBSTR	8
adChapter	136
adChar	129
adCurrency	6
adDate	7
adDBDate	133
adDBFileTime	137

Table 13-26. Parameter Data Types (continued)

CONSTANT	VALUE
adDBTime	134
adDBTimeStamp	135
adDecimal	14
adDouble	5
adEmpty	0
adError	10
adFileTime	64
adGUID	72
adIDispatch	9
adInteger	3
adIUnknown	13
adLongVarBinary	205
adLongVarChar	201
adLongVarWChar	203
adNumeric	131
adPropVariant	138
adSingle	4
adSmallInt	2
adTinyInt	16
adUnsignedBigInt	21
adUnsignedInt	19
adUnsignedSmallInt	18
adUnsignedTinyInt	17
adUserDefined	132
adVarBinary	204
adVarChar	200
adVariant	12
adVarNumeric	139
adVarWChar	202
adWChar	130

You can then append the Parameter object to the Parameters collection by calling the latter's Append method and passing it the parameter to be appended to the collection. For example, the following code fragment first creates a Parameter object and then appends it to the Parameters collection:

```
Set objParam = objCmd.CreateParameter("paramname", _
    adVarChar, , 40, "value")
objCmd.Parameters.Append objParam
```

You can also do this in a single step by appending the Parameter directly to the collection:

```
objCmd.Parameters.Append objCmd.CreateParameter("paramname", _
    adVarChar, , 40, "value")
```

One problem when passing parameters to SQL Server stored procedures is knowing exactly what ADO data type to specify. There are a large number of data types available and it can be difficult to know what data type maps to what stored procedure/SQL server type (e.g., Is it adSmallInt, adTinyInt, or adUnsignedTinyInt for a byte?).

The Parameters collection exposes a Refresh method. If a Command object is set to call a SQL Server stored procedure and the Refresh method is called on that object's Parameters collection, the Parameters collection is updated with all the correct parameter information for the stored procedure.

The Refresh method takes the guesswork out of determining the number of parameters to pass and the corresponding data types and lengths. You only need to set the parameters you require. If there are any optional parameters, they do not need to be set. The following code sample performs the same operation as the Solution script:

```
Const adCmdStoredProc = 4
Set objCmd = CreateObject("ADODB.Command")
Set objConn = CreateObject("ADODB.Connection")
'open the pubs data source
 objConn.Open _
  "Provider=SQLOLEDB.1;User ID=fred;Initial Catalog=pubs;Data Source=Odin"

'need to specify the command is a stored procedure
 objCmd.CommandType = adCmdStoredProc
 Set objCmd.ActiveConnection = objConn
'set the stored procedure name
objCmd.CommandText = "AddNewStore"
'refresh the parameters, this will update the Parameters collection
objCmd.Parameters.Refresh
```

```
'set the appropriate parameters
objCmd.Parameters("@StoreName").Value = "Acme Ltd."
objCmd.Parameters("@Address").Value = "123 Main Street"
objCmd.Parameters("@City").Value = "Somewhere"
objCmd.Execute
Wscript.Echo "The store id is" & objCmd.Parameters("@Storeid")
objCmd.ActiveConnection.Close
```

One requirement for the `Refresh` method to work is to specify that the `CommandType` is `adCmdStoredProc`. Parameter values can be read and set using the name specified in the stored procedure.

Unfortunately, using the `Refresh` method to get stored procedure parameters has a slight drawback. It requires an additional call to the server to refresh the `Parameters` collection. If performance is an issue, manually adding the parameters is the best method.

The `Refresh` method can be used to assist the building of these `Parameter` statements, which is demonstrated in the following command-line program, `buildparams.wsf`:

```
<?xml version="1.0" ?>
<job>
<reference object="ADODB.Recordset"/>
<!--comment
Script:buildparams.wsf
Builds Command object parameters from SQL Server stored procedures
-->
 <script language="VBScript" src="adoinc.vbs">
 <![CDATA[
   Option Explicit
   Dim strConn, objConn, objCmd
   If WScript.Arguments.Count <> 2 Then
    WScript.Echo "buildparams builds stored procedures ADO logic" _
       & vbCrLf &  "Syntax:" &  vbCrLf & _
       "buildparams.wsf connection storedproc" &  vbCrLf & _
       "connection Connection string to data source" & vbCrLf & _
       "storedproc stored procedure to build ADO parameter logic"
     Wscript.Quit
   End If

    Set objCmd = CreateObject("ADODB.Command")
    objCmd.ActiveConnection = Wscript.Arguments(0)
    'set stored procedure
    objCmd.CommandText = Wscript.Arguments(1)
```

```
        objCmd.CommandType = adCmdStoredProc
        objCmd.Parameters.Refresh
        BuildCommands objCmd

       Sub BuildCommands(objCmd)
        Dim objParameter, nF, strComm
        For nF = 0 To objCmd.Parameters.Count - 1
         Set objParameter = objCmd.Parameters(nF)
         strComm = "objCmd.Parameters.Append objCmd.CreateParameter(""" _
                    & objParameter.Name & """, " & _
                  GetDataType(objParameter.Type) & ","

           'if not default Direction, add value to statement
           If Not objParameter.Direction = adParamInput Then _
             strComm = strComm & objParameter.Direction

          'check if parameter type is not intput/output or return
          If objParameter.Direction <> adParamInputOutput And _
                objParameter.Direction <> adParamReturnValue Then

             strComm = strComm & ","
             If objParameter.Size > 0 Then
               strComm = strComm & objParameter.Size
             End If

             strComm = strComm & ","
            End If

           strComm = strComm & ")"
          Wscript.Echo strComm
       Next
     End Sub
     ]]>
     </script>
   </job>
```

The buildparams.wsf program requires two parameters: a valid connection string to the source and the name of a stored procedure to build the parameters for. It builds the statements required to build parameters for a Command object. buildparams.wsf uses the adoinc.vbs support library's GetDataType function to return the field type names:

```
'GetDataType
'Returns ADO data type.
'Parameter
'nType  ADO Data type value
'Returns string value representing data type name
Function GetDataType(nType)
 Dim strRet

Select Case nType
 Case 20
  strRet = "adBigInt"
 Case 128
  strRet = "adBinary"
 Case 11
  strRet = "adBoolean"
 Case 8
  strRet = "adBSTR"
 Case 136
  strRet = "adChapter"
 Case 129
  strRet = "adChar"
 Case 6
  strRet = "adCurrency"
 Case 7
  strRet = "adDate"
 Case 133
  strRet = "adDBDate"
 Case 137
  strRet = "adDBFileTime"
 Case 134
  strRet = "adDBTime"
 Case 135
  strRet = "adDBTimeStamp"
 Case 14
  strRet = "adDecimal"
 Case 5
  strRet = "adDouble"
 Case 0
  strRet = "adEmpty"
 Case 10
  strRet = "adError"
 Case 64
  strRet = "adFileTime"
```

```
Case 72
 strRet = "adGUID"
Case 9
 strRet = "adIDispatch"
Case 3
 strRet = "adInteger"
Case 13
 strRet = "adIUnknown"
Case 205
 strRet = "adLongVarBinary"
Case 201
 strRet = "adLongVarChar"
Case 203
 strRet = "adLongVarWChar"
Case 131
 strRet = "adNumeric"
Case 138
 strRet = "adPropVariant"
Case 4
 strRet = "adSingle"
Case 2
 strRet = "adSmallInt"
Case 16
 strRet = "adTinyInt"
Case 21
 strRet = "adUnsignedBigInt"
Case 19
 strRet = "adUnsignedInt"
Case 18
 strRet = "adUnsignedSmallInt"
Case 17
 strRet = "adUnsignedTinyInt"
Case 132
 strRet = "adUserDefined"
Case 204
 strRet = "adVarBinary"
Case 200
 strRet = "adVarChar"
Case 12
 strRet = "adVariant"
Case 139
 strRet = "adVarNumeric"
Case 202
```

```
  strRet = "adVarWChar"
 Case 130
  strRet = "adWChar"
 End Select

 GetDataType = strRet
End Function
```

The following command-line statement would build the parameter code for the AddNewStore stored procedure:

```
buildparams "Provider=SQLOLEDB;User Id=sa;Initial Catalog=pubs;
Data Source=THOR " addnewstore
```

> **NOTE** *The SQL Server provider will return a parameter called* RETURN_VALUE *for any stored procedure, which is not required when calling stored procedures. The* Refresh *method's action of updating the* Parameters *collection is provider specific and does not work with all providers, including the Jet provider.*

Note the following about passing Parameter objects to stored procedures:

- The stored procedure reads the parameters in the order they are added, not alphabetically by parameter name.
- You do not need to create parameter names that mirror the parameter names in the stored procedures you are calling. The parameter name is for reference and readability.

13.23 Transaction Processing

Problem

You want to perform database operations in which you are guaranteed data integrity is maintained during any operation that is performed.

Solution

You can use the Recordset object's BeginTrans and CommitTrans methods to start and complete transactions, and optionally you can use RollbackTrans to "roll back" any transactions.

The Solution script demonstrates the transaction commands by creating a history file from old orders in the Access Northwind sample database. Any order over a certain age is copied to the History tables. The order details are copied from the Order Details table into the Order Details History table, while the order master record is copied from the Orders table into the Orders History table.

Both Orders History and Order Details History do not exist in the Northwind database and must be created by using a copy of the structure from the Orders and Order Details History tables.

The script uses the WSHCB.CopyTable script from Solution 13.17 to copy the data to the History tables:

```
Const adCmdText = 1

Dim objConn
Dim objDestConn, objRst, objCopy, dDate
Set objCopy = CreateObject("ENTWSH.CopyTable")
Set objConn = CreateObject("ADODB.Connection")
Set objDestConn = CreateObject("ADODB.Connection")
Set objRst = CreateObject("ADODB.Recordset")
objConn.Open "Provider=Microsoft.Jet.OLEDB.4.0;" & _
    "Data Source=d:\data\access\samples\Northwind.mdb;"

objDestConn.Open "Provider=Microsoft.Jet.OLEDB.4.0;" & _
    "Data Source=d:\data\access\samples\Northwind.mdb;"
dDate = #1/1/1996#
'start transactions
objConn.BeginTrans
objDestConn.BeginTrans
objCopy.DESTINATION = objDestConn 'set the destination
'first get the order line items
Set objRst = objConn.Execute("SELECT [Order Details].* " & _
                "FROM Orders INNER JOIN [Order Details] ON " & _
                "Orders.OrderID =[Order Details].OrderID " & _
                "WHERE (ShippedDate<#" & dDate & "#)", , adCmdText)

objCopy.SOURCE = objRst
objCopy.Table = "[Order Details History]"
```

```
If Not objCopy.CopyTable() Then
    objConn.RollbackTrans
    objDestConn.RollbackTrans
End If

objConn.Execute "DELETE [Order Details].*, Orders.ShippedDate " & _
    "FROM Orders INNER JOIN [Order Details] ON Orders.OrderID = " & _
    "[Order Details].OrderID " & _
     "WHERE (((Orders.ShippedDate)<#" & dDate & "#));", , adCmdText

'get the details from order master
Set objRst = objConn.Execute("Select * From Orders Where ShippedDate<#" _
            & dDate & "#", , adCmdText)
objCopy.SOURCE = objRst
objCopy.Table = "OrderHist"

If Not objCopy.CopyTable() Then
    Debug.Print objCopy.Error
    objConn.RollbackTrans
    objDestConn.RollbackTrans
    Exit Sub
End If

Set objRst = objConn.Execute("Delete * From Orders Where ShippedDate<#" _
             & dDate & "#", , adCmdText)

objDestConn.CommitTrans
objConn.CommitTrans

objConn.Close
objDestConn.Close
```

Discussion

Transaction processing is a vital part of any mission-critical database system. It guarantees the integrity of data during the data transactions. Transaction processing is crucial especially when operations are performed on more than one table and the state of the tables must balance before and after the operation.

In the Solution, the order detail items are first copied and deleted, and then the order master records are copied and deleted. If the operation aborts before all steps are completed, you are left with tables in an incomplete state.

In this Solution, if there's a failure within any database operations while the data is being archived, the transaction is "rolled back." None of the operations take effect until the `CommitTrans` statements are executed. So if you set a breakpoint in the code halfway through the procedure and view the tables, it will appear as though nothing has actually changed in them.

There is error checking that will catch problems with the data transfer and roll back the data. But there is also a nonexplicit rollback, which guarantees if the database operations are interrupted by a critical failure, such as a power failure, system crash, or act of God, the database will be restored to the state before the transaction was started.

To start a transaction, invoke the `BeginTrans` method on the `Connection` object you want to perform the transaction on. Any operations performed with the `Connection` object, such as creation of recordsets or execution of commands, will be included in the transaction.

If a trappable error occurs during the transaction, the transaction can be rolled back by invoking the `RollbackTrans` method. If a critical system failure such as a power failure occurs, the database(s) in the transaction will be returned to its original state before the beginning of the transaction.

Transaction processing is provider specific. Some providers may not provide support for it.

See Also

For more information, search `http://msdn.microsoft.com` for the article "BeginTrans, CommitTrans, and RollbackTrans Methods."

CHAPTER 14

System Administration

TRADITIONALLY, ADMINISTRATORS have had to resort to system-specific application programming interfaces (APIs) to perform system maintenance—for example, manipulating network resources, user accounts, or mailboxes. Windows provides Win32 APIs to manipulate such resources. These interfaces are generally difficult to use and not directly accessible to scripting environments such as Windows Script Host (WSH).

The introduction of Active Directory Services Interface (ADSI) makes performing administrative tasks in the Windows environment much more accessible as well as easier.

ADSI on its own doesn't perform any system administrative tasks, such as creating a user account, but it provides an interface to directory services. A directory service exposes access to system administrative tasks through directory providers. A few directory providers are listed in Table 14-1.

Table 14-1. Directory Providers

PROVIDER	DESCRIPTION AND AVAILABILITY
WinNT	Windows NT 4.0 and later. Performs user account, group, domain, service, file share, and print queue operations.
LDAP	Exchange server and Windows. Performs user account and Active Directory administration under Windows and Exchange server administration, such as creating mailboxes and distribution lists.
IIS	Internet Information Server. Performs site creation, manipulation, and maintenance.
NWCOMPAT	Novell services.

Each provider, such as WinNT or LDAP, exposes a namespace. A namespace exposes the objects in the provider. A reference to the object must always start with the namespace it resides in, such as `WinNT://` for the Windows NT provider, `LDAP://` for Active Directory and Exchange administration, or `IIS://` for IIS servers.

Though ADSI is used to perform Active Directory operations in a Windows 2000 and later environment, having it installed does not mean you are using

Active Directory. Installing ADSI on Windows NT 4.0 or Windows 9*x*/ME does not provide them with Active Directory capabilities.

To use ADSI on Windows NT 4.0 and 95, you must download and install ADSI. This chapter makes references to the ADSI SDK/Resource kit, which contains valuable references and examples and can be downloaded from `http://www.microsoft.com/NTServer/nts/downloads/other/ADSI25/default.asp`. Select the SDK for Active Directory Services Interfaces 2.5 for download. An extensive ADSI help file is available for download at `http://www.microsoft.com/ntserver/downloads/bin/nts/adsi25.chm`.

The WinNT provider is installed on Windows NT 4.0 and Windows 2000 and later computers. There are operations and information that cannot be performed through LDAP and Active Directory on Windows 2000 and later that can be accessed through the WinNT provider.

> **NOTE** *For more information, refer to the following resources: search* `http://msdn.microsoft.com` *for "ADSI Scripting Primer"; read the article "Manage Directory Resources with Active Directory Services Interface"* (`http://ntmag.com/Articles/Index.cfm?ArticleID=258`)*; and access the Active Directory newsgroup at* `news://microsoft.public.activedirectory.interfaces`.

14.1 Setting Domain Properties

Problem

You want to set the password length for a Windows NT domain.

Solution

You can reference the domain using the WinNT ADSI provider and then set the required properties:

```
Dim objDomain
'get a reference to the Acme domain
Set objDomain = GetObject("WinNT://ACME")
objDomain. MinPasswordLength = 6
objDomain.SetInfo
```

For Active Directory, you can reference the domain using the LDAP provider and set the required properties:

```
Set objDomain = GetObject("LDAP://DC=Acme,DC=COM")
objDomain.minpwdlength = 6
objDomain.SetInfo
```

Discussion

The WinNT provider domain object exposes account policy information, such as password policies.

Use the `GetObject` function to bind to an NT domain object:

```
Set objDomain = GetObject("WinNT://DomainName")
```

`DomainName` represents the name of the Windows NT domain you are binding to. The WinNT provider name is case-sensitive, but object paths are not.

To get a reference to a Windows Active Directory domain object using ADSI, you must reference the domain's distinguished name (DN) using the LDAP provider:

```
Set objDomain = GetObject("LDAP://distinguishedname")
```

A DN is a path to an object, and it is composed of the relative distinguished name (RDN) separated by commas. The RDN is used to identify objects and is composed of the attribute ID (object type) followed by the object's name property. In the case of `dc=Acme`, the attribute is `dc` and the value is `Acme`.

One way of thinking of a DN is as an Internet domain name. For example, `microsoft.com` is a valid Internet DNS address. The DN for a Microsoft domain controller would be `dc=microsoft,dc=com`. The name of the highest level object is at the end of the string.

ADSI requires the `LDAP://` prefix for the DN so it knows what providers to use. The "LDAP" must be uppercase, while the DN is not case sensitive.

To get a reference to the Acme domain, use this code:

```
Set objDomain = GetObject("LDAP://dc=Acme,dc=com")
```

LDAP exposes a `RootDSE` directory service object. This object provides information about the directory services. To get the `RootDSE`, use the following line:

```
Set objRootDSE = GetObject("LDAP://RootDSE")
```

Using the RootDSE, you can automatically find the most available directory server to use. The RootDSE returns a defaultNameContext property, which identifies the name of the current domain:

```
'get a reference to the rootDSE
Set objRootDSE = GetObject("LDAP://RootDSE")
'get the domain
strDomain = objRootDSE.Get("defaultNamingContext")
'get a reference to the domain object
Set objDomain = GetObject("LDAP://" & strDomain)
```

Once you have a bound to a domain object, you can set any of the properties listed in Table 14-2. These properties correspond to the Account Policies option under Windows NT User Manager for NT 4.0 and Domain Group Policies under Windows Active Directory.

Table 14-2. WinNT Provider Domain Object Properties

WINNT PROPERTY	LDAP PROPERTY	DESCRIPTION
MinPasswordLength	minpwdlength	Minimum password length required for user. If 0, then no minimum password length is enforced.
MinPasswordAge	minpwdlength	Minimum time a password must be used before it can be changed. Stored in seconds for the WinNT provider and in nanoseconds for LDAP provider. If 0, a user can change his or her password immediately.
MaxPasswordAge	minPwdAge	The maximum time a password can be used before it expires and must be changed. Stored in seconds for the WinNT provider and in 100 nanosecond intervals for the LDAP provider. If 0, the password never expires.

Table 14-2. WinNT Provider Domain Object Properties (continued)

WINNT PROPERTY	LDAP PROPERTY	DESCRIPTION
MaxBadPasswordsAllowed	lockoutthreshold	Number of bad passwords that can be entered before the account is locked out.
PasswordHistoryLength	pwdhistorylength	Number of unique passwords a user must change before reusing a password. The maximum value is 24 passwords. If 0, no password history is kept.
AutoUnlockInterval	lockoutDuration	If the number of bad passwords a user enters exceeds the value set by MaxBadPasswordsAllowed, the user is "locked out" for the duration defined by AutoUnlockInterval. Stored in seconds for the WinNT provider and in 100 nanosecond intervals for the LDAP provider. If 0, the user account must be unlocked by an administrator.
LockoutObservationInterval	LockoutObservationWindow	Time that will elapse before the bad password counter is reset. Stored in seconds for the WinNT provider and in 100 nanosecond intervals for the LDAP provider.

The LDAP provider stores some of the time-related properties in 100 nanosecond intervals. One nanosecond is 10^–9, an almost immeasurably small number. One second in this format would be stored as 10000000. To complicate any time intervals over 6 minutes, create large numbers. A time interval of 500 seconds would represent over 5 billion nanoseconds. A long integer 32-bit value can store only a little more than 4 billion.

To solve this problem, the time intervals are stored in a 64-bit format known as *Int8*, which represents eight 8-bit numbers. Int8 values are actually stored as objects, so if you attempt to read an Int8 object property, you will get an error. The following example will return an error:

```
Wscript.Echo "Min domain password age:" & objDom.minPwdAge
```

The Int8 object stores two properties, `HighPart` and `LowPart`. `HighPart` represents the upper 32 bits, and `LowPart` stores the lower 32 bits of the 64-bit value. To get the 64-bit value from this, multiply the `HighPart` value by 2×32 and add `LowPart`. The following function `ConvToSeconds` converts an Int8 value to seconds:

```
Function ConvToSeconds(objTime)
Dim nLow

'get the lower 32 bits
nLow = objTime.LowPart
'if negative value add 2x32 to low value
If nLow < 0 Then
    nLow = nLow + 2 x 32
End If

ConvToSeconds = CDbl((objTime.HighPart * 2 x 32) + _
                      nLow) / CDbl(-10000000)
End Function
```

The function corrects an anomaly with the Int8 properties. The `LowPart` and `HighPart` properties return a signed long integer, which has a range of –2147483647 to 2147483648. Any values above 2147483648 are stored as the value minus 2×32. So 3 billion would be stored as the signed long integer value of –1294967296. If the `LowPart` property is less than 0, which indicates it is a large value, it is corrected by adding 2×32.

```
'list domain properties for LDAP and WinNT ADSI providers
Set objDom = GetObject("WinNT://Acme")
Set objDom2 = GetObject("LDAP://DC=Acme,DC=COM")

Wscript.Echo "Min password length " & objDom.MinPasswordLength & _
             " " & objDom2.minpwdlength
Wscript.Echo "Min password age " & objDom.MinPasswordAge & _
             " " & ConvToSeconds(objDom2.minPwdAge)
Wscript.Echo "Max password length " & objDom.MaxPasswordAge & _
             " " & ConvToSeconds(objDom2.maxPwdAge)
Wscript.Echo objDom.MaxBadPasswordsAllowed & _
             " " & objDom2.lockoutthreshold
```

```
Wscript.Echo objDom.PasswordHistoryLength & _
             " " & objDom2.pwdhistorylength
Wscript.Echo objDom.AutoUnlockInterval & _
             " " & ConvToSeconds(objDom2.lockoutDuration)
Wscript.Echo objDom.LockoutObservationInterval & _
             " " & ConvToSeconds(objDom2.LockoutObservationWindow
```

When any properties have been changed, you must invoke the domain object's SetInfo method for any of the changes to take effect.

To get a reference to a Windows domain object using ADSI, you must reference the domain's distinguished name (DN) using the Lightweight Directory Access Protocol (LDAP) provider:

```
Set objDomain = GetObject("LDAP://distinguishedname")
```

A DN is a path to an object, and it is composed of the relative distinguished name (RDN) separated by commas. The RDN is used to identify objects and is composed of the attribute ID (object type) followed by the object's name property. In the case of `dc=Acme`, the attribute is `dc` and the value is `Acme`.

One way of thinking of a DN is as an Internet domain name. For example, `microsoft.com` is a valid Internet DNS address. The DN for a Microsoft domain controller would be `dc=microsoft,dc=com`. The name of the highest level object is at the end of the string.

ADSI requires the `LDAP://` prefix for the DN so it knows what providers to use. The LDAP must be uppercase, while the DN is not case-sensitive.

To get a reference to the Acme domain, use this code:

```
Set objDomain = GetObject("LDAP://dc=Acme,dc=com")
```

LDAP exposes a `RootDSE` directory service object. This object provides information about the directory services. To get the `RootDSE`, use the following line:

```
Set objRootDSE = GetObject("LDAP://RootDSE")
```

Using the `RootDSE`, you can automatically find the most available directory server to use. The `RootDSE` returns a `defaultNameContext` property, which identifies the name of the current domain:

```
Dim objRootDSE, objDomain, strDomain
'get a reference to the rootDSE
Set objRootDSE = GetObject("LDAP://RootDSE")
'get the domain
strDomain = objRootDSE.Get("defaultNamingContext")
'get a reference to the domain object
Set objDomain = GetObject("LDAP://" & strDomain)
```

Windows 2000 and later implements the WinNT and LDAP providers, but only the WinNT provider is available to Windows NT 4.0. Windows NT 4.0 requires ADSI to be installed separately.

You can use the WinNT provider under Active Directory domains to read and set properties. In some instances, such as with the time-related properties `MinPasswordAge` and `MaxPasswordAge`, it's easier to use the WinNT provider to read and set values. The following sample sets the lockout interval to 40 minutes using the LDAP and WinNT providers under an Active Directory domain:

```
'set unlock interval to 40 minutes (2400 seconds)
Set objDom = GetObject("WinNT://Acme")
objDom.AutoUnlockInterval = 2400
objDom.SetInfo

'set unlock interval to 40 minutes (2400000000000 nano-seconds)
Set objDom = GetObject("LDAP://DC=Acme,DC=COM")
objDom.lockoutDuration.LowPart = 1769803776
objDom.lockoutDuration.HighPart = -6
objDom.SetInfo
```

Corresponding objects exposed by the different providers are not guaranteed to expose the same properties, so in the case of domain information for the LDAP and WinNT providers, the properties implemented are different.

See Also

Search the ADSI SDK for the topic "binding." For more information, search `http://msdn.microsoft.com` for "ADSI Scripting Tutorial, Binding."

14.2 Determining a Computer's OS

Problem

You want to determine a computer's OS.

Solution

You can reference an ADSI computer object using the WinNT provider and then reference the `OperatingSystem` property:

```
Set objComputer = GetObject("WinNT://odin,computer")
strOS = objComputer.OperatingSystem
```

Discussion

The Computer object represents an individual computer on your network. To get a reference to a computer object:

```
Set objComputer = GetObject("WinNT://computername,computer")
```

computername represents the name assigned to the computer. The ,computer that follows the computer name is optional, but it speeds the resolving of the object.

Table 14-3 lists the properties associated with the Computer object. These properties are read-only.

Table 14-3. Computer *Object Properties*

PROPERTY	DESCRIPTION
Owner	Name of individual/organization the OS was registered to.
Division	Name of individual/company the OS was registered to.
OperatingSystem	Operating system name (e.g., Windows NT).
OperatingSystemVersion	OS version (e.g., 4.0, 5.0).
Processor	Processor description (e.g., x86 Family 6 Model 5 Stepping 2). Doesn't directly correspond to a chip model such as Pentium II.
ProcessorCount	Number of processors (if supported).

To get a reference to a computer using the LDAP provider and Active Directory, use the following line:

```
Set objComputer = GetObject("LDAP://ComputerName")
```

The computer object returned by the LDAP provider exposes only the OperatingSystem and OperatingSystemVersion properties, but none of the other properties the WinNT provider does. However, because Windows 2000 and later implement the WinNT provider as well as the LDAP provider, this doesn't matter.

See Also

For more information, search http://msdn.microsoft.com for the articles "ADSI Scripting Tutorial, Binding" and "Provider Support of ADSI Interfaces."

14.3 Listing Users

Problem

You want to list all users from a computer or domain.

Solution

You can bind to a WinNT domain or computer object and then set the `Filter` property, filtering on the `User` class:

```
Dim objDomain, objUser

'get a reference to a domain ojbect
Set objDomain = GetObject("WinNT://Acme")
'filter on the user objects
objDomain.Filter = Array("user")
For Each objUser In objDomain
   Wscript.Echo objUser.Name
Next
```

Discussion

You can use the `Filter` property to filter ADSI objects. The property takes an array of class names, which allows for multiple class values to be specified. In the following example, all users and groups for the Acme domain are counted:

```
Set objDomain = GetObject("WinNT://Acme")
'filter on the user and group objects
objDomain.Filter = Array("user", "group")
For Each obj In objDomain
   Wscript.Echo obj.Name
Next
```

The class names specified in the array are not case-sensitive.

If the filter not is set, enumerating a computer or domain container object will return all objects in the container. This can be useful to determine all objects in that container.

```
'list all objects in the Acme domain and their type
Set objDomain = GetObject("WinNT://Acme")
```

```
'loop through each object, listing the name and object class
For Each obj In objDomain
   Wscript.Echo obj.Name, obj.Class
Next
```

Filters can be set on Active Directory container objects in exactly the same way as WinNT:

```
'list all users in the Users container
Set objCN = GetObject("LDAP://cn=Users,DC=acme,DC=com")
objCN.Filter=Array("User")

For Each obj In objCN
 Wscript.Echo obj.Name
Next
```

When an Active Directory container is enumerated, no attempt is made to enumerate subcontainers. In the following example, a reference is made to the container for the domain object for `Acme.com` and the `user` class is enumerated:

```
'list all users in the Users container
Set objCN = GetObject("LDAP://DC=acme,DC=com")
objCN.Filter=Array("User")

For Each obj In objCN
 Wscript.Echo obj.Name
Next
```

In this example, you would assume that all users belonging to the Acme domain would be listed, but only user objects from the domain container (and usually there shouldn't be any) will be listed. None of the containers below the domain container, such as the Users container, will be searched. Solution 14.16 provides a method of querying Active Directory containers using ADO.

You can use the WinNT provider to list all users in an Active Directory domain. The earlier example listing all users from the Windows NT 4.0 Acme domain would display all users from the corresponding Active Directory domain, but you would not be able to manipulate the native Active Directory object.

See Also

Solution 14.16. For more information, search `http://msdn.microsoft.com` for the article "Listing Users."

14.4 Creating a New User

Problem

You want to create a new user.

Solution

Using the WinNT provider, get an instance of a domain or computer object where you want to create a new user and invoke the `Create` method:

```
'bind to a domain
Set objDomain = GetObject("WinNT://ACME")
'create a new user - Fred Smith
Set objUser = objDomain.Create("User", "FredS")
objUser.SetPassword("iu12yt09")
objUser.SetInfo
```

Discussion

To create a new user with the WinNT provider, you first need to reference the domain or computer object in which you want to create the user.

Then invoke the object's `Create` method, specifying the `User` class as the object you want to create. When creating a user, you must be logged on with the appropriate administrative security level to create and manipulate user objects. The syntax is as follows:

```
Set objUser = objContainer.Create("User", strUserName)
```

`strUserName` represents the user name that is used to log on. The `objContainer` object represents the domain or computer in which you want to create the user.

Once the user has been created, invoke the object's `SetInfo` method to save the changes. No additional properties need be set once a new user has been created using the WinNT provider.

The solution demonstrates the `SetPassword` method. The `SetPassword` method sets the password for the current user object:

```
objUser.SetPasswordstrPassword
```

The `strPassword` parameter is the password you want to set for the user.

Creating an Active Directory user using the LDAP provider under Windows 2000 and later requires a similar procedure as using the WinNT provider:

```
'bind to the container to add user to. In this example the acme domain.
Set objContainer = GetObject("LDAP://cn=Users,dc=acme,dc=com")
Set objUser = objContainer.Create("User", "cn=Fred Smith ")
objUser.Put "samAccountName", "freds"
objUser.SetInfo

objUser.pwdLastSet = -1
objUser.SetPassword "we12oi90"
objUser.AccountDisabled = False

objUser.SetInfo
```

First, a reference to a container is required. Under Windows NT all users were added to a single list, essentially a single large container. Active Directory allows additional containers to be created to organize users. The commonly used container to perform this task is the organizational unit.

Windows Active Directory provides organizational units to organize objects into logical groupings. For example, users could be organized by departments, so you could create an organizational unit for accounting, finance, marketing, and so on.

To create an organizational unit, get a reference to the parent container, which is the container where the organizational unit will reside.

Then call the `Create` method, specifying `organizationalUnit` as the object class to be created followed by the organizational name in RDN format:

```
Set objCN = GetObject("LDAP://ou=Accounting,DC=Acme,DC=com")
Set objOU = objCN.Create("organizationalUnit","ou=Accounting")
```

To get a reference to a given organizational unit, you must specify the organizational unit name together with full domain DN:

```
'get a reference to account organizational unit container
Set objContainer = GetObject("LDAP://ou=accounting,dc=acme,dc=com")
```

Organizational units can be nested, allowing even greater organizational granularity:

```
Set objCN = GetObject("LDAP://ou=Accounting,DC=Acme,DC=com")
Set objOU = objCN.Create("organizationalUnit","ou=Taxation")
```

Users and groups can be created in organizational units. Organizational units may seem like a different way of creating a user group, but they allow for control of administrative delegation. For example, a user in the accounting department could be granted access to administer users in the accounting organizational unit, but nowhere else.

The Users container is a built-in container Windows 2000 and later provides for Windows NT 4.0 user compatibility. If you did not specify a specific container in the user string, the user would have been created at the root of the Active Directory domain tree. This is a perfectly valid, but not very logical place, to put users.

The LDAP user name specified for the `Create` method is a bit more involved than the user name specified for the WinNT provider. In the previous code snippet, `cn=Fred Smith` indicates the user name is Fred Smith.

The following example gets a reference to the Accounting organizational unit (OU) container and adds a user to it:

```
Set objContainer = GetObject("LDAP://OU=Accounting,DC=acme,DC=com")

Set objUser = objContainer.Create("User", "CN=Fred Smith")
objUser.Put "samAccountName", "freds"
objUser.SetInfo
```

The user name (Fred Smith) is not used to identify the person when logging on. The `samAccountName` property that is set after the creation of the user is used to identify the user when logging on, and it must be set when creating a new Active Directory user.

The `samAccountName` property represents the user ID that non–Windows 2000 and later clients (Windows 9*x*/ME, Windows NT) would use to log on. Windows 2000 and later uses this ID in NT domain or mixed-mode authentication, in a Windows Active Directory–only environment, Windows Active Directory clients would use a user principal name (UPN).

A UPN user ID looks like an Internet e-mail address. If not set, the UPN is created using the `samAccountName` property followed by the at sign (@) and an Internet-style fully qualified domain name representing the organizational domain. So in the previous example, the UPN for Fred Smith would be `freds@acme.com`.

You can set an alternative UPN for a user by setting the `userPrincipalName` property:

```
Set objContainer = GetObject("LDAP://OU=Accounting,DC=acme,DC=com")

Set objUser = objContainer.Create("User", "CN=Fred Smith")
objUser.Put "samAccountName", "freds"
objUser.Put "userPrincipalname", "fredsmith@acme.com"

objUser.SetInfo
```

See Also

For more information, search http://msdn.microsoft.com for the article "ADSI Scripting Tutorial, Binding."

14.5 Listing Object Properties

Problem

You want to list properties that are associated with an object and their corresponding set values.

Solution

You can bind to any instance of an ADSI object and then reference the Schema property. Enumerate the MandatoryProperties and OptionalProperties collections.

The following command-line script takes the path to an ADSI object (for any ADSI provider) and enumerates the mandatory and optional properties for the object:

```
'listprop.vbs
'lists schema properties for specified object
Dim objClass,varAttrib, aval, objObject, strLine
On Error Resume Next

 If Wscript.Arguments.Count <> 1 Then     ShowUsage
   Wscript.Quit
 End If

 'get the object
 Set objObject = GetObject(Wscript.Arguments (0))
If Err Then
  Wscript.Echo "Unable to get object " & Wscript.Arguments (0)
  Wscript.Quit
 End If

 Set objClass = GetObject(objObject.Schema)
 Wscript.Echo "Mandatory Attributes: "

 For Each varAttrib In objClass.MandatoryProperties
  strLine = "    " & varAttrib
```

```
        If IsArray(objObject.Get(varAttrib)) Then
            If Not Err Then
             For Each aval In objObject.Get(varAttrib)
                varAttrib = varAttrib & "," & aval
             Next
            End If
        Else
            strLine = strLine & " " & objObject.Get(varAttrib)
        End If
        If Err Then strLine = strLine & " No value"
Err.Clear
        Wscript.Echo strLine
 Next

 Wscript.Echo "Optional Attributes: "
 For Each varAttrib In objClass.OptionalProperties
   strLine = "    " & varAttrib
   objObject.GetInfoEx Array(varAttrib), 0
   'check if object is an array
    If IsArray(objObject.Get(varAttrib)) Then
        If Not Err Then
         For Each aval In objObject.Get(varAttrib)
            strLine = strLine & "," & aval
         Next
        End If
    Else
        strLine = strLine & " " & objObject.Get(varAttrib)
    End If
        If Err Then strLine = strLine & " No value"
    Err.Clear
  Wscript.Echo strLine
 Next

Sub ShowUsage
  WScript.Echo "listprop list properties for specified object" _
    & vbCrLf &  "Syntax:" &  vbCrLf & _
    "listprop.vbs objectpath" &  vbCrLf & _
     "objectpath Path to " & vbCrLf & _
     "Example: List details about computer Odin" & vbCrLf & _
     "listprop WinNT://Odin,computer"
End Sub
```

Discussion

The tables throughout this chapter list a number of important properties related to the various ADSI objects. However, there are literally hundreds of properties that are not listed here. And as a result of the extensible nature of Active Directory, additional attribute properties may be added to an object.

The class schema determines what objects and properties are exposed through the object. For each object, there may be many more properties than the ones that can be set using management applications for the underlying directory store, such as User Manager for Windows NT 4.0.

To get a reference to the schema, reference the `Schema` property of any given ADSI object.

The `Schema` object contains two properties that list the properties associated with the object: `MandatoryProperties` and `OptionalProperties`.

The `MandatoryProperties` property is a collection that stores the properties required to make the object functional.

The `OptionalProperties` property is a collection that stores the optional properties. This might not be always totally accurate, because there may be optional properties that are required to be set before an object is made functional.

To list the associated properties, you must get a reference to an object's schema:

```
'get an ADSI object
Set objClass = GetObject(strPath)
'get the schema for the object
Set objClass = GetObject(objObject.Schema)
```

Once you have the schema, you can enumerate the `MandatoryProperties` and `OptionalProperties` collections. They contain the name of each property.

Enumerating the `OptionalProperties` and `MandatoryProperties` collections lists all properties associated with an object. If you just need to list properties that contain values, use the object's `PropertyCount` property, which returns the number of set properties for an object.

The `PropertyCount` property returns the count for all properties that have been loaded into the cache. To ensure it gives an accurate count of properties, call the `GetInfo` method before using `PropertyCount`. The following script lists all set properties for the user freds:

```
Set objUser = GetObject("WinNT://Acme/freds,user")
objUser.GetInfo
For nF = 0 To objUser.PropertyCount - 1
    Wscript.Echo objUser.Item(nF).Name
Next
```

The solution lists all properties for a given ADSI path:

```
listprop ADSIpath
```

`ADSIpath` is the path to any ADSI object, so use the following line to list all properties for the computer Odin using the WinNT provider:

```
listprop WinNT://Odin,computer
```

If the ADSI path contains spaces, it must be surrounded by double quotes:

```
listprop "LDAP://CN=Fred Smith,OU=Accounting,DC=Acme,DC=com"
```

With the `listprop` command-line utility, you can easily determine all properties associated with an object. One way of determining what property is associated with a field in a management interface (such as User Manager or the Active Directory snap-in under Windows 2000 and later) is to fill in all of the fields with easily distinguishable values and then run `listprop` against the object.

See Also

For more information, search `http://msdn.microsoft.com` for the article "Modifying User Properties."

14.6 Setting Object Properties

Problem

You want to set user properties.

Solution

You can use the `dot` or `Put` method to set values.

The following sample sets the name and description properties for an NT user:

```
'get a reference to user
Set objUser = GetObject("WinNT://Acme/freds,user")
'set fullname and description properties
objUser.FullName = "Fred Smith"
```

```
objUser.Put "Description", "Accounting Manager"
objUser.SetInfo
```

Discussion

To set a property, use the dot method:

```
objUser.Property = Value
```

Alternatively, you can use the Put method to assign properties:

```
objUser.Put strProperty, value
```

strProperty represents the property name and value is the value to assign to the property.

When an object is bound, it is cached locally. When a property is read or set, the property values for the object are loaded into the local cache. Changing a property value updates the local cached copy of the object but not the underlying directory object.

Use the SetInfo method to update the underlying directory store, such as Windows NT security database, Windows Active Directory, Exchange server, and so on. Any changes to properties do not take effect until SetInfo is invoked:

```
'get a reference to user
Set objUser = GetObject("WinNT://Acme/freds,user")
'set fullname and description properties
objUser.FullName = "Fred Smith"
objUser.Put "Description", "Accounting Manager"
objUser.SetInfo
```

If you are setting a large number of properties, you should call SetInfo once after all the properties have been set instead of calling it after every single property has been set to limit traffic to the underlying directory store.

To get an object's property, use either the Get or dot method:

```
'get a reference to user
Set objUser = GetObject("WinNT://Acme/freds,user")
'read description using Get and dot method
Wscript.Echo objUser.Description
Wscript.Echo objUser.Get "Description"
```

Some properties do not automatically load into the ADSI cache, and when you reference a property it doesn't reflect any changes made by other uses since the object was created. The `GetInfo` method forces the reload of the cache:

```
objObject.GetInfo
```

Some properties fail to load even after using `GetInfo` and require the `GetInfoEx` method to read the information. The `GetInfoEx` method requires you to specify the properties you are attempting to reference:

```
objMailbox.GetInfoEx aProperties, nValue
```

The `aProperties` parameter is an array of property names you want to load. The `nValue` parameter is currently not used and must be set to 0.

```
Set objUser = GetObject("WinNT://Acme/freds,user")
objUser.GetInfoEx Array("Description"), 0
```

Unfortunately, there are no rules as to what properties require the `GetInfo` or `GetInfoEx` methods to load information.

Table 14-4 lists properties available through the WinNT provider.

Table 14-4. Windows NT `User` *Object Properties*

PROPERTY	DESCRIPTION
`AccountDisabled`	Boolean. Determines if the user account is disabled.
`AccountExpirationDate`	Date the account will expire. To disable account expiration date, set the property to `Empty`.
`BadPasswordAttempts`	Number of unsuccessful logon attempts.
`Description`	Account description.
`Fullname`	Full name of the user.
`HomeDirDrive`	Directory letter to associate with the user's home directory (e.g., `H:`).
`HomeDirectory`	User's home directory. If set to network share using UNC format, the network home directory is assumed and the `HomeDirDrive` property is required to be assigned a directory. If set to a local directory (e.g., `d:\data`), the `HomeDirDrive` setting is ignored.

Table 14-4. Windows NT `User` *Object Properties (continued)*

PROPERTY	DESCRIPTION
`IsAccountLocked`	Boolean. If the account becomes locked out due to login failure, this flag is set to `True`. An account cannot be manually locked out by setting this value (the value cannot be set to `True`). To unlock an account, set the property to `False`.
`LastLogin`	Date and time of last login. Read-only.
`LastLogoff`	Date and time of last logoff. Read-only.
`LoginHours`	Array of bytes. Hours a user is allowed to log in. See Solution 14.9 for how to set hours.
`LoginScript`	Name of the logon script/batch file to execute upon logon.
`LoginWorkstations`	Array of string values. Determines what machine a user can log on to. See Solution 14.10 for how to set the `LoginWorkstations` property.
`PasswordExpired`	Indicates if the user's password has expired. If set to 1, the password is flagged as expired and the user must change his or her password at next logon. This is the same as the "User Must Change Password at Next logon" flag under in the Windows NT User Manager.
`PasswordExpirationDate`	Date and time of password expiration. Read-only, cannot be changed.
`Profile`	Path to the directory where profile information is stored.
`UserFlags`	Integer. Combination of bitwise OR-ed values that determine options such as account status and password limitations. See Solution 14.11.

If you examine the ADSI `User` object using an object browser as shown in Figure 14-1, you will notice that more properties are available than listed in Table 14-4.

Some properties, such as `EmployeeID`, cannot be set under NT 4.0 using administrative tools such as User Manager. This is a result of the fact that the ADSI `User` object contains generic properties that might be applicable to users in other providers. So while it may seem as if there are more properties available than the provider exposes, they cannot all be used.

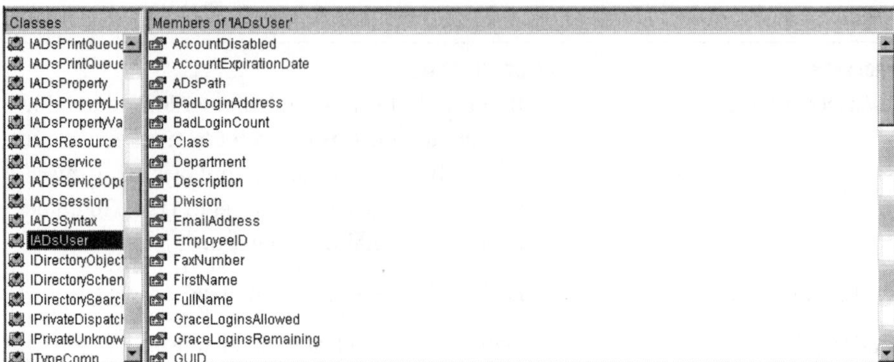

Figure 14-1. Active Directory Object Browser

When you work with properties, make sure the program has error handling (`On Error Resume Next`) enabled to catch any errors. Some properties are not set until certain operations take place, and referencing the property may generate an error because it doesn't exist in the cache for the object. For example, the `User` object does not set the `LastLogin` property until a user has logged on for the first time. Properties that are not set usually do not contain values to identify them as being empty, such as a Null or Empty value, so it is not easy to test for these conditions.

One way to determine the properties associated with directory objects is to use a directory browser application. This kind of application allows you to view, and in some cases set, values associated with directory objects.

The Windows 2000 and 2003 installation CDs include a utility called ADSIEdit. It is not installed with Windows 2000 or 2003 but it is included as part of a support tools installation located under the `support\tools` directory of the Windows installation CD.

The ADSI 2.5 SDK Resource Kit contains two visual browsers: Active Directory Browser and DSBrowse. The Active Directory Browser can browse any object and lists associated properties. You can download the ADSI SDK from `http://www.microsoft.com/NTServer/nts/downloads/other/ADSI25/default.asp`. Select the SDK for Active Directory Services Interfaces 2.5.

The Active Directory Browser is located under the `ADSI SDK\AdsVW\i386` directory, while DSBrowse is located under `ADSI SDK\Samples\General\DSbrowse`. Figure 14-2 shows a screen shot of the Active Directory Browser.

The Active Directory provider exposes more properties than the WinNT provider because there is much more information that can be stored in Windows Active Directory for each account:

```
'get a reference to a user object
Set objUser = GetObject("LDAP://CN=Fred Smith,OU=Accounting,DC=acme,DC=com")
'set a property
objUser.Put "samAccountName", "freds"
objUser.SetInfo
```

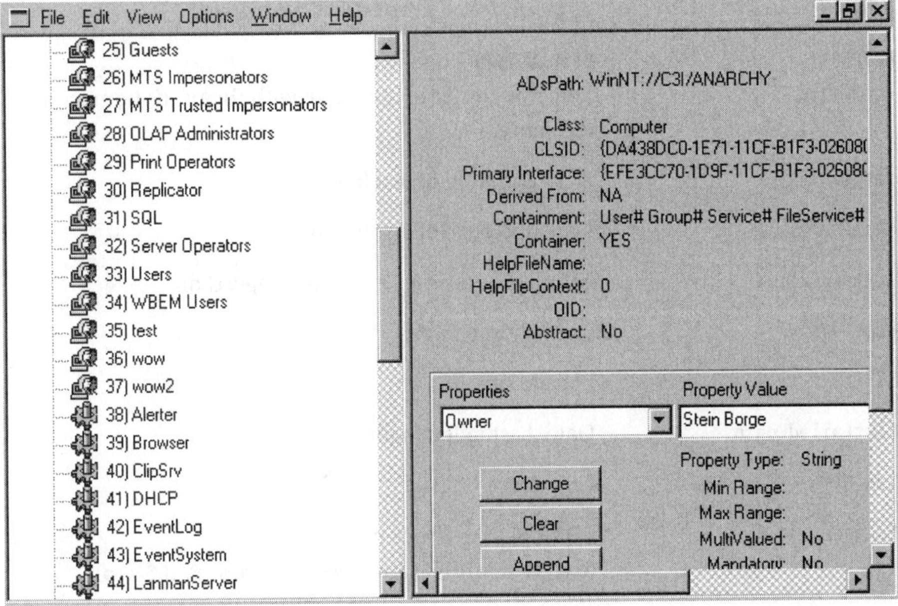

Figure 14-2. Active Directory Browser

Table 14-5 lists a number of Windows 2000 Active Directory properties.

Table 14-5. Active Directory Provider User Properties

PROPERTY	DESCRIPTION
`AccountExpirationDate`	Date the account will expire.
`BadLoginCount/badPwdCount`	Number of bad passwords.
`BadPasswordTime`	Date and time of last unsuccessful logon attempt. Stored in format.
`c`	Country code (e.g., US).
`Department`	User's department.
`Description`	Description.
`DisplayName`	Display name.
`Division`	Company division.
`EmailAddress/mail`	E-mail address.
`EmployeeID`	Employee ID.
`FaxNumber`	Fax number.
`FirstName`	User's first name.

continues

Table 14-5. Active Directory Provider User Properties (continued)

PROPERTY	DESCRIPTION
`HomeDrive`	Directory letter to associate with the user's home directory.
`LastLogin`	Date and time of last login.
`LastLogoff`	Date and time of last logoff.
`logonCount`	Number of times the user has logged on.
`HomePage`	User's home page.
`L`	Locale/city.
`LastFailedLogin`	Date. Last failed logon.
`LastName`	Last name.
`Manager`	LDAP path to user's manager (e.g., `CN=Administrator,CN=Users,DC=Acme,DC=com`).
`NamePrefix`	Name prefix (e.g., Mr.).
`Notes/Comment`	User notes.
`OfficeLocations`	Office address.
`PasswordLastChanged`	Date and time password last changed.
`PostalAddress`	User's address.
`PostOfficeBox`	User's post office box.
`PostalCode`	Postal code.
`Pwdlastset`	Date and time of last password change. Stored in INT8 format.
`Sn`	Surname.
`St`	State.
`StreetAddress`	Address property.
`TelephoneHome`	Home phone number.
`TelephoneMobile`	Mobile phone number.
`TelephoneNumber`	Mobile phone number.
`TelephonePager`	Pager number.
`Title`	Employee title.
`userSharedFolder`	User shared document folder.

Table 14-5. Active Directory Provider User Properties (continued)

PROPERTY	DESCRIPTION
`UserAccountControl`	Integer. Combination of bitwise OR-ed values that determine options such as account status and password limitations. See Solution 14.11 later in chapter. Same as the WinNT provider's `UserFlags` property.

A number of LDAP user object properties (`Pwdlastset` and `BadPasswordTime`) are stored as an `INT8` object, which represents a 64-bit value. The INT8 object stores two properties, `HighPart` and `LowPart`. `HighPart` represents the upper 32 bits, and `LowPart` stores the lower 32 bits of the 64-bit value. To get the 64-bit value from this INT8 object, multiply the `HighPart` value by 2^32 and add `LowPart`.

Many of the INT8 properties represent dates. To get the correct date, divide the 64-bit INT8 value by 864000000000. This represents the number of days since January 1, 1601.

The following `ConvToDate` function converts an INT8 object to a date:

```
Function ConvToDate(objTime)

ConvToDate = #1/1/1601# + ((objTime.HighPart * 2 ^ 32) + _
                    objTime.LowPart) / 864000000000

End Function
```

The parameter `objTime` represents an INT8 time object property, such as `Pwdlastset` or `BadPasswordTime`.

```
Set objUser = GetObject("LDAP://cn=Fred Smith,cn=Users,DC=Acme,DC=COM")

Wscript.Echo "Last login " & objUser.LastLogin
Wscript.Echo "Account expires " & objUser.AccountExpirationDate
Wscript.Echo "Password last set " & _
                ConvToDate(objUser.pwdlastset)
Wscript.Echo "Last bad password attempt " & _
                ConvToDate(objUser.badPasswordTime)


Function ConvToDate(objTime)
 ConvToDate = #1/1/1601# + ((objTime.HighPart * 2 ^ 32) + _
                    objTime.LowPart) / 864000000000
End Function
```

The `usermnt.wsf` script is a command-line utility that provides the ability to create or update users using the Windows NT ADSI provider:

```
<?xml version="1.0" ?>
<job>
<!--comment
Script:usermnt.wsf
Performs user maintenance operations
-->
 <script language="VBScript" src="adsilib.vbs">
 <![CDATA[
 Option Explicit
 Dim nF,objContainer, strContainer
 Dim aFields, aValues, objUser
 Dim bUpdate, strUserName
 ReDim aFields(0), aValues(0)

 If Not IsCscript Then
  ExitScript("This script must be run from command line using cscript.exe")
 End If
 bUpdate = False
  'get the command line arguments
  GetArguments
  Set objContainer = GetObject("WinNT://" & strContainer)
  If Err Then
    ExitScript("Can't find domain/computer" & strContainer)
  End If
  UpdateUser

 'Reads command line arguments and sets appropriate flags
 Sub GetArguments
 Dim nF, strArg
 'check the argument count
 If Wscript.Arguments.Count = 0 Then
  ShowUsage
  Wscript.Quit
 End If

  strContainer = Wscript.Arguments(0)
 'loop through command line parameters
 For nF = 1 to Wscript.Arguments.Count - 1
  strArg= Wscript.Arguments(nF)
  'check if parameter setting
```

```
 If Ucase(Left(strArg, 3))= "/P:" Then
   GetParameters(nF)
   nF=nF+1
 'check if update flag
 ElseIf Ucase(Left(strArg, 2)) = "/U" Then bUpdate = True

 Else 'otherwise assume it's a user id
   strUserName = strArg
 End If
Next

 'if the command line specifies a user get user
 If Not strUserName = "" Then aValues(0) = strUserName
End Sub

'populates array with command line property parameters
'Parameters nIndex command line parameter number to process
Sub GetParameters(nIndex)

 If nIndex+1> Wscript.Arguments.Count-1 Then _
              ExitScript("Not enough arguments")

 Redim Preserve aFields(Ubound(aFields)+1)
 Redim Preserve aValues(Ubound(aValues)+1)
 aFields(Ubound(aFields)) = Mid(Wscript.Arguments(nIndex),4)
 aValues(Ubound(aValues)) = Wscript.Arguments(nIndex+1)

End Sub

'Create or update a user
Sub UpdateUser
'check if it's user maintenance or creation mode
    If bUpdate Then 'get the user
       Set objUser = GetObject("WinNT://" & strContainer & "/" & aValues(0))
    Else
          'create a user using the first column value
           Set objUser = objContainer.Create("User", aValues(0))
           objUser.SetInfo
    End If

       'loop through and update all the properties
         For nF = 1 to Ubound(aFields)
        If IsNumeric(aValues(nF))  Then
```

```
                objUser.Put Trim(aFields(nF)), Clng(aValues(nF))
            ElseIf Ucase(aValues(nF))="TRUE" OR Ucase(aValues(nF))="FALSE" Then
                objUser.Put Trim(aFields(nF)), Cbool(aValues(nF))
            ElseIf IsDate(aValues(nF)) Then
                objUser.Put Trim(aFields(nF)), Cdate(aValues(nF))
                 ElseIf Ucase(aFields(nF))="PASSWORD" Then
                    objUser.SetPassword(aValues(nF))
                  Else
                    objUser.Put Trim(aFields(nF)), aValues(nF)
                  End If
             objUser.SetInfo
            Next
End Sub

'displays script usage information
Sub ShowUsage()
 WScript.Echo "Usermnt provides user creation and maintenance." & vbCrLf & _
     "Syntax:" &  vbCrLf & _
  "usermnt.wsf domain  [username] [/u] [/p:name value] " _
  & vbCrLf & "domain    user's domain " & vbCrLf & _
   "username user id to create or update" & vbCrLf & _
   "/u        indicates specified user(s) will be updated" & vbCrLf & _
   "/p:name  property name followed by corresponding value"
   WScript.Quit -1
End Sub
 ]]>
 </script>
</job>
```

For example, the following command sequence creates a new user, "freds," and sets the Fullname and Description properties:

```
usermnt.wsf Acme freds /p:fullname "Fred Smith" /p:description "Accountant"
```

If you want to update existing users, add the /u switch to the command line. The following command line updates the description for user freds:

```
usermnt.wsf Acme freds /u /p:description "Accountant"
```

The usermnt.wsf script includes an adsilib.vbs library of reusable support code. This code is used throughout the chapter:

```
'adsilib.vbs
'Description: Contains routines used by ADSI scripts
'Gets the value of a server object based on its server comment/name
'Parameters:
'objWebService  WebService object
'strSiteName    Site name you wish to get value
'Returns: Site number, blank string if not found
Function FindSiteNumber(objWebService, strSiteName, strType)
Dim nF, objSite
 nF = ""
 'loop through each site, find available site #
 For Each objSite In objWebService
    'check if the object is a web site
    If strcomp(objSite.Class,"IIs" & strType & "Server",1)=0 Then
     'check if server comment is same as specified server name
     If Ucase(objSite.ServerComment) = Ucase(strSiteName) Then
          nF = objSite.Name
      Exit For
     End If
    End If
 Next
FindSiteNumber = nF
End Function

'returns the
'Parameters
'strType     site type, web or FTP
Function GetSiteType(strType)
Select Case Ucase(strType)
  Case "FTP"
    GetSiteType = "MSFTPSVC"
  Case "SMTP"
    GetSiteType = "SmtpSvc"
  Case "NNTP"
    GetSiteType = "nntpSvc"
 Case Else
    GetSiteType = "W3SVC"
 End Select
End Function
```

```
'Find next available site number
'
Function FindNextSite(objService)
Dim nF, objSite
 nF = 0
'loop through each site, find available site #
 For Each objSite In objService
    'check if object is a IIS site
    If Left(objSite.Class,3) = "IIs" And _
                Right(objSite.Class,6)= "Server" Then
     If nF < objSite.Name Then nF = objSite.Name
End If
 Next
 FindNextSite = nF + 1
End Function

'check if script is being run interactively
'Returns:True if run from command line, otherwise False
Function IsCscript()
 If strcomp(Right(Wscript.Fullname,11),"cscript.exe",1)=0 Then
   IsCscript = True
 Else
   IsCscript = False
 End If
End Function

'display an error message and exits script
'Parameters:
'strMsg Message to display
Sub ExitScript(strMsg)
 Wscript.Echo strMsg
 Wscript.Quit -1
End Sub
```

See Also

Search for the topic “Getting Properties for Active Directory Objects” in the ADSI 2.5 SDK Help. For more information, search `http://msdn.microsoft.com` for the articles “WinNT Schema’s Mandatory and Optional Properties” and “Provider Support of ADSI Interfaces.”

14.7 Setting Multivalued Properties

Problem

You want to read and update multivalued properties.

Solution

You can use the PutEx method to set, update, and clear multivalued properties:

```
Const ADS_PROPERTY_CLEAR = 1
Const ADS_PROPERTY_UPDATE = 2
Const ADS_PROPERTY_APPEND = 3
Const ADS_PROPERTY_DELETE = 4
Set objUser = GetObject("LDAP://CN=Freds,CN=Users,DC=Acme,DC=com")
'add new home phone numbers to the user
objUser.PutEx ADS_PROPERTY_APPEND, "OtherhomePhone", _
               Array("555-1234", "222-2222")
objUser.SetInfo

'deletes a fax number
objUser.PutEx ADS_PROPERTY_DELETE, "otherFacsimileTelephoneNumber", _
               Array("555-3453")
objUser.SetInfo

'updates (sets) the addtional mailbox addresses for the user
objUser.PutEx ADS_PROPERTY_UPDATE, "otherMailbox", _
               Array("freddy@acme.com", "fred@acme.com")
objUser.SetInfo

'clear mobile phone
objUser.PutEx ADS_PROPERTY_CLEAR, "OtherMobile", Null
objUser.SetInfo
```

Discussion

Provider properties can be multivalued. Multivalued properties may contain one or more values. Use the GetEx method to reference values from multi-valued properties:

```
aValues = objADSI.GetEx(strProperty)
```

The GetEx method returns an array of values for the property specified by the strProperty argument.

```
Set objUser = GetObject("LDAP://cn=Fred Smith,cn=Users,dc=acme,dc=com")
aOtherPhone = objUser.GetEx("OtherTelephone")
For Each strPhone In aOtherPhone
    Wscript.Echo strPhone
Next
```

GetEx can return an error if the property hasn't been set in the underlying directory. For example, if no additional phone numbers have been set for an Active Directory user, an error will occur if you attempt to retrieve the OtherTelephone property.

The PutEx method adds, deletes, and sets multivalued properties:

```
objUser.PutEx intAction, strProperty, vValue
```

The intAction parameter determines how the value will be stored in the multivalued property array. Table 14-6 lists the valid intAction values.

Table 14-6. PutEx *Method Action Values*

ACTION VALUE	VALUE	DESCRIPTION
ADS_PROPERTY_CLEAR	1	Clears the property.
ADS_PROPERTY_UPDATE	2	Sets the property.
ADS_PROPERTY_APPEND	3	Appends a value to the property.
ADS_PROPERTY_DELETE	4	Deletes a value from the property. Error occurs if the value specified to delete does not exist.

The strProperty parameter is the property you want to maintain. The vValue parameter is the value(s) you are adding, setting, or removing from the property.

Table 14-7 contains a number of multivalued properties for the Active Directory provider.

Table 14-7. Active Directory Provider Multivalued Properties

PROPERTY	DESCRIPTION
OtherFacsimileTelephoneNumber	Additional fax numbers
OtherHomePhone	Additional home phone numbers
OtherIpPhone	Additional IP phone addresses
OtherMailbox	Additional mailboxes
OtherMobile	Additional mobile/cellular phone numbers
OtherPager	Additional pager numbers
OtherTelephone	Additional office phone numbers

See Also

Search for "Example Code for Using PutEx" in the ADSI 2.5 SDK Help file.

14.8 Deleting a User

Problem

You want to delete a user.

Solution

Using the WinNT ADSI provider, reference a computer or domain object in which the user resides and then invoke the `Delete` method:

```
Dim objDomain
'get a reference to the Acme domain
Set objDomain = GetObject("WinNT://Acme")
'delete a user
objDomain.Delete "user", "Freds"
```

For the Active Directory provider, you must get a reference to the container the object the user resides in and call the `Delete` method using the relative distinguished name (RDN) for the user you want to delete:

```
'delete a user using the Active Directory provider
Dim objContainer
'get a reference to the LDAP container that contains the object to delete
Set objContainer = GetObject("LDAP://OU=Accountants,DC=Acme,DC=com")

'delete Fred Smith by specifying his relative distinguished name
objContainer.delete "user", "CN=Fred Smith"
```

Discussion

To delete a user, get a reference to the container that you want to delete the user from. Under the Windows NT provider, the container is the domain or computer the user resides in.

Once you have a reference to the container, invoke the `Delete` method:

```
objContainer.Delete strClassName, strObjectName
```

`strClassName` specifies the object class type to delete, for a user the class name is "user." `strObjectName` represents the user to delete. For the Windows NT provider, this is the user ID.

See Also

For more information, search `http://msdn.microsoft.com` for the article "Removing Users."

14.9 Setting User Logon Time

Problem

You want to set user logon times.

Solution

The following command-line script sets the logon time for a specified user. It uses the WinNT provider to get a reference to a user and updates the LoginHours property with any changes specified from the command prompt:

```
<?xml version="1.0" ?>
<job>
<!--comment
Script:sethours.wsf
Description:sets logon hours for users
-->
 <script language="VBScript" src="adsilib.vbs">
 <![CDATA[
 Dim aLogonHours, objUser
 Dim strUser, strDay, strStart, strEnd, strFlag, strContainer

 If Not IsCscript() Then _
  ExitScript "This script must be run from command line using cscript.exe"

  If Wscript.Arguments.Count = 6 Then
    ShowUsage
   Wscript.Quit
  End If

  strContainer = Wscript.Arguments(0) 'WinNT domain or computer
  strUser = Wscript.Arguments(1)    'user id to set
  strDay = Wscript.Arguments(2)    ' day - starting from 1
  strStart = Wscript.Arguments(3) 'start hour
  strEnd = Wscript.Arguments(4)
  strFlag = Cbool(Wscript.Arguments(5))

  'get a reference to the user you wish to set logon times
  Set objUser = GetObject("WinNT://" & strContainer & "/" & strUser & ",user")

  'create a Byte Array Conversion (BAC) object
  Set objBAC = CreateObject("BAC.Convert")
  'convert login hours to an array of variants
  aLogonHours = objBAC.ByteToVariant(objUser.LoginHours)

  SetDay strDay, strStart, strEnd, strFlag, aLogonHours
  objuser.LoginHours = objBAC.VariantToByte(aLogonHours)
```

```
 objUser.SetInfo
Else

Sub ShowUsage
 WScript.Echo _
 "sethours.wsf sets logon hour for specified user" & vbCrLf & _
 "Syntax:" &  vbCrLf & _
 "sethours.wsf container user day hour duration onoff " &  vbCrLf & _
 "container computer or domain where user resides" & vbCrLf & _
 "user       user name to set logon hours " & vbCrLf & _
 "day        day to set, 1=Sunday, 2= Monday etc." & vbCrLf & _
 "hour       start hour in 24 hour clock format" & vbCrLf & _
 "duration  number of hours to set" & vbCrLf & _
 "access    Boolean value. True=grant access False=deny access" & vbCrLf &
 "Example:deny freds in Acme domain access on Sunday from 1-4PM" & vbCrLf & _
 "sethours.wsf Acme freds 1 13 3 False"
End Sub

Sub SetDay(nDay, nHour, nDuration, bOn, aHours)
Dim nHours, nF, nStart, nPos, nBitFlag
'calculate the hour of the week starting from Sunday
nHours = ((nDay - 1) * 24 + nHour) - 9

 'loop through all hours in range and change status
 For nF = nHours To (nHours + nDuration) - 1
    'since the period of Sunday 12AM to 9AM is stored
    'in the last array element we must change the array element
    'if the hour is in this range
    If nF < 0 Then
      nStart = nF + 168
    ElseIf nF > 168 Then
      nStart = nF - 168
    Else
      nStart = nF
    End If

   'determine the array element to start. each element
   'contains 8 hours
   nPos = Int(nStart / 8)

   'calculate the bit to set for the hour
   nBitFlag = 2 ^ (nStart Mod 8)
```

```
    If bOn Then
        'grant access to an hour
        aHours(nPos) = aHours(nPos) Or nBitFlag
    Else
        'deny access to hour
        aHours(nPos) = aHours(nPos) And Not nBitFlag
    End If
  Next
 End Sub
  ]]>
  </script>
</job>
```

Discussion

The logon hours allowed control of what hours a user can log on to the system. The user can be allowed/disallowed any 1-hour block within a 7-day period. This can be set from NT User Manager or the Windows 2000 Active Directory plug-in, as shown in Figure 14-3.

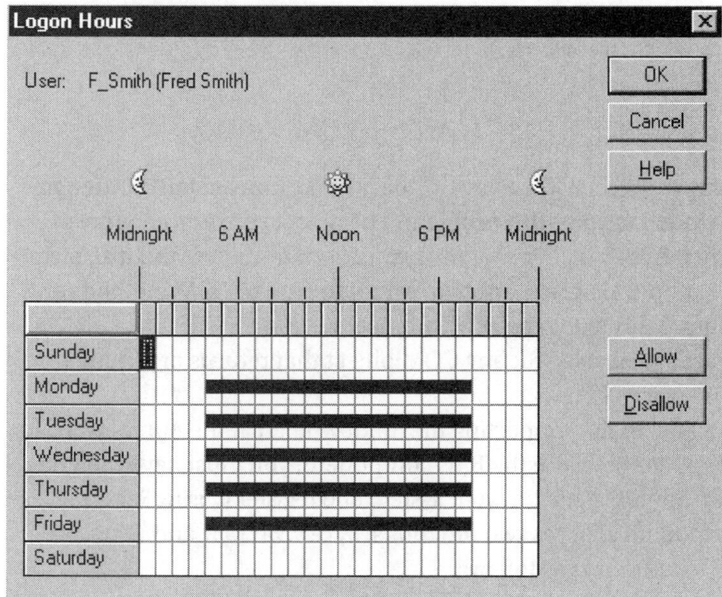

Figure 14-3. Logon Hours dialog box

The logon hours are represented by an array of byte (8-bit) values. Each bit represents 1 hour, so the entire week of 168 hours (7324) is represented by an array of 21-byte values (2138). If the bit is set to 1, access is allowed, if it is set to 0, access is disallowed during that period.

The LogonHours property returns the array of values, which has an offset of 0. The first element in the array stores the period of 8 hours from 9 AM Sunday to 5 PM Sunday. The second array element stores from 5 PM Sunday to 1 AM Monday, and so on.

Unfortunately, the LogonHours property is returned as an array of byte values. VBScript cannot handle this data type (it recognizes it, but can't deal with it). The following code binds to a user and returns the LoginHours property, but an error is generated when it tries to enumerate the array:

```
'get user
Set objuser = GetObject("WinNT://acme/freds,user")

'get the login hours
obj = objuser.LoginHours
'display data type
Wscript.Echo Vartype(obj)

'try to enumerate array, an error will occur:
For nF = Lbound (obj) to ubound (obj)
 Wscript.Echo obj(nF)
Next
```

A simple wrapper object BAC.Convert (Binary Array Conversion) written in Visual Basic is provided to solve this problem. The object converts an array of byte values returned from functions to an array of variant values, and it also converts an array of variants to an array of byte values to pass to COM methods and functions that require this data type as a parameter.

The BAC object can be used for any COM object that returns or requires a parameter as an array of bytes.

The DLL is located in the supporting file for download at the Apress Web site (http://www.apress.com/). To use the BAC component, you must have the VB5 runtime installed. Copy BAConv.DLL to your system and register it using Regsvr32.exe.

The BAC component exposes two functions: ByteToVariant and VariantToByte. Their syntax is as follows:

```
arrVar = ByteToVariant(arrByte)
arrByte = VariantToByte(arrVar)
```

ByteToVariant converts an array of byte values supplied by the arrByte parameter to an array of variants.

VariantToByte converts an array of variant values supplied by the arrVar parameter to an array of byte values.

The following snippet uses the BAC object to convert the array of bytes the LoginHours property returns to an array of variant values that VBScript can manipulate:

```
'get a user object
Set objUser = GetObject("WinNT://acme/freds,user")

'create a Byte array conversion object
Set objBAC = CreateObject("BAC.Convert")

'get the login hours using the BAC object
obj = objBAC.ByteToVariant(objUser.LoginHours)

'enumerate array
For nF = Lbound (obj) to ubound (obj)
 Wscript.Echo obj(nF)
Next
```

The BAC object works with LDAP and Active Directory as well. The following snippet sets all hours on for the Active Directory user Fred Smith:

```
'get a user object
Set objUser = GetObject("LDAP://cn=Fred Smith,cn=Users,DC=Acme,DC=COM")
'create a Byte array conversion object
Set objBAC = CreateObject("BAC.Convert")

'get the login hours using the BAC object
obj = objBAC.ByteToVariant(objUser.LoginHours)

'set all hours on
For nF = LBound(obj) To UBound(obj)
 Debug.Print obj(nF)
  obj(nF) = 255
Next

objUser.LoginHours = objBAC.VariantToByte(obj)
objUser.SetInfo
```

The `sethours.wsf` solution script sets the logon hours for a user:

```
sethours.wsf container user day hour duration onoff
```

The `container` parameter is a computer or domain in which the user resides. The `user` is the user ID for whom you set the logon hours. The `day` parameter is an integer value representing the day to set the logon access for: 1 is Sunday, 2 is Monday, and so on. `Hour` is the start hour to set the logon access for in 24-hour clock format: 0 is 12 AM, 13 is 1 PM, and so on. `Duration` is number of hours to set. `Onoff` is a Boolean value indicating whether to grant or deny access. If `onoff` is `True`, access is granted, and if `False`, access is denied.

To deny access to user freds in the Acme domain on Sunday from 1 PM to 4 PM, use the following line:

```
sethours.wsf Acme freds 1 13 3 False
```

See Also

Search `http://msdn.microsoft.com` for "Msvbvm50.exe Installs Visual Basic 5.0 Run-Time Files" for the VB 5.0 runtime download.

14.10 Limiting Computer Access

Problem

You want to limit the machines on which a user can log on.

Solution

Using the ADSI WinNT provider, you can set the `LoginWorkstations` property to limit the computers on which a user can log on:

```
'get a reference to the user
Set objUser = GetObject("WinNT://Acme/freds")

 'list the machines the users have access to
For Each station In objUser.LoginWorkstations
  Wscript.Echo station
Next
```

```
'set the machines a user is permitted to logon to
objUser.LoginWorkstations = Array("thor","odin","loki")
objUser.SetInfo
```

Discussion

Windows NT and later provide the ability to limit the machines users can log on to.

The WinNT provider's LoginWorkstations property returns an array of machine names that the user can access.

The ADSI provider can use the LoginWorkstations property, but it includes a UserWorkstations property as well. The UserWorkstations property is a string that contains workstation names separated by commas:

```
'set the workstations a user can log on to using the Active Directory provider
Dim objUser
'get a reference to a user object
Set objUser=GetObject("LDAP://CN=Fred Smith,OU=Accounting,DC=acme,DC=com")

objUser.UserWorkstations ="odin,thor,loki"
objUser.SetInfo 'update user settings
```

If workstation limitations have not been set under User Manager, an error will occur if you try to read the LoginWorkstations property.

14.11 Setting User Flags

Problem

You want to prevent a user's password from expiring.

Solution

You can set the UF_DONTEXPIRE_PASSWD bit of the UserFlags property for the WinNT provider:

```
Const UF_DONTEXPIRE_PASSWD = 65536
Set objUser = GetObject("WinNT://ACME/fsmith,user")
objUser.Put "userFlags", usr.Get("UserFlags") Or ADS_UF_DONTEXPIRE_PASSWD
objUser.SetInfo
```

The LDAP provider exposes the `userAccountControl` property. You can set the `UF_DONTEXPIRE_PASSWD` bit of the `userAccountControl` property as follows:

```
Const UF_DONTEXPIRE_PASSWD = 65536
Set objUser = GetObject("LDAP://CN=Fred Smith,CN=Users,DC=Acme,DC=com")
 objUser.userAccountControl = objUser.userAccountControl Or UF_DONTEXPIRE_PASSWD
objUser.SetInfo
```

Discussion

The Windows NT provider's `User` object's `UserFlags` property is a combination of values that control various user settings. Table 14-8 lists the WinNT provider's `UserFlags` values.

Table 14-8. WinNT Provider's `UserFlags` *and LDAP* `UserAccountControl` `Property` *Values*

FLAG	VALUE	DESCRIPTION
UF_SCRIPT	1	The logon script will be executed.
UF_ACCOUNTDISABLE	2	The user's account is disabled.
UF_LOCKOUT	16	The account is currently locked out.
UF_PASSWD_NOTREQD	32	No password is required.
UF_PASSWD_CANT_CHANGE	64	The user cannot change the password.
UF_ENCRYPTED_TEXT_PASSWORD_ALLOWED	128	Store password with reversible encryption. Active Directory only.
UF_TEMP_DUPLICATE_ACCOUNT	256	This is an account for users whose primary account is in another domain. This account provides user access to this domain, but not to any domain that trusts this domain. Sometimes it is referred to as a *local* user account.
UF_NORMAL_ACCOUNT	512	This is a default account type that represents a typical user.
UF_DONTEXPIRE_PASSWD	65536	Represents the password, which should never expire on the account.
UF_SMARTCARD_REQUIRED	262144	User requires smart card for logon. Active Directory only.

Table 14-8. WinNT Provider's `UserFlags` *and LDAP* `UserAccountControl` `Property` *Values (continued)*

FLAG	VALUE	DESCRIPTION
UF_TRUSTED_FOR_DELEGATION	524288	Account trusted for delegation. Active Directory only.
UF_NOT_DELEGATED	1048576	User account is sensitive and cannot be delegated. Active Directory only.
UF_USE_DES_KEY_ONLY	2097152	Use DES encryption types for this type of account. Active Directory only.
UF_DONT_REQUIRE_PREAUTH	4194304	Do not require Kerberos preauthentication. Active Directory only.

Use the logical operators OR and XOR to perform bitwise operations to set flags. To set a flag, OR the value against the `UserFlags` property:

```
'prevent user from changing their own password
Const UF_PASSWD_CANT_CHANGE = 65536
Set objUser = GetObject("WinNT://ACME/fsmith,user")
objUser.Put "userFlags", usr.Get("UserFlags") Or UF_PASSWD_CANT_CHANGE
objUser.SetInfo
```

To turn a flag off, use the AND NOT Boolean operation. If you want to "toggle" a flag, use the XOR operator. The XOR operator works like a toggle, so it can turn a bit on or off:

```
Const UF_PASSWD_CANT_CHANGE = 64
Const UF_DONTEXPIRE_PASSWD = 65536

Dim objUser
Set objUser = GetObject("WinNT://ACME/fsmith,user")
  'turn of the UF_PASSWD_CANT_CHANGE flag
   objUser.userFlags = objUser.userFlags And Not UF_PASSWD_CANT_CHANGE
  'toggle the UF_DONTEXPIRE_PASSWD flag
   objUser.userFlags = objUser.userFlags Xor UF_DONTEXPIRE_PASSWD
objUser.SetInfo
```

The majority of the bit flags listed in Table 14-8 are interchangeable between `UserAccountControl` and `UserFlags` except for the `UF_PASSWD_CANT_CHANGE (64)` flag. This flag controls if the user can change his or her own password. You can read the UF_PASSWD_CANT_CHANGE bit using the LDAP UserAccountControl property, but you cannot set the bit.

Active Directory assigns security on all objects using access control entries (ACE). The ability for a user to change his or her password is controlled by these entries. The following script contains a SetUserCannotChangePassword routine that can turn the UF_PASSWD_CANT_CHANGE flag on and off:

```
Set objUser = GetObject("LDAP://CN=fred smith,CN=Users,DC=Acme,DC=com")
SetUserCannotChangePassword objUser, False

Sub  SetUserCannotChangePassword(objUser, bChange)
Const CHANGE_PASSWORD_GUID = "{ab721a53-1e2f-11d0-9819-00aa0040529b}"
Const ADS_ACETYPE_ACCESS_DENIED_OBJECT = &H6
'get security descriptor and set trustees
Set objSD = objUser.Get("ntSecurityDescriptor")
Set objDACL = objSD.DiscretionaryAcl

For Each objACE In objDACL
  If objACE.ObjectType = CHANGE_PASSWORD_GUID Then
     If bChange Then
       objACE.AceType = ADS_ACETYPE_ACCESS_DENIED_OBJECT
     Else
       objACE.AceType = 5
     End If
  End If
Next

objSD.DiscretionaryAcl = objDACL
objUser.Put "nTSecurityDescriptor", objSD
objUser.SetInfo

End Sub
```

See Chapter 17 for more information on reading and setting security on Windows objects. You can use the WinNT provider to set the UF_PASSWD_CANT_CHANGE flag for Active Directory users for simpler code.

See Also

For more information, search http://msdn.microsoft.com for the article "Modifying User Properties."

14.12 Listing Groups

Problem

You want to list all objects from a group.

Solution

To list the members of a group using the WinNT provider, you can reference the group object and then loop through each member of the `Members` collection property:

```
Set objGroup = GetObject("WinNT://Acme/Domain Users,group")
'display name of each object in group
For Each objUser In objGroup.Members
    Wscript.Echo objUser.Name
Next
```

The LDAP provider allows for the enumeration of groups in the same way as the WinNT provider:

```
'get a reference to the Auditors group under the Accounting organizational unit
Set objGroup = GetObject("LDAP://cn=Auditors,ou=Accounting,DC=Acme,DC=com")

'display name of each object in group
For Each objUser In objGroup.Members
  Wscript.Echo objUser.Name
Next
```

Discussion

A group object exposes a `Members` collection, which contains all members of the group.

You may want to determine what groups a user is a member of. This is easily accomplished by enumerating the `Groups` collection property of the `User` object:

```
Set objUser = GetObject("LDAP://CN=Administrator,CN=Users,DC=Acme,DC=com")
'display name of each group user is member of
For Each objGroup In objUser.Groups
    Wscript.Echo objGroup.Name
Next
```

The preceding example demonstrates enumerating the Administrators groups using the LDAP provider. The WinNT provider exposes the same property.

See Also

For more information, read the 15 Seconds FAQ "How do I get all the users in a group using ADSI?" at `http://local.15seconds.com/faq/ADSI/623.htm`.

14.13 Creating or Deleting a User Group

Problem

You want to create or delete a user group.

Solution

Using the WinNT provider, you can reference a domain or computer and then invoke the `Create` method, specifying the group class as the object that you want to create:

```
Const ADS_GROUP_TYPE_DOMAIN_LOCAL_GROUP = 4

Set objDomain = GetObject("WinNT://Acme")
Set objGroup = objDomain.Create("group", "Acctusers")
objGroup.groupType = ADS_GROUP_TYPE_DOMAIN_LOCAL_GROUP
objGroup.Description = "Accounting Users"
objGroup.SetInfo
```

Discussion

To create a new group using the Windows NT provider, first reference the domain or computer object in which you want to create the user.

Then invoke the object's `Create` method, specifying the `Group` class as the object you want to create:

```
Set objGroup = objDomain.Create("Group", strGroupName)
```

`strGroupName` identifies the group.

A groupType property must be set for the new group being created. For the NT provider, there is either the global or local group. Table 14-9 lists the different group types and associated values.

Table 14-9. Group Types

PROPERTY	VALUE	DESCRIPTION
GROUP_TYPE_GLOBAL_GROUP	2	Can contain user accounts from the current domain.
GROUP_TYPE_LOCAL_GROUP	4	Can contain local accounts and global groups.
GROUP_TYPE_UNIVERSAL_GROUP	8	Active Directory domains only. Can contain accounts and account groups from any domain, but not local groups.

Once a group has been created, invoke the object's SetInfo method to save the changes. No additional properties are needed for the new group. An optional Description parameter can be set to provide a more detailed description of the group.

Creating a new group using the Active Directory provider is similar to creating one using the Windows NT provider.

First, get a reference to the container you want to add the new group in and create the group using the Create method, specifying the Group object as the class you want to create and the RDN for the group you want to create.

You need to set the samAccountName property for the new group. This property represents the name that appears to Windows NT and Windows 9*x* machines:

```
Const GROUP_TYPE_SECURITY_ENABLED = &h80000000
Dim objContainer, objGroup
Set objContainer = GetObject("LDAP://CN=Users,DC=Acme,DC=com")
'create the group
Set objGroup = objContainer.Create("Group", "CN=Accounting Group")

'set the SAM account name for compatibility with existing NT and
'Win9x clients
objGroup.samAccountName = "Acctusers"

objGroup.groupType = GROUP_TYPE_GLOBAL_GROUP Or GROUP_TYPE_SECURITY_ENABLED
objGroup.SetInfo
```

There are more group options available to Active Directory than to Windows NT. Active Directory has security groups and distribution groups. A security group is the same as a group in Windows NT. A distribution group is the same as a security group except it cannot be used to apply security access-control lists to Active Directory objects.

To create a security group, set the group type to local, global, or universal, and OR the GROUP_TYPE_SECURITY_ENABLED flag. The GROUP_TYPE_SECURITY_ENABLED flag has a value of –2147483648.

To delete a group using the WinNT provider, get a reference to the container the group exists in (domain or computer) and call the Delete method. You need to specify the group as the class type and the name of the group you are deleting:

```
Set objDomain = GetObject("WinNT://Acme")
Set objGroup = objDomain.Delete("group", "Acctusers")
```

Similar steps are required to delete an Active Directory group:

```
Set objCN = GetObject("LDAP://ou=Accounting,DC=Acme,DC=com")
objCN.Delete "group","cn=Accounting Group"
```

14.14 Adding a User or Group to a Group

Problem

You want to add a user or a group to a group.

Solution

You can reference the group object to which you want to add a user or local group and then invoke the Add method:

```
Dim objGroup

'get the group to add objects to..
Set objGroup = GetObject("WinNT://Acme/Acctusers")

objGroup.add "WinNT://Acme/freds,user" 'add a user
objGroup.add "WinNT://Acme/joeb" 'add a another user
'add a group - can only add other groups to Local groups, not Global
objGroup.add "WinNT://Acme/finance,group"
```

Discussion

To add groups or users to a group using the Windows NT provider, reference the group to which you want to add. Then invoke the Add method:

```
objGroup.add (strObjectPath)
```

strObjectPath represents the ADSI path to the user or group you want to add.

To add an object to an Active Directory group, get a reference to the container to which you want to add. Then invoke the Add method specifying the DN path to the object you want to add to the group:

```
'get the group to add objects to..
Set objGroup = _
                GetObject("LDAP://CN=Accounting Group,CN=Users,DC=Acme,DC=com")
'add a user
objGroup.add "LDAP://CN=Fred Smith,CN=Users,DC=Acme,DC=com"
```

To delete an object from a group using the WinNT provider, get a reference to the group you want to delete the object from and invoke the Remove method, specifying the ADSI path to the object you want to delete:

```
'get the group to remove objects from
Set objGroup = GetObject("WinNT://Acme/Acctusers")
objGroup.Remove("WinNT://Acme/freds ") 'remove the user freds
```

Removing an object from an Active Directory group using the LDAP provider involves the same steps as removing an object using the WinNT provider:

```
'get the group to remove the object from
Set objGroup = _
                GetObject("LDAP://CN=Accounting Group,CN=Users,DC=Acme,DC=com")
'remove a user from the group
objGroup.Remove "LDAP://CN=Fred Smith,CN=Users,DC=Acme,DC=com"
```

See Also

For more information, search http://msdn.microsoft.com for the article "Adding Domain Objects to Local Groups."

14.15 Determining Group Membership

Problem

You want to determine group membership at logon.

Solution

Use the Group object's IsMember method to check group membership:

```
Set objNetwork = Wscript.Create("Wscript.Network")

Set objGroup= GetObject("WinNT://Acme/Accounting Users,group")
'
If (objGroup.IsMember("WinNT://ACME/" & objNetwork.UserName)) Then
   'connect to printer
End If
```

Discussion

The IsMember method provides the ability to check if a user is a member of a specific group or not.

To use the IsMember method get a reference to the group you want to check the membership of. Invoke the IsMember method, specifying the name of the user you are checking the membership for:

```
bFlag = objGroup.IsMember(strMember)
```

The strMember parameter is the name of the user to check for. IsMember returns True if the user is a member of the group. For the WinNT provider, specify the full path to the name to check for (e.g., WinNT://Acme/Freds).

For Active Directory, get a reference to the group you want to check and invoke the IsMember method, specifying the full LDAP path to the object you are checking group membership for:

```
Set objGroup = _
         GetObject("LDAP://CN=Accounting Users,OU=Accounting,DC= Acme,DC=com")
'check group membership..
If (objGroup.IsMember("LDAP://CN=FredS,OU=Accounting,DC=Acme,DC=com")) Then
 'do something...
End If
```

See Also

For more information, search `http://msdn.microsoft.com` for the article "IADsGroup::IsMember."

14.16 Querying Active Directory Values

Problem

You want to query the Active Directory of a Windows Active Directory server.

Solution

You can use the ADSI ADO interface to execute queries against Active Directory:

```
<?xml version="1.0" ?>
<job>
<!--comment
Script:adsiqry.vbs
Description:executes queries against LDAP provider
-->
 <script language="VBScript" src="adsilib.vbs">
 <![CDATA[
Option Explicit
Const ADS_SCOPE_ONELEVEL = 1
Dim objRst, objConn, objCmd
Dim bShowFields, bSingleLevel, strQry
Dim strDelimiter, nF, strHeaders, strLine

If Not IsCscript() Then
 ExitScript "This script must be run from command line using cscript.exe"
End If

 strDelimiter = ","
 GetArguments
 Set objConn = CreateObject("ADODB.Connection")
 objConn.Provider = "ADsDSOObject"
 objConn.Open "Active Directory Provider"

 Set objCmd = CreateObject("ADODB.Command")
 Set objCmd.ActiveConnection = objConn
```

```
'check if only the single level is to be searched
If bSingleLevel Then objCmd.Properties("searchscope") = ADS_SCOPE_ONELEVEL

objCmd.CommandText = strQry

Set objRst = objCmd.Execute
'check if headers are to be outputted
If bShowFields Then
   'loop through
   For nF = 0 To objRst.Fields.Count - 1
       strHeaders = strHeaders & objRst.Fields(nF).Name & strDelimiter
   Next
 strHeaders = Left(strHeaders, Len(strHeaders) - 1)
 Wscript.StdOut.WriteLine strHeaders
End If

 Do While Not objRst.EOF
   strLine = ""

     For nF = 0 To objRst.Fields.Count - 1
       strLine = strLine & objRst.Fields(nF) & strDelimiter
     Next
   strLine = Left(strLine, Len(strLine) - 1)
   Wscript.StdOut.WriteLine strLine
   objRst.MoveNext
 Loop

objRst.Close
objConn.Close

'Reads command line arguments and sets appropriate flags
Sub GetArguments
 Dim nF, strArg
 If Wscript.Arguments.Count = 0 Then
  ShowUsage
  Wscript.Quit
 End If

 strQry = Wscript.Arguments(0)

 'loop through command line parameters
 For nF = 1 to Wscript.Arguments.Count - 1
  Select Case Ucase(Left(Wscript.Arguments(nF),2))
```

```
    Case "/H"
    bShowFields= True

    Case "/S"
    bSingleLevel = True

    Case "/D"
      strDelimiter = Mid(Wscript.Arguments(nF),4)
    End Select
 Next
End Sub

'displays script usage information
Sub ShowUsage()
WScript.Echo "adsiqry executes queries and LDAP provider." & vbLf & _
    "Syntax:" &  vbLf & _
    "adsiqry.ws query [/d:delimiter] [/s] [/h] " &  vbLf & _
    "/d:delimiter optional delimiter to separate output columns" & vbLf & _
    "/s    optional. If set then only single level is searched" & vbLf & _
    "/h    option flag. If set then field names are shown"
    WScript.Quit -1
 End Sub

 'display an error message and exist script
 Function ExitScript(strMsg)
  Wscript.Echo strMsg
  Wscript.Quit -1
 End Function
  ]]>
  </script>
</job>
```

Discussion

The Active Directory provider includes an OLE DB interface that can perform queries against the Active Directory namespace. Using this interface together with ADO, you can execute SQL queries to return information on Active Directory objects.

To use the provider, you must have a recent version of ADO installed. Before a query can be executed against the provider, you must create an ADO `Connection` object and specify the provider:

```
'create a ADO connection object
Set objConn = CreateObject("ADODB.Connection")

'select the provider
 objConn.Provider = "ADsDSOObject"
'open the connection - the string here can be anything
 objConn.Open "Active Directory Provider"
```

Once the Connection object is created, you can execute queries against the provider. The query contains standard SQL statements. The data source is the distinguished name of a LDAP container you want to search in (e.g., LDAP://ou=Sales,dc=Acme,dc=COM).

The query criteria can contain any Active Directory object properties. You can use the asterisk (*) wildcard to perform partial searches on fields:

```
Set objCmd = CreateObject("ADODB.Command")
Set objCmd.ActiveConnection = objConn
'Return all items where the name starts with F
objCmd.CommandText = "SELECT cn, name,sn, street, l, st FROM " & _
                     "'LDAP://OU=Sales,dc=acme,dc=COM' WHERE objectClass='user'" & _
                     " AND objectCategory='person' AND Name='F*'"
```

Initially when a search is performed, the source container and all containers below it are searched. If you only want to search a single container, set the SearchScope property of the ADO Command object to ADS_SCOPE_ONELEVEL, which has the value of 1. The default is ADS_SCOPE_SUBTREE, which has the value of 2.

The following sample searches the Sales organizational unit of the Acme domain for all objects in the container:

```
Const ADS_SCOPE_ONELEVEL = 1
'create a Connection object
Set objConn = CreateObject("ADODB.Connection")

objConn.Provider = "ADsDSOObject"
objConn.Open "Active Directory Provider"

'create a command object
Set objCmd = CreateObject("ADODB.Command")
Set objCmd.ActiveConnection = objConn

'search the one level only
objCmd.Properties("searchscope") = ADS_SCOPE_ONELEVEL objCmd.CommandText = _
   "SELECT cn FROM 'LDAP://OU=Sales,DC=Acme,DC=COM' WHERE objectClass='*'"
```

```
Set objRst = objCmd.Execute
While Not objRst.Eof
  Wscript.Echo objRst("cn")
    objRst.MoveNext
Wend

objRst.Close
objConn.Close
```

The ability to execute a query against the provider allows for the whole directory tree to be searched. If you specify the domain-level root object, the search starts from the root and iterates through all subcontainers (as long as the SearchScope property hasn't been changed).

Criteria must be specified in the search string, so if you want to list all object classes from the whole domain, you have to include criteria to include all objects:

```
SELECT name FROM 'LDAP://DC=Acme,DC=COM' WHERE objectClass='*'
```

The adsiqry.vbs script is a command-line script that executes a query against the Active Directory provider and outputs the results to standard output. It takes an Active Directory query as a parameter and outputs the results in comma-delimited format:

```
adsiqry.wsf "SELECT cn, name,sn, street, l, st FROM 'LDAP://OU=Sales,DC=Acme,
DC=COM' WHERE objectClass='user' AND objectCategory='person' ORDER BY NAME"
```

The script has three optional parameters. By default, all subcontainers are searched—if you specify /s, only the source container is searched. If you specify /h, the field names are included in the header. The default comma delimiter can be changed by specifying the /d:X parameter, where *X* represents an alternative delimiter:

```
adsiqry.wsf " SELECT name FROM 'LDAP://DC=Acme,DC=COM' WHERE
objectClass='*'" /s /h /d:;
```

You can't query the Windows NT provider using SQL queries through ADO. WinNT provider objects have a Filter property that allows the filtering of object types:

```
objObject.Filter = aPropArray
```

aPropArray is an array of object class names. Once a filter is applied to an object, any enumeration operations performed on the object will only return object types specified by the filter. You cannot specify detailed criteria.

```
'get a reference to a domain object
Set objDomain = GetObject("WinNT://Acme")
'filter on the user objects
objDomain.Filter = Array("user")
For Each objUser In objDomain
   Wscript.Echo objUser.Name
Next
```

See Also

For more information, search http://msdn.microsoft.com for the article "Searching with ActiveX Data Objects (ADO)."

14.17 Controlling NT Services

Problem

You want to check if a service has stopped.

Solution

You can use the WinNT ADSI provider to reference Windows NT and later services. Services can be queried, stopped, started, or paused. The following command-line script enumerates, starts, stops, or pauses services for a specified computer:

```
<?xml version="1.0" ?>
<job>
<!--comment
Script:svcmaint.vbs
Description:stops/starts/pauses/lists services
-->
 <script language="VBScript" src="adsilib.vbs">
 <![CDATA[
 Const ADS_SERVICE_STOPPED = 1
 Const ADS_SERVICE_START_PENDING = 2
 Const ADS_SERVICE_STOP_PENDING = 3
```

```
Const ADS_SERVICE_RUNNING = 4
Const ADS_SERVICE_CONTINUE_PENDING =5
Const ADS_SERVICE_PAUSE_PENDING = 6
Const ADS_SERVICE_PAUSED = 7
Const ADS_SERVICE_ERROR = 8
 Dim strService, strOperation, strComputer
Dim objService, objComputer
On Error Resume Next

If Not IsCscript() Then _
 ExitScript "This script must be run from command line using cscript.exe"

If Wscript.Arguments.Count < 2 Then
  ShowUsage
  Wscript.Quit
End If

 strComputer = Wscript.Arguments(0)
 strService = Wscript.Arguments(1)
If Wscript.Arguments.Count = 2 And Ucase(strService) = "/L" Then
 Set objComputer = GetObject("WinNT://" & strComputer)
 objComputer.Filter = Array("Service")

  For Each objService In objComputer
   Wscript.Echo objService.Name, objService.DisplayName, _
                SvcStatus(objService.Status)
  Next
Else

strOperation = Wscript.Arguments(2)
'get the specified service
Set objService = GetObject("WinNT://" & strComputer & "/" & strService)

If Err Then _
  ExitScript "Error getting reference to service " & strService

'check for operation
Select Case UCase(strOperation)
 Case "STOP"
  If objService.Status <> ADS_SERVICE_STOPPED Then
   objService.Stop
   WaitUntil ADS_SERVICE_STOPPED, objService
  End If
```

```
  Case "START"
   If objService.Status <> ADS_SERVICE_RUNNING Then
    objService.start
    WaitUntil ADS_SERVICE_RUNNING, objService
   End If
  Case "PAUSE"
   If objService.Status <> ADS_SERVICE_PAUSED Then
    objService.Pause
    WaitUntil ADS_SERVICE_PAUSED, objService
   End If
   End Select
End If

 Sub ShowUsage
   WScript.Echo _
    "svcmaint.ws stops/starts or pauses a specified service" & vbCrLf & _
    "Syntax:" &  vbCrLf & _
    "svcmaint.ws computer service [operation] [/l] " &  vbCrLf & _
    "computer  computer where service resides" & vbCrLf & _
    "service   name of service" & vbCrLf & _
    "operation start/stop or pause" & vbCrLf & _
    "/l        lists services on specified computer" & vbCrLf & _
    "Example:start SNMP on computer Odin" & vbCrLf & _
    "svcmaint.ws Odin SNMP start "
End Sub

 Sub WaitUntil(nStatus, objService)
  'wait until the service has changed
  While objService.Status <> nStatus
    Wscript.Sleep 100
  Wend
 End Sub

 Function SvcStatus(nStatus)
   Select Case nStatus
  Case ADS_SERVICE_STOPPED
   SvcStatus = "Stopped"
  Case ADS_SERVICE_START_PENDING
   SvcStatus = "Start pending"
  Case ADS_SERVICE_STOP_PENDING
   SvcStatus = "Stop pending"
  Case ADS_SERVICE_RUNNING
   SvcStatus = "Running"
```

```
  Case ADS_SERVICE_CONTINUE_PENDING
   SvcStatus = "Continue pending"
  Case ADS_SERVICE_PAUSE_PENDING
   SvcStatus = "Pause pending"
  Case ADS_SERVICE_PAUSED
   SvcStatus = "Paused"
  Case ADS_SERVICE_ERROR
   SvcStatus = "Error"
  End Select
End Function
 ]]>
  </script>
</job>
```

Discussion

The WinNT provider provides access to NT services. To get a reference to a service, use the following line:

```
objService = GetObject("WinNT://Computer/servicename,Service")
```

Servicename is the internally stored name of the service—it is not the name that appears under Control Panel > Services.

To list all services installed on a computer, get a reference to the computer and filter all class objects of type Service:

```
'list all services on the computer Odin
'get a reference to a computer
Set objComputer = GetObject("WinNT://Odin")
'filter on the Service object class
objComputer.Filter = Array("Service")
'enumerate the services
   For Each objService In objComputer
    Wscript.Echo objService.Name, objService.DisplayName
   Next
```

Table 14-10 lists Service object properties.

Table 14-10. Service *Object Properties*

PROPERTY	DESCRIPTION
DisplayName	Friendly name that appears in Control Panel.
Dependencies	Array of values. Lists all services that service is dependent upon.
LoadOrderGroup	Name of load order group.
Path	String. Path to service executable.
HostComputer	String. Computer the service resides on.
ServiceAccountName	String. Systems account used to log on user.
ServiceType	Service type. Combination of any value that is listed in Table 14-11.
StartType	Indicates how service is started. Valid values are listed in Table 14-12.
StartupParameters	Parameters pass to service executable at startup.
Status	Determines the operational status of the server (stopped, paused, and so on). Valid values are listed in Table 14-13.

Table 14-11 lists ServiceType values.

Table 14-11. ServiceType *Values*

NAME	VALUE
ADS_KERNEL_DRIVER	1
ADS_FILE_SYSTEM_DRIVER	2
ADS_OWN_PROCESS	16
ADS_SHARE_PROCESS	32

Table 14-12 lists service start type values.

Table 14-12. Service Start Type Values

NAME	VALUE	DESCRIPTION
ADS_BOOT_START	0	Starts by OS loader
ADS_SYSTEM_START	1	Starts during OS initialization
ADS_AUTO_START	2	Starts by Service Control Manager during system startup
ADS_DEMAND_START	3	Manual startup
ADS_DISABLED	4	Service disable

Table 14-13 lists service status values.

Table 14-13. Service Status Values

NAME	VALUE	DESCRIPTION
ADS_SERVICE_STOPPED	1	Service stopped
ADS_SERVICE_START_PENDING	2	Service start initialized
ADS_SERVICE_STOP_PENDING	3	Service stop initialized
ADS_SERVICE_RUNNING	4	Service is running
ADS_SERVICE_CONTINUE_PENDING	5	Service in the process of continuing
ADS_SERVICE_PAUSE_PENDING	6	Service in the process of pausing
ADS_SERVICE_PAUSED	7	Service paused
ADS_SERVICE_ERROR	8	Error occurred

A service can be started/stopped/paused by invoking the `Start`, `Stop`, or `Pause` method respectively on a `Service` object. Make sure that any dependant services are stopped before stopping the service. The `Stop` method provides the option to stop dependant services such as Control Panel.

When you perform multiple service operations (starting/stopping/pausing) where operations in the sequence are dependant on the successful completion of the previous service operation, checks should be made to determine that the service is in the assumed state before continuing.

For example, if a service is stopped using the Stop method, the code might continue executing before the service has been completely stopped. Following code might not execute correctly if it is dependant upon the service having been stopped.

```
'get a reference to the Exchange Internet Mail Connector service
Set objService = GetObject("WinNT://odin/MSExchangeIMC")
objService.Stop
'wait until the service has completely stopped
While objService.Status = ADS_SERVICE_STOPPED
Wscript.Sleep 100
Wend
```

The svcmaint.wsf script can stop, start, resume, and list services.

```
svcmaint.wsf computer [service] [operation] [/l]
```

Computer is the name of computer the service resides on. Service is the name of the service to manipulate. Operation represents start, stop, or pause. If you pass a /l switch, all services will be listed.

For example, the following stops Exchange server services:

```
svcmaint.wsf odin MSExchangeIMC stop
svcmaint.wsf odin MSExchangeMTA stop
svcmaint.wsf odin MSExchangeIS stop
svcmaint.wsf odin MSExchangeDS stop
svcmaint.wsf odin MSExchangeSA stop
```

See Also

For more information, search http://msdn.microsoft.com for the article "IADsServiceOperations."

14.18 Listing Connected Resources

Problem

You want to list all connected sessions.

Solution

Using the WinNT provider, you can enumerate connected resources through the `Sessions` collection of the `LanmanServer` object for a specified computer:

```
'lstcnusers.vbs
'list connected users to specified server
Dim objFileService, objSession, strComputer

'check argument count
If Not Wscript.Arguments.Count = 1 Then
 ShowUsage
 Wscript.Quit
End If

'get the file service object
strComputer = Wscript.Arguments(0)
'get a reference to the LanmanServer service
Set objFileService = GetObject("WinNT://" & strComputer & "/LanmanServer")

'loop through each session and display any connected users
For Each objSession In objFileService.sessions
 'check if the session user ID is not empty
 If Not objSession.user = "" Then [<> ?]
     Wscript.StdOut.WriteLine objSession.user
 End If
Next

Sub ShowUsage
    WScript.Echo "lstcnusers.vbs lists connected users " & vbCrLf & _
    "Syntax:"  &  vbCrLf & _
    "lstcnusers.vbs computer" & vbCrLf & _
    "computer computer to enumerate connected users"
End Sub
```

Discussion

The Windows NT provider exposes the connected session resources through the `FileService` object. A reference can be retrieved from the NT network management (Lanman) object of a server.

A connected session can represent either a user or a computer. To get a list of all connected sessions, get a reference to the LanmanServer service of the computer you want to check:

```
'list all sessions on computer odin
'get a reference to the LanmanServer service
Set objFileService = GetObject("WinNT://odin/LanmanServer")
'enumerate all sessions
For Each objSession In objFileService.sessions
   objTextStream.WriteLine objSession.Name
Next
```

Table 14-14 lists Session object's properties.

Table 14-14. Session *Object Properties*

PROPERTY	DESCRIPTION
Computer	Name of connected computer
ConnectTime	Time connected in seconds
Name	Name in format user\COMPUTER (e.g., administrator\ODIN)
IdleTime	Idle time in seconds
User	User name

See Also

For more information, search http://msdn.microsoft.com for the articles "IADsFileServiceOperations" and "IADsSession."

14.19 Determining User RAS Access

Problem

You want to determine all users' RAS access.

Solution

User RAS access is not directly exposed through the ADSI User object. The ADSI 2.5 SDK includes an extension DLL that allows for the setting of RAS access permissions. The following command-line script sets RAS settings for a specified user:

```
<?xml version="1.0" ?>
<job>
<!--comment
Script:rasusers.wsf
Description:lists all users with RAS access
-->
 <script language="VBScript" src="adsilib.vbs">
 <![CDATA[
   Option Explicit
   Const ADS_RAS_NOCALLBACK = 1
   Const ADS_RAS_ADMIN_SETCALLBACK = 2
   Const ADS_RAS_CALLER_SETCALLBACK = 4
   Dim objUser, strDomain, objDomain, strType, lFlag
   On Error Resume Next
   If Not Wscript.Arguments.Count = 1 Then
     ShowUsage
     Wscript.Quit
   End If

   'get a reference to a domain
   Set objDomain = GetObject("WinNT://" & Wscript.Arguments(0))

   If Err Then _
     ExitScript "Error getting reference to domain: " & Wscript.Arguments(0)

   'filter on user objects
   objDomain.Filter = Array("User")
   'loop through each user and check if they have RAS access
   For Each objUser In objDomain

    If objUser.DialinPrivilege Then

    lFlag = objUser.GetRasCallBack

    If lFlag And ADS_RAS_NOCALLBACK Then
      strType = "No Callback"
    ElseIf lFlag And ADS_RAS_CALLER_SETCALLBACK Then
      strType = "Call back set by caller"
```

```
    ElseIf lFlag And ADS_RAS_ADMIN_SETCALLBACK Then
      strType = "Call back number:" & objUser.GetRasPhoneNumber
    End If
          Wscript.Echo objUser.Name & ":" & strType
    End If
  Next

  Sub ShowUsage
    WScript.Echo "rasusers lists user RAS settings" & vbCrLf & _
    "Syntax:" &  vbCrLf & _
    "rasusers.wsf domain" &  vbCrLf & _
    "domain domain name to list users from"
  End Sub
    ]]>
  </script>
</job>
```

Active Directory native mode user objects expose properties that can control user dial-in access. The msNPAllowDialin property controls if a user has dial-in access:

```
Set objUser = GetObject("LDAP://CN=fred smith,CN=Users,DC=Acme,DC=com")
objUser.msNPAllowDialin = True
objUser.SetInfo
```

Discussion

To use the extensions, register the ADsRAS.dll file that is included with the ADSI 2.5 SDK.

The DLL extends the WinNT provider's User object with a number of RAS-related properties. Table 14-15 lists the ADsRAS properties.

Table 14-15. ADsRAS.dll *Properties*

PROPERTY	DESCRIPTION
DialinPrivilege	Boolean. If True, user has RAS dial-in access.
GetRasCallBack	Integer value. Determines user call back type.
ADS_RAS_NOCALLBACK	1
ADS_RAS_ADMIN_SETCALLBACK	2
ADS_RAS_CALLER_SETCALLBACK	4
GetRasPhoneNumber	Returns the RAS phone number used for call back.

To allow a user RAS, set the DialinPrivilege property to True. If you need to set specific call back access, invoke the SetCallBack method, specifying the type of call back the user has:

```
Dim objuser
Set objUser = GetObject("WinNT://acme/freds")
'all the user dial in access
objUser.DialinPrivilege = True
'set users call back access
objUser.SetRasCallBack ADS_RAS_CALLER_SETCALLBACK
objUser.SetInfo
```

The ADsRAS.dll works with Windows NT 4.0 and Active Directory mixed mode domains. Active Directory native mode domains can manipulate dial-in RAS settings via properties listed in Table 14-16.

Table 14-16. RAS Dial-in Settings

PROPERTY	DESCRIPTION
msNPAllowDialin	Boolean. If True, the user has RAS dial-in access.
msNPCallingStationID	Verify caller ID phone number.
msRADIUSCallbackNumber	Callback phone number.
msRADIUSServiceType	Determines if the callback number is used. If Empty, no callback is used. If 4, then use callback.
msRADIUSFramedIPAddress	Stores the dial-in user's optional static IP address. The address is stored as a long integer. The number is calculated by first octet × 16777216 + second octet × 65536 + third octet × 256 + fourth octet. If Empty, the IP address is not set.

The following snippet sets the callback number:

```
Set objUser = GetObject("LDAP://CN=fred smith,CN=Users,DC=Acme,DC=com")
objUser.msRADIUSServiceType = 4
objUser. msRADIUSCallbackNumber= "555-1245"
objUser.SetInfo
```

The following snippet sets the static IP address to 1.2.3.4:

```
Set objUser = GetObject("LDAP://CN=fred smith,CN=Users,DC=Acme,DC=com")
objUser. msRADIUSFramedIPAddress= 1 * 16777216 + 2 * 65536 + 3  * 256 + 4
objUser.SetInfo
```

To turn off the static IP address or callback number, set the appropriate properties to Empty. To do so, use the PutEx method to clear the properties:

```
Const ADS_PROPERTY_CLEAR = 1
Set objUser = GetObject("LDAP://CN=fred smith,CN=Users,DC=Acme,DC=com")
'turn off static IP address
objUser.PutEx ADS_PROPERTY_CLEAR, "msRADIUSFramedIPAddress", 0
'turn off callback
objUser.PutEx ADS_PROPERTY_CLEAR, "msRADIUSServiceType", 0
objUser.SetInfo
```

See Also

Search for the document Rtk.HTM in the ADSI 2.5 SDK directory.

14.20 Listing Network Shares

Problem

You want to list all network shares.

Solution

You can reference the computer on which the file shares reside and then enumerate all FileShare objects from the LanmanServer service object:

```
Dim objFileService, objSession

'get the file service object
Set objFileService = GetObject("WinNT://odin/LanmanServer")
'filter on file shares
objFileService.Filter = Array("FileShare")

'loop through and display description of all file shares
For Each objFileShare In objFileService
 Wscript.Echo objFileShare.Name
Next
```

Discussion

The WinNT provider exposes network share information. You can enumerate, create, and delete shares.

To reference a file share, reference the `LanmanServer` service on the computer on which the share resides, followed by the share name:

```
Set objFileShare = GetObject("WinNT://computer/LanmanServer/sharename")
```

`Sharename` is the name of the share you want to reference. The `Share` object returned exposes the properties listed in Table 14-17.

Table 14-17. `Share` *Object Properties*

PROPERTY	DESCRIPTION
`Name`	Name of share.
`Description`	Share description.
`Path`	Path share represents.
`CurrentUserCount`	Current connected users.
`MaxUserCount`	Maximum number of users allowed to connect to the share. For unlimited users, set to –1.

See Also

For more information, search `http://msdn.microsoft.com` for the article "IADsFileShare."

14.21 Creating or Deleting a Network Share

Problem

You want to create or delete a file share.

Solution

You can retrieve a reference to the LanmanServer service on the computer on which you want to create the share using the WinNT provider and then call the Create method, specifying the FileShare class as the object type you want to create:

```
'
'get the file service object
Set objFileService = GetObject("WinNT://Odin/LanmanServer")

Set objFileShare = objFileService.create("FileShare", "AcctData")
objFileShare.Path = "d:\data\accounting"
objFileShare.Description = "Accounting Data"
objFileShare.MaxUserCount = -1 'set unlimited users
objFileShare.SetInfo
```

Discussion

To create a file share, you can reference the LanmanServer service on the machine on which you want to create the share. Next, invoke the Create method, specifying the FileShare class as the object you want to create, followed by a share name. Then set the path the share will point to.

To delete a share, reference the LanmanServer service on the machine from which you want to delete the share. Invoke the Delete method, specifying the object class type as FileShare followed by the name of the share you want to delete:

```
'get the file service object
Set objFileService = GetObject("WinNT://odin/LanmanServer")
'delete the share AcctData
objFileService.Delete "FileShare", "AcctData"
```

See Also

For more information, search http://msdn.microsoft.com for the article "IADsFileShare."

14.22 Print Queue Operations

Problem

You want to purge a print queue of current print jobs.

Solution

You can reference the queue object using the WinNT provider and call the Purge method. The following command-line script pauses or resumes a specified print queue:

```
<?xml version="1.0" ?>
<job>
<!--comment
Script:pqmaint.wsf
Description:pauses or purges specified print queue
-->
 <script language="VBScript" src="adsilib.vbs">
 <![CDATA[
  Dim objPrintQ, strAction, strComputer, strPrinter

   If Not WScript.Arguments.Count = 3 Then
    ShowUsage
        Wscript.Quit
   End If

   strComputer = Wscript.Arguments(0)
   strPrinter = Wscript.Arguments(1)
   strAction = Wscript.Arguments(2)

   Set objPrintQ = GetObject("WinNT://" & strComputer & "/" & strPrinter)

    Select Case UCase(strAction)
     Case "PURGE"
      objPrintQ.Purge
     Case "PAUSE"
      objPrintQ.Pause
     Case "RESUME"
      objPrintQ.Resume
    End Select
```

```
  Sub ShowUsage
    WScript.Echo "pqmaint performs print queue maintenance" & vbCrLf & _
     "Syntax:" &  vbCrLf & _
    "pqmaint.wsf computer printer action" &  vbCrLf & _
    "computer computer printer is shared on" & vbCrLf & _
    "printer  name of printer" & vbCrLf & _
    "action   Purge, pause or resume" & vbCrLf & _
    "Example:purge " & vbCrLf & _
    "pqmaint.wsf odin web purge"
  End Sub
   ]]>
  </script>
</job>
```

Discussion

The Windows NT provider exposes computer-shared printers (print queues). To get a reference to a print queue, use the following line:

```
Set objPrintQ = GetObject("WinNT://Computer/PrintQ)
```

`Computer` is the name of the computer the print queue resides on. `PrintQ` is the name of the queue represented by the shared name of the printer.

The `PrintQueue` object provides a `Purge` method to remove all print jobs from the queue. The queue can also be paused using the `Pause` method, which prevents any further jobs from being printed. To resume a paused queue, invoke the `Resume` method.

The `PrintQueue` object exposes a `Status` property that identifies the current status of the printer servicing the queue. Table 14-18 lists the values the `Status` property can return.

Table 14-18. `Status` *Property Values*

CONSTANT	VALUE
ADS_PRINTER_PAUSED	1
ADS_PRINTER_PENDING_DELETION	2
ADS_PRINTER_ERROR	3
ADS_PRINTER_PAPER_JAM	4
ADS_PRINTER_PAPER_OUT	5
ADS_PRINTER_MANUAL_FEED	6

Table 14-18. `Status` *Property Values (continued)*

CONSTANT	VALUE
ADS_PRINTER_PAPER_PROBLEM	7
ADS_PRINTER_OFFLINE	8
ADS_PRINTER_IO_ACTIVE	256
ADS_PRINTER_BUSY	512
ADS_PRINTER_PRINTING	1024
ADS_PRINTER_OUTPUT_BIN_FULL	2048
ADS_PRINTER_NOT_AVAILABLE	4096
ADS_PRINTER_WAITING	8192
ADS_PRINTER_PROCESSING	16384
ADS_PRINTER_INITIALIZING	32768
ADS_PRINTER_WARMING_UP	65536
ADS_PRINTER_TONER_LOW	131072
ADS_PRINTER_NO_TONER	262144
ADS_PRINTER_PAGE_PUNT	524288
ADS_PRINTER_USER_INTERVENTION	&h00100000
ADS_PRINTER_OUT_OF_MEMORY	&h00200000
ADS_PRINTER_DOOR_OPEN	&h00400000
ADS_PRINTER_SERVER_UNKNOWN	&h00800000
ADS_PRINTER_POWER_SAVE	&h01000000

See Also

For more information, search `http://msdn.microsoft.com` for the article "IADsPrintQueueOperations."

14.23 Listing Print Jobs

Problem

You want to list current print jobs.

Solution

You can reference a queue object using the WinNT provider and enumerate the `PrintJobs` collection to list any jobs and related information:

```
<?xml version="1.0" ?>
<job>
<!--comment
Script:prjobs.wsf
Description:lists print jobs for specified print queue
-->
 <script language="VBScript" src="adsilib.vbs">
 <![CDATA[
  Dim objPrintQ, strComputer, strPrinter

  On Error Resume Next
  If Not Wscript.Arguments.Count = 2 Then
    ShowUsage
    Wscript.Quit
  End If
   strComputer = Wscript.Arguments(0)
   strPrinter = Wscript.Arguments(1)
   Set objPrintQ = GetObject("WinNT://" & strComputer & "/" & strPrinter)
   If Err Then _
     ExitScript "Error getting reference to printer : " & strPrinter

   For Each objPrintJob In objPrintQ.PrintJobs
    Wscript.Echo objPrintJob.Name & " " & objPrintJob.Description _
       & " " & Status(objPrintJob.Status) & " Pages " & _
      objPrintJob.TotalPages
   Next

  Sub ShowUsage
WScript.Echo "prjobs lists print jobs for specified queue" & vbLf & _
    "Syntax:" &  vbLf & _
    "prjobs.wsf computer printer " &  vbLf & _
    "computer computer printer is shared on" & vbLf & _
    "printer  name of printer"
  End Sub

  'returns a string
  'Parameter:
  'lFlag    long printer status value
  'Returns string representing print job status
  Function Status(lFlag)
    Dim sStat
```

```
    If lFlag And 1 Then sStat = sStat & "Paused "
    If lFlag And 2 Then    sStat = sStat & "Error "
    If lFlag And 4 Then    sStat = sStat & "Deleting "
    If lFlag And 16 Then sStat = sStat & "Printing "
    If lFlag And 32 Then sStat = sStat & "Offline "
    If lFlag And 64 Then sStat = sStat & "Paper out "
Status = sStat
  End Function
   ]]>
  </script>
</job>
```

Discussion

A print queue contains a list of print jobs currently being processed. Each job is represented as a `PrintJob` object and can be paused or resumed, but not deleted.

To enumerate a print queue, get a reference to the print queue you want to process. The `PrintQueue` object has a `PrintJobs` property that contains a list of active jobs in the form of a `PrintJob` object.

Table 14-19 lists the `PrintJob` object's properties.

Table 14-19. `PrintJob` *Object Properties*

PROPERTY	DESCRIPTION
User	User name of the user who submitted the print job.
TimeSubmitted	Time the job was submitted.
TotalPages	Number of pages in the document.
Size	Size in bytes.
Description	Name of the document being printed.
Priority	The higher the number, the greater the priority.
StartTime	Start of the time range when the document can be printed.
UntilTime	End of the time range when the document can be printed.
Notify	Name of the user to notify when the job is complete.
TimeElapsed	Time elapsed in seconds of the current active print job.
PagesPrinted	Number of pages in the current active job.
Position	Position of the job in the queue.
Status	Status of the job in the queue. Any combination of the status flag values listed in Table 14-20.

A PrintJob object can be paused by invoking the Pause method and resumed by invoking the Resume method. You cannot delete a print job.

PrintJob properties such as priority and start and end times can be modified. The following example increases the priority of jobs with less than 50 pages so they print before larger jobs:

```
Dim objPrintQ, objJob

'get a reference to a print queue
Set objPrintQ = GetObject("WinNT://Odin/HP5")

 'enumerate all print jobs
 For Each objJob In objPrintQ.printjobs
    'if the number of pages is less than 50, increase priority
    If objJob.TotalPages < 50 Then
        objJob.Priority = 10
        objJob.SetInfo
    End If
 Next
```

Table 14-20 lists PrintJob status flags.

Table 14-20. PrintJob *Status Flags*

NAME	VALUE	DESCRIPTION
ADS_JOB_PAUSED	1	Job is paused
ADS_JOB_ERROR	2	Job is in error status
ADS_JOB_DELETING	4	Job is being deleted
ADS_JOB_PRINTING	16	Job is being printed
ADS_JOB_OFFLINE	32	Printer offline
ADS_JOB_PAPEROUT	64	Printer is out of paper
ADS_JOB_PRINTED	128	Job is printed
ADS_JOB_DELETED	256	Job is deleted

See Also

For more information, search http://msdn.microsoft.com for the article "IADsPrintJobOperations."

14.24 Setting Windows Terminal Services Properties

Problem

You want to set Windows Terminal Services (WTS) client properties.

Solution

Windows 2003 supports setting WTS properties.

```
'set WTS properties for user Fred Smith
Set objUser = GetObject("LDAP://CN=fred smith,CN=Users,DC=Acme,DC=com")

'allow user to log on
objUser.AllowLogon = 1
'set profile and home directories
objUser.TerminalServicesProfilePath = "\\odin\profiles\freds"
objUser.TerminalServicesHomeDrive = "h:"
objUser.TerminalServicesHomeDirectory = "\\odin\freds$"
'set maximum session time to 10 hours
objUser.MaxConnectionTime = 600
objUser.SetInfo
```

Discussion

Windows 2003 includes an ADSI extension that allows WTS properties to be set. These properties are not available for Windows 2000 or WTS NT 4.0. A `WTSSupport` component is available to provide support for these earlier versions of Windows.

The DLL is located in the book's supporting file for download at the Apress Web site (`http://www.apress.com`). To use the `WTSSupport` component, you must have the VB 5.0 runtime installed. Copy `WTSLib.DLL` to your system and register it using `Regsvr32.exe`.

To use the `WTSSupport` object, create an object using the ProgID `WTSSupport.WTSLib`. The `WTSSupport` component exposes two properties that need to be set before any operations can be performed: `UserName` and `ServerName`. `ServerName` points to the Windows domain controller used to store user settings. The `UserName` property is the name of user to read or write.

Table 14-21 lists WTS Windows 2003 and `WTSSupport` component properties.

Table 14-21. WTS *Properties*

WINDOWS 2003 PROPERTY	WTSSUPPORT	DESCRIPTION
`TerminalServicesProfilePath`	`ProfilePath`	Path to terminal services roaming profile.
`TerminalServicesHomeDirectory`	`HomeDirectory`	User terminal services home directory. This is only used when the user logs onto a terminal services session.
`TerminalServicesHomeDrive`	`HomeDrive`	Home drive assigned to terminal services home directory. This is stored as drive letter followed by a colon.
`AllowLogon`	`AllowWTSLogon`	Allows logon to terminal services sessions. If the value is 1, logon is allowed; if the value is 0, logon is not allowed.
`EnableRemoteControl`	N/A	Determines issues related to user remote control sessions. Values include the following: 0: Disable remote control. 1 Require user's permission to connect. Allow session interaction. 2 Don't require user's permission to connect. Allow session interaction. 3 Require user's permission to connect. Don't allow session interaction. 4 Don't require user's permission to connect. Don't allow session interaction.
`MaxDisconnectionTime`	`DisconnectionTimeout`	Maximum time in minutes a disconnected terminal services session will remain active before being terminated.
`MaxConnectionTime`	`ConnectionTimeout`	Maximum time in minutes an active terminal services session will remain active. After this time has elapsed, the action specified by the `BrokenConnectionAction` is performed.
`MaxIdleTime`	`IdleTimeout`	Maximum time in minutes a terminal services session can remain idle before being disconnected or terminated.

Table 14-21. WTS Properties (continued)

WINDOWS 2003 PROPERTY	WTSSUPPORT	DESCRIPTION
BrokenConnectionAction	N/A	Determines the action to take when a terminal services session limit is reached. If the value is 1, the client session is terminated; if the value is 0, the client session is disconnected.
ReconnectionAction	N/A	Determines which computer a disconnected terminal services session can reconnect from. If the value is 1, only the original client can reconnect; if the value is 0, any client can reconnect.
ConnectClientDrivesAtLogon	ConnectClientDrives	Controls if client drives are connected at logon. If the value is 1, client drives are connected; if the value is 0, client drive connecting is disabled.
ConnectClientPrintersAtLogon	ConnectClientPrinters	Controls if client printers are connected at logon. If the value is 1, client printers are connected; if the value is 0, client printer connecting is disabled.
DefaultToMainPrinter	DefaultClientPrinter	Controls if a terminal services session defaults to client's default printer. If the value is 1, the client's default printer is used; if the value is 0, it is ignored.
TerminalServicesWorkDirectory	N/A	Working directory for the application set by the TerminalServicesInitialProgram property.
TerminalServicesInitialProgram	N/A	Application that runs when a terminal services session is started.

The following script sets WTS properties using the WTSSupport component:

```
Set objWTS = CreateObject("WTSSupport.WTSLib")
'set user and domain controller
objWTS.UserName = "freds"
objWTS.ServerName = "\\Odin"

'allow user to log on
objWTS.AllowWTSLogon = True
```

```
'set profile and home directories
objWTS.ProfilePath = "\\odin\profiles\freds"
objWTS.HomeDrive = "h:"
objWTS.HomeDirectory = "\\odin\freds$"

'set maximum session time to 2 hours
objWTS.ConnectionTimeout = 120
```

See Also

Search `http://msdn.microsoft.com` for "Msvbvm50.exe Installs Visual Basic 5.0 Run-Time Files" for the VB 5.0 runtime download.

CHAPTER 15

Internet Information Server

INTERNET INFORMATION SERVER (IIS) version 4.0 and later expose configuration information and operations through an ADSI interface.

Using this interface you can perform all of the administrative tasks that are normally accessed through the IIS MMC application, such as the creation and manipulation of Web, FTP, NNTP, and SMTP sites.

This can save time. For example, in a load-balanced environment, all the servers in a Web "farm" must contain identical configurations, or in an ISP environment, a single IIS server may host dozens or even hundreds of individual sites.

IIS configuration information is stored in a metabase that has a structure similar to the registry. The metabase is accessible through ADSI using the IIS namespace interface. The IIS namespace exposes objects in a hierarchical fashion.

The IIS ADSI provider is installed with IIS version 4.0 and later. A remote server can be accessed if and only if both computers have IIS installed. When you reference IIS objects, the path to the object must be prefixed with `IIS`. This indicates that the object resides in the IIS namespace and requires the IIS ADSI provider.

The top-level object in the IIS hierarchy represents the computer on which an IIS server resides. All IIS object paths must start with the name of the computer:

```
'get a reference to the IIS server on computer Odin
 Set objComputer = GetObject("IIS://Odin")
```

Once a reference has been made to the IIS computer, you can enumerate and manipulate any IIS resource that resides on that computer.

This chapter demonstrates how to perform IIS backup–related operations, resource enumeration, Web and FTP site creation, virtual directory manipulation, individual file and directory manipulation, and IP address assignment.

Most of the more complex command-line scripts in this chapter use the `adsilib.vbs` support include file listed in Chapter 14.

NOTE *For more information, read "Programming IIS 4.0 with ADSI"* (http://15seconds.com/issue/980304.htm) *and "An Introduction to the IIS Metabase"* (http://msdn.microsoft.com/library/en-us/iisref/html/psdk/asp/aint1aud.asp).

15.1 Backing Up and Restoring IIS Configuration Information

Problem

You want to back up and restore IIS configuration information.

Solution

You can reference the required IIS server using the IIS provider and then call the Backup or Restore method. The following script creates a backup called "Weekly Backup of the Metabase" for server Odin:

```
'weeklybackup.vbs
Const MD_BACKUP_NEXT_VERSION = &HFFFFFFFF
Const MD_BACKUP_FORCE_BACKUP = 4
Const MD_BACKUP_SAVE_FIRST = 2

Set objComputer = GetObject("IIS://odin")
'create a new backup. Assign the next available version number
objComputer.Backup "Weekly backup", MD_BACKUP_NEXT_VERSION _
        , MD_BACKUP_FORCE_BACKUP Or MD_BACKUP_SAVE_FIRST
```

Discussion

As with computer systems in general, it is important to back up IIS configuration information to ensure recovery in case of system failure. Incomplete creation of IIS objects and invalid property settings through code can cause problems in the operation of the IIS server, and in some cases they can disable access to the site through the MMC administrative interface.

For example, a Web site requires that a corresponding virtual root directory be created. If the root directory is not created or the Web site is not properly identified, it will not appear in the MMC administration console and cause error messages to appear.

To perform backup operations, first get a reference to the IIS computer you want to back up or restore:

```
'get a reference to the IIS server
 Set objComputer = GetObject("IIS://strServer")
```

The `strServer` part of the path represents the name of the IIS computer. The IIS ADSI provider is installed on machines with IIS server installed.

Once a reference to the computer is retrieved, you can perform backup operations. To back up server configuration, invoke the `Backup` method:

```
objComputer.Backup strName, nVersion, nFlag
```

IIS 6.0 provides a method for backing up the metabase with a password. To back up the IIS metabase under IIS 6.0 with a password, invoke the `BackupWithPassword` method:

```
objComputer.BackupWithPassword strName, nVersion, nFlag, strPassword
```

`strName` is the name of the backup. It can be up to 100 characters and contain spaces.

You can store multiple versions of a backup with the same name. The `nVersion` parameter identifies the version number. It can be any number between 0 and 9,999. Alternatively, you can pass one of the values listed in Table 15-1 to find the next version number automatically or replace the current version of the backup, which is specified by the `strName` parameter.

Table 15-1. Backup Version Options

NAME	VALUE	DESCRIPTION
MD_BACKUP_HIGHEST_VERSION	&HFFFFFFFE	Replace the current highest backup version for the specified backup
MD_BACKUP_NEXT_VERSION	&HFFFFFFFF	Find the next available backup version for the corresponding backup

The nFlag parameter can be a combination of the backup values in Table 15-2.

Table 15-2. Backup Values

PROPERTY	VALUE	DESCRIPTION
MD_BACKUP_OVERWRITE	1	Perform backup overwriting any existing versions with the same name and version number
MD_BACKUP_SAVE_FIRST	2	Save metabase data before performing backup
MD_BACKUP_FORCE_BACKUP	4	Force backup even if saving of configuration was not successful

The strPassword parameter is required for the BackupWithPassword method under IIS 6.0 and represents a password to protect the backup.

To restore a backup, invoke the Restore method:

```
objComputer.Restore strName, nVersion, nFlag
```

To restore a backup under IIS 6.0 that has been password protected, invoke the RestoreWithPassword method:

```
objComputer.RestoreWithPassword strName, nVersion, nFlag, strPassword
```

The strName parameter is the name of the backup to restore. nVersion is the version to restore. If you want to restore the latest version of the backup, pass the MD_BACKUP_HIGHEST_VERSION value, which will restore the highest version of the specified backup. The nFlag parameter is not used and must be 0.

```
objComputer.Restore "MyBackups", MD_BACKUP_HIGHEST_VERSION, 0
```

The IIS 6.0 RestoreWithPassword method requires the strPassword parameter to restore password-protected backups.

To delete a backup, invoke the Delete method:

```
objComputer.DeleteBackup strName, nVersion
```

The strName parameter is the name of the backup to delete, while nVersion is the version to delete. If you want to restore the latest version of the backup, pass the MD_BACKUP_HIGHEST_VERSION value.

The following script, iisbackup.wsf, provides a generic command-line utility that creates, restores, and deletes backups from a specified IIS computer:

```
<?xml version="1.0" ?>
<job>
<!--
iisbackup.wsf
creates, lists,restores and deletes IIS backup
-->
 <script language="VBScript" src="adsilib.vbs">
 <![CDATA[
  Option Explicit
  Const MD_BACKUP_MAX_VERSION = 9999
  Const MD_BACKUP_MAX_LEN = 100
  Const MD_BACKUP_HIGHEST_VERSION = &HFFFFFFFE
  Const MD_BACKUP_NEXT_VERSION = &HFFFFFFFF

  Const MD_BACKUP_OVERWRITE = 1
  Const MD_BACKUP_FORCE_BACKUP = 4
  Const MD_BACKUP_SAVE_FIRST = 2
  Dim strComputer, strType, strAction
  Dim strBackupName, nVersion, objComputer

  On Error Resume Next
  'check the argument count
   If Wscript.Arguments.Count < 1 Or Wscript.Arguments.Count > 2 Then
     ShowUsage
           Wscript.Quit
   End If

    strComputer = Wscript.Arguments(0)
strAction = Ucase(Wscript.Arguments(1))

    Set objComputer = GetObject("IIS://" & strComputer)
    If Err Then
            Wscript.Echo "Error connecting to computer " _
                                      & strComputer & vbCrLf & Err.Description
            Wscript.Quit
    End If

    Select Case strAction
      Case "/D" 'delete
        GetDetails
```

```
        objComputer.DeleteBackup strBackupName, nVersion
        If Err Then
         Wscript.Echo "Error deleting backup " & strBackupName _
                                                   & vbCrLf & Err.Description
        Else
         Wscript.Echo "Successfully deleted backup " & strBackupName
        End If

      Case "/L" 'list
        ListBackups

      Case "/B" 'backup
        GetDetails
        objComputer.Backup strBackupName, nVersion, _
                        MD_BACKUP_SAVE_FIRST Or MD_BACKUP_OVERWRITE

        If Err Then
         Wscript.Echo "Error creating backup " & strBackupName _
                                                     vbCrLf & Err.Description
        Else
         Wscript.Echo "Successfully created backup " & strBackupName
        End If

      Case "/R" 'restore
        GetDetails

        objComputer.Restore  strBackupName, nVersion,0

        If Err Then
         Wscript.Echo "Error restoring backup " & strBackupName _
                                                   & vbCrLf & Err.Description
        Else
         Wscript.Echo "Successfully restored backup " & strBackupName
        End If
     End Select

    Sub ShowUsage
     WScript.Echo "iisbackup.wsf performs IIS backup operations " & vbCrLf & _
    "Syntax:"  &  vbCrLf & _
    "iisbackup.wsf  computer /d | /b | /l | /r [name] [version] " &  vbCrLf & _
    "computer computer IIS server resides on" & vbCrLf & _
    "/d      deletes specified backup " & vbCrLf & _
    "/b      creates new backup " & vbCrLf & _
```

```
"/r       restores specified backup" & vbCrLf & _
"/l       list all backups for specified IIS server" & vbCrLf & _
"name     name of backup to delete/create/restore" & vbCrLf & _
"version optional version # of backup to delete/create/restore" & vbCrLf & _
"Example: create backup called newbackup for server acmeWeb" & vbCrLf & _
"iisbackup.wsf AcmeWeb /b newbackup"
End Sub

'GetDetails retrieves command line parameters and determines
'what operation to perform
 Sub GetDetails
   If Wscript.Arguments.Count < 3 Then ExitScript "Not enough parameters"
   strBackupName = Wscript.Arguments(2)
   'check if version # can be set
   If Wscript.Arguments.Count> 3 Then
      nVersion = Wscript.Arguments(3)
   Else
      'if action is backup then version # is next version
      'otherwise restore or delete highest version
      If strAction = "/B"  Then
       nVersion = MD_BACKUP_NEXT_VERSION
      Else
       nVersion = MD_BACKUP_HIGHEST_VERSION
      End If
   End If

  End Sub

 Sub ListBackups()
   Dim nIndex, dBackupTime
   nIndex= 0
   Do While True
    objComputer.EnumBackups "", nIndex, nVersion, _
           strBackupName, dBackupTime

    If Err Then
           Wscript.Echo "Error enumerating backup " & vbCrLf & _
                      Err.Description
            Wscript.Quit
    End If
    Wscript.Echo strBackupName, nVersion, dBackupTime
    nIndex = nIndex+1
   Loop
```

```
    End Sub
    ]]>
  </script>
</job>
```

The iisbackup script lists sites of a specified type for a given IIS server:

```
iisbackup.wsf computer /d | /b | /l | /r [name] [version]
```

Computer is the computer where IIS resides. This is followed by one of the following switches, which represent the operation you want to perform: /d to delete a backup, /b to perform a backup, /l to list an existing backup, or /r to restore a backup.

If you create, delete, or restore a backup, you must specify a name for the backup. You specify an optional version number for any of these operations. If you omit the version number, the backup option creates a new backup with the next available number while the restore or delete operations affect the backup with the highest version number.

See Also

For more information, search http://msdn.microsoft.com for the article "IIsComputer."

15.2 Listing Web Sites

Problem

You want to enumerate individual Web sites on a given IIS computer.

Solution

Reference the IIS Web service object for the computer and then list each site in the service:

```
'list all Web sites on the Thor Web server
Dim objWebService, objWebSite
WebSet objWebService = GetObject("IIS://Thor/W3SVC")
'loop through each site, find available site #
For Each objWebSite In objWebService
```

```
    'check if the object is a Web site
    If objWebSite.Class = "IIsWebServer" Then
     Wscript.Echo objWebSite.Name, objWebSite.ServerComment
    End If
Next
```

Discussion

The IIS computer object exposes IIS services that are installed on the server. These include news (NNTP), mail (SMTP), FTP, and Web servers.

To get a reference to a service, use the following:

```
Set objService = IIS://ComputerName/Servicename
```

`ComputerName` represents the name of the IIS server and `Servicename` identifies the service. Table 15-3 lists the IIS service names.

Table 15-3. IIS Service Names

SERVICE NAME	DESCRIPTION
W3SVC	Web service
MSFTPSVC	FTP service
SmtpSvc	SMTP mail service
NNTPSVC	NNTP news service

The following code snippet gets a reference to the Web service on computer Odin:

```
'get a reference to the Web service on server Odin
Set objService = GetObject("IIS://odin/W3SVC")
```

IIS allows the hosting of multiple sites for each service. The sites are identified with a site name, which is represented internally by a number. If you create a site using the Microsoft Management Console (MMC), you see a "friendly" server comment name assigned to the site in MMC, while internally the site is assigned an identifier number. The Windows 2003 IIS Admin console lists the identifier number under the column Identifier. Sites cannot be programmatically referenced using the server comment.

The default Web site installed with IIS is identified as site 1. The site object's `Name` property returns the number associated with the site, and the `ServerComment` property returns the descriptive name assigned to the site, which is what appears in the IIS MMC.

The Active Directory Browser that is included with the ADSI SDK can browse each IIS server metabase. A stand-alone application is available to view and edit IIS metabase information. The metabase application is called the Metabase Editor under Windows NT 4.0 and Windows 2000. Under Windows 2003, it is known as Metabase Explorer. Metabase Editor and Metabase Explorer are different applications, but they are functionaly equivalent.

The Metabase Editor displays the details of the IIS objects, as shown in Figure 15-1. To download Metabase Editor, search for "q232068" at `http://support.microsoft.com`.

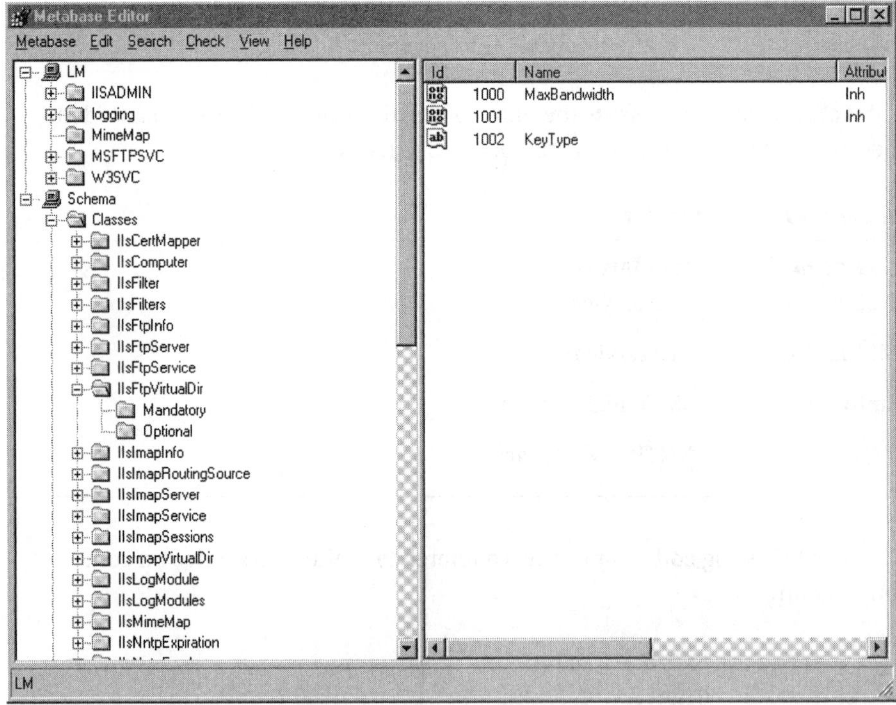

Figure 15-1. The Metabase Editor

Metabase Explorer is available from the IIS 6.0 Resource Kit. To download the IIS 6.0 Resource Kit, search for the phrase "IIS 6.0 resource kit download" at `http://www.microsoft.com`.

The following command-line script, `listsites.wsf`, lists the sites for a specified service on an IIS computer:

```
<?xml version="1.0" ?>
<job>
<!--
listsites.wsf
lists sites for specified service
-->
 <script language="VBScript" src="adsilib.vbs">
 <![CDATA[
  Option Explicit
  'check the argument count
   If Wscript.Arguments.Count <> 2 Then
    ShowUsage
    Wscript.Quit
   End If
    ListIIS Wscript.Arguments(0), Wscript.Arguments(1)

   Sub ShowUsage
     WScript.Echo "listsites lists sites for specific service " & vbCrLf & _
    "Syntax:" &  vbCrLf & _
    "listsites.wsf computer type" &  vbCrLf & _
    "computer computer IIS server resides on" & vbCrLf & _
    "type      site type - either Web,FTP, SMTP or NNTP" & vbCrLf & _
    "Example: List all Web sites" & vbCrLf & _
    "listsites.wsf Acme Web"
   End Sub

   'lists sites
   'Parameters
   'strComputer IIS server Computer name
   'strType      site type, Web or FTP
    Sub ListIIS(strComputer, strType)
    Dim objService, objItem, strSvc
    strSvc = GetSiteType(strType)

   'get the Web service from specified computer
    Set objService = GetObject("IIS://" & strComputer & "/" & strSvc )
   'loop through each site, find available site name
    For Each objItem In objService
    'check if object is a site
    If StrComp(objItem.Class, "IIs" & strType & "Server", vbTextCompare) = 0 Then
     'output site name and comment
```

```
      Wscript.Echo objItem.Name & "," & objItem.Servercomment
      End If
    Next
   End Sub
    ]]>
  </script>
</job>
```

The syntax for the `listsites.wsf` script is as follows:

```
listsites.wsf computer type
```

`Computer` is the server where IIS resides and `type` is the site type (Web, FTP, SMTP, or NNTP).

For example, to list all FTP sites on the IIS server odin, use this:

```
listsites.wsf odin FTP
```

See Also

For more information, search `http://msdn.microsoft.com` for the article "IIsComputer."

15.3 Creating a Site

Problem

You want to create an IIS Web or FTP site.

Solution

To create a Web site, you can reference the Web service (W3SVC) for the IIS server on which you want to create the site. Then call the `Create` method, specifying the `IIsWebServer` class. To make a Web site functional, you must create a root virtual directory and create it as a Web application. The following script creates a Web site called New Web site on server Odin:

```
Const MediumProtection = 2
Dim objService, objWebSite, objVirtDir
'get a reference to the Web service on server Odin
Set objService = GetObject("IIS://odin/W3SVC")
```

```
'create a new Web site and assign it the value of 5 as its 'name'
Set objWebSite = objService.create("IIsWebServer", 5)
'assign a friendly comment to appear in the IIS MMC
objWebSite.ServerComment = "New Web site"
objWebSite.SetInfo

'bind the site to an IP address and distinguished name
objWebSite.ServerBindings = Array("192.168.1.40:80:accounting.acme.com")
objWebSite.SetInfo

'create a virtual ROOT directory for the site
Set objVirtDir = objWebSite.create("IIsWebVirtualDir", "ROOT")
objVirtDir.Accessread = True
objVirtDir.AccessScript= True
objVirtDir.Path = "f:\inetpub\newsite" 'set the Web directory
objVirtDir.SetInfo

'create an application for the ROOT directory
objVirtDir.AppCreate2 MediumProtection
objVirtDir.AppFriendlyName = "Default Application"
objVirtDir.SetInfo
```

IIS 6.0 introduces a new method called `CreateNewSite` that makes creating new sites easier. The following script creates an equivalent site to the preceding solution script:

```
Set objWebService = GetObject("IIS://odin/W3SVC")
objWebService.CreateNewSite " New Web site", _
                Array("192.168.1.40:80:accounting.acme.com"),"f:\inetpub\newsite"
```

To create an FTP site, get a reference to either the FTP service (MSFTPSVC) or the IIS server on which you want to create the site. Then call the `Create` method, specifying the `IIsFTPVirtualDir` class:

```
Dim objService, objFTPSite, objVirtDir
'get a reference to the FTP service on server Thor
Set objService = GetObject("IIS://thor/MSFTPSVC")

'create a new FTP site and assign it the value of 6 as its 'name'
Set objFTPSite = objService.create("IIsFTPServer", 6)
'assign a friendly comment to appear in the IIS MMC
objFTPSite.ServerComment = "Accounting FTP Site"
```

```
'bind the site to an IP address and distinguished name
objFTPSite.ServerBindings = Array("192.168.1.40:21:ftp.accounting.acme.com")
objFTPSite.SetInfo

'create a virtual ROOT directory for the site
Set objVirtDir = objFTPSite.create("IIsFTPVirtualDir", "ROOT")
objVirtDir.Accessread = True
objVirtDir.Path = "f:\inetpub\ftp" 'set the FTP directory
objVirtDir.SetInfo
```

Discussion

IIS version 4.0 and later provide the ability to host multiple sites on a single computer. Each site can be accessed through a different URL. To create a Web site, get a reference to the particular service container (Web, FTP, or SMTP) for the server you want to create the site on:

```
Set objService = GetObject("IIS://server/service")
```

To get a reference to the Web service on server odin, use this:

```
Set objWebService = GetObject("IIS://odin/W3SVC")
```

To create the site, invoke the `Create` method on the service container object, specifying the object you want to create:

```
Set objSite = objWebService.Create(strObjectClass, nName)
```

`strObjectClass` is the site object type you want to create. Table 15-4 lists the available site object classes.

Table 15-4. IIS Site Object Classes

OBJECT CLASS	DESCRIPTION
WebIIsWebServer	Web server
IIsFTPServer	FTP server
IIsNNTPServer	News server
IIsSMTPServer	SMTP mail server

The site name specified by the `nName` parameter is not the name used to identify the site when accessing it via a browser, nor is it visible in the IIS MMC management interface for versions earlier than IIS 6.0. It appears as the Identifier column under IIS 6.0 MMC. The site name is a whole, positive numeric value. You must manually determine a name that has not already been used.

To simplify the process of determining a name, use the `FindNextSite` function, which is defined in the `adsilib.vbs` support file listed in Chapter 14:

```
FindNextSite(objService)
```

`objService` is an instance of an object for the service type you want to find the next site for, such as a Web or FTP service.

```
'get the next available site number for the FTP service:
Set objWebService = GetObject("IIS://Thor/MSFTPSVC")
Wscript.Echo FindNextSite(objWebService)
```

The following snippet of code creates a Web site with an internal ID of 5:

```
Set objWebSite = objWebService.Create("IIsWebServer", 5)
```

The new site requires that a server comment be assigned to it in order to appear in the IIS MMC application. The comment is set using the site object's `ServerComment` property:

```
objWebSite.ServerComment = "New Web site"
objWebSite.SetInfo
```

The site must be bound to at least one or more addresses. The address is in the format `address:port:domainname`.

The `address` is the IP address that is associated with the site. The `port` is the port number for the service. For a Web service, the default port is 80, and for an FTP service, the port is 21. The port number can be changed from the default port.

The `domainname` is an optional name that identifies the particular site. It is used if you want to host more than one site on a machine with a single IP address. The `ServerBindings` property stores the addresses and ports that are bound to the site:

```
objWebSite.ServerBindings = Array("10.0.0.1:80:accounting.acme.com")
```

NOTE *See Solution 15.9 for more details on setting server bindings.*

Once a site has been created, add a root directory to it. This is required for Web and FTP sites. The root folder provides entry-level access to the site and points to the first folder that appears in the site.

To create a root directory, invoke the `Create` method on the site container where the root will appear:

```
Set objVirtDir = objSite.Create(strVirtDirClass, "ROOT")
```

`strVirtDirClass` is the virtual directory class name. For a Web site, this is `WebIIsWebVirtualDir`, while for FTP this is `IIsFTPVirtualDir`.

To create a virtual root directory on a Web site, use this:

```
Set objVirtDir = objWebSite.Create("IIsWebVirtualDir", "ROOT")
```

A directory path must be set for the virtual directory. This path points to an existing server directory and is set using the `Path` property.

```
objVirtDir.Path = "d:\inetpub\wwwroot\intranet"
objVirtDir.Accessread = True
objVirtDir.AccessScript  = True
```

would allow for the execution of scripts and reading of data.

NOTE *See Solution 15.7 for more details on setting directory and file security.*

The root directory is also an IIS Web application. Use the `AppCreate` method to create the Web application:

```
Const MediumProtection = 2
objVirtDir.AppCreate2 MediumProtection
objVirtDir.AppFriendlyName = "Default Application"
objVirtDir.AppIsolated = 2
 objVirtDir.SetInfo
```

NOTE *See Solution 15.8 for more details on creating Web applications.*

IIS 6.0 introduces a new method called `CreateNewSite` that makes creating a site easier. To create a new site using the `CreateNewSite` method, get a reference to the W3SVC web service and invoke the `CreateNewSite` method:

```
objWebService.CreateNewSite strDescription, aBindings, strPath [, nID]
```

`strDescription` is the Web site description. The `aBindings` parameter is an array of server bindings and follows the same format as the `ServerBindings` property described earlier. The `strPath` argument is the path to the Web site root directory. `nID` is the optional site identifier. The site identifier is a number that describes the Web site internally to IIS. If the parameter is omitted, the number is generated by the method.

The following script creates a new site:

```
'get Web service
Set objWebService = GetObject("IIS://odin/W3SVC")
'create a new site
objService.CreateNewSite " New Web site", _
           Array("192.168.1.40:80:accounting.acme.com"), "f:\inetpub\newsite"
```

The following command-line script, `createsite.wsf`, creates a new FTP or Web site for a specified IIS server:

```
<?xml version="1.0" ?>
<job>
<!--comment
Script:createsite.wsf
Description:creates a new Web or FTP site
-->
 <script language="VBScript" src="adsilib.vbs">
 <![CDATA[
   Const MediumProtection = 2
   Dim objWebService, objWebSite, objVirtDir, nSiteNum, strSiteType
   Dim strComputer, strComment, strBinding, strPath, objService, strType
   On Error Resume Next

   If Not Wscript.Arguments.Count = 5 Then
      ShowUsage
      Wscript.Quit
   End If

    strComputer = Wscript.Arguments(0)
    strSiteType = Ucase(Wscript.Arguments(1))
    strType = GetSiteType(strSiteType)
```

```
strComment = Wscript.Arguments(2)
strBinding = Wscript.Arguments(3)
strPath = Wscript.Arguments(4)

'get the service from specified computer
Set objService = GetObject("IIS://" & strComputer & "/" & strType)

If Err Then
  ExitScript "Error getting reference to the server:" & strComputer & _
                 vbCrLf & "Error:" & Err.Description
 End If

'get number for new site using FindNextSite from adsilib
nSiteNum = FindNextSite(objService)

'create site with new number
Set objWebSite = _
 objService.Create("IIs" & strSiteType & "Server", nSiteNum)

If Err Then
   ExitScript "Error creating " & strSiteType & " site" & nSiteNum &  _
                 vbCrLf & "Error:" & Err.Description
 End If

'set the server comment and server bindings
objWebSite.ServerComment = strComment
objWebSite.ServerBindings = Array(strBinding)
objWebSite.SetInfo

If Err Then
  ExitScript "Error setting server bindings:" & strBinding & vbCrLf & _
               "Error:" & Err.Description
 End If

'create the root folder
Set objVirtDir = _
  objWebSite.Create("IIs" & strSiteType & "VirtualDir", "ROOT")
objVirtDir.Accessread = True
objVirtDir.Path = strPath

'only create Web application if site type is a Web server
If strSiteType= "WEB" Then
  objVirtDir. AccessScript = True
```

```
        objVirtDir.SetInfo
       If IISVersion(strComputer) = "4" Then
         objVirtDir.AppCreate False
       Else
         objVirtDir.AppCreate2 MediumProtection
       End If
        objVirtDir.AppFriendlyName = "Default Application"
       End If
        objVirtDir.SetInfo

        If Err Then
           ExitScript "Error creating virtual root on " & strComment & vbCrLf & _
                       "Error:" & Err.Description
        End If

       Wscript.Echo "Successfully created site " & strComment

      Sub ShowUsage
       WScript.Echo "createsite creates new Web and FTP sites" & vbCrLf & _
       "Syntax:"  &  vbCrLf & _
       "createsite.wsf computer type comment binding path" &  vbCrLf & _
       "computer computer IIS server resides on" & vbCrLf & _
       "type     type of server, either FTP or Web " & vbCrLf & _
       "comment  descriptive name of site" & vbCrLf & _
       "binding  " & vbCrLf & _
       "bindings server bindings in address:port:fqdn format" & vbCrLf & _
       "Example:" & vbCrLf & _
       "createsite.ws Acme Web ""Accounting Intranet" _
        & """ 10.0.0.1:80:accounting.acme.com d:\inetpub\wwwroot\acct"
      End Sub
      ]]>
    </script>
</job>
```

The `createsite.wsf` script is a command-line script that creates a new FTP or Web site. The syntax is as follows:

```
createsite.wsf computer type description connection path
```

`Computer` is the computer the IIS server resides on. `Type` is either FTP or Web. `Description` is the site's friendly name. `Connection` is the binding string and `path` is the local directory path to the site.

To create a Web site called "Accounting Site" bound to the IP address 10.0.0.1 on port 80 with a DNS address accounting.acme.com that is stored under the directory d:\Web\acct, execute the following command line:

```
createsite Odin Web "Accounting Site" 10.0.0.1:80:accounting.acme.com d:\Web\acct
```

To create a FTP site called "FTP Site" bound to the IP address 10.0.0.1 on port 21 with a DNS address ftp.accounting.acme.com that is stored under the directory d:\\ftp\acct, execute the following command line:

```
createsite Odin Web "FTP Site" 10.0.0.1:21:ftp.accounting.acme.com d:\ftp\acct
```

The createsite script works on IIS 4.0 and later. The default site protection that it assigns is High under IIS 4.0 and Medium (pooled) under IIS 5.0 and later. The createsite script uses WMI to determine what version of IIS is running on the computer. If you are running the script on an NT 4.0 computer, you must have WMI installed.

See Also

For more information, search for "IIsComputer" at http://msdn.microsoft.com and "Programming IIS 4.0 with ADSI" at http://15seconds.com/issue/980304.htm.

15.4 Starting an IIS Site

Problem

You want to start an IIS site.

Solution

You can bind to the site (FTP, Web, or SMTP) that you want to start and then invoke the Start method:

```
Web'get the Web service for Web site 1 for server ODIN
 Set objWebSite = GetObject("IIS://odin/W3SVC/1")
objWebSite.Start
```

Discussion

Each IIS site can be started, paused, or stopped using the `Start`, `Stop`, or `Pause` methods, respectively.

The state of a site can be determined by the `ServerState` property. It returns a numeric value that identifies the state. Table 15-5 lists values that are returned by the `ServerState` property.

Table 15-5. `ServerState` *Property Values*

STATE VALUE	DESCRIPTION
1	Site starting
2	Site started
3	Site stopping
4	Site stopped
5	Site pausing
6	Site paused
7	Site continuing

To continue a paused site, use the `Continue` method.

See Also

See the `startsrv.vbs`, `startWeb.vbs`, and `stopWeb.vbs` scripts supplied in the `System32\adminsamples\` directory installed with IIS.

15.5 Deleting a Site

Problem

You want to delete a site.

Solution

Bind to the service (FTP, Web, or SMTP) object for the site you want to delete. Call the Delete method, specifying the appropriate class and name of the site you want to remove:

```
Web'get the Web service from specified computer
Set objWebService = GetObject("IIS://odin/W3SVC")
'delete the Web server named 3
objWebService.delete "IIsWebServer", 3
```

Discussion

To delete an IIS object, reference the container object that holds the site you want to delete. Then invoke the Delete method:

```
objWebService.delete strClass, objectname
```

strClass represents the object class you want to delete, while objectname represents the name of the object you want to delete. For IIS site objects, the name is represented as a number. You cannot specify the "friendly" name of the site as the site you want to delete.

To simplify the process of determining a name, use the FindNextSite function, which is defined in the adsilib.vbs support file that is listed in Chapter 14:

```
FindSiteNumber(objWebService, strSiteName, strType)
```

objService is an instance of an object for the service type you want to find the next site for, such as Web or FTP service, strSiteName is the friendly site name that appears in the IIS MMC, and strType is the site type, which can be Web, FTP, SMTP, or NNTP.

```
<?xml version="1.0" ?>
<job>
<!--comment
 get the site number for the Web site Accounting Intranet
-->
 <script language="VBScript" src="adsilib.vbs">
 <![CDATA[
   Set objWebService = GetObject("IIS://Thor/W3SVC")
   nSiteName = FindSiteNumber(objWebService, "Accounting Intranet","Web")
```

```
  'delete the site
   objWebService.Delete "IIsWebServer", nSiteName
   ]]>
  </script>
</job>
```

The function returns an empty string if the specified site is not found.

Deleting a site does not delete the contents of the site—it only deletes site configuration information stored in the IIS metabase.

See Also

For more information, search `http://msdn.microsoft.com` for the article "ASDI Object Container Methods: Delete."

15.6 Creating Virtual Web Directories

Problem

You want to create and maintain virtual directories for your Web sites.

Solution

Bind to the parent directory container object where you want to create the virtual directory. Call the `Create` method, specifying `IIsWebVirtualDir` as the class to create and the name of the directory:

```
vget a reference to the root of the first Web site
Set objContainer = GetObject("IIS://odin/W3SVC/1/Root")
'create a virtual directory called AcctDir
Set objVirtDir = objContainer.Create("IIsWebVirtualDir", "AcctDir")
'set the virtual directory to point to a local folder
objVirtDir.Path = "d:\data\sites\intranet"
objVirtDir.SetInfo
```

Discussion

A virtual directory is a directory in a Web site that appears to be a physical directory but is actually a link to a separate location. The location may be a directory on the local server, a remote network connection, or a URL to a separate site. By providing a link to a separate location, information can be referenced on a Web site that does not physically reside in the Web site directory structure.

To create a virtual directory, get a reference to the parent directory for the directory you want to create. Then invoke the Create method with the name of the directory and virtual directory object class name. For Web sites the object class is WebIisWebVirtualDir, and for FTP sites it is IIsFTPVirtualDir:

```
'get a reference to the root of the first Web site
Set objContainer = GetObject("IIS://odin/W3SVC/1/Root")
'create a virtual directory called AcctDir
Set objVirtDir = objContainer.Create("IIsWebVirtualDir", "AcctDir")
```

The virtual directory requires a location to provide the information. This can be a physical path or a network share, or the location can be redirected to a different Web path.

To set a directory path, set the Path property to a valid directory path:

```
'set the virtual directory to point to a local folder
objVirtDir.Path = "d:\data\sites\intranet"
```

To reference a remote share, set the path property to a valid UNC path. You can associate a user name and password to the share name by setting the UNCUserName and UNCPassword properties:

```
'set the virtual directory to point to a local folder
objVirtDir.Path = "\\odin\acctsite"
objVirtDir.UNCUserName = "Webaccess"
objVirtDir.UNCPassword = "xy34ab32"
```

If you want to specify a domain user for the UNCUserName property, prefix the user name with the domain name separated by a backslash (\).

Note that the password properties are not encrypted. If you intend to use it, create a user ID with the minimum access rights.

The virtual directory can also be redirected to a different Web page. To redirect a virtual directory, set the HttpRedirect property to a valid URL. Access to the redirected page is controlled by the site hosting the URL.

```
'set the virtual directory to point different Web site
objVirtDir.HttpRedirect = "www.accounting.acme.com "
```

Once the location of the virtual directory is set, invoke the SetInfo method on the virtual directory object to update the settings.

See Also

See Solution 15.7 for more properties that you can apply to a virtual directory. For more information, read "Programming IIS 4.0 with ADSI" (http://15seconds.com/issue/980304.htm) and the mkWebdir.vbs script that you'll find in the System32\adminsamples\ directory under IIS 5.0 and earlier.

15.7 Setting File and Directory Properties

Problem

You want to set a property for a file or directory.

Solution

Get a reference to the object you want to set a property for. The SetInfo method must be called to store any property changes:

```
'get a reference to the file data.txt in Root directory of site 3 on Thor
Set objFile = GetObject("IIS://thor/W3SVC/3/Root/data.txt")
objFile.AccessWrite = False
objFile.SetInfo
```

Discussion

IIS allows you to change the properties of individual files and directories, enabling you to configure individual objects within a site differently than the default settings inherited from the root object.

There can be problems binding to directory or file objects. The IIS metabase is structured to inherit all base properties from root objects. For example, by default all files and directories in a new Web site contain the same properties as the root folder.

Instead of storing configuration information for all objects in a site in the metabase, only objects that have properties different than those inherited from root objects are stored.

As a result, any given file or directory in the hierarchy will inherit the settings from its root object. This means most files and directories will not be stored in the metabase, even if they physically exist on the site.

One easy way to see this is to use the Metabase Editor or Metabase Explorer (see Solution 15.2) to view the IIS metabase. Initially, it appears that the metabase mirrors most of the items that appear in the IIS MMC application, but any directory or file that does not have different properties than the root objects will not appear.

So even though all file and directories appear in the IIS MMC, they are not necessarily stored in the metabase. When you make a change to an object in MMC, an item is created for it in the metabase (if it doesn't already exist).

However, if you attempt to access an object programmatically that doesn't exist in the metabase, an error will occur. Before you can modify properties on any object that doesn't exist in the metabase, you must create it first in the metabase, even if it already physically exists in the Web site and appears in the IIS MMC application.

There is no ADSI method to check if a directory or file exists in the metabase. One way to check is to use error handling to determine if the object exists:

```
On Error Resume Next
'get a reference to the file data.txt in Root directory of site 3 on Thor
Set objFile = GetObject("IIS://thor/W3SVC/3/Root/data.txt")
'check to see if error occurred, object does not exist:
If Err Then Wscript.Echo "Object does not exist in Metabase"
```

To add a Web or directory object to the metabase, bind to the parent container the object will exist in. Invoke the `Create` method, specifying the object class and name of the object you are creating. The object class for a Web directory is `WebIIsWebDirectory` and for a Web file it is `WebIIsWebFile`.

To create a metabase entry for the `default.htm` file under the Web root directory for Web site number 3, use this:

```
'get a reference to the Root directory container for Website 3
Set objIIS = GetObject("IIS://thor/W3SVC/3/Root")
'create an IIsWebFile entry for default.htm
Set objWebFileDir = objIIS.create("IIsWebFile", "default.htm")
objWebFileDir.Setinfo
```

The following function checks for the existence of the object and attempts to add it to the metabase if it doesn't exist:

```
'Description
'Returns specified file or directory object
'Parameters
'strPath      File name to search for
'objIISPath  IIS object container to retrieve object from
Function GetFileDir(strPath, objIISPath)
Dim strObjectClass, objWebFileDir, objFSO

On Error Resume Next
```

```
'attempt to get the object from specified container
Set objWebFileDir = GetObject(objIISPath.ADsPath & "/" & strPath)

'check if error occured - could not get object
If Err Then
    Set objFSO = CreateObject("Scripting.FileSystemObject")
    'check if specified path is a file..
    If objFSO.FileExists(objIISPath.Path & "\" & strPath) Then
        'create the file object
        Set objWebFileDir = objIISPath.create("IIsWebFile",
strPath)objWebFileDir.Setinfo
    'check if specified path is a directory..
    ElseIf objFSO.FolderExists(objIISPath.Path & "\" & strPath) Then
       'create the directory object
       Set objWebFileDir = objIISPath.create("IIsWebDirectory", strPath)
objWebFileDir.Setinfo
    Else
        Set objWebFileDir = Nothing
    End If
End If

Set GetFileDir = objWebFileDir
End Function
```

When a file or directory object is added to the metabase, no checks are made to see if the file or directory actually physically exists. If the file or directory that is added doesn't exist, no error will occur. The entry will be added to the metabase, but a physical counterpart will not be created. This doesn't show up in the IIS MMC application or affect the server, but it is not good practice to have unused objects floating around.

The `GetFileDir` routine checks for the existence of a specified file or directory object. If an error occurs, it doesn't exist in the metabase and it attempts to create it, but first checks to determine if the file or directory actually exists. If the file or directory does exist, a new entry is created in the metabase; otherwise, the function returns `Nothing`.

```
Set objIIS = GetObject("IIS://Thor/W3SVC/1/Root")
Set objWebFile = GetFileDir("default.txt", objIIS)
```

Once you have a reference to the Web file object, you can manipulate its properties. All of the properties listed in Table 15-6 can be applied to Web and virtual directories, unless otherwise specified. A number of the properties apply to file objects as well as directories—this is indicated by an *X* in the File column.

The properties listed in Table 15-6 apply to values on the Directory tab that appears in the Directory Properties dialog box under IIS, as shown in Figure 15-2.

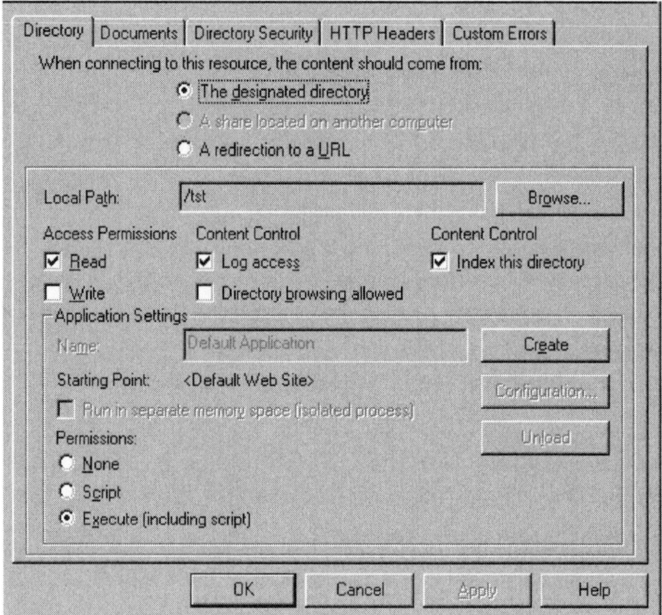

Figure 15-2. Directory tab

Table 15-6. File- and Directory-Related Properties

PROPERTY	DESCRIPTION	FILE
DontLog	Boolean. If True, don't log any access to directory.	
EnableDirBrowsing	Boolean. If True, browsers can browse the contents of the directory.	
EnableDefaultDoc	Boolean. Enables the default document for the directory if set to True.	
AccessRead	Boolean. Provides read access to a folder.	X
AccessWrite	Boolean. Provides write access to a folder.	X
AccessExecute	Boolean. Determines if files can be executed in the folder.	X
AccessScript	Boolean. If True, ASP script files can be executed.	X
ContentIndexed	Boolean. If True, IIS Index server indexes the contents of the folder.	

Web and virtual directories can control if default documents are assigned. Table 15-7 lists properties that are related to the Documents tab shown in Figure 15-3.

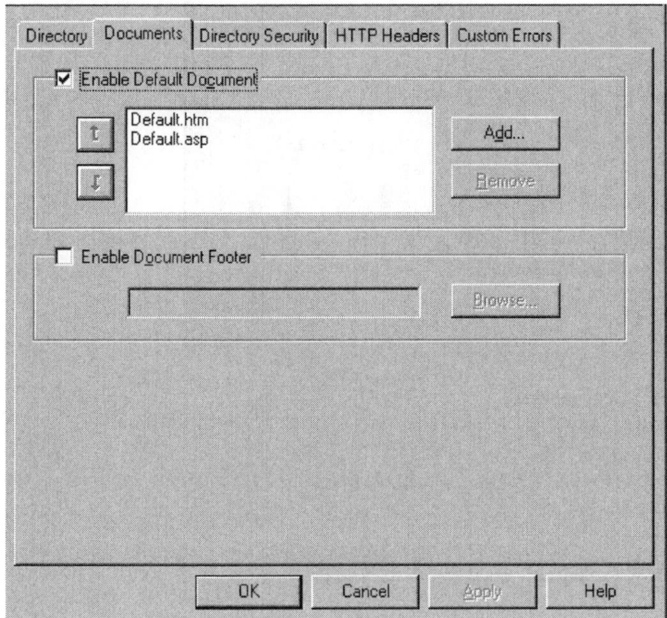

Figure 15-3. Documents tab

Table 15-7. Document Properties

PROPERTY	DESCRIPTION
`EnableDefaultDoc`	Boolean. Enables the default document for the directory if set to `True`.
`DefaultDoc`	Comma-delimited string identifying the default document names (e.g., `Default.htm`, `Default.asp`, and `iisstart.asp`). The `EnableDefaultDoc` property must be set to `True` to enable the documents.
`EnableDocFooter`	Boolean. Enables the document footer if set to `True`.
`DefaultDocFooter`	Path to HTML file containing document footer appended to the bottom of each document in the specified directory. The `EnableDefaultDoc` property must be set to `True` to enable the document footer.

All Web objects can have security settings applied to them. This provides very flexible security mechanisms and allows different levels of security to be applied.

Table 15-8 and Table 15-9 list properties that are related to the Authentication Methods dialog box shown in Figure 15-4.

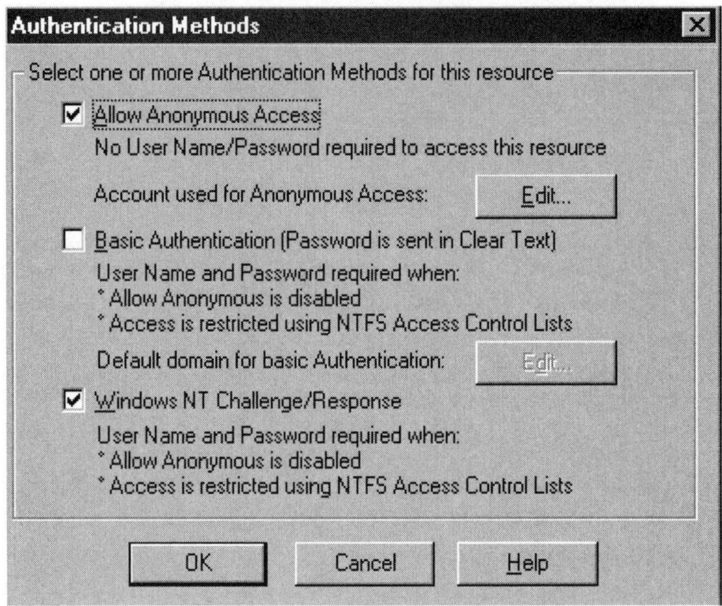

Figure 15-4. Authentication Methods dialog box

To configure Anonymous access, set the properties listed in Table 15-8.

Table 15-8. Anonymous Access Security Properties

PROPERTY	DESCRIPTION
`AnonymousUserName`	NT anonymous user account.
`AnonymousUserPass`	NT anonymous account password. This password is unencrypted and can be read as plain text, so create an account with minimal access.
`AnonymousPasswordSync`	Boolean. Determines if the anonymous user password specified by the `AnonymousUserPass` property is synchronized with the NT anonymous account specified by the `AnonymousUserName` property.
`AuthAnonymous`	Boolean. If set to `True`, IIS will allow anonymous authentication.

To configure basic (clear text) authentication, set the properties listed in Table 15-9.

Table 15-9. Basic Authentication Properties

PROPERTY	DESCRIPTION
DefaultLogonDomain	Default NT domain to authenticate clear-text user ID and passwords against.
AuthBasic	Boolean. If set to True, Basic authentication is enabled.

To configure Windows NT Challenge/Response authentication, set the AuthNTLM property to True.

You use the IPSecurity property to grant and deny access by IP address. (See Solution 15.9 for more information.)

The properties detailed in this section are some of the most used properties that can be applied to file and directory objects, but there are many more properties available to set.

One way to determine what properties map to what values in MMC is to set properties for a "dummy" object using MMC and enumerate the properties for the object. The listprop command-line utility (see Solution 14.5) lists all properties and associated values for any ADSI object:

```
listprop IIS://odin/W3SVC/1/Root/AppDir
```

15.8 Creating a Web Directory Application

Problem

You want to create a Web directory application.

Solution

You can reference the Web directory that you want to create as a Web application and then call the AppCreate method:

```
Const MediumProtection = 2
'get a reference to the directory NewApp under the root directory of the first site
Set objNewApp = GetObject("IIS://thor/W3SVC/1/Root/NewApp")
'create a new application for the directory
objNewApp.AppCreate True
objNewApp.AppFriendlyName = "Default Application"
objNewApp.AppIsolated = MediumProtection
objNewApp.SetInfo
```

Discussion

IIS allows different levels of "protection" to be applied to Web applications. This protection determines how Web application processes are organized in memory.

The lowest level of protection is called *in-process*. In-process applications run in the same memory space as the Web server itself. The advantage of running your Web site in-process is better performance, and the disadvantage is potential stability problems. If a part of a Web application (such as a DLL) performs an invalid operation, it can affect the operation of the whole Web server. If your Web site is only serving static Web pages and not performing any CGI or ASP operations, in-process can be suitable.

An *out-of-process* application is the highest level of protection that isolates the application's process from other applications. Each out-of-process application has its own memory space. If one crashes, it will not affect other applications or the operation of the Web server. This is useful for mission-critical applications. The disadvantage is worse performance.

In-process application protection and out-of-process application protection are available on IIS 4.0 and later. IIS version 5.0 and later provide an additional level of application protection called *pooled* out-of-process. Pooled applications run in a shared process that is separate from the Web server process. Pooling processes balance application integrity and performance, providing better application protection than in-process applications and better performance than out-of-process applications. IIS 6.0 was rewritten from scratch, and all applications are pooled by default. The changes in the IIS 6.0 architecture allow for processes to run in the protected confines of an application pool without any performance penalty. IIS 6.0 allows for multiple application pools to be configured for a Web server, and Web applications can be assigned to any application pool. Each application pool can be configured with specific resource priority levels.

In-process and out-of-process applications are available only under IIS 6.0 if you configure your IIS server to run in IIS 5.0 Isolation mode. To configure IIS 6.0 to run in IIS 5.0 Isolation mode, follow these steps:

1. Start Internet Information Services 6.0 Manager.

2. Display the properties for the Web Sites folder.

3. Select the Service tab.

4. Select the "Run WWW Service in IIS 5.0 isolation mode" check box.

IIS 6.0 Web servers should be set to 5.0 isolation mode only if there are applications that require backward compatibility with IIS 5.0.

The root folder of any IIS Web site is a Web application. All scripts and executables will run in the application protection defined for the site. A site can host multiple Web applications. Virtual and nonvirtual directories can be created as Web applications. Anything executed within the directory will run in the application protection defined for the directory. To create an application, get a reference to the directory object you want to create the application in and invoke the AppCreate method:

```
Set objVirtDir = GetObject("IIS:/odin/W3SVC/1/Root/AppDir")
objVirtDir.AppCreate bProcess
```

The bProcess parameter determines whether the application is an in-process or an out-of-process application. If bProcess is True, the application will run in-process; otherwise, it will run out-of-process. The AppCreate method is available for all versions of IIS. IIS 5.0 introduced the AppCreate2 method, which allows for pooled application security to be set. To use the AppCreate2 method, get a reference to the directory object you want to create the application in and invoke the AppCreate2 method:

```
objVirtDir.AppCreate2 nProtection
```

The nProtection parameter can be 0,1, or 2, which represent in-process, out-of-process, and pooled application protection.

IIS 6.0 introduces the AppCreate3 method, which allows for an application pool to be specified:

```
objVirtDir.AppCreate3 strPool, nProtection, bCreate
```

strPool is the name of application pool. Application pool names can be read from the Application Pools entry in IIS 6.0. nProtection represents the protection level the application directory will run in, and it takes the same values as the nProtection parameter used by the AppCreate2 method. The bCreate parameter is a Boolean value that controls if you want to create a virtual root directory.

Once the application is created, you can set the application-related properties listed in Table 15-10.

Table 15-10. Web Application–Related Properties

PROPERTY	DESCRIPTION
AspScriptTimeout	Maximum time in seconds an ASP script is allowed to execute.
AspSessionTimeout	Idle time in minutes before a user session is disconnected.
AspEnableParentPaths	Boolean. Determines if ASP can reference items below the root application folder.
AspAllowSessionState	Boolean. Determines if ASP can track user state.
AspScriptLanguage	Default script language for application, such as VBScript or JScript.
AspScriptErrorSentToBrowser	Boolean. If True, detailed error information is sent to the client browser. If False, the message stored in the AspScriptErrorMessage property is displayed.
AppIsolated	Determines how application will run in memory: 0 Low In-process 1 High Out-of-process 2 Medium (pooled resources, IIS 5.0 only) For IIS 4.0 AppIsolated is a Boolean property, where False sets protection to Low and True sets protection to High.

To delete an application, invoke the AppDelete method on the directory:

```
objDirectory.AppDelete
```

If you want to delete all applications associated with a specified directory and all directories below it, invoke the AppDeleteRecursive method:

```
objDirectory.AppDeleteRecursive
```

All applications below the specified directory will be deleted. Neither the AppDelete nor AppDeleteRecursive method deletes any files or directory structure.

See Also

For more information, search `http://msdn.microsoft.com` for the article "AppCreate."

15.9 Maintaining Server Bindings

Problem

You want to maintain server bindings.

Solution

You can bind the site for which you want to set the bindings and then set the `ServerBindings` property.

The following sample binds to the fourth Web site on server thor:

```
Set objSite = GetObject("IIS://thor/W3SVC/4")
'bind two domain names to the site
objSite.ServerBindings = Array("192.168.1.40:80:sales.acme.com", _
                               "192.168.1.40:80:marketing.acme.com")

objSite.SetInfo
```

Discussion

In order to host multiple sites on a server, each site must be associated with a unique access identifier. An IIS server may only have one physical IP address, but it can host multiple Web sites.

The ability to host multiple sites is accomplished by assigning a fully qualified domain name, such as `www.acme.com`, to identify sites. This allows any number of sites to be assigned to a server. Using this method, you specify one or more domain names for a site. When a browser makes a request using the domain name, it is sent with the request in the header. IIS checks the header and redirects the browser to the appropriate site.

The `ServerBindings` property is an array of strings. Each string element in the array contains an IP address, port, and optional site host name delimited by colons. For example, the string `10.0.1.1:80:sales.acme.com` represents a server binding for a site located on IP address 10.0.1.1, hosted on port 80, and assigned the domain name `sales.acme.com`.

If you want to list the server bindings for a site, enumerate each element from the ServerBindings array property. The following script lists all server bindings for the third Web site on server thor:

```
Set objSite = GetObject("IIS://thor/W3SVC/3")
For Each strBinding In objSite.ServerBindings
    Wscript.Echo strBinding
Next
```

To set the server bindings, reference the site for which you want to set the bindings. This may be a Web, FTP, NNTP, or SMTP site. Assign the bindings using an array with one or more bindings. The Solution script assigns two domain names to a site: sales.acme.com and marketing.acme.com. Both sites are bound to the same IP address and port.

Any domain names assigned to a site must be resolvable by client programs. The IIS server does not perform any name service (such as DNS or WINS) operations, nor does it check that the domain names assigned to a site are valid.

Setting the ServerBindings property overwrites any existing addresses assigned to the server. To add a new binding, resize the ServerBindings array and set the new binding. The following script adds a binding for marketing.acme.com to the fourth Web site on server thor:

```
Dim objSite, nF, aBindings
'get a reference to the fourth Web site on server Thor
Set objSite = GetObject("IIS://thor/W3SVC/4")
aBindings = objSite.ServerBindings
'resize the array of server bindings
ReDim Preserve aBindings(UBound(aBindings) + 1)
'add a new server binding to the last element in the resized array and set the
bindings
aBindings(UBound(aBindings)) = "192.168.1.40:80:marketing.acme.com"
objSite.ServerBindings = aBindings
objSite.SetInfo
```

If your IIS server is configured for Secure Sockets Layer (SSL) security, you can assign multiple security identities to your Web sites using the SecureBindings property. The SecureBindings property is similar to the ServerBindings property and contains an array of strings. Each string element in the array contains an IP address and port delimited by colons. The string 10.0.1.2:443 is a server binding for a site located at IP address 10.0.1.2 and hosted on SSL port 443.

```
Set objSite = GetObject("IIS://thor/W3SVC/4")
'set SSL addresses
objSite.ServerBindings = Array("192.168.1.40:443", _
                               "192.168.1.40:443")
objSite.SetInfo
```

See Also

For more information, search `http://msdn.microsoft.com` for the article "ServerBindings."

15.10 Setting IP Security

Problem

You want to use IP addresses or domain names to limit access to IIS resources.

Solution

You can bind to the object for which you want to set IP security and then get the `IPSecurity` property. You set the appropriate combination of properties for the `IPSecurity` object to grant or deny access to the resource.

The following sample restricts the IP address 10.5.5.1, the range of addresses 192.5.5.1 to 192.5.5.254, and any addresses from the domain `acme.com`:

```
Set objDir = GetObject("IIS://odin/W3SVC/1/ROOT/images")
'get the IPSecurity
Set objIPSecurity = objDir.IPSecurity
'allow all access to directory  by default
objIPSecurity.GrantByDefault = True
'deny the address 10.5.5.1 and range of address 192.5.5.x
objIPSecurity.IPDeny = _
              Array("10.5.5.1, 255.255.255.255", "192.5.5.0, 255.255.255.0")

'deny all computer from domain acme.com
objIPSecurity. DomainDeny= _
         Array("acme.com")

objDir.IPSecurity = objIPSecurity
objDir.SetInfo
```

Discussion

IIS provides security mechanisms to limit or allow access to resources by an individual IP address or a range of IP addresses. This can be applied at the server, site, folder, or file level. This security is provided by the `IPSecurity` property. By setting IP security, you can limit the access to resources to specific groups of machines based on their IP address or domain name.

With this security method a resource (site, directory, or file) provides either full access or no access. If full access is provided, the `IPSecurity` property contains a list of addresses that are denied access. If there is no access, the `IPSecurity` property contains a list of addresses that are allowed.

This method of applying security may sound confusing, but a look at the IIS MMC administration application can clarify things. The IIS MMC provides the ability to grant or deny IP addresses through the File or Directory Security tab. Figure 15-5 illustrates the restrictions applied after the Solution script has been executed on a directory.

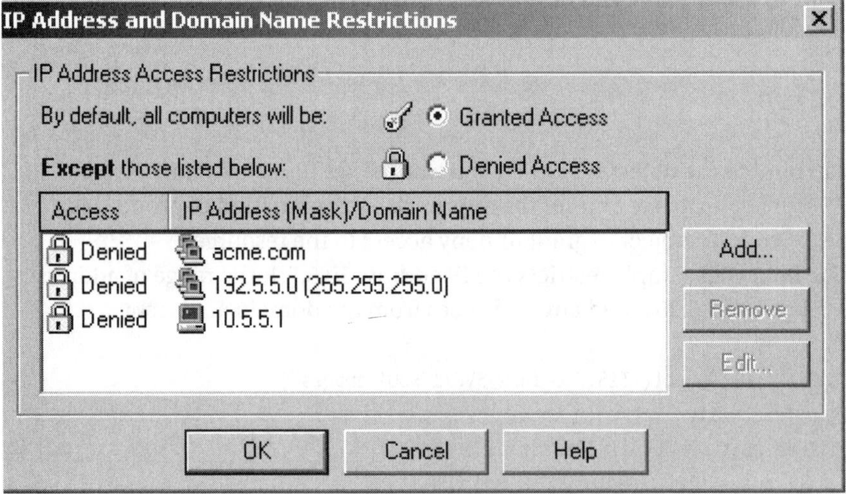

Figure 15-5. IP Address and Domain Name Restrictions dialog box

The `IPSecurity` property exposes a number of properties, which are listed in Table 15-11.

Table 15-11. IPSecurity *Property Structure*

PROPERTY	DESCRIPTION
DomainDeny	Array of domain addresses to deny.
DomainGrant	Array of domain addresses to deny.
GrantByDefault	Boolean. Determines if access is granted or denied by default.
IPDeny	Array of IP addresses to deny.
IPGrant	Array of IP addresses to grant.

If the GrantByDefault property is True, default access to the resource is allowed and the DomainDeny and IPDeny properties are read. If the GrantByDefault property is False, default access to the resource is denied and the DomainGrant and IPGrant properties are read.

IPGrant and IPDeny are arrays of IP addresses represented as a string in the format ipaddress, subnet. The IP address is the address associated with one or more machines you want to grant or deny access and the subnet is an IP subnet that can be used to narrow the access to the resource. The following script lists the security settings for the image directory for the first Web site on thor:

```
Set objDir = GetObject("IIS://thor/W3SVC/1/ROOT/images")
'if access is granted by default list the denied IP addresses and domains,
'otherwise list the granted IP adresses and domains
If objDir.IPSecurity.GrantByDefault Then
    Wscript.Echo "IP Addresses denied access"
    For Each obj In objDir.IPSecurity.IPDeny
        Wscript.Echo obj
    Next
    Wscript.Echo "Domains denied access"
    For Each obj In objDir.IPSecurity.DomainDeny
        Wscript.Echo obj
    Next
Else
    Wscript.Echo "IP Addresses granted access"
    For Each obj In objDir.IPSecurity.IPGrant
        Wscript.Echo obj
    Next
    Wscript.Echo "Domains granted access"
    For Each obj In objDir.IPSecurity.DomainGrant
        Wscript.Echo obj
    Next
End If
```

If you want to grant or deny access to a specific computer by IP address, add an entry to the array that starts with the IP address followed by a comma and the subnet mask 255.255.255.255. The string `10.0.0.1, 255.255.255.255` would specify the computer with the IP address 10.0.0.1.

If you want to grant or deny access to a group of computers by IP address, add an entry to the array that starts with the IP address followed by a comma and a subnet mask. The IP address in combination with the subnet mask would determine what range of computer addresses that would be granted or denied access to the resource.

`DomainGrant` and `DomainDeny` are arrays of domain names that can be granted or denied access to a resource.

The following snippet of code denies access to all computers except the IP address 10.5.5.1, the range of addresses 192.5.5.1 to 192.5.5.254, and any addresses from the domain `acme.com`:

```
Set objDir = GetObject("IIS://odin/W3SVC/1/ROOT/images")
'get the IPSecurity
Set objIPSecurity = objDir.IPSecurity
'deny all access to directory  by default
objIPSecurity.GrantByDefault = False
'grant the address 10.5.5.1 and range of address 192.5.5.1 to 192.5.5.254
objIPSecurity.IPGrant = _
             Array("10.5.5.1, 255.255.255.255", "192.5.5.0, 255.255.255.0")

'grant all computers from domain acme.com
objIPSecurity.DomainGrant = _
         Array("acme.com")
objDir.IPSecurity = objIPSecurity
objDir.SetInfo
```

See Also

For more information, search `http://msdn.microsoft.com` for the article "IIsIPSecurity."

CHAPTER 16

Exchange Server

ADSI TOGETHER WITH the LDAP provider can be used to perform operations against Exchange server 5.5, 2000, and 2003. Using this interface, most administrative tasks can be performed, such as mailbox, custom mailbox, and distribution list manipulation.

Administrative tasks are performed differently in Exchange 2000/2003 and Exchange 5.5. Code written for Exchange 5.5 will not work under Exchange 2000/2003 and vice versa. This chapter provides solution code and discussions for each platform.

16.1 Creating a Mailbox

Problem

You want to create a new Exchange mailbox.

Solution

To create a mailbox for Exchange 5.5, get a reference to the container you want to create the mailbox in and create an instance of an `organizationalPerson` object:

```
'createmailbox.vbs
Const ADS_RIGHT_EXCH_MODIFY_USER_ATT = 2
Const ADS_RIGHT_EXCH_MAIL_SEND_AS = 8
Const ADS_RIGHT_EXCH_MAIL_RECEIVE_AS = 16
Const ADS_SID_WINNT_PATH = 5
Const ADS_SID_HEXSTRING = 1
Dim objMailbox, objContainer, strServer
Dim strAlias, strMTA, strMDB, strSMTPAddr, strDisplayName
Dim objSid, strSidHex, strComputer, strSite, strOrg
Dim objComputer, strUserID, strDomain
Dim objSec, objSD, objDACL, objAce
strServer = "Odin"
strSite = "Office"
strDomain = "Acme"
strDisplayName = "Fred Smith"
strSMTPAddr = "FredSmith@acme.com"
```

```
strAlias = "Freds"
strUserID = "Freds"

Set objComputer = GetObject("LDAP://" & strServer)
'get the organization
strOrg = objComputer.o
'get the recipients container for the site
Set objContainer = _
            GetObject("LDAP://" & strServer & "/CN=Recipients,OU=" _
                     & strSite & ",o=" & strOrg)

'get the SID for the account to be associated with the new mailbox
Set objSid = CreateObject("ADsSID")
objSid.SetAs ADS_SID_WINNT_PATH, "WinNT://" & strDomain & "/" & strUserID
strSidHex = objSid.GetAs(ADS_SID_HEXSTRING)

'create a new MailBox
Set objMailbox = objContainer.create("organizationalPerson", "cn=" & strAlias)
'set display name and alias
objMailbox.Put "mailPreferenceOption", 0
objMailbox.Put "cn", strDisplayName
objMailbox.Put "uid", strAlias
objMailbox.Put "Home-MTA", _
     "cn=Microsoft MTA,cn=" & strServer & ",cn=Servers,cn=Configuration,ou=" _
  & strSite & ",o=" & strOrg

objMailbox.Put "Home-MDB", _
    "cn=Microsoft Private MDB,cn=" & strServer & _
    ",cn=Servers,cn=Configuration,ou=" _
    & strSite & ",o=" & strOrg
objMailbox.Put "MAPI-Recipient", True
'objMailbox.Put "rfc822Mailbox", strSMTPAddr
objMailbox.rfc822Mailbox = strSMTPAddr

objMailbox.Put "textEncodedORaddress", _
        "c=US;a= ;p=" & strSite & ";o=" & strOrg & ";s=" & strAlias

objMailbox.textEncodedORaddress = _
             "c=US;a= ;p=" & strSite & ";o=" & strOrg & ";s=" & strAlias
objMailbox.Put "Assoc-NT-Account", strSidHex
objMailbox.SetInfo
'create security objects
Set objSec = CreateObject("ADsSecurity")
Set objAce = CreateObject("AccessControlEntry")
```

```
Set objSD = objSec.GetSecurityDescriptor("LDAP://" & strServer & _
                              "/CN=Recipients,OU=" & strSite & ",o=" & strOrg)
Set objDACL = objSD.DiscretionaryAcl
objAce.Trustee = strDomain & "\" & strUserID
objAce.AccessMask = ADS_RIGHT_EXCH_MODIFY_USER_ATT Or _
                                     ADS_RIGHT_EXCH_MAIL_SEND_AS Or _
                                     ADS_RIGHT_EXCH_MAIL_RECEIVE_AS
objAce.AceType = ADS_ACETYPE_ACCESS_ALLOWED
objDACL.AddAce objAce
objSD.DiscretionaryAcl = objDACL
objSec.SetSecurityDescriptor objSD
```

To create an Exchange 2000/2003 mailbox, reference an Active Directory user and invoke the CreateMailbox method:

```
'create a Exchange 2000 mailbox
Dim strServer, strDomain, strOrganization, strAdminGroup
Dim strStorageGroup, strStoreName
Dim objPerson, objMailbox
strServer = "Odin "
strDomain = "acme.com"
strOrganization = "acme"
strAdminGroup = "First Administrative Group"
strStorageGroup = "First Storage Group"
strStoreName = "Mailbox Store (Odin)"

'get a user object from Active Directory to create mailbox for
 Set objMailbox = GetObject("LDAP://cn=Fred Smith,cn=Users,dc=acme,dc=com")
 ' create mailbox for specified server
 objMailbox.CreateMailbox "LDAP://" & _
                     strServer & _
                    "/CN=" & _
                    strStoreName & _
                    ",CN=" & _
                    strStorageGroup & ",CN=InformationStore,CN=" & _
                    strServer & _
                    ",CN=Servers,CN=" & _
                     strAdminGroup & "," & _
                    "CN=Administrative Groups,CN=" & _
                     strOrganization & "," & _
                    "CN=Microsoft Exchange,CN=Services," & _
                    "CN=Configuration,dc=acme,dc=com"
  objMailbox.SetInfo
```

Discussion

To create a new Exchange 5.5 object, you must first obtain a reference to a container:

```
Set objContainer = GetObject("LDAP://server/CN=container,OU=site,o=organization")
```

where the `server` is the name of the Exchange server and the `container` is the mailbox container. Exchange server creates a Recipients container by default. `Site` is the Exchange site name and `organization` is the Exchange organization.

To get a reference to the Recipients container for the office site in the Acme organization, use the following:

```
Set objContainer = _
GetObject("LDAP://odin/CN=Recipients,OU=office,o=acme")
```

The Exchange directory structure is hierarchical, so containers can be nested within containers, allowing groups of objects to be broken down and organized in a logical fashion. To reference a container in a hierarchy, prefix the LDAP path with the container names separated by commas. In the following example, a reference is made to the Accounting container, which has been created below the Recipients container:

```
Set objContainer = _
      GetObject("LDAP://odin/CN=Accounting,CN=Recipients,OU=office,o=acme")
```

Exchange mailboxes are created in mailbox containers. A mailbox is an `organizationalPerson` object class. To create a new mailbox, invoke the `Create` method on the container where the mailbox will reside. The mailbox is identified using a relative distinguished name (RDN), which in the case of a mailbox is `cn=` followed by the alias for the mailbox. The mailbox alias can be up to 64 characters and include spaces, but you should follow naming conventions used when creating accounts in the Exchange 5.5 Administrator program:

```
'Create a new MailBox for Fred smith using the alias Freds
Set objMailbox = objContainer.create("organizationalPerson", "cn=FredS")
```

A new object of type `organizationalPerson` is created in the container specified by the `objContainer` object and is assigned a container name (`cn`) of FredS. The `cn` property maps to the alias under the Exchange 5.5 administration piece.

Before a mailbox can become functional, the properties in Table 16-1 must be set.

Table 16-1. Default Mailbox Properties

PROPERTY	DESCRIPTION
cn	Descriptive mailbox display name (e.g., Accountant Fred Smith).
Uid	Unique mailbox alias, usually a combination of the first and last name of a user (e.g., Freds).

Home-MTA	Home-MTA is the default message transfer agent for the mailbox, which is the server the mailbox resides on. It has the following format:
	`Home-MTA, cn=Microsoft MTA,cn=Server,`
	`cn=Servers,cn=Configuration,ou=Site,o=Organization`

Server	Server name.
Organization	Exchange organization.

Site	Exchange site.
	For example:
	`Home-MTA, cn=Microsoft MTA,cn=Odin,`
	`cn=Servers,cn=Configuration,ou=HeadOffice,o=Acme`

Home-MDB	Home-MDB is the home server for the mailbox. It has the following format:
	`cn=Microsoft Private MDB,cn=Server,cn=Servers,`
	`cn=Configuration,ou=Site,o=Org`

Server	Server name.
Organization	Exchange organization.
Site	Exchange site.
MAPI-Recipient	Boolean value. Set to True if the mailbox is to be accessible by MAPI clients.
rfc822Mailbox	Default Internet address (e.g., freds@acme.com).
TextEncodedORaddress	X.400 address. This address is required for Exchange to perform global routing of messages. It has the following format: `c=CountryCode;a= ;p=Org;o=Site;s=Alias`
CountryCode	Country code (e.g., US).
Server	Server name.
Organization	Exchange organization.
Site	Exchange site. To determine how X.400 addresses are generated for your site, check the Site Addressing option under the Configuration container in the Exchange administration piece. Note that there must be an entry or a blank space for the a= component of an X.400 address (known as the *administrative management domain name*).

An NT user or group account must be associated with the mailbox to make it functional. The NT account's security identifier (SID) is used to identify what NT account is associated with the Exchange mailbox. The SID uniquely identifies the NT account and is represented as a string of hexadecimal values.

The SID can be retrieved from an ADSI Windows NT User object's objectSid property, which is a multivalued property that contains byte values representing the SID. The current version of VBScript cannot convert this data type.

Instead you will use an ADSI 2.5 SDK DLL to get the SID. This is a COM component called ADsSID that is part of the ADsSecurity DLL from the ADSI SDK. To use the DLL, register the ADsSecurity.dll using regsvr32.exe.

The ADsSecurity.dll doesn't depend upon the SDK for support libraries, so it can be copied from a machine that has the SDK installed to the required machine. It does require ADSI 2.5, which is installed by default on Windows 2000, 2003, and XP. ADSI is available as a separate installation on Windows NT 4.0.

An SID can be retrieved from a Windows NT user account using the ADsSID component. Create an instance of the component using the ProgID ADsSID and invoke the SetAs method:

```
objSid.SetAs nPath,strPath
```

The nPath parameter determines the path type for the object you are trying to get the SID from. ADS_SID_WINNT_PATH has the value 5 and indicates a Windows NT path, while ADS_SID_ACTIVE_DIRECTORY_PATH has the value 6 and indicates an LDAP Active Directory path.

The strPath parameter is the ADSI path to the object. For Windows NT user accounts, specify the path to the account using the ADSI WinNT provider path format, WinNT//domain/account. For the NT account Freds for the domain Acme, the path would be WinNT://acme/freds. See Chapter 14 for more information on the WinNT ADSI provider.

To return the SID in the appropriate format, use the GetAs method:

```
SID = objSid.GetAs (nType)
```

The nType parameter determines the format the SID is to be returned in. The Exchange server account requires it in a hexadecimal string format, which can be specified using the constant ADS_SID_HEXSTRING, which has the value 1.

The following code snippet returns the SID for account Freds from the Acme domain in a string format:

```
Const ADS_SID_HEXSTRING = 1
Const ADS_SID_WINNT_PATH = 5
Set objSid = CreateObject("ADsSID")
  objSid.SetAs ADS_SID_WINNT_PATH, "WinNT://acme/freds"
 strSidHex = objSid.GetAs(ADS_SID_HEXSTRING)
```

Once you have a user's SID string, assign it to the mailbox's Assoc-NT-Account property:

```
objMailbox.Put "Assoc-NT-Account", strSidHex 'set associated NT user
```

The final step in making the mailbox active is setting the mailbox security.

The user associated with the mailbox needs appropriate security access to the mailbox in order to use it. A standard Exchange mailbox allows a user to maintain his or her mailbox configuration, and send and receive messages. This security setting is automatically assigned to a mailbox created using the Exchange Server 5.5 Administrator. The option to view security details is not displayed in the Exchange Administrator by default, but it can be listed by changing the setting under the Options menu.

This security access is not directly accessible through ADSI. The security can be set using the AdsSecurity DLL provided by the ADSI 2.5 SDK. Like the ADsSID component, which also comes from the SDK, the SDK does not need to be installed on every computer using it, and the DLL can be copied and registered on any computer that requires it. The computer does require ADSI 2.5 or later to be installed.

The ProgID for the component is AdsSecurity. Get the security descriptor for the mailbox object you want to add the security to by invoking the security object's GetSecurityDescriptor method, specifying the path to the ADSI you want to retrieve the security details for.

The following code sample gets the security descriptor for the mailbox Freds:

```
'create an instance of the ADsSecurity object
   Set objSecurity = CreateObject("ADsSecurity")
   'get the security descriptor for a object
   strMailbox = "LDAP://odin/cn=Freds,cn=Recipients,ou=office,o=acme"
   Set objSD = objSecurity.GetSecurityDescriptor(strMailBox)
```

The object's security descriptor contains all security information related to the object, such as owner, access, and security auditing. The security access is stored in the Discretionary Access Control List (DACL). The DACL contains a list of Access Control Entries (ACEs). Each ACE either allows or denies access to a particular operation.

A general Exchange mailbox allows a user to send mail, receive mail, and modify mailbox settings. To achieve this, you must add a new ACE to the DACL that assigns the appropriate access to the mailbox.

First you get the DACL and create a new ACE, which you do by referencing the security descriptor object's DiscretionaryACL property:

```
'get discretionary ACL for the object
Set objDACL = objSD.DiscretionaryAcl
Set objAce = CreateObject("AccessControlEntry")
```

Set the ACE object's Trustee property to the account you want to assign to the mailbox. The trustee represents a NT user account in the format domain\accountname:

```
'set the user id to add security for
objAce.Trustee = "Acme\Freds"
```

The ACE object exposes an AccessMask property that determines what operations a particular user can perform against the mailbox. The AccessMask property is a numeric value, which consists of one or more values that identify what operations a user can perform.

A user by default has the ability to send and receive mail and modify his or her account. The values for these operations are 2, 8, and 16 for modify, send, and receive, respectively.

The AceType property determines if the user is granted or denied access to the operations specified by the AccessMask property. To grant access, set AceType to 0, and to deny access, set it to 1.

The following snippet demonstrates how to assign the rights to the AccessMask property:

```
Const ADS_RIGHT_EXCH_MODIFY_USER_ATT = &H2
Const ADS_RIGHT_EXCH_MAIL_SEND_AS = &H8
Const ADS_RIGHT_EXCH_MAIL_RECEIVE_AS = &H10
Const ADS_ACETYPE_ACCESS_ALLOWED = 0

'allow trustee to modify user attributes, send and receive mail
objAce.AccessMask = ADS_RIGHT_EXCH_MODIFY_USER_ATT Or _
    ADS_RIGHT_EXCH_MAIL_SEND_AS Or ADS_RIGHT_EXCH_MAIL_RECEIVE_AS
objAce.AceType =  ADS_ACETYPE_ACCESS_ALLOWED 'set access
```

Once the operations are complete, add the ACE to the DACL using the AddAce method. Update the security descriptor on the mailbox with the new settings by invoking the SetSecurityDescriptor method, specifying the updated security descriptor object:

```
objDACL.AddAce objAce 'add the ACE to DACL
objSD.DiscretionaryAcl = objDACL
objSecurity.SetSecurityDescriptor objSD
```

You can find more information on security operations in Chapter 17.

The following script, `createxusr.wsf`, allows for the creation of Exchange 5.5 mailboxes from the command line:

```
<?xml version="1.0" ?>
<job>
<!--comment
Script:createxusr.wsf
Description:creates new Exchange server mailboxes
-->
 <script language="VBScript" src="adsilib.vbs">
 <![CDATA[
   Option Explicit
   Const ADS_SID_WINNT_PATH = 5
   Const ADS_SID_HEXSTRING = 1
   Const ADS_RIGHT_EXCH_MODIFY_USER_ATT = 2
   Const ADS_RIGHT_EXCH_MAIL_SEND_AS = 8
   Const ADS_RIGHT_EXCH_MAIL_RECEIVE_AS = 16
   Const ADS_ACETYPE_ACCESS_ALLOWED = 0

   Dim objMailbox, objContainer, strServer
   Dim strAlias, strMTA, strMDB, strSMTPAddr, strDisplayName
   Dim objSid, strSidHex, strComputer, strSite, strOrg
   Dim objComputer, strUserID, strDomain
   Dim objSD, objACE, objSecurity, objDACL
  'On Error Resume Next

  If WScript.Arguments.Count <> 7 Then
   ShowUsage
    WScript.Quit
 End If
   strServer = WScript.Arguments(0) ' Exchange server name
   strSite = WScript.Arguments (1)  'Exchange site name
   strAlias = WScript.Arguments(2) 'mailbox alias
   strDisplayName = WScript.Arguments (3) 'mailbox displayname
   strSMTPAddr = WScript.Arguments(4) 'SMTP address
   strDomain = WScript.Arguments(5) ' user NT domain
   strUserID = WScript.Arguments(6) 'NT account name to associate with mailbox

   Set objComputer = GetObject("LDAP://" & strServer)
   If Err Then
```

```
        ExitScript "Error getting reference to Exchange server:" & strServer & _
                        vbCrLf & "Error " & Err.Description
    End If
    'get the organization
    strOrg = objComputer.o
Set objContainer = _
          GetObject("LDAP://" & strServer & _
              "/CN=Recipients,OU=" & strSite & ",o=" & strOrg)

    If Err Then
        ExitScript "Error getting reference to Recipients container for site " _
        & strSite & vbCrLf & "Error " & Err.Description
    End If

    'get the SID for
    Set objSid = CreateObject("ADsSID")
    If Err Then
       ExitScript "Unable to get reference to ADSSID object" & vbCrLf _
                        & "Error:" & Err.Description
    End If
    objSid.SetAs ADS_SID_WINNT_PATH, "WinNT://" _
                 & strDomain & "/" & strUserID
    If Err Then
         ExitScript "Error getting reference to user " & strUserID & _
        " from domain " & strDomain & vbCrLf & "Error " & Err.Description
    End If
    strSidHex = objSid.GetAs(ADS_SID_HEXSTRING)
'Create a new MailBox
    Set objMailbox = objContainer.create("organizationalPerson", _
                          "cn=" & strAlias)
    If Err Then
         ExitScript "Error creating mailbox " & strAlias & vbCrLf _
                          & "Error " & Err.Description
    End If
    objMailbox.Put "mailPreferenceOption", 0 ' set mail preference
    objMailbox.Put "cn", strDisplayName
    objMailbox.Put "uid", strAlias
    'set home server for MTA
    objMailbox.Put "Home-MTA", _
      "cn=Microsoft MTA,cn=" & strServer & _
        ",cn=Servers,cn=Configuration,ou=" & strSite & ",o=" & strOrg
    'set home server for MDB
```

```
objMailbox.Put "Home-MDB", "cn=Microsoft Private MDB,cn=" _
        & strServer & ",cn=Servers,cn=Configuration,ou=" _
        & strSite & ",o=" & strOrg

objMailbox.Put "MAPI-Recipient", True
objMailbox.rfc822Mailbox = strSMTPAddr 'set Internet SMTP address
'set X.400 address
objMailbox.Put "textEncodedORaddress", _
     "c=US;a= ;p=" & strSite & ";o=" & strOrg & ";s=" & strAlias
'set associated NT user account
objMailbox.Put "Assoc-NT-Account", strSidHex
objMailbox.SetInfo ' update settings

If Err Then
     ExitScript "Error creating mailbox:" & strDisplayName _
    & vbCrLF & Err.Description & vbCrLf & "Error " & Err.Description
End If

'mailbox has been created, now grant user permission to use mailbox
'create an instance of the ADsSecurity object
Set objSecurity = CreateObject("ADsSecurity")

'get the security descriptor for the object
Set objSD = objSecurity.GetSecurityDescriptor("LDAP://" & strServer & _
                  "/" & objMailbox.distinguishedName)

'get discretionary ACL for the object
Set objDACL = objSD.DiscretionaryAcl
'create a Access Control Entry (ACE)
Set objAce = WScript.CreateObject("AccessControlEntry")
'set the user id to add security for
objAce.Trustee = strDomain & "\" & strUserID

'allow trustee to modify user attributes, send and receive mail
objAce.AccessMask = ADS_RIGHT_EXCH_MODIFY_USER_ATT Or _
              ADS_RIGHT_EXCH_MAIL_SEND_AS Or ADS_RIGHT_EXCH_MAIL_RECEIVE_AS
objAce.AceType = ADS_ACETYPE_ACCESS_ALLOWED 'set access

objDACL.AddAce objAce 'add the ACE to DACL
objSD.DiscretionaryAcl = objDACL
```

```
    objSecurity.SetSecurityDescriptor objSD
 WScript.Echo "Successfully created mailbox:" & strDisplayName

 Sub ShowUsage
  WScript.Echo "createxuser.wsf creates new Exchange server mailboxes" & vbCrLf & _
    "Syntax:"  & vbCrLf & _
    "createxuser.wsf server site alias display SMTPAddress domain account" _
    & vbCrLf  & "server Exchange server " & vbCrLf & _
    "site   Exchange server site" & vbCrLf & _
    "alias  mailbox alias" & vbCrLf & _
    "display mailbox display name" & vbCrLf & _
    "SMTPAddress mailbox Internet address" & vbCrLf & _
    "domain domain to find associated user account" & vbCrLf & _
    "account NT user account"
   End Sub
   ]]>
  </script>
</job>
```

The script creates a new Exchange mailbox and associates it with a specified NT user account. The command-line syntax is as follows:

```
createxuser server site alias displayname SMTPAddress domain accountName
```

`server` is the name of the Exchange server, `site` is Exchange server site, `alias` is the Exchange mailbox alias, `displayname` is the Exchange mailbox display name, `SMTPAddress` is the Internet mail address, `domain` is the name of the NT domain to find associated user account, and `accountname` is the NT user account.

The following command line creates the Exchange mailbox for the user Fred Smith with an alias freds and the Internet address `freds@acme.com`, and associates the mailbox with the NT account freds on the Acme domain:

```
createxuser.wsf Odin Acme Freds "Fred Smith" freds@acme.com Acme freds
```

The script requires that ADSI version 2.5 or later is installed and also requires that the `AdsSecurity` DLL from the ADSI 2.5 SDK is installed and registered on the computer the script is run from. The script does not have to run on a computer where Exchange server is installed.

Creating a user for Exchange 2000 and 2003 is easier than in Exchange 5.5 because the mailbox is associated with an Active Directory user. Because Active Directory performs the directory operations implemented separately in Exchange 5.5, fewer steps are required than in Exchange 5.5, especially the tedious step of assigning a Windows NT account to the new mailbox.

Exchange 2000/2003 mailbox maintenance is made even easier by the introduction of Collaborative Data Objects for Exchange Management library (CDOEXM). CDOEXM provides a number of methods that help simplify Exchange 2000/2003 maintenance operations, such as the creation and deletion of mailboxes.

CDOEXM extends Active Directory, providing transparent functionality to Active Directory objects. You can use your existing knowledge of Active Directory objects and functionality while implementing new Exchange administrative functionality by calling methods and setting properties exposed by CDOEXM.

> **NOTE** *If you are running code that uses the CDOEXM library on a machine other than the Exchange 2000 server, you must install the Exchange Management Components from the Exchange 2000/2003 installation package.*

To create a new mailbox, reference the Active Directory user object you want to create a mailbox for and invoke the `CreateMailbox` method. `CreateMailbox` requires a single parameter: the path to Exchange 2000/2003 mailbox store where you want to create the mailbox. This consists of the Exchange server, directory, and mail store where you want the mailbox to reside.

This path is not very intuitive or easy to build and requires decent knowledge of your Exchange server installation. One way of assisting in building the path is to do a test user creation using the Microsoft Active Directory Users and Computer administration piece.

Right-click a user that has no mailbox enabled and select the Exchange Tasks option. From the Tasks dialog box, select the Create Mailbox option. A dialog box similar to the one in Figure 16-1 appears.

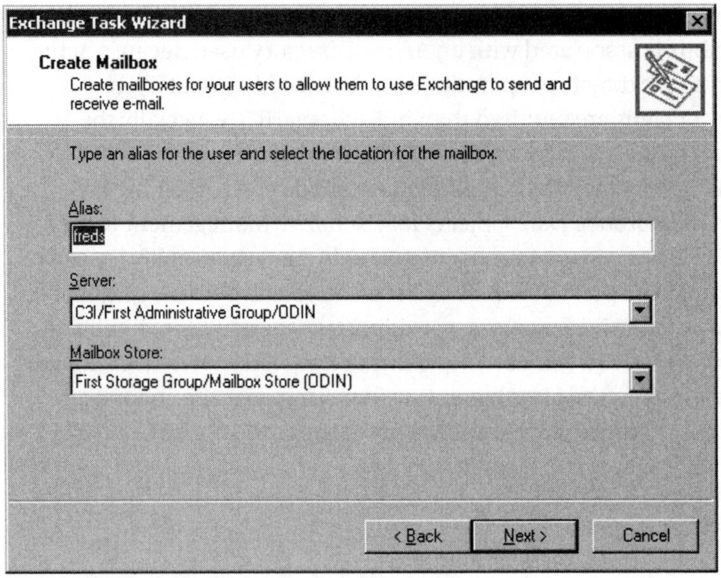

Figure 16-1. Create Mailbox dialog box

Select the server and mailbox store you want to create the mailbox in. The Server field consists of the organization, administration group, and server separated by forward slashes (/).

The Mailbox Store field contains the storage group and mailbox store separated by forward slashes. The following code builds the path to the mailbox store, as shown in Figure 16-1:

```
'these strings are built from the Server field
strOrganization = "acme"
strAdminGroup = "First Administrative Group"
strServer = "Odin " ' Exchange server name
'these strings are built from the Mailbox Store field
strStorageGroup = "First Storage Group" ' storage group
strStoreName = "Mailbox Store (Odin)" 'mail store name

strDomain = "acme.com" 'strPath =     "LDAP://" & _
                        strServer & _
                       "/CN=" & _
                       strStoreName & _
                       ",CN=" & _
                       strStorageGroup & ",CN=InformationStore,CN=" & _
                       strServer & _
                       ",CN=Servers,CN=" & _
```

```
strAdminGroup & "," & _
"CN=Administrative Groups,CN=" & _
strOrganization & "," & _
"CN=Microsoft Exchange,CN=Services," & _
"CN=Configuration,dc=acme,dc=com"
```

Another way of determining the mailbox store path is to use the Active Directory browser ADSI Edit to navigate the path. ASDI Edit is included under the `SUPPORT\TOOLS` directory on the Windows 2000 CD. Figure 16-2 shows the path to a mailbox store.

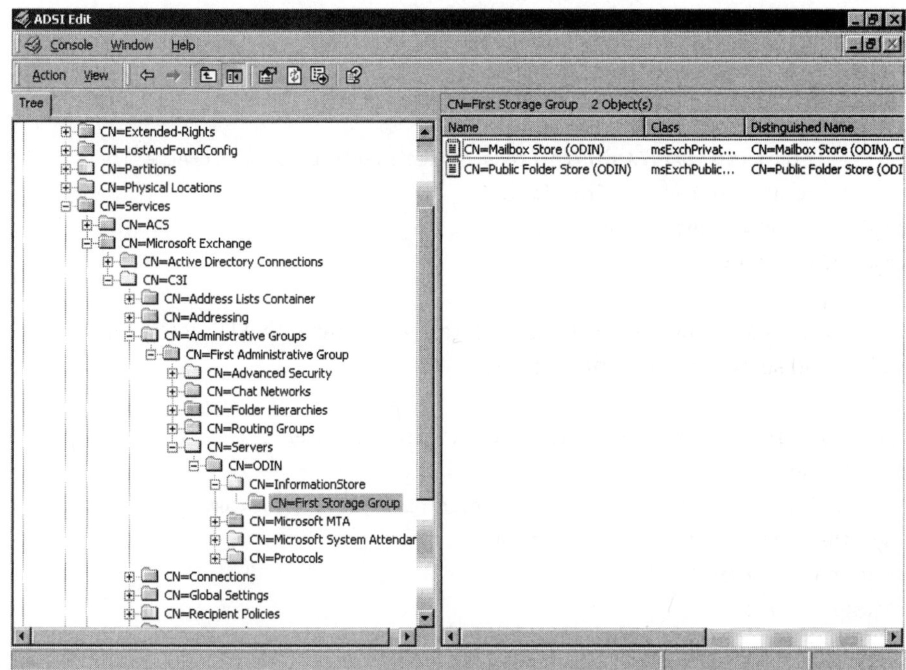

Figure 16-2. Path to the mailbox store in ASDI Edit

Once you find the mailbox store, double-click it and copy the path to the `CreateMailbox` method.

See Also

For more information, search `http://msdn.microsoft.com` for the article "CreateMailBox Method."

16.2 Setting Mailbox Properties

Problem

You want to set mailbox properties.

Solution

For Exchange 5.5, get a reference to the mailbox you want to set the property for, set the properties you want to change, and invoke the SetInfo method to write the changes back to the Exchange 5.5 directory:

```
'get a reference to the Freds mailbox
Set objMailbox = _
      GetObject("LDAP://odin/cn=Freds,cn=Recipients,ou=office,o=Acme")
'set the container name to Fred Smith
objMailBox.cn = "Fred Smith"
objMailBox.SetInfo
```

For Exchange 2000/2003 mailboxes, reference the Active Directory user object and set the required properties:

```
'get a reference to the Fred Smith Active Directory user object
Set objUser = _
      GetObject("LDAP://cn= Fred Smith,cn=Users,dc=acme,dc=com")
'set the container name to Fred Smith
objUser.cn = "Fred Smith"
objUser.SetInfo
```

Discussion

To set properties for an Exchange 5.5 object, get a reference to the Exchange 5.5 directory object you want to set properties for using the LDAP provider:

```
Set objMailbox = _
   GetObject("LDAP://server/cn=alias,cn=container,ou=site,o=organization")
```

You can set properties using the Put method or the dot method:

```
'the following statements perform the same operation
objMailBox.cn = "Fred Smith"
```

```
objMailBox.Put "cn", "Fred Smith"
objMailBox.SetInfo
```

Once you have set the properties, invoke the `SetInfo` method to set update the properties in the Exchange directory.

Exchange exposes many properties that contain hyphens (-). They require that the `Get`/`Put` method is used when referencing/setting values:

```
Wscript.Echo objMailBox.Get ("Submission-Cont-Length")
```

There are many properties that do not get loaded into the ADSI cache automatically. Referencing these properties using the `dot` or `Get` method generates a runtime error, even if the property is valid. To get a reference to these properties, you must use the `GetInfoEx` method to "force" them to be loaded:

```
objMailbox.GetInfoEx aProperties, nValue
```

The `aProperties` parameter is an array of property names you want to load. The `nValue` parameter is currently not used and must be set to 0:

```
objMailbox.GetInfoEx Array("Deliv-Cont-Length"), 0
Wscript.Echo objMailBox.Get ("Deliv-Cont-Length")
```

These properties can be set using the normal `Put` or `dot` methods. There are no specific rules as to which properties require `GetInfoEx` to read their value.

Objects stored in the Exchange directory, such as mailboxes and distribution lists, contain a large number of properties that can be manipulated.

The Microsoft Exchange Administrator application allows for the viewing and manipulation of these Exchange objects. It can be started in "raw" mode, which provides the ability to view Exchange object internal property names. This can be useful in determining the name of a property to modify using WSH and ADSI.

To start the Exchange administrator in raw mode, follow these steps:

1. Create a command prompt.

2. Find the location of the Exchange Administrator application. By default it is installed in the `c:\exchsrvr\bin` directory.

3. Enter the command `admin /r`. This starts the Exchange Administrator program in raw mode.

Select the object you want to view and select File > Raw Properties.

The attributes displayed in the dialog box are how the Exchange directory references the information. They do not all correspond to Active Directory/LDAP object properties.

To map the Exchange attribute name to its LDAP counterpart, note the attribute name and turn on raw directory mode by selecting View > Raw Directory.

You will notice that a Schema icon entry appears in the list of server containers. Selecting this icon will list Exchange directory attributes in the right-hand window pane.

Select the attribute name you want to reference through LDAP and view its property. View the Description of the attribute to get the LDAP name.

The result is the Exchange directory City attribute maps to the L property under LDAP, as shown in Figure 16-3.

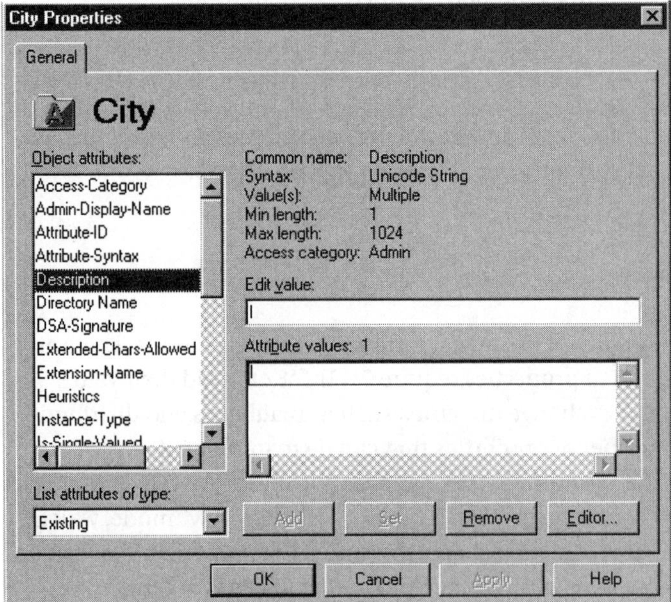

Figure 16-3. Exchange Administrator raw mode

Table 16-2 lists a number of commonly used Exchange mailbox properties and what field they map to in the Exchange Administrator program.

Table 16-2. Exchange Mailbox Properties

PROPERTY	DESCRIPTION
cn	Display name
co	Country code
Company	Company name
Department	Department name
FacsimileTelephoneNumber	Fax number
HomeFax	Home fax number
HomePhone	Home phone number
info	Notes
Initials	User initials
L	City
Mobile	Mobile phone number
Pager	Pager number
PhysicalDeliveryOfficeName	Office
PostalAddress	Address
PostalCode	Postal/ZIP code
Secretary/Telephone-Assistant	Assistant
sn	Last name
St	State
Telephone-Home2	Second home phone number
Telephone-Office2	Business phone number
TelephoneNumber	Primary phone number
title	Business title

The `mailbox` object exposes a great deal more properties than listed in the previous table. One way to list other properties and the corresponding entry in the Exchange Administrator is to create a "dummy" user, set properties using the Exchange Administrator, and then enumerate the object properties.

The `listprop` command-line script from Solution 14.5 requires a valid ADSI object. All properties and any related values are output. The following command line outputs all properties for the mailbox JoeB on the server Odin:

```
listprop LDAP://odin/cn=Joeb,cn=Recipients,ou=Office,o=Acme
```

The following script, xchgmaint.wsf, updates Exchange 5.5 mailbox properties from standard input:

```
<?xml version="1.0" ?>
<job>
<!--comment
'Script:xchgmaint.wsf
'Description:Updates Exchange mailboxes from standard input
-->
 <script language="VBScript" src="adsilib.vbs">
 <![CDATA[
 Dim nF, strLine, strServer, strSite
 Dim objContainer, strContainer
 Dim aFields, aValues
 Dim bUpdate, objComputer, strOrg
 ReDim aFields(0), aValues(0)

 If Not IsCscript Then
  ExitScript("This script must be run from command line using cscript.exe")
 End If
bUpdate = False
'check the argument count
 If Wscript.Arguments.Count <> 2 Then
     ShowUsage
 End If

  strServer = Wscript.Arguments(0)
 strSite = Wscript.Arguments(1)
On Error Resume Next
Set objComputer = GetObject("LDAP://" & strServer)
   If Err Then _
         ExitScript "Error getting reference to Exchange server: " & strServer
   'get the organization
   strOrg = objComputer.o
   ProcessStdIn
 'Process stdin for list of mailboxes to process
 Sub ProcessStdIn()

   'check if no standard input has been piped to the script
   If Wscript.StdIn.AtEndOfStream Then
      ExitScript "No standard input to process"
   End If
  'get the first line of the text stream - should be the column field names
   strLine = Wscript.StdIn.ReadLine
```

```
 'check if the stream has reached end of line, exit since no data found
  If Wscript.StdIn.AtEndOfStream Then _
              ExitScript("no data found in stream")
  'split the fields into an array
  aFields = Split(strLine, ",")

  'loop until the end of the text stream has been encountered
  Do While Not Wscript.StdIn.AtEndOfStream
    strLine = Wscript.StdIn.ReadLine
    aValues = Split(strLine, ",")
    UpdateMailbox
  Loop
 End Sub

Sub UpdateMailbox
 Dim objMailBox
   Set objMailBox = _
         GetObject("LDAP://" & strServer & "/cn=" & aValues(0) & _
             ",cn=Recipients,ou=" & strSite & ",o=" & strOrg)
   If Err Then
        ExitScript "Error getting reference to mailbox " & aValues(0)
   Else
         Wscript.Echo "---Setting properties for: " & aValues(0)
       'loop through and update all the properties
        For nF = 1 to Ubound(aFields)
'check if numeric value
        If IsNumeric(aValues(nF))  Then
           objMailbox.Put Trim(aFields(nF)), Clng(aValues(nF))
       ElseIF Ucase(aValues(nF))="TRUE" OR Ucase(aValues(nF))="FALSE" Then
           objMailbox.Put Trim(aFields(nF)), Cbool(aValues(nF))
       ElseIF IsDate(aValues(nF)) Then
           objMailbox.Put Trim(aFields(nF)), Cdate(aValues(nF))
            Else
              objMailbox.Put Trim(aFields(nF)), aValues(nF)
         End if
           Wscript.Echo "Setting " & Trim(aFields(nF)) & " to:" _
                   & aValues(nF)
         objMailbox.SetInfo
        Next
   End If
 End Sub

 'displays script usage information
```

```
Sub ShowUsage()
WScript.Echo "xchgmaint provides mailbox maintenance. " & vbCrLf & _
    "Syntax:" &  vbCrLf & _
  "xchgmaint.wsf server site " _
  & vbCrLf & "server Exchange server " & vbCrLf & _
   "site   Exchange site"
   WScript.Quit -1
End Sub
 ]]>
 </script>
</job>
```

The command line syntax is as follows:

```
xchgmaint.wsf server site [/d:delimiter]
```

in which `server` is the name of the Exchange 5.5 server, and `site` is the Exchange server site.

The standard input format requires input where the first column represents the mailbox alias and any following columns represent properties to be set. The first row must contain the property names. The following listing represents a text file that contains information to update mailboxes with:

```
alias,telephoneNumber,title, department
freds,555-1234,Accounting Manager, Accounting
```

To update the mailboxes, pipe the output of the file to the `xchgmaint.wsf` script. The following command-line sample pipes the file `mbupdate.txt` to the `xchgmaint.wsf` script for the Exchange site office on server Odin:

```
type mbupdate.txt | cscript xchgmaint.wsf Odin office
```

Because Exchange 2000 and 2003 rely on Active Directory, the bulk of the properties related to the mailbox, such as personal details and phone numbers, are associated with the Active Directory user object. See Chapter 14 for more details on setting these properties.

Any Exchange 2000 or 2003–specific properties can be listed using an Active Directory object browser or using the `listprop` method described earlier.

See Also

For more information, search http://msdn.microsoft.com for the article "The Microsoft Exchange Directory Schema."

16.3 Setting Mailbox Limits

Problem

You want to set mailbox storage and message limits.

Solution

You can get a reference to the mailbox object for which you want to set limitations and then set the appropriate property:

```
Set objMailbox = _
      GetObject("LDAP://odin/cn=Freds,cn=Accountants,ou=Office,o=Acme")
objMailBox.Put "MDB-Use-Defaults", False
'set the mailbox to send warnings at 10 megabytes
objMailBox.Put "MDB-Storage-Quota", 10000
objMailBox.SetInfo
```

Exchange 2000 mailboxes implement similar control over individual mailboxes but they use different property names than Exchange 5.5 mailboxes:

```
Set objMailbox = GetObject("LDAP://cn=Fred Smith,cn=Users,dc=acme,dc=com")
'set mailbox storage quota to 2 megabytes
objMailbox.mDBStorageQuota = 2000
objMailbox.SetInfo
```

Discussion

Table 16-3 lists properties for Exchange 5.5 and 2000/2003 that determine mailbox limits.

Table 16-3. Exchange Mailbox Limit Properties

EXCHANGE 5.5	EXCHANGE 2000/2003	DESCRIPTION
`MDB-Over-Quota-Limit`	`mDBOverQuotaLimit/OverQuotaLimit`	Maximum size of mailbox in kilobytes before sending of messages is prohibited.
`MDB-Storage-Quota`	`mDBStorageQuota/StoreQuota`	Maximum size of mailbox in kilobytes before warning messages are sent to mailbox.
`DXA-Task`	`mDBOverHardQuotaLimit/HardLimit`	Maximum size of mailbox in kilobytes before sending and receiving of messages is prohibited.
`MDB-Use-Defaults`	`mDBUseDefaults/EnableStoreDefaults`	Boolean. If set to `True`, default storage limits set under Private Information store configuration are used and the `MDB-Over-Quota-Limit`, `MDB-Storage-Quota`, and `DXA-Task` properties are ignored.
`Garbage-Coll-Period`	`garbageCollPeriod`	The maximum amount of time deleted messages are stored. For Exchange 5.5 this is stored in minutes, Exchange 2000 the value represents days.
`Submission-Cont-Length`	`submissionContLength`	The maximum size of an outgoing message
`Deliv-Cont-Length`	`delivContLength`	The maximum size of an incoming message.
Not supported	`msExchRecipLimit`	The maximum number of recipients a user can send a given message to.

A mailbox's default storage limits are inherited from the infostore. Properties such as mDBOverQuotaLimit, mDBStorageQuota, and mDBOverHardQuotaLimit appear empty on a newly created mailbox. When a value is assigned to one of these properties, the infostore default value is overridden. If you wish to reset a property to use default Exchange infostore values, you must use the PutEx method to clear the property:

```
Set ADS_PROPERTY_CLEAR = 1
Set objMailbox = GetObject("LDAP://cn=Fred Smith,cn=Users,dc=acme,dc=com")
'reset properties to force mailbox to use default Exchange infostore values
objMailbox.PutEx ADS_PROPERTY_CLEAR, " mDBStorageQuota ", 0
objMailbox.SetInfo
```

See Also

For more information, search http://msdn.microsoft.com for the article "Setting Mailbox Storage Limits."

16.4 Creating a Custom Recipient

Problem

You want to create a custom recipient.

Solution

To create a custom Exchange 5.5 recipient, get a reference to the container you want to create the recipient in. Create an object of Remote-Address type and assign a mailbox name, alias, and e-mail address:

```
Dim objContainer, objMailbox
'get a reference to the Recipients container. This is where the new custom
'recipient will be store
Set objContainer = GetObject("LDAP://odin/CN=Recipients,OU=Office,o=Acme")
'create an instance of a Remote-Address object. This is the class custom
'recipients are created
Set objMailbox = objContainer.create("Remote-Address", "cn=Fred Smith")

objMailbox.Put "cn", "Fred Smith at Hotmail"
objMailbox.Put "uid", "FredsHM"
objMailbox.Put "Target-Address", "SMTP:freds@hotmail.com"
objMailbox.SetInfo
```

To create an external e-mail address under Exchange 2000/2003, get a reference to either an Active Directory contact or user object and invoke the MailEnable method, specifying the e-mail address you want to associate with the object:

```
'get user Fred Smith
Set objUser = GetObject("LDAP://cn=Fred Smith,cn=Users,dc=acme,dc=com")
'mail enable user with a Internet SMTP address
objUser.MailEnable "smtp:freds@hotmail.com"
'update settings
objUser.SetInfo
```

Discussion

Exchange 5.5, 2000, and 2003 can contain addresses of external users that do not reside in the organization's Exchange servers. These "custom" recipients are assigned an e-mail address for the specific mail service and appear in the Exchange address list. Examples of this could be external e-mail addresses for customers.

Messages sent to these recipients are not stored on the Exchange server and custom recipients cannot log on to an Exchange server. Custom recipients do not require any associated NT account.

Table 16-4 lists the minimum required properties to make a customer recipient mailbox functional.

Table 16-4. Custom Recipient Required Properties

PROPERTY	DESCRIPTION
cn	Display name that appears in address list and Exchange Administrator.
Uid	Unique account alias.
Target-Address	Default address associated with account. This is in the format mailtype:address, where mailtype identifies the mail system and address is an address in the format of the specified mail system. Table 16-5 lists built-in address types available to Exchange. Example of Target-Address: SMTP:freds@hotmail.com

Once the properties have been set, invoke the `SetInfo` method to update the properties in the ADSI cache and Exchange 5.5 server.

Exchange 2000 and 2003 call custom recipients *mail-enabled contacts.* Exchange 2000 and 2003 introduce another type of custom recipient, a mail-enabled user, which is simply an Active Directory user that appears with an external e-mail address.

Using the CDOEXM library, objects can be mail-enabled objects by calling the `MailEnable` method. `MailEnable` requires a forwarding address in the same format as the Exchange 5.5 `Target-Address` property.

Mail-enabling an Active Directory user object is not the equivalent of an Exchange 5.5 custom recipient. This is accomplished by mail-enabling contact objects.

To create a contact, get a reference to the container that will contain the object and create an object using the `contact` class:

```
' get the container where the contact is to be stored
Set objContainer = GetObject("LDAP://ou=Contacts,dc=acme,dc=com")
'create the contact
Set objContact = objContainer.Create("contact", "CN=Joe SmithCX")

'set a few Active Directory contact object properties
objContact.givenName = "Joe"
objContact.sn = "Smith"
objContact.description = "Joe Smith, Salesperson Company X"
objContact.SetInfo
objContact.MailEnable "smtp:joes@companyx.com"
objContact.SetInfo
```

In the preceding example, an Active Directory contact is created for Joe Smith in the contacts container. A number of optional properties are set and the contact is mail-enabled using the address `joes@companyx.com`. The `MailEnable` method requires the CDOEXM to be installed on the computer where the code is running.

To change the recipient's e-mail address of an existing mail-enabled object, modify the `targetAddress` property:

```
'get contact Joe Smith
Set objUser = GetObject("LDAP://cn=Joe SmithCX,ou=Contacts,dc=acme,dc=com ")
'change the target address
objUser.TargetAddress = "joesmith@hotmail.com"
objUser.SetInfo
```

See Also

For more information, search http://msdn.microsoft.com for the articles "Creating a Mail-Enabled Recipient" and "Creating a Mail-Enabled Contact."

16.5 Maintaining Mailbox E-mail Addresses

Problem

You want to add a new e-mail address to a mailbox and delete an existing one.

Solution

For an Exchange 5.5 mailbox, get a reference to the mailbox you want to manipulate e-mail addresses for. Use the PutEx method to add or remove addresses from the mailbox's otherMailbox property:

```
Const ADS_PROPERTY_APPEND = 3
Const ADS_PROPERTY_DELETE = 4
Dim objMailbox
'get a reference to Freds mailbox
Set objMailbox = _
       GetObject("LDAP://odin/CN=FredS,CN=Recipients,OU=Office,o=Acme")

'add a new SMTP Internet address to a mailbox
objMailbox.PutEx ADS_PROPERTY_APPEND, "otherMailbox", _
           Array("smtp$freds@accounting.acme.com")
objMailbox.SetInfo

'delete a address from the mailbox
objMailbox.PutEx ADS_PROPERTY_DELETE, votherMailboxv, _
           Array("smtp$freds@finance.com ")
objMailBox.SetInfo
```

Discussion

An Exchange mailbox can have multiple addresses associated with it.
Under Exchange 5.5, mailbox object has the rfc822Mailbox/mail and textEncodedORaddress properties for the default SMTP and X.400 addresses, respectively. But you can have multiple Internet, X.400, MS Mail, and CC:Mail

addresses and any other mail service installed on your Exchange server. Different methods are required to perform these operations on Exchange 5.5 and 2000.

For Exchange 5.5 use the `otherMailbox` property to add custom addresses. The `otherMailbox` property is multivalued and contains all additional addresses associated with the mailbox. The format of the mail addresses is `addresstype$address`.

Table 16-5 lists built-in Exchange address types.

Table 16-5. Address Types

PREFIX	TYPE
SMTP	Internet e-mail
CCMAIL	CC:Mail
MS	Microsoft Mail
x400	X.400

The format for a new SMTP e-mail address for `freds@accounting.acme.com` would be `smtp$freds@accounting.acme.com`.

The address type identifies the transport agent that will be used to route and transmit the message.

Because `otherMailbox` is multivalued, use the `PutEx` method to update the `otherMailbox` property. You can add, update, and delete addresses. Call `SetInfo` each time you add or delete an address.

The following sample demonstrates how to add a new e-mail address for each user in a recipients container:

```
Const ADS_PROPERTY_APPEND = 3
Dim objContainer, objMailbox
'get a reference to the Recipients container.
Set objContainer = GetObject("LDAP://odin/CN=Recipients,OU=Office,o=Acme")

'set a filter on organizationalPerson objects - this will only return
'mailboxes in the container
 objContainer.Filter = Array("organizationalPerson")

'loop through each mailbox
 For Each objMailbox In objContainer
    'add a new Internet address to the mailbox, using the mailboxes
    'alias as the Internet address name
    objMailbox.PutEx ADS_PROPERTY_APPEND, "otherMailbox", _
            Array("smtp$" & objMailbox.uId & "@acmeus.com")
       objMailbox.SetInfo
 Next
```

Exchange 2000 and 2003 store all addresses in a proxyaddresses property. This property is similar to the otherMailbox property in Exchange 5.5 where addresses are stored in an array.

E-mail addresses are manipulated in a similar fashion to Exchange 5.5 using the PutEx method described earlier. The address format is similar to Exchange 5.5, but instead of a dollar sign ($) separating the e-mail type and address, there is a colon (:). The format for a new Exchange 2000 and 2003 Internet e-mail address for freds@accounting.acme.com would be smtp:freds@accounting.acme.com.

The case of the e-mail type is important. If the e-mail type is uppercase, it will become the default e-mail address for that e-mail type and will appear as the reply-to address in any mail sent using that mailbox. As a result, the address SMTP:freds@accounting.acme.com would show up as the default Internet e-mail address.

> **NOTE** *Setting a new primary e-mail address for a mailbox does not reset the preexisting primary address. This must be changed manually. Having multiple primary addresses for the same type in a mailbox may cause the mailbox to function incorrectly.*

In the following example, a new primary address is set for the Fred Smith mailbox and the current primary address is reset to a secondary SMTP address:

```
Const ADS_PROPERTY_APPEND = 3
Const ADS_PROPERTY_DELETE = 4
'get a reference to Fred's mailbox
Set objMailbox = _
      GetObject("LDAP://odin/cn=Freds,cn=Accountants,ou=Office,o=Acme")

'add a new SMTP Internet address to a mailbox
objMailbox.PutEx ADS_PROPERTY_APPEND, "proxyaddresses", _
            Array("SMTP:freds@accounting.acme.com")
objMailbox.SetInfo

'delete the current primary SMTP address from the mailbox
objMailbox.PutEx ADS_PROPERTY_DELETE, "proxyaddresses", _
            Array("SMTP:fred@acme.com")
objMailbox.SetInfo

'add the previously delete primary address back, but this time
'as a secondary SMTP address
```

```
objMailbox.PutEx ADS_PROPERTY_APPEND, "proxyaddresses", _
           Array("smtp:fred@acme.com")
objMailbox.SetInfo
```

In the preceding example, the existing primary address, `fred@acme.com`, is first deleted and then added again with the e-mail type in lowercase.

See Also

Solution 14.7. For more information, search `http://msdn.microsoft.com` for the article "Setting Proxy Addresses."

16.6 Creating a Distribution List

Problem

You want to create a distribution list.

Solution

To create a distribution list for Exchange 5.5, get a reference to the parent container where the distribution list will appear and create a `groupOfNames` object:

```
Dim objContainer, objDL
Dim strDisplayName, strAlias, strSMTPAddr
Set objContainer = GetObject("LDAP://odin/CN=Recipients,OU=Office,o=Acme")
'create a new distribution list
Set objDL = objContainer.create("groupOfNames", "cn=Acctusers")

'Set distribution  properties
objDL.cn = "Accounting Users" 'display name
objDL.uid = "Acctusers" 'alas
objDL.mail = "Acctusers@acme.com" ' default SMTP address

'X.400 address
objDL.textEncodedORaddress = _
           "c=US;a= ;p=HeadOffice;o=Acme;s=Acctusers"
objDL.SetInfo
```

The equivalent to a distribution list under Exchange 2000 is a mail-enabled group, which turns an Active Directory user group into a distribution list. Using CDOEXM, get a reference to the Active Directory group you want to enable and invoke the MailEnable method:

```
Dim objMember, objGroup
'get a reference to a group object list
Set objGroup = _
    GetObject("LDAP://cn=AG,cn=Users,dc=c3i,dc=com")
   objGroup.MailEnable
   objGroup.SetInfo
```

Discussion

Distribution lists allow the grouping of related recipients into lists. Distribution lists reside in the same containers as mailboxes.

To create a distribution list under Exchange 5.5, get a reference to the container you want to create the list in and create an object of groupOfNames type. The name of the distribution list is specified in RDN format:

```
'
Set objContainer = _
      GetObject("LDAP://odin/CN=Recipients,OU=office,O=Acme")
Set objDL = objContainer.Create("groupOfNames", "cn=Acctusers")
```

Before the distribution list can be made active, the properties listed in Table 16-6 must be set.

Table 16-6. Distribution List Required Properties

PROPERTY	DESCRIPTION
cn	Friendly display name.
Uid	Distribution list unique identifier.
TextEncodedORaddress	X.400 address. Used for message routing.

Once the Exchange 5.5 distribution has been created, you can add objects to it. To add an item to a distribution list, get a reference to a list and invoke the Add method. The syntax is as follows:

```
objDL.Add(strLDAPPath)
```

strLDAPPath is the full LDAP path to the object you want to add. You can add mailboxes, custom recipients, or other distribution lists.

```
'get a reference to an existing DL
Set objDL = _
   GetObject("LDAP://odin/cn=acctusers,cn=Recipients,ou=Office,o=Acme")

'add some mailboxes
objDL.Add "LDAP://odin/cn=jsmith,cn=Recipients,ou=Office,o=Acme"
objDL.Add "LDAP://odin/cn=joeb,cn=Recipients,ou=Office,o=Acme"
```

To delete an object from the list, invoke the Remove method on the distribution list object you want to remove an item from:

```
objDL.Remove(strLDAPPath)
```

strLDAPPath is the full LDAP path to the object you want to delete.

```
'get a reference to an existing DL
Set objDL = _
     GetObject("LDAP://odin/cn=acctusers,cn=Recipients,ou=Office,o=Acme")
'remove a mailbox
objDL.Remove "LDAP://odin/cn=jsmith,cn=Recipients,ou=Office,o=Acme "
```

Active Directory groups are used as distribution lists (mail-enabled groups) under Exchange 2000. Use the CDOEXM MailEnable method to mail-enable a group. See Solution 14.13 for an example of how to create an Active Directory group. The second Solution script mail-enables the Power Users group.

See Also

Solution 14.13. For more information, search http://msdn.microsoft.com for the article "Distribution List Manager Sample Code."

16.7 Enumerating a Distribution List

Problem

You want to enumerate a distribution list.

Solution

You can set a reference to the distribution list for which you want to enumerate and then iterate through the Members collection:

```
Dim objMember, objDL
'get a reference to a distribution list
Set objDL = _
      GetObject("LDAP://odin/cn=acctusers,cn=Recipients,ou=Office,o=Acme")
For Each objMember In objDL.Members
     Wscript.Echo objMember.Name
Next
```

The steps required to enumerate a distribution list under Exchange 2000 are pretty much the same as Exchange 5.5. Get a reference to the mail-enabled Active Directory group you want to enumerate and iterate the Members collection:

```
Dim objMember, objGroup
'get a reference to a group object list
Set objGroup = _
                    GetObject("LDAP://cn=AG,cn=Users,dc=c3i,dc=com")
'enumerate the group objects
For Each objMember In objGroup.Members
    If Not objMember.mailNickName = "" Then
     Wscript.Echo objMember.Name
    Else
     Wscript.Echo objMember.Name & " is not an Exchange enabled object"
    End If
Next
```

Discussion

To enumerate a distribution list, get a reference to a list and iterate through the Members property. The objects returned from the Members property may be a mailbox, custom recipient, or distribution list type objects.

Because Exchange 2000 uses the Active Directory to store mail recipients, distribution lists may contain objects that are not mail-enabled. One way of determining non-mail-enabled objects is to check if the mailNickName property is empty, as is demonstrated in the second Solution script.

See Also

For more information, search `http://msdn.microsoft.com` for the article "Enumerating Exchange Groups."

16.8 Creating a Recipients Container

Problem

You want to create an Exchange 5.5 recipients container or Exchange 2000 address list.

Solution

To create an Exchange 5.5 recipients container, get a reference to a container object you want to create the new container in. Create a new `Container` object, specifying an RDN name to identify the new container:

```
Dim objContainer, objNewContainer, objNewContainer2
Set objContainer = GetObject("LDAP://odin/OU=Office,O=Acme")
'create a root recipients container
Set objNewContainer = objContainer.create("Container", "cn=External Users")
objNewContainer.Put "Container-Info", &H80000001
objNewContainer.SetInfo

'nest a recipients container inside the new External users container
Set objNewContainer2 = objNewContainer.create("Container", "cn=ABC Ltd")
objNewContainer2.Put "Container-Info", &H80000001
objNewContainer2.SetInfo
```

For Exchange 2000 and 2003, get a reference to the container that will list the address list and create an object of the `addressBookContainer` class:

```
Dim objAddressContainer, objNewAddressContainer

'get a reference to the container the recipient list will reside in...
Set objAddressContainer = _
GetObject("LDAP://CN=All Address Lists," & _
                 "CN=Address Lists Container,CN=C3I,CN=Microsoft Exchange," & _
                  "CN=Services,CN=Configuration,DC=c3i,DC=com")
```

```
'create an object of addressBookContainer class, specifying the name
'using in RDN format
Set objNewAddressContainer = _
      objAddressContainer.Create("addressBookContainer", "CN=Company X")

'set display name
objNewAddressContainer.DisplayName = " Company X List"
objNewAddressContainer.instanceType = 4

'set the LDAP search criteria for the address list. The following criteria
' lists all contacts that are employees of Company XYZ
objNewAddressContainer.purportedSearch = "(&(&(&(&(& (mailnickname=*)(|" & _
                              "(&(objectCategory=person)(objectClass=contact)))))" & _
                              "(objectCategory=user)(company=Company X)))"
objNewAddressContainer.systemFlags = 1610612736
objNewAddressContainer.showInAdvancedViewOnly = True
objNewAddressContainer.SetInfo
```

Discussion

Containers are used to organize recipients under Exchange 5.5 servers. Initially the Recipients container is the only area available to store mailboxes, but additional containers can be created to organize recipients.

The `Container-Info` property must be set to the hexadecimal value of &H80000001, which identifies the container as a mailbox recipients container.

```
Set the objNewContainer.Put "Container-Info", &H80000001
```

Recipients containers can be nested.

Recipients containers are referred to as address lists under Exchange 2000 and 2003. While an address list is functionally equivalent to an Exchange 5.5 recipients container, they are implemented differently. Because the Active Directory contains the directory structure for Exchange 2000 and 2003, there is no real need for a separately maintained directory as in earlier versions of Exchange server.

The tricky part of creating an Exchange 2000 or 2003 address list is setting the search criteria through the `purportedSearch` property. This property determines what objects will appear in the address list based on search criteria using Lightweight Directory Access Protocol (LDAP) search criteria.

It is beyond the scope of this book to cover LDAP queries. Knowing how to build LDAP queries doesn't guarantee success setting the `purportedSearch` property, because Exchange 2000 and 2003 require a number of not-so-obvious properties to create enable function address list.

The easiest way to generate the LDAP queries is to use the Exchange System Manager to build a query and then copy and paste the query into code. To generate a query, follow these steps:

1. Start Exchange System Manager.

2. Select the address list you want to create a query for.

3. Display the properties for the address list.

A dialog box similar to the one in Figure 16-4 appears.

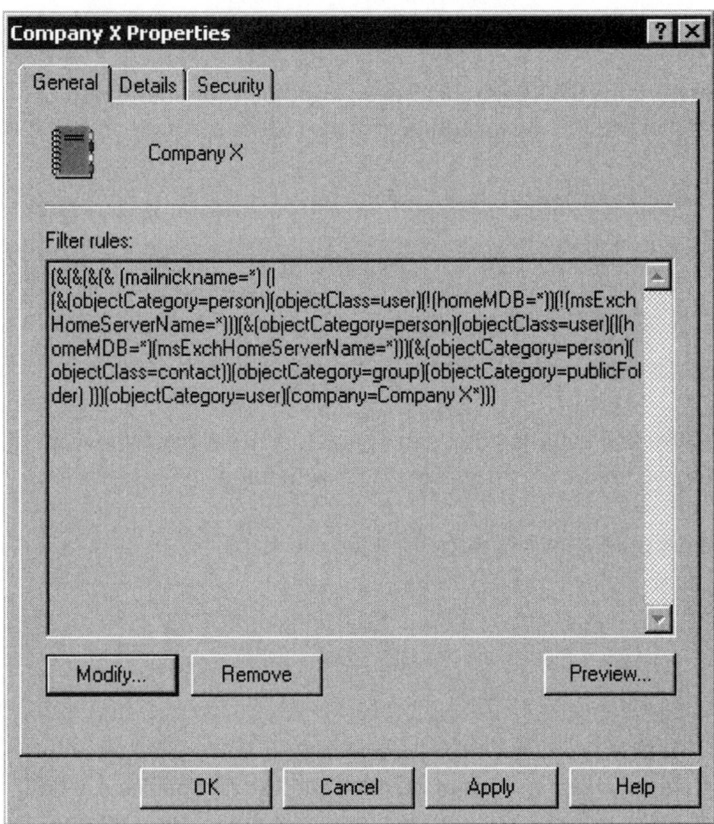

Figure 16-4. Address list properties

Modify the address list query. Once you have built the query, copy the resulting LDAP query string into your code.

Note that you won't be able to edit the query you created using code through System Manager. Exchange 2000 and 2003 store query builder information in the msExchPurportedSearchUI property, which is not a documented property.

16.9 Deleting an Exchange Object

Problem

You want to delete an Exchange mailbox.

Solution

To delete an object from the Exchange 5.5 directory, get the container that contains the object you want to delete and invoke the Delete method:

```
'get a reference to a container to remove object from
Set objContainer = _
    GetObject("LDAP://odin/cn=Recipients,ou=Office,o=Acme"

'delete an object
objContainer.Delete "organizationalPerson", "cn=freds"
```

For Exchange 2000 and 2003, get the Active Directory user object you want to remove the mailbox for and invoke the DeleteMailbox method:

```
Set objUser = GetObject("LDAP://cn=Fred,cn=Users,dc=c3i,dc=com")
 objUser.DeleteMailbox
 objUser.SetInfo
```

Discussion

Any item in an Exchange 5.5 server, such as a mailbox or distribution list, can be deleted using the Delete method. The Delete method operates on the container object, so you must first get a reference to the container where the object is located.

Once you have the container, invoke the Delete method. The syntax is as follows:

```
objContainer.Delete strClassName, strObjectName
```

strClassName specifies the object class type to delete—for a user, the class name is user. strObjectName represents the user ID to delete. This is organizationalPerson for a mailbox.

Exchange 2000 and 2003 are a bit different as a result of their reliance on Active Directory. CDOEXM exposes a DeleteMailbox method that deletes all Exchange resources associated with an Active Directory user. It does not delete the Active Directory user itself. See Solution 14.13 for information on deleting an Active Directory objects.

The DeleteMailbox method does not work on address lists or remote addresses under Exchange 2000 and 2003. Because no real resources such as messages are stored with these objects, they simply need to be disabled. Use the CDOEXM object's MailDisable method to disable an address list or remote address:

```
'get a reference to the group object you want to disable
   Set objGroup = GetObject("LDAP://cn=AGROUP,cn=Users,dc=c3i,dc=com")
    objGroup.MailDisable
    objGroup.SetInfo
```

See Also

For more information, search http://msdn.microsoft.com for the articles "Disabling a Mail Recipient" and "Deleting a Mailbox."

16.10 Searching an Exchange Server

Problem

You want to search all containers within an Exchange server.

Solution

You can create an ADO Connection object and set the provider to ADsDSOObject. Execute a query against the Exchange directory store using SQL to specify criteria for which objects to return.

The following example provides a generic function, ExecuteQuery, that can be used to execute Exchange 5.5:

```
'Exchange 2000/2003 query
ExecuteQuery "SELECT cn FROM " & _
     "'LDAP://DC=acme,DC=com' WHERE" & _
    " department='Accounting' AND objectCategory='person'"

'Exchange 5.5 query
ExecuteQuery "SELECT cn,TelephoneNumber  FROM " & _
     "'LDAP://Odin' WHERE objectClass='organizationalPerson'" & _
    " AND department='Accounting'"

Sub ExecuteQuery(strQuery)
  Dim objConn, objRst
  Set objConn = CreateObject("ADODB.Connection")
  objConn.Provider = "ADsDSOObject"
  objConn.Open "Active Directory Provider"

  'execute a query against the Exchange server Odin, listing all mailboxes
  'where the department is Accounting
  Set objRst = _
    objConn.Execute(strQuery)
    'loop through all mailboxes and output the display name
   Do While Not objRst.EOF
    Wscript.Echo objRst("cn")
    objRst.MoveNext
   Loop

   objRst.Close
   objConn.Close
End Sub
```

Discussion

Searching parts of or the entire Exchange 5.5 or 2000/2003 directory can be performed using the ADSI OLE DB provider. The steps required to initiate the ADO objects are the same for both versions of Exchange, the main difference being in how the source is specified.

Create an ADO Connection object and specify set the Provider property to ADsDSOObject. Open a connection by invoking the Connection object's Open method. The source here can be any string (something has to be passed) and it does not affect the Connection object.

```
Set objConn = CreateObject("ADODB.Connection")
  objConn.Provider = "ADsDSOObject"
  objConn.Open "Active Directory Provider"
```

Once the connection is open, you can execute queries against the Exchange directory. The query is in the form of a SQL query:

```
Set objRst = _
    objConn.Execute("SELECT adspath,cn,name,objectClass FROM " & _
            "'LDAP://odin'" & _
            " WHERE objectClass='organizationalPerson'")
```

You must specify the exact fields you want to select. You cannot specify the SQL * operator to get all fields, because you may be querying different objects in the directory that don't expose the same properties as other objects returned by the query. Specifying the SQL * operator only returns one field, the ADsPath, which is the LDAP path to the object.

The query source specified after the FROM clause is the LDAP path to the container you want to start the search. In Exchange 5.5 the source is specified by the LDAP path to the Exchange server, while in Exchange 2000 it's the path.

There must be a WHERE criteria clause to identify what is to be returned. The WHERE criteria cannot be omitted, even if you want to search for all objects in the directory. If you want to process all objects in the directory, set the criteria to match at least one string property to *, which is a wildcard and will return all matches:

```
SELECT adspath,cn,name,objectClass FROM 'LDAP://odin' WHERE objectClass='*'
```

Any string criteria must be surrounded in single quotes.

You cannot update the results returned by the query. All ADSI recordset results are read-only. If you need to modify the results, use the ADsPath field for the result to get a reference to the Exchange object using GetObject and modify the object properties directly.

Some Exchange directory objects properties cannot be easily queried. For example, each mailbox or distribution list can have multiple secondary e-mail addresses. These are stored as an array, which cannot be referenced using criteria.

The following sample demonstrates how to update values for Exchange 5.5 mailboxes returned by an ADO ADSI query. The code returns all mailboxes for the accounting department. References are made to the mailbox object. All the e-mail addresses are searched, and if any contain the domain `acme.com`, they are replaced with `accounting.acme.com`:

```
Dim objConn, objRst, aMailBoxes, nPos, objMailbox, nF
Set objConn = CreateObject("ADODB.Connection")
objConn.Provider = "ADsDSOObject"
objConn.Open "Active Directory Provider"

'execute a query against the Exchange server Odin, listing all mailboxes
'where the department is Accounting
Set objRst = _
  objConn.Execute("SELECT ADsPath FROM " & _
      "'LDAP://Odin" & _
      "' WHERE objectClass='organizationalPerson' AND department='Accounting'")

'loop through all mailboxes and output the display name
Do While Not objRst.EOF
 'get the mailbox object from directory using the object path
 Set objMailbox = GetObject(objRst("ADsPath"))
 aMailBoxes = objMailbox.otherMailbox

 'check if aMailBoxes returns an array of values
 If VarType(aMailBoxes) = 8204 Then
'loop through each E-mail address in array
    For nF = 0 To UBound(aMailBoxes)
   'check if E-mail address contains Acme.com, if so
   ' replace with accounting.acme.com

If StrComp(Right(aMailBoxes(nF), 9),"@acme.com",vbTextCompare) = 0
       nPos = InStr(aMailBoxes(nF), "@acme.com")
          aMailBoxes(nF) = Left(aMailBoxes(nF), nPos-1) &
"accounting.acme.com"
          objMailbox.Put "otherMailbox", aMailBoxes
          objMailbox.SetInfo
        End If
    Next
 End If

 objRst.MoveNext
Loop
objRst.Close
objConn.Close
```

The following command-line script, `exsearch.wsf`, searches a specified Exchange server and returns all results that meet the specified criteria:

```
<?xml version="1.0" ?>
<job>
<!--
exsearch.wsf
returns the ADS path of any objects that have an e-mail address that
contains a specified string
-->
 <script language="VBScript" src="adsilib.vbs">
 <![CDATA[
Option Explicit
 Dim objRst, objConn, nf
 Dim objArgs, strServer, strAddress, aMailBoxes
 Dim strQuery, strField, aFields
 If Not IsCscript Then
  ExitScript("This script must be run from command line using cscript.exe")
 End If

 If WScript.Arguments.Count <> 3 Then
   ShowUsage
   Wscript.Quit
 End If

  strServer = WScript.Arguments(0)
  strField = WScript.Arguments(1)
  strQuery = WScript.Arguments(2)
  Set objConn = CreateObject("ADODB.Connection")
objConn.Provider = "ADsDSOObject"
  objConn.Open "Active Directory Provider"

  Set objRst = _
    objConn.Execute("SELECT " & strField &  " FROM " & _
        "'LDAP://" & strServer & _
        "' WHERE objectClass='organizationalPerson' AND " & strQuery)

   aFields = Split(strField,",")
   Do While Not objRst.EOF
    For nF = 0 To UBound(aFields)
     WScript.Echo objRst(aFields(nF))
  Next
objRst.MoveNext
```

```
  Loop
 objRst.Close
  objConn.Close

 Sub ShowUsage
   WScript.Echo "exsearch lists all mailboxes that contain a specified" & vbLf
& _
   "search string. Syntax:"  &  vbCrLf & _
   "exsearch.wsf server fields query" & vbCrLf & _
   "server         Exchange server to search" & vbCrLf & _
   "fields         field values to returnfrom Exchange directory " & vbCrLf & _
   "query          SQL query to evaluate" & vbCrLf & _
   "Example: list all mailboxes that contain acme.com" & vbCrLf & _
   "exsearch.wsf Acme acme.com"
  End Sub
   ]]>
 </script>
</job>
```

The command-line syntax is as follows:

```
exsearch.wsf server fields query
```

`Server` is the name of the Exchange server, and `fields` is a list of LDAP property names you want to return. The results are separated by commas. `Query` is a query expression containing the search criteria to execute against the specified server.

The following command line would return the `cn,l` and `adspath` values from the Exchange server Odin for all objects where the city is Vancouver and the department is Accounting:

```
exsearch.wsf odin cn,l,adspath "l='Vancouver' AND department='Accounting'"
```

Exchange 2000 and 2003 information is stored in Active Directory under Windows 2000 or 2003. When you search Exchange 2000 or 2003, you are effectively searching Active Directory. Solution 14.6 provides a generic command-line script, `adsiqry.wsf`, that can execute queries against Active Directory.

See Also

Solution 14.16. For more information, search `http://msdn.microsoft.com` for the articles "Distribution List Manager Sample Code" and "Searching with ActiveX Data Objects (ADO)."

CHAPTER 17

Security

IN ANY NETWORKED environment where more than one user shares resources, security is of utmost importance.

The Windows NT and later environments provide security to files, network shares, registry, Active Directory services, Exchange, and IIS servers.

The underlying security for these services is implemented using a *security descriptor.* A security descriptor contains security permissions that limit the types of operations that users and/or groups can perform. Security descriptors also contain auditing information. Auditing information can be used to report access to resources.

These permissions are stored in Access Control Lists (ACLs). The permissions ACL is called the Discretionary ACL (DACL), while object auditing is stored in the System Access Control List (SACL).

An ACL contains a list of Access Control Entries (ACEs). An ACE determines the individual permissions set for the object. An ACE object stores the *access mask,* which is a numeric value that determines the object permissions, access type (which either grants or denies access), and a trustee. The *trustee* is the user account or group that the permission is being applied to.

There are a few ways to manipulate Windows object security information. The ADSI 2.5 SDK includes an object that performs security operations by manipulating object security descriptors. This object can modify permissions on files, directory, and registry entries, but not file shares. It requires ADSI 2.5 to be installed.

WMI version 1.5 can manipulate security on file, directory, and network shares. WMI also can manipulate these resources on local and remote computers, as long as the remote computers are running WMI 1.5.

Choosing which technology to use depends upon the operations you are performing. The ADSI permissions object can perform registry security operations and is fast, but it requires the permissions object library from the ADSI 2.5 SDK/Resource kit to be installed on any machine to run. You can download this from `http://www.microsoft.com/NTServer/nts/downloads/other/ADSI25/default.asp`. Select the SDK for Active Directory Services Interfaces 2.5 for download.WMI can manipulate shares, access remote resources, and requires no additional component files to be installed, but it is slower and slightly more cumbersome to use.

17.1 Setting NT Share Security

Problem

You want to set share security.

Solution

Windows Management Instrumentation (WMI) version 1.1 and later provide classes to manipulate Windows NT and later share and file security.

The following sample grants the user Freds change permissions for the Data share on remote machine Odin. It requires the include file `wmiinc.vbs`, which is listed in Chapter 10:

```
<?xml version="1.0" ?>
<job>
<!--comment
Script:setacl.wsf
example on how to grant network share permissions
-->
 <script language="VBScript" src="wmiinc.vbs">
 <![CDATA[
 Option Explicit
Const CHANGE = 1245631    Const ACCESS_DENIED = 0
Dim objShare, objDescriptor, objACE, retval, aDACL
 Dim objTrustee, objService
'get a reference to WMI service on the remote machine Odin
 Set objService = GetObject( _
              "winmgmts:{impersonationLevel=impersonate}!\\Odin")
'get a reference to the data share on the remote machine Odin
 Set objShare = _
     objService.Get("Win32_LogicalShareSecuritySetting.Name='data'")

 'get the security descriptor and DACL
 retval = objShare.GetSecurityDescriptor(objDescriptor)
aDACL = objDescriptor.DACL
'create a new instance of an ACE and Trustee object
 Set objACE = objService.Get("Win32_ACE")
 Set objTrustee = objService.Get("Win32_Trustee")

 'set trustee information
 objTrustee.Name = "Acme\Freds"
```

```
 'assign the binary SID value for user account Freds
 objTrustee.SID = GetBinarySID("Freds")

 objACE.AccessMask = CHANGE
 objACE.AceType = ACCESS_DENIED
 objACE.Trustee = objTrustee

 'resize DACL array and assign to security descriptor
 ReDim Preserve aDACL(UBound(aDACL) + 1)
 Set aDACL(UBound(aDACL)) = objACE
objDescriptor.dacl = aDACL
'set the security descriptor
 retval = objShare.SetSecurityDescriptor(objDescriptor)
]]>
 </script>
</job>
```

Discussion

The WMI `Win32_LogicalShareSecuritySetting` class exposes security details for network shares under Windows NT and later. Permissions can be set and revoked using the `GetSecurityDescriptor` and `SetSecurityDescriptor` methods.

The ability to access share and file permissions is available in the latest WMI service (version 1.1 and later) for Windows NT and later. WMI version 1.5 is automatically installed on Windows 2000 and later, whereas a separate installation is required under Windows NT.

While the security provider files are installed automatically with WMI, they must be manually registered by running the `mofcomp` utility on the `secrcw32.mof` for Windows NT. The `mofcomp` utility is located under the WBEM directory, which you can find under the Windows NT/2000 system32 directory:

1. Go to the command prompt.
2. Change the directory to the WBEM directory located under your computer's system32 directory.
3. Enter the following command line:

```
mofcomp secrcw32.mof
```

Once the MOF file is compiled, instances of the `Win32_LogicalShareSecuritySetting` class can be created. The security classes are stored under the `root\cimv2` namespace.

Use the Win32_LogicalShareSecuritySetting class to manipulate share security. If you have connected to a WMI namespace using a WMI Services object, use the object's Get method to retrieve a Win32_LogicalShareSecuritySetting object by specifying the relative path to the share:

```
'create an instance of the WMI Services object, connecting to the
' root\cimv2 namespace on the local machine
Set objServices = _
    GetObject("winmgmts:{impersonationLevel=impersonate}!root\cimv2")
'get a reference to the share 'sharename'
Set objShare = _
    objServices.Get("Win32_LogicalShareSecuritySetting.Name='sharename'")
```

Chapter 10 provides more detailed information on how to connect to WMI Service objects.

References to shares can be retrieved using the GetObject method:

```
Const WMIMoniker = "winmgmts:{impersonationLevel=impersonate}!root\cimv2:"
Set objShare = GetObject(WMIMoniker & _
                  "Win32_LogicalShareSecuritySetting.Name='sharename'")
```

This method bypasses the step of first creating a Services object. If you intend to manipulate more than one share, it's preferable to use the Services object's Get method, because it requires the establishment of a connection to a WMI namespace only once.

Remote shares can be manipulated by specifying the name of the remote computer in the WMI connection string:

```
Const WMIMoniker = "winmgmts:{impersonationLevel=impersonate}!"
'reference the 'data' share on remote computer odin.
Set objShare = GetObject(WMIMoniker & _
        "\\odin\root\cimv2:Win32_LogicalShareSecuritySetting.Name='data'")
```

The only difference between this example and previous examples is the computer name is specified in the WMI connection string. You must have appropriate administrative security permissions to access resources on remote computers.

The share name referenced is not case-sensitive. If the share doesn't exist, a runtime error is generated. Note that the share must have a valid user or group assigned to it. If a share only has the Everyone group assigned to it, a "not found" error will occur when you attempt to reference it.

The Win32_LogicalShareSecuritySetting class exposes a GetSecurityDescriptor method that returns a reference to a security descriptor for the share. A security descriptor contains information about object ownership and security permissions. The syntax is as follows:

```
nResult = objInstance.GetSecurityDescriptor(objDescriptor)
```

If successful, the GetSecurityDescriptor method returns a Win32_SecurityDescriptor security descriptor object to the objDescriptor parameter. The GetSecurityDescriptor method returns 0 if a security descriptor is successfully returned.

Share permission information is exposed through the Discretionary Access Control List (DACL) collection property of the Win32_SecurityDescriptor class. The DACL property is a collection of Access Control Entry (ACE) Win32_ACE objects that determine the permissions assigned to the share.

Table 17-1 describes some of the properties exposed through the Win32_ACE class.

Table 17-1. Win32_ACE *Properties*

PROPERTY	DESCRIPTION
AccessMask	Numeric value that determines permissions granted to trustee
AceType	0 = access allowed, 1 = access denied
Trustee	Win32_Trustee object

The Win32_Trustee object identifies to whom the permission is granted. It exposes a Name property, which contains the trustee name in the format Domain\Accountname. A SID property contains an array of binary values representing the unique SID for the account.

The following script gets a reference to a share called "data" on the local machine and lists the permissions for the share:

```
Dim objShare, objDescriptor, objACE, retval

Const WMIMoniker = "winmgmts:{impersonationLevel=impersonate}!"
'get a reference to the data share
Set objShare = _
    GetObject(WMIMoniker & "Win32_LogicalShareSecuritySetting.Name='Data'")

retval = objShare.GetSecurityDescriptor(objDescriptor)
'loop through each ACE in the DACL and output the trustee's access
For Each objACE In objDescriptor.dacl
 'list the trustee (account) name and associated permission
 Wscript.Echo objACE.Trustee.Name, objACE.AccessMask
Next
```

The permissions are determined by a combination of the AccessMask and AceType. Table 17-2 lists AccessMask and AceType values for NT share permissions.

Table 17-2. AccessMask *and* AceType *Permission Settings*

PERMISSION	ACETYPE	ACCESSMASK
No Access	1	2032127
Full Access	0	2032127
Change	0	1245631
Read	0	1179817

Share permissions are set using the SetSecurityDescriptor method. This method updates the security descriptor for the specified share security object. The syntax is as follows:

```
avar = objInstance.SetSecurityDescriptor(objDescriptor)
```

The objDescriptor parameter is the Win32_SecurityDescriptor to set for the share. SetSecurityDescriptor returns 0 if a security descriptor was successfully returned.

Unfortunately, there are no methods that provide simple addition or removal of trustee permissions. To add a new trustee, a new ACE must be added to the DACL array. To remove an entry, the DACL entry must be removed and the array resized accordingly.

When adding a new ACE to the DACL, you must set the SID for the account you want add to the DACL. The SID is stored as an array of bytes. The tricky part is to get the binary of representation of the SID for the particular account.

Account SIDs are exposed through the Win32_Account class as a string, but the Win32_Account class isn't keyed on the account name, so a sequential search of the class is required to find the appropriate account.

String representations of the SID cannot be used by the ACE SID property, but they can be used to reference a binary representation of the SID value from the Win32_SID class. The Win32_SID class stores the binary representation of the SID and is keyed on the SID string representation.

The GetBinarySID function defined in the wmiinc.vbs include file returns the SID of an account as an array of bytes. The syntax is as follows:

```
aSID = GetBinarySID(strAccount)
```

strAccount is the name of the account you want to return the SID for. It can be in format Domain\Account, Computer\Account, or just the account name. If you do not specify a domain or computer, it will pick the first occurrence of the name if the name occurs for a domain and computer.

Windows NT and later do not include a command-line utility to manipulate share permissions. The following script, `shrmaint.wsf`, is a command-line script that performs share permissions maintenance on local and remote shares:

```
<?xml version="1.0" ?>
<job>
<!--comment
Script:shrmaint.wsf
Description:
Performs network share maintenance
-->
 <script language="VBScript" src="wmiinc.vbs">
 <![CDATA[
Option Explicit
Dim avar, objDescriptor, objACE, objACE2, objTrustee, aDACL, objArgs
 Dim strShareName, objInstance, strMachine,  strPermission
 Dim objService, strAccountName, nF, bFound, nI
'check if script is being run from command prompt
 If Not IsCscript Then
  ExitScript _
      "This script must be run from command line using cscript.exe",False
 End If

 'check the argument count
 If Wscript.Arguments.Count = 0 Then
   ShowUsage
 End If
   GetArguments
  On Error Resume Next
  'get reference to local or remote computer
  Set objService = GetObject( _
              "winmgmts:{impersonationLevel=impersonate}" & strMachine)
  If Err Then
     ExitScript "Unable to connect to computer " & strMachine, False
  End If
  'check if share name specified
  If  strShareName = "" Then
    ShowUsage
  End If

  Set objInstance = _
```

```
objService.Get("Win32_LogicalShareSecuritySetting.Name='" _
         &  strShareName & "'")
  If Err Then
   ExitScript "Unable to connect to share '" & strShareName & "'", False
  End If
  avar = objInstance.GetSecurityDescriptor(objDescriptor)
aDACL = objDescriptor.dacl
  'if no actions specified then list existing permissions for share
  If strPermission = "" Then
'loop through each ACE in the DACL
    For Each objACE In aDACL
            Wscript.Echo objACE.Trustee.Name, _
                GetPermissionString(objACE.AccessMask, objACE.AceType)
    Next
   Else 'set permissions for share

    'loop through each ACE in the DACL
    For nF = Lbound(aDACL) To Ubound(aDACL)
      Set objACE = aDACL(nF)
      'check if ACL exists for specfied account name..
      If StrComp(objACE.Trustee.Name, strAccountName, vbTextCompare) = 0 Then
         bFound = True
          Exit For
      End If
    Next

'are we revoking the permissions?
    If strPermission = "REVOKE" Then
     'does the account specified to revoke exist?
     If bFound Then
       'check if array needs resizing to remove account
       If UBound(aDACL)>nF Then
        'resize the DACL array to remove the revoked account
        For nI = nF To UBound(aDACL)-1
          Set aDACL(nI) = aDACL(nI+1)
        Next
       End If
       ReDim Preserve aDACL(UBound(aDACL)-1)
     Else
        ExitScript "Could not find user " & strAccountName, False
     End If
    Else
     'get instances of WMI Win32 ACE and Trustee objects
```

```
 Set objACE2 = objService.Get("Win32_ACE")
 Set objTrustee = objService.Get("Win32_Trustee")
 If Err Then
            ExitScript "Error occurred creating Win32_ACE " _
                    & "and Win32_Trustee objects" & vbCrLf _
                          & "Error" & Err.Description , False
 End If
'set trustee information
objTrustee.Name = strAccountName
'attempt to get binary SID value for account
objTrustee.SID = GetBinarySID(strAccountName)
'check if user was found
If IsNull(objTrustee.SID) Then
    ExitScript "Could not find user " & strAccountName, False
End If

'set ACE information
objACE2.Trustee = objTrustee
objACE2.AceType = 0
 'check if no access is specified - then AceType must be 1
  If Ucase(strPermission) = "NOACCESS" Then
    objACE2.AceType = 1
  Else
     objACE2.AceType = 0
 End If

 objACE2.AccessMask = GetPermissionValue(strPermission)
 If objACE2.AccessMask = 0 Then
        ExitScript "Invalid permission " & strPermission, False
 End If
 'if user exists in DACL, then update existing ACE
 If bFound Then
  Set aDACL(nF) = objACE2
 Else
  'resize DACL array and assign to security descriptor
  ReDim Preserve aDACL(UBound(aDACL) + 1)
  Set aDACL(UBound(aDACL)) = objACE2
 End If
End If
objDescriptor.dacl = aDACL
'set the security descriptor
avar = objInstance.SetSecurityDescriptor(objDescriptor)
If avar<>0 Or Err Then
```

```
            ExitScript "Error occurred setting security descriptor",False
    End If
  End If

'Reads command line arguments and sets appropriate flags
Sub GetArguments
Dim nF, strArg
'loop through command line parameters
For nF = 0 to Wscript.Arguments.Count - 1
 Select Case Ucase(Wscript.Arguments(nF))
   Case "/MACHINE" 'gets machine name
            strMachine = "!\\" & GetParameter(nF)
Case "/SHARE"
            strShareName = GetParameter(nF)
   Case "/GRANT"
      strAccountName = GetParameter(nF)
      nF = nF+1
      strPermission = GetParameter(nF)
   Case "/REVOKE"
      strAccountName = GetParameter(nF)
      strPermission = "REVOKE"
  End Select
 Next
End Sub

'gets next command line argument
'Parameters nIndex command line argument number to process
Function GetParameter(nIndex)
 If nIndex+1> Wscript.Arguments.Count-1 Then
   ExitScript "Not enough arguments", True
 End If
 GetParameter = Wscript.Arguments(nIndex+1)
End Function

Sub ShowUsage
 WScript.Echo "shrmaint performs network share maintenance" & vbCrLf & _
 "Syntax:"  &  vbCrLf & _
 "shrmaint.wsf /SHARE name [/MACHINE name] [/GRANT account " & vbCrLf & _
 "permissions | REVOKE account]" & vbCrLf & _
 "/SHARE   name of share to process" & vbCrLf & _
 "/MACHINE optional name of machine where shares reside" & vbCrLf & _
 "/GRANT   optional permissions to grant: NOACCESS," & vbCrLf & _
 " FULL, READ or CHANGE" & vbCrLf & _
```

```
"               the account is the name of a user or group accountv  _
 & vbCrLf & "Example: list permissions for DATA share:" & vbCrLf & _
 "shrmaint.wsf /SHARE data" & vbCrLf & _
 "Example:grant freds permissions for admin share on machine Thor:" & _
  vbCrLf & "shrmaint.wsf /SHARE admin /MACHINE Thor /GRANT freds read "
  Wscript.Quit
End Sub

 'GetPermissionString returns a descriptive string for specified
 'numeric permissions value.
 'Parameters:
 'nPermission  Permission value to evaluate
 'Returns:
 'string value representing security permission. Empty string if
 '           permission value not found
 Function GetPermissionString(nPermission, nType)
 If nType = 1 Then
     GetPermissionString = "No Access"
   Exit Function
 End If

 Select Case nPermission
   Case 2032127, 268435456
       GetPermissionString = "Full Access"
   Case 1245631
       GetPermissionString = "Change"
   Case 1179817
       GetPermissionString = "Read"
   Case Else
       GetPermissionString = ""
  End Select
 End Function

 'GetPermissionValue returns a numeric value for specified
 'permissions string.
 'Parameters:
 'strPermission value to evaluate
 'Returns:
 'numeric value representing security permission. Returns 0
 'if invalid permissions string
 Function GetPermissionValue(strPermission)

 Select Case Ucase(strPermission)
```

```
        Case "FULL", "NOACCESS"
            GetPermissionValue = 2032127
        Case "CHANGE", "C"
            GetPermissionValue = 1245631
        Case "READ","R"
            GetPermissionValue = 1179817
        Case Else
            GetPermissionValue = 0
      End Select
    End Function
    ]]>
  </script>
</job>
```

The syntax for the script is as follows:

```
shrmaint.wsf /SHARE name [/MACHINE computer] [/GRANT user perms | REVOKE account]
```

The share for maintenance is specified by the `name` parameter. If the share resides on a remote computer, pass the `computer` parameter. To list the current permissions for a share, specify the share and optionally the name of the computer upon which the share resides:

```
shrmaint.wsf /SHARE Data /MACHINE Odin
```

If you want to modify share permissions, specify the `/GRANT` switch followed by the user or group name to modify followed by the permissions you want to apply. The following command-line statement would grant the user Joeb full access to the share Data on computer Odin:

```
shrmaint.wsf /SHARE Data /MACHINE Odin /GRANT Joeb Full
```

Share permissions can be Full, Change, Read, or NoAccess.

To revoke share permissions, use the `/Revoke` switch followed by the account you want to revoke permissions for:

```
shrmaint.wsf /SHARE Data /Revoke Joeb
```

WMI 1.1 or later must be installed on any local or remote machine you intend to manipulate shares on. You must have appropriate security access to set share security on local and remote computers.

See Also

The topic "Setting Security Descriptors" in the WMI SDK documentation. For more information, search http://msdn.microsoft.com for "Win32_LogicalFileSecuritySetting," "Win32_ACE," and "Win32_Trustee."

17.2 Setting File Permissions

Problem

You want to set file permissions.

Solution

The ADsSecurity.dll library that is included with the ADSI 2.5 SDK allows the manipulation of file and directory security for Windows NT and 2000. Windows XP and 2003 provide the built-in ADSI ADsSecurityUtility interface to manipulate file, share, and registry security.

The following sample sets Read/Execute permissions on the file report.doc for the user Freds. It demonstrates the use of the ADsSecurityUtility and ADsSecurity objects:

```
'grant the user Freds Read/Execute permissions on the report.doc file
Const RIGHT_GENERIC_READ = 1179785
Const RIGHT_GENERIC_EXECUTE = 1179808
Const ACETYPE_ACCESS_ALLOWED = 0
Const ADS_PATH_FILE = 1
Const ADS_SD_FORMAT_IID = 1

Dim objDACL, objNewAce, objACE
Dim objSecurity, objSD, strFile

strFile = "c:\data\report.doc"

'if bADsSecurity is True, then use ADsSecurity object from
'ADSI 2.5 resource kit. If False, then use ADsSecurityUtility object
'available in Windows XP and 2003
bADsSecurity = True

If bADsSecurity Then
    Set objSecurity = CreateObject("ADsSecurity")
```

```
    Set objSD = objSecurity.GetSecurityDescriptor("FILE://" & strFile)
Else
    Set objSecurity = CreateObject("ADsSecurityUtility")
    Set objSD = objSecurity.GetSecurityDescriptor(strFile, _
                ADS_PATH_FILE, ADS_SD_FORMAT_IID)
End If

Set objDACL = objSD.DiscretionaryAcl 'get the Discretionary ACL DACL
Set objNewAce = CreateObject("AccessControlEntry")

'Set the properties for the ACE. Set the trustee to be the Freds account,
objNewAce.Trustee = "Acme\Freds "
'allow permissions to read and execute file
objNewAce.AccessMask = RIGHT_GENERIC_READ Or RIGHT_GENERIC_EXECUTE
'allow access to file
objNewAce.AceType = ACETYPE_ACCESS_ALLOWED

'add ACE to DACL
objDACL.AddAce objNewAce
'assign the DACL back to the security descriptor
objSD.DiscretionaryAcl = objDACL

'set the security descriptor for the file
If bADsSecurity Then
    objSecurity.SetSecurityDescriptor objSD
Else
    objSecurity.SetSecurityDescriptor strFile, _
                  ADS_PATH_FILE, objSD, ADS_SD_FORMAT_IID
End If
```

Discussion

ADSI does not provide built-in file security maintenance for Windows NT and 2000. The ADSI 2.5 SDK contains a Resource Kit DLL called ADsSecurity that implements file and directory permissions maintenance. You can download this from http://www.microsoft.com/NTServer/nts/downloads/other/ADSI25/default.asp. Select the SDK for Active Directory Services Interfaces 2.5 for download.

Windows XP and later implement the ADsSecurityUtility object to perform security operations. The ADsSecurity and ADsSecurityUtility objects are very similar in implementation.

To use the ADsSecurity DLL, install the ADSI 2.5 SDK and register the ADsSecurity.dll using regsvr32.exe.

The ADsSecurity.dll doesn't depend upon the SDK for support libraries, so it can be copied to a machine without the SDK installed. It does, however, require ADSI 2.5, which is installed by default on Windows 2000 and later and is a separate installation on Windows NT 4.0.

A Security object performs the retrieval and application of the security descriptors to files. The ProgID used to create a Security object for the ADsSecurity object is AdsSecurity. The ProgID used to create a Security object under XP and later is ADsSecurityUtility.

To get a reference to the security descriptor of a file, invoke the GetSecurityDescriptor method. The syntax is slightly different for the two Security objects. The GetSecurityDescriptor syntax using the ADsSecurity object is

```
Set objSD = objSecurity.GetSecurityDescriptor(strPath)
```

The GetSecurityDescriptor syntax using the ADsSecurityUtility object is

```
Set objSD = objSecurity.GetSecurityDescriptor(strPath, nPathType, nPathFormat)
```

The strPath parameter is the path to the file or directory. For the ADsSecurity object, this is prefixed with FILE://. It has to be prefixed with FILE:// in order for the method to know what namespace to reference.

The ADsSecurityUtility GetSecurityDescriptor method requires the nPathType and nPathFormat parameters. nPathType identifies the type of path specified by the strPath parameter. These values are listed in Table 17-3. The nPathFormat parameter specifies what format the method will return the security descriptor. These values are listed in Table 17-4. You should use the ADS_SD_FORMAT_IID format to set permissions using ADSI.

Table 17-3. Path Type

PATH TYPE	VALUE	DESCRIPTION
ADS_PATH_FILEADS_PATH_FILEI	1	File or directory path
ADS_PATH_FILESHAREADS_PATH_FILESHARE	2	File share
ADS_PATH_REGISTRYADS_PATH_REGISTRY	3	Registry key path

Table 17-4. Path Type Format

PATH FORMAT	VALUE	DESCRIPTION
ADS_SD_FORMAT_IID	1	Return or pass an ADSI security object.
ADS_SD_FORMAT_RAW	2	Return or pass an array of byte values in the security descriptor format.
ADS_SD_FORMAT_HEXSTRING	3	Return or pass a security descriptor in the hex string format.

The following snippet creates an instance of the `ADsSecurity` object and retrieves the security descriptor for the file `report.doc`:

```
'create security object and get file security descriptor
'for Windows NT/2000 and AD resource kit ADSSecurity object
Set objSecurity = CreateObject("ADsSecurity")
Set objSD = objSecurity.GetSecurityDescriptor("FILE://d:\data\report.doc")
Set objDACL = objSD.DiscretionaryAcl
```

The following snippet creates an instance of the `ADsSecurityUtility` object and retrieves the security descriptor for the file `report.doc`:

```
'create security object and get file security descriptor
'for Windows XP and later
Const ACETYPE_ACCESS_ALLOWED = 0
Const ADS_PATH_FILE = 1
Const ADS_SD_FORMAT_IID =1
Set objSecurity = CreateObject("AdsSecurityUtility")
Set objSD = objSecurity.GetSecurityDescriptor("c:\data\report.doc", _
                                        ADS_PATH_FILE, ADS_SD_FORMAT_IID)
Set objDACL = objSD.DiscretionaryAcl
```

A runtime error will occur if the file or directory specified by strPath is not found.

The file's Discretionary ACL (DACL) contains a list of Access Control Entries (ACEs) for the file. An ACE contains the permission settings required for an NT account. Each ACE contains a `Trustee`, `AccessMask`, and `AceType` property, which must be set before adding to the DACL.

The Trustee property is the name of the NT account associated with the security setting. This is in the format of the account name prefixed by the domain name:

```
'set the trustee to the account Fred for the Acme domain
objNewAce.Trustee = "Acme\Fred"
```

The AccessMask property is a numeric value that determines the permissions applied to the file and is a combination of the access flag values in Table 17-5.

Table 17-5. File Access Rights

SECURITY RIGHT	VALUE	DESCRIPTION
FILE_GENERIC_READ	1179785	File read access
FILE_GENERIC_WRITE	1179926	File write access
FILE_GENERIC_EXECUTE	1179808	Allows execution of files
FILE_GENERIC_DELETE	65536	Allows deletion of files
FILE_FULL_ACCESS	2032127	Allows all access to file
FILE_PERMISSION_ACCESS	262144	Allows the user to change permission on file
FILE_OWNERSHIP_ACCESS	524288	Allows the user to change ownership off file

The file access permissions can be combined to grant specific permissions, such as read and execute permissions:

```
objNewAce.AccessMask = FILE_GENERIC_READ Or FILE_GENERIC_EXECUTE
```

The ACE object's AceType property determines if the ACE permissions are granted or denied. The valid values are ACETYPE_ACCESS_ALLOWED (0) or ACETYPE_ACCESS_DENIED (1).

The AceType property should only be set to ACETYPE_ACCESS_DENIED for the Windows No Access permission, which denies the specified account any access to the file.

Apart from the No Access permission, the AceType should always be set to ACETYPE_ACCESS_ALLOWED.

Once the ACL has been set, add it to the DACL. To do so, use the DACL object's AddAce method:

```
objDACL.AddAce objNewAce
```

If an ACL already exists for the user, it will not replace the existing ACL. No error will occur if an ACL for a user is added that already exists.

If you require multiple accounts assignments to be added to the file, repeat the previous steps for each account required. Once all required permissions have been added to the DACL, assign it to the file's security descriptor object. Then use the Security object's SetSecurityDescriptor method to set the security descriptor for the file. The syntax is slightly different for the two objects. The SetSecurityDescriptor syntax using the ADsSecurity object is

```
objSecurity.SetSecurityDescriptor objSecurityDescriptor
```

The SetSecurityDescriptor syntax using the ADsSecurityUtility object is

```
objSecurity.SetSecurityDescriptor strPath, nPathType, _
                                        objSecurityDescriptor ,nPathFormat
```

The objSecurityDescriptor parameter is the security descriptor to set. The ADsSecurityUtility SetSecurityDescriptor method requires the nPathType, strPath, and nPathFormat parameters. strPath is the path to the object to set security. nPathType identifies the type of path specified by the strPath parameter. These values are listed in Table 17-3. The nPathFormat parameter specifies what format the objSecurityDescriptor is being passed in. These values are listed in Table 17-4. You should use the ADS_SD_FORMAT_IID format to set permissions using ADSI.

The following code sets the security descriptor using the ADsSecurity object:

```
'set the security descriptor for the file using the ADsSecurity object
objSecurity.SetSecurityDescriptor objSD
```

The following code sets the security descriptor using the ADsSecurityUtility object:

```
'set the security descriptor for the file using the ADsSecurityUtility object
objSecurity.SetSecurityDescriptor "c:\data",
                    ADS_PATH_FILE, objSD, ADS_SD_FORMAT_IID
objSecurity.SetSecurityDescriptor objSD
```

Note that you can only manipulate security permissions on files and directories that are stored on NTFS partitions. If you want to remove an existing ACL, invoke the Remove method. The Remove method requires the ACE you want to remove as the parameter. You cannot remove an ACE by user account, so you must check the Trustee property for each ACE object in the DACL for the account you want to remove:

```
'remove user Freds from file data.doc
Set objSecurity = CreateObject("ADsSecurity")
Set objSD = objSecurity.GetSecurityDescriptor("FILE://d:\data\data.doc")
Set objDACL = objSD.DiscretionaryAcl For Each objACE In objDACL
  If objACE.Trustee = "Acme\FredS" Then
     objDACL.RemoveAce objACE
  End If
Next
 objSD.DiscretionaryAcl = objDACL
 'set the security descriptor for the file
 objSecurity.SetSecurityDescriptor objSD
```

The following code sample performs the same operations as the Solution script but uses WMI instead of ADSI:

```
<?xml version="1.0" ?>
<job>
<!--comment
Script:filesec.wsf
Description:
Sets security permissions on a file
-->
 <script language="VBScript" src="wmiinc.vbs">
 <![CDATA[
 Option Explicit
Const RIGHT_GENERIC_READ = 1179785
 Const RIGHT_GENERIC_EXECUTE = 1179808
 Const ACETYPE_ACCESS_ALLOWED = 0
Dim objDescriptor, objACE, retval, objServices
 Dim objFileSec, objTrustee, aDACL
Set objServices = GetObject("winmgmts:{impersonationLevel=impersonate}")
 Set objFileSec = objServices.Get( _
        "Win32_LogicalFileSecuritySetting.Path='d:\data\report.doc'")

Set objACE = objServices.Get("Win32_ACE")
 Set objTrustee = objServices.Get("Win32_Trustee")
 Set objDescriptor = objServices.Get("Win32_SecurityDescriptor")
  retval = objFileSec.GetSecurityDescriptor(objDescriptor)
 aDACL = objDescriptor.dacl

 'set trustee information
 objTrustee.Name = "Acme\Freds"
  objTrustee.Sid = GetBinarySID("Freds")
```

```
objACE.AccessMask = RIGHT_GENERIC_READ Or RIGHT_GENERIC_EXECUTE
 objACE.AceType = 0
 objACE.Trustee = objTrustee

ReDim Preserve aDACL(UBound(aDACL) + 1)
 Set aDACL(UBound(aDACL)) = objACE
objDescriptor.dacl = aDACL
 retval = objFileSec.SetSecurityDescriptor(objDescriptor)
]]>
 </script>
</job>
```

The script requires the GetBinarySID function from the include file wmiinc.vbs, which is listed in Chapter 10. The values that are used when setting permissions for the file are the same as those listed in Table 17-5.

WMI uses the Win32_LogicalFileSecuritySetting class to retrieve file security settings. You can retrieve the security settings from a file by specifying the path of the file:

```
Set objServices = GetObject("winmgmts:{impersonationLevel=impersonate}")
'get a reference to the security settings for d:\data\report.doc
 Set objFileSec = objServices.Get( _
        "Win32_LogicalFileSecuritySetting.Path='d:\data\report.doc'")
```

The path can be to any file on local or mapped network drives. The path cannot be in UNC format, such as \\odin\d$\data\report.doc.

You can access files on a remote machine that does not have any shared drives. For example, suppose you want to access the file d:\data\report.doc on the remote computer Thor. Thor does not have the d: drive shared. Connect to the WMI Services on the computer Thor, and then get a reference to the file:

```
 Set objServices = _
  GetObject("winmgmts:{impersonationLevel=impersonate}!\\Thor")
'get a reference to the security settings for d:\data\report.doc
 Set objFileSec = objServices.Get( _
        "Win32_LogicalFileSecuritySetting.Path='d:\data\report.doc'")
```

Once you have reference to the remote file, you can change the security settings using the same steps as for a local computer.

You must be logged on with the appropriate security credentials to perform any operation that requires file or directory permission modification.

See Also

For more information, search `http://msdn.microsoft.com` for articles "SetSecurityDescriptor Method in Class Win32_LogicalFileSecuritySetting" and "SetSecurityDescriptor file."

17.3 Setting Directory Security

Problem

You want to set security permissions for a directory.

Solution

To set directory permissions, two ACLs must be added: one for directory security and one to determine the permissions for files within the directory.

The following sample grants the user account "Freds" add and read access to the directory `d:\data`. It uses either `ADsSecurity` or `ADsSecurityUtility`, depending upon the `bADsSecurity` variable set in the code:

```
Const OBJECT_INHERIT_ACE = 1
Const CONTAINER_INHERIT_ACE = 2
Const INHERIT_ONLY_ACE = 8
Const ACETYPE_ACCESS_ALLOWED = 0

'file access types
Const FILE_GENERIC_READ = &H120089
Const FILE_GENERIC_WRITE = &H120116
Const FILE_GENERIC_EXECUTE = &H1200A0
Dim objDACL, objNewAce, objACE, objNewAce2
Dim objSecurity, objSD, strTrustee, bADsSecurity

'if bADsSecurity is True, then use ADsSecurity object from
'ADSI 2.5 resource kit. If False, then use ADsSecurityUtility object
'available in Windows XP and 2003
bADsSecurity = False

If bADsSecurity Then
    Set objSecurity = CreateObject("ADsSecurity")
    Set objSD = objSecurity.GetSecurityDescriptor("FILE://c:\data")
Else
```

```
    Set objSecurity = CreateObject("ADsSecurityUtility")
    Set objSD = objSecurity.GetSecurityDescriptor("c:\data", _
                ADS_PATH_FILE, ADS_SD_FORMAT_IID)
End If

Set objDACL = objSD.DiscretionaryAcl
Set objNewAce = CreateObject("AccessControlEntry")
strTrustee = "Acme\Freds"
'set file access to directory so any FredS can
'read existing file in the directory.
Set objNewAce = CreateObject("AccessControlEntry")
objNewAce.Trustee = strTrustee
objNewAce.AccessMask = FILE_GENERIC_READ Or FILE_GENERIC_EXECUTE
objNewAce.AceType = ACETYPE_ACCESS_ALLOWED
'permissions are to be inherited to any new files in the directory
objNewAce.AceFlags = INHERIT_ONLY_ACE Or OBJECT_INHERIT_ACE
objDACL.AddAce objNewAce

'set directory permissions so FredS can add files
Set objNewAce2 = CreateObject("AccessControlEntry")
objNewAce2.Trustee = strTrustee
objNewAce2.AccessMask = FILE_GENERIC_READ Or _
                   FILE_GENERIC_EXECUTE Or FILE_GENERIC_WRITE
objNewAce2.AceType = ACETYPE_ACCESS_ALLOWED
objNewAce2.AceFlags = CONTAINER_INHERIT_ACE
objDACL.AddAce objNewAce2
objSD.DiscretionaryAcl = objDACL

If bADsSecurity Then
    objSecurity.SetSecurityDescriptor objSD
Else
    objSecurity.SetSecurityDescriptor "c:\data", _
                ADS_PATH_FILE, objSD, ADS_SD_FORMAT_IID
End If
```

Discussion

A Windows NT or later directory contains two ACLs: One determines directory permissions and one determines permissions to the files within the directory.

The file permissions determine the access to files in the directory. Any file copied, moved, or created in the directory is automatically assigned the file access permissions.

> **NOTE** *The* `AccessMask` *property can be set to any combination of file access rights that are specified in Table 17-7.*

The `AceFlags` property must be set so that file properties are inherited by all files that are created or copied to the directory. To do this, the `AceFlags` property of the ACE object must be set to `INHERIT_ONLY_ACE` (8) or `OBJECT_INHERIT_ACE` (1).

The directory rights are similar to file rights. They determine the access a user has to the directory container object. A directory requires a separate ACE object to be applied to the DACL.

Set the `AccessMask` to determine what access the trustee has. (The rights that can be combined in the `AccessMask` can be any of the rights listed in Table 17-7 except for file generic read, write, execute, or delete permissions.) These are replaced with values that are listed in Table 17-6.

Table 17-6. File Access Rights

DIRECTORY CONTAINER RIGHT	VALUE
GENERIC_ALL	&H10000000
GENERIC_EXECUTE	&H20000000
GENERIC_WRITE	&H40000000
GENERIC_READ	&H80000000

The `AceFlags` property must be set so that the properties are inherited by all directories exist in the directory. To do this, the `AceFlags` property of the ACE object must be set to `CONTAINER_INHERIT_ACE`.

Setting directory permissions using WMI requires the same steps to be taken. The following script performs the same operation as the Solution script using WMI:

```
<?xml version="1.0" ?>
<job>
<!--comment
Script:dirsec.wsf
Description:
Sets security permissions on a directory
-->
 <script language="VBScript" src="wmiinc.vbs">
 <![CDATA[
 Option Explicit
Const OBJECT_INHERIT_ACE = 1
```

```
Const CONTAINER_INHERIT_ACE = 2
Const INHERIT_ONLY_ACE = 8
Const ACETYPE_ACCESS_ALLOWED = 0

'file access types
Const FILE_GENERIC_READ = &H120089
Const FILE_GENERIC_WRITE = &H120116
Const FILE_GENERIC_EXECUTE = &H1200A0
 Dim objDescriptor, objACE, retval, objServices
 Dim objFileSec, objTrustee, aDACL, objACE2
Set objServices = GetObject("winmgmts:{impersonationLevel=impersonate,(Security)}")

 Set objFileSec = objServices.Get( _
      "Win32_LogicalFileSecuritySetting.Path='d:\data'")

Set objACE = objServices.Get("Win32_ACE")
 Set objACE2 = objServices.Get("Win32_ACE")
Set objTrustee = objServices.Get("Win32_Trustee")
 Set objDescriptor = objServices.Get("Win32_SecurityDescriptor")

  retval = objFileSec.GetSecurityDescriptor(objDescriptor)
 aDACL = objDescriptor.dacl
'set trustee information
 objTrustee.Name = "Acme\Freds"
objTrustee.sid = GetBinarySID("Freds")

 'set the file permissions for the directory
 objACE.AccessMask = FILE_GENERIC_READ Or FILE_GENERIC_EXECUTE
 objACE.AceType = ACETYPE_ACCESS_ALLOWED
 objACE.AceFlags = INHERIT_ONLY_ACE Or OBJECT_INHERIT_ACE
 objACE.Trustee = objTrustee

 'set directory permissions
 objACE2.AccessMask = FILE_GENERIC_READ Or _
                      FILE_GENERIC_EXECUTE Or FILE_GENERIC_WRITE
 objACE2.AceType = ACETYPE_ACCESS_ALLOWED
 objACE2.AceFlags = CONTAINER_INHERIT_ACE
 objACE2.Trustee = objTrustee

 'resize DACL array and add new ACEs to DACL
 ReDim Preserve aDACL(UBound(aDACL) + 2)
 Set aDACL(UBound(aDACL) - 1) = objACE
 Set aDACL(UBound(aDACL)) = objACE2
objDescriptor.dacl = aDACL
```

```
'set the security descriptor
 retval = objFileSec.SetSecurityDescriptor(objDescriptor)
]]>
 </script>
</job>
```

The rules and limitations for referencing directories and applying security to them using WMI are the same that apply to setting file security using WMI, as outlined in Solution 17.2.

To simplify permissions management, the following script component, `ADSIFileSecurity.wsc`, provides file security operations. The component performs permissions setting and enumeration on any specified file or directory using either the `ADsSecurity` or `ADsSecurityUtility` object:

```
<?xml version="1.0"?>
<component>

<registration
   description="ADSIFileSecurity"
   progid="ENTWSH.FileSecurity"
   version="1.00"
   classid="{f27d40d0-7a43-11d3-bc2c-00104b164591}"
>
</registration>

<public>
   <method name="SetSecurity">
   </method>
   <method name="ListSecurity">
      <PARAMETER name="strPath"/>
   </method>
    <property name=" "><put/>
  </property>

 </public>

<script language="VBScript">
<![CDATA[
'ADSIFileSecurity.wsc
'Description: Sets and lists file/folder security

Option Explicit
```

```
Const OBJECT_INHERIT_ACE = 1
Const CONTAINER_INHERIT_ACE = 2
Const NO_PROPAGATE_INHERIT_ACE = 4
Const INHERIT_ONLY_ACE = 8
Const VALID_INHERIT_FLAGS = 15

Const GENERIC_ALL = &H10000000
Const GENERIC_EXECUTE = &H20000000
Const GENERIC_WRITE = &H40000000
Const GENERIC_READ = &H80000000

Const ACETYPE_ACCESS_DENIED = 1
Const ACETYPE_ACCESS_ALLOWED = 0

'file access types
Const FILE_GENERIC_READ = 1179785
Const FILE_GENERIC_WRITE = 1179926
Const FILE_GENERIC_EXECUTE = 1179808
Const FILE_GENERIC_DELETE = 65536
Const FILE_FULL_ACCESS = 2032127
Const FILE_PERMISSION_ACCESS = 262144
Const FILE_OWNERSHIP_ACCESS = 524288
Const ADS_PATH_FILE = 1
Const ADS_SD_FORMAT_IID = 1

Dim objSecurity, objSD, objDACL, objAce
Dim ErrorString, bADsSecurity
bADsSecurity = False

Function get_Error()
   get_Error = ErrorString
End Function

'Description:Sets specified file or folder security
Function SetSecurity(strPath, strRights, strTrustee)

Dim objNewAce, objNewAce2
Dim strType, strRights2, nF
Dim objfolder, objFSO

Set objFSO = CreateObject("Scripting.FileSystemObject")

'determine if the path is a file or a folder
```

```
If objFSO.FileExists(strPath) Then
    strType = "F" 'file
ElseIf objFSO.FolderExists(strPath) Then
    strType = "D" 'folder/directory
Else ' not found
    SetSecurity = False
    ErrorString = CreateErrMsg(Err, _
        "File " & strPath & " does not exist")
    Exit Function
End If

'if bADsSecurity is True, then use ADsSecurity object from
'ADSI 2.5 resource kit. If False, then use ADsSecurityUtility object
'available in Windows XP and 2003
If bADsSecurity Then
    Set objSecurity = CreateObject("ADsSecurity")'create security object
    'get reference to specified file/folder path
    Set objSD = objSecurity.GetSecurityDescriptor("FILE://" & strPath)
Else
    Set objSecurity = CreateObject("ADsSecurityUtility")
    Set objSD = objSecurity.GetSecurityDescriptor(strPath, _
                ADS_PATH_FILE, ADS_SD_FORMAT_IID)
End If

Set objDACL = objSD.DiscretionaryAcl 'get the Discretionary ACL

 'check if object is a file
 If strType = "F" Then
    Set objNewAce = CreateObject("AccessControlEntry")
    objNewAce.Trustee = strTrustee 'set trustee

    objNewAce.AccessMask = FileRightsID(strRights, "F")

    'remove the trustee from the existing ACL
    FileSetSecurityRemove strTrustee, strPath

    'check if no access is specified
    If strRights = "N" Then
        objNewAce.AceType = ACETYPE_ACCESS_DENIED
    Else
        objNewAce.AceType = ACETYPE_ACCESS_ALLOWED
    End If
    'add the new ACE to the DACL
```

```
    objDACL.AddAce objNewAce
 Else 'set security on a folder
    'check if folder container and file access rights are specified
    nF = InStr(strRights, ":")
    If nF > 0 Then
        strRights2 = Mid(strRights, nF + 1)
        strRights = Left(strRights, nF - 1)
    Else
        strRights2 = strRights
    End If

    'remove the trustee from the existing ACL
    FileSetSecurityRemove strTrustee, strPath

    'set file access
    Set objNewAce = CreateObject("AccessControlEntry")
    objNewAce.Trustee = strTrustee 'set file trustee
    objNewAce.AccessMask = FileRightsID(strRights2, "F")
    objNewAce.AceType = ACETYPE_ACCESS_ALLOWED
    objNewAce.AceFlags = INHERIT_ONLY_ACE Or OBJECT_INHERIT_ACE

    objDACL.AddAce objNewAce

    'set folder container access
    Set objNewAce2 = CreateObject("AccessControlEntry")
    objNewAce2.Trustee = strTrustee
    objNewAce2.AccessMask = FileRightsID(strRights, "D")
    objNewAce2.AceType = ACETYPE_ACCESS_ALLOWED
    objNewAce2.AceFlags = CONTAINER_INHERIT_ACE

    objDACL.AddAce objNewAce2 'add ACE to DACL

  End If

    objSD.DiscretionaryAcl = objDACL 'set the DACL

If bADsSecurity Then
    objSecurity.SetSecurityDescriptor objSD
Else
    objSecurity.SetSecurityDescriptor strPath, _
                        ADS_PATH_FILE, objSD, ADS_SD_FORMAT_IID
End If
```

```
    SetSecurity = True
    Set objSD = Nothing
    Set objSecurity = Nothing
    Set objAce = Nothing
    Set objNewAce = Nothing
    Set objNewAce2 = Nothing
    Set objFSO = Nothing

End Function

Function put_UseADSUtility(bFlag)
  bADsSecurity = bFlag
End Function


Function ListSecurity(strPath)
   Dim objSecurity
   Dim objSD, objDACL, objAce
   Dim strUser, strLastUser, strLine, strRights

  ' Set objSecurity = CreateObject("ADsSecurity")

   'On Error Resume Next

   'Set objSD = objSecurity.GetSecurityDescriptor("FILE://" & strPath)



   'if bADsSecurity is True, then use ADsSecurity object from
    'ADSI 2.5 resource kit. If False, then use ADsSecurityUtility object
    'available in Windows XP and 2003
    If bADsSecurity Then
       Set objSecurity = CreateObject("ADsSecurity")'create security object
       'get reference to specified file/folder path
       Set objSD = objSecurity.GetSecurityDescriptor("FILE://" & strPath)
    Else
       Set objSecurity = CreateObject("ADsSecurityUtility")
       Set objSD = objSecurity.GetSecurityDescriptor(strPath, _
                ADS_PATH_FILE, ADS_SD_FORMAT_IID)
    End If

   Set objDACL = objSD.DiscretionaryAcl
```

```
   If Not Err Then
    strUser = ""
    For Each objAce In objDACL

     strUser = objAce.Trustee

     If strUser <> strLastUser And strLastUser <> "" Then
       strRights = strRights & vbCrLf & objAce.Trustee & "," & _
                   FileRights(objAce.AccessMask, objAce.AceType)
     ElseIf strLastUser = "" Then
      strRights = strRights & objAce.Trustee & "," & _
               FileRights(objAce.AccessMask, objAce.AceType)
     Else
       strRights = strRights & ":" & _
               FileRights(objAce.AccessMask, objAce.AceType)
     End If
     strLastUser = strUser
    Next
   End If

   ListSecurity = strRights
   Set objSecurity = Nothing
   Set objSD = Nothing
   Set objDACL = Nothing
   Set objAce = Nothing

end function

'Description:removes trustee from DACL
'Parameters:
'strTrustee  Name of trustee account to remove from DACL
Sub FileSetSecurityRemove(strTrustee, strPath)
Dim bChange

bChange = False

For Each objAce In objDACL
    If StrComp(strTrustee, objAce.Trustee, 1) = 0 Or strTrustee = "" Then
        objDACL.RemoveAce objAce
        bChange = True
    End If
Next
```

```
If bChange Then
     objSD.DiscretionaryAcl = objDACL
     'objSecurity.SetSecurityDescriptor objSD

   If bADsSecurity Then
objSecurity.SetSecurityDescriptor objSD
   Else
     objSecurity.SetSecurityDescriptor strPath, _
                    ADS_PATH_FILE, objSD, ADS_SD_FORMAT_IID
   End If

End If

End Sub

'Description:returns a string of security settings for specified value
'Parameters:
'rights   access rights
'nType    Access type. 0 = access allowed, 1 - access denied
'Returns: String containing security flags
Function FileRights(rights, nType)
Dim strRet
strRet = ""
Select Case rights

        Case FILE_FULL_ACCESS, GENERIC_ALL
            If nType = ACETYPE_ACCESS_DENIED Then
                strRet = "N"
            Else
                strRet = "F"
            End If

        Case FILE_GENERIC_READ Or FILE_GENERIC_EXECUTE Or _
         FILE_GENERIC_DELETE Or FILE_GENERIC_READ _
         Or FILE_GENERIC_WRITE, GENERIC_READ _
            Or GENERIC_WRITE Or GENERIC_EXECUTE Or FILE_GENERIC_DELETE
            strRet = "C"
        Case Else

            If rights = (rights Or FILE_GENERIC_READ) Or _
            rights = (rights Or GENERIC_READ) Then strRet = strRet & "R"

            If rights = (rights Or FILE_GENERIC_EXECUTE) Or _
```

```
            rights = (rights Or GENERIC_EXECUTE) Then strRet= strRet & "X"

            If rights = (rights Or FILE_GENERIC_WRITE) Or _
            rights = (rights Or GENERIC_WRITE) Then strRet = strRet & "W"

            If rights = (rights Or FILE_GENERIC_DELETE) Then _
                strRet = strRet & "D"

            If rights = (rights Or 524288) Then strRet = strRet & "O"

            If rights = (rights Or 262144) Then strRet = strRet & "P"

End Select

FileRights = strRet

End Function


'Description:returns the access value for specified string type
'Parameters:
'rights   string of access rights
'strType  object . F = file, D - folder/directory
'Returns: value for specified access string
Function FileRightsID(rights, strType)

    Dim lret, counter

    For counter = 1 To Len(rights)

        Select Case Mid(rights, counter, 1)

        Case "F", "N"
            If strType = "F" Then
                lret = lret Or FILE_FULL_ACCESS
            Else
            lret = lret Or GENERIC_ALL
            End If

        Case "W"
            If strType = "F" Then
                lret = lret Or FILE_GENERIC_WRITE
            Else
```

```
                lret = lret Or GENERIC_WRITE
            End If

        Case "X"
            If strType = "F" Then
                lret = lret Or FILE_GENERIC_EXECUTE
            Else
                lret = lret Or GENERIC_EXECUTE
            End If

        Case "D"
                lret = lret Or FILE_GENERIC_DELETE

        Case "C"
            If strType = "F" Then
                lret = lret Or FILE_GENERIC_READ Or FILE_GENERIC_EXECUTE _
                Or FILE_GENERIC_DELETE Or FILE_GENERIC_WRITE
            Else
                lret = lret Or GENERIC_READ Or GENERIC_WRITE _
                Or GENERIC_EXECUTE Or FILE_GENERIC_DELETE
            End If

        Case "P"
                lret = lret Or FILE_PERMISSION_ACCESS
        Case "O"
                lret = lret Or FILE_OWNERSHIP_ACCESS
        Case "R"
            If strType = "F" Then
                lret = lret Or FILE_GENERIC_READ
            Else
                lret = lret Or GENERIC_READ
            End If
    End Select
    Next

FileRightsID = lret
End Function


Function  CreateErrMsg(objErr,sMsg)
Dim sTemp
 sTemp = "Error# [" & Err & "] " & Err.Description
 If Not sMsg = "" Then sTemp = sTemp & vbCrLf & sMsg
```

```
 CreateErrMsg = sTemp
End Function
]]>
</script>
</component>
```

The ProgID for the component is ENTWSH.FileSecurity. The component exposes two methods: ListSecurity and SetSecurity. ListSecurity returns file and directory permissions in a similar format displayed using the Windows NT command-line permissions CACLS.EXE. To list security permissions, create an instance of the FileSecurity object and invoke the ListSecurity method:

```
strRights = objWS.ListSecurity(strPath)
```

The strPath parameter represents the path to a file or directory.

ListSecurity returns the account(s) with access followed by associated permissions on a separate line for each account:

```
'list the permissions for a file
'create an instance of the ENTWSH.FileSecurity object
Set objWS = CreateObject("ENTWSH.FileSecurity")
'list the permissions associated with a file
Wscript.Echo objWS.ListSecurity("D:\data\reports.htm")
```

Permissions are represented with a single letter code that corresponds to a level of security access, as listed in Table 17-7.

Table 17-7. File and Directory Rights

ATTRIBUTE	DESCRIPTION
F	Full access
C	Change—read, write, execute
R	Read
W	Write
D	Delete
O	Ownership
P	Permissions
N	None

To set permissions, invoke the SetSecurity method:

```
bSuccess =objWS.SetSecurity(strPath, strPermissions, strTrustee)
```

The strPath parameter is the path to the directory of the file to set the security for. strPermissions is a string of one or more permissions to be assigned to the file or directory. The strTrustee parameter represents the user or group to be assigned the rights, and it must be in the format Domain\Accountname.

To set the read, execute, delete, ownership, and permissions rights for the file d:\data\reports.doc for account ACME\Freds, use the following:

```
bSuccess = objWS.SetSecurity("d:\data\reports.doc", "RXDOP", "ACME\Freds")
```

SetSecurity returns True if the security was successfully set; otherwise, it returns False.

If you are setting or listing permissions for a directory, you can specify two sets of security. One is the directory container access, which determines the access a trustee has to the directory. The second is file rights. The following example grants the user account Freds add and read permissions to the directory d:\data:

```
bSuccess = objWS.SetSecurity("d:\data ", "RWX:RX", "ACME\Freds")
```

By default, the ENTWSH.FileSecurity component uses the ADsSecurityUtility object that Windows XP and 2003 implement. If you are using Windows NT or 2000 with the ADsSecurity component, set the ENTWSH.FileSecurity component's UseADSUtility to True.

```
'create an instance of the ENTWSH.FileSecurity object and set UseADSUtility
property
Set objWS = CreateObject("ENTWSH.FileSecurity")
'list the permissions associated with a file
objWS.UseADSUtility = True
bSuccess = objWS.SetSecurity("c:\data\report.doc ", "RXDO", "acme\Freds ")
```

17.4 Changing User Access to the Exchange 5.5 Recipients Container

Problem

You want to change user access to an Exchange server 5.5 Recipients container.

Solution

You can use the AdsSecurity component included in the ADSI 2.5 SDK to retrieve a reference to the Exchange server container you want to manipulate. Add an ACE object for each account you want to grant or deny additional permissions to the container:

```
'Exchangesec.vbs
'sets Admin access to the Recipients container for the account Freds
Dim objSecurity, objSD, objDACL, objAce
Const ADS_ACETYPE_ACCESS_ALLOWED = 0
Const ADS_RIGHT_EXCH_ADD_CHILD = 1
Const ADS_RIGHT_EXCH_DELETE = 65536
Const ADS_RIGHT_EXCH_MAIL_ADMIN_AS = 32
Const ADS_RIGHT_EXCH_MODIFY_ADMIN_ATT = 4
Const ADS_RIGHT_EXCH_MODIFY_USER_ATT = 2

Set objSecurity = CreateObject("ADsSecurity")

Set objSD = objSecurity.GetSecurityDescriptor _
   ("LDAP://odin/cn=Recipients,ou=office,o=acme")
Set objDACL = objSD.DiscretionaryAcl
Set objAce = CreateObject("AccessControlEntry")
objAce.Trustee = "acme\Freds"
'set the access mask to provide admin access
objAce.AccessMask = ADS_RIGHT_EXCH_ADD_CHILD Or ADS_RIGHT_EXCH_DELETE Or _
    ADS_RIGHT_EXCH_MODIFY_ADMIN_ATT Or ADS_RIGHT_EXCH_MODIFY_USER_ATT Or _
    ADS_RIGHT_EXCH_MAIL_ADMIN_AS
objAce.AceType = ADS_ACETYPE_ACCESS_ALLOWED

objDACL.AddAce objAce
objSD.DiscretionaryAcl = objDACL
objSecurity.SetSecurityDescriptor objSD
```

Discussion

Exchange server allows for different levels of access to be set to different containers and objects. You might want to provide an administrative access to specific containers for certain users to maintain the objects in the container.

Different levels of security can be added to containers. To view container permissions under the Exchange Administrator application, select the container and choose File > Properties.

This will show the object's general "role" permissions, such as Admin access. These roles are combination of permission rights.

To view the actual rights in Exchange Admin, select Tools > Options, choose the Permissions tab, and select Show Permissions Page for all objects. When you view any object, including a mailbox, you will be able to see and modify the individual rights assigned to the object.

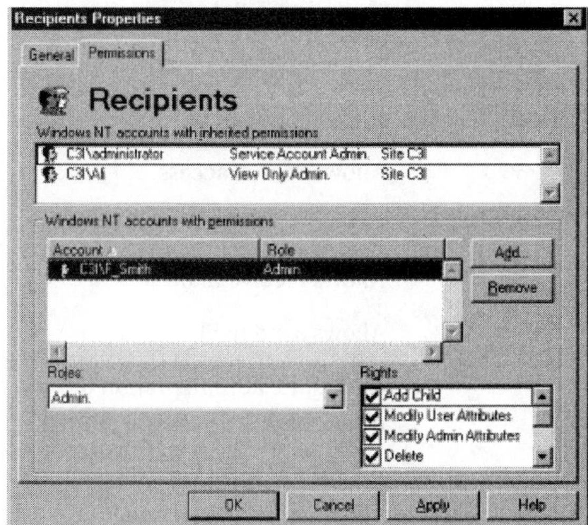

Figure 17-1. Exchange 5.5 Recipients properties

Get a reference to the security descriptor for the object you want to change the access to. Retrieve the DACL from the security descriptor:

```
Set objSD = objSecurity.GetSecurityDescriptor _
    ("LDAP://odin/cn=Recipients,ou=office,o=acme")
Set objDACL = objSD.DiscretionaryAcl
```

Add a new ACE with the access to be provided to the DACL:

```
objAce.Trustee = "acme\freds" 'specify trustee to set security for
objAce.AccessMask = ADS_RIGHT_EXCH_ADD_CHILD Or ADS_RIGHT_EXCH_DELETE Or _
    ADS_RIGHT_EXCH_MODIFY_ADMIN_ATT Or ADS_RIGHT_EXCH_MODIFY_USER_ATT Or _
    ADS_RIGHT_EXCH_MAIL_ADMIN_AS

objAce.AceType = ADS_ACETYPE_ACCESS_ALLOWED 'allow access
'add the ACE to the DACL
objDACL.AddAce objAce
objSD.DiscretionaryAcl = objDACL
objSecurity.SetSecurityDescriptor objSD
```

The AccessMask determines the access to the object. It is a combination of the Exchange security rights listed in Table 17-8.

Table 17-8. AccessMask *Security Values*

CONSTANT	VALUE	DESCRIPTION
ADS_RIGHT_EXCH_ADD_CHILD	1	Adds a new child object in container
ADS_RIGHT_EXCH_DELETE	65536	Deletes objects
ADS_RIGHT_EXCH_DS_REPLICATION	64	Allows replication
ADS_RIGHT_EXCH_DS_SEARCH	256	Allows search access
ADS_RIGHT_EXCH_MAIL_ADMIN_AS	32	Provides administrative rights
ADS_RIGHT_EXCH_MAIL_RECEIVE_AS	16	Allows receive mail
ADS_RIGHT_EXCH_MAIL_SEND_AS	8	Allows send mail
ADS_RIGHT_EXCH_MODIFY_ADMIN_ATT	4	Allows the administration of object administrative attributes
ADS_RIGHT_EXCH_MODIFY_SEC_ATT	128	Allows the administration of object security (permission) attributes
ADS_RIGHT_EXCH_MODIFY_USER_ATT	2	Allows the administration of object user attributes

To enumerate the security settings from an object, get a reference to the security descriptor on the object you want to check. Retrieve the DACL and loop through each ACE in the DACL:

```
Dim objSecurity, objSD, objDACL, objAce
Set objSecurity = CreateObject("ADsSecurity")

Set objSD = _
objSecurity.GetSecurityDescriptor("LDAP://odin/cn=Recipients,ou=acme,o=com")
Set objDACL = objSD.DiscretionaryAcl

For Each objAce In objDACL
    Wscript.Echo  objAce.AccessMask, objAce.Trustee, _
     objAce.AceFlags, objAce.AceType
Next
```

It can be useful enumerating existing objects to determine the right values to be used for the objects you are setting access to.

See Also

Solution 15.1. `Exchange.htm` from the ADSI 2.5 SDK.

17.5 Copying a File with Its Security Settings

Problem

You want to copy a file together with file security settings.

Solution

You can use the FSO object to copy the specified file to a new destination, and then use either the ADSI Resource Kit's `AdsSecurity` DLL for Windows NT/2000 or the ADsSecurityUtility for Windows XP and later to copy the security to the new file.

The following code snippet copies the file `report.doc` from one directory to another and then sets the security descriptor of the copied file to the security descriptor of the original:

```
Dim objSecurity, objSD, strSource, strDest, objFSO, bADsSecurity
Set objFSO = CreateObject("Scripting.FileSystemObject")

'if bADsSecurity is True, then use ADsSecurity object from
'ADSI 2.5 resource kit. If False, then use ADsSecurityUtility object
'available in Windows XP and 2003
 bADsSecurity = False

Set objSecurity = CreateObject("ADsSecurity")
strSource = "d:\data\report.doc"
strDest = " d:\backup\report.doc"

'copy the file to the destination
objFSO.CopyFile strSource, strDest
' get the security descriptor for the file

 If bADsSecurity Then
  Set objSecurity = CreateObject("ADsSecurity")
```

```
  Set objSD = _
       objSecurity.GetSecurityDescriptor("FILE://" & strSource)
  'copy the security descriptor from the original file to the copied file
  objSecurity.SetSecurityDescriptor objSD, "FILE://" & strDest
Else
   Set objSecurity = CreateObject("ADsSecurityUtility")
   Set objSD = objSecurity.GetSecurityDescriptor(strSource, _
             ADS_PATH_FILE, ADS_SD_FORMAT_IID)
   objSecurity.SetSecurityDescriptor strDest, _
                 ADS_PATH_FILE, objSD, ADS_SD_FORMAT_IID
End If
```

Discussion

When you copy a file from one directory to another, the file inherits the security from the directory container it is being copied into.

The Resource Kit's AdsSecurity DLL's SetSecurityDescriptor method provides an optional parameter where you can specify the destination of the security descriptor you are setting:

```
objSecurity.SetSecurityDescriptor objSD[, path]
```

By default, the AdsSecurity object's SetSecurityDescriptor sets the security descriptor on the objSecurity object that it was read from. If the path parameter is specified, the security descriptor will be set on the object specified in the path. This can be used to duplicate security access from one object to another.

The AdsSecurity SetSecurityDescriptor method can be used to duplicate ADSI security from file, Exchange, LDAP, and registry objects.

The Windows XP and 2000 ADsSecurityUtility object requires that you specify the destination path by default.

The following script, frcopy.wsf, provides a command-line interface to copy files and security using the AdsSecurity DLL:

```
<?xml version="1.0" ?>
<job>
<!--comment
Script:frcopy.wsf
Description:copies files with permissions
-->
 <script language="VBScript" src="adsilib.vbs">
 <![CDATA[
Dim strUser, strLastUser, strLine, strRights, strPath
```

```
Dim objSrcFile, objFSO
Dim objSecurity, objSD
Dim strSrcFolder, strDstFolder, objArgs
Set objFSO = CreateObject("Scripting.FileSystemObject")

If Wscript.Arguments.Count <> 2 Then
  ShowUsage
  Wscript.Quit
End If
 strSource = Wscript.Arguments(0)
 strDstFolder = Wscript.Arguments(1)
 Set objSecurity = CreateObject("ADsSecurity")
 'get a reference to the file to copy
 Set objSrcFile = objFSO.GetFile(strSource)
If Err Then
     ExitScript "File " & strSource & " not found"
 End If

'copy the file to the destination folder
 objSrcFile.Copy strDstFolder & "\" & objSrcFile.Name
 If Err Then
     ExitScript "Unable to copy " & _
          strSource & " to " & strDstFolder & vbCrLf & Err.Description
 End If

 ' get the security descriptor for the file
  Set objSD = _
       objSecurity.GetSecurityDescriptor("FILE://" & objSrcFile.Path)
 'copy the security descriptor from the original file to the copied file
 objSecurity.SetSecurityDescriptor objSD, "FILE://" & _
       strDstFolder & "\" & objSrcFile.Name
 Wscript.Echo strSource & " copied to " & strDstFolder & "\" & objSrcFile.Name

 Sub ShowUsage
  WScript.Echo "frcopy.wsf copies files together with file rights" _
    & vbCrLf & "Syntax:" & vbCrLf & _
    "frcopy.wsf file destination" & vbCrLf & _
    "file            name of file to copy"  & vbLf & _
    "destination    destination directory to copy to"
 End Sub
]]>
  </script>
</job>
```

See Also

Rtk.htm from the ADSI 2.5 SDK.

17.6 Taking Ownership of Files

Problem

You want to take ownership of files.

Solution

You can get a reference to the file you want to take ownership of through the WMI CIM_DataFile class and invoke the TakeOwnership method:

```
'connect to WMI namespace on local machine
Set objServices = GetObject("winmgmts:{impersonationLevel=impersonate}")
'get a reference to data file
Set objFile = objServices.Get("CIM_DataFile.Name='d:\data\report.doc")
If  objFile.TakeOwnership = 0 Then
 Wscript.Echo "File ownership successfully changed"
Else
 Wscript.Echo "File ownership transfer operation"
End If
```

Discussion

File and directory ownership can be set using the TakeOwnership method of the CIM_DataFile class. Ownership reverts to the account ID of the user executing the method. The syntax is as follows:

```
nResult = objFileDirectory.TakeOwnership
```

TakeOwnership returns 0 if successful. The objFileDirectory object represents either an instance of a CIM_DataFile class for a file or Win32_Directory or a CIM_Directory for a directory.

If the ownership of a directory is taken, the ownership of all files and subdirectories within the directory are set.

File and directory ownership can be determined through the Owner property of a Win32_SecurityDescriptor object. Get a reference to a file or directory object through the Win32_LogicalFileSecuritySetting class. Use the object's GetSecurityDescriptor method to return the Win32_SecurityDescriptor object.

The Owner property returns a Win32_Trustee object. The name of the owner account can be returned through the Name property:

```
Set objServices = GetObject("winmgmts:{impersonationLevel=impersonate}")
 Set objFileSec = objServices.Get( _
          "Win32_LogicalFileSecuritySetting.Path='d:\data\report.doc'")
nResult = objFileSec.GetSecurityDescriptor(objSD)
Wscript.Echo objSD.Owner.Name
```

See Also

For more information, search http://msdn.microsoft.com for articles "Win32_Directory" and "Win32_NTEventlogFile."

17.7 Setting Active Directory Permissions

Problem

You want to grant security access to an Active Directory container.

Solution

The following script grants the user Fred Smith full access to the User container:

```
Const FULL_ACCESS = 983551
Dim objSecurity
Dim objContainer, objDACL , objACE
Set objACE = CreateObject("AccessControlEntry")
'get a reference to the users container for the Acme domain
Set objContainer = GetObject("LDAP://cn=users,dc=acme,dc=com")

Set objSecurity = objContainer.Get("ntSecurityDescriptor")
Set objDACL = objSecurity.DiscretionaryAcl
objACE.Trustee = "Acme\Freds"
objACE.AccessMask = FULL_ACCESS

objDACL.AddAce objACE
objSecurity.DiscretionaryAcl = objDACL
'write security descriptor back to container
objContainer.Put "ntSecurityDescriptor", objSecurity
objContainer.SetInfo
```

Discussion

Under Windows NT 4.0 and earlier, there was essentially a single list of users and groups. Only administrators or users who had been granted the appropriate permissions could manipulate accounts. Under NT 4.0 there is no way to delegate different levels of access to different groups of users. For example, you might want Fred in accounting to be able to create new users or modify existing accounting users' details.

Active Directory provides for delegation of administrative tasks. This allows for the account structure to be organized in a hierarchical fashion. Groups of users can be split into organizational units (not to be confused with user groups). See Chapter 14 for more information on organizational units.

Specific accounts can be granted varying levels of administrative access to the organizational units. So, for example, Fred Smith could be granted access to perform specific administrative tasks to the Accounting organizational unit.

Active Directory is not limited to storing user account details. Applications such as Exchange 2000 and 2003 server use Active Directory to store configuration information and mailbox details.

As a result of the complexity and expandable nature of Active Directory, it is difficult to determine what properties and values are required when setting object permissions.

The easiest way to get an overview with permissions is to use a graphical interface such as the ADSI Edit program. ADSI Edit is included on the Windows 2000/2003 CD. It is not installed with Windows 2000, but it is included as part of a support tools installation located under the `support\tools` directory of the Windows 2000/2003 installation CD.

To use the program, run the `Adsiedit.msc` management console application. Using this program, you can manipulate object permissions. Figure 17-2 shows ADSI Edit.

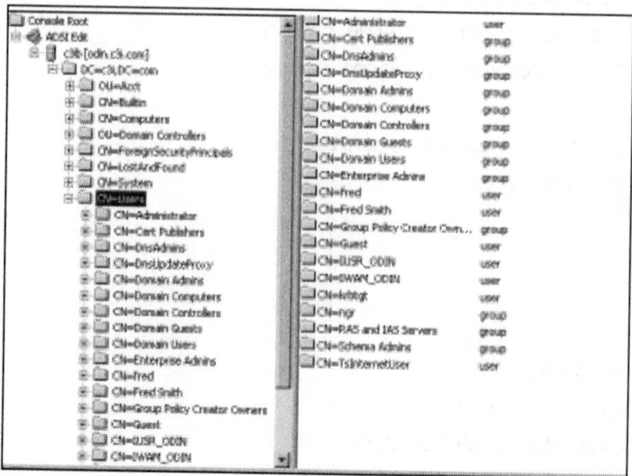

Figure 17-2. ADSI Edit

Right-click the object you want to view permissions for and select the Properties option, which will display the Object Properties dialog box. From this dialog box, select the Security tab, as shown in Figure 17-3.

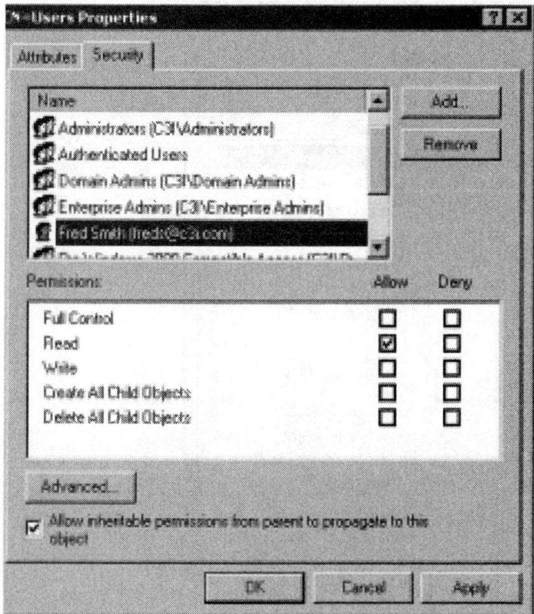

Figure 17-3. User object's Security properties

The dialog box displays a number of generic permission that can be set: Full Control, Read, Write, Delete All Child Objects, and Create All Child Objects. To set these permissions on an object using the Solution script as a model, change the `AccessMask` property of the ACE object to one of the values listed in Table 17-9.

Table 17-9. Active Directory Object Permissions

ATTRIBUTE	VALUE
Full Control	983551
Read	131092
Write	40
Create All Child Objects	1
Delete All Child Objects	2

Most of the operations in this table are combinations of different levels of security permissions. For example, the Read permission is a combination of listing and reading properties.

To view these and other permissions, click the Advanced button on the Security tab. A dialog box appears that lists all of the advanced permissions associated with the object, as shown in Figure 17-4.

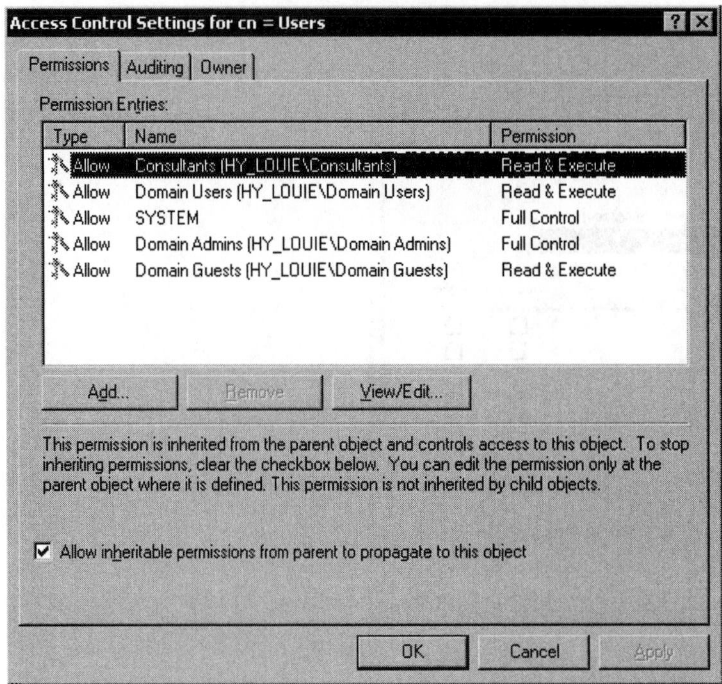

Figure 17-4. User object's Advanced properties

This dialog box lists the same accounts and groups as the "normal" security dialog box as well as additional individual permissions.

Clicking the View/Edit button for any account in the list brings up a dialog box similar to the one in Figure 17-5.

This dialog box shows all permissions set for the object. You can set any of the individual permissions from this list.

For example, say you want to allow an account read access as well as the ability to create and delete user accounts. From the advanced user permissions dialog box, edit the permissions for the appropriate account and set the appropriate permissions, as shown in Figure 17-6.

Once you set a specific combination of permissions, such as in the previous example, multiple entries will appear.

The Solution script demonstrates how to apply Full Access permissions for a user. This requires simply adding an ACE with the `AccessMask` property set to a specific value.

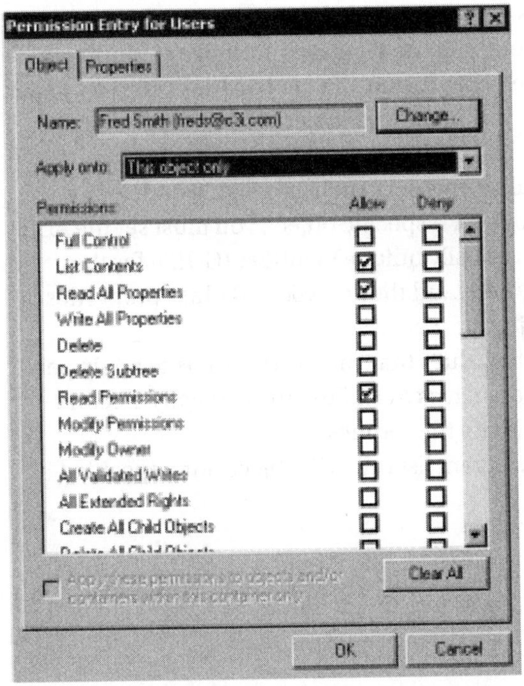

Figure 17-5. User object's Advanced permissions

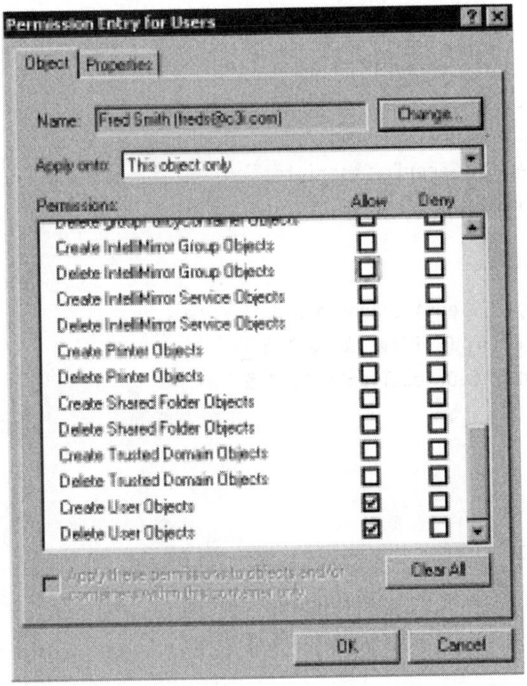

Figure 17-6. Setting advanced permissions

Setting individual permissions on objects complicates matters. For each permission you may get a specific entry in the security list. Unlike setting a permission such as Full or Read that requires the only the AccessMask property to be set, individual permissions require you specify the object you are applying the permissions to.

An object can be any individual permission, such as creating or deleting a user or file share. To set permissions for a specific object, you must set the ACE object's ObjectType property to the globally unique identifier (GUID) for the object. Getting the GUID is no easy task, and the AceType and Flags properties must have specific values to set object properties.

The easiest way to determine the values that you need to set is to apply permissions using a graphical interface, such as ADSI Edit, to an Active Directory object and programmatically enumerate the settings.

The following command-line program lists all ACE objects for a specified Active Directory object:

```
'listperms.vbs
'lists all permissions for a specified Active Directory object
Dim objSecurity, objArgs
Dim objContainer, objDACL , objACE
If Wscript.Arguments.Count <> 1 Then
  Wscript.Echo "Usage: listperms ADPath"
End If

 Set objACE = CreateObject("AccessControlEntry")
 'get a reference to users container
 Set objContainer = GetObject(Wscript.Arguments (0))
  Set objSecurity = objContainer.Get("ntSecurityDescriptor")
Set objDACL = objSecurity.DiscretionaryAcl

 For Each objACE In objDACL
   Wscript.Echo objACE.Trustee & ", " & objACE.AceFlags & _
     ", " & objACE.AceType & ", " & objACE.Flags & ", " & _
     objACE.AccessMask  & ", " & objACE.ObjectType & ", " & _
     objACE.InheritedObjectType
 Next
```

To use the command-line script, specify the LDAP path to an Active Directory object. To list the permissions for the Users organizational unit container for the Acme domain, use the following:

```
listperms "LDAP://cn=users,dc=acme,dc=com"
```

Use the enumerated ACE objects to determine what properties are set for a specific permission entry.

Table 17-10 lists the ACE property values for different permission settings. One is for Full Access and the second is if the Create and Delete user object permissions are granted to a user.

Table 17-10. ACE Property Values

PERMISSION	ACEFLAGS OBJECTTYPE	ACETYPE	FLAGS	ACCESSMASK
Full Access	0	0	0	983551
Create and Delete user objects	5	1	3	{BF967ABA-0DE6-11D0-A285-00AA003049E2}

Next, I'll cover the individual ACE properties and how they apply to the different permission settings. `AceFlags` determines how the ACE is inherited, and it can have any of the values listed in Table 17-11.

Table 17-11. `AceFlag` *Values*

CONSTANT	VALUE
ADS_ACEFLAG_INHERIT_ACE	2
ADS_ACEFLAG_NO_PROPAGATE_INHERIT_ACE	4
ADS_ACEFLAG_INHERIT_ONLY_ACE	8
ADS_ACEFLAG_INHERITED_ACE	16
ADS_ACEFLAG_VALID_INHERIT_FLAGS	31
ADS_ACEFLAG_SUCCESSFUL_ACCESS	64
ADS_ACEFLAG_FAILED_ACCESS	128

Both of the sample entries set the AceFlag to 0, and this indicates that the permission is not inherited and only applies to the current container object. If you want the permissions to be inherited to subcontainers, set the value to 2.

The AceType property values listed in Table 17-12 determine how the ACE permissions are applied.

Table 17-12. AceType *Property Values*

CONSTANT	VALUE
ADS_ACETYPE_ACCESS_ALLOWED	0
ADS_ACETYPE_ACCESS_DENIED	1
ADS_ACETYPE_SYSTEM_AUDIT	2
ADS_ACETYPE_ACCESS_ALLOWED_OBJECT	5
ADS_ACETYPE_ACCESS_DENIED_OBJECT	6
ADS_ACETYPE_SYSTEM_AUDIT_OBJECT	7

If you are permitting access to a nonobject, set the value to 0. This applies to the Full Access or Read access type permissions. Setting the value to 1 will deny access. So if you want to deny all access to a user, set the AccessMask to 983551 (Full Access) and the AceType to 1. Table 17-14 lists AccessMask values.

If you are setting permissions on a specific object, you must either specify 5, which will grant access, or 6, which will deny access to the specific object.

The Flags property only needs to be set if you are setting permissions for an object, and you can have the values listed in Table 17-13.

Table 17-13. Flags *Property Values*

CONSTANT	VALUE
ADS_FLAG_OBJECT_TYPE_PRESENT	1
ADS_FLAG_INHERITED_OBJECT_TYPE_PRESENT	2

Setting the Flags property to 1 indicates the security permissions apply to the object specified by the ObjectType property. If the value is 2, permissions are applied to the object specified by the InheritedObjectType property. Flags can be a combination, so the value 3 would apply the permissions to the object specified by the ObjectType and InheritedObjectType properties.

Table 17-14. AccessMask *Values*

CONSTANT	VALUE
ADS_RIGHT_DS_CREATE_CHILD	1
ADS_RIGHT_DS_DELETE_CHILD	2
ADS_RIGHT_ACTRL_DS_LIST	4
ADS_RIGHT_DS_SELF	8
ADS_RIGHT_DS_READ_PROP	16
ADS_RIGHT_DS_WRITE_PROP	32
ADS_RIGHT_DS_DELETE_TREE	64
ADS_RIGHT_DS_LIST_OBJECT	128
ADS_RIGHT_DS_CONTROL_ACCESS	256
ADS_RIGHT_DELETE	65536
ADS_RIGHT_READ_CONTROL	131072
ADS_RIGHT_WRITE_DAC	262144
ADS_RIGHT_WRITE_OWNER	524288
ADS_RIGHT_SYNCHRONIZE	1048576
ADS_RIGHT_ACCESS_SYSTEM_SECURITY	&H1000000
ADS_RIGHT_GENERIC_READ	&H80000000
ADS_RIGHT_GENERIC_WRITE	&H40000000
ADS_RIGHT_GENERIC_EXECUTE	&H20000000
ADS_RIGHT_GENERIC_ALL	&H10000000

The following sample permits the user Fred Smith to delete and create objects in the Users container:

```
<?xml version="1.0" ?>
<job>
<reference guid="{97D25DB0-0363-11CF-ABC4-02608C9E7553}"/>
<!--comment
Script:adsiacl.wsf
-->
 <script language="VBScript">
 <![CDATA[
  Option Explicit
  Const FULL_ACCESS = 983551
  Dim objSecurity
  Dim objContainer, objDACL , objACE
  Set objACE = CreateObject("AccessControlEntry")
  'get a reference to users container
  Set objContainer = GetObject("LDAP://cn=users,dc=acme,dc=com")
  Set objSecurity = objContainer.Get("ntSecurityDescriptor")
  Set objDACL = objSecurity.DiscretionaryAcl

  'set ACE properties
  objACE.Trustee = "Acme\Freds" 'trustee account
  'allow access to object
  objACE.AceType = ADS_ACETYPE_ACCESS_ALLOWED_OBJECT
  'specify to look at ObjectType field for GUID
  objACE.Flags = ADS_FLAG_OBJECT_TYPE_PRESENT
  'Set permissions to create and delete user objects
  objACE.AccessMask = ADS_RIGHT_DS_CREATE_CHILD + _
                      ADS_RIGHT_DS_DELETE_CHILD
  objACE.ObjectType =  "{BF967ABA-0DE6-11D0-A285-00AA003049E2}"
  objDACL.AddAce objACE
  objSecurity.DiscretionaryAcl = objDACL

  objContainer.Put "ntSecurityDescriptor", objSecurity
  objContainer.SetInfo
]]>
  </script>
</job>
```

The script references constants from the ADSI type library by referencing it by GUID.

To remove permissions from an object, you must check each ACE in the ACL for the account you want to remove. Once you have found the user you want to remove, call the ACL object's RemoveAce method, specifying the ACE object that you want to remove as a parameter. The following sample removes Fred Smith's permissions from the Users container:

```
Set objACE = CreateObject("AccessControlEntry")
'get a reference to users container
Set objContainer = "LDAP://cn=users,dc=acme,dc=com"
Set objSecurity = objContainer.Get("ntSecurityDescriptor")
Set objDACL = objSecurity.DiscretionaryAcl
'check each ACE for the account or permission you want to delete
For Each objACE In objDACL
   If objACE.Trustee =  "Acme\Freds " Then
    objDACL.RemoveAce objACE
  End If
 Next
End If
objSecurity.DiscretionaryAcl = objDACL
objContainer.Put "ntSecurityDescriptor", objSecurity
objContainer.SetInfo
```

Index

Symbols

- (hyphen) character, 711
$ (dollar sign) metacharacter, 198–99, 210, 212, 235, 724
% character, 69
% (percent symbol), 46, 181
%windir%\Tasks folder, 84
* wildcard, 146, 148
. (period) metacharacter, 199, 200
/ (forward slash) character, 202, 708
: (colon) character, 250, 255, 724
? (question mark) metacharacter, 198
? wildcard, 146, 148
?xml declaration element, 20
[] (square brackets), 201
\ (backslash) character, 250, 313, 678
\\ (double backslash) character, 250
^ (caret) metacharacter, 198–99
^ character, 69
` (grave accent) character, 231, 298
{} (brace brackets), 68, 201, 254
| (vertical bar) character, 36, 159, 199
+ character, 69
+ (plus sign) metacharacter, 198
<!-- --> comment tag, 11
</ /> tags, 297, 298
<?XML> element, 10
> (redirection symbol), 36, 53
" " (parentheses), 198

A

A (address or host) record, 344
aBindings parameter, 671
Access Control Entities (ACEs), 617, 701, 739, 743, 754
Access Control Lists (ACLs), 739
access mask, 739
access parameter query, executing, 556–58
access reports, generating electronic copies of, 246–48
access rights, 761
access to data. *See* data access
Access97 Service Release 2 (SR2), 247
AccessMask property, 702, 744, 754, 755, 761, 776, 783, 784, 786, 788, 789
ACE object, 702, 787
AceFlags property, 761, 787–88
AceType property, 702, 744, 754, 755, 786, 788
ACETYPE_ACCESS_ALLOWED value, 755
ACETYPE_ACCESS_DENIED value, 755
ACL object, 791
Active Directory, 707, 716
Active Directory Browser, 596–99, 664
Active Directory Domains, 73, 88, 89, 97
active directory permissions, setting, 781–91
Active Directory Services Interface (ADSI), 88, 95, 96, 575–76
active directory values, querying, 625–30
Active Server Pages (ASP), 1
ActiveX Data Object (ADO), 363
ActiveXObject method, 9
Add method, 135, 235, 622, 623, 726
AddAce method, 702, 755
AddPrinterConnection method, 116, 119
address book recipient, retrieving, 468–72
Address parameter, 399
address parameter, 669
address type, 723
addressBookContainer class, 729
address:port:domainname format, 669
addresstype$address format, 723
AddURL method, 33
AddWindowsPrinterConnection method, 115
admin /r, 711
administration, system. *See* system administration
ADO, 478–80
ADO (ActiveX Data Object), 363
ADO interface, 625, 627
ADS_SCOPE_ONELEVEL value, 628
ADS_SCOPE_SUBTREE value, 628
ADS_SD_FORMAT_IID format, 753, 756
ADS_SID_ACTIVE_DIRECTORY_PATH type, 700
ADS_SID_HEXSTRING constant, 700
ADS_SID_WINNT_PATH type, 700
AdsDSOObject provider, 733, 734

ADSI 2.5 SDK DLL, 700, 739
ADSI (Active Directory Services Interface), 88, 95, 96, 575–76
ADSI Edit, 709, 782–86
ADSI SDK/Resource Kit, 576, 596
ADSIEdit utility, 596
Adsiedit.msc application, 782
ADSIFileSecurity.wsc script, 763
adsilib.vbs library, 603, 669, 676
ADSIpath path, 592
adsiqry.vbs script, 629
adsiqry.wsf script, 738
ADsPath field, 735
adspath value, 738
ADsRAS.dlll file, 640, 641
ADsSecurity component, 773, 774
ADsSecurity DLL, 700, 701, 706, 753, 777, 778
ADsSecurity object, 753, 754, 756, 759, 763
ADsSecurity ProgID, 701, 753
ADsSecurity.dll file, 700, 751, 752–53
ADsSecurityUtility interface, 751, 777
ADsSecurityUtility object, 752, 753, 754, 756, 759, 763, 773, 778
ADsSecurityUtility ProgID, 753
ADsSID component, 700, 701
ADsSID ProgID, 700
aIpAddress array, 280
alias parameter, 706
All property, 380
AND NOT Boolean operation, 618
And operator, 129–30
Anonymous access, 684
Anonymous level, 253
anonymous mail, sending, 411–13
APIs (application programming interfaces), 575
AppActivate method, 67
AppCreate method, 670, 685, 687
AppCreate2 method, 687
AppCreate3 method, 687
AppDelete method, 688
AppDeleteRecursive method, 688
append symbol (>>), 36
Application object, 220
application programming interfaces (APIs), 575
Application reference, 238
applications. *See also* Internet applications
  automation of, 215–48
    building Web page rollover images, 244–46
    creating formatted Word documents, 215–26
    generating electronic copies of access reports, 246–48
    generating thumbnail images for Web pages, 240–43
    identifying office documents by their properties, 227–31
    importing data into Excel, 231–39
    overview, 215
  running, 52–58
  starting on remote computers, 304–9
aPropArray array, 630
aProperties parameter, 594, 711
Arguments collection, 41, 42
Arguments property, 39
arrByte parameter, 613
arrVar parameter, 613
ASP (Active Server Pages), 1
ASPInet FTP control, 394–95
Assoc-NT-Account property, 701
asterisk (*) wildcard, 628, 735
aSubnetMask array, 280
at (@) sign, 588
AT command, 83
attachments
  attaching files to messages, 436–39
  extracting, 444–45
Attributes property, 128
AType record object, 344, 352
authentication methods, 684
AuthNTLM property, 685
Autoexec.bat command file, 50
automation of applications. *See* applications, automation of

B

BAC.Convert (Binary Array Conversion) object, 612
backing up and restoring IIS configuration information, 656–62
backslash (\) character, 250, 313, 678
Backup method, 656, 657–58
BackupEventlog method, 327
BackupEventLog method, 328, 329
BackupWithPassword method, 657, 658
BAConv.DLL file, 612
bADsSecurity variable, 759
batch files, 71
bCreate parameter, 687
bDefragRecommended parameter, 339
bDone variable, 371
bForce parameter, 144, 145, 149
Binary Array Conversion (BAC.Convert) object, 612
bitwise Or operator, 130
Blue Screen of Death (BSOD), 276

bookmarks, 216
bOverwrite parameter, 150
bOverWriteFiles flag, 146
bOverwriteFiles parameter, 146, 147, 148
bProcess parameter, 687
brace brackets ({}), 68, 201, 254
bRunRepeat parameter, 305
BSOD (Blue Screen of Death), 276
BufferSize property, 400
BuiltinDocumentProperties collection, 226, 227
BuiltinDocumentProperties property, 228
ByteToVariant function, 612–13

C

CACLS.EXE permission, 772
Canonical Names (CNAME) records, 352
Caption property, 301
caret (^) metacharacter, 198–99
CDOEXM (Collaborative Data Objects for Exchange Management) library, 707
Cells property, 237
Change method, 333, 334–35
ChangeDir method, 394
CIM_DataFile class, 310, 311, 312, 313, 780
CIM_Directory class, 780
CIM_LogicalFile class, 310
CIMV2 (Common Information Model Version 2) namespace, 250
Cimv2 namespace, 250
CIMV2 provider, 331
CIMWIN32.MOF file, 278
class ID (CLSID), 8, 223
class object, 250
Class_Initialize subroutine, 262
Class_Terminate subroutine, 262
classid attribute, 18
ClearEventlog method, 329
Close method, 150
closing tag, 4
CLSID (class ID), 8, 223
CMD.EXE command shell, 53
cn value, 738
CNAME (Canonical Names) records, 352
Collaborative Data Objects for Exchange Management library (CDOEXM), 707
colon (:) character, 250, 255, 724
COM automation, 2–3
COM components, 90
COM interface, 241
COM objects, 240
Command object, 628
COMMAND.COM command shell, 53
command-line arguments, reading, 39–46
<comment> element, 11
compacting access databases, 495–99
component registration, 20–21
<component> element, 18
Compress method, 310
compressing folders and files, 309–11
computer components, inventorying, 288–92
Computer object, 583
computer parameter, 636, 646, 662, 666, 673, 750
computer status notification, 433–34
Computer\Account format, 744
ComputerName function, 297
ComputerName parameter, 663
COMSPEC environment variable, 53
connected resources, listing, 636–38
Connection object, 627, 628, 733, 734, 735
connection parameter, 673
ConnectObject method, 29, 57, 58
ConnectServer method, 252, 254
constants, 220
contact class, 721
container name (cn), 698
Container object, 729
container parameter, 614, 698
CONTAINER_INHERIT_ACE setting, 761
Container-Info property, 730
Continue method, 675
Controls collections, 248
Convert2DMTFDate function, 298, 323, 338
ConvToDate function, 599
ConvToSeconds function, 580
Copy method, 145, 146, 147, 148, 314
CopyFile method, 146
CopyFolder method, 147, 148
copying
    files, 145–46
        on remote computers, 312–16
        with security settings, 777–80
    folders, 147–48, 462–64
    messages, 459–62
Corel PHOTO-PAINT, 240, 241–42, 244, 245
CorelDRAW version 8, 240
Count property, 41, 109, 118, 207
Create method, 304, 305, 586, 587, 588, 620, 621, 644, 666, 667, 668, 670, 677, 678, 680, 698
CreateDir method, 394

CreateFolder method, 135
CreateInstance FromPropertyData method, 351–52, 353
CreateKey method, 183, 185
CreateMailbox method, 697, 707–8, 709
CreateNewSite method, 667, 671
CreateObject method, 9, 21–22, 24, 29, 31, 39, 41, 89
CreatePath subroutine, 136–37
CreateScript method, 55–56
CreateShortcut method, 60, 62
createsite.wsf script, 671, 673, 674
CreateTextFile method, 149, 150
createxusr.wsf script, 703
CreateZone method, 346
CreateZone parameters, 346
Creation date property, 230
cscript command, 12
Cscript host, 160
cscript.exe application, 1, 7
cscript.exe file, 77, 83
Ctrl-Break command, 160
Ctrl-Z command, 160, 164
CurrentTimeZone property, 323

D

DACL (Discretionary Access Control List), 701, 739, 743, 754
DACL object, 755
data access, 477–574
  accessing Excel data, 510–13
  accessing HTML data, 520–24
  accessing internet resources, 525–35
  adding data, 515–18
  compacting access databases, 495–99
  data source name connection strings, 480–84
  deleting data, 524–25
  DSN-less connection strings, 487–92
  executing access parameter query, 556–58
  executing stored procedures, 552–55
  exporting data, 535–37
  File DSN connection, 485–87
  importing data, 537–52
  manipulating text files, 508–10
  modifying command results, 559–61
  ODBC, 477
  OLE DB, 477–78
  opening secure databases, 492–95
  opening table for writing, 504–8
  overview, 477
  processing multiple recordsets, 558–59
  querying Index Server, 513–15
  querying tables, 500–503
  returning parameter value from stored procedure, 561–71
  transaction processing, 571–74
  updating data, 518–20
  using ADO, 478–80
data source name connection strings, 480–84
data.htm page, 363
data.txt file, 363
day parameter, 614
DCOM (Distributed Component Object Model), 25, 26, 55
dcomcnfg.exe configuration utility, 26–27
dDate parameter, 323
debug attribute, 30–31
debug functionality, 30
DebugFilePath property, 275
default.htm file, 680
defaultNameContext property, 578, 581
Defrag method, 338, 339
DefragAnalysis method, 339
defragging drives, 338–41
Delegate level, 253
Delete method, 144–45, 148, 149, 313, 314, 355, 607, 608, 622, 644, 658, 676, 732
DeleteFile method, 148, 149
DeleteFile operation, 149
DeleteFolder method, 144–45
DeleteKey method, 185
DeleteMailbox method, 732, 733
DeleteValue method, 185, 187
deleting
  DNS resources, 355–56
  Exchange objects, 732–33
  files, 148–49
  folders, 144–45, 464–65
  messages, 464–65
  network shares, 643–44
  registry entry, 184–86
  temporary files, 137–40
  users, 607–8
description attribute, 18
Description parameter, 621, 673
Description property, 301, 602
<description> element, 42, 43
Desktop Management Task Force (DMTF), 249
Destination parameter, 243
DestinationPath parameter, 245
DHTML (dynamic HTML), 359
DialinPrivilege property, 641
dir command, 160
directory security, setting, 759–73

directory service, 575
Discretionary Access Control List (DACL), 701, 739, 743, 754
DiscretionaryACL property, 701
dispid attribute, 30
displayname parameter, 706
distinguished name (DN), 577, 581
Distributed Component Object Model (DCOM), 25, 26, 55
distribution group, 622
distribution lists, 474–75
DMTF (Desktop Management Task Force), 249
DMTFDate2String function, 323
DN (distinguished name), 577, 581
DNS addresses
  creating, 351–55
  modifying, 356–58
DNS resources, deleting, 355–56
DNS zone
  creating, 345–49
  modifying properties, 350
DNSLookup method, 396
dnsprov.dll file, 342
dnsschema.mof file, 342
.doc extension, 218
Doc property, 35
DoCmd.OpenForm method, 248
DoCmd.OutputTo procedure, 247
DocPath parameter, 230
Document object, 364, 365, 378, 379, 380
Document Object Model (DOM), 359, 375
Document property, 371
Document Type Definition (DTD), 10
Documents, 220
Documents collection, 221
dollar sign ($) metacharacter, 198–99, 210, 212, 235, 724
DOM (Document Object Model), 359, 375
domain name resolution, 396–98
Domain object, 578–79
domain parameter, 706
domain properties, setting, 576–82
Domain\Account format, 744
domain\accountname format, 702, 743, 773
DomainDeny property, 693, 694
DomainGrant property, 693, 694
DomainName name, 577
domainname parameter, 669
dot method, 592, 593, 710, 711
double backslash (\\) character, 250
Drive object, 122, 123, 124
DriveExists method, 108, 125
drives
  defragging, 338–41
  floppy, determining readiness of, 122–23
  listing on system, 124–25
Drives collection, 124
DSN-less connection strings, 487–92
DSNs, file-based, 485–87
DTD (Document Type Definition), 10
DTDflag parameter, 10
duration parameter, 614
dynamic HTML (DHTML), 359

E

Edir.vbs solution script, 140, 142
e-mail addresses, maintaining (Exchange server), 722–25
Empty object, 276
EnableStatic method, 280
EnableWINS method, 281–82
End event, 57
end of file (EOF) sequence, 160, 164
EndTable function, 368
Enterprise WSH. *See* ENTWSH (Enterprise WSH)
ENTWSH (Enterprise WSH), 35
  .HTMLGen scripting component, 86
  .ListFiles component, 23, 24
  .RecurseDir component, 137, 139, 142, 394
  .RecurseDir object, 139–40
  .SysInfo Windows Script component, 235
ENTWSH.FileSecurity component, 773
ENTWSH.FileSecurity ProgID, 772
ENTWSH.HTMLGen ProgID, 367
ENTWSH.SysInfo component, 289
EnumKey method, 187, 188
EnumNetworkDrives collection, 114
EnumNetworkDrives property, 109
EnumPrinterConnections collection, 118
EnumPrinterConnections property, 117
EnumValues method, 187, 188
Environment collection, 47, 48, 51
Environment object, 52, 299
environment variables
  changing, 298–300
  creating or updating, 48–51
  deleting, 51–52
  reading, 46–48
EOF (end of file) sequence, 160, 164
error attribute, 30
Error event, 57
error functionality, 30
error handling, 596

Error property, 56
ERRORLEVEL environment variable, 264
Eval function, 143
event log, checking, 432–33
event object, 326
event parameter, 377
event sink, 371
Event Viewer
backing up events, 327–29
checking for unauthorized access, 320–27
processing events, 329–33
<event> element, 22
events, 12, 22–25
events attribute, 9
EventSource object, 331
EWX_FORCE constant, 319
EWX_SHUTDOWN constant, 319
Excel
accessing data, 510–13
importing data into, 231–39
Exchange Administrator, 711–12, 713
Exchange Management Components, 707
Exchange server, 695–738
5.5 recipients container, changing user access to, 773–77
creating custom recipient, 719–22
creating distribution list, 725–27
creating mailbox, 695–709
creating recipients container, 729–32
deleting exchange objects, 732–33
enumerating distribution list, 727–29
maintaining mailbox e-mail addresses, 722–25
overview, 695
public folder, posting messages to, 456–57
searching, 733–38
setting mailbox limits, 717–19
setting mailbox properties, 710–17
exclamation point (!) character, 254
Exec command, 54
Exec method, 54–55, 55, 56
ExecNotificationQuery method, 330, 331
ExecQuery method, 265, 267
ExecQuery statement, 321
ExecutablePath property, 301
Execute method, 56, 204
ExecuteQuery function, 734
Exists method, 44
ExpandEnvironmentStrings method, 46, 47, 48, 53, 78, 181
ExpandEnvironmentVariables method, 46
exsearch.wsf script, 737
Extensible Markup Language (XML), 4
ExtractCSV function, 226

F

fields parameter, 738
file access permissions, 755
File object, 127–28, 145, 146, 147, 148, 149, 152
file operations, 121–56
comparing files by version number, 133–35
copying and moving folders, 147–48
copying files, 145–46
creating and writing to text files, 149–50
creating folders, 135–37
deleting files, 148–49
deleting folders, 144–45
determining existence of a file or folder, 131–32
determining readiness of floppy drives, 122–23
determining size of files, 127–28
finding and deleting temporary files, 137–40
finding files that meet criteria, 140–43
finding size of user directory, 125–26
listing drives on system, 124–25
opening and reading a file, 151–53
overview, 121–22
reading and changing file attributes, 128–31
renaming files or folders, 132–33
updating a text file, 153–56
File Scripting Object (FSO), 363
file services, migrating from one server to another, 112–14
File System Object (FSO), 121–22, 144, 146, 147, 148, 149, 150, 151, 156
file transfer protocol (FTP), 390–95
FILE:// prefix, 753
file-based DSNs, 485–87
FileExists method, 131–32
FilePath path, 239
FileSecurity object, 772
FileService object, 637
FileShare class, 644
FileShare object, 642
Filter property, 140, 584, 629
filtering mail, 441–44
FindNextSite function, 669, 676
fireEvent subroutine, 24
Firstindex property, 204
Flags property, 788–89
floppy drives, determining readiness of, 122–23

Folder object, 125, 126, 135, 136, 144, 147, 156
FolderExists method, 132, 137
folders
- compressing, 309–11
- copying, 462–64
- creating, 135–37, 457–59
- deleting, 144–45, 464–65
- determining existence of, 131–32
- retrieving, 451–56

Font property, 236
For Each statement, 113
forward slash (/) character, 202, 708
FoundFile event, 24, 25, 140
FQDN (fully qualified domain name), 343
FQDN parameter, 353, 354
frcopy.wsf, 778
FSO (File System Object), 121–22, 144, 146, 147, 148, 149, 150, 151, 156
FTP COM (FTP/X) object, 390
FTP (file transfer protocol), 390–95
FTP protocol, 359
FTP service (MSFTPSVC), 667
FTPGetFile method, 395
FTPPutFile method, 395
FullName property, 62
Fullname property, 602
fully qualified domain name (FQDN), 343

G

g switch, 203
Get method, 178, 593, 711, 742
get_function, 19, 29
GetAs method, 700
GetBinarySID function, 744, 758
GetDrive method, 122
GetEx method, 605–6
GetFile method, 127
GetFileDir routine, 681
GetFileVersion method, 93, 133–35
GetFolder method, 125, 126
GetImage function, 378
GetInfo method, 591, 594
GetInfoEx method, 594, 711
GetObject function, 253, 255
GetObject method, 21, 22, 89, 218, 577, 735, 742
Get/Put method, 711
GetRef function, 212, 377
getResource function, 9
GetSecurityDescriptor method, 701, 741, 742–43, 753, 780
GetSpecialFolder method, 156
GetStringValue method, 179
GetTempName method, 155
Global property, 203, 204
globally unique identifier (GUID), 8, 786
Goto method, 235
gpedit.msc application, 76
GrantByDefault property, 693
graphical user interface (GUI) capability, 359
grave accent (`) character, 231, 298
Greenwich Mean Time (GMT), 323
Group class, 620
Group object, 96, 621, 624
Group Policies, 73–76, 97
groupOfNames object, 725, 726
groups
- determining group membership, 624–25
- listing, 619–20
- performing operations based on group membership, 95–101

Groups collection, 619
groupType property, 621
GUI (graphical user interface) capability, 359
GUI menu, creating, 387–90
GUID (globally unique identifier), 8, 786
GUID parameter, 9, 35
guid type library, 8

H

Handle property, 301
handle/process ID (PID), 301
helpstring attribute, 43
HighPart property, 580, 599
HKEY_CLASS_ROOT registry key, 28
HKEY_CURRENT_USER\ Environment registry key, 49
HKEY_CURRENT_USER registry root, 185
HKEY_CURRENT_USER\Volatile Environment registry key, 49
HKEY_LOCAL_MACHINE root key, 183, 185, 187
hour parameter, 614
HTML
- accessing HTML data, 520–24
- creating HTML form, 373–78
- displaying, 364–69
- displaying HTML logon message, 369–73
- enumerating HTML elements, 378–87
- retrieving HTML data, 359–64

HTML documents, 167
HTML events, 377

htmlelem.vbs script, 380
HTMLGen component, 89, 365, 368
HTTP protocol, 359
HttpRedirect property, 678
HyperText Markup Language. *See* HTML
hyphen (-) character, 711

I

i switch, 203
id attribute, 7, 31
Identify level, 253
IE events, 372
IE methods, 372
IE properties, 372
ie_OnQuit subroutine, 371
ie_prefix, 371
ieadmin.vbs script, 381
IgnoreCase property, 197, 199
IIS. *See* Internet Information Server (IIS)
IIS 5.0, Isolation mode, 686–87
iisbackup.wsf script, 659, 662
IIsFTPVirtualDir class, 667, 670, 678
IIsWebServer class, 666
IIsWebVirtualDir class, 677
images
  rollover images, 244–46
  thumbnail, 240–43
Impersonate level, 254
impersonation level, 252–53
impersonationLevel property, 252–53, 254
include file, 5–6
Index Server, querying, 513–15
index value, 254
INHERIT_ONLY_ACE setting, 761
InheritedObjectType property, 789
in-process application, 686
InputLine function, 364
input/output streams, 157–73
  creating multiple-user prompts, 170–73
  generating template-based data, 164–70
  overview, 157
  reading keyboard input, 163–64
  using regular expressions to filter contents of input stream, 157–63
InsertionStrings property, 323–24
_instancemodificationevent statement, 331
InstancesOf method, 254, 267
Int8 format, 580
INT8 object, 599
INT8 property, 599
intAction parameter, 606
Interior property, 236
internalName attribute, 29, 30
Internet applications, 359–401
  creating GUI menu, 387–90
  creating HTML form, 373–78
  displaying HTML, 364–69
  displaying HTML logon message, 369–73
  domain name resolution, 396–98
  enumerating HTML elements, 378–87
  overview, 359
  pinging computers, 398–401
  retrieving HTML data, 359–64
  transferring files using FTP, 390–95
Internet Explorer (IE), 1, 89, 359, 364, 365, 369, 370, 371, 373, 375, 389
Internet Information Server (IIS), 655–94
  backing up and restoring configuration information, 656–62
  creating sites, 666–74
  creating virtual Web directories, 677–79
  creating Web directory application, 685–89
  deleting sites, 675–77
  listing Web sites, 662–66
  maintaining server bindings, 689–91
  overview, 655–56
  setting file and directory properties, 679–85
  setting IP security, 691–94
  starting an IIS site, 674–75
InternetExplorer.Application ProgID, 364
intIOMode parameter, 152
intTriState parameter, 150, 152
inventory.wsf script, 292
inventory.xlt template, 235
IP address, 693–94
IP information, obtaining, 265–75
IP subnet, 693
IPAddress parameter, 352
IPAddress property, 344
ipaddress, subnet format, 693
ipconfig utility, 271
IPDeny property, 693
IPEnabled Boolean property, 266
IPGrant property, 693
ipinfo.wsf command-line script, 268, 271
ipmaint.wsf script, 283, 288
IPSecurity object, 691
IPSecurity property, 685, 691, 692–93
ISchedulingAgent_ScheduleTask method, 84
IsMember method, 95, 96, 624
Isolation mode, IIS 5.0, 686–87

ispdc.vbs script, 263
IsPhone function, 195
IsReady property, 122

J

.job files, 84, 85
<job> element, 4–5, 7
Join function, 154
JScript, 202, 210, 377–78
JScript scripting engine, 1

K

keyboard input, reading, 163–64
keystroke codes, 68
keystrokes to applications, sending, 65–69

L

L property, 712
language attribute, 5, 19
LanmanServer object, 637, 638, 642, 643, 644
LastError method, 394
LastLogin property, 596
Lbound function, 265
LDAP (Lightweight Directory Access Protocol), 88, 581, 730–31
LDAP provider, 582
LDAP:// prefix, 577, 581
LDIR environment variable, 78, 79
length property, 41
_lf prefix, 25
lf_ prefix, 24
lf_FoundFile function, 24, 25
Lightweight Directory Access Protocol (LDAP), 88, 581, 730–31
ListFiles object, 25
listing
  DNS resources, 341–44
  groups, 619–20
listprop command-line script, 713
listprop method, 716
listprop utility, 592, 685
ListSecurity method, 772
listsites.wsf script, 665, 666
.lnk extension, 61
Locator object, 252
log month-date-year hh-mm.evt event name, 327
LogEvent method, 94
LogFileName property, 328
logging, 405–9
LoginHours property, 609, 612, 613
LoginWorkstations property, 614, 615
Logoff parameter, 76
logoff script, 75–76
logon hours, 611–12
logon message, displaying, 86–95
logon scripts and scheduling, 71–106
  connecting network resources at logon, 71–79
  creating inventory of computers at logon, 101–6
  displaying logon message, 86–95
  overview, 71
  performing operations based on group membership, 95–101
  scheduling scripts, 79–86
LogonHours property, 612
LowPart property, 580, 599

M

mail
  creating mail messages, 416–17
  filtering, 441–44
Mail Exchange (MX) records, 353
mail (SMTP) servers, 663
mailbox (Exchange server)
  creating, 695–709
  maintaining mailbox e-mail addresses, 722–25
  setting mailbox limits, 717–19
  setting mailbox properties, 710–17
mailbox object, 713
MailDisable method, 733
MailEnable method, 720, 721, 726, 727
mail-enabled contacts, 721
mail-enabled group, 726
mailNickName property, 728
MakeDirPath subroutine, 394
Managed Object Format (MOF) file, 278
MandatoryProperties collection, 589, 591
MandatoryProperties property, 591
MapNetworkDrive method, 72, 110, 111, 112
mapping network drives, 110–12
Marby FTP object
  .FtpXObj, 391
  Account parameter, 391
  Connect method, 391
  GetFile method, 391, 392
  Host property, 391
  LogonName parameter, 391
  LogonPassword parameter, 391
  PutFile method, 391, 392
Match element, 207
Match object, 204, 207

Matches collection, 204, 206, 210
mbupdate.txt, 716
MD_BACKUP_HIGHEST_VERSION value, 658
Members collection, 619, 728
Members property, 728
Menus parameter, 246
Message property, 326
messaging operations, 403–75
- adding distribution lists, 474–75
- attaching files to messages, 436–39
- checking event log, 432–33
- copying and moving folders, 462–64
- copying or moving messages, 459–62
- creating folders, 457–59
- creating mail messages, 416–17
- creating message recipients, 419–22
- creating new message fields, 465–68
- creating recipient entries, 472–74
- deleting messages and folders, 464–65
- determining default profile, 409–10
- extracting attachments, 444–45
- filtering mail, 441–44
- getting computer status notification, 433–34
- logging on, 405–9
- overview, 403–5
- posting messages to exchange server public folder, 456–57
- processing messages, 439–41
- retrieving an address book recipient, 468–72
- retrieving folders, 451–56
- running message scripts using NT scheduler service, 413–15
- sending anonymous mail, 411–13
- sending messages, 422–26
- setting message properties, 417–19
- using command-line script to send e-mail, 426–32
- using Performance Monitor event, 435–36
- using WSH script mail agent, 446–51

Metabase Editor, 664, 679
Metabase Explorer, 664, 679
metacharacters, 198, 200
<method> element, 19, 30
methods, 2, 12
Microsoft Access, 246, 247
MicrosoftDNS namespace, 342
MicrosoftDNS_AType object, 352
MicrosoftDNS_CNAMEType object, 352, 353
MicrosoftDNS_PTRType object, 353
MicrosoftDNS_Zone object, 345, 346
microsoft.public.scripting.wsh newsgroup, 37
Microsoft.XMLHTTP ProgId, 360
MMC (Microsoft Management Console), 663
Modify method, 357
MOF (Managed Object Format) file, 278
mofcomp utility, 741
moniker, 253
more command, 160
more program, 36
Move method, 145, 146, 147, 148
MoveFile method, 146
MoveFolder method, 147, 148
moving
- folders, 147–48, 462–64
- messages, 459–62

MSDN (Microsoft Developers Network), 37
msExchPurportedSearchUI property, 732
MSFTPSVC (FTP service), 667
MsgBox function, 364
msNPAllowDialin property, 640
mstask.chm file, 86
multiple recordsets, processing, 558–59
multiple site hosting, 689
multiple-user prompts, creating, 170–73
multivalued properties, setting, 605–7
MX (Mail Exchange) records, 353

N

name attribute, 19, 30, 43
Name collection, 235
name parameter, 750
Name property, 35, 132–33, 255, 299, 301, 663, 743, 781
Named object, 45
<named> element, 42, 43, 45
namespaces, 249, 250, 575
nanosecond, 579
nArgument position, 46
Navigate method, 365, 371, 375
nChars characters, 153
nConstant parameter, 318
nDelay parameter, 331
net use command, 116, 119
net use /h command-line, 112
network administration/WMI, 249–358
- accessing information about a computer, 251–62
- backing up Event Viewer events, 327–29
- changing environment variables, 298–300
- changing location of NT dump file, 275–78
- changing NT service account information, 333–36

changing system time, 336–38
checking Event Viewer for unauthorized access, 320–27
compressing folders and files, 309–11
copying files on remote computer, 312–16
creating DNS address, 351–55
creating DNS zone, 345–49
defragging drives, 338–41
deleting DNS resources, 355–56
determining role of a computer, 263–65
executing generic WMI queries, 292–98
inventorying computer components, 288–92
listing DNS resources, 341–44
modifying DNS addresses, 356–58
modifying DNS zone properties, 350
obtaining IP information, 265–75
overview, 249–50
processing Event Viewer events, 329–33
rebooting computer, 316–20
setting TCP/IP information, 279–88
starting application on remote computer, 304–9
terminating system processes, 300–304
Network object, 107–8, 109, 111, 112, 115, 117, 118
network shares
creating or deleting, 643–44
listing, 642–43
networking resources, 107–19
connecting at logon, 71–79
connecting to network printers, 115–17
disconnecting network printers, 118–19
finding available network drive, 108–10
identifying users, 107–8
listing connected network printers, 117–18
mapping network drives, 110–12
migrating file services from one server to another, 112–14
overview, 107
New operator, 197
news (NNTP) servers, 663
NextEvent method, 331
nFlag parameter, 657, 658
nFlags parameter, 267
nID parameter, 671
nMonthDay parameter, 306
nName parameter, 669
NNTP (news) servers, 663
Not And bitwise operation, 130
nPath parameter, 700
nPathFormat parameter, 753, 756
nPathType parameter, 753–54, 756
nProcID parameter, 305
nProtection parameter, 687
nReason parameter, 301
nRootKey parameter, 178, 183, 185, 187
nSpecialFolder parameter, 156
nStyle parameter, 53
NT dump file, changing location of, 275–78
NT scheduler service, running message scripts using, 413–15
NT service account information, changing, 333–36
NT services, controlling, 630–36
NT share security, setting, 740–51
nType parameter, 700
Null value, 265
NumberOfRecords property, 328
nuser.bat batch file, 173
nuser.txt template, 172, 173
nusr.txt file, 172
nValue parameter, 594, 711
nVersion parameter, 657, 658
nWaitOnReturn parameter, 53
nWeekDay parameter, 305

O

o3.o2.o1.in-addr.arpa format, 347
objContainer object, 586, 698
objDefragAnalysis parameter, 339
objDescripter parameter, 743, 744
objDOMElement object, 377
object browser, 221–22
object classes, 249
object parameter, 25
object properties
listing, 589–92
setting, 592–604
object references, 222–23
OBJECT_INHERIT_ACE setting, 761
<object> element, 9
objectname parameter, 676
objectSID property, 700
ObjectType property, 786, 789
objFileDirectory object, 780
objID parameter, 9
objProcessStartInfo parameter, 305
objRegExp object, 204
objRegExp parameter, 213
objSecurity object, 778

objSecurityDescriptor parameter, 756
objService parameter, 669, 676
objTime parameter, 599
ODBC, 477
office documents, identifying by their properties, 227–31
offprops.vbs script, 229, 230
Offset property, 238
OLE DB, 477–78
OLE DB interface, 627
OLE/COM Object Viewer, 223–24, 238–39
On Error Resume Next statement, 111
ON extension, 246
onchange event, 377
onclick event, 377
onoff parameter, 614
OnQuit event, 371
Open method, 360–61, 734–35
OpenAsTextStream method, 152
opening
  files, 151–53
  tables for writing, 504–8
opening tag, 4
OpenTextFile method, 151, 152
operating system (OS), determining, 582–83
OperatingSystem property, 582
operation parameter, 636
OptionalProperties collection, 589, 591
OptionalProperties property, 591
OR logical operator, 617
ORDER BY statements, 267
organization parameter, 698
organizational units, 587–88
organizationalPerson object, 695, 698, 733
organizationalUnit class, 587
otherMailbox property, 722, 723, 724
out-of-process application, 686
output streams. *See* input/output streams
Owner property, 781
OwnerAddress parameter, 352, 354
ownership of files, taking, 780–81

P

<p> (paragraph) tag, 368
<package> element, 7, 31
paragraph tag (<p>), 368
parameter attribute, 19
<parameter> element, 19, 22
parentheses (" "), 198
path, 250
PATH environment variable, 53
Path object, 276
path parameter, 673, 778
Path property, 24, 670, 678
Pattern property, 196, 197, 203
Pause method, 635, 646, 650, 675
percent symbol (%), 46, 181
Performance Monitor event, 435–36
period (.) metacharacter, 199, 200
permissions, setting, 751–59, 781–91
PHOTO-PAINT, 240, 241–42, 244, 245
PHOTO-PAINT object, 243
ping command, 400
Ping method, 398–99
pinging computers, 398–401
piping, 36
plus sign (+) metacharacter, 198
pointer (PTR) records, 353
pooled application, 686
Popup method, 64–65
port parameter, 669
Preference parameter, 353
Presentations, 220
Primary property, 318
Primary_Domain_Controller, 263
PrimaryWINSServer parameter, 281
printers
  connecting to network printers, 115–17
  disconnecting network printers, 118–19
  listing connected network printers, 117–18
  listing print jobs, 647–50
  print queue operations, 645–47
PrintJob object, 649–50
PrintJob property, 650
PrintJobs collection, 648
PrintJobs property, 649
PrintQ parameter, 646
PrintQueue object, 646, 649
Privileges qualifier, 318
Process environment, 48
process environment variables, 47, 52
Process method, 140
processes, system. *See* system processes
processing messages, 439–41
procmaint.wsf script, 301, 304
ProgID attribute, 13, 18, 20, 22, 28, 33
ProgID parameter, 9
ProgID type library, 8
prompt.wsf script, 171, 173
Proper function, 213
properties, 2, 12
<property> element, 19, 30
  <get/>, 29
  <put/>, 29
PropertyCount property, 591

Provider property, 734
proxyaddresses property, 724
PTR (pointer) records, 353
<public> element, 18, 19, 22, 24
Purge method, 645, 646
purportedSearch property, 730
Put method, 592, 593, 710, 711
Put_ method, 276
put_function, 19, 29
PutEx method, 605, 606, 642, 719, 722, 723, 724

Q

QADNA (Quick and Dirty Network Administration), 97–98, 101, 102, 105
quantifiers, 198
Query parameter, 230
query parameter, 738
querying
  active directory values, 625–30
  Index Server, 513–15
  tables, 500–503
question mark (?) metacharacter, 198
Quick and Dirty Network Administration (QADNA), 97–98, 101, 102, 105

R

range names, 216
Range object, 234, 236, 237, 238
Range Object, Borders property, 236
RangeName name, 239
RAS access, determining, 638–42
RDN (relative distinguished name), 577, 581, 608, 698
Read method, 151, 152, 163, 164, 179
ReadAll method, 152
ReadAll method, AtEndOfStream property, 152
reading
  files, 151–53
  keyboard input, 163–64
  value from registry, 176–79
ReadLine method, 151, 152
Reboot method, 316, 317, 318, 319
rebooting computer, 316–20
recipient entries, creating, 472–74
Recipients container, 698
RecurseDir component, 140
redirection symbol (>), 36, 53
<reference> element, 8, 9, 220
.reg extension, 29
REG_EXPAND_SZ values, 181
REG_SZ values, 181
RegDelete method, 184–85, 186
RegEdit.exe registry editing tool, 28, 181, 182
RegExp class, 210
RegExp object, 196, 197, 202, 203
RegExp program ID, 203
regflt script, 209
regflt.vbs script, 207
Register function, 20, 21, 34
<registration> element, 18, 21, 26, 34
registry operations, 175–93
  accessing remote registry, 192–93
  deleting registry entry, 184–86
  listing registry key values, 186–88
  overview, 175–76
  reading value from registry, 176–79
  searching and replacing registry values, 188–92
  writing value to registry, 180–84
registry root key, 176–77
Regmon utility, 175
regobj.dll registry component, 90
RegRead method, 176, 177, 181
Regsvr32.exe file, 612, 651, 700
regsvr32.exe program, 20, 90, 262, 395, 396
Regular expression object, 204, 206
regular expressions, 195–214
  </ /> search replace tags, 167
  back-references, 202
  matching multiple patterns, 203–5
  matching subexpressions, 206–11
  overview, 195–96
  replacing values, 211–14
  using to filter contents of input stream, 157–63
  validating strings, 196–203
RegWrite method, 180, 181, 182, 184
relative distinguished name (RDN), 577, 581, 608, 698
remote automation, 25–29
remote computers
  copying files on, 312–16
  starting application on, 304–9
Remote object, 56
remote registry, accessing, 192–93
remote scripting, 55
remoteable attribute, 26
Remote-Address object, 719
Remove method, 51, 52, 623, 727, 756
RemoveAce method, 791
RemoveNetworkDrive method, 111
RemovePrinterConnection method, 118–19
Rename method, 314
renaming files or folders, 132–33

Replace method, 212, 213, 327
report.doc file, 754, 777
ResetSecondaries method, 348
ResetSecondaryIpArray method, 348
Resource Record Objects, 343–44
resource records (RRs), 343
<resource> element, 9–10
responseBody property, 363
responseText property, 361, 363
Restore method, 656, 658
RestoreWithPassword method, 658
Resume method, 646, 650
ReturnNextDrive function, 109
Reverse lookup, 396
rfc822Mailbox/mail property, 722
rmtcopy.wsf script, 314
rmtexecute.wsf script, 307
Roles property, 263, 265
rollover images, 244–46
root\cimv2 namespace, 253, 254, 278, 741
root\default namespace, 178
RootDSE directory service object, 577–78, 581
Route Print command, 161
Run command, 53
Run method, 49, 52, 53, 54, 56, 304
<runtime> element, 42, 44, 45

S

/s parameter, 629
SACL (System Access Control List), 739
samAccountName property, 588, 621
Save method, 62
Scheduled Tasks feature, 79, 80–82, 83–85
scheduling. *See* logon scripts and scheduling
SchedulingAgent.NTScheduler class, 83
Schema property, 589, 591
script piping, 159
script: prefix, 22, 89
<script> element, 4–5, 6, 9, 10, 19, 21
scripting components, 12–35
  advanced script component topics, 29–32
  component registration, 20–21
  creating type libraries, 32–35
  events, 22–25
  overview, 12
  remote automation, 25–29
  using, 21–22
  Windows Script Component wizard, 12–20
scripts. *See* logon scripts and scheduling
scrobj.dll file, 12
Search method, 24
searching
  Exchange server, 733–38
  registry values, 188–92
SearchScope property, 628, 629
secrcw32.mof file, 741
secure database, opening, 492–95
Secure Sockets Layer (SSL) security, 690
SecureBindings property, 690
security, 739–91
  changing user access to Exchange 5.5 recipients container, 773–77
  copying file with its security settings, 777–80
  overview, 739
  setting active directory permissions, 781–91
  setting directory security, 759–73
  setting file permissions, 751–59
  setting IP security, 691–94
  setting NT share security, 740–51
  taking ownership of files, 780–81
security descriptor, 739, 743
security group, 622
security identifier (SID), 700–701
Security object, 753, 756
Security privilege, 323, 328
.Security_ property, 252
Select method, 238
SELECT statement, 267
send method, 361
SendKeys method, 65, 67
SePRIVILEGEPNAMEPrivilege format, 318
server bindings, maintaining, 689–91
server parameter, 698, 706, 716, 738
ServerBindings array, 690
ServerBindings property, 669, 671, 689, 690
ServerComment property, 663–64, 669
ServerName property, 651
ServerState property, 675
Service object, 252, 253, 633–35
service parameter, 636
servicename parameter, 633, 663
Services object, 251, 253, 254, 255, 256, 317, 742
SeShutdownPrivilege qualifier, 318
Session object, 638
Sessions collection, 637
Set method, 183
SET statement, 49, 50, 52
SetAs method, 700
SetBinaryValue method, 184
SetCallBack method, 641

SetDateTime method, 336, 338
SetGateways method, 281
sethours.wsf script, 614
SetInfo method, 581, 586, 593, 621, 678, 679, 710, 711, 721, 723
SetPassword method, 586
SetSecurity method, 772, 773
SetSecurityDescriptor method, 702, 741, 744, 756, 778
SetUserCannotChangePassword routine, 617
SetWINSServer method, 280, 281
Share object, 643
Sharename parameter, 643
Shell object, 46, 49, 94, 175, 176, 178, 180, 181, 184, 187, 192, 193, 299, 304
shell operations
  accessing Windows-related folders, 58–60
  creating Windows shortcut, 60–62
  displaying message prompt, 63–65
  environment variables
    creating or updating, 48–51
    deleting, 51–52
    reading, 46–48
  overview, 39
  reading command-line arguments, 39–46
  running applications, 52–58
  sending keystrokes to applications, 65–69
Shortcut object, 61, 62
shrmaint.wsf script, 745
Shutdown method, 317, 318, 319
Shutdown privilege, 317
SID (security identifier), 700–701
sinking, 24, 371
site object, 668
site parameter, 698, 706, 716
Size property, 127
Skip method, 152–53
SkipLine method, 152–53
SML attribute, 5
SMTP servers, 663
SMTPAddress parameter, 706
Snapshot Viewer, 247
sort program, 36
Source parameter, 243
SpecialFolders collection, 58–60
SpecialFolders parameters, 59–60
Split function, 154
square brackets ([]), 201
src attribute, 5
src property, 380
<src> element, 19
SScripting.IPNetwork, 396
SSL (Secure Sockets Layer) security, 690
standard input and output, 36
Start method, 57, 635, 674, 675
StartDoc function, 368
StartTable function, 368
static methods, 281
Static qualifier, 282
Status property, 55, 56, 646–47
statusText property, 361
StdErr output stream, 170, 173
StdErr property, 157
StdErr stream, 54
StdIn object, 158, 159
StdIn property, 157, 159
Stdin stream, 54
StdIn stream, 159, 160, 161, 164, 169, 173
StdOut object, 159
StdOut property, 157, 159
Stdout stream, 54
StdOut stream, 159, 160, 161, 169, 170
StdRegProv class, 178, 183, 192, 193
STE50EN.EXE installation file, 77
Stop method, 635, 636, 675
stored procedures
  executing, 552–55
  returning parameter value from, 561–71
straccount parameter, 744
strApp parameter, 305
strAppPath parameter, 305
strClass parameter, 676
strClassName parameter, 254, 608, 733
strCurrentDir parameter, 305
strDateTime parameter, 305, 338
strDescription parameter, 671
strDestination parameter, 313
strDMTFDate parameter, 323
Stream object, 363
streams, 35–36
strEventQuery parameter, 331
strFile parameter, 329
strFunction parameter, 377
strGroupName parameter, 620
strHost parameter, 396
strLanguage parameter, 267
strLDAPPath parameter, 727
strMember parameter, 624
strName parameter, 657, 658
strObjectClass parameter, 668
strObjectName parameter, 608, 733
strObjectPath parameter, 623
strPassword parameter, 586, 658
strPath argument, 671
strPath parameter, 700, 753, 756, 772, 773
strPermissions parameter, 773
strPool parameter, 687

strPrimaryServer server argument, 280
strProperty argument, 606
strProperty parameter, 593, 606
strQuery parameter, 267
strSecondaryServer argument, 280
strServer parameter, 657
strSiteName parameter, 676
strTimeZone parameter, 323
strTrustee parameter, 773
strType parameter, 676
strUserName parameter, 586
strVirtDirClass parameter, 670
Style property, 236
styles, 216
SubFolders collection, 125
SubMatches property, 206, 207
svcmaint.wsf script, 636
SwbemLocator object, 251–52
sysdiff.exe utility, 175
SysInfo class, 258
SysInfo.ENTWSHWindows script component, 102
SysInfo.wsc scripting component, 262
System Access Control List (SACL), 739
system administration, 575–654
  adding user or group to a group, 622–23
  controlling NT services, 630–36
  creating new user, 586–89
  creating or deleting network shares, 643–44
  creating or deleting user groups, 620–22
  deleting users, 607–8
  determining computer's OS, 582–83
  determining group membership, 624–25
  determining user RAS access, 638–42
  limiting computer access, 614–15
  listing connected resources, 636–38
  listing groups, 619–20
  listing network shares, 642–43
  listing object properties, 589–92
  listing print jobs, 647–50
  listing users, 583–85
  overview, 575–76
  print queue operations, 645–47
  querying active directory values, 625–30
  setting domain properties, 576–82
  setting multivalued properties, 605–7
  setting object properties, 592–604
  setting user flags, 615–18
  setting user logon time, 608–14
  setting windows terminal services properties, 651–54
System environment variables, 48
system processes, terminating, 300–304
System Scripting Runtime object, 396, 398
System temp environment variable, 47
system time, changing, 336–38
System variable, 47

T

<table> element, 167
tables
  opening for writing, 504–8
  querying, 500–503
TakeOwnership method, 780
Target-Address property, 721
targetAddress property, 721
TargetPath property, 62
TCP/IP information, setting, 279–88
temp environment variable, 47
templates, 216
temporary files, finding and deleting, 137–40
Terminate method, 55, 300, 301
terminating system processes, 300–304
Test method, 196, 197
text files
  creating and writing to, 149–50
  manipulating, 508–10
textEncodedORaddress property, 722
TextStream object, 149, 150, 152, 154, 159, 164, 173
thumbnail images, 240–43
time, system, changing, 336–38
Timeout property, 400
TimeToLive property, 400
TimeWritten property, 323
.tmp extension, 139
tn extension, 243
transaction processing, 571–74
transferring files, using FTP, 390–95
trustee, 739
Trustee object, 781
Trustee property, 702, 754, 755, 756
TTL parameter, 357
txt prefix, 376
txtDescription element, 377
txtDescription_OnChange subroutine, 377
type attribute, 43
type libraries, creating, 32–35
type library, 8
type parameter, 666, 673
TypeName function, 380

U

/u command, 20
Ubound function, 265
UF_DONTEXPIRE_PASSWD bit, 615, 616
UF_PASSWD_CANT_CHANGE flag, 617, 618
Uncompress method, 310, 311
UNCPassword property, 678
UNCUserName property, 678
Universal Time Coordinates (UTC), 323
Unnamed collection, 45–46
Unregister function, 20, 21
updating text files, 153–56
UPN (user principal name), 588
.url extension, 61
URL parameter, 363
URL shortcuts, 62
UseADSUtility, 773
User class, 584, 585, 586, 733
user directory, finding size of, 125–26
User environment, 48
User environment variable, 49, 52
User object, 88, 594–95, 596, 616, 619, 639, 640, 700
user PrincipalName property, 588
user principal name (UPN), 588
user prompts, multiple, creating, 170–73
User variable, 47
userAccountControl property, 616–17
UserFlags property, 615, 616–17
usermnt.wsf script, 600, 603
UserName property, 107, 108, 112, 299, 651
users
- adding to group, 622–23
- creating new, 586–89
- creating or deleting user groups, 620–22
- deleting, 607–8
- determining user RAS access, 638–42
- identifying, 107–8
- listing, 583–85
- setting user flags, 615–18
- setting user logon time, 608–14

Users container, 588
UserWorkstations property, 615
UTC (Universal Time Coordinates), 323

V

value parameter, 593
Value property, 204, 376
variables, environment, 48–51
- deleting, 51–52
- reading, 46–48

VariantToByte function, 612–13
VBA code, 219
VBScript, 143, 195, 197, 203, 206–7, 377–78
VBScript (Visual Basic Scripting Edition) scripting engine, 1
version argument, 10
version attribute, 18
version number, comparing files by, 133–35
vertical bar (|) character, 36, 159, 199
virtual Web directories, creating, 677–79
Visual Basic Scripting Edition (VBScript) scripting engine, 1
Volatile environment, 48
Volatile environment variable, 49, 52
vValue parameter, 178, 183, 606

W

WBEM (Web-Based Enterprise Management), 249
Web directory application, creating, 685–89
Web service (W3SVC), 666
Web-Based Enterprise Management (WBEM), 249
WebIIsWebDirectory class, 680
WebIIsWebFile class, 680
WebIIsWebVirtualDir class, 670, 678
Win32_Account class, 744
Win32_ACE class, 743
Win32_ACE objects, 743
Win32_ComputerSystem class, 263, 264, 297, 323
Win32_ComputerSystem object, 250, 265
Win32_ComputerSystemWMI class, 251, 255, 256, 257
Win32_DefragAnalysis object, 339–40
Win32_Directory class, 310, 313, 780
Win32_Environment class, 298, 299
Win32_LocalTime class, 307, 337
Win32_LogicalFileSecuritySetting class, 758, 780
Win32_LogicalShareSecuritySetting class, 741, 742
Win32_LogicalShareSecuritySetting object, 742
Win32_NetworkAdapterConfiguration class, 265, 266–68, 279, 280, 282
Win32_NTEventLog provider, 331
Win32_NTEventLogFile class, 327, 328, 329
Win32_NTLogEvent class, 320, 321, 322, 331
Win32_NTLogEvent object, 322

Win32_OperatingSystem class, 254, 316, 318, 336, 338
Win32_OSRecoveryConfiguration class, 275, 276, 278
Win32_OSRecoveryOption class, 277
Win32_PingStatus class, 399
Win32_PingStatus properties, 400
Win32_Process class, 301, 304, 305
Win32_Process object, 304, 305
Win32_ProcessStartup class, 305
Win32_ScheduledJob object, 305
Win32_SecurityDescriptor class, 743, 744
Win32_SecurityDescriptor object, 743, 780
Win32_Service class, 333, 334
Win32_Service value, 336
Win32_SID class, 744
Win32_Trustee object, 743
Win32_Volume class, 338, 339
Win32Shutdown method, 318–19
Windows 9x, 27, 49, 50, 52, 53, 55, 77, 94, 108, 185
Windows 95, 77, 80, 115
Windows 98, 72, 79, 115
Windows 2000, 47, 48, 52, 53, 72, 73, 74–76, 79, 82, 83, 85, 88, 93, 94, 97, 116, 160
Windows 2000 WMI DNS provider, 342
Windows 2003, 72, 73, 74–76, 79, 83, 85, 88, 94, 97, 160
Windows Management Instrumentation (WMI), 175, 399, 739, 740, 741. *See also* network administration/WMI
Windows Management Interface (WMI), 83, 102, 105, 178, 182, 186, 187, 192, 193
Windows ME, 27, 49, 50, 52, 53, 55, 72, 77, 79, 94, 108, 115, 185
Windows NT, 47, 48, 52, 53, 73, 77, 80, 82, 83, 85, 88, 93, 94, 116, 185
Windows Script Components (WSC), 4, 12, 365
Windows Script Component wizard, 12–20
Windows Script File (WSF) files, 4–11
Windows shortcut, creating, 60–62
Windows terminal services, setting properties, 651–54
Windows XP, 47, 48, 52, 53, 72, 73, 74–76, 79, 83, 85, 88, 93, 94, 97, 160
Windows-related folders, accessing, 58–60
winmgmts (Windows Management) prefix, 254
WinNT provider, 576–77, 582
WinNT//domain/account format, 700
Winset.exe application, 49–50
With statement, 220, 243
WITHIN clause, 331
wkst prefix, 354
WMI CIM Studio, 256–58, 276–77, 317–18
WMI Computer Information Classes, 292
WMI connection string, 742
WMI DNS provider, 342
WMIExec command-line switches, 298
wmiexec script, 297
wmiinc.vbs file, 271, 298, 323, 338, 740, 744, 758
Word documents, creating formatted, 215–26
Word.Application, ProgID, 218, 220
Word.Document
  application ProgID, 220
  class ID (CLSID), 238
Worksheets collection, 220
Write method, 34, 149, 150, 182
write method, 365
WriteBlankLines method, 150
WriteLine method, 149, 150, 368
writeln method, 365
WritePara function, 368
WriteRow function, 368
writing value to registry, 180–84
WSC object, 89
wscript command, 12
WScript Echo statement, 42
Wscript host, 160, 161
WScript object, 12, 39, 41, 159, 164
WScript.Arguments.Named object, 44, 45
WScript.Arguments.ShowUsage method, 45
WScript.Arguments.Unnamed collection, 46
WScript.Arguments.Unnamed.Count property, 46
WScript.CreateObject method, 369, 371
WScript.DisconnectObject method, 25
wscript.exe application, 1, 7
WScript.Network object, 72
WScript.Quit method, 264
WScript.Shell argument, 39
WScript.Shell object, 48, 52, 54, 58, 60, 65
.wsf script, 7, 161
WSH
  script mail agent, 446–51
  version 2.0 features, 4–11
    overview, 4
    Windows Script File (WSF) files, 4–11
  what it is, 1
WSH 1.0, 35

WSH 2.0, 35, 36, 55
WSH 5.6, 40, 42, 45, 54, 55
WSH Shell object, 39
WSHCB.HTMLGen component, 368
WSHController object, 55
WSH.log file, 94
WSH.RecurseDir scripting component, 231
WshRemote object, 56, 57
WshRemoteError object, 56–57
WshScriptExec object, 54
WshShortCut object, 61
WSscript.Create method, 377
WSscript.Sleep statement, 371
WTSLib.DLL file, 651
WTSSupport component, 651–53
WTSSupport.WTSLib ProgID, 651

X

xchgmaint.wsf script, 714, 716
xlimport script, 239
xlimport.wsf script, 231, 239
XML element, 4
XML (Extensible Markup Language), 4
XMLHTTP component, 360, 363
Xor bitwise operation, 130
XOR logical operator, 617, 618

Z

zones, 343